ACADEMY AWARDS

The publisher and the compiler acknowledge the kind cooperation of the Academy of Motion Picture Arts and Sciences in the preparation of this work. The book is not a publication of the Academy of Motion Picture Arts and Sciences.

ACADEMY AWARDS

AN UNGAR REFERENCE INDEX

Compiled and introduced by Richard Shale

Foreword by Howard W. Koch
President, Academy of Motion Picture Arts and Sciences

With the 50th Anniversary Winners and Nominees

FREDERICK UNGAR PUBLISHING CO.
New York

Copyright © 1978 by Frederick Ungar Publishing Co., Inc.
Printed in the United States of America
Designed by Jacqueline Schuman

Library of Congress Cataloging in Publication Data

Shale, Richard, 1947–
  Academy awards.

  (Ungar film library)
  Bibliography: p.
  1. Academy awards (Moving-pictures) 2. Moving-
pictures—United States—Catalogs. I. Title.
PN1993.5.U6S47   791.43′7′079   78-4296
ISBN 0-8044-2819-0
ISBN 0-8044-6860-5 pbk.

Contents

Foreword

The Academy of Motion Picture Arts and Sciences was founded in May 1927. The organizers believed that by recognizing outstanding achievements in filmmaking further excellence would be stimulated. Louis B. Mayer, one of the founders of Metro-Goldwyn-Mayer, suggested, "What we need to do is focus new attention on movie achievement. Academies and institutions reward excellence in other fields, why shouldn't we?"

And so . . . Oscar was born.

In the intervening half century, he has been sought and spurned, revered and reviled, called an incentive for excellence and a commercial tool. But throughout his first fifty years, the integrity of the Academy members who bestow him, and the honesty of the voting process, have rarely been questioned.

From an initial membership of less than three hundred, the Academy has grown into a professional honorary organization composed of four thousand motion picture craftsmen and artists.

Its stature has grown to the point where it provides unparalleled incentives for higher levels of technical and professional achievement among all branches of filmmaking throughout the world. And, in so doing, it has become motion pictures' most effective ambassador.

Richard Shale's *Academy Awards: An Ungar Reference Index* offers a comprehensive study of Oscar and the evolution of the Academy Awards over the past fifty years. Since the Academy itself is dedicated to the advancement of the arts and sciences of motion pictures, we are pleased to see serious study given to the Awards of Merit we bestow upon film artists and craftsmen.

The book was written for both the serious historian and film buff. I believe anyone interested in motion pictures will find it well worth his time.

Howard W. Koch
President
Academy of Motion Picture Arts & Sciences

ACADEMY AWARDS

Introduction

There is a fascinating parallel between the history of film and the evolution of the Oscars over the past fifty years. The advent of talkies, the age of the Hollywood musical, and the growing popularity of color, for example, have all been reflected by changes in the award categories. Those who examine motion pictures through the achievements of the Academy will literally find a story with a cast of thousands, and this index has been compiled to make more accessible the names of those performers, craftsmen, and scientists—all artists in their respective fields— and the films they created.

To underscore when each category was established and when those no longer in existence were discontinued, the first major section of the book is indexed according to award category, each introduced by a brief explanation of its history and voting procedure. The same information is repeated, in chronological arrangement, in the second major section of the book. The details for each entry have been determined by official lists supplied by the Academy. Beginning in 1951, for example, I list the name of the producer of the Best Picture as well as the studio because that is when the Academy began to include that information.

Some critics of the Academy argue that the awards are self-serving and that the competition is meaningless since comparisons of different roles and different films are impossible. The complaints that a comedy cannot be judged against a dramatic picture, that no single achievement can be termed "best," and that the winners don't always coincide with the public's choice seem to me beside the point. The Oscars are and always have been a means by which film industry people recognize their fellow workers, and they have attained a popularity and significance far beyond the dreamiest expectations of the Academy founders. If sentiment or questionable judgment have occasionally been used to choose the winners, then so be it. It is not my intention to debate the validity of the Oscars but to record the results. Those who wish to defend or attack the choices may find the ammunition for their arguments in these pages. My aim is to offer a complete account of the Academy and to provide easy access to the names of the nominees and winners of the past fifty years.

Acknowledgments: I would like to thank several people who helped me as I prepared this book. Marty Cooper of Harshe-Rotman & Druck, Sam Gill and Tony Slide of the Academy of Motion Picture Arts and Sciences, Howard Walls, Kemp Niver, Three Tyler of *American Cinematographer,* and Rich Mason all assisted in various ways. I am also grateful to my editor, Stan Hochman, for guiding the project from conception to birth and to Howard W. Koch, President of the Academy, for providing the foreword.

My special gratitude goes to Mildred Simpson and her excellent staff at the

Academy's Margaret Herrick Library who responded with patience, warmth, and efficiency to my seemingly endless requests.

My thanks to the Academy of Motion Picture Arts and Sciences and the many individual companies who graciously provided the photographs used in this book.

The Academy:
How It Started, What It Is, What It Does

To the general public, the Academy of Motion Picture Arts and Sciences simply means the Oscars. But to the founders fifty years ago and to the more than four thousand present members, the Academy has always meant much more. To place the birth of Oscar in proper perspective, it is necessary first to examine the Academy itself and its many other important activities in addition to the annual awards.

Origins of the Academy

When the idea for an Academy of Motion Picture Arts and Sciences (AMPAS) was developed in the late 1920s, the movie industry was in the midst of its greatest period of change. Potentially revolutionary experiments in sound had begun which would seriously threaten and finally doom the silent picture. Repercussions from scandals which had rocked Hollywood earlier in the decade were still being felt, and the industry, particularly sensitive to outside attacks and cries for censorship, searched for a manageable way to protect itself.

Less known to the public but of great concern within the industry was the growing mood of unionism. There had been a strike by studio craftsmen in 1918, and by the mid-twenties the labor struggle had intensified. Los Angeles was a stronghold of the open shop and, as such, presented a challenge to organized labor. On November 29, 1926, nine major studios and five unions signed the Studio Basic Agreement, and the motion picture industry became unionized after a ten-year struggle. The pact, however, covered only stagehands, carpenters, musicians, electricians, and painters; the major talent groups were still without bargaining power, and the producers could only anticipate that the actors, writers, and directors would also soon press for standardized contracts.

In such a climate the seeds of the Academy were sown. During the first week of January 1927, five weeks after the Studio Basic Agreement was signed, the idea for a new organization was suggested over dinner at the home of MGM chief Louis B. Mayer. Present as Mayer's guests were actor Conrad Nagel and director Fred Niblo. Several sources also claim Fred Beetson of the Association of Motion Picture Producers was present, and Beetson himself later wrote in an *Academy Bulletin* of his good fortune "to be one of the original four to discuss the value to the industry of forming an organization for the benefit of all in the industry." The prospect of such an institution prompted the men to plan a dinner the following week to which they would invite representatives from all creative branches of the motion picture industry.

On January 11, 1927 thirty-six people gathered at the Ambassador Hotel in Los

Among the thirty-six founders of the Academy were: (standing, L to R) Cedric Gibbons, J. A. Ball, Carey Wilson, George Cohen, Edwin Loeb, Fred Beetson, Frank Lloyd, Roy Pomeroy, John Stahl, Harry Rapf; (seated, L to R) Louis B. Mayer, Conrad Nagel, Mary Pickford, Douglas Fairbanks, Frank Woods, M. C. Levee, Joseph M. Schenck, and Fred Niblo.© *1978 A.M.P.A.S.*

Angeles and enthusiastically endorsed the idea of an association which would be mutually beneficial. These persons became the founders of the Academy of Motion Picture Arts and Sciences (see Appendix I). By March 19, 1927, articles of incorporation had been presented and the first officers elected. Douglas Fairbanks was chosen as president, with Fred Niblo as vice-president, M. C. Levee as treasurer, and Frank Woods as secretary. The Academy was granted a charter as a non-profit corporation by the State of California on May 4, 1927, and a week later on May 11, an organizational banquet was held at the Biltmore Hotel. Three hundred persons attended, and, according to the Academy's 1929 *Annual Report*, 231 people joined the new Academy that night.

Because it was not limited to a single studio or to a specific talent group, the newly created organization had great potential as a forum for exchanging ideas and settling differences. "Each of the talent classes had grievances with no medium for their adjustment," wrote Frank Woods. "But more than this and of greater importance as some of us viewed it, the screen and all its people were under a great and alarming cloud of public censure and contempt. . . . Some constructive action seemed imperative to halt the attacks and establish the industry in the public mind as a respectable, legitimate institution, and its people as reputable individuals."

Shortly after the organizational banquet, the Academy published on June 20, 1927, a statement of aims which read in part:

> The Academy will take aggressive action in meeting outside attacks that are unjust.

6

It will promote harmony and solidarity among the membership and among the different branches.

It will reconcile internal differences that may exist or arise.

It will adopt such ways and means as are proper to further the welfare and protect the honor and good repute of the profession.

It will encourage the improvement and advancement of the arts and sciences of the profession by the interchange of constructive ideas and by awards of merit for distinctive achievements.

It will take steps to develop the greater power and influence of the screen.

In a word, the Academy proposes to do for the motion picture profession in all its branches what other great national and international bodies have done for other arts and sciences and industries.

Labor Relations

Despite the positive and nobly stated purposes of the Academy, critics would later charge that the organization was nothing more than a company union conceived by the wily Mayer as a means by which the producers could control the talent groups and forestall unionization. Murray Ross wrote in *Stars and Strikes,* his 1941 study of Hollywood's labor struggle: "The founding of the Academy was a master stroke of producer ingenuity; its successful operation resulted from actor acquiescence in its policies." Others vehemently denied the charges and pointed out that the structure of the Academy offered equal representation to all. The producers constituted only one of the five branches of the Academy—actors, directors, technicians, and writers had equal status—and the Board of Directors which ran the organization was made up of three representatives from each branch.

A labor dispute became the first order of business for the new Academy. In the summer of 1927 the studios, claiming pressure from their New York bankers, tried to impose a 10 percent salary cut as a response to charges of financial mismanagement and extravagance. When the talent groups protested loudly and threatened to strike, the studios quickly suggested that the producers' branch of the Academy hold conferences with the other branches to air grievances and suggest ways of cutting costs. The sessions were held, and the result was a decision to withdraw the proposed salary cut. But when this announcement was made at an Academy dinner on July 28, 1927, the producers let the other branches accept the blame for soaring motion picture costs. The talent branches felt double-crossed, and though the Academy claimed credit for averting the salary cut, this episode marked the beginning for many of a distrust of the Academy's impartiality in labor-management disputes.

The realization that sound pictures would become more than a passing fad prompted many legitimate stage actors to come to Hollywood and switch to film work. Many of these stage players belonged to the Actors' Equity Association which had won a closed shop on Broadway in 1919, and a controversy soon developed over who should represent film actors. In December 1927 the Academy announced the successful negotiation of a contract for free-lance actors, which

Academy
of
Motion Picture Arts and Sciences
Organization Banquet
May 11. 1927.
Los Angeles Biltmore.

The Academy's organizational banquet was held May 11, 1927, at the Biltmore Hotel in Los Angeles.
© 1978 A.M.P.A.S.

was the first standard actor-producer agreement in the history of Hollywood. For the next two years Equity battled the Academy for the right to represent actors, but AMPAS gained the advantage after a 1929 strike by Equity failed to generate sufficient support.

The novelty of talking pictures had sustained movie box-office receipts after the crash of 1929, but in 1931 the depression caught up with the film industry. By 1933 Paramount was bankrupt, RKO and Universal were in receivership, and Fox had been forced to reorganize. The crisis came in March 1933 when President Roosevelt declared a nationwide bank holiday. Hollywood reeled. Some studios immediately suspended salaries; others talked of closing, and production schedules were suddenly uncertain. The Academy quickly formed an Emergency Committee

which suggested temporary 50 percent pay cuts as an alternative to a complete shutdown. The committee worked out a scale making the cuts more equitable for low income workers, and no salary cuts were to last longer than the eight-week period from March 6th to April 30th. Many studios restored salaries immediately; others were to resume full pay on a timetable worked out by the Academy committee.

The Academy was given the right to inspect the studios' financial records, and Price Waterhouse and Company was hired to conduct the audits. (Three years later the firm would be retained by the Academy on a permanent basis to tabulate the Academy Award voting.) The stumbling block arose when Warner Brothers refused to restore salaries on the date set by the Academy. Darryl Zanuck, then with

Warners, had promised his employees that the studio would abide by the Academy decision, and when it refused, Zanuck resigned his $5,000-a-week job in protest.

The Warners controversy also precipitated the resignation of Conrad Nagel as Academy president when his actions met with the disapproval of the Board. The Los Angeles *Times* quoted Nagel as saying he worked through Will Hays to persuade Harry Warner to accept the Academy decision, but another paper claimed Nagel supported Warner's stand and in doing so drew a vote of no confidence from the Academy directors. The Academy issued a statement simply saying "the intensive struggle within the industry within the last few weeks has resulted in many questions of Academy policy with some of which Mr. Nagel felt he could not agree."

The Academy survived this crisis but with a further erosion of its reputation, because the salary waiver plan had not been popular with the talent groups. Despite the Academy's attempt to deal equitably with a difficult situation, "it marked," one labor historian noted, "the beginning of the end of the usefulness of the AMPAS in the labor relations field."

J. T. Reed replaced Nagel as president and immediately speeded up work on a new constitution which would reorganize the Academy. After less than a month in office Reed sent "An Open Letter To Every Member of the Academy" in which he outlined the changes in structure and policy. "Every effort has been made," he wrote, "to guarantee that both the election system and the Academy as a whole will be free from politics, and from any taint of self-preservation in office."

Further trouble erupted that summer. Already pressured by internal strife and the growing militancy of Hollywood unionization, the Academy nearly capsized in the troubled waters of the National Recovery Administration. On June 16, 1933, Roosevelt signed the National Industrial Recovery Act which suspended anti-trust laws and allowed industries to regulate themselves through "codes of fair competition." The NRA Motion Picture Code became the longest of more than six hundred industry codes drawn up. Though J. T. Reed was a member of the code committee, the Academy lacked enough internal unity to be much of a factor in the code hearings. The studios saw the code as a first step toward government control of the industry, and the talent groups saw it as a tool for further producer dominance.

Convinced that the Academy was not acting in their best interests, several actors quit to form the Screen Actors Guild in July 1933, and the new group gained further impetus that fall when the provisions of the code became known. As Murray Ross noted: "The final draft of the NRA code published in September contained the agency-licensing, salary-control, and antiraiding provisions which aroused instant and widespread indignation. The knowledge that Reed, the president of the Academy, was a member of the committee which drafted the obnoxious provisions intensified the actors' resentment."

Thus began an exodus of actors. In October, fourteen prominent stars, including James Cagney, Gary Cooper, Fredric March, Frank Morgan, Paul Muni, and

The first awards were presented at the Academy's second anniversary banquet, held May 16, 1929. © 1978 A.M.P.A.S.

George Raft, resigned from the Academy. By November the fledgling Screen Actors Guild had over a thousand members. A rejuvenated Screen Writers Guild, whose aims were similar, joined with the actors and jointly published *The Screen Guild's Magazine,* which constantly editorialized against the Academy and called it a company union.

At issue was the power struggle for the right to represent the talent groups in negotiations with the producers. "Hidden behind the mask of an arbiter of taste," the Screen Actors Guild charged, "and obscured under the cloak of research, what the Academy is really trying to do is destroy the possibility of an honest actor organization—of, by, and for actors. . . . The Guild is not going to be destroyed. But the Academy cannot exist and claim jurisdiction over actors without throwing a constant harpoon into Guild efforts for betterment of actor conditions."

On May 27, 1935, the U.S. Supreme Court unanimously declared that Roosevelt's National Recovery Administration was unconstitutional. The removal of the controversial Code of Fair Competition left labor relations in Hollywood even more chaotic than before. And so the battle raged.

The low point in Academy-Guild relations came at the Eighth Awards banquet held March 5, 1936. A few days before the dinner the Screen Guilds sent their members the following telegram:

> You have probably been asked by your producer to go to the Academy dinner stop we find that this is a concerted move to make people think that Guild members are supporting the Academy stop the Board feels that since the Academy is definitely inimical to the best interests of the Guilds you should not attend.

The boycott was successful, and only a handful of actors and writers attended the Oscar ceremony. Dudley Nichols, a militant member of the Screen Writers Guild who had resigned from the Academy three years earlier, won the Oscar for Best Screenplay and became the first person to refuse an Academy Award. "I realize," Nichols wrote, "the awards were voted by a generous membership who had no thought of personal partiality or political interest. But a writer who accepts an Academy award tacitly supports the Academy, and I believe it to be the duty of every screen writer to stand with his own, and to strengthen the Guild."

In 1937 the Academy rewrote its by-laws and withdrew completely from labor-movement negotiations. W. S. Van Dyke, who chaired the Academy's Reorganization Committee, pointed out that the change allowed the Academy "to return to its first principles and be non-economic and non-political in theory and in fact."

Though finally divisive, the Academy's ten-year involvement with labor problems was by no means a complete failure. In the early days the Conciliation Committee had successfully settled a number of disputes between individuals of different branches, and the Academy's efforts in negotiating provided a foundation on which the Guilds could later build. In their detailed study of the labor movement in Los Angeles, Louis and Richard Perry concluded:

> The AMPAS had been an innovation in industrial relations, and seemed to be a reasonable idea for successful industry-wide employee representation. Through the Academy a number of talent groups obtained standard contracts and developed codes covering various practices which worked to their benefit. Although the AMPAS was not a true union, it introduced the principle of collective bargaining. Thus when opportunities to develop labor unions came along, the talent groups were able to use the experience gained in Academy relationships to good advantage in establishing collective bargaining through various guilds.

Only once after 1937 did the Academy reenter the stormy world of politics, and that occurred during the blacklist period of the 1950s. On February 6, 1957, the Academy enacted the following rule: "Any person who, before any duly constituted Federal legislative committee or body, shall have admitted that he is a member of the Communist Party (and has not since publicly renounced the party) or who shall have refused to answer whether or not he is, or was, a member of the Communist Party or shall have refused to respond to a subpoena to appear before such a committee or body, shall be ineligible for any Academy Award so long as he persists in such a refusal."

One person affected by the rule was screenwriter Michael Wilson, who had won an Oscar for *A Place in the Sun* (1951) before being blacklisted. He appeared certain to be nominated for *Friendly Persuasion* (which was released in 1956 without screenplay credit), but when the nominations were announced February 18th the film was listed without Wilson's name. That same year blacklisted writer Dalton Trumbo won an Oscar for writing *The Brave One* but was unable to claim it since he had written the film under the pseudonym Robert Rich.

Late in 1958 several Academy members, including George Seaton and Valentine Davies, began a campaign to repeal the rule. Among that year's possible nominations for Best Story and Screenplay was *The Defiant Ones,* written by

Nathan E. Douglas and Harold Jacob Smith. Smith was "clean" but Douglas (a pseudonym for blacklisted screenwriter Ned Young) had once taken the Fifth Amendment. The Academy, faced with the embarrassing prospect of having to declare half of a writing team ineligible, revoked the rule on January 12, 1959, six weeks before the 1958 nominations were announced. Denying any specific connection to *The Defiant Ones* (for which Douglas and Smith did win Oscars), the Board of Governors issued a statement calling the rule "unworkable and impractical to administer and enforce." In the future the Academy would simply "honor achievements as presented."

Dalton Trumbo hailed the Academy decision as the equivalent of an official end to the blacklist. In a letter to Michael Wilson he wrote, "How can an industry officially rescind a blacklist which legally it cannot admit the existence of? There *was*, however, the Academy rule. Revocation of the Academy rule was the nearest thing to an official rescission of the blacklist that could or will occur." (Trumbo finally received his 1956 Oscar in 1975 after Frank and Maurice King, producers of *The Brave One*, sent the Academy an affidavit verifying that the mysterious Robert Rich was in fact Trumbo.)

Technical Activities

The Academy's role in technical research was far more successful and harmonious than its labor relations. The advent of talking pictures required an enormous amount of technical study, for not only sound but lighting, camera operation, and set construction were affected. From January through April 1928 the Academy's technicians' branch co-sponsored with the American Society of Cinematographers and the Association of Motion Picture Producers a series of lectures on incandescent lighting. The demonstrations and papers read approximated the scholarly function of a true academy, and 150 cinematographers received training. A similar school in sound fundamentals was organized in 1929, and over nine hundred persons were instructed in the latest techniques.

The Academy could draw upon the talent of all studios, and many technical problems were first handled by special committees such as the Aperture Committee and the Screen Illumination Committee, but in 1929 these groups were consolidated into the Academy Producers-Technicians Joint Committee. In January 1930 the Technical Bureau of the Association of Motion Picture Producers, which duplicated many of the Joint Committee's activities, was transferred to Academy jurisdiction. It was absorbed into the Producers-Technicians Committee but continued to receive financial support from the producers' association. A further indication of the Academy's growing involvement in research was the establishment of a category for Scientific or Technical achievement for the third year of awards.

In 1932 the Academy reorganized its technical activities into a Research Council which included members from all five branches and representatives from the major companies manufacturing motion picture equipment. Under the reorganiza-

L to R: Frank Capra, winner of three Oscars for Directing; James Cagney, 1942 Best Actor; Darryl Zanuck, who received three Thalberg Awards; and Jack Warner, Academy founder and Thalberg Award winner.© *1978 A.M.P.A.S.*

tion of the Academy following the 1933 bank holiday crisis, the companies and studios engaged in production became Corporate (non-voting) Members of the Academy, and their dues were used solely to finance the work of the Research Council.

The Research Council became quite prominent during World War II. The Academy had maintained a training course for Signal Corps officers since 1930, and during World War II the Council sponsored a series of schools for motion-picture cameramen and still photographers in the Signal Corps and the Marines. Even before war was declared, the Signal Corps turned to Hollywood for help in preparing training films. Under the leadership of Darryl Zanuck, the Research Council in October 1940 volunteered to negotiate the contracts for government films. The studios and guilds pledged their support, and by November 1940 the Council had become the body which would distribute the projects to the studios. The agreement was to assign the projects alphabetically, but frequent exceptions were made, and smaller producers not a party to the Research Council's plan complained they were being frozen out. As Harry Truman's Senate committee on the war effort discovered in 1943, the assignments had not always been parceled out evenly—of the $1.4 million spent by the government in this period more than 70 percent went to four major studios: Paramount, Twentieth-Century-Fox, MGM, and RKO. The Research Council delivered 330 reels to the War Department before the contract was canceled in December 1942.

The Research Council was also responsible for determining officers' commissions for motion picture people who joined the Armed Forces. The Military Personnel Selection Committee considered over fifteen hundred applicants, recommending 105 for commissions and 610 for enlistment.

The invaluable work performed during the war was the last major activity of the Academy's Research Council. To facilitate its acceptance of funding from commercial companies, the Council was transferred to the Association of Motion Picture Producers in January 1948 and renamed the Motion Picture Research Council.

Publications and Educational Activities

When the Academy was founded in 1927 no one could imagine that the annual awards would eventually overshadow all of the organization's other activities. That these other projects are less publicized than the Oscar does not diminish their importance. The record in the field of education, for instance, is nearly as old as the Academy itself.

The early investigations in lighting resulted in the Academy's first book, *Report On Incandescent Illumination,* published in 1928, and the sound school resulted in two volumes: *Recording Sound For Motion Pictures* in 1931 and the updated, more authoritative *Motion Picture Sound Engineering* in 1938.

The College Affairs Committee had cooperated with the University of Southern California in 1928 to present a film course, and these lectures were published the following year as *Introduction To the Photoplay.* Several universities began their cinema departments with help from the Academy, and the practice of assisting college students and faculty members is continued today by the National Film Information Service, a mail service to researchers, and the Visiting Artists Program.

The Academy has made four attempts to publish a magazine. The first effort, *Motion Picture Arts and Sciences,* which lasted for only a single issue, was published in November 1927 and circulated only to Academy members. It featured articles, Academy news, a lithograph by Cedric Gibbons, and an artistic photograph by Karl Struss. The following year the Board signed a contract to purchase an existing periodical called *Hollywood,* but when it became apparent that the magazine could not be turned into a national publication the contract was canceled by mutual consent. A third try in 1939 was titled *Montage.* Intended as a monthly, only one issue was printed. According to Academy executive secretary Donald Gledhill, it was to have contained film information "upon a level comparable to the academic and professional journals in other fields." The most recent attempt at an Academy magazine came in 1972. *Academy Leader* offered a mix of film news and reviews and featured excellent reproductions of stills. Intended as a quarterly, it ceased publication after three issues.

Several other Academy publications have been more lasting. The *Screen Achievement Records Bulletin* began in slightly different form in 1933 as a list of film productions and credits for writers and directors. It is currently published three times a year and provides an authoritative list of complete credits indexed by film title, company, craft, and individual.

Equally important to the industry is the *Academy Players Directory,* also published three times a year, which serves as a casting director's bible. Pictures of the player and the name of the player's agent are included, and everyone gets the

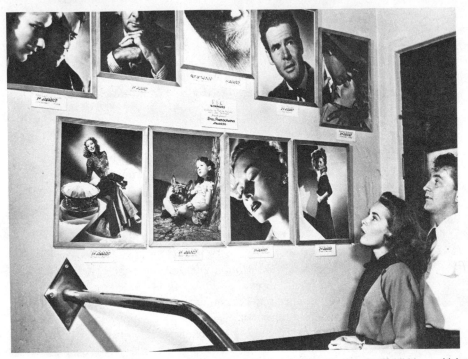

Janet Leigh and Robert Mitchum look at the RKO winners in a Still Photography Exhibition, which was at one time an annual event sponsored by the Academy. *RKO Photo*

same amount of space, regardless of rank or reputation. The publication, begun in 1937 as an alternative to the many private casting directories which exploited actors, now includes nearly twelve entries.

In 1970 the Academy and the Writers Guild of America jointly published *Who Wrote the Movie and What Else Did He Write?*, a comprehensive directory of screenwriting credits from 1936 through 1969.

The Academy Foundation was created in the early 1940s to oversee educational and cultural activities of the motion picture industry. First discussed in September 1942 by Charles Coburn, George Stevens, Farciot Edouart, Walter Wanger, and Darryl Zanuck, the Foundation filed articles of incorporation on January 31, 1944. It is incorporated separately from the Academy in order to qualify for certain tax exemption privileges and to receive state, federal, and private funding.

One of the first and most valuable projects of the Foundation was the restoration of the Library of Congress Paper Prints Collection. Motion pictures made between 1894 and 1912 were copyrighted as a series of still photographs by reproducing a paper print of the celluloid original. Approximately 2.5 million feet of these prints were stored and forgotten in Washington until discovered in the early 1940s by Howard Walls, then working for the Copyright Office. Walls subsequently was appointed Curator of the Motion Picture Collection of the Library of Congress, and he set about to find a means of transferring the paper prints back to film. With

In 1951 Mack Sennett donated to the Academy an extensive collection of stills, scripts, financial records, and correspondence. L to R: Executive Director Margaret Herrick, Sennett, and Academy president Charles Brackett. © *1978 A.M.P.A.S.*

the help of Carl Gregory he started the restoration process but was forced to stop in 1947 when Congress voted to discontinue the Motion Picture Division. The Academy Foundation was persuaded to undertake the project, and Walls was hired as curator of the film archives. After Walls left the Academy in the early 1950s, Kemp Niver took over the restoration work and successfully devised an economical way of transferring the priceless paper prints to 16mm film. When the Academy's funds for the project ran out after two and a half years, Senator Thomas Kuchel (R-Calif.) successfully pushed through a government appropriation to complete the work. Niver received an Honorary Oscar in 1954 for his Renovare process which made possible the completion of the ten-year project.

In 1965 the Academy began a scholarship program for film students, and, in cooperation with the American Film Institute and the Society of Motion Picture and Television Engineers, it now also sponsors an internship program for young filmmakers. In 1973 competition for Student Film Awards was begun, and a year later the annual Marvin Borowsky Memorial Lectureship in Screenwriting was inaugurated.

The Academy headquarters in Beverly Hills houses the 1,111-seat Samuel Goldwyn Theater, a custom-designed facility capable of handling every known projection and sound system. It sets the standard for the industry and is regarded as one of the technically finest movie theaters in the world.

L to R: Best Actor Gary Cooper, Best Actress Joan Fontaine, guest speaker Wendell Willkie, Supporting Actress Mary Astor, and Supporting Actor Donald Crisp at the 14th Awards ceremony. © *1978 A.M.P.A.S.*

The Margaret Herrick Library is named for the woman who served as executive director of the Academy from 1943 until 1970 when she retired. The research facility, begun in 1931, is open to the public and holds one of the world's most complete collections of film-related material.

The Academy Awards

When the Academy of Motion Picture Arts and Sciences was organized in 1927, among the several general committees formed was one named Awards of Merit. The original seven members of this group were Sid Grauman, Bess Meredyth, J. Stuart Blackton, Richard Barthelmess, D. W. Griffith, and Henry King, with Cedric Gibbons as chairman. (Charles Rosher and George Fawcett subsequently replaced Griffith, Gibbons, and Barthelmess.) An awards presentation was considered by this committee, and a 1928 *Academy Bulletin* reported that "a partial plan was worked out, but, in the press of other business, no definite action was taken by the Board."

By May 1928 interest in the awards had been revived, and that summer the procedure for nominations was worked out. In July the Academy Board authorized awards in twelve categories and, anticipating that the contest would become a yearly event, decided to limit the nominations to achievements in pictures released in a specific twelve-month period. August 1, 1927, to July 31, 1928, was declared the period of eligibility, and the studios happily furnished the Academy with a list of pictures released within those dates. To refresh the memories of its members, the Academy sent this reminder list of eligible films to everyone, a practice which has been maintained to the present.

Five Boards of Judges—one for each Academy branch—were appointed to consider the nominations made by the general membership, and by the August 15, 1928, deadline nearly one thousand nominations had been received. The rules stated "no national or Academy membership distinctions are to be considered."

A list of the ten achievements in each category receiving the highest number of votes was turned over to the Boards of Judges which narrowed the ten choices down to three recommendations for each award. A Central Board of Judges consisting of one member from each branch examined these three finalists in each class and decided who was to receive the first place and honorable mentions. The five men who decided these first awards were: Alec Francis, representing the Actors Branch: Frank Lloyd, Directors; Sid Grauman, Producers; Tom Geraghty, Writers; and A. George Volck, Technicians. The results were announced immediately, though the presentations were not made until three months later at the Academy's second anniversary banquet.

The period of eligibility remained August 1st to July 31st for the next four years but was changed to the calendar year for the Sixth Awards. The adjustment required the addition of five months to the eligibility period, so the 1932/33 Awards covered August 1, 1932, to December 31, 1933. Since 1934 the eligibility period has remained January 1st to December 31st. (The one current exception is the Foreign Language Film Award whose year of eligibility runs from November 1st to October 31st.)

The selection of winners by Branch and Central Boards of Judges was used again for the Second Awards, though the number of categories was pared to seven and the practice of awarding honorable mentions was dropped. Sound pictures were eligible for the first time, having been excluded from consideration the first year because their development was too recent to insure competitive results.

The selection process was broadened the following year, and for the Third through the Eighth Awards nominations and final voting were by the full Academy membership. In 1936 (9th year) nominations were made by a special Awards Nominating Committee appointed by the Academy president, but the final vote was retained by the full membership.

The problems in labor relations which plagued the Academy in the mid-thirties had resulted in the resignation of nearly half of the members, so, in an attempt to get a more representative vote and also to appear more democratic, nominating and final voting privileges were extended to the motion picture guilds and unions as well as to Academy members. This expansion of eligible voters remained in effect from 1937 (10th year) through 1945 (18th year). Class B of the Screen Actors' Guild—the extras—was dropped in 1944, and in 1946 (19th year) the final vote was again limited to Academy members. Guilds and unions continued to vote for nominees until 1957 (30th year) when the current rule of nominating and final voting by Academy members only was put back into effect.

Each branch of the Academy makes its own rules. Most achievements are not "entered" in competition; they are simply eligible if they have met the following general rule:

> Academy Awards of Merit shall be bestowed for achievements in connection with motion pictures first publicly exhibited by means of 35mm film or larger for paid admission (previews excluded) in a commercial motion picture theater in the Los Angeles area, defined as Los Angeles, West Los Angeles, or Beverly Hills, between January 1 [year] and midnight of December 31 [same year], such exhibition being for a consecutive run of not less than a week after an opening prior to midnight of December 31st, following normal exploitation and advertising utilized by the producer for his other pictures within the dates specified.

Four categories allow exceptions to this general rule: Documentaries and Short Films are entered by their producers, and Music Awards require the creator of the achievement to file an Official Submission Form. Foreign Language Films are submitted by each country's equivalent to AMPAS (limit: one film per country). The three current exceptions to the location rule are Documentaries and Foreign Language Films, which need not play in the Los Angeles area (the latter need not have opened in the United States but must have English subtitles), and Short Films, which may play anywhere in Los Angeles County.

Rules are sometimes created or clarified as a result of a controversy or confusion. Many Academy members, for instance, felt Bette Davis's 1934 performance in *Of Human Bondage* was the best of the year, and a furor erupted when her name was not listed among the nominees for Best Actress. The Academy was forced to accept write-in candidates, but the confusion eventually brought about a rule prohibiting write-ins.

With the creation of the Supporting Actor and Actress categories in 1936, it was only a matter of time before clarifying rules would be needed. Paulette Goddard's 1943 nomination for Supporting Actress in *So Proudly We Hail* left many members asking if she really belonged under Best Actress since she had received co-star billing for the role. The following year Barry Fitzgerald, who co-starred with Bing Crosby in *Going My Way,* found himself nominated in two categories for the same role. (He lost the Best Actor award to Crosby but won the Supporting Actor Oscar.) The Academy finally asked the studios to designate which category the performance belonged in, and thereafter the yearly reminder lists to members carried a designation distinguishing the leads from the supporting roles. In 1964 the Academy Board of Governors voted to omit this differentiation, and the rule now in effect says the "determination as to whether a role is a lead or a support shall be made individually by members of the [Actors'] branch at the time of balloting."

An actor or actress can no longer be nominated in both categories for the same performance, but the rules have never prevented a nomination in lead and supporting categories for two different roles. This happened to Fay Bainter in 1938 and Teresa Wright in 1942. (Both ladies lost the Best Actress award but won for Supporting Actress.) Nor can actors and actresses compete against themselves. Should two different performances by the same person receive enough votes for a nomination, only one will be accepted.

For several years it was possible for a film to be eligible for both Documentary Short Subject and Short Subject–Live Action, but when *Sentinels of Silence* won the 1971 Oscars in *both* categories the rule was changed to allow a film to compete in *either* but not both classifications. The choice is left to the producer of the film.

One cannot, it appears, refuse Academy recognition. Actor George C. Scott declined his 1970 Best Actor nomination for *Patton,* just as he had done in 1961 for a Supporting Actor nomination in *The Hustler.* Daniel Taradash, president of the Academy, tersely explained that it was Scott's *performance,* not Scott, that was involved and that the nomination would stand. It did, and Scott won. Two years later Marlon Brando refused his Best Actor award won for *The Godfather* on the grounds that Hollywood had not treated the American Indian fairly in its pictures. Neither Scott nor Brando's action was without precedent, since Dudley Nichols had previously refused a 1935 Oscar for writing *The Informer.* Despite such refusals, all men are still listed as winners.

Oscars have occasionally been awarded to persons who have died before their achievement can be recognized. The most recent posthumous award went to Peter Finch, named Best Actor for his 1976 role in *Network,* but the tradition goes all the way back to the first awards ceremony when an honorable mention for Title Writing was presented to Gerald Duffy who had died some months before. Due to unusual circumstances, composer Raymond Rasch didn't win his Oscar until eight years after he died. Rasch, Larry Russell (who had also died before winning the award), and Charlie Chaplin had collaborated on the musical score of Chaplin's 1952 film *Limelight.* The film was never released in the Los Angeles area until 1972 when it qualified for and won the award for Best Original Dramatic Score.

Price Waterhouse and Company, the firm of certified public accountants which had first worked with the Academy during the 1933 bank moratorium salary crisis, began counting Oscar ballots in 1936, the year a preferential system of voting was begun:

> Under the preferential system of voting, each member has one vote, which may be expressed in several alternate choices, in the order of his preference. If his first choice agrees with that of a sufficient majority, that achievement becomes one of the nominations. However, should his first choice be in the minority, his vote is applied to his second choice, or his third, and so on until the voter has helped to select one of the achievements. In this way, the entire voting group has a voice in the ultimate selections. Voters are not obligated to list more choices than they really have, but if only one choice is expressed, and it is in the minority, the ballot becomes void and cannot help in the selection of another achievement.

For the first twelve years of the Academy Awards, the final results of the balloting were released to the press prior to the ceremony to accommodate newspaper deadlines, but when one paper broke the pledge not to print the winners' names until after the ceremony the practice of advance notice ended. With the 1940

L to R: Director George Roy Hill, Liza Minnelli, screenwriter David Ward, Elizabeth Taylor, producers Michael Phillips, Julia Phillips, and Tony Bill. Liza and Liz were both presenters; the others were all winners for *The Sting* (1973). © 1978 A.M.P.A.S.

Awards came sealed envelopes and secrecy. The names of *all* winners were withheld until the actual awards presentation from 1940 to 1955. Since 1956 (29th Awards) the Honorary, Scientific or Technical, Hersholt, and Thalberg Award winners have been announced in advance, but the names of all other winners remain secret until the presentation.

The Academy Award statuette was designed in 1928 by MGM Art Director Cedric Gibbons. Once his sketches (which, contrary to the popular myth, were not first drawn on the tablecloth during an Academy banquet) were approved by the Academy Board, Los Angeles sculptor George Stanley created the trophy. The figure represents a knight holding a crusader's sword standing on a reel of film whose spokes represent the five original branches of the Academy—Actors, Directors, Producers, Technicians, and Writers. The nickname Oscar dates from the early 1930s, and several people, including Margaret Herrick (then the Academy's librarian, later Executive Director), actress Bette Davis, and Hollywood columnist Sidney Skolsky, have claimed credit for the nickname. Verification of who really named Oscar isn't possible, so the Academy supports Herrick's claim. The Oscar is thirteen and a half inches tall and weighs eight and a half pounds. It is made of britannium and is gold plated. The statuettes have been numbered since 1949 (starting with #501).

The Awards were first televised in 1953, and for five years (1953–57) the Academy staged simultaneous ceremonies in Los Angeles and New York. Here, Claudette Colbert (right) in New York presents the 1955 Oscar for Documentary Feature to Nancy Hamilton. © *1978 A.M.P.A.S.*

Academy Awards may take several forms. Recipients of all Annual Awards, Class I Scientific or Technical Awards, Special Achievement Awards, and the Jean Hersholt Humanitarian Awards receive the Oscar statuette. Class II Scientific winners receive a plaque, and the Class III winners a certificate. The Irving G. Thalberg Memorial Award is a bronze head of Thalberg. Honorary Awards may be a statuette, scroll, life membership, or any design ordered by the Board of Governors. Walt Disney, for example, received one large statuette and seven miniatures for *Snow White and the Seven Dwarfs,* and Edgar Bergen got a wooden statuette when honored for the creation of Charlie McCarthy. On the eleven occasions when an Honorary Juvenile Award was given, the winner received a miniature statuette. All nominees receive Certificates of Nomination.

World War II produced one temporary change in the Oscar: plaster statuettes were awarded in 1942, 1943, and 1944 when all metals were needed for the war effort. These ersatz Oscars were replaced by the genuine metal ones after the war. Another tradition, however, ended permanently during World War II. The Academy banquet, a yearly event since the first organizational dinner in 1927, was discontinued in 1944. A banquet seemed inappropriate during wartime, especially in a country that was rationing its food, and, more practically, the crowds had grown too large to be comfortably accommodated at a dinner.

After alternating between the Ambassador and Biltmore Hotels for several years, the awards ceremony switched to a theater setting in 1944 when the banquet was discontinued. After three years at Grauman's Chinese Theatre, two at the Shrine Auditorium, and one at the Academy's own Academy Awards Theatre, the Oscar ceremony settled in for eleven straight years at RKO's Pantages Theatre. In 1961 (33rd year) the ceremony moved to the Santa Monica Civic Auditorium where it remained until 1969 when it switched to its present site, the Dorothy Chandler Pavilion at the Los Angeles County Music Center.

The publicity achieved through radio and television has helped immeasurably to popularize the Oscar and the people who win them. The first awards drew little coverage, but the second awards caused enough interest to prompt Los Angeles radio station KNX to broadcast an hour of the ceremonies. The entire ceremony was broadcast for the first time in 1945 over the ABC network and the Armed Forces Radio Service. Such exposure may be one reason why the Academy has frequently asked a comedian to host the presentations. Will Rogers and humorist Irvin S. Cobb were among the hosts during the first decade of awards, and since World War II Bob Hope has served as emcee more than a dozen times.

The Academy had always depended upon the Hollywood studios to underwrite the cost of the awards presentations, but in 1949 the studios announced the end of their financial support. Some said the pullout was due to the British film *Hamlet* being named Best Picture in 1948, but *Newsweek* reported that the decision had been reached months before the 1948 winners were announced. By the early 1950s the Academy faced a financial crisis but ironically was rescued by television, a medium then regarded with great suspicion by Hollywood. RCA Victor agreed to sponsor the 1952 Awards which NBC would televise for the first time. *Life* magazine noted wryly that television "bought the rights to the ceremony for $100,000, used it for a one-and-a-half-hour show which presumably kept millions of TV-viewers from going to the movies that night." Despite criticisms that the awards had been tainted by commercialism, the marriage of Oscar and television was successful, and *Variety* headlined "1st MAJOR PIX-TV WEDDING BIG CLICK." The national TV hookup allowed the Academy to experiment with simultaneous ceremonies in Los Angeles and New York; viewers would be switched back and forth according to which city the winner was in. For five years, 1953 through 1957, this practice of holding presentations on both coasts was continued. The Oscar ceremonies were telecast in color for the first time in 1966 (by ABC); radio broadcasts were dropped in favor of television coverage only in 1969.

In its first fifty years the Academy of Motion Picture Arts and Sciences has grown from thirty-six founders (see Appendix I) to an organization of over four thousand members. Of this total, over thirty-four hundred are active members and six hundred are associate (non-voting) members. Dues for all are $100.00 a year. The Academy has always been an honorary organization. Membership is by invitation only, and proposed members must be sponsored by two members of the branch which they will join.

LISTING BY
ACADEMY AWARD
CATEGORIES

(1927–1977)

BEST PICTURE

The Best Picture is one of the original categories established for the 1927/28 awards. Only three times, in 1928/29, 1931/32, and 1935, has the film named Best Picture failed to win any other awards. *Ben Hur,* named Best Picture in 1959, holds the record for the most awards with eleven Oscars out of twelve nominations. *West Side Story* (1961) with ten awards and *Gigi* (1958) with nine are the closest runners-up. *All About Eve* (1950) holds the record for the most nominations with fourteen.

The Best Picture award is the only category where the nominations are voted by the entire Academy membership.

1927/28   First Year
THE LAST COMMAND, Paramount
THE RACKET, Caddo, Paramount
SEVENTH HEAVEN, Fox
THE WAY OF ALL FLESH, Paramount
WINGS, Paramount

1928/29   Second Year
ALIBI, Feature Prod., UA
BROADWAY MELODY, Metro-Goldwyn-Mayer
HOLLYWOOD REVUE, Metro-Goldwyn-Mayer
IN OLD ARIZONA, Fox
THE PATRIOT, Paramount

1929/30   Third Year
ALL QUIET ON THE WESTERN FRONT, Universal
THE BIG HOUSE, Metro-Goldwyn-Mayer
DISRAELI, Warner Bros.
THE DIVORCEE, Metro-Goldwyn-Mayer
THE LOVE PARADE, Paramount

1930/31   Fourth Year
CIMARRON, RKO Radio
EAST LYNNE, Fox
THE FRONT PAGE, Caddo, UA
SKIPPY, Paramount
TRADER HORN, Metro-Goldwyn-Mayer
LARGE CAPITAL LETTERS DENOTE WINNER

1931/32   Fifth Year
ARROWSMITH, Goldwyn, UA
BAD GIRL, Fox
THE CHAMP, Metro-Goldwyn-Mayer
FIVE STAR FINAL, First National
GRAND HOTEL, Metro-Goldwyn-Mayer
ONE HOUR WITH YOU, Paramount
SHANGHAI EXPRESS, Paramount
SMILING LIEUTENANT, Paramount

1932/33   Sixth Year
CAVALCADE, Fox
A FAREWELL TO ARMS, Paramount
FORTY-SECOND STREET, Warner Bros.
I AM A FUGITIVE FROM A CHAIN GANG, Warner Bros.
LADY FOR A DAY, Columbia
LITTLE WOMEN, RKO Radio
THE PRIVATE LIFE OF HENRY VIII, London Films, UA (British)
SHE DONE HIM WRONG, Paramount
SMILIN' THRU, Metro-Goldwyn-Mayer
STATE FAIR, Fox

1934   Seventh Year
THE BARRETTS OF WIMPOLE STREET, Metro-Goldwyn-Mayer
CLEOPATRA, Paramount
FLIRTATION WALK, First National
THE GAY DIVORCEE, RKO Radio
HERE COMES THE NAVY, Warner Bros.

L to R: Charles "Buddy" Rogers, Clara Bow, and Richard Arlen starred in *Wings* (1927), the first film to win the award for Best Picture. *Paramount Photo*

THE HOUSE OF ROTHSCHILD, 20th Century, UA

IMITATION OF LIFE, Universal

IT HAPPENED ONE NIGHT, Columbia

ONE NIGHT OF LOVE, Columbia

THE THIN MAN, Metro-Goldwyn-Mayer

VIVA VILLA, Metro-Goldwyn-Mayer

THE WHITE PARADE, Fox

1935   Eighth Year

ALICE ADAMS, RKO Radio

BROADWAY MELODY OF 1936, Metro-Goldwyn-Mayer

CAPTAIN BLOOD, Warner Bros.-Cosmopolitan

DAVID COOPERFIELD, Metro-Goldwyn-Mayer

THE INFORMER, RKO Radio

LES MISERABLES, 20th Century, UA

LIVES OF A BENGAL LANCER, Paramount

A MIDSUMMER NIGHT'S DREAM, Warner Bros.

MUTINY ON THE BOUNTY, Metro-Goldwyn-Mayer

NAUGHTY MARIETTA, Metro-Goldwyn-Mayer

RUGGLES OF RED GAP, Paramount

TOP HAT, RKO Radio

1936   Ninth Year

ANTHONY ADVERSE, Warner Bros.

DODSWORTH, Goldwyn, UA

THE GREAT ZIEGFELD, Metro-Goldwyn-Mayer

LIBELED LADY, Metro-Goldwyn-Mayer

MR. DEEDS GOES TO TOWN, Columbia

ROMEO AND JULIET, Metro-Goldwyn-Mayer

30

SAN FRANCISCO, Metro-Goldwyn-Mayer
THE STORY OF LOUIS PASTEUR, Warner Bros.
A TALE OF TWO CITIES, Metro-Goldwyn-Mayer
THREE SMART GIRLS, Universal

1937   Tenth Year

THE AWFUL TRUTH, Columbia
CAPTAINS COURAGEOUS, Metro-Goldwyn-Mayer
DEAD END, Goldwyn, UA
THE GOOD EARTH, Metro-Goldwyn-Mayer
IN OLD CHICAGO, 20th Century-Fox
THE LIFE OF EMILE ZOLA, Warner Bros.
LOST HORIZON, Columbia
ONE HUNDRED MEN AND A GIRL, Universal
STAGE DOOR, RKO Radio
A STAR IS BORN, Selznick International, UA

1938   Eleventh Year

THE ADVENTURES OF ROBIN HOOD, Warner Bros.
ALEXANDER'S RAGTIME BAND, 20th Century-Fox
BOYS TOWN, Metro-Goldwyn-Mayer
THE CITADEL, Metro-Goldwyn-Mayer (British)
FOUR DAUGHTERS, Warner Bros.-First National
GRAND ILLUSION, R.A.O., World Pictures (French)
JEZEBEL, Warner Bros.
PYGMALION, Metro-Goldwyn-Mayer (British)
TEST PILOT, Metro-Goldwyn-Mayer
YOU CAN'T TAKE IT WITH YOU, Columbia

1939   Twelfth Year

DARK VICTORY, Warner Bros.
GONE WITH THE WIND, Selznick, M-G-M

GOODBYE, MR. CHIPS, Metro-Goldwyn-Mayer (British)
LOVE AFFAIR, RKO Radio
MR. SMITH GOES TO WASHINGTON, Columbia
NINOTCHKA, Metro-Goldwyn-Mayer
OF MICE AND MEN, Roach, UA
STAGECOACH, Wanger, UA
WIZARD OF OZ, Metro-Goldwyn-Mayer
WUTHERING HEIGHTS, Goldwyn, UA

1940   Thirteenth Year

ALL THIS, AND HEAVEN TOO, Warner Bros.
FOREIGN CORRESPONDENT, Wanger, UA
THE GRAPES OF WRATH, 20th Century-Fox
THE GREAT DICTATOR, Chaplin, UA
KITTY FOYLE, RKO Radio
THE LETTER, Warner Bros.
THE LONG VOYAGE HOME, Argosy-Wanger, UA
OUR TOWN, Lesser, UA
THE PHILADELPHIA STORY, Metro-Goldwyn-Mayer
REBECCA, Selznick International, UA

1941   Fourteenth Year

BLOSSOMS IN THE DUST, Metro-Goldwyn-Mayer
CITIZEN KANE, Mercury, RKO Radio
HERE COMES MR. JORDAN, Columbia
HOLD BACK THE DAWN, Paramount
HOW GREEN WAS MY VALLEY, 20th Century-Fox
THE LITTLE FOXES, Goldwyn, RKO Radio
THE MALTESE FALCON, Warner Bros.
ONE FOOT IN HEAVEN, Warner Bros.
SERGEANT YORK, Warner Bros.
SUSPICION, RKO Radio

1942   Fifteenth Year

THE INVADERS, Ortus, Columbia (British)
KINGS ROW, Warner Bros.

THE MAGNIFICENT AMBERSONS, Mercury, RKO Radio
MRS. MINIVER, Metro-Goldwyn-Mayer
THE PIED PIPER, 20th Century-Fox
THE PRIDE OF THE YANKEES, Goldwyn, RKO Radio
RANDOM HARVEST, Metro-Goldwyn-Mayer
THE TALK OF THE TOWN, Columbia
WAKE ISLAND, Paramount
YANKEE DOODLE DANDY, Warner Bros.

1943   Sixteenth Year
CASABLANCA, Warner Bros.
FOR WHOM THE BELL TOLLS, Paramount
HEAVEN CAN WAIT, 20th Century-Fox
THE HUMAN COMEDY, Metro-Goldwyn-Mayer
IN WHICH WE SERVE, Two Cities, UA (British)
MADAME CURIE, Metro-Goldwyn-Mayer
THE MORE THE MERRIER, Columbia
THE OX-BOW INCIDENT, 20th Century-Fox
THE SONG OF BERNADETTE, 20th Century-Fox
WATCH ON THE RHINE, Warner Bros.

1944   Seventeenth Year
DOUBLE INDEMNITY, Paramount
GASLIGHT, Metro-Goldwyn-Mayer
GOING MY WAY, Paramount
SINCE YOU WENT AWAY, Selznick International, UA
WILSON, 20th Century-Fox

1945   Eighteenth Year
ANCHORS AWEIGH, Metro-Goldwyn-Mayer
THE BELLS OF ST. MARY'S, Rainbow, RKO Radio
THE LOST WEEKEND, Paramount
MILDRED PIERCE, Warner Bros.
SPELLBOUND, Selznick International, UA

1946   Nineteenth Year
THE BEST YEARS OF OUR LIVES, Goldwyn, RKO Radio
HENRY V, Rank-Two-Cities, UA (British)
IT'S A WONDERFUL LIFE, Liberty, RKO Radio
THE RAZOR'S EDGE, 20th Century-Fox
THE YEARLING, Metro-Goldwyn-Mayer

1947   Twentieth Year
THE BISHOP'S WIFE, Goldwyn, RKO Radio
CROSSFIRE, RKO Radio
GENTLEMAN'S AGREEMENT, 20th Century-Fox
GREAT EXPECTATIONS, Rank-Cineguild, U-I (British)
MIRACLE ON 34TH STREET, 20th Century-Fox

1948   Twenty-first Year
HAMLET, Rank-Two Cities, U-I (British)
JOHNNY BELINDA, Warner Bros.
THE RED SHOES, Rank-Archers, Eagle-Lion (British)
THE SNAKE PIT, 20th Century-Fox
TREASURE OF SIERRA MADRE, Warner Bros.

1949   Twenty-second Year
ALL THE KING'S MEN, Rossen, Columbia
BATTLEGROUND, Metro-Goldwyn-Mayer
THE HEIRESS, Paramount
A LETTER TO THREE WIVES, 20th Century-Fox
TWELVE O'CLOCK HIGH, 20th Century-Fox

1950   Twenty-third Year
ALL ABOUT EVE, 20th Century-Fox
BORN YESTERDAY, Columbia
FATHER OF THE BRIDE, Metro-Goldwyn-Mayer

KING SOLOMON'S MINES, Metro-
Goldwyn-Mayer
SUNSET BOULEVARD, Paramount

1951 Twenty-fourth Year
AN AMERICAN IN PARIS, Metro-
Goldwyn-Mayer. Arthur Freed, Pro-
ducer
DECISION BEFORE DAWN, 20th Century-
Fox. Anatole Litvak & Frank Mc-
Carthy, Producers
A PLACE IN THE SUN, Paramount.
George Stevens, Producer
QUO VADIS, Metro-Goldwyn-Mayer.
Sam Zimbalist, Producer
A STREETCAR NAMED DESIRE, Charles
K. Feldman Group Prods., Warner
Bros. Charles K. Feldman, Producer

1952 Twenty-fifth Year
THE GREATEST SHOW ON
EARTH, Cecil B. DeMille, Para-
mount. Cecil B. DeMille, Producer
HIGH NOON, Stanley Kramer Prods.,
UA. Stanley Kramer, Producer
IVANHOE, Metro-Goldwyn-Mayer. Pan-
dro S. Berman, Producer
MOULIN ROUGE, Romulus Films, UA
THE QUIET MAN, Argosy Pictures
Corp., Republic. John Ford and
Merian C. Cooper, Producers

1953 Twenty-sixth Year
FROM HERE TO ETERNITY, Colum-
bia. Buddy Adler, Producer
JULIUS CAESAR, Metro-Goldwyn-
Mayer. John Houseman, Producer
THE ROBE, 20th Century-Fox. Frank
Ross, Producer
ROMAN HOLIDAY, Paramount. William
Wyler, Producer
SHANE, Paramount. George Stevens,
Producer.

1954 Twenty-seventh Year
THE CAINE MUTINY, A Stanley Kramer
Prod., Columbia. Stanley Kramer,
Producer

THE COUNTRY GIRL, Perlberg-Seaton,
Paramount. William Perlberg, Pro-
ducer
ON THE WATERFRONT, Horizon-
American Corp., Columbia. Sam
Spiegel, Producer
SEVEN BRIDES FOR SEVEN BROTHERS,
Metro-Goldwyn-Mayer. Jack Cum-
mings, Producer
THREE COINS IN THE FOUNTAIN, 20th
Century-Fox. Sol C. Siegel, Pro-
ducer

1955 Twenty-eighth Year
LOVE IS A MANY-SPLENDORED THING,
20th Century-Fox. Buddy Adler,
Producer
MARTY, Hecht and Lancaster's Ste-
ven Prods., UA. Harold Hecht, Pro-
ducer
MISTER ROBERTS, An Orange Prod.,
Warner Bros. Leland Hayward, Pro-
ducer
PICNIC, Columbia. Fred Kohlmar, Pro-
ducer
THE ROSE TATTOO, Hal Wallis, Para-
mount. Hal B. Wallis, Producer

1956 Twenty-ninth Year
AROUND THE WORLD IN 80
DAYS, The Michael Todd Co., Inc.,
UA. Michael Todd, Producer
FRIENDLY PERSUASION Allied Artists.
William Wyler, Producer
GIANT, Giant Prod., Warner Bros.,
George Stevens & Henry Ginsberg,
Producers
THE KING AND I, 20th Century-Fox.
Charles Brackett, Producer
THE TEN COMMANDMENTS, Motion Pic-
ture Assocs., Inc., Paramount. Cecil
B. DeMille, Producer

1957 Thirtieth Year
THE BRIDGE ON THE RIVER
KWAI, A Horizon Picture, Colum-
bia. Sam Spiegel, Producer

From the MGM release *Ben Hur* (1959) which won a record eleven awards, including Best Picture, out of twelve nominations. © *1959 Loews Incorporated*

PEYTON PLACE, Jerry Wald Prods., Inc., 20th Century-Fox. Jerry Wald, Producer

SAYONARA, William Goetz, Prod., Warner Bros. William Goetz, Producer

12 ANGRY MEN, Orion-Nova Prod., UA. Henry Fonda & Reginald Rose, Producers

WITNESS FOR THE PROSECUTION, Edward Small-Arthur Hornblow Prod., UA. Arthur Hornblow, Jr., Producer

1958 Thirty-first Year

AUNTIE MAME, Warner Bros.

CAT ON A HOT TIN ROOF, Avon Prods., Inc. M-G-M, Lawrence Weingarten, Producer

THE DEFIANT ONES, Stanley Kramer, UA. Stanley Kramer, Producer

GIGI, Arthur Freed Prods., Inc., M-G-M. Arthur Freed, Producer

SEPARATE TABLES, Clifton Prods., Inc., UA. Harold Hecht, Producer

1959 Thirty-second Year

ANATOMY OF A MURDER, Otto Preminger, Columbia. Otto Preminger, Producer

BEN-HUR, Metro-Goldwyn-Mayer. Sam Zimbalist, Producer

THE DIARY OF ANNE FRANK, 20th Century-Fox. George Stevens, Producer

THE NUN'S STORY, Warner Bros. Henry Blanke, Producer

ROOM AT THE TOP, Romulus Films, Ltd., Continental Distr., Inc., (British). John & James Woolf, Producers.

1960 Thirty-third Year

THE ALAMO, Batjac Prod., UA. John Wayne, Producer

THE APARTMENT, The Mirisch Co., Inc., UA. Billy Wilder, Producer

ELMER GANTRY, Burt Lancaster-Richard Brooks Prod., UA. Bernard Smith, Producer

SONS AND LOVERS, Company of Artists, Inc., 20th Century-Fox. Jerry Wald, Producer

THE SUNDOWNERS, Warner Bros. Fred Zinnemann, Producer

1961   Thirty-fourth Year

FANNY, Mansfield Prod., Warner Bros. Joshua Logan, Producer

THE GUNS OF NAVARONE, Carl Foreman Prod., Columbia. Carl Foreman, Producer

THE HUSTLER, Robert Rossen Prod., 20th Century-Fox. Robert Rossen, Producer

JUDGMENT AT NUREMBERG, Stanley Kramer Prod., UA. Stanley Kramer, Producer

WEST SIDE STORY, Mirisch Pictures, Inc. and B and P Enterprises, Inc., UA. Robert Wise, Producer

1962   Thirty-fifth Year

LAWRENCE OF ARABIA, Horizon Pictures (G.B.), Ltd.-Sam Spiegel-David Lean Prod., Columbia. Sam Spiegel, Producer

THE LONGEST DAY, Darryl F. Zanuck Prod., 20th Century-Fox. Darryl F. Zanuck, Producer

Meredith Willson's THE MUSIC MAN, Warner Bros. Morton Da Costa, Producer

MUTINY ON THE BOUNTY, Arcola Prod., M-G-M. Aaron Rosenberg, Producer

TO KILL A MOCKINGBIRD, Universal-International-Pakula-Mulligan-Brentwood Prod., U-I. Alan J. Pakula, Producer

1963   Thirty-sixth Year

AMERICA AMERICA, Athena Enterprises Prod., Warner Bros. Elia Kazan, Producer

CLEOPATRA, 20th Century-Fox Ltd.,-MCL Films S.A.-WALWA Films

S.A. Prod., 20th Century-Fox. Walter Wanger, Producer

HOW THE WEST WAS WON, Metro-Goldwyn-Mayer & Cinerama. Bernard Smith, Producer

LILIES OF THE FIELD, Rainbow Prod., UA. Ralph Nelson, Producer

TOM JONES, Woodfall Prod., UA-Lopert Pictures. Tony Richardson, Producer

1964   Thirty-seventh Year

BECKET, Hal Wallis Prod., Paramount. Hal B. Wallis, Producer

DR. STRANGELOVE OR: HOW I LEARNED TO STOP WORRYING AND LOVE THE BOMB, Hawk Films, Ltd. Prod., Columbia. Stanley Kubrick, Producer

MARY POPPINS, Walt Disney Prods. Walt Disney and Bill Walsh, Producers

MY FAIR LADY, Warner Bros. Jack L. Warner, Producer

ZORBA THE GREEK, Rochley, Ltd. Prod., International Classics. Michael Cacoyannis, Producer

1965   Thirty-eighth Year

DARLING, Anglo-Amalgamated,Ltd. Prod., Embassy. Joseph Janni, Producer

DOCTOR ZHIVAGO, Sostar S.A.-Metro-Goldwyn-Mayer British Studios, Ltd. Prod., M-G-M. Carlo Ponti, Producer

SHIP OF FOOLS, Columbia. Stanley Kramer, Producer

THE SOUND OF MUSIC, Argyle Enterprises Prod., 20th Century-Fox. Robert Wise, Producer

A THOUSAND CLOWNS, Harrell Prod., United Artists. Fred Coe, Producer

1966   Thirty-ninth Year

ALFIE, Sheldrake Films, Ltd. Prod., Paramount. Lewis Gilbert, Producer

A MAN FOR ALL SEASONS, Highland Films, Ltd. Prod., Columbia. Fred Zinnemann, Producer

THE RUSSIANS ARE COMING THE RUSSIANS ARE COMING, Mirisch Corp. of Delaware Prod., U.A. Norman Jewison, Producer

THE SAND PEBBLES, Argyle-Solar Prod., 20th Century-Fox. Robert Wise, Producer

WHO'S AFRAID OF VIRGINIA WOOLF?, Chenault Prod., Warner Bros. Ernest Lehman, Producer

1967   Fortieth Year

BONNIE AND CLYDE, Tatira-Hiller Prod., Warner Bros.-Seven Arts. Warren Beatty, Producer

DOCTOR DOLITTLE, Apjac Prods., 20th Century-Fox. Arthur P. Jacobs, Producer

THE GRADUATE, Mike Nichols-Lawrence Turman Prod., Embassy. Lawrence Turman, Producer

GUESS WHO'S COMING TO DINNER, Columbia. Stanley Kramer, Producer

IN THE HEAT OF THE NIGHT, Mirisch Corp. Prod., United Artists. Walter Mirisch, Producer

1968   Forty-first Year

The Franco Zeffirelli production of ROMEO & JULIET, B.H.E. Film-Verona Prod.-Dino De Laurentiis Cinematografica Prod., Paramount. Anthony Havelock-Allan and John Brabourne, Producers

FUNNY GIRL, Rastar Prods., Columbia. Ray Stark, Producer

THE LION IN WINTER, Haworth Prods., Avco Embassy. Martin Poll, Producer

OLIVER!, Romulus Films, Columbia. John Woolf, Producer

RACHEL, RACHEL, Kayos Prod., Warner Bros.-Seven Arts. Paul Newman, Producer

1969   Forty-second Year

ANNE OF THE THOUSAND DAYS, Hal B. Wallis-Universal Pictures, Ltd. Production, Universal. Hal B. Wallis, Producer

BUTCH CASSIDY AND THE SUNDANCE KID, George Roy Hill-Paul Monash Prod., 20th Century-Fox. John Foreman, Producer

HELLO, DOLLY!, Chenault Productions, 20th Century-Fox. Ernest Lehman, Producer

MIDNIGHT COWBOY, Jerome Hellman-John Schlesinger Production. United Artists. Jerome Hellman, Producer

Z, Reggane Films-O.N.C.I.C. Production, Cinema V. Jacques Perrin and Hamed Rachedi, Producers

1970   Forty-third Year

AIRPORT, Ross-Hunter-Universal Prod., Universal. Ross Hunter, Producer

FIVE EASY PIECES, BBS Prods., Columbia. Bob Rafelson and Richard Wechsler, Producers

LOVE STORY, The Love Story Company Prod., Paramount. Howard G. Minsky, Producer

M*A*S*H, Aspen Prods., 20th Century-Fox. Ingo Preminger, Producer

PATTON, 20th Century-Fox. Frank McCarthy, Producer

1971   Forty-fourth Year

A CLOCKWORK ORANGE, A Hawks Films, Ltd. Prod., Warner Bros. Stanley Kubrick, Producer

FIDDLER ON THE ROOF, Mirisch-Cartier Prods., UA. Norman Jewison, Producer

THE FRENCH CONNECTION, A Philip D'Antoni Prod. in association with Schine-Moore Prods., 20th Century-Fox. Philip D'Antoni, Producer

The Corleone family in 1972's Best Picture *The Godfather*. L to R: Al Pacino, Best Actor Marlon Brando, James Caan, and John Cazale. *Paramount Photo*

THE LAST PICTURE SHOW, BBS Prods., Columbia. Stephen J. Friedman, Producer

NICHOLAS AND ALEXANDRA, A Horizon Pictures Prod., Columbia. Sam Spiegel, Producer

1972   Forty-fifth Year

CABARET, An ABC Pictures Production, Allied Artists. Cy Feuer, Producer

DELIVERANCE, Warner Bros. John Boorman, Producer

THE EMIGRANTS, A Svensk Filmindustri Production, Warner Bros. Bengt Furslund, Producer

THE GODFATHER, An Albert S. Ruddy Production, Paramount. Albert S. Ruddy, Producer

SOUNDER, Radnitz/Mattel Productions, 20th Century-Fox. Robert B. Radnitz, Producer

1973   Forty-sixth Year

AMERICAN GRAFFITI, A Universal-Lucasfilm, Ltd.-Coppola Company Prod., Universal. Francis Ford Coppola, Producer. Gary Kurtz, Co-Producer

CRIES AND WHISPERS, A Svenka Filminstitutet-Cinematograph AB Prod., New World Pictures. Ingmar Bergman, Producer

THE EXORCIST, Hoya Prods., Warner Bros. William Peter Blatty, Producer

THE STING, A Universal-Bill/Phillips-George Roy Hill Film Prod., Zanuck/Brown Presentation, Universal. Tony Bill, Michael and Julia Phillips, Producers

A TOUCH OF CLASS, Brut Prods., Avco Embassy. Melvin Frank, Producer

1974   Forty-seventh Year

CHINATOWN, A Robert Evans Production, Paramount. Robert Evans, Producer

THE CONVERSATION, A Directors Company Production, Paramount. Francis Ford Coppola, Producer. Fred Roos, Co-Producer

THE GODFATHER PART II, A Coppola Company Production, Paramount. Francis Ford Coppola, Producer. Gray Frederickson and Fred Roos, Co-Producers

LENNY, A Marvin Worth Production, United Artists. Marvin Worth, Producer

THE TOWERING INFERNO, An Irwin Allen Production, 20th Century-Fox/Warner Bros. Irwin Allen, Producer

1975   Forty-eighth Year

BARRY LYNDON, A Hawk Films, Ltd. Production, Warner Bros. Stanley Kubrick Producer

DOG DAY AFTERNOON, Warner Bros. Martin Bregman and Martin Elfand, Producers

JAWS, A Universal-Zanuck/Brown Production, Universal. Richard D. Zanuck and David Brown, Producers

NASHVILLE, An ABC Entertainment-Jerry Weintraub-Robert Altman Production, Paramount. Robert Altman, Producer

ONE FLEW OVER THE CUCKOO'S NEST, A Fantasy Films Production, United Artists. Saul Zaentz and Michael Douglas, Producers

1976   Forty-ninth Year

ALL THE PRESIDENT'S MEN, A Wildwood Enterprises Production, Warner Bros. Walter Coblenz, Producer

BOUND FOR GLORY, The Bound For Glory Company Production, United Artists. Robert F. Blumofe and Harold Leventhal, Producers

NETWORK, A Howard Gottfried/Paddy Chayefsky Production, Metro-Goldwyn-Mayer/United Artists. Howard Gottfried, Producer

ROCKY, A Robert Chartoff-Irwin Winkler Production, United Artists. Irwin Winkler and Robert Chartoff, Producers

TAXI DRIVER, A Bill/Phillips Production of a Martin Scorsese Film, Columbia Pictures. Michael Phillips and Julia Phillips, Producers

1977   Fiftieth Year

ANNIE HALL, Jack Rollins-Charles H. Joffe Productions, United Artists. Charles H. Joffe, Producer

THE GOODBYE GIRL, A Ray Stark Production, Metro-Goldwyn-Mayer/Warner Bros. Ray Stark, Producer

JULIA, A Twentieth Century-Fox Production, Twentieth Century-Fox. Richard Roth, Producer

STAR WARS, A Twentieth Century-Fox Production, Twentieth Century-Fox. Gary Kurtz, Producer

THE TURNING POINT, Hera Productions, Twentieth Century-Fox. Herbert Ross and Arthur Laurents, Producers

ACTOR

When nominations for the first acting awards were solicited in 1928, Academy members were asked to name the actor and actress who "gave the best performance in acting, with special reference to character portrayal and effectiveness of dramatic or comedy rendition." Emil Jannings won the first Actor award, effectively demonstrating that one need not be an Academy member or even an American to win.

Four actors have won the award twice: Spencer Tracy (1937, 1938), Fredric March (1931/32, 1946), Gary Cooper (1941, 1952), and Marlon Brando (1954, 1972). Tracy has the highest number of Best Actor nominations with nine, followed by Laurence Olivier with eight and Brando with seven. A tie occurred during the fifth year of competition. Wallace Beery came within a vote of Fredric March, and, in those days before an independent accounting firm tabulated the votes, when a nominee came within three votes of another a tie was declared. In 1944 Barry Fitzgerald was nominated for Best Actor and Best Supporting Actor for the same performance. The rules now prevent this, though an actor may still be nominated in both categories for two different roles. The present rules also limit an actor to one nomination per category.

Achievements in this category are nominated by members of the Academy Actors Branch who decide individually at the time of balloting whether a role is a lead or support.

1927/28   First Year
RICHARD BARTHELMESS in *The Noose*, First National
RICHARD BARTHELMESS in *The Patent Leather Kid*, First National
CHARLES CHAPLIN in *The Circus*, Chaplin, UA
EMIL JANNINGS in *The Last Command*, Paramount
EMIL JANNINGS in *The Way of All Flesh*, Paramount

1928/29   Second Year
GEORGE BANCROFT in *Thunderbolt*, Paramount
WARNER BAXTER in *In Old Arizona*, Fox
CHESTER MORRIS in *Alibi*, UA

LARGE CAPITAL LETTERS DENOTE WINNER

PAUL MUNI in *The Valiant*, Fox
LEWIS STONE in *The Patriot*, Paramount

1929/30   Third Year
GEORGE ARLISS in *Disraeli*, Warner Bros.
GEORGE ARLISS in *The Green Goddess*, Warner Bros.
WALLACE BEERY in *The Big House*, Metro-Goldwyn-Mayer
MAURICE CHEVALIER in *The Love Parade*, Paramount
MAURICE CHEVALIER in *The Big Pond*, Paramount
RONALD COLMAN in *Bulldog Drummond*, Goldwyn, UA
RONALD COLMAN in *Condemned*, Goldwyn, UA
LAWRENCE TIBBETT in *The Rogue Song*, Metro-Goldwyn-Mayer

A stately D. W. Griffith (right) presents the 1935 Oscars for Best Actor and Actress to Victor Mc-Laglen (*The Informer*) and Bette Davis (*Dangerous*). © *1978 A.M.P.A.S.*

1930/31 Fourth Year

LIONEL BARRYMORE in *A Free Soul*, Metro-Goldwyn-Mayer

JACKIE COOPER in *Skippy*, Paramount

RICHARD DIX in *Cimarron*, RKO Radio

FREDRIC MARCH in *The Royal Family Of Broadway*, Paramount

ADOLPHE MENJOU in *The Front Page*, Caddo, UA

1931/32 Fifth Year

WALLACE BEERY in *The Champ*, Metro-Goldwyn-Mayer

ALFRED LUNT in *The Guardsman*, Metro-Goldwyn-Mayer

FREDRIC MARCH in *Dr. Jekyll And Mr. Hyde*, Paramount

1932/33 Sixth Year

LESLIE HOWARD in *Berkeley Square*, Fox

CHARLES LAUGHTON in *The Private Life Of Henry VIII*, London Films, UA. (British)

PAUL MUNI in *I Am A Fugitive From A Chain Gang*, Warner Bros.

1934 Seventh Year

CLARK GABLE in *It Happened One Night*, Columbia

FRANK MORGAN in *Affairs Of Cellini*, 20th Century, UA

WILLIAM POWELL in *The Thin Man*, Metro-Goldwyn-Mayer

1935 Eighth Year

CLARK GABLE in *Mutiny On The Bounty*, Metro-Goldwyn-Mayer

CHARLES LAUGHTON in *Mutiny On The Bounty*, Metro-Goldwyn-Mayer

VICTOR McLAGLEN in *The Informer*, RKO Radio

FRANCHOT TONE in *Mutiny On The Bounty*, Metro-Goldwyn-Mayer

1936   Ninth Year

GARY COOPER in *Mr. Deeds Goes To Town*, Columbia

WALTER HUSTON in *Dodsworth*, Goldwyn, UA

PAUL MUNI in *The Story Of Louis Pasteur*, Warner Bros.

WILLIAM POWELL in *My Man Godfrey*, Universal

SPENCER TRACY in *San Francisco*, Metro-Goldwyn-Mayer

1937   Tenth Year

CHARLES BOYER in *Conquest*, Metro-Goldwyn-Mayer

FREDRIC MARCH in *A Star Is Born*, Selznick, UA

ROBERT MONTGOMERY in *Night Must Fall*, Metro-Goldwyn-Mayer

PAUL MUNI in *The Life Of Emile Zola*, Warner Bros.

SPENCER TRACY in *Captains Courageous*, Metro-Goldwyn-Mayer

1938   Eleventh Year

CHARLES BOYER in *Algiers*, Wanger, UA

JAMES CAGNEY in *Angels With Dirty Faces*, Warner Bros.

ROBERT DONAT in *The Citadel*, Metro-Goldwyn-Mayer. (British)

LESLIE HOWARD in *Pygmalion*, Metro-Goldwyn-Mayer. (British)

SPENCER TRACY in *Boys Town*, Metro-Goldwyn-Mayer

1939   Twelfth Year

ROBERT DONAT in *Goodbye, Mr. Chips*, Metro-Goldwyn-Mayer. (British)

CLARK GABLE in *Gone With The Wind*, Selznick, M-G-M

LAURENCE OLIVIER in *Wuthering Heights*, Goldwyn, UA

MICKEY ROONEY in *Babes In Arms*, Metro-Goldwyn-Mayer

JAMES STEWART in *Mr. Smith Goes To Washington*, Columbia

1940   Thirteenth Year

CHARLES CHAPLIN in *The Great Dictator*, Chaplin, UA

HENRY FONDA in *The Grapes Of Wrath*, 20th Century-Fox

RAYMOND MASSEY in *Abe Lincoln In Illinois*, RKO Radio

LAURENCE OLIVIER in *Rebecca*, Selznick-UA

JAMES STEWART in *The Philadelphia Story*, Metro-Goldwyn-Mayer

1941   Fourteenth Year

GARY COOPER in *Sergeant York*, Warner Bros.

CARY GRANT in *Penny Serenade*, Columbia

WALTER HUSTON in *All That Money Can Buy*, RKO Radio

ROBERT MONTGOMERY in *Here Comes Mr. Jordan*, Columbia

ORSON WELLES in *Citizen Kane*, Mercury, RKO Radio

1942   Fifteenth Year

JAMES CAGNEY in *Yankee Doodle Dandy*, Warner Bros.

RONALD COLMAN in *Random Harvest*, Metro-Goldwyn-Mayer

GARY COOPER in *The Pride Of The Yankees*, Goldwyn, RKO Radio

WALTER PIDGEON in *Mrs. Miniver*, Metro-Goldwyn-Mayer

MONTY WOOLLEY in *The Pied Piper*, 20th Century-Fox

1943   Sixteenth Year

HUMPHREY BOGART in *Casablanca*, Warner Bros.

GARY COOPER in *For Whom The Bell Tolls*, Paramount

PAUL LUKAS in *Watch On The Rhine*, Warner Bros.

WALTER PIDGEON in *Madame Curie*, Metro-Goldwyn-Mayer

MICKEY ROONEY in *The Human Comedy*, Metro-Goldwyn-Mayer

1944   Seventeenth Year

CHARLES BOYER in *Gaslight*, Metro-Goldwyn-Mayer

BING CROSBY in *Going My Way*, Paramount

BARRY FITZGERALD in *Going My Way*, Paramount

CARY GRANT in *None But The Lonely Heart*, RKO Radio

ALEXANDER KNOX in *Wilson*, 20th Century-Fox

1945   Eighteenth Year

BING CROSBY in *The Bells Of St. Mary's*, Rainbow, RKO Radio

GENE KELLY in *Anchors Aweigh*, Metro-Goldwyn-Mayer

RAY MILLAND in *The Lost Weekend*, Paramount

GREGORY PECK in *The Keys Of The Kingdom*, 20th Century-Fox

CORNEL WILDE in *A Song To Remember*, Columbia

1946   Nineteenth Year

FREDRIC MARCH in *The Best Years Of Our Lives*, Goldwyn, RKO Radio

LAURENCE OLIVIER in *Henry V*, J. Arthur Rank-Two Cities, UA. (British)

LARRY PARKS in *The Jolson Story*, Columbia

GREGORY PECK in *The Yearling*, Metro-Goldwyn-Mayer

JAMES STEWART in *It's A Wonderful Life*, Liberty Films, RKO Radio

1947   Twentieth Year

RONALD COLMAN in *A Double Life*, Kanin, U-I

JOHN GARFIELD in *Body And Soul*, Enterprise, UA

GREGORY PECK in *Gentleman's Agreement*, 20th Century-Fox

WILLIAM POWELL in *Life With Father*, Warner Bros.

MICHAEL REDGRAVE in *Mourning Becomes Electra*, RKO Radio

1948   Twenty-first Year

LEW AYRES in *Johnny Belinda*, Warner Bros.

MONTGOMERY CLIFT in *The Search*, Praesens Films, M-G-M. (Swiss)

DAN DAILEY in *When My Baby Smiles At Me*, 20th Century-Fox

LAURENCE OLIVIER in *Hamlet*, J. Arthur Rank-Two Cities, U-I. (British)

CLIFTON WEBB in *Sitting Pretty*, 20th Century-Fox

1949   Twenty-second Year

BRODERICK CRAWFORD in *All The King's Men*, Robert Rossen, Columbia

KIRK DOUGLAS in *Champion*, Screen Plays Corp., UA

GREGORY PECK in *Twelve O'Clock High*, 20th Century-Fox

RICHARD TODD in *The Hasty Heart*, Warner Bros.

JOHN WAYNE in *Sands Of Iwo Jima*, Republic

1950   Twenty-third Year

LOUIS CALHERN in *The Magnificent Yankee*, Metro-Goldwyn-Mayer

JOSE FERRER in *Cyrano De Bergerac*, Stanley Kramer, UA

WILLIAM HOLDEN in *Sunset Boulevard*, Paramount

JAMES STEWART in *Harvey*, Universal-International

SPENCER TRACY in *Father Of The Bride*, Metro-Goldwyn-Mayer

1951   Twenty-fourth Year
HUMPHREY BOGART in *The African Queen*, Horizon, UA
MARLON BRANDO in *A Streetcar Named Desire*, Charles K. Feldman Group Prods., Warner Bros.
MONTGOMERY CLIFT in *A Place In The Sun*, Paramount
ARTHUR KENNEDY in *Bright Victory*, Universal-International
FREDRIC MARCH in *Death Of A Salesman*, Stanley Kramer, Columbia

1952   Twenty-fifth Year
MARLON BRANDO in *Viva Zapata!*, 20th Century-Fox
GARY COOPER in *High Noon*, Stanley Kramer, UA
KIRK DOUGLAS in *The Bad And The Beautiful*, Metro-Goldwyn-Mayer
JOSE FERRER in *Moulin Rouge,* Romulus Films, UA
ALEC GUINNESS in *The Lavender Hill Mob*, J. Arthur Rank Presentation-Ealing Studios, U-I. (British)

1953   Twenty-sixth Year
MARLON BRANDO in *Julius Caesar*, Metro-Goldwyn-Mayer
RICHARD BURTON in *The Robe*, 20th Century-Fox
MONTGOMERY CLIFT in *From Here To Eternity*, Columbia
WILLIAM HOLDEN in *Stalag 17*, Paramount
BURT LANCASTER in *From Here To Eternity*, Columbia

1954   Twenty-seventh Year
HUMPHREY BOGART in *The Caine Mutiny*, Kramer, Columbia
MARLON BRANDO in *On The Waterfront*, Horizon-American, Columbia
BING CROSBY in *The Country Girl*, Perlberg-Seaton, Paramount

JAMES MASON in *A Star Is Born*, Transcona, Warner Bros.
DAN O'HERLIHY in *Adventures Of Robinson Crusoe*, Dancigers-Ehrlich, UA

1955   Twenty-eighth Year
ERNEST BORGNINE in *Marty*, Hecht & Lancaster's Steven Prods., UA
JAMES CAGNEY in *Love Me Or Leave Me*, Metro-Goldwyn-Mayer
JAMES DEAN in *East Of Eden*, Warner Bros.
FRANK SINATRA in *The Man With The Golden Arm*, Preminger, UA
SPENCER TRACY in *Bad Day At Black Rock*, Metro-Goldwyn-Mayer

1956   Twenty-ninth Year
YUL BRYNNER in *The King And I*, 20th Century-Fox
JAMES DEAN in *Giant*, Giant Prod., Warner Bros.
KIRK DOUGLAS in *Lust For Life*, Metro-Goldwyn-Mayer
ROCK HUDSON in *Giant*, Giant Prod., Warner Bros.
SIR LAURENCE OLIVIER in *Richard III*, Laurence Olivier Prod., Lopert Films Dist. Corp. (British)

1957   Thirtieth Year
MARLON BRANDO in *Sayonara*, William Goetz Prod., Warner Bros.
ANTHONY FRANCIOSA in *A Hatful Of Rain*, 20th Century-Fox
ALEC GUINNESS in *The Bridge On The River Kwai*, A Horizon Picture, Columbia
CHARLES LAUGHTON in *Witness For The Prosecution*, Edward Small-Arthur Hornblow Prod., UA
ANTHONY QUINN in *Wild Is The Wind*, A Hal Wallis Prod., Paramount

1958   Thirty-first Year
TONY CURTIS in *The Defiant Ones*, Stanley Kramer, UA

PAUL NEWMAN in *Cat On A Hot Tin Roof*, Avon Prods., Inc., M-G-M
DAVID NIVEN in *Separate Tables*, Clifton Prods., Inc., UA
SIDNEY POITIER in *The Defiant Ones*, Stanley Kramer, UA
SPENCER TRACY in *The Old Man And The Sea*, Leland Hayward, Warner Bros.

1959   Thirty-second Year
LAURENCE HARVEY in *Room At The Top*, Romulus Films, Ltd., Continental Dist., Inc. (British)
CHARLTON HESTON in *Ben-Hur*, Metro-Goldwyn-Mayer
JACK LEMMON in *Some Like It Hot*, Ashton Prods. & The Mirisch Co., UA
PAUL MUNI in *The Last Angry Man*, Fred Kohlmar Prods., Columbia
JAMES STEWART in *Anatomy Of A Murder*, Otto Preminger, Columbia

1960   Thirty-third Year
TREVOR HOWARD in *Sons And Lovers*, Company of Artists, Inc., 20th Century-Fox
BURT LANCASTER in *Elmer Gantry*, Burt Lancaster-Richard Brooks Prod., UA
JACK LEMMON in *The Apartment*, The Mirisch Company, Inc., UA
LAURENCE OLIVIER in *The Entertainer*, Woodfall Prod., Continental Dist., Inc. (British)
SPENCER TRACY in *Inherit The Wind*, Stanley Kramer, UA

1961   Thirty-fourth Year
CHARLES BOYER in *Fanny*, Mansfield Prod., Warner Bros.
PAUL NEWMAN in *The Hustler*, Robert Rossen Prod., 20th Century-Fox
MAXIMILIAN SCHELL in *Judgment At Nuremberg*, Stanley Kramer Prod., UA

SPENCER TRACY in *Judgment At Nuremberg*, Stanley Kramer Prod., UA
STUART WHITMAN in *The Mark*, Raymond Stross-Sidney Buchman Prod., Continental Dist., Inc. (British)

1962   Thirty-fifth Year
BURT LANCASTER in *Bird Man Of Alcatraz*, Harold Hecht Prod., UA
JACK LEMMON in *Days Of Wine And Roses*, Martin Manulis-Jalem Prod., Warner Bros.
MARCELLO MASTROIANNI in *Divorce-Italian Style*, Lux-Vides-Galatea Film Prod., Embassy Pictures
PETER O'TOOLE in *Lawrence Of Arabia*, Horizon Pictures (G.B.), Ltd.-Sam Spiegel-David Lean Prod., Columbia
GREGORY PECK in *To Kill A Mockingbird*, Universal-International-Pakula-Mulligan-Brentwood Prod., U-I

1963   Thirty-sixth Year
ALBERT FINNEY in *Tom Jones*, Woodfall Prod., UA-Lopert Pictures
RICHARD HARRIS in *This Sporting Life*, Julian Wintle-Leslie Parkyn Prod., Walter Reade-Sterling-Continental Dist.
REX HARRISON in *Cleopatra*, 20th Century-Fox Ltd.-MCL Films S.A.-WALWA Films S.A. Prod., 20th Century-Fox
PAUL NEWMAN in *Hud*, Salem-Dover Prod., Paramount
SIDNEY POITIER in *Lilies Of The Field*, Rainbow Prod., UA

1964   Thirty-seventh Year
RICHARD BURTON in *Becket*, Hal Wallis Prod., Paramount
REX HARRISON in *My Fair Lady*, Warner Bros.
PETER O'TOOLE in *Becket*, Hal Wallis Prod., Paramount
ANTHONY QUINN in *Zorba The Greek*,

Rochley, Ltd. Prod., International Classics

PETER SELLERS in *Dr. Strangelove Or: How I Learned To Stop Worrying And Love The Bomb*, Hawk Films, Ltd. Prod., Columbia

1965   Thirty-eighth Year

RICHARD BURTON in *The Spy Who Came In From The Cold*, Salem Films, Ltd. Prod., Paramount

LEE MARVIN in *Cat Ballou*, Harold Hecht Prod., Columbia

LAURENCE OLIVIER in *Othello*, B.H.E. Prod., Warner Bros.

ROD STEIGER in *The Pawnbroker*, Ely Landau Prod., American Intl.

OSKAR WERNER in *Ship Of Fools*, Columbia

1966   Thirty-ninth Year

ALAN ARKIN in *The Russians Are Coming The Russians Are Coming*, Mirisch Corp. of Delaware Prod., UA

RICHARD BURTON in *Who's Afraid Of Virginia Woolf?*, Chenault Prod., Warner Bros.

MICHAEL CAINE in *Alfie*, Sheldrake Films, Ltd. Prod., Paramount

STEVE MC QUEEN in *The Sand Pebbles*, Argyle-Solar Prod., 20th Century-Fox

PAUL SCOFIELD in *A Man For All Seasons*, Highland Films, Ltd. Prod., Columbia

1967   Fortieth Year

WARREN BEATTY in *Bonnie And Clyde*, Tatira-Hiller Prod., Warner Bros.-Seven Arts

DUSTIN HOFFMAN in *The Graduate*, Mike Nichols-Lawrence Turman Prod., Embassy

PAUL NEWMAN in *Cool Hand Luke*, Jalem Prod., Warner Bros.-Seven Arts

ROD STEIGER in *In The Heat Of The Night*, Mirisch Corp. Prod., United Artists

SPENCER TRACY in *Guess Who's Coming To Dinner*, Columbia

1968   Forty-first Year

ALAN ARKIN in *The Heart Is A Lonely Hunter*, Warner Bros.-Seven Arts

ALAN BATES in *The Fixer*, John Frankenheimer-Edward Lewis Prods., Metro-Goldwyn-Mayer

RON MOODY in *Oliver!*, Romulus Films, Ltd., Columbia

PETER O'TOOLE in *The Lion In Winter*, Haworth Prods., Ltd., Avco Embassy

CLIFF ROBERTSON in *Charly*, American Broadcasting Companies-Selmur Pictures Prod., Cinerama

1969   Forty-second Year

RICHARD BURTON in *Anne Of The Thousand Days*, Hal B. Wallis-Universal Pictures, Ltd. Prod., Universal

DUSTIN HOFFMAN in *Midnight Cowboy*, Jerome Hellman-John Schlesinger Prod., United Artists

PETER O'TOOLE in *Goodbye, Mr. Chips*, APJAC Prod., Metro-Goldwyn-Mayer

JON VOIGHT in *Midnight Cowboy*, Jerome Hellman-John Schlesinger Prod., United Artists

JOHN WAYNE in *True Grit*, Hal Wallis Prod., Paramount

1970   Forty-third Year

MELVYN DOUGLAS in *I Never Sang For My Father*, Jamel Prods., Columbia

JAMES EARL JONES in *The Great White Hope*, Lawrence Turman Films Prod., 20th Century-Fox

JACK NICHOLSON in *Five Easy Pieces*, BBS Prods., Columbia

RYAN O'NEAL in *Love Story*, The Love Story Company Prod., Paramount

GEORGE C. SCOTT in *Patton*, 20th Century-Fox

1971 Forty-fourth Year

PETER FINCH in *Sunday Bloody Sunday*, A Joseph Janni Prod., UA

GENE HACKMAN in *The French Connection*, A Philip D'Antoni Prod. in association with Schine-Moore Prods., 20th Century-Fox

WALTER MATTHAU in *Kotch*, A Kotch Company Prod., ABC Pictures Presentation, Cinerama

GEORGE C. SCOTT in *The Hospital*, A Howard Gottfried-Paddy Chayefsky Prod. in association with Arthur Hiller, UA

TOPOL in *Fiddler On The Roof*, A Mirisch-Cartier Prod., UA

1972 Forty-fifth Year

MARLON BRANDO in *The Godfather*, An Albert S. Ruddy Production, Paramount

MICHAEL CAINE in *Sleuth*, A Palomar Pictures International Production, 20th Century-Fox

LAURENCE OLIVIER in *Sleuth*, A Palomar Pictures International Production, 20th Century-Fox

PETER O'TOOLE in *The Ruling Class*, A Keep Films, Ltd. Production, Avco Embassy

PAUL WINFIELD in *Sounder*, Radnitz/Mattel Productions, 20th Century-Fox

1973 Forty-sixth Year

MARLON BRANDO in *Last Tango In Paris*, A PEA Produzioni Europee Associate S.A.S.-Les Productions Artistes Associes S.A. Prod., UA

JACK LEMMON in *Save The Tiger*, Filmways-Jalem-Cirandinha Prods., Paramount

JACK NICHOLSON in *The Last Detail*, An Acrobat Films Prod., Columbia

AL PACINO in *Serpico*, A Produzioni De Laurentiis International Manufacturing Company S.p.A. Prod., Paramount

ROBERT REDFORD in *The Sting*, A Universal-Bill/Phillips-George Roy Hill Film Production, Zanuck/Brown Presentation, Universal

1974 Forty-seventh Year

ART CARNEY in *Harry And Tonto*, 20th Century-Fox

ALBERT FINNEY in *Murder On The Orient Express*, A G.W. Films, Ltd. Production, Paramount

DUSTIN HOFFMAN in *Lenny*, A Marvin Worth Production, United Artists

JACK NICHOLSON in *Chinatown*, A Robert Evans Production, Paramount

AL PACINO in *The Godfather Part II*, A Coppola Company Production, Paramount

1975 Forty-eighth Year

WALTER MATTHAU in *The Sunshine Boys*, A Ray Stark Production, Metro-Goldwyn-Mayer

JACK NICHOLSON in *One Flew Over The Cuckoo's Nest*, A Fantasy Films Production, United Artists

AL PACINO in *Dog Day Afternoon*, Warner Bros.

MAXIMILIAN SCHELL in *The Man In The Glass Booth*, An Ely Landau Organization Production, AFT Distributing

JAMES WHITMORE in *Give 'em Hell, Harry!*, A Theatrovision Production, Avco Embassy

1976 Forty-ninth Year

ROBERT DE NIRO in *Taxi Driver*, A Bill/Phillips Production of a Martin Scorsese Film, Columbia Pictures

PETER FINCH in *Network*, A Howard Gottfried/Paddy Chayefsky Production, Metro-Goldwyn-Mayer/United Artists

Oscar winners Louise Fletcher and Jack Nicholson in *One Flew Over the Cuckoo's Nest* (1975). Not since *It Happened One Night* (1934) had a single film won the Picture, Actor, Actress, Directing and Writing awards. *United Artists Photo*

GIANCARLO GIANNINI in *Seven Beauties,* A Medusa Distribuzione Production, Cinema 5, Ltd.

WILLIAM HOLDEN in *Network,* A Howard Gottfried/Paddy Chayefsky Production, Metro-Goldwyn-Mayer/United Artists

SYLVESTER STALLONE in *Rocky,* A Robert Chartoff-Irwin Winkler Production, United Artists

1977 Fiftieth Year

WOODY ALLEN in *Annie Hall,* Jack Rollins-Charles H. Joffe Productions, United Artists

RICHARD BURTON in *Equus,* A Winkast Company, Ltd./P.B., Ltd. Production, United Artists

RICHARD DREYFUSS in *The Goodbye Girl,* A Ray Stark Production, Metro-Goldwyn-Mayer/Warner Bros.

MARCELLO MASTROIANNI in *A Special Day,* A Canafox Films Production, Cinema 5, Ltd.

JOHN TRAVOLTA in *Saturday Night Fever,* A Robert Stigwood Production, Paramount

ACTRESS

The rules governing actors also apply to the Best Actress category. A tie for Best Actress occurred in 1968, but, unlike the 1931/32 tie between actors, the rules now required Katharine Hepburn and Barbra Streisand to compile identical vote totals. It was Hepburn's third Oscar in this category (1932/33, 1967, 1968). Seven actresses have won twice: Luise Rainer (1936, 1937), Bette Davis (1935, 1938), Vivien Leigh (1939, 1951), Olivia De Havilland (1946, 1949), Ingrid Bergman (1944, 1956, plus a 1974 Supporting Actress award), Elizabeth Taylor (1960, 1966), and Glenda Jackson (1970, 1973). The most nominated actresses are Katharine Hepburn with eleven, Bette Davis with ten, and Greer Garson with seven nominations.

Achievements in this category are nominated by members of the Academy Actors Branch who decide individually at the time of balloting whether a role is a lead or support.

1927/28   First Year

LOUISE DRESSER in *A Ship Comes In*, Pathe-RKO Radio
JANET GAYNOR in *Seventh Heaven*, Fox
JANET GAYNOR in *Street Angel*, Fox
JANET GAYNOR in *Sunrise*, Fox
GLORIA SWANSON in *Sadie Thompson*, United Artists

1928/29   Second Year

RUTH CHATTERTON in *Madame X*, Metro-Goldwyn-Mayer
BETTY COMPSON in *The Barker*, First National
JEANNE EAGELS in *The Letter*, Paramount
BESSIE LOVE in *The Broadway Melody*, Metro-Goldwyn-Mayer
MARY PICKFORD in *Coquette*, Pickford, UA

1929/30   Third Year

NANCY CARROLL in *The Devil's Holiday*, Paramount

LARGE CAPITAL LETTERS DENOTE WINNER

RUTH CHATTERTON in *Sarah And Son*, Paramount
GRETA GARBO in *Anna Christie*, Metro-Goldwyn-Mayer
GRETA GARBO in *Romance*, Metro-Goldwyn-Mayer
NORMA SHEARER in *The Divorcee*, Metro-Goldwyn-Mayer
NORMA SHEARER in *Their Own Desire*, Metro-Goldwyn-Mayer
GLORIA SWANSON in *The Trespasser*, Kennedy, UA

1930/31   Fourth Year

MARLENE DIETRICH in *Morocco*, Paramount
MARIE DRESSLER in *Min And Bill*, Metro-Goldwyn-Mayer
IRENE DUNNE in *Cimarron*, RKO Radio
ANN HARDING in *Holiday*, RKO Pathe
NORMA SHEARER in *A Free Soul*, Metro-Goldwyn-Mayer

1931/32   Fifth Year

MARIE DRESSLER in *Emma*, Metro-Goldwyn-Mayer

LYNN FONTANNE in *The Guardsman*, Metro-Goldwyn-Mayer

HELEN HAYES in *The Sin of Madelon Claudet*, Metro-Goldwyn-Mayer

1932/33   Sixth Year

KATHARINE HEPBURN in *Morning Glory*, RKO Radio

MAY ROBSON in *Lady For A Day*, Columbia

DIANA WYNYARD in *Cavalcade*, Fox

1934   Seventh Year

CLAUDETTE COLBERT in *It Happened One Night*, Columbia

GRACE MOORE in *One Night of Love*, Columbia

NORMA SHEARER in *The Barretts Of Wimpole Street*, Metro-Goldwyn-Mayer

1935   Eighth Year

ELISABETH BERGNER in *Escape Me Never*, British & Dominions, UA (British)

CLAUDETTE COLBERT in *Private Worlds*, Paramount

BETTE DAVIS in *Dangerous*, Warner Bros.

KATHARINE HEPBURN in *Alice Adams*, RKO Radio

MIRIAM HOPKINS in *Becky Sharp*, Pioneer, RKO Radio

MERLE OBERON in *The Dark Angel*, Goldwyn, UA

1936   Ninth Year

IRENE DUNNE in *Theodora Goes Wild*, Columbia

GLADYS GEORGE in *Valiant Is The Word For Carrie*, Paramount

CAROLE LOMBARD in *My Man Godfrey*, Universal

LUISE RAINER in *The Great Ziegfeld*, Metro-Goldwyn-Mayer

NORMA SHEARER in *Romeo And Juliet*, Metro-Goldwyn-Mayer

1937   Tenth Year

IRENE DUNNE in *The Awful Truth*, Columbia

GRETA GARBO in *Camille*, Metro-Goldwyn-Mayer

JANET GAYNOR in *A Star Is Born*, Selznick, UA

LUISE RAINER in *The Good Earth*, Metro-Goldwyn-Mayer

BARBARA STANWYCK in *Stella Dallas*, Goldwyn, UA

1938   Eleventh Year

FAY BAINTER in *White Banners*, Warner Bros.

BETTE DAVIS in *Jezebel*, Warner Bros.

WENDY HILLER in *Pygmalion*, Metro-Goldwyn-Mayer. (British)

NORMA SHEARER in *Marie Antoinette*, Metro-Goldwyn-Mayer

MARGARET SULLAVAN in *Three Comrades*, Metro-Goldwyn-Mayer

1939   Twelfth Year

BETTE DAVIS in *Dark Victory*, Warner Bros.

IRENE DUNNE in *Love Affair*, RKO Radio

GRETA GARBO in *Ninotchka*, Metro-Goldwyn-Mayer

GREER GARSON in *Goodbye, Mr. Chips*, Metro-Goldwyn-Mayer. (British)

VIVIEN LEIGH in *Gone With The Wind*, Selznick, M-G-M

1940   Thirteenth Year

BETTE DAVIS in *The Letter*, Warner Bros.

JOAN FONTAINE in *Rebecca*, Selznick, UA

KATHARINE HEPBURN in *The Philadelphia Story*, Metro-Goldwyn-Mayer

GINGER ROGERS in *Kitty Foyle*, RKO Radio

MARTHA SCOTT in *Our Town*, Lesser, UA

Vivien Leigh and Hattie McDaniel won the Actress and Supporting Actress Oscars for their memorable performances in *Gone With the Wind* (1939). *From the MGM release* Gone With the Wind © *1939 Selznick International Pictures, Inc. Copyright renewed 1963 by Metro-Goldwyn-Mayer, Inc.*

1941   Fourteenth Year

BETTE DAVIS in *The Little Foxes*, Goldwyn, RKO Radio

OLIVIA DE HAVILLAND in *Hold Back The Dawn*, Paramount

JOAN FONTAINE in *Suspicion*, RKO Radio

GREER GARSON in *Blossoms In The Dust*, Metro-Goldwyn-Mayer

BARBARA STANWYCK in *Ball Of Fire*, Goldwyn, RKO Radio

1942   Fifteenth Year

BETTE DAVIS in *Now, Voyager*, Warner Bros.

GREER GARSON in *Mrs. Miniver*, Metro-Goldwyn-Mayer

KATHARINE HEPBURN in *Woman Of The Year*, Metro-Goldwyn-Mayer

ROSALIND RUSSELL in *My Sister Eileen*, Columbia

TERESA WRIGHT in *The Pride Of The Yankees*, Goldwyn, RKO Radio

1943   Sixteenth Year

JEAN ARTHUR in *The More The Merrier*, Columbia

INGRID BERGMAN in *For Whom The Bell Tolls*, Paramount

JOAN FONTAINE in *The Constant Nymph*, Warner Bros.

GREER GARSON in *Madame Curie*, Metro-Goldwyn-Mayer

JENNIFER JONES in *The Song Of Bernadette*, 20th Century-Fox

Sibling rivalry: sisters Joan Fontaine (left) and Olivia De Havilland wish each other luck as they compete for the 1941 Best Actress Award. Fontaine won for *Suspicion*. © 1978 A.M.P.A.S.

1944   Seventeenth Year
INGRID BERGMAN in *Gaslight*,
  Metro-Goldwyn-Mayer
CLAUDETTE COLBERT in *Since You
  Went Away*, Selznick, UA
BETTE DAVIS in *Mr. Skeffington*,
  Warner Bros.
GREER GARSON in *Mrs. Parkington*,
  Metro-Goldwyn-Mayer
BARBARA STANWYCK in *Double Indemnity*, Paramount

1945   Eighteenth Year
INGRID BERGMAN in *The Bells Of St.
  Mary's*, Rainbow, RKO Radio
JOAN CRAWFORD in *Mildred
  Pierce*, Warner Bros.
GREER GARSON in *The Valley Of Decision*, Metro-Goldwyn-Mayer
JENNIFER JONES in *Love Letters*, Wallis, Paramount
GENE TIERNEY in *Leave Her To
  Heaven*, 20th Century-Fox

1946   Nineteenth Year
OLIVIA DE HAVILLAND in *To Each
  His Own*, Paramount
CELIA JOHNSON in *Brief Encounter*,
  Rank, U-I. (British)
JENNIFER JONES in *Duel In The Sun*,
  Selznick International
ROSALIND RUSSELL in *Sister Kenny*,
  RKO Radio
JANE WYMAN in *The Yearling*, Metro-Goldwyn-Mayer

1947   Twentieth Year
JOAN CRAWFORD in *Possessed*, Warner
  Bros.
SUSAN HAYWARD in *Smash Up—The
  Story Of A Woman*, Wanger, U-I
DOROTHY MCGUIRE in *Gentleman's
  Agreement*, 20th Century-Fox
ROSALIND RUSSELL in *Mourning Becomes Electra*, RKO Radio
LORETTA YOUNG in *The Farmer's
  Daughter*, RKO Radio

1948   Twenty-first Year
INGRID BERGMAN in *Joan Of Arc*,
  Sierra, RKO Radio
OLIVIA DE HAVILLAND in *The Snake
  Pit*, 20th Century-Fox
IRENE DUNNE in *I Remember Mama*,
  RKO Radio
BARBARA STANWYCK in *Sorry, Wrong
  Number*, Wallis, Paramount
JANE WYMAN in *Johnny Belinda*,
  Warner Bros.

1949   Twenty-second Year
JEANNE CRAIN in *Pinky*, 20th Century-Fox
OLIVIA DE HAVILLAND in *The
  Heiress*, Paramount
SUSAN HAYWARD in *My Foolish Heart*,
  Goldwyn, RKO Radio
DEBORAH KERR in *Edward, My Son*,
  Metro-Goldwyn-Mayer
LORETTA YOUNG in *Come To The Stable*, 20th Century-Fox

1950   Twenty-third Year
ANNE BAXTER in *All About Eve*, 20th
  Century-Fox
BETTE DAVIS in *All About Eve*, 20th
  Century-Fox
JUDY HOLLIDAY in *Born Yesterday*,
  Columbia
ELEANOR PARKER in *Caged*, Warner
  Bros.
GLORIA SWANSON in *Sunset Boulevard*,
  Paramount

1951   Twenty-fourth Year
KATHARINE HEPBURN in *The African
  Queen*, Horizon, UA
VIVIEN LEIGH in *A Streetcar Named
  Desire*, Charles K. Feldman Group
  Prods., Warner Bros.
ELEANOR PARKER in *Detective Story*,
  Paramount
SHELLEY WINTERS in *A Place In The
  Sun*, Paramount

52

JANE WYMAN in *The Blue Veil*, Wald-Krasna, RKO Radio

1952   Twenty-fifth Year

SHIRLEY BOOTH in *Come Back, Little Sheba*, Hal Wallis, Paramount

JOAN CRAWFORD in *Sudden Fear*, Joseph Kaufman Prods., RKO Radio

BETTE DAVIS in *The Star*, Bert E. Friedlob, 20th Century-Fox

JULIE HARRIS in *The Member Of The Wedding*, Stanley Kramer, Columbia

SUSAN HAYWARD in *With A Song In My Heart*, 20th Century-Fox

1953   Twenty-sixth Year

LESLIE CARON in *Lili*, Metro-Goldwyn-Mayer

AVA GARDNER in *Mogambo*, Metro-Goldwyn-Mayer

AUDREY HEPBURN in *Roman Holiday*, Paramount

DEBORAH KERR in *From Here To Eternity*, Columbia

MAGGIE MCNAMARA in *The Moon Is Blue*, Preminger-Herbert, UA

1954   Twenty-seventh Year

DOROTHY DANDRIDGE in *Carmen Jones*, Otto Preminger, 20th Century-Fox

JUDY GARLAND in *A Star Is Born*, Transcona, Warner Bros.

AUDREY HEPBURN in *Sabrina*, Paramount

GRACE KELLY in *The Country Girl*, Perlberg-Seaton, Paramount

JANE WYMAN in *The Magnificent Obsession*, Universal-International

1955   Twenty-eighth Year

SUSAN HAYWARD in *I'll Cry Tomorrow*, Metro-Goldwyn-Mayer

KATHARINE HEPBURN in *Summertime*, Ilya Lopert-David Lean, UA.(Anglo-American)

JENNIFER JONES in *Love Is A Many-Splendored Thing*, 20th Century-Fox

ANNA MAGNANI in *The Rose Tattoo*, Hal B. Wallis, Paramount

ELEANOR PARKER in *Interrupted Melody*, Metro-Goldwyn-Mayer

1956   Twenty-ninth Year

CARROLL BAKER in *Baby Doll*, A Newtown Prod., Warner Bros.

INGRID BERGMAN in *Anastasia*, 20th Century-Fox

KATHARINE HEPBURN in *The Rainmaker*, Hal Wallis Prods., Paramount

NANCY KELLY in *The Bad Seed*, Warner Bros.

DEBORAH KERR in *The King And I*, 20th Century-Fox

1957   Thirtieth Year

DEBORAH KERR in *Heaven Knows, Mr. Allison*, 20th Century-Fox

ANNA MAGNANI in *Wild Is The Wind*, Hal Wallis Prod., Paramount

ELIZABETH TAYLOR in *Raintree County*, Metro-Goldwyn-Mayer

LANA TURNER in *Peyton Place*, Jerry Wald Prods. Inc., 20th Century-Fox

JOANNE WOODWARD in *The Three Faces Of Eve*, 20th Century-Fox

1958   Thirty-first Year

SUSAN HAYWARD in *I Want To Live!*, Figaro, Inc., UA

DEBORAH KERR in *Separate Tables*, Clifton Prods., Inc., UA

SHIRLEY MACLAINE in *Some Came Running*, Sol C. Siegel Prods., Inc., M-G-M

ROSALIND RUSSELL in *Auntie Mame*, Warner Bros.

ELIZABETH TAYLOR in *Cat On A Hot Tin Roof*, Avon Prods., Inc., M-G-M

1959   Thirty-second Year

DORIS DAY in *Pillow Talk*, Arwin Prods., Inc., U-I

AUDREY HEPBURN in *The Nun's Story*, Warner Bros.

KATHARINE HEPBURN in *Suddenly, Last Summer*, Horizon Prod., Columbia

SIMONE SIGNORET in *Room At The Top*, Romulus Films, Ltd., Continental Dist., Inc. (British)

ELIZABETH TAYLOR in *Suddenly, Last Summer*, Horizon Prod., Columbia

1960   Thirty-third Year

GREER GARSON in *Sunrise At Campobello*, Schary Prod., Warner Bros.

DEBORAH KERR in *The Sundowners*, Warner Bros.

SHIRLEY MACLAINE in *The Apartment*, The Mirisch Co., Inc., UA

MELINA MERCOURI in *Never On Sunday*, Melinafilm Prod., Lopert Pictures Corp. (Greek)

ELIZABETH TAYLOR in *Butterfield 8*, Afton-Linebrook Prod., M-G-M

1961   Thirty-fourth Year

AUDREY HEPBURN in *Breakfast At Tiffany's*, Jurow-Shepherd Prod., Paramount

PIPER LAURIE in *The Hustler*, Robert Rossen Prod., 20th Century-Fox

SOPHIA LOREN in *Two Women*, Champion-Les Films Marceau-Cocinor and Société Generale de Cinematographie Prod., Embassy Pictures Corp. (Italo-French)

GERALDINE PAGE in *Summer And Smoke*, Hal Wallis Prod., Paramount

NATALIE WOOD in *Splendor In The Grass*, NBI Prod., Warner Bros.

1962   Thirty-fifth Year

ANNE BANCROFT in *The Miracle Worker*, Playfilms Prod., UA

BETTE DAVIS in *What Ever Happened To Baby Jane?*, Seven Arts-Associates & Aldrich Co. Prod., Warner Bros.

KATHARINE HEPBURN in *Long Day's Journey Into Night*, Ely Landau Prods., Embassy Pictures

GERALDINE PAGE in *Sweet Bird of Youth*, Roxbury Prod., M-G-M

LEE REMICK in *Days Of Wine And Roses*, Martin Manulis-Jalem Prod., Warner Bros.

1963   Thirty-sixth Year

LESLIE CARON in *The L-Shaped Room*, Romulus Prods., Ltd., Columbia

SHIRLEY MACLAINE in *Irma La Douce*, Mirisch-Phalanx Prod., UA

PATRICIA NEAL in *Hud*, Salem-Dover Prod., Paramount

RACHEL ROBERTS in *This Sporting Life*, Julian Wintle-Leslie Parkyn Prod., Walter Reade-Sterling-Continental Dist.

NATALIE WOOD in *Love With The Proper Stranger*, Boardwalk-Rona Prod., Paramount

1964   Thirty-seventh Year

JULIE ANDREWS in *Mary Poppins*, Walt Disney Prods.

ANNE BANCROFT in *The Pumpkin Eater*, Romulus Films, Ltd. Prod., Royal Films International

SOPHIA LOREN in *Marriage Italian Style*, Champion-Concordia Prod., Embassy Pictures

DEBBIE REYNOLDS in *The Unsinkable Molly Brown*, Marten Prod., M-G-M

KIM STANLEY in *Seance On A Wet Afternoon*, Richard Attenborough-Bryan Forbes Prod., Artixo Prods., Ltd.

1965   Thirty-eighth Year

JULIE ANDREWS in *The Sound Of Music*, Argyle Enterprises Prod., 20th Century-Fox

JULIE CHRISTIE in *Darling*, Anglo-Amalgamated, Ltd. Prod., Embassy

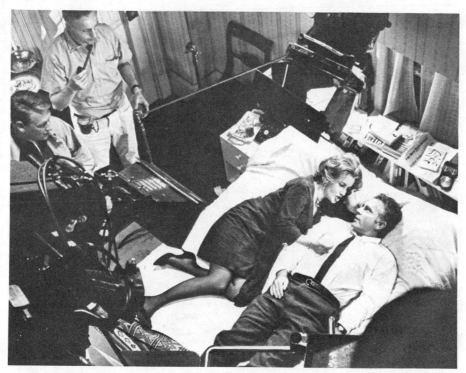

L to R: Director Mike Nichols, cinematographer Haskell Wexler, Elizabeth Taylor, and Richard Burton on the set of *Who's Afraid of Virginia Woolf?* (1966). Wexler and Taylor won Oscars for their work. *American Cinematographer Photo*

SAMANTHA EGGAR in *The Collector*, The Collector Company, Columbia

ELIZABETH HARTMAN in *A Patch Of Blue*, Pandro S. Berman-Guy Green Prod., M-G-M

SIMONE SIGNORET in *Ship Of Fools*, Columbia

1966   Thirty-ninth Year

ANOUK AIMEE in *A Man And A Woman*, Les Films 13 Prod., Allied Artists

IDA KAMINSKA in *The Shop On Main Street*, Ceskoslovensky Film Company Prod., Prominent Films

LYNN REDGRAVE in *Georgy Girl*, Everglades Prods., Ltd., Columbia

VANESSA REDGRAVE in *Morgan!*, Quintra Films, Ltd. Prod., Cinema V

ELIZABETH TAYLOR in *Who's Afraid Of Virginia Woolf?*, Chenault Prod., Warner Bros.

1967   Fortieth Year

ANNE BANCROFT in *The Graduate*, Mike Nichols-Lawrence Turman Prod., Embassy

FAYE DUNAWAY in *Bonnie And Clyde*, Tatira-Hiller Prod., Warner Bros.-Seven Arts

DAME EDITH EVANS in *The Whisperers*, Seven Pines Prods., Ltd., United Artists

AUDREY HEPBURN in *Wait Until Dark*, Warner Bros.-Seven Arts

KATHARINE HEPBURN in *Guess Who's Coming To Dinner*, Columbia

1968   Forty-first Year

KATHARINE HEPBURN in *The Lion In Winter*, Haworth Prods., Ltd., Avco Embassy.

Katharine Hepburn won her third Best Actress award for *The Lion in Winter* (1968). © *1968 by Haworth Productions Ltd.* Photo courtesy of Avco Embassy Pictures Corp.

PATRICIA NEAL in *The Subject Was Roses*, Metro-Goldwyn-Mayer

VANESSA REDGRAVE in *Isadora*, Robert and Raymond Hakim-Universal, Ltd. Prod., Universal

BARBRA STREISAND in *Funny Girl*, Rastar Prods., Columbia

JOANNE WOODWARD in *Rachel, Rachel*, Kayos Prod., Warner Bros.-Seven Arts

1969   Forty-second Year

GENEVIEVE BUJOLD in *Anne Of The Thousand Days*, Hal B. Wallis-Universal Pictures, Ltd. Prod., Universal

JANE FONDA in *They Shoot Horses, Don't They?*, Chartoff-Winkler-Pollack Prod., ABC Pictures Presentation, Cinerama

LIZA MINNELLI in *The Sterile Cuckoo*, Boardwalk Prods., Paramount

JEAN SIMMONS in *The Happy Ending*, Pax Films Prod., United Artists

MAGGIE SMITH in *The Prime Of Miss Jean Brodie*, 20th Century-Fox Prods., Ltd., 20th Century-Fox

1970 Forty-third Year

JANE ALEXANDER in *The Great White Hope*, Lawrence Turman Films Prod., 20th Century-Fox

GLENDA JACKSON in *Women In Love*, Larry Kramer-Martin Rosen Prod., United Artists

ALI MacGRAW in *Love Story*, The Love Story Company Prod., Paramount

SARAH MILES in *Ryan's Daughter*, Faraway Prods., Metro-Goldwyn-Mayer

CARRIE SNODGRESS in *Diary Of A Mad Housewife*, Frank Perry Films Prod., Universal

1971 Forty-fourth Year

JULIE CHRISTIE in *McCabe & Mrs. Miller*, A Robert Altman-David Foster Prod., Warner Bros.

JANE FONDA in *Klute*, A Gus Prod., Warner Bros.

GLENDA JACKSON in *Sunday Bloody Sunday*, A Joseph Janni Prod., UA

VANESSA REDGRAVE in *Mary, Queen Of Scots*, A Hal Wallis-Universal Pictures, Ltd. Prod., Universal

JANET SUZMAN in *Nicholas And Alexandra*, A Horizon Pictures Prod., Columbia

1972 Forty-fifth Year

LIZA MINNELLI in *Cabaret*, An ABC Pictures Production, Allied Artists

DIANA ROSS in *Lady Sings The Blues*, A Motown-Weston-Furie Production, Paramount

MAGGIE SMITH in *Travels With My Aunt*, Robert Fryer Productions, Metro-Goldwyn-Mayer

CICELY TYSON in *Sounder*, Radnitz/Mattel Productions, 20th Century-Fox

LIV ULLMANN in *The Emigrants*, A Svensk Filmindustri Production, Warner Bros.

1973 Forty-sixth Year

ELLEN BURSTYN in *The Exorcist*, Hoya Prods., Warner Bros.

GLENDA JACKSON in *A Touch Of Class*, Brut Prods., Avco Embassy

MARSHA MASON in *Cinderella Liberty*, A Sanford Prod., 20th Century-Fox

BARBRA STREISAND in *The Way We Were*, Rastar Prods., Columbia

JOANNE WOODWARD in *Summer Wishes, Winter Dreams*, A Rastar Pictures Prod., Columbia

1974 Forty-seventh Year

ELLEN BURSTYN in *Alice Doesn't Live Here Anymore*, Warner Bros.

DIAHANN CARROLL in *Claudine*, Third World Cinema Productions in association with Joyce Selznick and Tina Pine, 20th Century-Fox

FAYE DUNAWAY in *Chinatown*, A Robert Evans Production, Paramount

VALERIE PERRINE in *Lenny*, A Marvin Worth Production, United Artists

GENA ROWLANDS in *A Woman Under The Influence*, A Faces International Films Production

1975 Forty-eighth Year

ISABELLE ADJANI in *The Story of Adele H.*, A Les Films du Carrosse-Les Productions Artistes Associes Production, New World Pictures

ANN-MARGRET in *Tommy*, A Robert Stigwood Organisation, Ltd. Production, Columbia

LOUISE FLETCHER in *One Flew Over The Cuckoo's Nest*, A Fantasy Films Production, United Artists

GLENDA JACKSON in *Hedda,* A Royal Shakespeare-Brut Productions-George Barrie/Robert Enders Film Production, Brut Productions

CAROL KANE in *Hester Street,* Midwest Film Productions

1976 Forty-ninth Year

MARIE-CHRISTINE BARRAULT in *Cousin, Cousine,* Les Films Pomereu-Gaumont Production, Northal Film Distributors Ltd.

FAYE DUNAWAY in *Network,* A Howard Gottfried/Paddy Chayefsky Production, Metro-Goldwyn-Mayer/United Artists

TALIA SHIRE in *Rocky,* A Robert Chartoff-Irwin Winkler Production, United Artists

SISSY SPACEK in *Carrie,* A Redbank Films Production, United Artists

LIV ULLMANN in *Face To Face,* A Cinematograph A.B. Production, Paramount

1977 Fiftieth Year

ANNE BANCROFT in *The Turning Point,* Hera Productions, Twentieth Century-Fox

JANE FONDA in *Julia,* A Twentieth Century-Fox Production, Twentieth Century-Fox

DIANE KEATON in *Annie Hall,* Jack Rollins-Charles H. Joffe Productions, United Artists

SHIRLEY MACLAINE in *The Turning Point,* Hera Productions, Twentieth Century-Fox

MARSHA MASON in *The Goodbye Girl,* A Ray Stark Production, Metro-Goldwyn-Mayer/Warner Bros.

SUPPORTING ACTOR

In 1936 the acting awards were expanded to recognize supporting roles. Within five years Walter Brennan had won three Oscars, and no one has since matched this total in the Supporting Actor category.

Confusion eventually developed over the distinction between a lead and supporting role, and for several years the studios decided to which category an acting performance belonged. This designation was announced prior to balloting in the Academy's annual reminder lists. In 1964 the Academy Board of Governors voted to eliminate the designation and leave the decision up to each voter.

Achievements in this category are nominated by members of the Academy Actors Branch who decide individually at the time of balloting whether a role is a lead or support.

1936 Ninth Year
MISCHA AUER in *My Man Godfrey*, Universal
WALTER BRENNAN in *Come And Get It*, Goldwyn, UA
STUART ERWIN in *Pigskin Parade*, 20th Century-Fox
BASIL RATHBONE in *Romeo And Juliet* Metro-Goldwyn-Mayer
AKIM TAMIROFF in *The General Died At Dawn*, Paramount

1937 Tenth Year
RALPH BELLAMY in *The Awful Truth*, Columbia
THOMAS MITCHELL in *Hurricane*, Goldwyn, UA
JOSEPH SCHILDKRAUT in *The Life Of Emile Zola*, Warner Bros.
H. B. WARNER in *Lost Horizon*, Columbia
ROLAND YOUNG in *Topper*, Roach, M-G-M

1938 Eleventh Year
WALTER BRENNAN in *Kentucky*, 20th Century-Fox
JOHN GARFIELD in *Four Daughters*, Warner Bros.
LARGE CAPITAL LETTERS DENOTE WINNER

GENE LOCKHART in *Algiers*, Wanger, UA
ROBERT MORLEY in *Marie Antoinette*, Metro-Goldwyn-Mayer
BASIL RATHBONE in *If I Were King*, Paramount

1939 Twelfth Year
BRIAN AHERNE in *Juarez*, Warner Bros.
HARRY CAREY in *Mr. Smith Goes To Washington*, Columbia
BRIAN DONLEVY in *Beau Geste*, Paramount
THOMAS MITCHELL in *Stagecoach*, Wanger, UA
CLAUDE RAINS in *Mr. Smith Goes To Washington*, Columbia

1940 Thirteenth Year
ALBERT BASSERMANN in *Foreign Correspondent*, Wanger, UA
WALTER BRENNAN in *The Westerner*, Goldwyn, UA
WILLIAM GARGAN in *They Knew What They Wanted*, RKO Radio
JACK OAKIE in *The Great Dictator*, Chaplin, UA
JAMES STEPHENSON in *The Letter*, Warner Bros.

For his role in *Kentucky* (1938) Walter Brennan, pictured here with Loretta Young, won the second of his three Supporting Actor Oscars. *Twentieth Century-Fox Photo*

1941   Fourteenth Year

WALTER BRENNAN in *Sergeant York*, Warner Bros.

CHARLES COBURN in *The Devil And Miss Jones*, RKO Radio

DONALD CRISP in *How Green Was My Valley*, 20th Century-Fox

JAMES GLEASON in *Here Comes Mr. Jordan*, Columbia

SYDNEY GREENSTREET in *The Maltese Falcon*, Warner Bros.

1942   Fifteenth Year

WILLIAM BENDIX in *Wake Island*, Paramount

VAN HEFLIN in *Johnny Eager*, Metro-Goldwyn Mayer

WALTER HUSTON in *Yankee Doodle Dandy*, Warner Bros.

FRANK MORGAN in *Tortilla Flat*, Metro-Goldwyn-Mayer

HENRY TRAVERS in *Mrs. Miniver*, Metro-Goldwyn-Mayer

1943   Sixteenth Year

CHARLES BICKFORD in *The Song Of Bernadette*, 20th Century-Fox

CHARLES COBURN in *The More The Merrier*, Columbia

J. CARROL NAISH in *Sahara*, Columbia

CLAUDE RAINS in *Casablanca*, Warner Bros.

AKIM TAMIROFF in *For Whom The Bell Tolls*, Paramount

1944   Seventeenth Year

HUME CRONYN in *The Seventh Cross*, Metro-Goldwyn-Mayer

BARRY FITZGERALD in *Going My Way*, Paramount

CLAUDE RAINS in *Mr. Skeffington*, Warner Bros.

CLIFTON WEBB in *Laura*, 20th Century-Fox

MONTY WOOLLEY in *Since You Went Away*, Selznick, UA

1945   Eighteenth Year

MICHAEL CHEKHOV in *Spellbound*, Selznick, UA

JOHN DALL in *The Corn Is Green*, Warner Bros.

JAMES DUNN in *A Tree Grows In Brooklyn*, 20th Century-Fox

ROBERT MITCHUM in *G. I. Joe*, Cowan, UA

J. CARROL NAISH in *A Medal For Benny*, Paramount

1946   Nineteenth Year

CHARLES COBURN in *The Green Years*, Metro-Goldwyn-Mayer

WILLIAM DEMAREST in *The Jolson Story*, Columbia

CLAUDE RAINS in *Notorious*, RKO Radio

HAROLD RUSSELL in *The Best Years Of Our Lives*, Goldwyn, RKO Radio

CLIFTON WEBB in *The Razor's Edge*, 20th Century-Fox

1947   Twentieth Year

CHARLES BICKFORD in *The Farmer's Daughter*, RKO Radio

THOMAS GOMEZ in *Ride The Pink Horse*, Universal-International

EDMUND GWENN in *Miracle On 34th Street*, 20th Century-Fox

ROBERT RYAN in *Crossfire*, RKO Radio

RICHARD WIDMARK in *Kiss Of Death*, 20th Century-Fox

1948   Twenty-first Year

CHARLES BICKFORD in *Johnny Belinda*, Warner Bros.

JOSE FERRER in *Joan Of Arc*, Sierra, RKO Radio

OSCAR HOMOLKA in *I Remember Mama*, RKO Radio

WALTER HUSTON in *Treasure Of Sierra Madre*, Warner Bros.

CECIL KELLAWAY in *The Luck Of The Irish*, 20th Century-Fox

1949   Twenty-second Year

JOHN IRELAND in *All The King's Men*, Rossen, Columbia

DEAN JAGGER in *Twelve O'Clock High*, 20th Century-Fox

ARTHUR KENNEDY in *Champion*, Screen Plays Corp., UA

RALPH RICHARDSON in *The Heiress*, Paramount

JAMES WHITMORE in *Battleground*, Metro-Goldwyn-Mayer

1950   Twenty-third Year

JEFF CHANDLER in *Broken Arrow*, 20th Century-Fox

EDMUND GWENN in *Mister 880*, 20th Century-Fox

SAM JAFFE in *The Asphalt Jungle*, Metro-Goldwyn-Mayer

GEORGE SANDERS in *All About Eve*, 20th Century-Fox

ERICH VON STROHEIM in *Sunset Boulevard*, Paramount

1951   Twenty-fourth Year

LEO GENN in *Quo Vadis*, Metro-Goldwyn-Mayer

KARL MALDEN in *A Streetcar Named Desire*, Charles K. Feldman Group Prods., Warner Bros.

KEVIN MCCARTHY in *Death Of A Salesman*, Kramer, Columbia

PETER USTINOV in *Quo Vadis*, Metro-Goldwyn-Mayer

GIG YOUNG in *Come Fill The Cup*, Warner Bros.

1952   Twenty-fifty Year

RICHARD BURTON in *My Cousin Rachel*, 20th Century-Fox

ARTHUR HUNNICUTT in *The Big Sky*, Winchester, RKO Radio

VICTOR MCLAGLEN in *The Quiet Man*, Argosy, Republic

JACK PALANCE in *Sudden Fear*, Kaufman, RKO Radio

ANTHONY QUINN in *Viva Zapata!*, 20th Century-Fox

1953   Twenty-sixth Year

EDDIE ALBERT in *Roman Holiday*, Paramount

BRANDON DE WILDE in *Shane*, Paramount

JACK PALANCE in *Shane*, Paramount

FRANK SINATRA in *From Here To Eternity*, Columbia

ROBERT STRAUSS in *Stalag 17*, Paramount

1954   Twenty-seventh Year

LEE J. COBB in *On The Waterfront*, Horizon-American, Columbia

KARL MALDEN in *On The Waterfront*, Horizon-American, Columbia

EDMOND O'BRIEN in *The Barefoot Contessa*, Figaro, UA

ROD STEIGER in *On The Waterfront*, Horizon-American, Columbia

TOM TULLY in *The Caine Mutiny*, Kramer, Columbia

1955   Twenty-eighth Year

ARTHUR KENNEDY in *Trial* Metro-Goldwyn-Mayer

JACK LEMMON in *Mister Roberts*, An Orange Prod., Warner Bros.

JOE MANTELL in *Marty*, Hecht & Lancaster's Steven Prods., UA

SAL MINEO in *Rebel Without A Cause*, Warner Bros.

ARTHUR O'CONNELL in *Picnic*, Columbia

1956   Twenty-ninth Year

DON MURRAY in *Bus Stop*, 20th Century-Fox

ANTHONY PERKINS in *Friendly Persuasion*, Allied Artists

ANTHONY QUINN in *Lust For Life*, Metro-Goldwyn-Mayer

MICKEY ROONEY in *The Bold And The Brave*, Filmakers Releasing Org., RKO Radio

ROBERT STACK in *Written On The Wind*, Universal-International

1957   Thirtieth Year

RED BUTTONS in *Sayonara*, William Goetz Prod., Warner Bros.

VITTORIO DE SICA in *A Farewell To Arms*, The Selznick Co., Inc., 20th Century-Fox

SESSUE HAYAKAWA in *The Bridge On The River Kwai*, A Horizon Picture, Columbia

ARTHUR KENNEDY in *Peyton Place*, Jerry Wald Prods., Inc., 20th Century-Fox

RUSS TAMBLYN in *Peyton Place*, Jerry Wald Prods., Inc., 20th Century-Fox

1958   Thirty-first Year

THEODORE BIKEL in *The Defiant Ones*, Stanley Kramer, UA

LEE J. COBB in *The Brothers Karamazov*, Avon Prods., Inc., M-G-M

BURL IVES in *The Big Country*, Anthony-Worldwide Prods., UA

ARTHUR KENNEDY in *Some Came Running*, Sol C. Siegel Prods., Inc., M-G-M

GIG YOUNG in *Teacher's Pet*, Perlberg-Seaton, Paramount

1959   Thirty-second Year

HUGH GRIFFITH in *Ben-Hur*, Metro-Goldwyn-Mayer

ARTHUR O'CONNELL in *Anatomy Of A Murder*, Otto Preminger, Columbia

GEORGE C.SCOTT in *Anatomy Of A Murder*, Otto Preminger, Columbia

ROBERT VAUGHN in *The Young Philadelphians*, Warner Bros.

ED WYNN in *The Diary Of Anne Frank*, 20th Century-Fox

1960   Thirty-third Year

PETER FALK in *Murder, Inc.*, 20th Century-Fox

JACK KRUSCHEN in *The Apartment*, The Mirisch Co., Inc., UA

SAL MINEO in *Exodus*, Carlyle-Alpina S.A. Prod., UA

PETER USTINOV in *Spartacus*, Bryna Prods., Inc., U-I

CHILL WILLS in *The Alamo*, Batjac Prod., UA

1961 Thirty-fourth Year

GEORGE CHAKIRIS in *West Side Story*, Mirisch Pictures, Inc. and B and P Enterprises, Inc., UA

MONTGOMERY CLIFT in *Judgment At Nuremberg*, Stanley Kramer Prod., UA

PETER FALK in *Pocketful Of Miracles*, Franton Prod., UA

JACKIE GLEASON in *The Hustler*, Robert Rossen Prod., 20th Century-Fox

GEORGE C. SCOTT in *The Hustler*, Robert Rossen Prod., 20th Century Fox

1962 Thirty-fifth Year

ED BEGLEY in *Sweet Bird Of Youth*, Roxbury Prod., M-G-M

VICTOR BUONO in *What Ever Happened To Baby Jane?*, Seven Arts-Associates & Aldrich Co. Prod., Warner Bros.

TELLY SAVALAS in *Bird Man Of Alcatraz*, Harold Hecht Prod., UA

OMAR SHARIF in *Lawrence Of Arabia*, Horizon Pictures (G.B.), Ltd.-Sam Spiegel-David Lean Prod., Columbia

TERENCE STAMP in *Billy Budd*, Harvest Prods., Allied Artists

1963 Thirty-sixth Year

NICK ADAMS in *Twilight Of Honor*, Perlberg-Seaton Prod., M-G-M

BOBBY DARIN in *Captain Newman, M.D.*, Universal-Brentwood-Reynard Prod., Universal

MELVYN DOUGLAS in *Hud*, Salem-Dover Prod., Paramount

HUGH GRIFFITH in *Tom Jones*, Woodfall Prod., UA-Lopert Pictures

JOHN HUSTON in *The Cardinal*, Gamma Prod., Columbia

1964 Thirty-seventh Year

JOHN GIELGUD in *Becket*, Hal Wallis Prod., Paramount

STANLEY HOLLOWAY in *My Fair Lady*, Warner Bros.

EDMOND O'BRIEN in *Seven Days In May*, Joel Prods., Paramount

LEE TRACY in *The Best Man*, Millar-Turman Prod., United Artists

PETER USTINOV in *Topkapi*, Filmways Prod., United Artists

1965 Thirty-eighth Year

MARTIN BALSAM in *A Thousand Clowns*, Harrell Prod., United Artists

IAN BANNEN in *The Flight Of The Phoenix*, Associates & Aldrich Company Prod., 20th Century-Fox

TOM COURTENAY in *Doctor Zhivago*, Sostar S.A.-Metro-Goldwyn-Mayer British Studios, Ltd. Prod. M-G-M

MICHAEL DUNN in *Ship Of Fools*, Columbia

FRANK FINLAY in *Othello*, B.H.E. Prod., Warner Bros.

1966 Thirty-ninth Year

MAKO in *The Sand Pebbles*, Argyle-Solar Prod., 20th Century-Fox

JAMES MASON in *Georgy Girl*, Everglades Prods., Ltd., Columbia

WALTER MATTHAU in *The Fortune Cookie*, Phalanx-Jalem-Mirisch Corp. of Delaware Prod., UA

GEORGE SEGAL in *Who's Afraid Of Virginia Woolf?*, Chenault Prod., Warner Bros.

ROBERT SHAW in *A Man For All Seasons*, Highland Films, Ltd., Prod., Columbia

1967 Fortieth Year

JOHN CASSAVETES in *The Dirty Dozen*, MKH Prods., Ltd., Metro-Goldwyn-Mayer

GENE HACKMAN in *Bonnie And Clyde*, Tatira-Hiller Prod., Warner Bros.-Seven Arts

CECIL KELLAWAY in *Guess Who's Coming To Dinner*, Columbia

GEORGE KENNEDY in *Cool Hand Luke*, Jalem Prod., Warner Bros.-Seven Arts

MICHAEL J. POLLARD in *Bonnie And Clyde*, Tatira-Hiller Prod., Warner Bros.-Seven Arts.

1968 Forty-first Year

JACK ALBERTSON in *The Subject Was Roses*, Metro-Goldwyn-Mayer

SEYMOUR CASSEL in *Faces*, John Cassavetes Prod., Walter Reade-Continental Distributing

DANIEL MASSEY in *Star!*, Robert Wise Prod., 20th Century-Fox

JACK WILD in *Oliver!*, Romulus Films, Ltd., Columbia

GENE WILDER in *The Producers*, Sidney Glazier Prod., Avco Embassy.

1969 Forty-second Year

RUPERT CROSSE in *The Reivers*, Irving Ravetch-Arthur Kramer-Solar Prods., Cinema Center Films Presentation, National General

ELLIOTT GOULD in *Bob & Carol & Ted & Alice*, Frankovich Prods., Columbia

JACK NICHOLSON in *Easy Rider*, Pando-Raybert Prod., Columbia

ANTHONY QUAYLE in *Anne Of The Thousand Days* Hal B. Wallis-Universal Pictures, Ltd. Prod., Universal

GIG YOUNG in *They Shoot Horses, Don't They?*, Chartoff-Winkler-Pollack Prod., ABC Pictures Presentation, Cinerama

1970 Forty-third Year

RICHARD CASTELLANO in *Lovers And Other Strangers*, ABC Pictures Prod., Cinerama

CHIEF DAN GEORGE in *Little Big Man*, Hiller Prods., Ltd.-Stockbridge Prods., Cinema Center Films Presentation, National General

GENE HACKMAN in *I Never Sang For My Father*, Jamel Prods., Columbia

JOHN MARLEY in *Love Story*, The Love Story Company Prod., Paramount

JOHN MILLS in *Ryan's Daughter*, Faraway Prods., Metro-Goldwyn-Mayer

1971 Forty-fourth Year

JEFF BRIDGES in *The Last Picture Show*, BBS Prods., Columbia

LEONARD FREY in *Fiddler On The Roof*, Mirisch-Cartier Prods., UA

RICHARD JAECKEL in *Sometimes A Great Notion*, A Universal-Newman-Foreman Company Prod., Universal

BEN JOHNSON in *The Last Picture Show*, BBS Prods., Columbia

ROY SCHEIDER in *The French Connection*, A Philip D'Antoni Prod. in association with Schine-Moore Prods., 20th Century-Fox

1972 Forty-fifth Year

EDDIE ALBERT in *The Heartbreak Kid*, A Palomar Pictures International Production, 20th Century-Fox

JAMES CAAN in *The Godfather*, An Albert S. Ruddy Production, Paramount

ROBERT DUVALL in *The Godfather*, An Albert S. Ruddy Production, Paramount

JOEL GREY in *Cabaret*, An ABC Pictures Production, Allied Artists

AL PACINO in *The Godfather*, An Albert S. Ruddy Production, Paramount

1973 Forty-sixth Year

VINCENT GARDENIA in *Bang The Drum Slowly*, A Rosenfield Production, Paramount

JACK GILFORD in *Save The Tiger*, Filmways-Jalem- Cirandinha Productions, Paramount

JOHN HOUSEMAN in *The Paper Chase,* Thompson-Paul Productions, 20th Century-Fox

JASON MILLER in *The Exorcist,* Hoya Productions, Warner Bros.

RANDY QUAID in *The Last Detail,* An Acrobat Films Prod., Columbia

1974   Forty-seventh Year

FRED ASTAIRE in *The Towering Inferno,* An Irwin Allen Production, 20th Century-Fox/Warner Bros.

JEFF BRIDGES in *Thunderbolt And Lightfoot,* A Malpaso Company Film Production, United Artists

ROBERT DE NIRO in *The Godfather Part II,* A Coppola Company Production, Paramount

MICHAEL V. GAZZO in *The Godfather Part II,* A Coppola Company Production, Paramount

LEE STRASBERG in *The Godfather Part II,* A Coppola Company Production, Paramount

1975   Forty-eighth Year

GEORGE BURNS in *The Sunshine Boys,* A Ray Stark Production, Metro-Goldwyn-Mayer

BRAD DOURIF in *One Flew Over The Cuckoo's Nest,* A Fantasy Films Production, United Artists

BURGESS MEREDITH in *The Day Of The Locust,* A Jerome Hellman Production, Paramount

CHRIS SARANDON in *Dog Day Afternoon,* Warner Bros.

JACK WARDEN in *Shampoo,* Rubeeker Productions, Columbia

1976   Forty-ninth Year

NED BEATTY in *Network,* A Howard Gottfried/Paddy Chayefsky Production, Metro-Goldwyn-Mayer/United Artists

BURGESS MEREDITH in *Rocky,* A Robert Chartoff-Irwin Winkler Production, United Artists

LAURENCE OLIVIER in *Marathon Man,* A Robert Evans-Sidney Beckerman Production, Paramount

JASON ROBARDS in *All The President's Men,* A Wildwood Enterprises Production, Warner Bros.

BURT YOUNG in *Rocky,* A Robert Chartoff-Irwin Winkler Production, United Artists

1977   Fiftieth Year

MIKHAIL BARYSHNIKOV in *The Turning Point,* Hera Productions, Twentieth Century-Fox

PETER FIRTH in *Equus,* A Winkast Company, Ltd./P.B., Ltd. Production, United Artists

ALEC GUINNESS in *Star Wars,* A Twentieth Century-Fox Production, Twentieth Century-Fox

JASON ROBARDS in *Julia,* A Twentieth Century-Fox Production, Twentieth Century-Fox

MAXIMILIAN SCHELL in *Julia,* A Twentieth Century-Fox Production, Twentieth Century-Fox

SUPPORTING ACTRESS

The Supporting Actress category, created in 1936 with the Supporting Actor award, is marked by a surprising lack of multiple winners. Only Shelley Winters, with Oscars in 1959 and 1965, has received more than one Supporting Actress award, though Ingrid Bergman and Helen Hayes have won acting awards in both the lead and supporting categories. Ten-year-old Tatum O'Neal, 1973's Best Supporting Actress, is the youngest to win an award in *any* of the acting categories. In 1938 Fay Bainter was nominated for Best Actress and Best Supporting Actress for two different roles, as was Teresa Wright in 1942.

Achievements in this category are nominated by members of the Academy Actors Branch who decide individually at the time of balloting whether a role is a lead or support.

1936   Ninth Year
BEULAH BONDI in *The Gorgeous Hussy*, Metro-Goldwyn-Mayer
ALICE BRADY in *My Man Godfrey*, Universal
BONITA GRANVILLE in *These Three*, Goldwyn, UA
MARIA OUSPENSKAYA in *Dodsworth*, Goldwyn, UA
GALE SONDERGAARD in *Anthony Adverse*, Warner Bros.

1937   Tenth Year
ALICE BRADY in *In Old Chicago*, 20th Century-Fox
ANDREA LEEDS in *Stage Door*, RKO Radio
ANNE SHIRLEY in *Stella Dallas*, Goldwyn, UA
CLAIRE TREVOR in *Dead End*, Goldwyn, UA
DAME MAY WHITTY in *Night Must Fall*, Metro-Goldwyn-Mayer

1938   Eleventh Year
FAY BAINTER in *Jezebel*, Warner Bros.
BEULAH BONDI in *Of Human Hearts*, Metro-Goldwyn-Mayer

LARGE CAPITAL LETTERS DENOTE WINNER

BILLIE BURKE in *Merrily We Live*, Roach, M-G-M
SPRING BYINGTON in *You Can't Take It With You*, Columbia
MILIZA KORJUS in *The Great Waltz*, Metro-Goldwyn-Mayer

1939   Twelfth Year
OLIVIA DE HAVILLAND in *Gone With The Wind*, Selznick, M-G-M
GERALDINE FITZGERALD in *Wuthering Heights*, Goldwyn, UA
HATTIE McDANIEL in *Gone With The Wind*, Selznick, M-G-M
EDNA MAY OLIVER in *Drums Along The Mohawk*, 20th Century-Fox
MARIA OUSPENSKAYA in *Love Affair*, RKO Radio

1940   Thirteenth Year
JUDITH ANDERSON in *Rebecca*, Selznick, UA
JANE DARWELL in *The Grapes Of Wrath*, 20th Century-Fox
RUTH HUSSEY in *The Philadelphia Story*, Metro-Goldwyn-Mayer
BARBARA O'NEIL in *All This, And Heaven Too*, Warner Bros.
MARJORIE RAMBEAU in *Primrose Path*, RKO Radio

1941 Fourteenth Year

SARA ALLGOOD in *How Green Was My Valley*, 20th Century-Fox
MARY ASTOR in *The Great Lie*, Warner Bros.
PATRICIA COLLINGE in *The Little Foxes*, Goldwyn, RKO Radio
TERESA WRIGHT in *The Little Foxes*, Goldwyn, RKO Radio
MARGARET WYCHERLY in *Sergeant York*, Warner Bros.

1942 Fifteenth Year

GLADYS COOPER in *Now, Voyager*, Warner Bros.
AGNES MOOREHEAD in *The Magnificent Ambersons*, Mercury, RKO Radio
SUSAN PETERS in *Random Harvest*, Metro-Goldwyn-Mayer
DAME MAY WHITTY in *Mrs. Miniver*, Metro-Goldwyn-Mayer
TERESA WRIGHT in *Mrs. Miniver*, Metro-Goldwyn-Mayer

1943 Sixteenth Year

GLADYS COOPER in *The Song Of Bernadette*, 20th Century-Fox
PAULETTE GODDARD in *So Proudly We Hail*, Paramount
KATINA PAXINOU in *For Whom The Bell Tolls*, Paramount
ANNE REVERE in *The Song Of Bernadette*, 20th Century-Fox
LUCILE WATSON in *Watch On The Rhine*, Warner Bros.

1944 Seventeenth Year

ETHEL BARRYMORE in *None But The Lonely Heart*, RKO Radio
JENNIFER JONES in *Since You Went Away*, Selznick, UA
ANGELA LANSBURY in *Gaslight*, Metro-Goldwyn-Mayer
ALINE MacMAHON in *Dragon Seed*, Metro-Goldwyn-Mayer
AGNES MOOREHEAD in *Mrs. Parkington*, Metro-Goldwyn-Mayer

1945 Eighteenth Year

EVE ARDEN in *Mildred Pierce*, Warner Bros.
ANN BLYTH in *Mildred Pierce*, Warner Bros.
ANGELA LANSBURY in *The Picture Of Dorian Gray*, Metro-Goldwyn-Mayer
JOAN LORRING in *The Corn Is Green*, Warner Bros.
ANNE REVERE in *National Velvet*, Metro-Goldwyn-Mayer

1946 Nineteenth Year

ETHEL BARRYMORE in *The Spiral Staircase*, RKO Radio
ANNE BAXTER in *The Razor's Edge*, 20th Century-Fox
LILLIAN GISH in *Duel In The Sun*, Selznick International
FLORA ROBSON in *Saratoga Trunk*, Warner Bros.
GALE SONDERGAARD in *Anna And The King Of Siam*, 20th Century-Fox

1947 Twentieth Year

ETHEL BARRYMORE in *The Paradine Case*, Selznick
GLORIA GRAHAME in *Crossfire*, RKO Radio
CELESTE HOLM in *Gentleman's Agreement*, 20th Century-Fox
MARJORIE MAIN in *The Egg And I*, Universal-International
ANNE REVERE in *Gentleman's Agreement*, 20th Century-Fox

1948 Twenty-first Year

BARBARA BEL GEDDES in *I Remember Mama*, RKO Radio
ELLEN CORBY in *I Remember Mama*, RKO Radio
AGNES MOOREHEAD in *Johnny Belinda*, Warner Bros.
JEAN SIMMONS in *Hamlet*, Rank-Two Cities, U-I. (British)
CLAIRE TREVOR in *Key Largo*, Warner Bros.

1949   Twenty-second Year

ETHEL BARRYMORE in *Pinky*, 20th Century-Fox

CELESTE HOLM in *Come To The Stable*, 20th Century-Fox

ELSA LANCHESTER in *Come To The Stable*, 20th Century-Fox

MERCEDES McCAMBRIDGE in *All The King's Men*, Rossen, Columbia

ETHEL WATERS in *Pinky*, 20th Century-Fox

1950   Twenty-third Year

HOPE EMERSON in *Caged*, Warner Bros.

CELESTE HOLM in *All About Eve*, 20th Century-Fox

JOSEPHINE HULL in *Harvey*, Universal-International

NANCY OLSON in *Sunset Boulevard*, Paramount

THELMA RITTER in *All About Eve*, 20th Century-Fox

1951   Twenty-fourth Year

JOAN BLONDELL in *The Blue Veil*, Wald-Krasna, RKO Radio

MILDRED DUNNOCK in *Death Of A Salesman*, Kramer, Columbia

LEE GRANT in *Detective Story*, Paramount

KIM HUNTER in *A Streetcar Named Desire*, Charles K. Feldman Group Prods, Warner Bros.

THELMA RITTER in *The Mating Season*, Paramount

1952   Twenty-fifth Year

GLORIA GRAHAME in *The Bad And The Beautiful*, Metro-Goldwyn-Mayer

JEAN HAGEN in *Singin' In The Rain*, Metro-Goldwyn-Mayer

COLETTE MARCHAND in *Moulin Rouge*, Romulus, UA

TERRY MOORE in *Come Back, Little Sheba*, Wallis, Paramount

THELMA RITTER in *With A Song In My Heart*, 20th Century-Fox

1953   Twenty-sixth Year

GRACE KELLY in *Mogambo*, Metro-Goldwyn-Mayer

GERALDINE PAGE in *Hondo*, Wayne-Fellows, Warner Bros.

MARJORIE RAMBEAU in *Torch Song*, Metro-Goldwyn-Mayer

DONNA REED in *From Here To Eternity*, Columbia

THELMA RITTER in *Pickup On South Street*, 20th Century-Fox

1954   Twenty-seventh Year

NINA FOCH in *Executive Suite*, Metro-Goldwyn-Mayer

KATY JURADO in *Broken Lance*, 20th Century-Fox

EVA MARIE SAINT in *On The Waterfront*, Horizon-American, Columbia

JAN STERLING in *The High And The Mighty*, Wayne-Fellows, Warner Bros.

CLAIRE TREVOR in *The High And The Mighty*, Wayne-Fellows, Warner Bros.

1955   Twenty-eighth Year

BETSY BLAIR in *Marty*, Hecht & Lancaster's Steven Prods., UA

PEGGY LEE in *Pete Kelly's Blues*, A Mark VIII Ltd. Prod., Warner Bros.

MARISA PAVAN in *The Rose Tattoo*, Hal Wallis, Paramount

JO VAN FLEET in *East of Eden*, Warner Bros.

NATALIE WOOD in *Rebel Without A Cause*, Warner Bros.

1956   Twenty-ninth Year

MILDRED DUNNOCK in *Baby Doll*, A Newtown Prod., Warner Bros.

EILEEN HECKART in *The Bad Seed*, Warner Bros.

MERCEDES MCCAMBRIDGE in *Giant*, Giant Prod., Warner Bros.

PATTY MCCORMACK in *The Bad Seed*, Warner Bros.

DOROTHY MALONE in *Written On The Wind*, Universal-International

1957 Thirtieth Year

CAROLYN JONES in *The Bachelor Party*, Norma Prod., UA

ELSA LANCHESTER in *Witness For The Prosecution*, Edward Small-Arthur Hornblow Prod., UA

HOPE LANGE in *Peyton Place*, Jerry Wald Prods., Inc., 20th Century-Fox

MIYOSHI UMEKI in *Sayonara*, William Goetz Prod., Warner Bros.

DIANE VARSI in *Peyton Place*, Jerry Wald Prods., Inc., 20th Century-Fox

1958 Thirty-first Year

PEGGY CASS in *Auntie Mame*, Warner Bros.

WENDY HILLER in *Separate Tables*, Clifton Prods., Inc., UA

MARTHA HYER in *Some Came Running*, Sol C. Siegel Prods., Inc., Metro-Goldwyn-Mayer

MAUREEN STAPLETON in *Lonelyhearts*, Schary Prods., Inc., UA

CARA WILLIAMS in *The Defiant Ones*, Stanley Kramer, UA

1959 Thirty-second Year

HERMIONE BADDELEY in *Room At The Top*, Romulus Films, Ltd., Continental Distributing, Inc. (British)

SUSAN KOHNER in *Imitation Of Life*, Universal-International

JUANITA MOORE in *Imitation Of Life*, Universal-International

THELMA RITTER in *Pillow Talk*, Arwin Prods., Inc., U-I

SHELLEY WINTERS in *The Diary Of Anne Frank*, 20th Century-Fox

1960 Thirty-third Year

GLYNIS JOHNS in *The Sundowners*, Warner Bros.

SHIRLEY JONES in *Elmer Gantry*, Burt Lancaster-Richard Brooks Prod., UA

SHIRLEY KNIGHT in *The Dark At The Top Of The Stairs*, Warner Bros.

JANET LEIGH in *Psycho*, Alfred J. Hitchcock Prods., Paramount

MARY URE in *Sons And Lovers*, Company of Artists, Inc., 20th Century-Fox

1961 Thirty-fourth Year

FAY BAINTER in *The Children's Hour*, Mirisch-Worldwide Prod., UA

JUDY GARLAND in *Judgment At Nuremberg*, Stanley Kramer Prod., UA

LOTTE LENYA in *The Roman Spring Of Mrs. Stone*, Seven Arts Presentation, Warner Bros.

UNA MERKEL in *Summer And Smoke*, Hal Wallis Prod., Paramount

RITA MORENO in *West Side Story*, Mirisch Pictures, Inc. and B and P Enterprises, Inc., UA

1962 Thirty-fifth Year

MARY BADHAM in *To Kill A Mockingbird*, Universal-International-Pakula-Mulligan-Brentwood Prod., U-I

PATTY DUKE in *The Miracle Worker*, Playfilms Prod., UA

SHIRLEY KNIGHT in *Sweet Bird Of Youth*, Roxbury Prod., M-G-M

ANGELA LANSBURY in *The Manchurian Candidate*, M. C. Prod., UA

THELMA RITTER in *Bird Man Of Alcatraz*, Harold Hecht Prod., UA

1963 Thirty-sixth Year

DIANE CILENTO in *Tom Jones*, Woodfall Prod., UA-Lopert Pictures

DAME EDITH EVANS in *Tom Jones*, Woodfall Prod., UA-Lopert Pictures

JOYCE REDMAN in *Tom Jones*, Woodfall Prod., UA-Lopert Pictures

MARGARET RUTHERFORD in *The V.I.P.s*, Metro-Goldwyn-Mayer

LILIA SKALA in *Lilies of The Field*, Rainbow Prod., UA

1964　Thirty-seventh Year

GLADYS COOPER in *My Fair Lady*, Warner Bros.

DAME EDITH EVANS in *The Chalk Garden*, Quota Rentals, Ltd.-Ross Hunter Prod., Universal

GRAYSON HALL in *The Night Of The Iguana*, Seven Arts Prod., M-G-M

LILA KEDROVA in *Zorba The Greek*, Rochley, Ltd. Prod., International Classics

AGNES MOOREHEAD in *Hush . . . Hush, Sweet Charlotte*, Associates & Aldrich Co. Prod., 20th Century-Fox

1965　Thirty-eighth Year

RUTH GORDON in *Inside Daisy Clover*, Park Place Prod., Warner Bros.

JOYCE REDMAN in *Othello*, B.H.E. Prod., Warner Bros.

MAGGIE SMITH in *Othello*, B.H.E. Prod., Warner Bros.

SHELLEY WINTERS in *A Patch Of Blue*, Pandro S. Berman-Guy Green Prod., M-G-M

PEGGY WOOD in *The Sound Of Music*, Argyle Enterprises Prod., 20th Century-Fox

1966　Thirty-ninth Year

SANDY DENNIS in *Who's Afraid Of Virginia Woolf?*, Chenault Prod., Warner Bros.

WENDY HILLER in *A Man For All Seasons*, Highland Films, Ltd. Prod., Columbia

JOCELYNE LAGARDE in *Hawaii*, Mirisch Corp. of Delaware Prod., UA

VIVIEN MERCHANT in *Alfie*, Sheldrake Films, Ltd. Prod., Paramount

GERALDINE PAGE in *You're A Big Boy Now*, Seven Arts

1967　Fortieth Year

CAROL CHANNING in *Thoroughly Modern Millie*, Ross Hunter-Universal Prod., Universal

MILDRED NATWICK in *Barefoot In The Park*, Hal Wallis Prod., Paramount

ESTELLE PARSONS in *Bonnie And Clyde*, Tatira-Hiller Prod., Warner Bros.-Seven Arts

BEAH RICHARDS in *Guess Who's Coming To Dinner*, Columbia

KATHARINE ROSS in *The Graduate*, Mike Nichols-Lawrence Turman Prod., Embassy

1968　Forty-first Year

LYNN CARLIN in *Faces*, John Cassavetes Prod., Walter Reade-Continental Distributing

RUTH GORDON in *Rosemary's Baby*, William Castle Enterprises Prod., Paramount

SONDRA LOCKE in *The Heart Is A Lonely Hunter*, Warner Bros.-Seven Arts

KAY MEDFORD in *Funny Girl*, Rastar Prods., Columbia

ESTELLE PARSONS in *Rachel, Rachel*, Kayos Prod., Warner Bros.-Seven Arts

1969　Forty-second Year

CATHERINE BURNS in *Last Summer*, Frank Perry-Alsid Prod., Allied Artists

DYAN CANNON in *Bob & Carol & Ted & Alice*, Frankovich Prods., Columbia

GOLDIE HAWN in *Cactus Flower*, Frankovich Prods., Columbia

SYLVIA MILES in *Midnight Cowboy*, A Jerome Hellman-John Schlesinger Prod., United Artists

SUSANNAH YORK in *They Shoot Horses, Don't They?*, Chartoff-Winkler-Pollack Prod., ABC Pictures Presentation, Cinerama

1970　Forty-third Year

KAREN BLACK in *Five Easy Pieces*, BBS Prods., Columbia

From the MGM release *A Patch of Blue* (1966). Shelley Winters (left) won her second Supporting Actress Award while newcomer Elizabeth Hartman received a Best Actress nomination for her portrayal of a blind girl. © *1965 Metro-Goldwyn-Mayer, Inc. and Pandro S. Berman Productions, Inc.*

LEE GRANT in *The Landlord*, A Mirisch-Cartier II Prod., United Artists

HELEN HAYES in *Airport*, Ross-Hunter-Universal Prod., Universal

SALLY KELLERMAN in *M*A*S*H*, Aspen Prods., 20th Century-Fox

MAUREEN STAPLETON in *Airport*, Ross Hunter-Universal Prod., Universal

1971   Forty-fourth Year

EŁLEN BURSTYN in *The Last Picture Show*, BBS Prods., Columbia

BARBARA HARRIS in *Who Is Harry Kellerman, And Why Is He Saying Those Terrible Things About Me?*, A Who Is Harry Kellerman Company Prod., Cinema Center Films Presentation, National General

CLORIS LEACHMAN in *The Last Picture Show*, BBS Prods., Columbia

MARGARET LEIGHTON in *The Go-Between*, A World Film Services, Ltd. Prod., Columbia

ANN-MARGRET in *Carnal Knowledge*, Icarus Prods., Avco Embassy

1972   Forty-fifth Year

JEANNIE BERLIN in *The Heartbreak Kid*, A Palomar Pictures International Production, 20th Century-Fox

EILEEN HECKART in *Butterflies Are Free*, Frankovich Productions, Columbia

GERALDINE PAGE in *Pete 'n' Tillie*, A Universal-Martin Ritt-Julius J. Epstein Production, Universal

SUSAN TYRRELL in *Fat City*, Rastar Productions, Columbia

SHELLEY WINTERS in *The Poseidon Adventure*, An Irwin Allen Production, 20th Century-Fox

1973   Forty-sixth Year

LINDA BLAIR in *The Exorcist*, Hoya Prods., Warner Bros.

CANDY CLARK in *American Graffiti*, A Universal-Lucasfilm, Ltd.-Coppola Company Prod., Universal

MADELINE KAHN in *Paper Moon*, A Directors Company Prod., Paramount

TATUM O'NEAL in *Paper Moon*, A Directors Company Prod., Paramount

SYLVIA SIDNEY in *Summer Wishes, Winter Dreams*, A Rastar Pictures Prod., Columbia

1974   Forty-seventh Year

INGRID BERGMAN in *Murder On The Orient Express*, A G.W. Films, Ltd. Production, Paramount

VALENTINA CORTESE in *Day For Night*, A Les Films Du Carrosse and P.E.C.F., Paris; P.I.C., Rome Prod., Warner Bros.

MADELINE KAHN in *Blazing Saddles*, Warner Bros.

DIANE LADD in *Alice Doesn't Live Here Anymore*, Warner Bros.

TALIA SHIRE in *The Godfather Part II*, A Coppola Company Prod., Paramount

1975   Forty-eighth Year

RONEE BLAKLEY in *Nashville*, An ABC Entertainment-Jerry Weintraub-Robert Altman Production, Paramount

LEE GRANT in *Shampoo*, Rubeeker Productions, Columbia

SYLVIA MILES in *Farewell, My Lovely*, An Elliott Kastner-ITC Production, Avco Embassy

LILY TOMLIN in *Nashville*, An ABC Entertainment-Jerry Weintraub-Robert Altman Production, Paramount

BRENDA VACCARO in *Jacqueline Susann's Once Is Not Enough*, A Howard W. Koch Production, Paramount

1976   Forty-ninth Year

JANE ALEXANDER in *All The President's Men*, A Wildwood Enterprises Production, Warner Bros.

JODIE FOSTER in *Taxi Driver*, A Bill/Phillips Production of a Martin Scorsese Film, Columbia Pictures

LEE GRANT in *Voyage Of The Damned*, An ITC Entertainment Production, Avco Embassy

PIPER LAURIE in *Carrie*, A Redbank Films Production, United Artists

BEATRICE STRAIGHT in *Network*, A Howard Gottfried/Paddy Chayefsky Production, Metro-Goldwyn-Mayer/United Artists

1977   Fiftieth Year

LESLIE BROWNE in *The Turning Point*, Hera Productions, Twentieth Century-Fox

QUINN CUMMINGS in *The Goodbye Girl*, A Ray Stark Production, Metro-Goldwyn-Mayer/Warner Bros.

MELINDA DILLON in *Close Encounters Of The Third Kind*, Close Encounter Productions, Columbia

VANESSA REDGRAVE in *Julia*, A Twentieth Century-Fox Production, Twentieth Century-Fox

TUESDAY WELD in *Looking For Mr. Goodbar*, A Freddie Fields Production, Paramount

DIRECTING

The category for Directing was begun in 1927/28, and for that year only there were two awards, one for direction of a dramatic film, another for comedy direction. The latter was dropped the following year. John Ford with four Oscars (1935, 1940, 1941, 1952) and Frank Capra (1934, 1936, 1938) and William Wyler (1942, 1946, 1959) with three each are the most frequent winners in this category. Though the categories are completely separate, voting patterns indicate a correlation between the Best Picture and Directing awards. Only three times in the last twenty-five years has the film voted Best Picture not been directed by the person named Best Director.

Achievements in this category are nominated by members of the Academy Directors Branch.

1927/28   First Year

FRANK BORZAGE for *Seventh Heaven*, Fox

HERBERT BRENON for *Sorrell And Son*, United Artists

KING VIDOR for *The Crowd*, Metro-Goldwyn-Mayer

Comedy Direction
Note: Not given after this year.
CHARLES CHAPLIN for *The Circus*, Chaplin, UA

LEWIS MILESTONE for *Two Arabian Knights*, United Artists

TED WILDE for *Speedy*, Paramount

1928/29   Second Year

LIONEL BARRYMORE for *Madame X*, Metro-Goldwyn-Mayer

HARRY BEAUMONT for *Broadway Melody*, Metro-Goldwyn-Mayer

IRVING CUMMINGS for *In Old Arizona*, Fox

FRANK LLOYD for *The Divine Lady*, First National

FRANK LLOYD for *Weary River*, First National

FRANK LLOYD for *Drag*, First National

ERNST LUBITSCH for *The Patriot*, Paramount

1929/30   Third Year

CLARENCE BROWN for *Anna Christie*, Metro-Goldwyn-Mayer

CLARENCE BROWN for *Romance*, Metro-Goldwyn-Mayer

ROBERT LEONARD for *The Divorcee*, Metro-Goldwyn-Mayer

ERNST LUBITSCH for *The Love Parade*, Paramount

LEWIS MILESTONE for *All Quiet On The Western Front*, Universal

KING VIDOR for *Hallelujah*, Metro-Goldwyn-Mayer

1930/31   Fourth Year

CLARENCE BROWN for *A Free Soul*, Metro-Goldwyn-Mayer

LEWIS MILESTONE for *The Front Page*, Caddo, UA

WESLEY RUGGLES for *Cimarron*, RKO Radio

NORMAN TAUROG for *Skippy*, Paramount

JOSEF VON STERNBERG for *Morocco*, Paramount

1931/32 Fifth Year
FRANK BORZAGE for *Bad Girl*, Fox
KING VIDOR for *The Champ*, Metro-
Goldwyn-Mayer
JOSEF VON STERNBERG for *Shanghai
Express*, Paramount

1932/33 Sixth Year
FRANK CAPRA for *Lady For A Day*, Co-
lumbia
GEORGE CUKOR for *Little Women*, RKO
Radio
FRANK LLOYD for *Cavalcade*, Fox

1934 Seventh Year
FRANK CAPRA for *It Happened One
Night*, Columbia
VICTOR SCHERTZINGER for *One Night
Of Love*, Columbia
W. S. VAN DYKE for *The Thin Man*,
Metro-Goldwyn-Mayer

1935 Eighth Year
JOHN FORD for *The Informer*, RKO
Radio
HENRY HATHAWAY for *Lives Of A
Bengal Lancer*, Paramount
FRANK LLOYD for *Mutiny On The Boun-
ty*, Metro-Goldwyn-Mayer

1936 Ninth Year
FRANK CAPRA for *Mr. Deeds Goes
To Town*, Columbia
GREGORY LA CAVA for *My Man God-
frey*, Universal
ROBERT Z. LEONARD for *The Great
Ziegfeld*, Metro-Goldwyn-Mayer
W. S. VAN DYKE for *San Francisco*,
Metro-Goldwyn-Mayer
WILLIAM WYLER for *Dodsworth*, Gold-
wyn, UA

1937 Tenth Year
WILLIAM DIETERLE for *The Life Of
Emile Zola*, Warner Bros.
SIDNEY FRANKLIN for *The Good Earth*,
Metro-Goldwyn-Mayer

GREGORY LA CAVA for *Stage Door*,
RKO Radio
LEO McCAREY for *The Awful Truth*,
Columbia
WILLIAM WELLMAN for *A Star Is Born*,
Selznick, UA

1938 Eleventh Year
FRANK CAPRA for *You Can't Take It
With You*, Columbia
MICHAEL CURTIZ for *Angels With Dirty
Faces*, Warner Bros.
MICHAEL CURTIZ for *Four Daughters*,
Warner Bros.
NORMAN TAUROG for *Boys Town*,
Metro-Goldwyn-Mayer
KING VIDOR for *The Citadel*, Metro-
Goldwyn-Mayer

1939 Twelfth Year
FRANK CAPRA for *Mr. Smith Goes To
Washington*, Columbia
VICTOR FLEMING for *Gone With
The Wind*, Selznick, M-G-M
JOHN FORD for *Stagecoach*, Wanger,
UA
SAM WOOD for *Goodbye, Mr. Chips*,
Metro-Goldwyn-Mayer (British)
WILLIAM WYLER for *Wuthering
Heights*, Goldwyn, UA

1940 Thirteenth Year
GEORGE CUKOR for *The Philadelphia
Story*, Metro-Goldwyn-Mayer
JOHN FORD for *The Grapes Of
Wrath*, 20th Century-Fox
ALFRED HITCHCOCK for *Rebecca*, Selz-
nick, UA
SAM WOOD for *Kitty Foyle*, RKO Radio
WILLIAM WYLER for *The Letter*, Warner
Bros.

1941 Fourteenth Year
JOHN FORD for *How Green Was My
Valley*, 20th Century-Fox
ALEXANDER HALL for *Here Comes Mr.
Jordan*, Columbia

HOWARD HAWKS for *Sergeant York,* Warner Bros.

ORSON WELLES for *Citizen Kane,* Mercury, RKO Radio

WILLIAM WYLER for *The Little Foxes,* Goldwyn, RKO Radio

1942   Fifteenth Year

MICHAEL CURTIZ for *Yankee Doodle Dandy,* Warner Bros.

JOHN FARROW for *Wake Island,* Paramount

MERVYN LEROY for *Random Harvest,* Metro-Goldwyn-Mayer

SAM WOOD for *Kings Row,* Warner Bros.

WILLIAM WYLER for *Mrs. Miniver,* Metro-Goldwyn-Mayer

1943   Sixteenth Year

CLARENCE BROWN for *The Human Comedy,* Metro-Goldwyn-Mayer

MICHAEL CURTIZ for *Casablanca,* Warner Bros.

HENRY KING for *The Song Of Bernadette,* 20th Century-Fox

ERNST LUBITSCH for *Heaven Can Wait,* 20th Century-Fox

GEORGE STEVENS for *The More The Merrier,* Columbia

1944   Seventeenth Year

ALFRED HITCHCOCK for *Lifeboat,* 20th Century-Fox

HENRY KING for *Wilson,* 20th Century-Fox

LEO McCAREY for *Going My Way,* Paramount

OTTO PREMINGER for *Laura,* 20th Century-Fox

BILLY WILDER for *Double Indemnity,* Paramount

1945   Eighteenth Year

CLARENCE BROWN for *National Velvet,* Metro-Goldwyn-Mayer

ALFRED HITCHCOCK for *Spellbound,* Selznick, UA

LEO McCAREY for *The Bells of St. Mary's,* Rainbow, RKO Radio

JEAN RENOIR for *The Southerner,* Loew-Hakim, UA

BILLY WILDER for *The Lost Weekend,* Paramount

1946   Nineteenth Year

CLARENCE BROWN for *The Yearling,* Metro-Goldwyn-Mayer

FRANK CAPRA for *It's A Wonderful Life,* Liberty, RKO Radio

DAVID LEAN for *Brief Encounter,* Rank, U-I (British)

ROBERT SIODMAK for *The Killers,* Hellinger, Universal

WILLIAM WYLER for *The Best Years Of Our Lives,* Goldwyn, RKO Radio

1947   Twentieth Year

GEORGE CUKOR for *A Double Life,* Kanin, U-I

EDWARD DMYTRYK for *Crossfire,* RKO Radio

ELIA KAZAN for *Gentleman's Agreement,* 20th Century-Fox

HENRY KOSTER for *The Bishop's Wife,* Goldwyn, RKO Radio

DAVID LEAN for *Great Expectations,* Rank-Cineguild, U-I (British)

1948   Twenty-first Year

JOHN HUSTON for *Treasure Of Sierra Madre,* Warner Bros.

ANATOLE LITVAK for *The Snake Pit,* 20th Century-Fox

JEAN NEGULESCO for *Johnny Belinda,* Warner Bros.

LAURENCE OLIVIER for *Hamlet,* Rank-Two Cities, U-I (British)

FRED ZINNEMANN for *The Search,* Praesens Films, M-G-M (Swiss)

1949   Twenty-second Year

JOSEPH L. MANKIEWICZ for *A Letter To Three Wives,* 20th Century-Fox

Walter Huston (left) told his son, "If you ever become a writer or director, please find a good part for your old man." John Huston did, and both won Oscars for *Treasure of Sierra Madre* (1948). © 1978 *A.M.P.A.S.*

CAROL REED for *The Fallen Idol*, London Films, SRO (British)

ROBERT ROSSEN for *All The King's Men*, Rossen, Columbia

WILLIAM A. WELLMAN for *Battleground*, Metro-Goldwyn-Mayer

WILLIAM WYLER for *The Heiress*, Paramount

1950 *Twenty-third Year*

GEORGE CUKOR for *Born Yesterday*, Columbia

JOHN HUSTON for *The Asphalt Jungle*, Metro-Goldwyn-Mayer

JOSEPH L. MANKIEWICZ for *All About Eve*, 20th Century-Fox

CAROL REED for *The Third Man*, Selz-

nick-London Films, SRO (British)
BILLY WILDER for *Sunset Boulevard*, Paramount

1951   Twenty-fourth Year

JOHN HUSTON for *The African Queen*, Horizon, UA
ELIA KAZAN for *A Streetcar Named Desire*, Charles K. Feldman Group Prods., Warner Bros.
VINCENTE MINNELLI for *An American In Paris*, Metro-Goldwyn-Mayer
GEORGE STEVENS for *A Place In The Sun*, Paramount
WILLIAM WYLER for *Detective Story*, Paramount

1952   Twenty-fifth Year

CECIL B. DEMILLE for *The Greatest Show On Earth*, Cecil B. DeMille, Paramount
JOHN FORD for *The Quiet Man*, Argosy, Republic
JOHN HUSTON for *Moulin Rouge*, Romulus Films, UA
JOSEPH L. MANKIEWICZ for *Five Fingers*, 20th Century-Fox
FRED ZINNEMANN for *High Noon*, Stanley Kramer, UA

1953   Twenty-sixth Year

GEORGE STEVENS for *Shane*, Paramount
CHARLES WALTERS for *Lili*, Metro-Goldwyn-Mayer
BILLY WILDER for *Stalag 17*, Paramount
WILLIAM WYLER for *Roman Holiday*, Paramount
FRED ZINNEMANN for *From Here To Eternity*, Columbia

1954   Twenty-seventh Year

ALFRED HITCHCOCK for *Rear Window*, Patron, Inc., Paramount
ELIA KAZAN for *On The Waterfront*, Horizon-American, Columbia

GEORGE SEATON for *The Country Girl*, Perlberg-Seaton, Paramount
WILLIAM WELLMAN for *The High And The Mighty*, Wayne-Fellows, Warner Bros.
BILLY WILDER for *Sabrina*, Paramount

1955   Twenty-eighth Year

ELIA KAZAN for *East Of Eden*, Warner Bros.
DAVID LEAN for *Summertime*, Ilya Lopert-David Lean, UA (Anglo-American)
JOSHUA LOGAN for *Picnic*, Columbia
DELBERT MANN for *Marty*, Hecht & Lancaster's Steven Prods., UA
JOHN STURGES for *Bad Day At Black Rock*, Metro-Goldwyn-Mayer

1956   Twenty-ninth Year

MICHAEL ANDERSON for *Around The World In 80 Days*, The Michael Todd Co., Inc., UA
WALTER LANG for *The King And I*, 20th Century-Fox
GEORGE STEVENS for *Giant*, Giant Prod., Warner Bros.
KING VIDOR for *War And Peace*, A Ponti-DeLaurentiis Prod., Paramount (Italo-American)
WILLIAM WYLER for *Friendly Persuasion*, Allied Artists

1957   Thirtieth Year

DAVID LEAN for *The Bridge On The River Kwai*, A Horizon Picture, Columbia
JOSHUA LOGAN for *Sayonara*, William Goetz Prod., Warner Bros.
SIDNEY LUMET for *12 Angry Men*, Orion-Nova Prod., UA
MARK ROBSON for *Peyton Place*, Jerry Wald Prods., Inc., 20th Century-Fox
BILLY WILDER for *Witness For The Prosecution*, Edward Small-Arthur Hornblow Prod., UA

1958   Thirty-first Year

RICHARD BROOKS for *Cat On A Hot Tin Roof*, Avon Prods., Inc., M-G-M

STANLEY KRAMER for *The Defiant Ones*, Stanley Kramer, UA

VINCENTE MINNELLI for *Gigi*, Arthur Freed Prods., Inc., M-G-M

MARK ROBSON for *The Inn Of The Sixth Happiness*, 20th Century-Fox

ROBERT WISE for *I Want To Live!*, Figaro, Inc., UA

1959   Thirty-second Year

JACK CLAYTON for *Room At The Top*, Romulus Films, Ltd., Continental Dist. Inc., (British)

GEORGE STEVENS for *The Diary Of Anne Frank*, 20th Century-Fox

BILLY WILDER for *Some Like It Hot*, Ashton Prods. & The Mirisch Co., UA

WILLIAM WYLER for *Ben-Hur*, Metro-Goldwyn-Mayer

FRED ZINNEMANN for *The Nun's Story*, Warner Bros.

1960   Thirty-third Year

JACK CARDIFF for *Sons And Lovers*, Company of Artists, Inc., 20th Century-Fox

JULES DASSIN for *Never On Sunday*, Melinafilm Prod., Lopert Pictures Corp. (Greek)

ALFRED HITCHCOCK for *Psycho*, Alfred J. Hitchcock Prods., Paramount

BILLY WILDER for *The Apartment*, The Mirisch Co., Inc., UA

FRED ZINNEMANN for *The Sundowners*, Warner Bros.

1961   Thirty-fourth Year

FEDERICO FELLINI for *La Dolce Vita*, Riama Film Prod., Astor Pictures, Inc. (Italian)

STANLEY KRAMER for *Judgment At Nuremberg*, Stanley Kramer Prod., UA

JEROME ROBBINS for *West Side Story*, Mirisch Pictures, Inc. and B and P Enterprises, Inc., UA

ROBERT ROSSEN for *The Hustler*, Robert Rossen Prod., 20th Century-Fox

J. LEE THOMPSON for *The Guns Of Navarone*, Carl Foreman Prod., Columbia

ROBERT WISE for *West Side Story*, Mirisch Pictures, Inc. and B and P Enterprises, Inc., UA

1962   Thirty-fifth Year

PIETRO GERMI for *Divorce—Italian Style*, Lux-Vides-Galatea Film Prod., Embassy Pictures

DAVID LEAN for *Lawrence Of Arabia*, Horizon Pictures (G.B.), Ltd.-Sam Spiegel-David Lean Prod., Columbia

ROBERT MULLIGAN for *To Kill A Mockingbird*, Universal-International-Pakula-Mulligan-Brentwood Prod., U-I

ARTHUR PENN for *The Miracle Worker*, Playfilms Prod., UA

FRANK PERRY for *David And Lisa*, Heller-Perry Prods., Continental Dist.

1963   Thirty-sixth Year

FEDERICO FELLINI for *Federico Fellini's 8½*, Cineriz Prod., Embassy Pictures

ELIA KAZAN for *America America*, Athena Enterprises Prod., Warner Bros.

OTTO PREMINGER for *The Cardinal*, Gamma Prod., Columbia

TONY RICHARDSON for *Tom Jones*, Woodfall Prod., UA-Lopert Pictures.

MARTIN RITT for *Hud*, Salem-Dover Prod., Paramount

1964   Thirty-seventh Year

MICHAEL CACOYANNIS for *Zorba The*

Greek, Rochley, Ltd. Prod., Intl. Classics

GEORGE CUKOR for *My Fair Lady*, Warner Bros.

PETER GLENVILLE for *Becket*, Hal Wallis Prod., Paramount

STANLEY KUBRICK for *Dr. Strangelove Or: How I Learned To Stop Worrying And Love The Bomb*, Hawk Films, Ltd. Prod., Columbia

ROBERT STEVENSON for *Mary Poppins*, Walt Disney Prods.

1965 Thirty-eighth Year

DAVID LEAN for *Doctor Zhivago*, Sostar S.A.-Metro-Goldwyn-Mayer British Studios, LTD. Prod., M-G-M

JOHN SCHLESINGER for *Darling*, Anglo-Amalgamated, Ltd. Prod., Embassy

HIROSHI TESHIGAHARA for *Woman In The Dunes*, Teshigahara Prod., Pathe Contemporary Films

ROBERT WISE for *The Sound Of Music*, Argyle Enterprises Prod., 20th Century-Fox

WILLIAM WYLER for *The Collector*, The Collector Company, Columbia

1966 Thirty-ninth Year

MICHELANGELO ANTONIONI for *Blow-Up*, Carlo Ponti Prod., Premier Productions

RICHARD BROOKS for *The Professionals*, Pax Enterprises Prod., Columbia

CLAUDE LELOUCH for *A Man And A Woman*, Les Films 13 Prod., Allied Artists

MIKE NICHOLS for *Who's Afraid Of Virginia Woolf?*, Chenault Prod., Warner Bros.

FRED ZINNEMANN for *A Man For All Seasons*, Highland Films, Ltd. Prod., Columbia

1967 Fortieth Year

RICHARD BROOKS for *In Cold Blood*, Pax Enterprises Prod., Columbia

NORMAN JEWISON for *In The Heat Of The Night*, Mirisch Corp. Prod., United Artists

STANLEY KRAMER for *Guess Who's Coming To Dinner*, Columbia

MIKE NICHOLS for *The Graduate*, Mike Nichols-Lawrence Turman Prod., Embassy

ARTHUR PENN for *Bonnie And Clyde*, Tatira-Hiller Prod., Warner Bros.-Seven Arts

1968 Forty-first Year

ANTHONY HARVEY for *The Lion In Winter*, Haworth Prods., Avco Embassy

STANLEY KUBRICK for *2001: A Space Odyssey*, Polaris Prod., Metro-Goldwyn-Mayer

GILLO PONTECORVO for *The Battle Of Algiers*, Igor-Casbah Film Prod., Allied Artists

CAROL REED for *Oliver!*, Romulus Films, Columbia

FRANCO ZEFFIRELLI for *The Franco Zeffirelli production of Romeo & Juliet*, B.H.E. Film-Verona Prod.-Dino De Laurentiis Cinematografica Prod., Paramount

1969 Forty-second Year

COSTA-GAVRAS for *Z*, Reggane Films-O.N.C.I.C. Prod., Cinema V

GEORGE ROY HILL for *Butch Cassidy And The Sundance Kid*, George Roy Hill-Paul Monash Prod., 20th Century-Fox

ARTHUR PENN for *Alice's Restaurant*, Florin Prod., United Artists

SYDNEY POLLACK for *They Shoot Horses, Don't They?*, Chartoff-Winkler-Pollack Prod., ABC Pictures Presentation, Cinerama

JOHN SCHLESINGER for *Midnight Cowboy*, Jerome Hellman-John Schlesinger Prod., United Artists

1970   *Forty-third Year*

ROBERT ALTMAN for *M*A*S*H*, Aspen
Prods., 20th Century-Fox

FEDERICO FELLINI for *Fellini Satyricon*,
Alberto Grimaldi Prod., United Artists

ARTHUR HILLER for *Love Story*, The
Love Story Company Prod., Paramount

KEN RUSSELL for *Women In Love*, Larry
Kramer-Martin Rosen Prod., United
Artists

FRANKLIN J. SCHAFFNER for *Patton*, 20th Century-Fox

1971   *Forty-fourth Year*

PETER BOGDANOVICH for *The Last Picture Show*, BBS Prods., Columbia

WILLIAM FRIEDKIN for *The French
Connection*, A Philip D'Antoni
Prod. in association with Schine-
Moore Prods., 20th Century-Fox

NORMAN JEWISON for *Fiddler On The
Roof*, Mirisch-Cartier Prods., UA

STANLEY KUBRICK for *A Clockwork
Orange*, A Hawks Films, Ltd.,
Prod., Warner Bros.

JOHN SCHLESINGER for *Sunday Bloody
Sunday*, A Joseph Janni Prod., UA

1972   *Forty-fifth Year*

JOHN BOORMAN for *Deliverance*,
Warner Bros.

FRANCIS FORD COPPOLA for *The Godfather*, An Albert S. Ruddy Production, Paramount

BOB FOSSE for *Cabaret*, An ABC
Pictures Production, Allied Artists

JOSEPH L. MANKIEWICZ for *Sleuth*, A
Palomar Pictures International Production, 20th Century-Fox

JAN TROELL for *The Emigrants*, A
Svensk Filmindustri Production,
Warner Bros.

1973   *Forty-sixth Year*

INGMAR BERGMAN for *Cries And Whis-
pers*, A Svenska Filminstitutet-
Cinematograph AB Prod., New
World Pictures

BERNARDO BERTOLUCCI for *Last Tango
In Paris*, A PEA Produzioni Europee
Associate S.A.S.-Les Productions
Artistes Associes S.A. Prod., UA

WILLIAM FRIEDKIN for *The Exorcist*,
Hoya Prods., Warner Bros.

GEORGE ROY HILL for *The Sting*, A
Universal-Bill/Phillips-George Roy
Hill Film Prod., Zanuck/Brown Pre-
sentation, Universal

GEORGE LUCAS for *American Graffiti*, A
Universal-Lucasfilm, Ltd.-Coppola
Company Prod., Universal

1974   *Forty-seventh Year*

JOHN CASSAVETES for *A Woman Under
The Influence*, A Faces International
Films Prod.

FRANCIS FORD COPPOLA for *The
Godfather Part II*, A Coppola Company Prod., Paramount

BOB FOSSE for *Lenny*, A Marvin Worth
Prod., United Artists

ROMAN POLANSKI for *Chinatown*, A
Robert Evans Prod., Paramount

FRANCOIS TRUFFAUT for *Day For
Night*, A Les Films Du Carrosse and
P.E.C.F., Paris; P.I.C., Rome
Prod., Warner Bros.

1975   *Forty-eighth Year*

ROBERT ALTMAN for *Nashville*, An
ABC Entertainment-Jerry Weintraub-
Robert Altman Production, Para-
mount

FEDERICO FELLINI for *Amarcord*, An
F.C. Productions-P.E.C.F. Production, New World Pictures

MILOS FORMAN for *One Flew Over
The Cuckoo's Nest*, A Fantasy Films
Production, United Artists

STANLEY KUBRICK for *Barry Lyndon,* A Hawk Films, Ltd. Production, Warner Bros.

SIDNEY LUMET for *Dog Day Afternoon,* Warner Bros.

1976   Forty-ninth Year

JOHN G. AVILDSEN for *Rocky,* A Robert Chartoff-Irwin Winkler Production, United Artists

INGMAR BERGMAN for *Face To Face,* A Cinematograph A.B. Production, Paramount

SIDNEY LUMET for *Network,* A Howard Gottfried/Paddy Chayefsky Production, Metro-Goldwyn-Mayer/United Artists

ALAN J. PAKULA for *All The President's Men,* A Wildwood Enterprises Production, Warner Bros.

LINA WERTMULLER for *Seven Beauties,* A Medusa Distribuzione Production, Cinema 5, Ltd.

1977   Fiftieth Year

WOODY ALLEN for *Annie Hall,* Jack Rollins/Charles H. Joffe Productions, United Artists

STEVEN SPIELBERG for *Close Encounters Of The Third Kind,* Close Encounter Productions, Columbia

FRED ZINNEMANN for *Julia,* A Twentieth Century-Fox Production, Twentieth Century-Fox

GEORGE LUCAS for *Star Wars,* A Twentieth Century-Fox Production, Twentieth Century-Fox

HERBERT ROSS for *The Turning Point,* Hera Productions, Twentieth Century-Fox

WRITING

Established as one of the original categories in 1927/28, the Writing awards have undergone considerable changes in the past fifty years. An award for Title Writing was added at the last minute in 1927/28, but the rapid demise of silent films rendered the job of the title writer obsolete, and the category was dropped after the first awards. A single Writing award was given the second and third years, but since 1930/31 at least two and for several years three awards have been made annually. The division of the category has usually depended upon whether a screenplay was original or adapted, and the wording of these divisions has changed frequently. The present rule allows two awards: Best Screenplay Written Directly for the Screen—based on factual material or on story material not previously published or produced, and Best Screenplay—based on material from another medium.

The Writing awards have been marked by occasional controversy. Dudley Nichols, embroiled in a dispute between the Academy and the Screen Writers' Guild, refused a 1935 Oscar for *The Informer*. Blacklisted writer Dalton Trumbo won a 1956 Oscar under the pseudonym Robert Rich, and the same year another blacklisted writer, Michael Wilson, a previous Oscar winner, was declared ineligible for political reasons. Two films with the same title caused further confusion in 1956. Both pictures were titled *High Society;* one was a Cole Porter musical from MGM, the other a low-budget Bowery Boys film from Allied Artists. Edward Bernds and Elwood Ullman, the writers of the Allied Artists film, asked that their names be withdrawn when it became apparent that members of the Writers branch and the Writers Guild had meant to nominate the other film. Even so, MGM's *High Society* would only have been eligible for adapted screenplay.

Achievements in this category are nominated by members of the Academy Writers Branch.

1927/28 First Year

(Adaptation)

GLORIOUS BETSY, Warner Bros.: ANTHONY COLDEWAY

THE JAZZ SINGER, Warner Bros.: ALFRED COHN

SEVENTH HEAVEN, Fox: BENJAMIN GLAZER

(Original Story)

THE LAST COMMAND, Paramount: LAJOS BIRO

LARGE CAPITAL LETTERS DENOTE WINNER

THE PATENT LEATHER KID, First National: RUPERT HUGHES

UNDERWORLD, Paramount: BEN HECHT

(Title Writing—Not given after this year)

THE PRIVATE LIFE OF HELEN OF TROY, First National: GERALD DUFFY

THE FAIR CO-ED, Metro-Goldwyn-Mayer: JOSEPH FARNHAM

LAUGH, CLOWN, LAUGH, Metro-Goldwyn-Mayer: JOSEPH FARNHAM

TELLING THE WORLD, Metro-
Goldwyn-Mayer: JOSEPH FARN-
HAM
OH KAY!, First National: GEORGE
MARION, JR.

1928/29 Second Year
(Achievement)
IN OLD ARIZONA, Fox: TOM BARRY
THE LEATHERNECK, Pathe: ELLIOTT
CLAWSON
OUR DANCING DAUGHTERS, Metro-
Goldwyn-Mayer: JOSEPHINE LOVETT
THE PATRIOT, Paramount: HANS
KRALY
THE VALIANT, Fox: TOM BARRY
WONDER OF WOMEN, Metro-Goldwyn-
Mayer: BESS MEREDYTH

1929/30 Third Year
(Achievement-
—Not given after this year)
ALL QUIET ON THE WESTERN FRONT,
Universal: GEORGE ABBOTT, MAX-
WELL ANDERSON and DELL ANDREWS
THE BIG HOUSE, Metro-Goldwyn-
Mayer: FRANCES MARION
DISRAELI, Warner Bros.: JULIAN JO-
SEPHSON
THE DIVORCEE, Metro-Goldwyn-Mayer:
JOHN MEEHAN
STREET OF CHANCE, Paramount. HOW-
ARD ESTABROOK

1930/31 Fourth Year
(Adaptation)
CIMARRON, RKO Radio: HOWARD
ESTABROOK
THE CRIMINAL CODE, Columbia: SETON
MILLER and FRED NIBLO, JR.
HOLIDAY, RKO Pathe: HORACE JACK-
SON
THE LITTLE CAESAR, Warner Bros.:
FRANCIS FARAGOH and ROBERT N. LEE
SKIPPY, Paramount: JOSEPH MANKIE-
WICZ and SAM MINTZ

(Original Story)
THE DAWN PATROL, Warner Bros.-
First National: JOHN MONK
SAUNDERS
DOORWAY TO HELL, Warner Bros.-First
National: ROWLAND BROWN
LAUGHTER, Paramount: HARRY D'AB-
BADIE D'ARRAST, DOUGLAS DOTY and
DONALD OGDEN STEWART
THE PUBLIC ENEMY, Warner Bros.-First
National: JOHN BRIGHT and KUBEC
GLASMON
SMART MONEY, Warner Bros.-First Na-
tional: LUCIEN HUBBARD and JOSEPH
JACKSON

1931/32 Fifth Year
(Adaptation)
ARROWSMITH, Goldwyn, UA: SIDNEY
HOWARD
BAD GIRL, Fox: EDWIN BURKE
DR. JEKYLL AND MR. HYDE, Paramount:
PERCY HEATH and SAMUEL HOFFEN-
STEIN
(Original Story)
THE CHAMP, Metro-Goldwyn-Mayer:
FRANCES MARION
LADY AND GENT, Paramount: GROVER
JONES and WILLIAM SLAVENS MCNUTT
STAR WITNESS, Warner Bros.: LUCIEN
HUBBARD
WHAT PRICE HOLLYWOOD, RKO Radio:
ADELA ROGERS ST. JOHN

1932/33 Sixth Year
(Adaptation)
LADY FOR A DAY, Columbia: ROBERT
RISKIN
LITTLE WOMEN, RKO Radio: VIC-
TOR HEERMAN and SARAH Y.
MASON
STATE FAIR, Fox: PAUL GREEN and
SONYA LEVIEN
(Original Story)
ONE WAY PASSAGE, Warner Bros.:
ROBERT LORD

THE PRIZEFIGHTER AND THE LADY, Metro-Goldwyn-Mayer: FRANCES MARION

RASPUTIN AND THE EMPRESS, Metro-Goldwyn-Mayer: CHARLES MacARTHUR

1934 Seventh Year

(Adaptation)

IT HAPPENED ONE NIGHT, Columbia: ROBERT RISKIN

THE THIN MAN, Metro-Goldwyn-Mayer: FRANCES GOODRICH and ALBERT HACKETT

VIVA VILLA, Metro-Goldwyn-Mayer: BEN HECHT

(Original Story)

HIDE-OUT, Metro-Goldwyn-Mayer: MAURI GRASHIN

MANHATTAN MELODRAMA, Metro-Goldwyn-Mayer: ARTHUR CAESAR

THE RICHEST GIRL IN THE WORLD, RKO Radio: NORMAN KRASNA

1935 Eighth Year

(Original Story)

BROADWAY MELODY OF 1936, Metro-Goldwyn-Mayer: MOSS HART

THE GAY DECEPTION, Lasky, Fox: DON HARTMAN and STEPHEN AVERY

THE SCOUNDREL, Paramount: BEN HECHT and CHARLES MacARTHUR

(Screenplay)

THE INFORMER, RKO Radio: DUDLEY NICHOLS

LIVES OF A BENGAL LANCER, Paramount: ACHMED ABDULLAH, JOHN L. BALDERSTON, GROVER JONES, WILLIAM SLAVENS MCNUTT and WALDEMAR YOUNG

MUTINY ON THE BOUNTY, Metro-Goldwyn-Mayer: JULES FURTHMAN, TALBOT JENNINGS and CAREY WILSON

1936 Ninth Year

(Original Story)

FURY, Metro-Goldwyn-Mayer: NORMAN KRASNA

THE GREAT ZIEGFELD, Metro-Goldwyn-Mayer: WILLIAM ANTHONY MCGUIRE

SAN FRANCISCO, Metro-Goldwyn-Mayer: ROBERT HOPKINS

THE STORY OF LOUIS PASTEUR, Warner Bros.: PIERRE COLLINGS and SHERIDAN GIBNEY

THREE SMART GIRLS, Universal: ADELE COMMANDINI

(Screenplay)

AFTER THE THIN MAN, Metro-Goldwyn-Mayer: FRANCES GOODRICH and ALBERT HACKETT

DODSWORTH, Goldwyn, UA: SIDNEY HOWARD

MR. DEEDS GOES TO TOWN, Columbia: ROBERT RISKIN

MY MAN GODFREY, Universal: ERIC HATCH and MORRIS RYSKIND

THE STORY OF LOUIS PASTEUR, Warner Bros.: PIERRE COLLINGS and SHERIDAN GIBNEY

1937 Tenth Year

(Original Story)

BLACK LEGION, Warner Bros.: ROBERT LORD

IN OLD CHICAGO, 20th Century-Fox: NIVEN BUSCH

THE LIFE OF EMILE ZOLA, Warner Bros.: HEINZ HERALD and GEZA HERCZEG.

100 MEN AND A GIRL, Universal: HANS KRALY

A STAR IS BORN, Selznick, UA: WILLIAM A. WELLMAN and ROBERT CARSON

(Screenplay)

THE AWFUL TRUTH, Columbia: VINA DELMAR

CAPTAINS COURAGEOUS, Metro-Goldwyn-Mayer: MARC CONNOLLY,

JOHN LEE MAHIN and DALE VAN EVERY
THE LIFE OF EMILE ZOLA, Warner Bros.: HEINZ HERALD, GEZA HERCZEG and NORMAN REILLY RAINE
STAGE DOOR, RKO Radio: MORRIS RYSKIND and ANTHONY VEILLER
A STAR IS BORN, Selznick, UA: ALAN CAMPBELL, ROBERT CARSON and DOROTHY PARKER

1938   Eleventh Year
(Adaptation)
PYGMALION, Metro-Goldwyn-Mayer (British): IAN DALRYMPLE, CECIL LEWIS and W. P. LIPSCOMB

(Original Story)
ALEXANDER'S RAGTIME BAND, 20th Century-Fox: IRVING BERLIN
ANGELS WITH DIRTY FACES, Warner Bros.: ROWLAND BROWN
BLOCKADE, Wanger, UA: JOHN HOWARD LAWSON
BOYS TOWN, Metro-Goldwyn-Mayer: ELEANORE GRIFFIN and DORE SCHARY
MAD ABOUT MUSIC, Universal: MARCELLA BURKE and FREDERICK KOHNER
TEST PILOT, Metro-Goldwyn-Mayer: FRANK WEAD

(Screenplay)
BOYS TOWN, Metro-Goldwyn-Mayer: JOHN MEEHAN and DORE SCHARY
THE CITADEL, Metro-Goldwyn-Mayer (British): IAN DALRYMPLE, ELIZABETH HILL and FRANK WEAD
FOUR DAUGHTERS, Warner Bros.: LENORE COFFEE and JULIUS J. EPSTEIN
PYGMALION, Metro-Goldwyn-Mayer (British): GEORGE BERNARD SHAW
YOU CAN'T TAKE IT WITH YOU, Columbia: ROBERT RISKIN

1939   Twelfth Year
(Original Story)
BACHELOR MOTHER, RKO Radio: FELIX JACKSON
LOVE AFFAIR, RKO Radio: MILDRED CRAM and LEO MCCAREY
MR. SMITH GOES TO WASHINGTON, Columbia: LEWIS R. FOSTER
NINOTCHKA, Metro-Goldwyn-Mayer: MELCHIOR LENGYEL
YOUNG MR. LINCOLN, 20th Century-Fox: LAMAR TROTTI

(Screenplay)
GONE WITH THE WIND, Selznick, M-G-M: SIDNEY HOWARD
GOODBYE, MR. CHIPS, Metro-Goldwyn-Mayer (British): ERIC MASCHWITZ, R. C. SHERRIFF and CLAUDINE WEST
MR. SMITH GOES TO WASHINGTON, Columbia: SIDNEY BUCHMAN
NINOTCHKA, Metro-Goldwyn-Mayer: CHARLES BRACKETT, WALTER REISCH and BILLY WILDER
WUTHERING HEIGHTS, Goldwyn, UA: BEN HECHT and CHARLES MacARTHUR

1940   Thirteenth Year
(Original Story)
ARISE, MY LOVE, Paramount: BENJAMIN GLAZER and JOHN S. TOLDY
COMRADE X, Metro-Goldwyn-Mayer: WALTER REISCH
EDISON THE MAN, Metro-Goldwyn-Mayer: HUGO BUTLER and DORE SCHARY
MY FAVORITE WIFE, RKO Radio: LEO MCCAREY, BELLA SPEWACK & SAMUEL SPEWACK
THE WESTERNER, Goldwyn, UA: STUART N. LAKE

(Original Screenplay)
ANGELS OVER BROADWAY, Columbia: BEN HECHT

DR. EHRLICH'S MAGIC BULLET, Warner
Bros.: NORMAN BURNSIDE, HEINZ
HERALD and JOHN HUSTON
FOREIGN CORRESPONDENT, Wanger,
UA: CHARLES BENNETT and JOAN
HARRISON
THE GREAT DICTATOR, Chaplin, UA:
CHARLES CHAPLIN
THE GREAT McGINTY, Paramount:
PRESTON STURGES

(Screenplay)

THE GRAPES OF WRATH, 20th Century-
Fox: NUNNALLY JOHNSON
KITTY FOYLE, RKO Radio: DALTON
TRUMBO
THE LONG VOYAGE HOME, Argosy-
Wanger, UA: DUDLEY NICHOLS
THE PHILADELPHIA STORY,
Metro-Goldwyn-Mayer: DONALD
OGDEN STEWART
REBECCA, Selznick, UA: ROBERT E.
SHERWOOD and JOAN HARRISON

1941   Fourteenth Year
(Original Story)

BALL OF FIRE, Goldwyn, RKO Radio:
THOMAS MONROE and BILLY WILDER
HERE COMES MR. JORDAN, Colum-
bia: HARRY SEGALL
THE LADY EVE, Paramount: MONCKTON
HOFFE
MEET JOHN DOE, Warner Bros. RICHARD
CONNELL & ROBERT PRESNELL
NIGHT TRAIN, 20th Century-Fox. GOR-
DON WELLESLEY

(Original Screenplay)

CITIZEN KANE, Mercury, RKO
Radio: HERMAN J. MANKIEWICZ
and ORSON WELLES
THE DEVIL AND MISS JONES, RKO
Radio: NORMAN KRASNA
SERGEANT YORK, Warner Bros: HARRY
CHANDLEE, ABEM FINKEL, JOHN
HUSTON and HOWARD KOCH
TALL, DARK AND HANDSOME, 20th Cen-

tury-Fox: KARL TUNBERG and DAR-
RELL WARE
TOM, DICK AND HARRY, RKO Radio:
PAUL JARRICO

(Screenplay)

HERE COMES MR. JORDAN, Colum-
bia: SIDNEY BUCHMAN and
SETON I. MILLER
HOLD BACK THE DAWN, Paramount:
CHARLES BRACKETT and BILLY
WILDER
HOW GREEN WAS MY VALLEY, 20th Cen-
tury-Fox: PHILIP DUNNE
THE LITTLE FOXES, Goldwyn, RKO
Radio: LILLIAN HELLMAN
THE MALTESE FALCON, Warner Bros:
JOHN HUSTON

1942   Fifteenth Year
(Original Story)

HOLIDAY INN, Paramount: IRVING BER-
LIN
THE INVADERS, Ortus, Columbia
(British): EMERIC PRESSBURGER
THE PRIDE OF THE YANKEES, Goldwyn,
RKO Radio: PAUL GALLICO
THE TALK OF THE TOWN, Columbia:
SIDNEY HARMON
YANKEE DOODLE DANDY, Warner Bros:
ROBERT BUCKNER

(Original Screenplay)

ONE OF OUR AIRCRAFT IS MISSING, Po-
well, UA (British): MICHAEL POWELL
and EMERIC PRESSBURGER
THE ROAD TO MOROCCO, Paramount:
FRANK BUTLER and DON HARTMAN
WAKE ISLAND, Paramount: W. R. BUR-
NETT and FRANK BUTLER
THE WAR AGAINST MRS. HADLEY,
Metro-Goldwyn-Mayer: GEORGE OP-
PENHEIMER
WOMAN OF THE YEAR, Metro-
Goldwyn-Mayer: MICHAEL
KANIN and RING LARDNER, JR.

(Screenplay)

THE INVADERS, Ortus, Columbia (British): RODNEY ACKLAND and EMERIC PRESSBURGER

MRS. MINIVER, Metro-Goldwyn-Mayer: GEORGE FROESCHEL, JAMES HILTON, CLAUDINE WEST and ARTHUR WIMPERIS

THE PRIDE OF THE YANKEES, Goldwyn, RKO Radio: HERMAN J. MANKIEWICZ and JO SWERLING

RANDOM HARVEST, Metro-Goldwyn-Mayer: GEORGE FROESCHEL, CLAUDINE WEST and ARTHUR WIMPERIS

THE TALK OF THE TOWN, Columbia: SIDNEY BUCHMAN and IRWIN SHAW

1943 Sixteenth Year

(Original Story)

ACTION IN THE NORTH ATLANTIC, Warner Bros: GUY GILPATRIC

DESTINATION TOKYO, Warner Bros: STEVE FISHER

THE HUMAN COMEDY, Metro-Goldwyn-Mayer: WILLIAM SAROYAN

THE MORE THE MERRIER, Columbia: FRANK ROSS and ROBERT RUSSELL

SHADOW OF A DOUBT, Universal: GORDON MCDONELL

(Original Screenplay)

AIR FORCE, Warner Bros: DUDLEY NICHOLS

IN WHICH WE SERVE, Two Cities, UA (British): NOEL COWARD

THE NORTH STAR, Goldwyn, RKO Radio: LILLIAN HELLMAN

PRINCESS O'ROURKE, Warner Bros: NORMAN KRASNA

SO PROUDLY WE HAIL, Paramount: ALLAN SCOTT

(Screenplay)

CASABLANCA, Warner Bros:

JULIUS J. EPSTEIN, PHILIP G. EPSTEIN and HOWARD KOCH

HOLY MATRIMONY, 20th Century-Fox: NUNNALLY JOHNSON

THE MORE THE MERRIER, Columbia: RICHARD FLOURNOY, LEWIS R. FOSTER, FRANK ROSS and ROBERT RUSSELL

THE SONG OF BERNADETTE, 20th Century-Fox: GEORGE SEATON

WATCH ON THE RHINE, Warner Bros.: DASHIELL HAMMETT

1944 Seventeenth Year

(Original Story)

GOING MY WAY, Paramount: LEO McCAREY

A GUY NAMED JOE, Metro-Goldwyn-Mayer: DAVID BOEHM and CHANDLER SPRAGUE

LIFEBOAT, 20th Century-Fox: JOHN STEINBECK

NONE SHALL ESCAPE, Columbia: ALFRED NEUMANN and JOSEPH THAN

THE SULLIVANS, 20th Century-Fox: EDWARD DOHERTY and JULES SCHERMER

(Original Screenplay)

HAIL THE CONQUERING HERO, Paramount: PRESTON STURGES

THE MIRACLE OF MORGAN'S CREEK, Paramount: PRESTON STURGES

TWO GIRLS AND A SAILOR, Metro-Goldwyn-Mayer: RICHARD CONNELL and GLADYS LEHMAN

WILSON, 20th Century-Fox: LAMAR TROTTI

WING AND A PRAYER, 20th Century-Fox: JEROME CADY

(Screenplay)

DOUBLE INDEMNITY, Paramount: RAYMOND CHANDLER and BILLY WILDER

GASLIGHT, Metro-Goldwyn-Mayer: JOHN L. BALDERSTON, WALTER REISCH and JOHN VAN DRUTEN

Howard Koch (left), no relation to the current Academy president, accepts his Oscar for co-writing *Casablanca* (1943). At the right is James Hilton who had won an Oscar the previous year for co-writing *Mrs. Miniver.* © *1978 A.M.P.A.S.*

GOING MY WAY, Paramount:
FRANK BUTLER and FRANK CA-
VETT
LAURA, 20th Century-Fox: JAY DRAT-
LER, SAMUEL HOFFENSTEIN and
BETTY REINHARDT
MEET ME IN ST. LOUIS, Metro-Goldwyn-
Mayer: IRVING BRECHER and FRED F.
FINKELHOFFE

1945 Eighteenth Year
(Original Story)
THE AFFAIRS OF SUSAN, Wallis, Para-
mount: LASZLO GOROG and THOMAS
MONROE
THE HOUSE ON 92ND STREET, 20th
Century-Fox: CHARLES G. BOOTH
A MEDAL FOR BENNY, Paramount: JOHN
STEINBECK and JACK WAGNER

OBJECTIVE-BURMA, Warner Bros:
ALVAH BESSIE
A SONG TO REMEMBER, Columbia:
ERNST MARISCHKA

(Original Screenplay)
DILLINGER, Monogram: PHILIP YORDAN
MARIE-LOUISE, Praesens Films
(Swiss): RICHARD SCHWEIZER
MUSIC FOR MILLIONS, Metro-Goldwyn-
Mayer: MYLES CONNOLLY
SALTY O'ROURKE, Paramount: MILTON
HOLMES
WHAT NEXT, CORPORAL HARGROVE?,
Metro-Goldwyn-Mayer: HARRY
KURNITZ

(Screenplay)
G. I. JOE, Cowan, UA: LEOPOLD ATLAS,
GUY ENDORE and PHILIP STEVENSON

THE LOST WEEKEND, Paramount: CHARLES BRACKETT and BILLY WILDER

MILDRED PIERCE, Warner Bros: RANALD MacDOUGALL

PRIDE OF THE MARINES, Warner Bros: ALBERT MALTZ

A TREE GROWS IN BROOKLYN, 20th Century-Fox: FRANK DAVIS and TESS SLESINGER

1946   Nineteenth Year

(Original Story)

THE DARK MIRROR, Universal-International: VLADIMIR POZNER

THE STRANGE LOVE OF MARTHA IVERS, Wallis, Paramount: JACK PATRICK

THE STRANGER, International, RKO Radio: VICTOR TRIVAS

TO EACH HIS OWN, Paramount: CHARLES BRACKETT

VACATION FROM MARRIAGE, London Films, M-G-M (British): CLEMENCE DANE

(Original Screenplay)

THE BLUE DAHLIA, Paramount: RAYMOND CHANDLER

CHILDREN OF PARADISE, Pathe-Cinema, Tricolore (French): JACQUES PREVERT

NOTORIOUS, RKO Radio: BEN HECHT

THE ROAD TO UTOPIA, Paramount: NORMAN PANAMA and MELVIN FRANK

THE SEVENTH VEIL, Rank, Universal (British): MURIEL BOX and SYDNEY BOX

(Screenplay)

ANNA AND THE KING OF SIAM, 20th Century-Fox: SALLY BENSON and TALBOT JENNINGS

THE BEST YEARS OF OUR LIVES, Goldwyn, RKO Radio: ROBERT E. SHERWOOD

BRIEF ENCOUNTER, Rank, U-I (British): ANTHONY HAVELOCK-ALLAN, DAVID LEAN and RONALD NEAME

THE KILLERS, Hellinger, U-I: ANTHONY VEILLER

OPEN CITY, Minerva Films (Italian): SERGIO AMIDEI and F. FELLINI

1947   Twentieth Year

(Original Story)

A CAGE OF NIGHTINGALES, Gaumont, Lopert Films (French): GEORGES CHAPEROT and RENE WHEELER

IT HAPPENED ON FIFTH AVENUE, Roy Del Ruth, Allied Artists: HERBERT CLYDE LEWIS and FREDERICK STEPHANI

KISS OF DEATH, 20th Century-Fox: ELEAZAR LIPSKY

MIRACLE ON 34TH STREET, 20th Century-Fox: VALENTINE DAVIES

SMASH-UP—THE STORY OF A WOMAN, Wanger, U-I: DOROTHY PARKER and FRANK CAVETT

(Original Screenplay)

THE BACHELOR AND THE BOBBY-SOXER, RKO Radio: SIDNEY SHELDON

BODY AND SOUL, Enterprise, UA: ABRAHAM POLONSKY

A DOUBLE LIFE, Kanin Prod., U-I: RUTH GORDON & GARSON KANIN

MONSIEUR VERDOUX, Chaplin, UA: CHARLES CHAPLIN

SHOE-SHINE, Lopert Films (Italian): SERGIO AMIDEI, ADOLFO FRANCI, C. G. VIOLA and CESARE ZAVATTINI

(Screenplay)

BOOMERANG!, 20th Century-Fox: RICHARD MURPHY

CROSSFIRE, RKO Radio: JOHN PAXTON

GENTLEMAN'S AGREEMENT, 20th Century-Fox: MOSS HART

GREAT EXPECTATIONS, Rank-Cineguild, U-I (British): DAVID LEAN, RONALD NEAME and ANTHONY HAVELOCK-ALLAN

MIRACLE ON 34TH STREET, 20th Century-Fox: GEORGE SEATON

1948   Twenty-first Year

(Motion Picture Story)

THE LOUISIANA STORY, Robert Flaherty, Lopert: FRANCES FLAHERTY and ROBERT FLAHERTY

THE NAKED CITY, Hellinger, U-I: MALVIN WALD

RED RIVER, Monterey Productions, UA: BORDEN CHASE

THE RED SHOES, Rank-Archers, Eagle-Lion (British): EMERIC PRESSBURGER

THE SEARCH, Praesens Films, M-G-M (Swiss): RICHARD SCHWEIZER and DAVID WECHSLER

(Screenplay)

A FOREIGN AFFAIR, Paramount: CHARLES BRACKETT, BILLY WILDER and RICHARD L. BREEN

JOHNNY BELINDA, Warner Bros: IRMGARD VON CUBE and ALLEN VINCENT

THE SEARCH, Praesens Films, M-G-M (Swiss): RICHARD SCHWEIZER and DAVID WECHSLER

THE SNAKE PIT, 20th Century-Fox: FRANK PARTOS and MILLEN BRAND

TREASURE OF SIERRA MADRE, Warner Bros: JOHN HUSTON

1949   Twenty-second Year

(Motion Picture Story)

COME TO THE STABLE, 20th Century-Fox: CLARE BOOTHE LUCE

IT HAPPENS EVERY SPRING, 20th Century-Fox: SHIRLEY W. SMITH and VALENTINE DAVIES

SANDS OF IWO JIMA, Republic: HARRY BROWN

THE STRATTON STORY, Metro-Goldwyn-Mayer: DOUGLAS MORROW

WHITE HEAT, Warner Bros: VIRGINIA KELLOGG

(Screenplay)

ALL THE KING'S MEN, a Robert Rossen Prod., Columbia: ROBERT ROSSEN

THE BICYCLE THIEF, De Sica, Mayer-Burstyn (Italian): CESARE ZAVATTINI

CHAMPION, Screen Plays Corp., UA: CARL FOREMAN

THE FALLEN IDOL, London Films, SRO (British): GRAHAM GREENE

A LETTER TO THREE WIVES, 20th Century-Fox: JOSEPH L. MANKIEWICZ

(Story and Screenplay)

BATTLEGROUND, Metro-Goldwyn-Mayer: ROBERT PIROSH

JOLSON SINGS AGAIN, Columbia: SIDNEY BUCHMAN

PAISAN, Roberto Rossellini, Mayer-Burstyn (Italian): ALFRED HAYES, FEDERICO FELLINI, SERGIO AMIDEI, MARCELLO PAGLIERO and ROBERTO ROSSELLINI

PASSPORT TO PIMLICO, Rank-Ealing, Eagle-Lion (British): T.E.B. CLARKE

THE QUIET ONE, Film Documents, Mayer-Burstyn: HELEN LEVITT, JANICE LOEB and SIDNEY MEYERS

1950   Twenty-third Year

(Motion Picture Story)

BITTER RICE, Lux Films (Italian): GIUSEPPE DE SANTIS and CARLO LIZZANI

THE GUNFIGHTER, 20th Century-Fox: WILLIAM BOWERS and ANDRE DE TOTH

MYSTERY STREET, Metro-Goldwyn-Mayer: LEONARD SPIGELGASS

PANIC IN THE STREETS, 20th Century-Fox: EDNA ANHALT and EDWARD ANHALT

WHEN WILLIE COMES MARCHING HOME, 20th Century-Fox: SY GOMBERG

(Screenplay)

ALL ABOUT EVE, 20th Century-Fox: JOSEPH L. MANKIEWICZ

THE ASPHALT JUNGLE, Metro-Goldwyn-Mayer: BEN MADDOW and JOHN HUSTON

BORN YESTERDAY, Columbia: ALBERT MANNHEIMER

BROKEN ARROW, 20th Century-Fox: MICHAEL BLANKFORT

FATHER OF THE BRIDE, Metro-Goldwyn-Mayer: FRANCES GOODRICH and ALBERT HACKETT

(Story and Screenplay)

ADAM'S RIB, Metro-Goldwyn-Mayer: RUTH GORDON and GARSON KANIN

CAGED, Warner Bros: VIRGINIA KELLOGG and BERNARD C. SCHOENFELD

THE MEN, Kramer, UA: CARL FOREMAN

NO WAY OUT, 20th Century-Fox: JOSEPH L. MANKIEWICZ and LESSER SAMUELS

SUNSET BOULEVARD, Paramount: CHARLES BRACKETT, BILLY WILDER and D. M. MARSHMAN, JR.

1951   Twenty-fourth Year

(Motion Picture Story)

BULLFIGHTER AND THE LADY, Republic: BUDD BOETTICHER and RAY NAZARRO

THE FROGMEN, 20th Century-Fox: OSCAR MILLARD

HERE COMES THE GROOM, Paramount: ROBERT RISKIN and LIAM O'BRIEN

SEVEN DAYS TO NOON, Boulting Bros., Mayer-Kingsley-Distinguished Films (British): PAUL DEHN and JAMES BERNARD

TERESA, Metro-Goldwyn-Mayer: ALFRED HAYES and STEWART STERN

(Screenplay)

THE AFRICAN QUEEN, Horizon, UA: JAMES AGEE and JOHN HUSTON

DETECTIVE STORY, Paramount: PHILIP YORDAN and ROBERT WYLER

LA RONDE, Sacha Gordine, Commercial Pictures (French): JACQUES NATANSON and MAX OPHULS

A PLACE IN THE SUN, Paramount: MICHAEL WILSON and HARRY BROWN

A STREETCAR NAMED DESIRE, Charles K. Feldman Group Prods., Warner Bros: TENNESSEE WILLIAMS

(Story and Screenplay)

AN AMERICAN IN PARIS, Metro-Goldwyn-Mayer: ALAN JAY LERNER

THE BIG CARNIVAL, Paramount: BILLY WILDER, LESSER SAMUELS and WALTER NEWMAN

DAVID AND BATHSHEBA, 20th Century-Fox: PHILIP DUNNE

GO FOR BROKE!, Metro-Goldwyn-Mayer: ROBERT PIROSH

THE WELL, Popkin, UA: CLARENCE GREENE and RUSSELL ROUSE

1952   Twenty-fifth Year

(Motion Picture Story)

THE GREATEST SHOW ON EARTH, DeMille, Paramount: FREDERIC M. FRANK, THEODORE ST. JOHN and FRANK CAVETT

MY SON JOHN, Rainbow, Paramount: LEO MCCAREY

THE NARROW MARGIN, RKO Radio: MARTIN GOLDSMITH and JACK LEONARD

THE PRIDE OF ST. LOUIS, 20th Century-Fox: GUY TROSPER

THE SNIPER, Kramer, Columbia: EDNA ANHALT and EDWARD ANHALT

(Screenplay)

THE BAD AND THE BEAUTIFUL, Metro-Goldwyn-Mayer: CHARLES SCHNEE

FIVE FINGERS, 20th Century-Fox: MICHAEL WILSON

HIGH NOON, Kramer, UA: CARL FORE-
MAN

THE MAN IN THE WHITE SUIT, Rank-
Ealing, U-I (British): ROGER MAC-
DOUGALL, JOHN DIGHTON and ALEX-
ANDER MACKENDRICK

THE QUIET MAN, Argosy, Republic:
FRANK S. NUGENT

(Story and Screenplay)

THE ATOMIC CITY, Paramount: SYDNEY
BOEHM

BREAKING THE SOUND BARRIER, London
Films, UA (British): TERENCE
RATTIGAN

THE LAVENDER HILL MOB, Rank-
Ealing, U-I (British): T.E.B.
CLARKE

PAT AND MIKE, Metro-Goldwyn-Mayer:
RUTH GORDON and GARSON KANIN

VIVA ZAPATA!, 20th Century-Fox: JOHN
STEINBECK

1953   Twenty-sixth Year

(Motion Picture Story)

ABOVE AND BEYOND, Metro-Goldwyn-
Mayer: BEIRNE LAY, JR.

THE CAPTAIN'S PARADISE, London
Films, Lopert-UA (British): ALEC
COPPEL

LITTLE FUGITIVE, Little Fugitive Prod.
Co., Joseph Burstyn, Inc.: RAY ASH-
LEY, MORRIS ENGEL and RUTH ORKIN

ROMAN HOLIDAY, Paramount: IAN
McLELLAN HUNTER

(Screenplay)

THE CRUEL SEA, Rank-Ealing, U-I (British): ERIC AMBLER

FROM HERE TO ETERNITY, Columbia: DANIEL TARADASH

LILI, Metro-Goldwyn-Mayer: HELEN
DEUTSCH

ROMAN HOLIDAY, Paramount: IAN
MCLELLAN HUNTER and JOHN
DIGHTON

SHANE, Paramount: A. B. GUTHRIE, JR.

(Story and Screenplay)

THE BAND WAGON, Metro-Goldwyn-
Mayer: BETTY COMDEN and ADOLPH
GREEN

THE DESERT RATS, 20th Century-Fox:
RICHARD MURPHY

THE NAKED SPUR, Metro-Goldwyn-
Mayer: SAM ROLFE and HAROLD JACK
BLOOM

TAKE THE HIGH GROUND, Metro-
Goldwyn-Mayer: MILLARD KAUFMAN

TITANIC, 20th Century-Fox:
CHARLES BRACKETT, WALTER
REISCH and RICHARD BREEN

1954   Twenty-seventh Year

(Motion Picture Story)

BREAD, LOVE AND DREAMS, Titanus,
I.F.E. Releasing Corp. (Italian): ET-
TORE MARGADONNA

BROKEN LANCE, 20th Century-Fox:
PHILIP YORDAN

FORBIDDEN GAMES, Silver Films, Times
Film Corp. (French): FRANÇOIS
BOYER

NIGHT PEOPLE, 20th Century-Fox: JED
HARRIS and TOM REED

THERE'S NO BUSINESS LIKE SHOW BUSI-
NESS, 20th Century-Fox: LAMAR
TROTTI

(Screenplay)

THE CAINE MUTINY, A Stanley Kramer
Prod., Columbia: STANLEY ROBERTS

THE COUNTRY GIRL, Perlberg-Seaton, Paramount: GEORGE SEATON

REAR WINDOW, Patron Inc., Paramount:
JOHN MICHAEL HAYES

SABRINA, Paramount: BILLY WILDER,
SAMUEL TAYLOR and ERNEST LEHMAN

SEVEN BRIDES FOR SEVEN BROTHERS,
Metro-Goldwyn-Mayer: ALBERT
HACKETT, FRANCES GOODRICH and
DOROTHY KINGSLEY

(Story and Screenplay)

THE BAREFOOT CONTESSA, A Figaro,

Inc., Prod. UA: JOSEPH MANKIEWICZ

GENEVIEVE, A J. Arthur Rank Presentation-Sirius Prods., Ltd., U-I (British): WILLIAM ROSE

THE GLENN MILLER STORY, Universal-International: VALENTINE DAVIES and OSCAR BRODNEY

KNOCK ON WOOD, Dena Prods., Paramount: NORMAN PANAMA and MELVIN FRANK

ON THE WATERFRONT, Horizon-American Corp., Columbia: BUDD SCHULBERG

1955 Twenty-eighth Year
(Motion Picture Story)

LOVE ME OR LEAVE ME, Metro-Goldwyn-Mayer: DANIEL FUCHS

THE PRIVATE WAR OF MAJOR BENSON, U-I: JOE CONNELLY and BOB MOSHER

REBEL WITHOUT A CAUSE, Warner Bros.: NICHOLAS RAY

THE SHEEP HAS 5 LEGS, Raoul Ploquin, United Motion Picture Organization (French): JEAN MARSAN, HENRY TROYAT, JACQUES PERRET, HENRI VERNEUIL and RAOUL PLOQUIN

STRATEGIC AIR COMMAND, Paramount: BEIRNE LAY, JR.

(Best Screenplay)

BAD DAY AT BLACK ROCK, Metro-Goldwyn-Mayer: MILLARD KAUFMAN

BLACKBOARD JUNGLE, Metro-Goldwyn-Mayer: RICHARD BROOKS

EAST OF EDEN, Warner Bros.: PAUL OSBORN

LOVE ME OR LEAVE ME, Metro-Goldwyn-Mayer: DANIEL FUCHS and ISOBEL LENNART

MARTY, Hecht and Lancaster's Steven Prods., UA: PADDY CHAYEFSKY

(Story and Screenplay)

THE COURT-MARTIAL OF BILLY MITCHELL, A United States Pictures Prod., Warner Bros.: MILTON SPERLING and EMMET LAVERY

INTERRUPTED MELODY, Metro-Goldwyn-Mayer: WILLIAM LUDWIG and SONYA LEVIEN

IT'S ALWAYS FAIR WEATHER, Metro-Goldwyn-Mayer: BETTY COMDEN and ADOLPH GREEN

MR. HULOT'S HOLIDAY, Fred Orain Prod., GBD International Releasing Corp. (French): JACQUES TATI and HENRI MARQUET

THE SEVEN LITTLE FOYS, Hope Enterprises, Inc. and Scribe Prods.: MELVILLE SHAVELSON and JACK ROSE

1956 Twenty-ninth Year
(Motion Picture Story)

THE BRAVE ONE, King Bros. Prods., Inc., RKO Radio: ROBERT RICH (pseudonym for Dalton Trumbo)

THE EDDY DUCHIN STORY, Columbia: LEO KATCHER

HIGH SOCIETY, Allied Artists: EDWARD BERNDS and ELWOOD ULLMAN (withdrawn from final ballot)

THE PROUD AND THE BEAUTIFUL, La Compagnie Industrielle Commerciale Cinematographique, Kingsley International (French): JEAN-PAUL SARTRE

UMBERTO D., Rizzoli-De Sica-Amato Prod. Harrison & Davidson (Italian): CESARE ZAVATTINI

(Best Screenplay—adapted)

AROUND THE WORLD IN 80 DAYS, The Michael Todd Co., Inc., UA: JAMES POE, JOHN FARROW and S. J. PERELMAN

BABY DOLL, A Newtown Prod., Warner Bros.: TENNESSEE WILLIAMS

FRIENDLY PERSUASION, Allied Artists: (Writer Michael Wilson ineligible for nomination under Academy By-laws.)

GIANT, Giant Prod., Warner Bros.: FRED GUIOL and IVAN MOFFAT

LUST FOR LIFE, Metro-Goldwyn-Mayer: NORMAN CORWIN

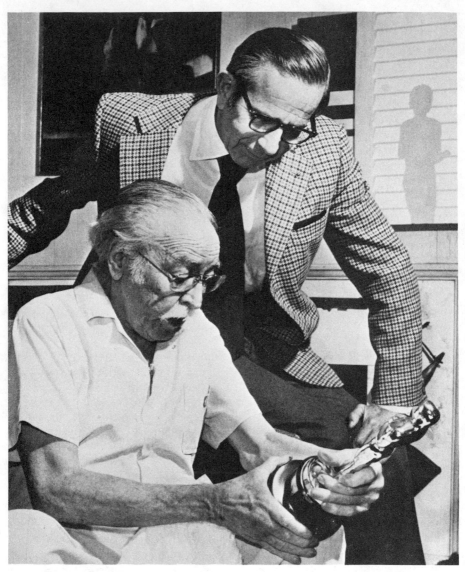

Blacklisted writer Dalton Trumbo (seated) won—but was unable to accept—a 1956 Academy Award for writing *The Brave One* under the pseudonym Robert Rich. Eighteen years later, on May 2, 1975, Academy president Walter Mirisch presented Trumbo with his Oscar. © *1978 A.M.P.A.S.*

(Best Screenplay—original)

THE BOLD AND THE BRAVE, Filmakers Releasing Organization, RKO Radio: ROBERT LEWIN

JULIE, Arwin Prods., M-G-M: ANDREW L. STONE

LA STRADA, Ponti-De Laurentiis Prod., Trans-Lux Dist. Corp. (Italian): FEDERICO FELLINI and TULLIO PINELLI

THE LADY KILLERS, Ealing Studios Ltd., Continental Dist., Inc. (British): WILLIAM ROSE

THE RED BALLOON, Films Montsouris, Lopert Films Dist. Corp.
(French): ALBERT LAMORISSE

1957   *Thirtieth Year*

Note: Rules changed this year to two
awards for Writing instead of
three awards as previously
given.

(Best Screenplay—based on material
from another medium)

THE BRIDGE ON THE RIVER
KWAI, A Horizon Picture, Columbia: PIERRE BOULLE

HEAVEN KNOWS, MR. ALLISON, 20th
Century-Fox: JOHN LEE MAHIN and
JOHN HUSTON

PEYTON PLACE, Jerry Wald Prods.,
Inc., 20th Century-Fox: JOHN
MICHAEL HAYES

SAYONARA, William Goetz Prod.,
Warner Bros.: PAUL OSBORN

12 ANGRY MEN, Orion-Nova Prod., UA:
REGINALD ROSE

(Best Story and Screenplay—written directly for the screen)

DESIGNING WOMAN, Metro-
Goldwyn-Mayer: GEORGE WELLS

FUNNY FACE, Paramount: LEONARD
GERSHE

MAN OF A THOUSAND FACES, Universal-
International: Story by RALPH
WHEELRIGHT. Screenplay by R.
WRIGHT CAMPBELL, IVAN GOFF and
BEN ROBERTS

THE TIN STAR, The Perlberg-Seaton
Prod., Paramount: Story by BARNEY
SLATER and JOEL KANE. Screenplay
by DUDLEY NICHOLS

VITELLONI, Peg Films/Cite Films, API-
Janus Films (Italian): Story by FE-
DERICO FELLINI, ENNIO FLAIANO and
TULLIO PINELLI. Screenplay by FE-
DERICO FELLINI and ENNIO FLAIANO

1958   *Thirty-first Year*

(Best Screenplay—based on material
from another medium)

CAT ON A HOT TIN ROOF, Avon Prods.,
Inc., M-G-M: RICHARD BROOKS and
JAMES POE

GIGI, Arthur Freed Prods., Inc.,
M-G-M: ALAN JAY LERNER

THE HORSE'S MOUTH, Knightsbridge,
UA (British): ALEC GUINNESS

I WANT TO LIVE!, Figaro, Inc., UA:
NELSON GIDDING and DON MANKIE-
WICZ

SEPARATE TABLES, Clifton Prods., Inc.,
UA: TERENCE RATTIGAN and JOHN
GAY

(Best Story and Screenplay—written directly for the screen)

THE DEFIANT ONES, Stanley Kramer, UA: NATHAN E. DOUGLAS
and HAROLD JACOB SMITH

THE GODDESS, Carnegie Prods., Inc.,
Columbia: PADDY CHAYEFSKY

HOUSEBOAT, Paramount and Scribe,
Paramount: MELVILLE SHAVELSON
and JACK ROSE

THE SHEEPMAN, Metro-Goldwyn-
Mayer: Story by JAMES EDWARD
GRANT. Screenplay by WILLIAM
BOWERS and JAMES EDWARD GRANT

TEACHER'S PET, Perlberg-Seaton, Paramount: FAY and MICHAEL KANIN

1959   *Thirty-second Year*

(Best Screenplay—based on material
from another medium)

ANATOMY OF A MURDER, Otto Preminger, Columbia: WENDELL MAYES

BEN-HUR, Metro-Goldwyn-Mayer:
KARL TUNBERG

THE NUN'S STORY, Warner Bros.: ROB-
ERT ANDERSON

ROOM AT THE TOP, Romulus Films,
Ltd., Continental Dist., Inc. (British): NEIL PATERSON

SOME LIKE IT HOT, Ashton Prods. & The Mirisch Co., UA: BILLY WILDER and I.A.L. DIAMOND.

(Best Story and Screenplay—written directly for the screen)

THE 400 BLOWS, Les Films du Carrosse & SEDIF, Zenith International (French): FRANÇOIS TRUFFAUT and MARCEL MOUSSY

NORTH BY NORTHWEST, Metro-Goldwyn-Mayer: ERNEST LEHMAN

OPERATION PETTICOAT, Granart Co., U-I: Story by PAUL KING and JOSEPH STONE. Screenplay by STANLEY SHAPIRO and MAURICE RICHLIN

PILLOW TALK, Arwin Prods., Inc., U-I: Story by RUSSEL ROUSE and CLARENCE GREENE. Screenplay by STANLEY SHAPIRO and MAURICE RICHLIN

WILD STRAWBERRIES, Svensk Filmindustri, Janus Films (Swedish): INGMAR BERGMAN

1960   Thirty-third Year

(Best Screenplay—based on material from another medium)

ELMER GANTRY, Burt Lancaster-Richard Brooks Prod., UA: RICHARD BROOKS

INHERIT THE WIND, Stanley Kramer Prod., UA: NATHAN E. DOUGLAS and HAROLD JACOB SMITH

SONS AND LOVERS, Company of Artists, Inc., 20th Century-Fox: GAVIN LAMBERT and T.E.B. CLARKE

THE SUNDOWNERS, Warner Bros.: ISOBEL LENNART

TUNES OF GLORY, H. M. Films Limited Prod., Lopert Pictures Corp. (British): JAMES KENNAWAY

(Best Story and Screenplay—written directly for the screen)

THE ANGRY SILENCE, Beaver Films Limited Prod., Joseph Harris–Sig Shore (British): Story by RICHARD GREGSON and MICHAEL CRAIG. Screenplay by BRYAN FORBES

THE APARTMENT, The Mirisch Co., Inc., UA: BILLY WILDER and I.A.L. DIAMOND

THE FACTS OF LIFE, Panama & Frank Prod., UA: NORMAN PANAMA and MELVIN FRANK

HIROSHIMA, MON AMOUR, Argos Films-Como Films-Daiei Pictures, Ltd.-Pathe Overseas Prod., Zenith International Film Corp. (French-Japanese): MARGUERITE DURAS

NEVER ON SUNDAY, Melinafilm Prod., Lopert Pictures Corp. (Greek): JULES DASSIN

1961   Thirty-fourth Year

(Best Screenplay—based on material from another medium)

BREAKFAST AT TIFFANY'S, Jurow-Shepherd Prod., Paramount: GEORGE AXELROD

THE GUNS OF NAVARONE, Carl Foreman Prod., Columbia: CARL FOREMAN

THE HUSTLER, Robert Rossen Prod., 20th Century-Fox: SIDNEY CARROLL and ROBERT ROSSEN

JUDGMENT AT NUREMBERG, Stanley Kramer Prod., UA: ABBY MANN

WEST SIDE STORY, Mirisch Pictures, Inc. and B and P Enterprises, Inc., UA: ERNEST LEHMAN

(Best Story and Screenplay—written directly for the screen)

BALLAD OF A SOLDIER, Mosfilm Studio Prod., Kingsley International-M.J.P. Enterprises, Inc. (Russian): VALENTIN YOSHOV and GRIGORI CHUKHRAI

GENERAL DELLA ROVERE, Zebra & S.N.E. Gaumont Prod., Continental Dist., Inc. (Italian): SERGIO AMIDEI, DIEGO FABBRI and INDRO MONTANELLI

LA DOLCE VITA, Riama Film Prod., Astor Pictures, Inc. (Italian): FEDERICO FELLINI, TULLIO PINELLI, ENNIO FLAIANO and BRUNELLO RONDI

LOVER COME BACK, Universal-International-The 7 Pictures Corp., Nob Hill Prods., Inc., Arwin Prods., Inc., U-I: STANLEY SHAPIRO and PAUL HENNING

SPLENDOR IN THE GRASS, NBI Prod., Warner Bros.: WILLIAM INGE

1962   Thirty-fifth Year

(Best Screenplay—based on material from another medium)

DAVID AND LISA, Heller-Perry Prods., Continental Distributing: ELEANOR PERRY

LAWRENCE OF ARABIA, Horizon Pictures (G.B.), Ltd.-Sam Spiegel-David Lean Prod., Columbia: ROBERT BOLT

LOLITA, Seven Arts Prods., M-G-M: VLADIMIR NABOKOV

THE MIRACLE WORKER, Playfilms Prod., UA: WILLIAM GIBSON

TO KILL A MOCKINGBIRD, Universal-International-Pakula-Mulligan-Brentwood Prod., U-I: HORTON FOOTE

(Best Story and Screenplay—written directly for the screen)

DIVORCE—ITALIAN STYLE, Lux-Vides-Galatea Film Prod., Embassy Pictures: ENNIO DE CONCINI, ALFREDO GIANNETTI and PIETRO GERMI

FREUD, Universal-International-John Huston Prod., U-I: Story by CHARLES KAUFMAN. Screenplay by CHARLES KAUFMAN and WOLFGANG REINHARDT

LAST YEAR AT MARIENBAD, Preceitel-Terra Film Prod., Astor Pictures: ALAIN ROBBE-GRILLET

THAT TOUCH OF MINK, Universal-International-Granley-Arwin-Nob Hill Prod., U-I: STANLEY SHAPIRO and NATE MONASTER

THROUGH A GLASS DARKLY, Svensk Filmindustri Prod., Janus Films: INGMAR BERGMAN

1963   Thirty-sixth Year

(Best Screenplay—based on material from another medium)

CAPTAIN NEWMAN, M.D., Universal-Brentwood-Reynard Prod., Universal: RICHARD L. BREEN, PHOEBE and HENRY EPHRON

HUD, Salem-Dover Prod., Paramount: IRVING RAVETCH and HARRIET FRANK, JR.

LILIES OF THE FIELD, Rainbow Prod., UA: JAMES POE

SUNDAYS AND CYBELE, Terra-Fides-Orsay-Films Trocadero Prods., Columbia: SERGE BOURGUIGNON and ANTOINE TUDAL

TOM JONES, Woodfall Prod., UA-Lopert Pictures: JOHN OSBORNE

(Best Story and Screenplay—written directly for the screen)

AMERICA AMERICA, Athena Enterprises Prod., Warner Bros.: ELIA KAZAN

FEDERICO FELLINI'S 8½, Cineriz Prod., Embassy Pictures. FEDERICO FELLINI, ENNIO FLAIANO, TULLIO PINELLI and BRUNELLO RONDI

THE FOUR DAYS OF NAPLES, Titanus Prod., M-G-M: Story by PASQUALE FESTA CAMPANILE, MASSIMO FRANCIOSA, NANNI LOY and VASCO PRATOLINI. Screenplay by CARLO BERNARI, PASQUALE FESTA CAMPANILE, MASSIMO FRANCIOSA and NANNI LOY

HOW THE WEST WAS WON, Metro-Goldwyn-Mayer & Cinerama: JAMES R. WEBB

LOVE WITH THE PROPER STRANGER, Boardwalk-Rona Prod., Paramount: ARNOLD SCHULMAN

1964 Thirty-seventh Year

(Best Screenplay—based on material from another medium)

BECKET, Hal Wallis Prod., Paramount: EDWARD ANHALT

DR. STRANGELOVE OR: HOW I LEARNED TO STOP WORRYING AND LOVE THE BOMB, Hawk Films, Ltd. Prod., Columbia: STANLEY KUBRICK, PETER GEORGE and TERRY SOUTHERN

MARY POPPINS, Walt Disney Prods.: BILL WALSH and DON DaGRADI

MY FAIR LADY, Warner Bros.: ALAN JAY LERNER

ZORBA THE GREEK, Rochley, Ltd. Prod., International Classics: MICHAEL CACOYANNIS

(Best Story and Screenplay—written directly for the screen)

FATHER GOOSE, Universal-Granox Prod., Universal: Story by S. H. BARNETT. Screenplay by PETER STONE and FRANK TARLOFF

A HARD DAY'S NIGHT, Walter Shenson Prod., United Artists: ALUN OWEN

ONE POTATO, TWO POTATO, Bawalco Picture Prod., Cinema V Distributing: Story by ORVILLE H. HAMPTON. Screenplay by RAPHAEL HAYES and ORVILLE H. HAMPTON

THE ORGANIZER, Lux-Vides-Mediterranee Cinema Prod., Walter Reade-Sterling-Continental Distributing: AGE, SCARPELLI and MARIO MONICELLI

THAT MAN FROM RIO, Ariane-Les Artistes Prod., Lopert Pictures: JEAN-PAUL RAPPENEAU, ARIANE MNOUCHKINE, DANIEL BOULANGER and PHILIPPE DE BROCA

1965 Thirty-eighth Year

(Best Screenplay—based on material from another medium)

CAT BALLOU, Harold Hecht Prod., Columbia: WALTER NEWMAN and FRANK R. PIERSON

THE COLLECTOR, The Collector Company, Columbia: STANLEY MANN and JOHN KOHN

DOCTOR ZHIVAGO, Sostar S.A.-Metro-Goldwyn-Mayer British Studios, Ltd. Prod., M-G-M: ROBERT BOLT

SHIP OF FOOLS, Columbia: ABBY MANN

A THOUSAND CLOWNS, Harrell Prod., United Artists: HERB GARDNER

(Best Story and Screenplay—written directly for the screen)

CASANOVA '70, C. C. Champion-Les Films Concordia Prod., Embassy: AGE, SCARPELLI, MARIO MONICELLI, TONINO GUERRA, GIORGIO SALVIONI and SUSO CECCHI D'AMICO

DARLING, Anglo-Amalgamated, Ltd. Prod., Embassy: FREDERIC RAPHAEL

THOSE MAGNIFICENT MEN IN THEIR FLYING MACHINES, 20th Century-Fox, Ltd. Prod., 20th Century-Fox: JACK DAVIES and KEN ANNAKIN

THE TRAIN, Les Prods. Artistes Associes, United Artists: FRANKLIN COEN and FRANK DAVIS

THE UMBRELLAS OF CHERBOURG, Parc-Madeleine Films Prod., American International: JACQUES DEMY

1966 Thirty-ninth Year

(Best Screenplay—based on material from another medium)

ALFIE, Sheldrake Films, Ltd. Prod., Paramount: BILL NAUGHTON

A MAN FOR ALL SEASONS, Highland Films, Ltd. Prod., Columbia: ROBERT BOLT

THE PROFESSIONALS, Pax Enterprises Prod., Columbia: RICHARD BROOKS

THE RUSSIANS ARE COMING THE RUSSIANS ARE COMING, Mirisch Corp. of Delaware Prod., UA: WILLIAM ROSE

WHO'S AFRAID OF VIRGINIA WOOLF?, Chenault Prod., Warner Bros.: ERNEST LEHMAN

(Best Story and Screenplay—written directly for the screen)

BLOW-UP, Carlo Ponti Prod., Premier Productions: Story by MICHELANGELO ANTONIONI. Screenplay by MICHELANGELO ANTONIONI, TONINO GUERRA and EDWARD BOND

THE FORTUNE COOKIE, Phalanx-Jalem-Mirisch Corp. of Delaware Prod., UA: BILLY WILDER and I.A.L. DIAMOND

KHARTOUM, Julian Blaustein Prod., UA: ROBERT ARDREY

A MAN AND A WOMAN, Les Films 13 Prod., Allied Artists: Story by CLAUDE LELOUCH. Screenplay by PIERRE UYTTERHOEVEN and CLAUDE LELOUCH

THE NAKED PREY, Theodora Prod., Paramount: CLINT JOHNSTON and DON PETERS

1967 Fortieth Year

(Best Screenplay—based on material from another medium)

COOL HAND LUKE, Jalem Prod., Warner Bros.-Seven Arts.: DONN PEARCE and FRANK R. PIERSON

THE GRADUATE, Mike Nichols/Lawrence Turman Prod., Embassy: CALDER WILLINGHAM and BUCK HENRY

IN COLD BLOOD, Pax Enterprises Prod., Columbia: RICHARD BROOKS

IN THE HEAT OF THE NIGHT, Mirisch Corp. Prod., United Artists: STIRLING SILLIPHANT

ULYSSES, Walter Reade, Jr.-Joseph Strick Prod., Walter Reade-Continental Distributing: JOSEPH STRICK and FRED HAINES

(Best Story and Screenplay—written directly for the screen)

BONNIE AND CLYDE, Tatira-Hiller Prod., Warner Bros.-Seven Arts: DAVID NEWMAN and ROBERT BENTON

DIVORCE AMERICAN STYLE, Tandem Prods. for National General Prods., Columbia: Story by ROBERT KAUFMAN. Screenplay by NORMAN LEAR

GUESS WHO'S COMING TO DINNER, Columbia: WILLIAM ROSE

LA GUERRE EST FINIE Sofracima and Europa-Film Prod., Brandon Films: JORGE SEMPRUN

TWO FOR THE ROAD, Stanley Donen Films Prod., 20th Century-Fox: FREDERIC RAPHAEL

1968 Forty-first Year

(Best Screenplay—based on material from another medium)

THE LION IN WINTER Haworth Prods., Avco Embassy: JAMES GOLDMAN

THE ODD COUPLE, Howard W. Koch Prod., Paramount: NEIL SIMON

OLIVER!, Romulus Films, Columbia: VERNON HARRIS

RACHEL, RACHEL, Kayos Prod., Warner Bros.-Seven Arts: STEWART STERN

ROSEMARY'S BABY, William Castle Enterprises Prod., Paramount: ROMAN POLANSKI

(Best Story and Screenplay—written directly for the screen)

THE BATTLE OF ALGIERS, Igor-Casbah Film Prod., Allied Artists: FRANCO SOLINAS and GILLO PONTECORVO

FACES, John Cassavetes Prod., Walter Reade-Continental Dist.: JOHN CASSAVETES

HOT MILLIONS, Mildred Freed Albert Prod., Metro-Goldwyn-Mayer: IRA WALLACH and PETER USTINOV

THE PRODUCERS, Sidney Glazier Prod., Avco Embassy: MEL BROOKS

2001: A SPACE ODYSSEY, Polaris Prod.,
Metro-Goldwyn-Mayer: STANLEY
KUBRICK and ARTHUR C. CLARKE

1969 Forty-second Year
(Best Screenplay—based on material
from another medium)

ANNE OF THE THOUSAND DAYS, Hal B.
Wallis-Universal Pictures, Ltd.
Prod., Universal: JOHN HALE and
BRIDGET BOLAND. Adaptation by
RICHARD SOKOLOVE

GOODBYE, COLUMBUS, Willow Tree
Prods., Paramount: ARNOLD SCHUL-
MAN

MIDNIGHT COWBOY, Jerome
Hellman-John Schlesinger Prod.,
United Artists: WALDO SALT

THEY SHOOT HORSES, DON'T THEY?,
Chartoff-Winkler-Pollack Prod.,
ABC Pictures Presentation, Cinera-
ma: JAMES POE and ROBERT E.
THOMPSON

Z, Reggane Films-O.N.C.I.C. Prod.,
Cinema V: JORGE SEMPRUN and
COSTA-GAVRAS

(Best Story and Screenplay—based on
material not previously published or
produced.)

BOB & CAROL & TED & ALICE, Frankovich Prods., Columbia: PAUL MA-
ZURSKY and LARRY TUCKER

BUTCH CASSIDY AND THE SUN-
DANCE KID, George Roy Hill-Paul
Monash Prod., 20th Century-Fox:
WILLIAM GOLDMAN

THE DAMNED, Pegaso-Praesidens Film
Prod., Warner Bros.: Story by NI-
COLA BADALUCCO. Screenplay by
NICOLA BADALUCCO, ENRICO MEDIOLI
and LUCHINO VISCONTI

EASY RIDER, Pando-Raybert Prods., Columbia: PETER FONDA, DENNIS HOP-
PER and TERRY SOUTHERN

THE WILD BUNCH, Phil Feldman Prod.,
Warner Bros.: Story by WALON

GREEN and ROY N. SICKNER. Screenplay by WALON GREEN and SAM
PECKINPAH

1970 Forty-third Year
(Best Screenplay—based on material
from another medium)

AIRPORT Ross Hunter-Universal Prod.,
Universal: GEORGE SEATON

I NEVER SANG FOR MY FATHER, Jamel
Prods., Columbia: ROBERT ANDERSON

LOVERS AND OTHER STRANGERS, ABC
Pictures Prod., Cinerama: RENEE
TAYLOR, JOSEPH BOLOGNA and DAVID
ZELAG GOODMAN

M*A*S*H, Aspen Prods., 20th Century-Fox: RING LARDNER, JR.

WOMEN IN LOVE, Larry Kramer-Martin
Rosen Prod., UA: LARRY KRAMER

(Best Story and Screenplay—based on
factual material or material not previously published or produced)

FIVE EASY PIECES, BBS Prods., Colum-
bia: Story by BOB RAFELSON and
ADRIEN JOYCE. Screenplay by ADRIEN
JOYCE.

JOE, Cannon Group Prod., Cannon Releasing: NORMAN WEXLER

LOVE STORY, The Love Story Company
Prod., Paramount: ERICH SEGAL

MY NIGHT AT MAUD'S, Films du
Losange-Carrosse-Renn-Deux
Mondes-La Gueville-Simar-La
Pleiade-F.F.P. Prod., Pathe Contem-
porary: ERIC ROHMER

PATTON, 20th Century-Fox:
FRANCIS FORD COPPOLA and
EDMUND H. NORTH

1971 Forty-fourth Year
(Best Screenplay—based on material
from another medium)

A CLOCKWORK ORANGE, A Hawks
Films, Ltd. Prod., Warner Bros.:
STANLEY KUBRICK

THE CONFORMIST, Mars Film Produzione, S.P.A.-Marianne Prods., Paramount: BERNARDO BERTOLUCCI

THE FRENCH CONNECTION, A Philip D'Antoni Prod. in association with Schine-Moore Prods., 20th Century-Fox: ERNEST TIDYMAN

THE GARDEN OF THE FINZI-CONTINIS, A Gianni Hecht Lucari–Arthur Cohn Prod., Cinema 5, Ltd.: UGO PIRRO and VITTORIO BONICELLI

THE LAST PICTURE SHOW, BBS Prods., Columbia: LARRY MCMURTRY and PETER BOGDANOVICH

(Best Story and Screenplay—based on factual material or material not previously published or produced)

THE HOSPITAL, A Howard Gottfried-Paddy Chayefsky Prod. in association with Arthur Hiller, UA: PADDY CHAYEFSKY

INVESTIGATION OF A CITIZEN ABOVE SUSPICION, A Vera Films, S.P.A. Prod., Columbia: ELIO PETRI and UGO PIRRO

KLUTE, A Gus Prod., Warner Bros.: ANDY and DAVE LEWIS

SUMMER OF '42, A Robert Mulligan-Richard Alan Roth Prod., Warner Bros.: HERMAN RAUCHER

SUNDAY BLOODY SUNDAY, A Joseph Janni Prod., UA: PENELOPE GILLIATT

1972   Forty-fifth Year

(Best Screenplay—based on material from another medium)

CABARET, An ABC Pictures Prod., Allied Artists. JAY ALLEN

THE EMIGRANTS, A Svensk Filmindustri Prod., Warner Bros.: JAN TROELL and BENGT FORSLUND

THE GODFATHER, An Albert S. Ruddy Prod., Paramount: MARIO PUZO and FRANCIS FORD COPPOLA

PETE 'N' TILLIE, A Universal-Martin Ritt-Julius J. Epstein Prod., Universal: JULIUS J. EPSTEIN

SOUNDER, Radnitz/Mattel Prods., 20th Century-Fox: LONNE ELDER, III

(Best Story and Screenplay—based on factual material or material not previously published or produced)

THE CANDIDATE, A Redford-Ritchie Prod., Warner Bros.: JEREMY LARNER

THE DISCREET CHARM OF THE BOURGEOISIE, A Serge Silberman Prod., 20th Century-Fox: LUIS BUÑUEL in collaboration with JEAN-CLAUDE CARRIERE

LADY SINGS THE BLUES, A Motown-Weston-Furie Prod., Paramount: TERENCE MCCLOY, CHRIS CLARK and SUZANNE DE PASSE

MURMUR OF THE HEART, A Nouvelles Editions De Films-Marianne Productions-Vides Cinematografica-Franz Seitz Filmproduktion, Continental Distributing: LOUIS MALLE

YOUNG WINSTON, An Open Road Films, Ltd. Prod., Columbia: CARL FOREMAN

1973   Forty-sixth Year

(Best Screenplay—based on material from another medium)

THE EXORCIST, Hoya Prods., Warner Bros.: WILLIAM PETER BLATTY

THE LAST DETAIL, An Acrobat Films Prod., Columbia: ROBERT TOWNE

THE PAPER CHASE, Thompson-Paul Prods., 20th Century-Fox: JAMES BRIDGES

PAPER MOON, A Directors Company Prod., Paramount: ALVIN SARGENT

SERPICO, A Produzioni De Laurentiis International Manufacturing Company S.p.A. Prod., Paramount: WALDO SALT and NORMAN WEXLER

(Best Story and Screenplay—based on factual material or material not previously published or produced)

AMERICAN GRAFFITI, A Universal-Lucasfilm, Ltd.-Coppola Company Prod., Universal: GEORGE LUCAS, GLORIA KATZ and WILLARD HUYCK

CRIES AND WHISPERS, A Svenska Filminstitutet-Cinematograph AB Prod., New World Pictures: INGMAR BERGMAN

SAVE THE TIGER, Filmways-Jalem-Cirandinha Prods., Paramount: STEVE SHAGAN

THE STING, A Universal-Bill/Phillips-George Roy Hill Film Prod., Zanuck/Brown Presentation, Universal: DAVID S. WARD

A TOUCH OF CLASS, Brut Productions, Avco Embassy: MELVIN FRANK and JACK ROSE

1974 Forty-seventh Year

(Best Original Screenplay)

ALICE DOESN'T LIVE HERE ANYMORE, Warner Bros.: ROBERT GETCHELL

CHINATOWN, A Robert Evans Production, Paramount: ROBERT TOWNE

THE CONVERSATION, A Directors Company Production, Paramount: FRANCIS FORD COPPOLA

DAY FOR NIGHT, A Les Films Du Carrosse and P.E.C.F., Paris; P.I.C., Rome Production, Warner Bros.: FRANÇOIS TRUFFAUT, JEAN-LOUIS RICHARD, and SUZANNE SCHIFFMAN

HARRY AND TONTO, 20th Century-Fox: PAUL MAZURSKY and JOSH GREENFELD

(Best Screenplay adapted from other material)

THE APPRENTICESHIP OF DUDDY KRAVITZ, An International Cinemedia Centre, Ltd. Prod., Paramount: Screenplay by MORDECAI RICHLER.

Adaptation by LIONEL CHETWYND

THE GODFATHER PART II, A Coppola Company Prod., Paramount: Screenplay by FRANCIS FORD COPPOLA and MARIO PUZO

LENNY, A Marvin Worth Production, United Artists: Screenplay by JULIAN BARRY

MURDER ON THE ORIENT EXPRESS, A G.W. Films, Ltd. Prod., Paramount: Screenplay by PAUL DEHN

YOUNG FRANKENSTEIN, A Gruskoff/Venture Films-Crossbow Prods.-Jouer, Ltd. Production, 20th Century-Fox: Screenplay by GENE WILDER and MEL BROOKS

1975 Forty-eighth Year

(Best Original Screenplay)

AMARCORD, An F.C. Productions-P.E.C.F. Production, New World Pictures: FEDERICO FELLINI and TONINO GUERRA

AND NOW MY LOVE, A Rizzoli Film-Les Films 13 Production, Avco Embassy: CLAUDE LELOUCH and PIERRE UYTTERHOEVEN

DOG DAY AFTERNOON, Warner Bros.: FRANK PIERSON

LIES MY FATHER TOLD ME, Pentimento Productions, Ltd.-Pentacle VIII Productions, Ltd., Columbia: TED ALLAN

SHAMPOO, Rubeeker Productions, Columbia: ROBERT TOWNE and WARREN BEATTY

(Best Screenplay adapted from other material)

BARRY LYNDON, A Hawk Films, Ltd. Production, Warner Bros.: Screenplay by STANLEY KUBRICK

THE MAN WHO WOULD BE KING, An Allied Artists-Columbia Pictures Production, Allied Artists: Screenplay by JOHN HUSTON and GLADYS HILL

ONE FLEW OVER THE CUCKOO'S NEST, A Fantasy Films Production,

United Artists: Screenplay by
LAWRENCE HAUBEN and BO
GOLDMAN

SCENT OF A WOMAN, A Dean Film Production, 20th Century-Fox: Screenplay by RUGGERO MACCARI and DINO RISI

THE SUNSHINE BOYS, A Ray Stark Production, Metro-Goldwyn-Mayer: Screenplay by NEIL SIMON

1976   Forty-ninth Year

(Best Screenplay Written Directly For the Screen)

COUSIN, COUSINE, Les Films Pomereu-Gaumont Production, Northal Film Distributors Ltd.: Story and Screenplay by JEAN-CHARLES TACCHELLA. Adaptation by DANIELE THOMPSON

THE FRONT, Columbia Pictures: Story and Screenplay by WALTER BERNSTEIN

NETWORK, A Howard Gottfried/Paddy Chayefsky Production, Metro-Goldwyn-Mayer/United Artists: Story and Screenplay by PADDY CHAYEFSKY

ROCKY, A Robert Chartoff-Irwin Winkler Production, United Artists: Story and Screenplay by SYLVESTER STALLONE

SEVEN BEAUTIES, A Medusa Distribuzione Production, Cinema 5, Ltd.: Story and Screenplay by LINA WERTMULLER

(Best Screenplay Based On Material From Another Medium)

ALL THE PRESIDENT'S MEN, A Wildwood Enterprises Production, Warner Bros.: Screenplay by WILLIAM GOLDMAN

BOUND FOR GLORY, The Bound For Glory Company Production, United Artists: Screenplay by ROBERT GETCHELL

FELLINI'S CASANOVA, A P.E.A.-

Produzioni Europee Associate S.p.A. Production, Universal: Screenplay by FEDERICO FELLINI and BERNADINO ZAPPONI

THE SEVEN-PER-CENT SOLUTION, A Herbert Ross Film/Winitsky-Sellers Production, A Universal Release: Screenplay by NICHOLAS MEYER

VOYAGE OF THE DAMNED, An ITC Entertainment Production, Avco Embassy: Screenplay by STEVE SHAGAN and DAVID BUTLER

1977   Fiftieth Year

(Best Original Screenplay)

ANNIE HALL, Jack Rollins-Charles H. Joffe Productions, United: Story and screenplay by WOODY ALLEN and MARSHALL BRICKMAN

THE GOODBYE GIRL, A Ray Stark Production, Metro-Goldwyn-Mayer/Warner Bros.: Story and screenplay by NEIL SIMON

THE LATE SHOW, A Lion's Gate Film Production, Warner Bros.: Story and screenplay by ROBERT BENTON

STAR WARS, A Twentieth Century-Fox Production, Twentieth Century-Fox: Story and screenplay by GEORGE LUCAS

THE TURNING POINT, Hera Productions, Twentieth Century-Fox: Story and screenplay by ARTHUR LAURENTS

(Best Screenplay—based on material from another medium)

EQUUS, A Winkast Company, Ltd./P.B., Ltd. Production, United Artists: Screenplay by PETER SHAFFER

I NEVER PROMISED YOU A ROSE GARDEN, A Scherick/Blatt Production, New World Pictures: Screenplay by GAVIN LAMBERT and LEWIS JOHN CARLINO

JULIA, A Twentieth Century-Fox Production, Twentieth Century-Fox: Screenplay by ALVIN SARGENT

OH, GOD!, A Warner Bros. Production, Warner Bros.: Screenplay by
LARRY GELBART

THAT OBSCURE OBJECT OF DESIRE, A Greenwich-Les Films Galaxie-In Cine Production, First Artists: Screenplay by LUIS BUÑUEL and JEAN-CLAUDE CARRIERE

CINEMATOGRAPHY

Cinematography is one of three categories (with Costume Design and Art Direction-Set Decoration) that has in certain years been split into separate awards for black-and-white films and color films. When the category was begun at the first awards color cinematography was still in an experimental stage. By the mid-1930s, however, Technicolor had perfected its three-color process, and the use of color became more widespread. Special awards for color cinematography were given by the Academy in 1936, 1937, and 1938, and in 1939 the Cinematography award was officially divided into black-and-white and color categories. Except for 1957, the practice of giving separate awards continued through 1966. As late as 1964 black-and-white films outnumbered color by a narrow margin among the year's eligible pictures, but within three years only one film in five was made in black and white. In 1967 the Academy voted to eliminate the separate categories and give only a single award.

Achievements in this category are nominated by the members of the Academy Cinematographers Branch.

1927/28   First Year
DEVIL DANCER, United Artists: GEORGE BARNES
DRUMS OF LOVE, United Artists: KARL STRUSS
MAGIC FLAME, United Artists: GEORGE BARNES
MY BEST GIRL, Pickford, UA: CHARLES ROSHER
SADIE THOMPSON, United Artists: GEORGE BARNES
SUNRISE, Fox: CHARLES ROSHER and KARL STRUSS
THE TEMPEST, United Artists: CHARLES ROSHER

1928/29   Second Year
THE DIVINE LADY, First National: JOHN SEITZ
FOUR DEVILS, Fox: ERNEST PALMER
IN OLD ARIZONA, Fox: ARTHUR EDESON
OUR DANCING DAUGHTERS, Metro-Goldwyn-Mayer: GEORGE BARNES
STREET ANGEL, Fox: ERNEST PALMER
LARGE CAPITAL LETTERS DENOTE WINNER

WHITE SHADOWS IN THE SOUTH SEAS, Metro-Goldwyn-Mayer: CLYDE DE VINNA

1929/30   Third Year
ALL QUIET ON THE WESTERN FRONT, Universal: ARTHUR EDESON
ANNA CHRISTIE, Metro-Goldwyn-Mayer: WILLIAM DANIELS
HELL'S ANGELS, United Artists: GAETANO GAUDIO and HARRY PERRY
THE LOVE PARADE, Paramount: VICTOR MILNER
WITH BYRD AT THE SOUTH POLE, Paramount: JOSEPH T. RUCKER and WILLARD VAN DER VEER

1930/31   Fourth Year
CIMARRON, RKO Radio: EDWARD CRONJAGER
MOROCCO, Paramount: LEE GARMES
THE RIGHT TO LOVE, Paramount: CHARLES LANG

SVENGALI, Warners-First National:
BARNEY "CHICK" MCGILL
TABU, Paramount: FLOYD CROSBY

1931/32   Fifth Year
ARROWSMITH, Goldwyn, UA: RAY
JUNE
DR. JEKYLL AND MR. HYDE, Paramount:
KARL STRUSS
SHANGHAI EXPRESS, Paramount:
LEE GARMES

1932/33   Sixth Year
A FAREWELL TO ARMS, Para-
mount: CHARLES BRYANT
LANG, JR.
REUNION IN VIENNA, Metro-Goldwyn-
Mayer: GEORGE J. FOLSEY, JR.
SIGN OF THE CROSS, Paramount: KARL
STRUSS

1934   Seventh Year
THE AFFAIRS OF CELLINI, 20th Century,
UA: CHARLES ROSHER
CLEOPATRA, Paramount: VICTOR
MILNER
OPERATION 13, Metro-Goldwyn-Mayer:
GEORGE FOLSEY

1935   Eighth Year
BARBARY COAST, Goldwyn, UA: RAY
JUNE
THE CRUSADES, Paramount: VICTOR
MILNER
LES MISERABLES, 20th Century, UA:
GREGG TOLAND
A MIDSUMMER NIGHT'S DREAM,
Warner Bros.: HAL MOHR

1936   Ninth Year
ANTHONY ADVERSE, Warner
Bros.: GAETANO GAUDIO
THE GENERAL DIED AT DAWN, Para-
mount: VICTOR MILNER
THE GORGEOUS HUSSY, Metro-
Goldwyn-Mayer: GEORGE FOLSEY

1937   Tenth Year
DEAD END, Goldwyn, UA: GREGG TO-
LAND
THE GOOD EARTH, Metro-Goldwyn-
Mayer: KARL FREUND
WINGS OVER HONOLULU, Universal:
JOSEPH VALENTINE

1938   Eleventh Year
ALGIERS, Wanger, UA: JAMES WONG
HOWE
ARMY GIRL, Republic: ERNEST MILLER
and HARRY WILD
THE BUCCANEER, Paramount: VICTOR
MILNER
THE GREAT WALTZ, Metro-
Goldwyn-Mayer: JOSEPH RUT-
TENBERG
JEZEBEL, Warner Bros.: ERNEST HAL-
LER
MAD ABOUT MUSIC, Universal: JOSEPH
VALENTINE
MERRILY WE LIVE, Roach, M-G-M:
NORBERT BRODINE
SUEZ, 20th Century-Fox: PEVERELL
MARLEY
VIVACIOUS LADY, RKO Radio: ROBERT
DE GRASSE
YOU CAN'T TAKE IT WITH YOU, Colum-
bia: JOSEPH WALKER
THE YOUNG IN HEART, Selznick, UA:
LEON SHAMROY

1939   Twelfth Year
(Black-and-White)
STAGECOACH, Wanger, UA: BERT
GLENNON
WUTHERING HEIGHTS, Goldwyn,
UA: GREGG TOLAND

(Color)
GONE WITH THE WIND, Selznick,
M-G-M: ERNEST HALLER and
RAY RENNAHAN
THE PRIVATE LIVES OF ELIZABETH AND
ESSEX, Warner Bros.: SOL POLITO
and W. HOWARD GREENE

1940   Thirteenth Year

(Black-and-White)

ABE LINCOLN IN ILLINOIS, RKO Radio: JAMES WONG HOWE

ALL THIS, AND HEAVEN TOO, Warner Bros.: ERNEST HALLER

ARISE, MY LOVE, Paramount: CHARLES B. LANG, JR.

BOOM TOWN, Metro-Goldwyn-Mayer: HAROLD ROSSON

FOREIGN CORRESPONDENT, Wanger, UA: RUDOLPH MATE

THE LETTER, Warner Bros.: GAETANO GAUDIO

THE LONG VOYAGE HOME, Argosy-Wanger, UA: GREGG TOLAND

REBECCA, Selznick, UA: GEORGE BARNES

SPRING PARADE, Universal: JOSEPH VALENTINE

WATERLOO BRIDGE, Metro-Goldwyn-Mayer: JOSEPH RUTTENBERG

(Color)

BITTER SWEET, Metro-Goldwyn-Mayer: OLIVER T. MARSH and ALLEN DAVEY

THE BLUE BIRD, 20th Century-Fox: ARTHUR MILLER and RAY RENNAHAN

DOWN ARGENTINE WAY, 20th Century-Fox: LEON SHAMROY and RAY RENNAHAN

NORTH WEST MOUNTED POLICE, Paramount: VICTOR MILNER and W. HOWARD GREENE

NORTHWEST PASSAGE, Metro-Goldwyn-Mayer: SIDNEY WAGNER and WILLIAM V. SKALL

THIEF OF BAGDAD, Korda, UA (British): GEORGE PERINAL

1941   Fourteenth Year

(Black-and-White)

THE CHOCOLATE SOLDIER, Metro-Goldwyn-Mayer: KARL FREUND

CITIZEN KANE, Mercury, RKO Radio: GREGG TOLAND

DR. JEKYLL AND MR. HYDE, Metro-Goldwyn-Mayer: JOSEPH RUTTENBERG

HERE COMES MR. JORDAN, Columbia: JOSEPH WALKER

HOLD BACK THE DAWN, Paramount: LEO TOVER

HOW GREEN WAS MY VALLEY, 20th Century-Fox: ARTHUR MILLER

SERGEANT YORK, Warner Bros.: SOL POLITO

SUN VALLEY SERENADE, 20th Century-Fox: EDWARD CRONJAGER

SUNDOWN, Wanger, UA: CHARLES LANG

THAT HAMILTON WOMAN, Korda, UA: RUDOLPH MATE

(Color)

ALOMA OF THE SOUTH SEAS, Paramount: WILFRED M. CLINE, KARL STRUSS and WILLIAM SNYDER

BILLY THE KID, Metro-Goldwyn-Mayer: WILLIAM V. SKALL and LEONARD SMITH

BLOOD AND SAND, 20th Century-Fox: ERNEST PALMER and RAY RENNAHAN

BLOSSOMS IN THE DUST, Metro-Goldwyn-Mayer: KARL FREUND and W. HOWARD GREENE

DIVE BOMBER, Warner Bros.: BERT GLENNON

LOUISIANA PURCHASE, Paramount: HARRY HALLENBERGER and RAY RENNAHAN

1942   Fifteenth Year

(Black-and-White)

KINGS ROW, Warner Bros.: JAMES WONG HOWE

THE MAGNIFICENT AMBERSONS, Mercury, RKO Radio: STANLEY CORTEZ

MRS. MINIVER, Metro-Goldwyn-Mayer: JOSEPH RUTTENBERG

Director of Photography Leon Shamroy has received a remarkable eighteen nominations and four Oscars for Cinematography. *American Cinematographer Photo*

Joseph Ruttenberg has won four Academy Awards for his cinematography. *American Cinematographer Photo*

MOONTIDE, 20th Century-Fox: CHARLES CLARKE

THE PIED PIPER, 20th Century-Fox: EDWARD CRONJAGER

THE PRIDE OF THE YANKEES, Goldwyn, RKO Radio: RUDOLPH MATE

TAKE A LETTER, DARLING, Paramount: JOHN MESCALL

THE TALK OF THE TOWN, Columbia: TED TETZLAFF

TEN GENTLEMEN FROM WEST POINT, 20th Century-Fox: LEON SHAMROY

THIS ABOVE ALL, 20th Century-Fox: ARTHUR MILLER

(color)

ARABIAN NIGHTS, Wanger, Universal: MILTON KRASNER, WILLIAM V. SKALL and W. HOWARD GREENE

THE BLACK SWAN, 20th Century-Fox: LEON SHAMROY

CAPTAINS OF THE CLOUDS, Warner Bros.: SOL POLITO

JUNGLE BOOK, Korda, UA: W. HOWARD GREENE

REAP THE WILD WIND, Paramount: VICTOR MILNER and WILLIAM V. SKALL

TO THE SHORES OF TRIPOLI, 20th Century-Fox: EDWARD CRONJAGER and WILLIAM V. SKALL

1943   Sixteenth Year

(Black-and-White)

AIR FORCE, Warner Bros.: JAMES WONG HOWE, ELMER DYER and CHARLES MARSHALL

CASABLANCA, Warner Bros.: ARTHUR EDESON

CORVETTE K-225, Universal: TONY GAUDIO

FIVE GRAVES TO CAIRO, Paramount: JOHN SEITZ

THE HUMAN COMEDY, Metro-Goldwyn-Mayer: HARRY STRADLING

MADAME CURIE, Metro-Goldwyn-Mayer: JOSEPH RUTTENBERG

THE NORTH STAR, Goldwyn, RKO Radio: JAMES WONG HOWE

SAHARA, Columbia: RUDOLPH MATE

SO PROUDLY WE HAIL, Paramount: CHARLES LANG

THE SONG OF BERNADETTE, 20th Century-Fox: ARTHUR MILLER

(color)

FOR WHOM THE BELL TOLLS, Paramount: RAY RENNAHAN

HEAVEN CAN WAIT, 20th Century-Fox: EDWARD CRONJAGER

HELLO, FRISCO, HELLO, 20th Century-Fox: CHARLES G. CLARKE and ALLEN DAVEY

LASSIE COME HOME, Metro-Goldwyn-Mayer: LEONARD SMITH

PHANTOM OF THE OPERA, Universal: HAL MOHR and W. HOWARD GREENE

THOUSANDS CHEER, Metro-Goldwyn-Mayer: GEORGE FOLSEY

1944   Seventeenth Year

(Black-and-White)

DOUBLE INDEMNITY, Paramount: JOHN SEITZ

DRAGON SEED, Metro-Goldwyn-Mayer: SIDNEY WAGNER

GASLIGHT, Metro-Goldwyn-Mayer: JOSEPH RUTTENBERG

GOING MY WAY, Paramount: LIONEL LINDON

LAURA, 20th Century-Fox: JOSEPH LaSHELLE

LIFEBOAT, 20th Century-Fox: GLEN MacWILLIAMS

SINCE YOU WENT AWAY, Selznick, UA: STANLEY CORTEZ and LEE GARMES

THIRTY SECONDS OVER TOKYO, Metro-Goldwyn-Mayer: ROBERT SURTEES and HAROLD ROSSON

THE UNINVITED, Paramount: CHARLES LANG

THE WHITE CLIFFS OF DOVER, Metro-Goldwyn-Mayer: GEORGE FOLSEY

(Color)

COVER GIRL, Columbia: RUDY MATE and ALLEN M. DAVEY

HOME IN INDIANA, 20th Century-Fox: EDWARD CRONJAGER

KISMET, Metro-Goldwyn-Mayer: CHARLES ROSHER

LADY IN THE DARK, Paramount: RAY RENNAHAN

MEET ME IN ST. LOUIS, Metro-Goldwyn-Mayer: GEORGE FOLSEY

WILSON, 20th Century-Fox: LEON SHAMROY

1945   Eighteenth Year

(Black-and-White)

THE KEYS OF THE KINGDOM, 20th Century-Fox: ARTHUR MILLER

THE LOST WEEKEND, Paramount: JOHN F. SEITZ

MILDRED PIERCE, Warner Bros.: ERNEST HALLER

THE PICTURE OF DORIAN GRAY, Metro-Goldwyn-Mayer: HARRY STRADLING

SPELLBOUND, Selznick, UA: GEORGE BARNES

(Color)

ANCHORS AWEIGH, Metro-Goldwyn-Mayer: ROBERT PLANCK and CHARLES BOYLE

LEAVE HER TO HEAVEN, 20th Century-Fox: LEON SHAMROY

NATIONAL VELVET, Metro-Goldwyn-Mayer: LEONARD SMITH

A SONG TO REMEMBER, Columbia: TONY GAUDIO and ALLEN M. DAVEY

THE SPANISH MAIN, RKO Radio: GEORGE BARNES

1946   Nineteenth Year

(Black-and-White)

ANNA AND THE KING OF SIAM, 20th Century-Fox: ARTHUR MILLER

THE GREEN YEARS, Metro-Goldwyn-Mayer: GEORGE FOLSEY

(Color)

THE JOLSON STORY, Columbia: JOSEPH WALKER

THE YEARLING, Metro-Goldwyn-Mayer: CHARLES ROSHER, LEONARD SMITH and ARTHUR ARLING

1947   Twentieth Year

(Black-and-White)

THE GHOST AND MRS. MUIR, 20th Century-Fox: CHARLES LANG, JR.

GREAT EXPECTATIONS, Rank-Cineguild, U-I (British): GUY GREEN

GREEN DOLPHIN STREET, Metro-Goldwyn-Mayer: GEORGE FOLSEY

(Color)

BLACK NARCISSUS, Rank-Archers, U-I (British): JACK CARDIFF

LIFE WITH FATHER, Warner Bros.: PEVERELL MARLEY and WILLIAM V. SKALL

MOTHER WORE TIGHTS, 20th Century-Fox: HARRY JACKSON

1948   Twenty-first Year

(Black-and-White)

A FOREIGN AFFAIR, Paramount: CHARLES B. LANG, JR.

I REMEMBER MAMA, RKO Radio: NICHOLAS MUSURACA

JOHNNY BELINDA, Warner Bros.: TED MCCORD

THE NAKED CITY, Hellinger, U-I: WILLIAM DANIELS

PORTRAIT OF JENNIE, The Selznick Studio: JOSEPH AUGUST

(Color)

GREEN GRASS OF WYOMING, 20th Century-Fox: CHARLES G. CLARKE

JOAN OF ARC, Sierra Pictures, RKO Radio: JOSEPH VALENTINE, WILLIAM V. SKALL and WINTON HOCH

THE LOVES OF CARMEN, Beckworth Corporation, Columbia: WILLIAM SNYDER

THE THREE MUSKETEERS, Metro-Goldwyn-Mayer: ROBERT PLANCK

1949   Twenty-second Year

(Black-and-White)

BATTLEGROUND, Metro-Goldwyn-Mayer: PAUL C. VOGEL

CHAMPION, Screen Plays Corp., UA: FRANK PLANER

COME TO THE STABLE, 20th Century-Fox: JOSEPH LASHELLE

THE HEIRESS, Paramount: LEO TOVER

PRINCE OF FOXES, 20th Century-Fox: LEON SHAMROY

(color)

THE BARKLEYS OF BROADWAY, Metro-Goldwyn-Mayer: HARRY STRADLING

JOLSON SINGS AGAIN, Columbia: WILLIAM SNYDER

LITTLE WOMEN, Metro-Goldwyn-Mayer: ROBERT PLANCK and CHARLES SCHOENBAUM

SAND, 20th Century-Fox: CHARLES G. CLARKE

SHE WORE A YELLOW RIBBON, Argosy, RKO Radio: WINTON HOCH

1950   Twenty-third Year

(Black-and-White)

ALL ABOUT EVE, 20th Century-Fox. MILTON KRASNER

THE ASPHALT JUNGLE, Metro-Goldwyn-Mayer: HAROLD ROSSON

THE FURIES, Wallis, Paramount: VIC-
TOR MILNER

SUNSET BOULEVARD, Paramount: JOHN
F. SEITZ

THE THIRD MAN, Selznick-London
Films, SRO (British): ROBERT
KRASKER

(Color)

ANNIE GET YOUR GUN, Metro-
Goldwyn-Mayer: CHARLES ROSHER

BROKEN ARROW, 20th Century-Fox:
ERNEST PALMER

THE FLAME AND THE ARROW, Norma-
F.R., Warner Bros.: ERNEST HALLER

KING SOLOMON'S MINES, Metro-
Goldwyn-Mayer: ROBERT SUR-
TEES

SAMSON AND DELILAH, DeMille, Paramount: GEORGE BARNES

1951   Twenty-fourth Year

(Black-and-White)

DEATH OF A SALESMAN, Kramer, Columbia: FRANK PLANER

THE FROGMEN, 20th Century-Fox:
NORBERT BRODINE

A PLACE IN THE SUN, Paramount:
WILLIAM C. MELLOR

STRANGERS ON A TRAIN, Warner Bros.:
ROBERT BURKS

A STREETCAR NAMED DESIRE, Charles
K. Feldman Group Prods., Warner
Bros.: HARRY STRADLING

(Color)

AN AMERICAN IN PARIS, Metro-
Goldwyn-Mayer: ALFRED GILKS;
Ballet photographed by JOHN
ALTON

DAVID AND BATHSHEBA, 20th Century-
Fox: LEON SHAMROY

QUO VADIS, Metro-Goldwyn-Mayer:
ROBERT SURTEES and WILLIAM V.
SKALL

SHOW BOAT, Metro-Goldwyn-Mayer:
CHARLES ROSHER

WHEN WORLDS COLLIDE, Paramount:
JOHN F. SEITZ and W. HOWARD
GREENE

1952   Twenty-fifth Year

(Black-and-White)

THE BAD AND THE BEAUTIFUL,
Metro-Goldwyn-Mayer: ROBERT
SURTEES

THE BIG SKY, Winchester, RKO Radio:
RUSSELL HARLAN

MY COUSIN RACHEL, 20th Century-Fox:
JOSEPH LASHELLE

NAVAJO, Bartlett-Foster, Lippert:
VIRGIL E. MILLER

SUDDEN FEAR, Joseph Kaufman,
RKO Radio: CHARLES B.LANG, JR.

(Color)

HANS CHRISTIAN ANDERSEN, Goldwyn,
RKO Radio: HARRY STRADLING

IVANHOE, Metro-Goldwyn-Mayer:
F. A. YOUNG

MILLION DOLLAR MERMAID, Metro-
Goldwyn-Mayer: GEORGE J. FOLSEY

THE QUIET MAN, Argosy, Republic:
WINTON C. HOCH and ARCHIE
STOUT

THE SNOWS OF KILIMANJARO, 20th Century-Fox: LEON SHAMROY

1953   Twenty-sixth Year

(Black-and-White)

THE FOUR POSTER, Kramer, Columbia:
HAL MOHR

FROM HERE TO ETERNITY, Columbia: BURNETT GUFFEY

JULIUS CAESAR, Metro-Goldwyn-
Mayer: JOSEPH RUTTENBERG

MARTIN LUTHER, Louis de Rochemont
Associates: JOSEPH C. BRUN

ROMAN HOLIDAY, Paramount: FRANK
PLANER and HENRY ALEKAN

(Color)

ALL THE BROTHERS WERE VALIANT,
Metro-Goldwyn-Mayer: GEORGE
FOLSEY

BENEATH THE TWELVE-MILE REEF, 20th Century-Fox: EDWARD CRONJAGER

LILI, Metro-Goldwyn-Mayer: ROBERT PLANCK

THE ROBE, 20th Century-Fox: LEON SHAMROY

SHANE, Paramount: LOYAL GRIGGS

1954   Twenty-seventh Year

(Black-and-White)

THE COUNTRY GIRL, Perlberg-Seaton, Paramount: JOHN F. WARREN

EXECUTIVE SUITE, Metro-Goldwyn-Mayer: GEORGE FOLSEY

ON THE WATERFRONT, Horizon-American Corp., Columbia: BORIS KAUFMAN

ROGUE COP, Metro-Goldwyn-Mayer: JOHN SEITZ

SABRINA, Paramount: CHARLES LANG, JR.

(Color)

THE EGYPTIAN, 20th Century-Fox: LEON SHAMROY

REAR WINDOW, Patron Inc., Paramount: ROBERT BURKS

SEVEN BRIDES FOR SEVEN BROTHERS, Metro-Goldwyn-Mayer: GEORGE FOLSEY

THE SILVER CHALICE, A Victor Saville Prod., Warner Bros.: WILLIAM V. SKALL

THREE COINS IN THE FOUNTAIN, 20th Century-Fox: MILTON KRASNER

1955   Twenty-eighth Year

(Black-and-White)

BLACKBOARD JUNGLE, Metro-Goldwyn-Mayer: RUSSELL HARLAN

I'LL CRY TOMORROW, Metro-Goldwyn-Mayer: ARTHUR E. ARLING

MARTY, Hecht and Lancaster's Steven Prods., UA: JOSEPH LASHELLE

QUEEN BEE, Columbia: CHARLES LANG

THE ROSE TATTOO, Hal Wallis, Paramount: JAMES WONG HOWE

(Color)

GUYS AND DOLLS, Samuel Goldwyn Prods., Inc., M-G-M: HARRY STRADLING

LOVE IS A MANY-SPLENDORED THING, 20th Century-Fox: LEON SHAMROY

A MAN CALLED PETER, 20th Century-Fox: HAROLD LIPSTEIN

OKLAHOMA!, Rodgers & Hammerstein Pictures, Inc., Magna Theatre Corp.: ROBERT SURTEES

TO CATCH A THIEF, Paramount: ROBERT BURKS

1956   Twenty-ninth Year

(Black-and-White)

BABY DOLL, A Newtown Prod., Warner Bros.: BORIS KAUFMAN

THE BAD SEED, Warner Bros.: HAL ROSSON

THE HARDER THEY FALL, Columbia: BURNETT GUFFEY

SOMEBODY UP THERE LIKES ME, Metro-Goldwyn-Mayer: JOSEPH RUTTENBERG

STAGECOACH TO FURY, Regal Films, Inc. Prod., 20th Century-Fox: WALTER STRENGE

(Color)

AROUND THE WORLD IN 80 DAYS, The Michael Todd Co., Inc., UA: LIONEL LINDON

THE EDDY DUCHIN STORY, Columbia: HARRY STRADLING

THE KING AND I, 20th Century-Fox: LEON SHAMROY

THE TEN COMMANDMENTS, Motion Picture Assoc., Paramount: LOYAL GRIGGS

WAR AND PEACE, A Ponti-De Laurentiis Prod., Paramount (Italo-American): JACK CARDIFF

1957 Thirtieth Year

Note: Rules changed this year to one award for Cinematography instead of separate awards for black-and-white and color.

AN AFFAIR TO REMEMBER, Jerry Wald Prods., Inc., 20th Century-Fox: MILTON KRASNER

THE BRIDGE ON THE RIVER KWAI, A Horizon Picture, Columbia: JACK HILDYARD

FUNNY FACE, Paramount: RAY JUNE

PEYTON PLACE, Jerry Wald Prods., Inc., 20th Century-Fox: WILLIAM MELLOR

SAYONARA, William Goetz Prod., Warner Bros.: ELLSWORTH FREDERICKS

1958 Thirty-first Year

Note: Rules changed this year to two awards for Cinematography: One for black-and-white and one for color.

(Black-and-White)

THE DEFIANT ONES, Stanley Kramer, UA: SAM LEAVITT

DESIRE UNDER THE ELMS, Don Hartman, Paramount: DANIEL L. FAPP

I WANT TO LIVE!, Figaro, Inc., UA: LIONEL LINDON

SEPARATE TABLES, Clifton Prods., Inc., UA: CHARLES LANG, JR.

THE YOUNG LIONS, 20th Century-Fox: JOE MacDONALD

(Color)

AUNTIE MAME, Warner Bros.: HARRY STRADLING, SR.

CAT ON A HOT TIN ROOF, Avon Prods., Inc., M-G-M: WILLIAM DANIELS

GIGI, Arthur Freed Prods., Inc., M-G-M: JOSEPH RUTTENBERG

THE OLD MAN AND THE SEA, Leland Hayward, Warner Bros.: JAMES WONG HOWE

SOUTH PACIFIC, South Pacific Enterprises, Inc., Magna Theatre Corp.: LEON SHAMROY

1959 Thirty-second Year

(Black-and-White)

ANATOMY OF A MURDER, Otto Preminger, Columbia: SAM LEAVITT

CAREER, Hal Wallis Prods., Paramount: JOSEPH LASHELLE

THE DIARY OF ANNE FRANK, 20th Century-Fox: WILLIAM C. MELLOR

SOME LIKE IT HOT, Ashton Prods. & The Mirisch Co., UA: CHARLES LANG, JR.

THE YOUNG PHILADELPHIANS, Warner Bros.: HARRY STRADLING, SR.

(Color)

BEN-HUR, Metro-Goldwyn-Mayer: ROBERT L. SURTEES

THE BIG FISHERMAN, Rowland V. Lee Prods., Buena Vista Film Dist. Co., Inc.: LEE GARMES

THE FIVE PENNIES, Dena Prod., Paramount: DANIEL L. FAPP

THE NUN'S STORY, Warner Bros.: FRANZ PLANER

PORGY AND BESS, Samuel Goldwyn Prods., Columbia: LEON SHAMROY

1960 Thirty-third Year

(Black-and-White)

THE APARTMENT, The Mirisch Co., UA: JOSEPH LASHELLE

THE FACTS OF LIFE, Panama & Frank Prod., UA: CHARLES B. LANG, JR.

INHERIT THE WIND, Stanley Kramer Prod., UA: ERNEST LASZLO

PSYCHO, Alfred J. Hitchcock Prods., Paramount: JOHN L. RUSSELL

SONS AND LOVERS, Company of Artists, Inc., 20th Century-Fox: FREDDIE FRANCIS

Robert Surtees has received fifteen nominations and three Oscars for Cinematography. *American Cinematographer Photo*

(Color)

THE ALAMO, Batjac Prod., UA: WILLIAM H. CLOTHIER

BUTTERFIELD 8, Afton-Linebrook Prod., M-G-M: JOSEPH RUTTENBERG and CHARLES HARTEN

EXODUS, Carlyle-Alpina S. A. Prod., UA: SAM LEAVITT

PEPE, G. S.-Posa Films International Prod., Columbia: JOE MacDONALD

SPARTACUS, Bryna Prods., Inc., U-I: RUSSELL METTY.

1961   Thirty-fourth Year

(Black-and-White)

THE ABSENT MINDED PROFESSOR, Walt Disney Prods., Buena Vista Distribution Co., Inc.: EDWARD COLMAN

THE CHILDREN'S HOUR, Mirisch-Worldwide Prod., UA: FRANZ F. PLANER

THE HUSTLER, Robert Rossen Prod., 20th Century-Fox: EUGEN SHUFTAN

JUDGMENT AT NUREMBERG, Stanley Kramer Prod., UA: ERNEST LASZLO

ONE, TWO, THREE, Mirisch Company, Inc. in association with Pyramid Prods., A. G., UA: DANIEL L. FAPP

(Color)

FANNY, Mansfield Prod., Warner Bros.: JACK CARDIFF

FLOWER DRUM SONG, Universal-International-Ross Hunter Prod. in association with Joseph Fields, U-I: RUSSELL METTY

A MAJORITY OF ONE, Warner Bros.: HARRY STRADLING, SR.

ONE-EYED JACKS, Pennebaker Prod., Paramount: CHARLES LANG, JR.

WEST SIDE STORY, Mirisch Pictures, Inc. and B and P Enteprises Inc., UA: DANIEL L. FAPP

1962   Thirty-fifth Year
(Black-and-White)

BIRD MAN OF ALCATRAZ, Harold Hecht Prod., UA: BURNETT GUFFEY

THE LONGEST DAY, Darryl F. Zanuck Prods., 20th Century-Fox: JEAN BOURGOIN and WALTER WOTTITZ

TO KILL A MOCKINGBIRD, Universal-International-Pakula-Mulligan-Brentwood Prod., U-I: RUSSELL HARLAN

TWO FOR THE SEESAW, Mirisch-Argyle-Talbot Prod. in association with Seven Arts Prods., UA: TED MCCORD

WHAT EVER HAPPENED TO BABY JANE?, Seven Arts-Associates & Aldrich Co. Prod., Warner Bros.: ERNEST HALLER

(Color)

GYPSY, Warner Bros.: HARRY STRADLING, SR.

HATARI!, Malabar Prods., Paramount: RUSSELL HARLAN

LAWRENCE OF ARABIA, Horizon Pictures (G.B.), Ltd.-Sam Spiegel-David Lean Prod., Columbia: FRED A. YOUNG

MUTINY ON THE BOUNTY, Arcola Prod., M-G-M: ROBERT L. SURTEES

THE WONDERFUL WORLD OF THE BROTHERS GRIMM, Metro-Goldwyn-Mayer & Cinerama. PAUL C. VOGEL

1963   Thirty-sixth Year
(Black-and-White)

THE BALCONY, Walter Reade-Sterling-Allen-Hodgdon Prod., Walter Reade-Sterling-Continental Dist.: GEORGE FOLSEY

THE CARETAKERS, Hall Bartlett Prod., UA: LUCIEN BALLARD

HUD, Salem-Dover Prod., Paramount. JAMES WONG HOWE

LILIES OF THE FIELD, Rainbow Prod., UA: ERNEST HALLER

LOVE WITH THE PROPER STRANGER, Boardwalk-Rona Prod., Paramount: MILTON KRASNER

(Color)

THE CARDINAL, Gamma Prod., Columbia: LEON SHAMROY

CLEOPATRA, 20th Century-Fox Ltd.-MCL Films S.A.-WALWA Films S.A. Prod., 20th Century-Fox: LEON SHAMROY

HOW THE WEST WAS WON, Metro-Goldwyn-Mayer & Cinerama: WILLIAM H. DANIELS, MILTON KRASNER, CHARLES LANG, JR. and JOSEPH LaSHELLE

IRMA LA DOUCE, Mirisch-Phalanx Prod., UA: JOSEPH LaSHELLE

IT'S A MAD, MAD, MAD, MAD WORLD, Casey Prod., UA. ERNEST LASZLO

1964   Thirty-seventh Year
(Black-and-White)

THE AMERICANIZATION OF EMILY, Martin Ransohoff Prod., M-G-M: PHILIP H. LATHROP

FATE IS THE HUNTER, Arcola Pictures Prod., 20th Century-Fox: MILTON KRASNER

HUSH. . . HUSH, SWEET CHARLOTTE, Associates & Aldrich Prod., 20th Century-Fox: JOSEPH BIROC

THE NIGHT OF THE IGUANA, Seven Arts Prod., M-G-M: GABRIEL FIGUEROA

ZORBA THE GREEK, Rochley, Ltd. Prod., International Classics: WALTER LASSALLY

(Color)

BECKET, Hal Wallis Prod., Paramount: GEOFFREY UNSWORTH

CHEYENNE AUTUMN, John Ford-Bernard Smith Prod., Warner Bros.: WILLIAM H. CLOTHIER

MARY POPPINS, Walt Disney Prods.: EDWARD COLMAN

MY FAIR LADY, Warner Bros.: HARRY STRADLING

THE UNSINKABLE MOLLY BROWN, Marten Prod., M-G-M: DANIEL L. FAPP

1965   Thirty-eighth Year

(Black-and-White)

IN HARM'S WAY, Sigma Prods., Paramount: LOYAL GRIGGS

KING RAT, Coleytown Prod., Columbia: BURNETT GUFFEY

MORITURI, Arcola-Colony Prod., 20th Century-Fox: CONRAD HALL

A PATCH OF BLUE, Pandro S. Berman-Guy Green Prod., M-G-M: ROBERT BURKS

SHIP OF FOOLS, Columbia: ERNEST LASZLO

(Color)

THE AGONY AND THE ECSTASY, International Classics Prod., 20th Century-Fox: LEON SHAMROY

DOCTOR ZHIVAGO, Sostar S.A.-Metro-Goldwyn-Mayer British Studios, Ltd. Prod., M-G-M: FREDDIE YOUNG

THE GREAT RACE, Patricia-Jalem-Reynard Prod., Warner Bros.: RUSSELL HARLAN

THE GREATEST STORY EVER TOLD, George Stevens Prod., United Artists: WILLIAM C. MELLOR and LOYAL GRIGGS

THE SOUND OF MUSIC, Argyle Enterprises Prod., 20th Century-Fox: TED MCCORD

1966   Thirty-ninth Year

(Black-and-White)

THE FORTUNE COOKIE, Phalanx-Jalem-Mirisch Corp. of Delaware Prod., U.S.: JOSEPH LaSHELLE

GEORGY GIRL, Everglades Prods., Ltd., Columbia: KEN HIGGINS

IS PARIS BURNING?, Transcontinental Films-Marianne Prod., Paramount: MARCEL GRIGNON

SECONDS, The Seconds Company, Paramount: JAMES WONG HOWE

WHO'S AFRAID OF VIRGINIA WOOLF?, Chenault Prod., Warner Bros.: HASKELL WEXLER

(Color)

FANTASTIC VOYAGE, 20th Century-Fox: ERNEST LASZLO

HAWAII, Mirisch Corp. of Delaware Prod., U.A.: RUSSELL HARLAN

A MAN FOR ALL SEASONS, Highland Films, Ltd. Prod., Columbia: TED MOORE

THE PROFESSIONALS, Pax Enterprises Prod., Columbia: CONRAD HALL

THE SAND PEBBLES, Argyle-Solar Prod., 20th Century-Fox: JOSEPH MacDONALD

1967   Fortieth Year

Note: Rules changed this year to one award for Cinematography instead of separate awards for black-and-white and color.

BONNIE AND CLYDE, Tatira-Hiller

Director of Photography Freddie Young (left) and director David Lean on location filming *Ryan's Daughter* (1970). Young has won three Oscars for Cinematography, all for David Lean pictures. *American Cinematographer Photo*

Prod., Warner Bros.-Seven Arts: BURNETT GUFFEY

CAMELOT, Warner Bros.-Seven Arts: RICHARD H. KLINE

DOCTOR DOLITTLE, Apjac Prods., 20th Century-Fox: ROBERT SURTEES

THE GRADUATE, Mike Nichols-Lawrence Turman Prod., Embassy: ROBERT SURTEES

IN COLD BLOOD, Pax Enterprises Prod., Columbia: CONRAD HALL

1968 Forty-first Year

The Franco Zeffirelli production of ROMEO & JULIET, B.H.E. Film-Verona Prod.-Dino De Laurentiis Cinematografica Prod., Paramount: PASQUALINO DE SANTIS

FUNNY GIRL, Rastar Prods., Columbia: HARRY STRADLING

ICE STATION ZEBRA, Filmways Prod., Metro-Goldwyn-Mayer: DANIEL L. FAPP

OLIVER!, Romulus Films, Columbia: OSWALD MORRIS

STAR!, Robert Wise Prod., 20th Century-Fox: ERNEST LASZLO

1969 Forty-second Year

ANNE OF THE THOUSAND DAYS, Hal B. Wallis-Universal Pictures, Ltd. Prod., Universal: ARTHUR IBBETSON

BOB & CAROL & TED & ALICE, Frankovich Prods., Columbia: CHARLES B. LANG

BUTCH CASSIDY AND THE SUNDANCE KID, George Roy Hill-Paul Monash Prod., 20th Century-Fox: CONRAD HALL

HELLO, DOLLY!, Chenault Prods., 20th Century-Fox: HARRY STRADLING

MAROONED, Frankovich-Sturges Prod., Columbia: DANIEL FAPP

1970   Forty-third Year

AIRPORT, Ross Hunter-Universal Prod., Universal: ERNEST LASZLO

PATTON, 20th Century-Fox: FRED KOENEKAMP

RYAN'S DAUGHTER, Faraway Prods., Metro-Goldwyn-Mayer: FREDDIE YOUNG

TORA! TORA! TORA!, 20th Century-Fox: CHARLES F. WHEELER, OSAMI FURUYA, SINSAKU HIMEDA and MASAMICHI SATOH

WOMEN IN LOVE, Larry Kramer-Martin Rosen Prod., United Artists: BILLY WILLIAMS

1971   Forty-fourth Year

FIDDLER ON THE ROOF, Mirisch-Cartier Prods., UA: OSWALD MORRIS

THE FRENCH CONNECTION, A Philip D'Antoni Prod. in association with Schine-Moore Prods., 20th Century-Fox: OWEN ROIZMAN

THE LAST PICTURE SHOW, BBS Prods., Columbia: ROBERT SURTEES

NICHOLAS AND ALEXANDRA, A Horizon Pictures Prod., Columbia: FREDDIE YOUNG

SUMMER OF '42, A Robert Mulligan-Richard Alan Roth Prod., Warner Bros.: ROBERT SURTEES

1972   Forty-fifth Year

BUTTERFLIES ARE FREE, Frankovich Productions, Columbia: CHARLES B. LANG

CABARET, An ABC Pictures Production, Allied Artists: GEOFFREY UNSWORTH

THE POSEIDON ADVENTURE, An Irwin Allen Production, 20th Century-Fox: HAROLD E. STINE

1776, A Jack L. Warner Production, Columbia: HARRY STRADLING, JR.

TRAVELS WITH MY AUNT, Robert Fryer Productions, Metro-Goldwyn-Mayer: DOUGLAS SLOCOMBE

1973   Forty-sixth Year

CRIES AND WHISPERS, A Svenska Filminstitutet-Cinematograph AB Prod., New World Pictures: SVEN NYKVIST

THE EXORCIST, Hoya Prods., Warner Bros.: OWEN ROIZMAN

JONATHAN LIVINGSTON SEAGULL, A JLS Limited Partnership Prod., Paramount: JACK COUFFER

THE STING, A Universal-Bill/Phillips-George Roy Hill Film Prod., Zanuck/Brown Presentation, Universal: ROBERT SURTEES

THE WAY WE WERE, Rastar Prods., Columbia: HARRY STRADLING, JR.

1974   Forty-seventh Year

CHINATOWN, A Robert Evans Prod., Paramount: JOHN A. ALONZO

EARTHQUAKE, A Universal-Mark Robson-Filmakers Group Prod., Universal: PHILIP LATHROP

LENNY, A Marvin Worth Prod., United Artists: BRUCE SURTEES

MURDER ON THE ORIENT EXPRESS, A G.W. Films, Ltd. Prod., Paramount: GEOFFREY UNSWORTH

THE TOWERING INFERNO, An Irwin Allen Prod., 20th Century-Fox/Warner Bros.: FRED KOENEKAMP and JOSEPH BIROC

1975   Forty-eighth Year

BARRY LYNDON, A Hawk Films, Ltd. Production, Warner Bros.: JOHN ALCOTT

Haskell Wexler won his second Oscar for Cinematography in 1976 for *Bound For Glory*. *American Cinematographer Photo*

THE DAY OF THE LOCUST, A Jerome Hellman Production, Paramount: CONRAD HALL

FUNNY LADY, A Rastar Pictures Production, Columbia: JAMES WONG HOWE

THE HINDENBURG, A Robert Wise-Filmakers Group-Universal Production, Universal: ROBERT SURTEES

ONE FLEW OVER THE CUCKOO'S NEST, A Fantasy Films Production, United Artists: HASKELL WEXLER and BILL BUTLER

1976   Forty-ninth Year

BOUND FOR GLORY, The Bound For Glory Company Production, United Artists: HASKELL WEXLER

KING KONG, A Dino De Laurentiis Production, Paramount: RICHARD H. KLINE

LOGAN'S RUN, A Saul David Production, Metro-Goldwyn-Mayer: ERNEST LASZLO

NETWORK, A Howard Gottfried/Paddy Chayefsky Production, Metro-Goldwyn-Mayer/United Artists: OWEN ROIZMAN

A STAR IS BORN, A Barwood/Jon Peters Production, First Artists Presentation, Warner Bros.: ROBERT SURTEES

1977   Fiftieth Year

CLOSE ENCOUNTERS OF THE THIRD KIND, Close Encounter Pro-

ductions, Columbia: VILMOS ZSIG-
MOND
ISLANDS IN THE STREAM, A Peter
Bart/Max Palevsky Production, Para-
mount: FRED J. KOENEKAMP
JULIA, A Twentieth Century-Fox Pro-
duction, Twentieth Century-Fox:

DOUGLAS SLOCOMBE
LOOKING FOR MR. GOODBAR, A Freddie
Fields Production, Paramount: WIL-
LIAM A. FRAKER
THE TURNING POINT, Hera Productions,
Twentieth Century-Fox: ROBERT
SURTEES

ART DIRECTION -
SET DECORATION

An art director not only designs the sets and backgrounds but works with the director, cinematographer, and costume designer to create the visual character of a film. A set decorator supplies the appropriate decor for a set—furniture, draperies, and decorative details for the interiors.

Art Direction, or Interior Decoration, as it was called until 1947, is one of the original categories begun with the first awards. As originally defined, the award honored "the best achievement in set designing, with special reference to art quality, correct detail, story application, and originality." In 1941 the category was expanded to provide an award for the set decorator as well as the art director, but this was not considered a new category since the two winners must work together on the same film. For twenty-five years (1940–67 except for 1957–58) this category was divided into separate awards for black and white films and color films. The most frequent winners in this category are Cedric Gibbons, with eleven awards for Art Direction, and Edwin B. Willis, who worked with Gibbons, with eight Set Decoration Oscars.

Achievements in this category are nominated by all members of the Academy Art Directors Branch except the Costume Designers.

1927/28   First Year
THE DOVE, United Artists: WIL-
LIAM CAMERON MENZIES
SEVENTH HEAVEN, Fox: HARRY OLIVER
SUNRISE, Fox: ROCHUS GLIESE
THE TEMPEST, United Artists: WIL-
LIAM CAMERON MENZIES

1928/29   Second Year
THE BRIDGE OF SAN LUIS REY,
Metro-Goldwyn-Mayer: CEDRIC
GIBBONS
DYNAMITE, Pathe: MITCHELL LEISEN
HOLLYWOOD REVUE, Metro-Goldwyn-
Mayer: CEDRIC GIBBONS
THE IRON MASK, United Artists: WIL-
LIAM CAMERON MENZIES
THE PATRIOT, Paramount: HANS DREIER
STREET ANGEL, Fox: HARRY OLIVER

LARGE CAPITAL LETTERS DENOTE WINNER

1929/30   Third Year
BULLDOG DRUMMOND, Goldwyn, UA:
WILLIAM CAMERON MENZIES
KING OF JAZZ, Universal: HERMAN
ROSSE
THE LOVE PARADE, Paramount: HANS
DREIER
SALLY, First National: JACK OKEY
THE VAGABOND KING, Paramount:
HANS DREIER

1930/31   Fourth Year
CIMARRON, RKO Radio: MAX REE
JUST IMAGINE, Fox: STEPHEN GOOSSON
and RALPH HAMMERAS
MOROCCO, Paramount: HANS DREIER
SVENGALI, Warner Bros.-First Na-
tional: ANTON GROT
WHOOPEE, Goldwyn, UA: RICHARD
DAY

1931/32   Fifth Year

A NOUS LA LIBERTÉ (French): LAZARE MEERSON

ARROWSMITH, Goldwyn, UA: RICHARD DAY

TRANSATLANTIC, Fox: GORDON WILES

1932/33   Sixth Year

CAVALCADE, Fox: WILLIAM S. DARLING

A FAREWELL TO ARMS, Paramount: HANS DREIER and ROLAND ANDERSON

WHEN LADIES MEET, Metro-Goldwyn-Mayer: CEDRIC GIBBONS

1934   Seventh Year

AFFAIRS OF CELLINI, 20th Century, UA: RICHARD DAY

THE GAY DIVORCEE, RKO Radio: VAN NEST POLGLASE and CARROLL CLARK

THE MERRY WIDOW, Metro-Goldwyn-Mayer: CEDRIC GIBBONS and FREDERIC HOPE

1935   Eighth Year

THE DARK ANGEL, Goldwyn, UA: RICHARD DAY

LIVES OF A BENGAL LANCER, Paramount: HANS DREIER and ROLAND ANDERSON

TOP HAT, RKO Radio: CARROLL CLARK and VAN NEST POLGLASE

1936   Ninth Year

ANTHONY ADVERSE, Warner Bros.: ANTON GROT

DODSWORTH, Goldwyn, UA: RICHARD DAY

THE GREAT ZIEGFELD, Metro-Goldwyn-Mayer: CEDRIC GIBBONS, EDDIE IMAZU and EDWIN B. WILLIS

LLOYDS OF LONDON, 20th Century-Fox: WILLIAM S. DARLING

THE MAGNIFICENT BRUTE, Universal: ALBERT S. D'AGOSTINO and JACK OTTERSON

ROMEO AND JULIET, Metro-Goldwyn-Mayer: CEDRIC GIBBONS, FREDERIC HOPE and EDWIN B. WILLIS

WINTERSET, RKO Radio: PERRY FERGUSON

1937   Tenth Year

CONQUEST, Metro-Goldwyn-Mayer: CEDRIC GIBBONS and WILLIAM HORNING

A DAMSEL IN DISTRESS, RKO Radio: CARROLL CLARK

DEAD END, Goldwyn, UA: RICHARD DAY

EVERY DAY'S A HOLIDAY, Major Prods., Paramount: WIARD IHNEN

THE LIFE OF EMILE ZOLA, Warner Bros.: ANTON GROT

LOST HORIZON, Columbia: STEPHEN GOOSSON

MANHATTAN MERRY-GO-ROUND, Republic: JOHN VICTOR MACKAY

THE PRISONER OF ZENDA, Selznick, UA: LYLE WHEELER

SOULS AT SEA, Paramount: HANS DREIER and ROLAND ANDERSON

VOGUES OF 1938, Wanger, UA: ALEXANDER TOLUBOFF

WEE WILLIE WINKIE, 20th Century-Fox: WILLIAM S. DARLING and DAVID HALL

YOU'RE A SWEETHEART, Universal: JACK OTTERSON

1938   Eleventh Year

ADVENTURES OF ROBIN HOOD, Warner Bros.: CARL J. WEYL

ADVENTURES OF TOM SAWYER, Selznick, UA: LYLE WHEELER

ALEXANDER'S RAGTIME BAND, 20th Century-Fox: BERNARD HERZBRUN and BORIS LEVEN

ALGIERS, Wanger, UA: ALEXANDER TOLUBOFF

CAREFREE, RKO Radio: VAN NEST POLGLASE

GOLDWYN FOLLIES, Goldwyn, UA: RICHARD DAY

HOLIDAY, Columbia: STEPHEN GOOSSON and LIONEL BANKS

IF I WERE KING, Paramount: HANS DREIER and JOHN GOODMAN

MAD ABOUT MUSIC, Universal: JACK OTTERSON

MARIE ANTOINETTE, Metro-Goldwyn-Mayer: CEDRIC GIBBONS

MERRILY WE LIVE, Roach, M-G-M: CHARLES D. HALL

1939 Twelfth Year

BEAU GESTE, Paramount: HANS DREIER and ROBERT ODELL

CAPTAIN FURY, Roach, UA: CHARLES D. HALL

FIRST LOVE, Universal: JACK OTTERSON and MARTIN OBZINA

GONE WITH THE WIND, Selznick, M-G-M: LYLE WHEELER

LOVE AFFAIR, RKO Radio: VAN NEST POLGLASE and AL HERMAN

MAN OF CONQUEST, Republic: JOHN VICTOR MACKAY

MR. SMITH GOES TO WASHINGTON, Columbia: LIONEL BANKS

THE PRIVATE LIVES OF ELIZABETH AND ESSEX, Warner Bros.: ANTON GROT

THE RAINS CAME, 20th Century-Fox: WILLIAM DARLING and GEORGE DUDLEY

STAGECOACH, Wanger, UA: ALEXANDER TOLUBOFF

THE WIZARD OF OZ, Metro-Goldwyn-Mayer: CEDRIC GIBBONS and WILLIAM A. HORNING

WUTHERING HEIGHTS, Goldwyn, UA: JAMES BASEVI

1940 Thirteenth Year
(Black-and-White)

ARISE, MY LOVE, Paramount: HANS DREIER and ROBERT USHER

ARIZONA, Columbia: LIONEL BANKS and ROBERT PETERSON

THE BOYS FROM SYRACUSE, Universal: JOHN OTTERSON

DARK COMMAND, Republic: JOHN VICTOR MACKAY

FOREIGN CORRESPONDENT, Wanger, UA: ALEXANDER GOLITZEN

LILLIAN RUSSELL, 20th Century-Fox: RICHARD DAY and JOSEPH C. WRIGHT

MY FAVORITE WIFE, RKO Radio: VAN NEST POLGLASE and MARK-LEE KIRK

MY SON, MY SON, Small, UA: JOHN DuCASSE SCHULZE

OUR TOWN, Lesser, UA: LEWIS J. RACHMIL

PRIDE AND PREJUDICE, Metro-Goldwyn-Mayer: CEDRIC GIBBONS and PAUL GROESSE

REBECCA, Selznick, UA: LYLE WHEELER

SEA HAWK, Warner Bros.: ANTON GROT

THE WESTERNER, Goldwyn, UA: JAMES BASEVI

(Color)

BITTER SWEET, Metro-Goldwyn-Mayer: CEDRIC GIBBONS and JOHN S. DETLIE

DOWN ARGENTINE WAY, 20th Century-Fox: RICHARD DAY and JOSEPH C. WRIGHT

NORTHWEST MOUNTED POLICE, Paramount: HANS DREIER and ROLAND ANDERSON

THIEF OF BAGDAD, Korda, UA: VINCENT KORDA

1941 Fourteenth Year
(Black-and-White)

CITIZEN KANE, Mercury, RKO Radio: PERRY FERGUSON and VAN NEST POLGLASE
Interior Decoration: AL FIELDS and DARRELL SILVERA

FLAME OF NEW ORLEANS, Universal: MARTIN OBZINA and JACK OTTERSON
Interior Decoration: RUSSELL A. GAUSMAN

HOLD BACK THE DAWN, Paramount:

HANS DREIER and ROBERT USHER
Interior Decoration: SAM COMER
HOW GREEN WAS MY VALLEY,
20th Century-Fox: RICHARD DAY
and NATHAN JURAN
Interior Decoration: THOMAS LIT-
TLE
LADIES IN RETIREMENT, Columbia:
LIONEL BANKS
Interior Decoration: GEORGE
MONTGOMERY
THE LITTLE FOXES, Goldwyn, RKO
Radio: STEPHEN GOOSSON
Interior Decoration: HOWARD BRISTOL
SERGEANT YORK, Warner Bros.: JOHN
HUGHES
Interior Decoration: FRED MacLEAN
SON OF MONTE CRISTO, Small, UA:
JOHN DuCASSE SCHULZE
Interior Decoration: EDWARD G.
BOYLE
SUNDOWN, Wanger, UA: ALEXANDER
GOLITZEN
Interior Decoration: RICHARD IRVINE
THAT HAMILTON WOMAN, Korda, UA:
VINCENT KORDA
Interior Decoration: JULIA HERON
WHEN LADIES MEET, Metro-Goldwyn-
Mayer: CEDRIC GIBBONS and RAN-
DALL DUELL
Interior Decoration: EDWIN B. WILLIS

(Color)

BLOOD AND SAND, 20th Century-Fox:
RICHARD DAY and JOSEPH C. WRIGHT
Interior Decoration: THOMAS LITTLE
BLOSSOMS IN THE DUST, Metro-
Goldwyn-Mayer: CEDRIC GIB-
BONS and URIE McCLEARY
Interior Decoration: EDWIN B.
WILLIS
LOUISIANA PURCHASE, Paramount:
RAOUL PENE DU BOIS
Interior Decoration: STEPHEN A.
SEYMOUR

1942   Fifteenth Year
(Black-and-White)

GEORGE WASHINGTON SLEPT HERE,
Warner Bros.: MAX PARKER and
MARK-LEE KIRK
Interior Decoration: CASEY ROBERTS
THE MAGNIFICENT AMBERSONS, Mer-
cury, RKO Radio: ALBERT S.
D'AGOSTINO
Interior Decoration: AL FIELDS and
DARRELL SILVERA
THE PRIDE OF THE YANKEES, Goldwyn,
RKO Radio: PERRY FERGUSON
Interior Decoration: HOWARD BRIS-
TOL
RANDOM HARVEST, Metro-Goldwyn-
Mayer: CEDRIC GIBBONS and RAN-
DALL DUELL
Interior Decoration: EDWIN B. WILLIS
and JACK MOORE
THE SHANGHAI GESTURE, Arnold, UA:
BORIS LEVEN
Interior Decoration: BORIS LEVEN
SILVER QUEEN, Sherman, UA: RALPH
BERGER
Interior Decoration: EMILE KURI
THE SPOILERS, Universal: JOHN B.
GOODMAN and JACK OTTERSON
Interior Decoration: RUSSELL A.
GAUSMAN and EDWARD R. ROBINSON
TAKE A LETTER, DARLING, Paramount:
HANS DREIER and ROLAND ANDERSON
Interior Decoration: SAM COMER
THE TALK OF THE TOWN, Columbia:
LIONEL BANKS and RUDOLPH STER-
NAD
Interior Decoration: FAY BABCOCK
THIS ABOVE ALL, 20th Century-
Fox: RICHARD DAY and JOSEPH
WRIGHT
Interior Decoration: THOMAS LIT-
TLE

(Color)

ARABIAN NIGHTS, Universal: ALEX-
ANDER GOLITZEN and JACK OTTER-
SON
Interior Decoration: RUSSELL A.
GAUSMAN and IRA S. WEBB

CAPTAINS OF THE CLOUDS, Warner Bros.: TED SMITH
Interior Decoration: CASEY ROBERTS

JUNGLE BOOK, Korda, UA: VINCENT KORDA
Interior Decoration: JULIA HERON

MY GAL SAL, 20th Century-Fox: RICHARD DAY and JOSEPH WRIGHT
Interior Decoration: THOMAS LITTLE

REAP THE WILD WIND, Paramount: HANS DREIER and ROLAND ANDERSON
Interior Decoration: GEORGE SAWLEY

1943   Sixteenth Year
(Black-and-White)

FIVE GRAVES TO CAIRO, Paramount: HANS DREIER and ERNST FEGTE
Interior Decoration: BERTRAM GRANGER

FLIGHT FOR FREEDOM, RKO Radio: ALBERT S. D'AGOSTINO and CARROLL CLARK
Interior Decoration: DARRELL SILVERA and HARLEY MILLER

MADAME CURIE, Metro-Goldwyn-Mayer: CEDRIC GIBBONS and PAUL GROESSE
Interior Decoration: EDWIN B. WILLIS and HUGH HUNT

MISSION TO MOSCOW, Warner Bros.: CARL WEYL
Interior Decoration: GEORGE J. HOPKINS

THE NORTH STAR, Goldwyn, RKO Radio: PERRY FERGUSON
Interior Decoration: HOWARD BRISTOL

THE SONG OF BERNADETTE, 20th Century-Fox: JAMES BASEVI and WILLIAM DARLING
Interior Decoration: THOMAS LITTLE

(Color)

FOR WHOM THE BELL TOLLS, Paramount: HANS DREIER and HALDANE DOUGLAS
Interior Decoration: BERTRAM GRANGER

THE GANG'S ALL HERE, 20th Century-Fox: JAMES BASEVI and JOSEPH C. WRIGHT
Interior Decoration: THOMAS LITTLE

PHANTOM OF THE OPERA, Universal: ALEXANDER GOLITZEN and JOHN B. GOODMAN
Interior Decoration: RUSSELL A. GAUSMAN and IRA S. WEBB

THIS IS THE ARMY, Warner Bros.: JOHN HUGHES and LT. JOHN KOENIG
Interior Decoration: GEORGE J. HOPKINS

THOUSANDS CHEER, Metro-Goldwyn-Mayer: CEDRIC GIBBONS and DANIEL CATHCART
Interior Decoration: EDWIN B. WILLIS and JACQUES MERSEREAU

1944   Seventeenth Year
(Black-and-White)

ADDRESS UNKNOWN, Columbia: LIONEL BANKS and WALTER HOLSCHER
Interior Decoration: JOSEPH KISH

THE ADVENTURES OF MARK TWAIN, Warner Bros.: JOHN J. HUGHES
Interior Decoration: FRED MacLEAN

CASANOVA BROWN, International, RKO Radio: PERRY FERGUSON
Interior Decoration: JULIA HERON

GASLIGHT, Metro-Goldwyn-Mayer: CEDRIC GIBBONS and WILLIAM FERRARI
Interior Decoration: EDWIN B. WILLIS and PAUL HULDSCHINSKY

LAURA, 20th Century-Fox: LYLE WHEELER and LELAND FULLER
Interior Decoration: THOMAS LITTLE

NO TIME FOR LOVE, Paramount: HANS DREIER and ROBERT USHER
Interior Decoration: SAM COMER

SINCE YOU WENT AWAY, Selznick, UA: MARK-LEE KIRK
Interior Decoration: VICTOR A. GANGELIN
STEP LIVELY, RKO Radio: ALBERT S. D'AGOSTINO and CARROLL CLARK
Interior Decoration: DARRELL SILVERA and CLAUDE CARPENTER

(Color)

THE CLIMAX, Universal: JOHN B. GOODMAN and ALEXANDER GOLITZEN
Interior Decoration: RUSSELL A. GAUSMAN and IRA S. WEBB
COVER GIRL, Columbia: LIONEL BANKS and CARY ODELL
Interior Decoration: FAY BABCOCK
THE DESERT SONG, Warner Bros.: CHARLES NOVI
Interior Decoration: JACK MC-CONAGHY
KISMET, Metro-Golwyn-Mayer: CEDRIC GIBBONS and DANIEL B. CATHCART
Interior Decoration: EDWIN B. WILLIS and RICHARD PEFFERLE
LADY IN THE DARK, Paramount: HANS DREIER and RAOUL PENE DU BOIS
Interior Decoration: RAY MOYER
THE PRINCESS AND THE PIRATE, Goldwyn, RKO Radio: ERNST FEGTE
Interior Decoration: HOWARD BRISTOL
WILSON, 20th Century-Fox: WIARD IHNEN
Interior Decoration: THOMAS LITTLE

1945   Eighteenth Year
(Black-and-White)
BLOOD ON THE SUN, Cagney, UA: WIARD IHNEN
Interior Decoration: A. ROLAND FIELDS
EXPERIMENT PERILOUS, RKO Radio: ALBERT S. D'AGOSTINO and JACK OKEY

Interior Decoration: DARRELL SILVERA and CLAUDE CARPENTER
THE KEYS OF THE KINGDOM, 20th Century-Fox: JAMES BASEVI and WILLIAM DARLING
Interior Decoration: THOMAS LITTLE and FRANK E. HUGHES
LOVE LETTERS, Hal Wallis, Paramount: HANS DREIER and ROLAND ANDERSON
Interior Decoration: SAM COMER and RAY MOYER
THE PICTURE OF DORIAN GRAY, Metro-Goldwyn-Mayer: CEDRIC GIBBONS and HANS PETERS
Interior Decoration: EDWIN B. WILLIS, JOHN BONAR and HUGH HUNT

(Color)

FRENCHMAN'S CREEK, Paramount: HANS DREIER and ERNST FEGTE
Interior Decoration: SAM COMER
LEAVE HER TO HEAVEN, 20th Century-Fox: LYLE WHEELER and MAURICE RANSFORD
Interior Decoration: THOMAS LITTLE
NATIONAL VELVET, Metro-Goldwyn-Mayer: CEDRIC GIBBONS and URIE MCCLEARY
Interior Decoration: EDWIN B. WILLIS and MILDRED GRIFFITHS
SAN ANTONIO, Warner Bros.: TED SMITH
Interior Decoration: JACK MC-CONAGHY
THOUSAND AND ONE NIGHTS, Columbia: STEPHEN GOOSSON and RUDOLPH STERNAD
Interior Decoration: FRANK TUTTLE

1946   Nineteenth Year
(Black-and-White)

ANNA AND THE KING OF SIAM, 20th Century-Fox: LYLE WHEELER and WILLIAM DARLING
Interior Decoration: THOMAS LITTLE and FRANK E. HUGHES

KITTY, Paramount: HANS DRIER and WALTER TYLER
Interior Decoration: SAM COMER and RAY MOYER
THE RAZOR'S EDGE, 20th Century-Fox: RICHARD DAY and NATHAN JURAN
Interior Decoration: THOMAS LITTLE and PAUL S. FOX

(Color)

CAESAR AND CLEOPATRA, Rank, UA (British): JOHN BRYAN
Interior Decoration: No credits listed.
HENRY V, Rank, UA (British): PAUL SHERIFF and CARMEN DILLON
Interior Decoration: No credits listed.
THE YEARLING, Metro-Goldwyn-Mayer: CEDRIC GIBBONS and PAUL GROESSE
Interior Decoration: EDWIN B. WILLIS

1947 Twentieth Year
Note: Name of category changed from Interior Decoration to Art Direction–Set Direction

(Black-and-White)

THE FOXES OF HARROW, 20th Century-Fox: LYLE WHEELER and MAURICE RANSFORD
Set Decoration: THOMAS LITTLE and PAUL S. FOX
GREAT EXPECTATIONS, Rank-Cineguild, U-I (British): JOHN BRYAN
Set Decoration: WILFRED SHINGLETON.

(Color)

BLACK NARCISSUS, Rank-Archers, U-I (British): ALFRED JUNGE
Set Decoration: ALFRED JUNGE
LIFE WITH FATHER, Warner Bros.: ROBERT M. HAAS
Set Decoration: GEORGE JAMES HOPKINS

1948 Twenty-first Year
(Black-and-White)

HAMLET, Rank-Two Cities, U-I (British): ROGER K. FURSE
Set Decoration: CARMEN DILLON
JOHNNY BELINDA, Warner Bros.: ROBERT HAAS
Set Decoration: WILLIAM WALLACE

(Color)

JOAN OF ARC, Sierra Pictures, RKO Radio: RICHARD DAY
Set Decoration: EDWIN CASEY ROBERTS and JOSEPH KISH
THE RED SHOES, Rank-Archers, Eagle-Lion (British): HEIN HECKROTH
Set Decoration: ARTHUR LAWSON

1949 Twenty-second Year
(Black-and-White)

COME TO THE STABLE, 20th Century-Fox: LYLE WHEELER and JOSEPH C. WRIGHT
Set Decoration: THOMAS LITTLE and PAUL S. FOX
THE HEIRESS, Paramount: JOHN MEEHAN and HARRY HORNER
Set Decoration: EMILE KURI
MADAME BOVARY, Metro-Goldwyn-Mayer: CEDRIC GIBBONS and JACK MARTIN SMITH
Set Decoration: EDWIN B. WILLIS and RICHARD A. PEFFERLE

(Color)

ADVENTURES OF DON JUAN, Warner Bros.: EDWARD CARRERE
Set Decoration: LYLE REIFSNIDER
LITTLE WOMEN, Metro-Goldwyn-Mayer: CEDRIC GIBBONS and PAUL GROESSE
Set Decoration: EDWIN B. WILLIS and JACK D. MOORE
SARABAND, Rank-Ealing, Eagle-Lion (British): JIM MORAHAN, WILLIAM

KELLNER and MICHAEL RELPH
Set Decoration: No credits listed.

1950   Twenty-third Year
(Black-and-White)

ALL ABOUT EVE, 20th Century-Fox:
LYLE WHEELER and GEORGE DAVIS
Set Decoration: THOMAS LITTLE and
WALTER M. SCOTT

THE RED DANUBE, Metro-Goldwyn-
Mayer: CEDRIC GIBBONS and HANS
PETERS
Set Decoration: EDWIN B. WILLIS and
HUGH HUNT

SUNSET BOULEVARD, Paramount:
HANS DREIER and JOHN
MEEHAN
Set Decoration: SAM COMER and
RAY MOYER

(Color)

ANNIE GET YOUR GUN, Metro-Goldwyn-
Mayer: CEDRIC GIBBONS and PAUL
GROESSE
Set Decoration: EDWIN B. WILLIS and
RICHARD A. PEFFERLE

DESTINATION MOON, George Pal, Eagle-
Lion Classics: ERNST FEGTE
Set Decoration: GEORGE SAWLEY

SAMSON AND DELILAH, DeMille-
Paramount: HANS DREIER and
WALTER TYLER
Set Decoration: SAM COMER and
RAY MOYER

1951   Twenty-fourth Year
(Black-and-White)

FOURTEEN HOURS, 20th Century-Fox:
LYLE WHEELER and LELAND FULLER
Set Decoration: THOMAS LITTLE and
FRED J. RODE

HOUSE ON TELEGRAPH HILL, 20th Cen-
tury-Fox: LYLE WHEELER and JOHN
DeCUIR
Set Decoration: THOMAS LITTLE and
PAUL S. FOX

LA RONDE, Sacha Gordine Prod., Com-
mercial Pictures (French): D'EAU-
BONNE
Set Decoration: No credits listed

A STREETCAR NAMED DESIRE,
Chas. K. Feldman Group Prods.,
Warner Bros.: RICHARD DAY
Set Decoration: GEORGE JAMES
HOPKINS

TOO YOUNG TO KISS, Metro-Goldwyn-
Mayer: CEDRIC GIBBONS and PAUL
GROESSE
Set Decoration: EDWIN B. WILLIS and
JACK D. MOORE

(Color)

AN AMERICAN IN PARIS, Metro-
Goldwyn-Mayer: CEDRIC GIB-
BONS and PRESTON AMES
Set Decoration: EDWIN B. WILLIS
and KEOGH GLEASON

DAVID AND BATHSHEBA, 20th Century-
Fox: LYLE WHEELER and GEORGE
DAVIS
Set Decoration: THOMAS LITTLE and
PAUL S. FOX

ON THE RIVIERA, 20th Century-Fox:
LYLE WHEELER and LELAND FULLER
Musical Settings: JOSEPH C. WRIGHT
Set Decoration: THOMAS LITTLE and
WALTER M. SCOTT

QUO VADIS, Metro-Goldwyn-Mayer:
WILLIAM A. HORNING, CEDRIC GIB-
BONS and EDWARD CARFAGNO
Set Decoration: HUGH HUNT

TALES OF HOFFMAN, Powell-Press-
burger, Lopert (British): HEIN
HECKROTH
Set Decoration: No credits listed.

1952   Twenty-fifty Year
(Black-and-White)

THE BAD AND THE BEAUTIFUL,
Metro-Goldwyn-Mayer: CEDRIC
GIBBONS and EDWARD CAR-
FAGNO

Cedric Gibbons, Academy founder and designer of the Oscar statuette, poses here with nine of the eleven awards he won for Art Direction.

Set Decoration: EDWIN B. WILLIS
and KEOGH GLEASON
CARRIE, Paramount: HAL PEREIRA and
ROLAND ANDERSON
Set Decoration: EMILE KURI
MY COUSIN RACHEL, 20th Century-Fox:
LYLE WHEELER AND JOHN DeCUIR
Set Decoration: WALTER M. SCOTT

RASHOMON, Daiei, RKO Radio (Japanese): MATSUYAMA
Set Decoration: H. MOTSUMOTO
VIVA ZAPATA!, 20th Century-Fox: LYLE
WHEELER and LELAND FULLER
Set Decoration: THOMAS LITTLE and
CLAUDE CARPENTER

129

(Color)

HANS CHRISTIAN ANDERSEN, Goldwyn, RKO Radio: RICHARD DAY and CLAVE
Set Decoration: HOWARD BRISTOL

THE MERRY WIDOW, Metro-Goldwyn-Mayer: CEDRIC GIBBONS and PAUL GROESSE
Set Decoration: EDWIN B. WILLIS and ARTHUR KRAMS

MOULIN ROUGE, Romulus Films, UA: PAUL SHERIFF
Set Decoration: MARCEL VERTES

THE QUIET MAN, Argosy, Republic: FRANK HOTALING
Set Decoration: JOHN MCCARTHY, JR. and CHARLES THOMPSON

THE SNOWS OF KILIMANJARO, 20th Century-Fox: LYLE WHEELER and JOHN DeCUIR
Set Decoration: THOMAS LITTLE and PAUL S. FOX

1953   Twenty-Sixth Year

(Black-and-White)

JULIUS CAESAR, Metro-Goldwyn-Mayer: CEDRIC GIBBONS and EDWARD CARFAGNO
Set Decoration: EDWIN B. WILLIS and HUGH HUNT

MARTIN LUTHER, Louis de Rochemont Assocs.: FRITZ MAURISCHAT and PAUL MARKWITZ
Set Decoration: No credits listed

THE PRESIDENT'S LADY, 20th Century-Fox: LYLE WHEELER and LELAND FULLER
Set Decoration: PAUL S. FOX

ROMAN HOLIDAY, Paramount: HAL PEREIRA and WALTER TYLER
Set Decoration: No credits listed

TITANIC, 20th Century-Fox: LYLE WHEELER and MAURICE RANSFORD
Set Decoration: STUART REISS

(Color)

KNIGHTS OF THE ROUND TABLE, Metro-Goldwyn-Mayer: ALFRED JUNGE and HANS PETERS
Set Decoration: JOHN JARVIS

LILI, Metro-Goldwyn-Mayer: CEDRIC GIBBONS and PAUL GROESSE
Set Decoration: EDWIN B. WILLIS and ARTHUR KRAMS

THE ROBE, 20th Century-Fox: LYLE WHEELER and GEORGE W. DAVIS
Set Decoration: WALTER M. SCOTT and PAUL S. FOX

THE STORY OF THREE LOVES, Metro-Goldwyn-Mayer: CEDRIC GIBBONS, PRESTON AMES, EDWARD CARFAGNO and GABRIEL SCOGNAMILLO
Set Decoration: EDWIN B. WILLIS, KEOGH GLEASON, ARTHUR KRAMS and JACK D. MOORE

YOUNG BESS, Metro-Goldwyn-Mayer: CEDRIC GIBBONS and URIE MCCLEARY
Set Decoration: EDWIN B. WILLIS and JACK D. MOORE

1954   Twenty-seventh Year

(Black-and-White)

THE COUNTRY GIRL, Perlberg-Seaton, Paramount: HAL PEREIRA and ROLAND ANDERSON
Set Decoration: SAM COMER and GRACE GREGORY

EXECUTIVE SUITE, Metro-Goldwyn-Mayer: CEDRIC GIBBONS and EDWARD CARFAGNO
Set Decoration: EDWIN B. WILLIS and EMILE KURI

LE PLAISIR, Stera Film-CCFC Prod., Arthur Meyer-Edward Kingsley (French): MAX OPHULS
Set Decoration: No credits listed

ON THE WATERFRONT, Horizon-American Corp., Columbia: RICHARD DAY
Set Decoration: No credits listed

SABRINA, Paramount: HAL PEREIRA and WALTER TYLER
Set Decoration: SAM COMER and RAY MOYER

(Color)

BRIGADOON, Metro-Goldwyn-Mayer: CEDRIC GIBBONS and PRESTON AMES
Set Decoration: EDWIN B. WILLIS and KEOGH GLEASON

DESIREE, 20th Century-Fox: LYLE WHEELER and LELAND FULLER
Set Decoration: WALTER M. SCOTT and PAUL S. FOX

RED GARTERS, Paramount: HAL PEREIRA and ROLAND ANDERSON
Set Decoration: SAM COMER and RAY MOYER

A STAR IS BORN, A Transcona Enterprises Prod., Warner Bros.: MALCOLM BERT, GENE ALLEN and IRENE SHARAFF
Set Decoration: GEORGE JAMES HOPKINS

20,000 LEAGUES UNDER THE SEA, Walt Disney Prods., Buena Vista Film Dist. Co., Inc.: JOHN MEEHAN
Set Decoration: EMILE KURI

1955   Twenty-eighth Year

(Black-and-White)

BLACKBOARD JUNGLE, Metro-Goldwyn-Mayer: CEDRIC GIBBONS and RANDALL DUELL
Set Decoration: EDWIN B. WILLIS and HENRY GRACE

I'LL CRY TOMORROW, Metro-Goldwyn-Mayer: CEDRIC GIBBONS and MALCOLM BROWN
Set Decoration: EDWIN B. WILLIS and HUGH B. HUNT

THE MAN WITH THE GOLDEN ARM, Otto Preminger Prod., UA: JOSEPH C. WRIGHT
Set Decoration: DARRELL SILVERA

MARTY, Hecht and Lancaster's Steven Prods., UA: EDWARD S. HAWORTH and WALTER SIMONDS
Set Decoration: ROBERT PRIESTLEY

THE ROSE TATTOO, Hal Wallis, Paramount: HAL PEREIRA and TAMBI LARSEN
Set Decoration: SAM COMER and ARTHUR KRAMS

(Color)

DADDY LONG LEGS, 20th Century-Fox: LYLE WHEELER and JOHN DeCUIR
Set Decoration: WALTER M. SCOTT and PAUL S. FOX

GUYS AND DOLLS, Samuel Goldwyn Prods., Inc., M-G-M: OLIVER SMITH and JOSEPH C. WRIGHT
Set Decoration: HOWARD BRISTOL

LOVE IS A MANY-SPLENDORED THING, 20th Century-Fox: LYLE WHEELER and GEORGE W. DAVIS
Set Decoration: WALTER M. SCOTT and JACK STUBBS

PICNIC, Columbia: WILLIAM FLANNERY and JO MIELZINER
Set Decoration: ROBERT PRIESTLEY

TO CATCH A THIEF, Paramount: HAL PEREIRA and JOSEPH MCMILLAN JOHNSON
Set Decoration: SAM COMER and ARTHUR KRAMS

1956   Twenty-ninth Year

(Black-and-White)

THE MAGNIFICENT SEVEN, A Toho Prod., Kingsley International (Japanese): TAKASHI MATSUYAMA
Set Decoration: No credits listed

THE PROUD AND THE PROFANE, The Perlberg-Seaton Prod., Paramount: HAL PEREIRA and A. EARL HEDRICK
Set Decoration: SAMUEL M. COMER and FRANK R. MCKELVY

THE SOLID GOLD CADILLAC, Columbia: ROSS BELLAH
Set Decoration: WILLIAM R. KIERNAN and LOUIS DIAGE

SOMEBODY UP THERE LIKES ME, Metro-Goldwyn-Mayer: CEDRIC

GIBBONS and MALCOLM F. BROWN
Set Decoration: EDWIN B. WILLIS and F. KEOGH GLEASON

TEENAGE REBEL, 20th Century-Fox: LYLE R. WHEELER and JACK MARTIN SMITH
Set Decoration: WALTER M. SCOTT and STUART A. REISS

(Color)

AROUND THE WORLD IN 80 DAYS, The Michael Todd Co., Inc., UA: JAMES W. SULLIVAN and KEN ADAM
Set Decoration: ROSS J. DOWD

GIANT, Giant Prod., Warner Bros.: BORIS LEVEN
Set Decoration: RALPH S. HURST

THE KING AND I, 20th Century-Fox: LYLE R. WHEELER and JOHN De-CUIR
Set Decoration: WALTER M. SCOTT and PAUL S. FOX

LUST FOR LIFE, Metro-Goldwyn-Mayer: CEDRIC GIBBONS, HANS PETERS and PRESTON AMES
Set Decoration: EDWIN B. WILLIS and F. KEOGH GLEASON

THE TEN COMMANDMENTS, Motion Picture Assocs., Inc., Paramount: HAL PEREIRA, WALTER H. TYLER and ALBERT NOZAKI
Set Decoration: SAM M. COMER and RAY MOYER

1957 Thirtieth Year

Note: Rules changed this year to one award for Art Direction instead of separate awards for black-and-white and color.

FUNNY FACE, Paramount: HAL PEREIRA and GEORGE W. DAVIS
Set Decoration: SAM COMER and RAY MOYER

LES GIRLS, Sol C. Siegel Prods., Inc., M-G-M: WILLIAM A. HORNING and GENE ALLEN

Set Decoration: EDWIN B. WILLIS and RICHARD PEFFERLE

PAL JOEY, Essex-George Sidney Prod., Columbia: WALTER HOLSCHER
Set Decoration: WILLIAM KIERNAN and LOUIS DIAGE

RAINTREE COUNTY, Metro-Goldwyn-Mayer: WILLIAM A. HORNING and URIE MCCLEARY
Set Decoration: EDWIN B. WILLIS and HUGH HUNT

SAYONARA, William Goetz Prod., Warner Bros.: TED HAWORTH
Set Decoration: ROBERT PRIESTLEY

1958 Thirty-first Year

AUNTIE MAME, Warner Bros.: MALCOLM BERT
Set Decoration: GEORGE JAMES HOPKINS

BELL, BOOK AND CANDLE, Phoenix Prods., Inc., Columbia: CARY ODELL
Set Decoration: LOUIS DIAGE

A CERTAIN SMILE, 20th Century-Fox: LYLE R. WHEELER and JOHN DeCUIR
Set Decoration: WALTER M. SCOTT and PAUL S. FOX

GIGI, Arthur Freed Prods., Inc., M-G-M: WILLIAM A. HORNING and PRESTON AMES
Set Decoration: HENRY GRACE and KEOGH GLEASON

VERTIGO, Alfred J. Hitchcock Prods., Inc., Paramount: HAL PEREIRA and HENRY BUMSTEAD
Set Decoration: SAM COMER and FRANK MCKELVY

1959 Thirty-second Year

Note: Rules changed this year to two awards for Art Direction: one for black-and-white and one for color.

(Black-and-White)

CAREER, Hal Wallis Prods., Paramount:

HAL PEREIRA and WALTER TYLER
Set Decoration: SAM COMER and AR-
THUR KRAMS
THE DIARY OF ANNE FRANK, 20th
Century-Fox: LYLE R. WHEELER
and GEORGE W. DAVIS
Set Decoration: WALTER M.
SCOTT and STUART A. REISS
THE LAST ANGRY MAN, Fred Kohlmar
Prods., Columbia: CARL ANDERSON
Set Decoration: WILLIAM KIERNAN
SOME LIKE IT HOT, Ashton Prods. & The
Mirisch Co., UA: TED HAWORTH
Set Decoration: EDWARD G. BOYLE
SUDDENLY, LAST SUMMER, Horizon
Prod., Columbia: OLIVER MESSELL
and WILLIAM KELLNER
Set Decoration: SCOT SLIMON

(Color)

BEN-HUR, Metro-Goldwyn-Mayer:
WILLIAM A. HORNING and ED-
WARD CARFAGNO
Set Decoration: HUGH HUNT
THE BIG FISHERMAN, Rowland V. Lee
Prods., Buena Vista Film Dist. Co.,
Inc.: JOHN DeCUIR
Set Decoration: JULIA HERON
JOURNEY TO THE CENTER OF THE
EARTH, Joseph M. Schenck En-
terprises, Inc. & Cooga Mooga Film
Prods., Inc., 20th Century-Fox: LYLE
R. WHEELER, FRANZ BACHELIN and
HERMAN A. BLUMENTHAL
Set Decoration: WALTER M. SCOTT
and JOSEPH KISH
NORTH BY NORTHWEST, Metro-
Goldwyn-Mayer: WILLIAM A. HORN-
ING, ROBERT BOYLE and MERRILL PYE
Set Decoration: HENRY GRACE and
FRANK MCKELVY
PILLOW TALK, Arwin Prods., Inc., U-I:
RICHARD H. RIEDEL
Set Decoration: RUSSELL A. GAUSMAN
and RUBY R. LEVITT

1960 Thirty-third Year
(Black-and-White)

THE APARTMENT, The Mirisch Co.,
Inc., UA: ALEXANDER TRAUNER
Set Decoration: EDWARD G.
BOYLE
THE FACTS OF LIFE, Panama & Frank
Prod., UA: JOSEPH MCMILLAN JOHN-
SON and KENNETH A. REID
Set Decoration: ROSS DOWD
PSYCHO, Alfred J. Hitchcock Prods.,
Paramount: JOSEPH HURLEY and
ROBERT CLATWORTHY
Set Decoration: GEORGE MILO
SONS AND LOVERS, Company of Artists,
Inc., 20th Century-Fox: TOM MORA-
HAN
Set Decoration: LIONEL COUCH
VISIT TO A SMALL PLANET, Hal Wallis
Prods., Paramount: HAL PEREIRA and
WALTER TYLER
Set Decoration: SAM COMER and AR-
THUR KRAMS

(Color)

CIMARRON, Metro-Goldwyn-Mayer:
GEORGE W. DAVIS and ADDISON HEHR
Set Decoration: HENRY GRACE, HUGH
HUNT and OTTO SIEGEL
IT STARTED IN NAPLES, Paramount and
Capri Prod., Paramount: HAL
PEREIRA and ROLAND ANDERSON
Set Decoration: SAM COMER and AR-
RIGO BRESCHI
PEPE, G.S.-Posa Films International
Prod., Columbia: TED HAWORTH
Set Decoration: WILLIAM KIERNAN
SPARTACUS, Bryna Prods., Inc., U-I:
ALEXANDER GOLITZEN and
ERIC ORBOM
Set Decoration: RUSSELL A.
GAUSMAN and JULIA HERON
SUNRISE AT CAMPOBELLO, Schary Prod.,
Warner Bros.: EDWARD CARRERE
Set Decoration: GEORGE JAMES HOP-
KINS

1961 Thirty-fourth Year
(Black-and-White)

133

THE ABSENT-MINDED PROFESSOR, Walt Disney Prod., Buena Vista Distribution Co., Inc.: CARROLL CLARK
Set Decoration: EMILE KURI and HAL GAUSMAN

THE CHILDREN'S HOUR, Mirisch-Worldwide Prod., UA: FERNANDO CARRERE
Set Decoration: EDWARD G. BOYLE

THE HUSTLER, Robert Rossen Prod., 20th Century-Fox: HARRY HORNER
Set Decoration: GENE CALLAHAN

JUDGMENT AT NUREMBERG, Stanley Kramer Prod., UA: RUDOLPH STERNAD
Set Decoration: GEORGE MILO

LA DOLCE VITA, Riama Film Prod., Astor Pictures, Inc. (Italian): PIERO GHERARDI

(Color)

BREAKFAST AT TIFFANY'S, Jurow-Shepherd Prod., Paramount: HAL PEREIRA and ROLAND ANDERSON
Set Decoration: SAM COMER and RAY MOYER

EL CID, Samuel Bronston Prod. in association with Dear Film Prod., Allied Artists: VENIERO COLASANTI and JOHN MOORE

FLOWER DRUM SONG, Universal-International-Ross Hunter Prod. in association with Joseph Fields, U-I: ALEXANDER GOLITZEN and JOSEPH WRIGHT
Set Decoration: HOWARD BRISTOL

SUMMER AND SMOKE, Hal Wallis Prod., Paramount: HAL PEREIRA and WALTER TYLER
Set Decoration: SAM COMER and ARTHUR KRAMS

WEST SIDE STORY, Mirisch Pictures, Inc. and B and P Enterprises, Inc., UA: BORIS LEVEN
Set Decoration: VICTOR A. GANGELIN

1962   Thirty-fifth Year
(Black-and-White)

DAYS OF WINE AND ROSES, Martin Manulis-Jalem Prod., Warner Bros.: JOSEPH WRIGHT
Set Decoration: GEORGE JAMES HOPKINS

THE LONGEST DAY, Darryl F. Zanuck Prods., 20th Century-Fox: TED HAWORTH, LEON BARSACQ and VINCENT KORDA
Set Decoration: GABRIEL BECHIR

PERIOD OF ADJUSTMENT, Marten Prod., M-G-M: GEORGE W. DAVIS and EDWARD CARFAGNO
Set Decoration: HENRY GRACE and DICK PEFFERLE

THE PIGEON THAT TOOK ROME, Llenroc Prods., Paramount: HAL PEREIRA and ROLAND ANDERSON
Set Decoration: SAM COMER and FRANK R. MCKELVY

TO KILL A MOCKINGBIRD, Universal-International-Pakula-Mulligan-Brentwood Prod., U-I: ALEXANDER GOLITZEN and HENRY BUMSTEAD
Set Decoration: OLIVER EMERT

(Color)

LAWRENCE OF ARABIA, Horizon Pictures (G.B.), Ltd.-Sam Spiegel-David Lean Prod., Columbia: JOHN BOX and JOHN STOLL
Set Decoration: DARIO SIMONI

Meredith Willson's THE MUSIC MAN, Warner Bros.: PAUL GROESSE
Set Decoration: GEORGE JAMES HOPKINS

MUTINY ON THE BOUNTY, Arcola Prod., M-G-M: GEORGE W. DAVIS and J. MCMILLAN JOHNSON
Set Decoration: HENRY GRACE and HUGH HUNT

THAT TOUCH OF MINK, Universal-International-Granley-Arwin-Nob Hill

Prod., U-I: ALEXANDER GOLITZEN and ROBERT CLATWORTHY
Set Decoration: GEORGE MILO
THE WONDERFUL WORLD OF THE BROTHERS GRIMM, Metro-Goldwyn-Mayer & Cinerama: GEORGE W. DAVIS and EDWARD CARFAGNO
Set Decoration: HENRY GRACE and DICK PEFFERLE

1963   Thirty-sixth Year
(Black-and-White)
AMERICA AMERICA, Athena Enterprises Prod., Warner Bros.: GENE CALLAHAN
FEDERICO FELLINI'S 8½, Cineriz Prod., Embassy Pictures: PIERO GHERARDI
HUD, Salem-Dover Prod., Paramount: HAL PEREIRA and TAMBI LARSEN
Set Decoration: SAM COMER and ROBERT BENTON
LOVE WITH THE PROPER STRANGER, Boardwalk-Rona Prod., Paramount: HAL PEREIRA and ROLAND ANDERSON
Set Decoration: SAM COMER and GRACE GREGORY
TWILIGHT OF HONOR, Perlberg-Seaton Prod., M-G-M: GEORGE W. DAVIS and PAUL GROESSE
Set Decoration: HENRY GRACE and HUGH HUNT

(Color)
THE CARDINAL, Gamma Production, Columbia: LYLE WHEELER
Set Decoration: GENE CALLAHAN
CLEOPATRA, 20th Century-Fox Ltd.-MCL Films S.A.-WALWA Films S.A. Prod., 20th Century Fox: JOHN DeCUIR, JACK MARTIN SMITH, HILYARD BROWN, HERMAN BLUMENTHAL, ELVEN WEBB, MAURICE PELLING and BORIS JURAGA
Set Decoration: WALTER M. SCOTT, PAUL S. FOX and RAY MOYER

COME BLOW YOUR HORN, Essex-Tandem Enterprises Prod., Paramount: HAL PEREIRA and ROLAND ANDERSON
Set Decoration: SAM COMER and JAMES PAYNE
HOW THE WEST WAS WON, Metro-Goldwyn-Mayer & Cinerama: GEORGE W. DAVIS, WILLIAM FERRARI and ADDISON HEHR
Set Decoration: HENRY GRACE, DON GREENWOOD, JR. and JACK MILLS
TOM JONES, Woodfall Production, UA-Lopert Pictures: RALPH BRINTON, TED MARSHALL and JOCELYN HERBERT
Set Decoration: JOSIE MacAVIN

1964   Thirty-seventh Year
(Black-and-White)
THE AMERICANIZATION OF EMILY, Martin Ransohoff Prod., M-G-M: GEORGE W. DAVIS, HANS PETERS and ELLIOT SCOTT
Set Decoration: HENRY GRACE and ROBERT R. BENTON
HUSH . . . HUSH, SWEET CHARLOTTE, Associates & Aldrich Prod., 20th Century-Fox: WILLIAM GLASGOW
Set Decoration: RAPHAEL BRETTON
THE NIGHT OF THE IGUANA, Seven Arts Prod., M-G-M: STEPHEN GRIMES
SEVEN DAYS IN MAY, Joel Prods., Paramount: CARY ODELL
Set Decoration: EDWARD G. BOYLE
ZORBA THE GREEK, Rochley, Ltd. Prod., International Classics: VASSILIS FOTOPOULOS

(Color)
BECKET, Hal Wallis Prod., Paramount: JOHN BRYAN and MAURICE CARTER
Set Decoration: PATRICK MCLOUGHLIN and ROBERT CARTWRIGHT
MARY POPPINS, Walt Disney Prods.: CARROLL CLARK and WILLIAM H. TUNTKE
Set Decoration: EMILE KURI and HAL GAUSMAN

MY FAIR LADY, Warner Bros.: GENE ALLEN and CECIL BEATON
Set Decoration: GEORGE JAMES HOPKINS

THE UNSINKABLE MOLLY BROWN, Marten Prod., M-G-M: GEORGE W. DAVIS and PRESTON AMES
Set Decoration: HENRY GRACE and HUGH HUNT

WHAT A WAY TO GO, Apjac-Orchard Prod., 20th Century-Fox: JACK MARTIN SMITH and TED HAWORTH
Set Decoration: WALTER M. SCOTT and STUART A. REISS

1965 Thirty-eighth Year

(Black-and-White)

KING RAT, Coleytown Prod., Columbia: ROBERT EMMET SMITH
Set Decoration: FRANK TUTTLE

A PATCH OF BLUE, Pandro S. Berman-Guy Green Prod., M-G-M: GEORGE W. DAVIS and URIE MCCLEARY
Set Decoration: HENRY GRACE and CHARLES S. THOMPSON

SHIP OF FOOLS, Columbia: ROBERT CLATWORTHY
Set Decoration: JOSEPH KISH

THE SLENDER THREAD, Paramount: HAL PEREIRA and JACK POPLIN
Set Decoration: ROBERT BENTON and JOSEPH KISH

THE SPY WHO CAME IN FROM THE COLD, Salem Films, Ltd. Prod., Paramount: HAL PEREIRA, TAMBI LARSEN and EDWARD MARSHALL
Set Decoration: JOSIE MacAVIN

(Color)

THE AGONY AND THE ECSTASY, International Classics Prod., 20th Century-Fox: JOHN DeCUIR and JACK MARTIN SMITH
Set Decoration: DARIO SIMONI

DOCTOR ZHIVAGO, Sostar S.A.-Metro-Goldwyn-Mayer British Studios, Ltd. Prod., M-G-M: JOHN BOX and TERRY MARSH
Set Decoration: DARIO SIMONI

THE GREATEST STORY EVER TOLD, George Stevens Prod., United Artists: RICHARD DAY, WILLIAM CREBER and DAVID HALL
Set Decoration: RAY MOYER, FRED MacLEAN and NORMAN ROCKETT

INSIDE DAISY CLOVER, Park Place Prod., Warner Bros.: ROBERT CLATWORTHY
Set Decoration: GEORGE JAMES HOPKINS

THE SOUND OF MUSIC, Argyle Enterprises Prod., 20th Century-Fox: BORIS LEVEN
Set Decoration: WALTER M. SCOTT and RUBY LEVITT

1966 Thirty-ninth Year

(Black-and-White)

THE FORTUNE COOKIE, Phalanx-Jalem-Mirisch Corp. of Delaware Prod., U.A.: ROBERT LUTHARDT
Set Decoration: EDWARD G. BOYLE

THE GOSPEL ACCORDING TO ST. MATTHEW, Arco-Lux Cie Cinematografique de France Prod., Walter Reade-Continental Distributing: LUIGI SCACCIANOCE

IS PARIS BURNING?, Transcontinental Films-Marianne Prod., Paramount: WILLY HOLT
Set Decoration: MARC FREDERIX and PIERRE GUFFROY

MISTER BUDDWING, DDD-Cherokee Prod., M-G-M: GEORGE W. DAVIS and PAUL GROESSE
Set Decoration: HENRY GRACE and HUGH HUNT

WHO'S AFRAID OF VIRGINIA WOOLF?, Chenault Prod., Warner Bros.: RICHARD SYLBERT
Set Decoration: GEORGE JAMES HOPKINS

(Color)

FANTASTIC VOYAGE, 20th Century-Fox: JACK MARTIN SMITH and DALE HENNESY
Set Decoration: WALTER M. SCOTT and STUART A. REISS

GAMBIT, Universal: ALEXANDER GOLITZEN and GEORGE C. WEBB
Set Decoration: JOHN McCARTHY and JOHN AUSTIN

JULIET OF THE SPIRITS, Rizzoli Films S.P.A. Prod., Rizzoli Films: PIERO GHERARDI

THE OSCAR, Greene-Rouse Prod., Embassy: HAL PEREIRA and ARTHUR LONERGAN
Set Decoration: ROBERT BENTON and JAMES PAYNE

THE SAND PEBBLES, Argyle-Solar Prod., 20th Century-Fox: BORIS LEVEN
Set Decoration: WALTER M. SCOTT, JOHN STURTEVANT and WILLIAM KIERNAN

1967 Fortieth Year

Note: Rules changed this year to one award for Art Direction instead of separate awards for black-and-white and color.

CAMELOT, Warner Bros.-Seven Arts: JOHN TRUSCOTT and EDWARD CARRERE
Set Decoration: JOHN W. BROWN

DOCTOR DOLITTLE, Apjac Prods., 20th Century-Fox: MARIO CHIARI, JACK MARTIN SMITH and ED GRAVES
Set Decoration: WALTER M. SCOTT and STUART A. REISS

GUESS WHO'S COMING TO DINNER, Columbia: ROBERT CLATWORTHY
Set Decoration: FRANK TUTTLE

THE TAMING OF THE SHREW, Royal Films International-Films Artistici Internazionali S.r.L. Prod., Columbia: RENZO MONGIARDINO, JOHN DeCUIR, ELVEN WEBB and GIUSEPPE MARIANI

Set Decoration: DARIO SIMONI and LUIGI GERVASI

THOROUGHLY MODERN MILLIE, Ross Hunter-Universal Prod., Universal: ALEXANDER GOLITZEN and GEORGE C. WEBB
Set Decoration: HOWARD BRISTOL

1968 Forty-first Year

OLIVER!, Romulus Films, Ltd., Columbia. JOHN BOX and TERENCE MARSH.
Set Decoration: VERNON DIXON and KEN MUGGLESTON

THE SHOES OF THE FISHERMAN, George Englund Prod., Metro-Goldwyn-Mayer: GEORGE W. DAVIS and EDWARD CARFAGNO

STAR!, Robert Wise Prod., 20th Century-Fox: BORIS LEVEN
Set Decoration: WALTER M. SCOTT and HOWARD BRISTOL

2001: A SPACE ODYSSEY, Polaris Prod., Metro-Goldwyn-Mayer: TONY MASTERS, HARRY LANGE and ERNIE ARCHER

WAR AND PEACE, Mosfilm Prod., Walter Reade-Continental Dist.: MIKHAIL BOGDANOV and GENNADY MYASNIKOV
Set Decoration: G. KOSHELEV and V. UVAROV

1969 Forty-second Year

ANNE OF THE THOUSAND DAYS, Hal B. Wallis-Universal Pictures, Ltd. Prod., Universal: MAURICE CARTER and LIONEL COUCH
Set Decoration: PATRICK MCLOUGHLIN

GAILY, GAILY, Mirisch-Cartier Prod., United Artists: ROBERT BOYLE and GEORGE B. CHAN
Set Decoration: EDWARD BOYLE and CARL BIDDISCOMBE

HELLO, DOLLY!, Chenault Prods., 20th Century-Fox: JOHN DeCUIR,

JACK MARTIN SMITH and HERMAN BLUMENTHAL
Set Decoration: WALTER M. SCOTT, GEORGE HOPKINS and RAPHAEL BRETTON
SWEET CHARITY, Universal: ALEXANDER GOLITZEN and GEORGE C. WEBB
Set Decoration: JACK D. MOORE
THEY SHOOT HORSES, DON'T THEY?, Chartoff-Winkler-Pollack Prod., ABC Pictures Presentation, Cinerama: HARRY HORNER
Set Decoration: FRANK MCKELVEY

1970 Forty-third Year

AIRPORT, Ross Hunter-Universal Prod., Universal: ALEXANDER GOLITZEN and E. PRESTON AMES
Set Decoration: JACK D. MOORE and MICKEY S. MICHAELS
THE MOLLY MAGUIRES, Tamm Prods., Paramount: TAMBI LARSEN
Set Decoration: DARRELL SILVERA
PATTON, 20th Century-Fox: URIE McCLEARY and GIL PARRONDO
Set Decoration: ANTONIO MATEOS and PIERRE-LOUIS THEVENET
SCROOGE, Waterbury Films, Ltd. Prod., Cinema Center Films Presentation, National General: TERRY MARSH and BOB CARTWRIGHT
Set Decoration: PAMELA CORNELL
TORA! TORA! TORA!, 20th Century-Fox: JACK MARTIN SMITH, YOSHIRO MURAKI, RICHARD DAY and TAIZOH KAWASHIMA
Set Decoration: WALTER M. SCOTT, NORMAN ROCKETT and CARL BIDDISCOMBE

1971 Forty-fourth Year

THE ANDROMEDA STRAIN, A Universal-Robert Wise Prod., Universal: BORIS LEVEN and WILLIAM TUNTKE
Set Decoration: RUBY LEVITT

BEDKNOBS AND BROOMSTICKS, Walt Disney Prods., Buena Vista Distribution Company: JOHN B. MANSBRIDGE and PETER ELLENSHAW
Set Decoration: EMILE KURI and HAL GAUSMAN
FIDDLER ON THE ROOF, Mirisch-Cartier Prods., UA: ROBERT BOYLE and MICHAEL STRINGER.
Set Decoration: PETER LAMONT
MARY, QUEEN OF SCOTS, Hal Wallis-Universal Pictures, Ltd. Prod., Universal: TERENCE MARSH and ROBERT CARTWRIGHT
Set Decoration: PETER HOWITT
NICHOLAS AND ALEXANDRA, A Horizon Pictures Prod., Columbia: JOHN BOX, ERNEST ARCHER, JACK MAXSTED and GIL PARRONDO
Set Decoration: VERNON DIXON

1972 Forty-fifth Year

CABARET, An ABC Pictures Production, Allied Artists: ROLF ZEHETBAUER and JURGEN KIEBACH
Set Decoration: HERBERT STRABEL
LADY SINGS THE BLUES, A Motown-Weston-Furie Production, Paramount: CARL ANDERSON
Set Decoration: REG ALLEN.
THE POSEIDON ADVENTURE, An Irwin Allen Production, 20th Century-Fox: WILLIAM CREBER
Set Decoration: RAPHAEL BRETTON
TRAVELS WITH MY AUNT, Robert Fryer Productions, Metro-Goldwyn-Mayer: JOHN BOX, GIL PARRONDO and ROBERT W. LAING
YOUNG WINSTON, An Open Road Films, Ltd. Production, Columbia: DON ASHTON, GEOFFREY DRAKE, JOHN GRAYSMARK and WILLIAM HUTCHINSON
Set Decoration: PETER JAMES

1973   Forty-sixth Year

BROTHER SUN SISTER MOON, Euro International Films-Vic Film (Prods.), Ltd., Paramount: LORENZO MONGIARDINO and GIANNI QUARANTA
Set Decoration: CARMELO PATRONO
THE EXORCIST, Hoya Prods., Warner Bros.: BILL MALLEY
Set Decoration: JERRY WUNDERLICH
THE STING, A Universal-Bill/ Phillips-George Roy Hill Film Prod., Zanuck/Brown Presentation, Universal: HENRY BUMSTEAD
Set Decoration: JAMES PAYNE
TOM SAWYER, An Arthur P. Jacobs Prod., Reader's Digest Presentation, UA: PHILIP JEFFERIES
Set Decoration: ROBERT de VESTEL
THE WAY WE WERE, Rastar Prods., Columbia: STEPHEN GRIMES
Set Decoration: WILLIAM KIERNAN

1974   Forty-seventh Year

CHINATOWN, A Robert Evans Prod., Paramount: RICHARD SYLBERT and W. STEWART CAMPBELL
Set Decoration: RUBY LEVITT
EARTHQUAKE, A Universal-Mark Robson-Filmakers Group Prod., Universal: ALEXANDER GOLITZEN and E. PRESTON AMES
Set Decoration: FRANK MCKELVY
THE GODFATHER PART II, A Coppola Company Prod., Paramount DEAN TAVOULARIS and ANGELO GRAHAM
Set Decoration: GEORGE R. NELSON
THE ISLAND AT THE TOP OF THE WORLD, Walt Disney Prods., Buena Vista Distribution Company: PETER ELLENSHAW, JOHN B. MANSBRIDGE, WALTER TYLER and AL ROELOFS
Set Decoration: HAL GAUSMAN
THE TOWERING INFERNO, An Irwin Allen Prod., 20th Century-Fox/Warner Bros.: WILLIAM CREBER and WARD PRESTON
Set Decoration: RAPHAEL BRETTON

1975   Forty-eighth Year

BARRY LYNDON, A Hawk Films, Ltd. Production, Warner Bros.: KEN ADAM and ROY WALKER
Set Decoration: VERNON DIXON
THE HINDENBURG, A Robert Wise-Filmakers Group-Universal Production, Universal: EDWARD CARFAGNO
Set Decoration: FRANK MCKELVY
THE MAN WHO WOULD BE KING, An Allied Artists-Columbia Pictures Production, Allied Artists: ALEXANDER TRAUNER and TONY INGLIS
Set Decoration: PETER JAMES
SHAMPOO, Rubeeker Productions, Columbia: RICHARD SYLBERT and W. STEWART CAMPBELL
Set Decoration: GEORGE GAINES
THE SUNSHINE BOYS, A Ray Stark Production, Metro-Goldwyn-Mayer: ALBERT BRENNER
Set Decoration: MARVIN MARCH

1976   Forty-ninth Year

ALL THE PRESIDENT'S MEN, A Wildwood Enterprises Production, Warner Bros.: GEORGE JENKINS
Set Decoration: GEORGE GAINES
THE INCREDIBLE SARAH, A Helen M. Strauss-Reader's Digest Films, Ltd. Production, Seymour Borde & Associates: ELLIOT SCOTT and NORMAN REYNOLDS
THE LAST TYCOON, A Sam Spiegel-Elia Kazan Film Production, Paramount: GENE CALLAHAN and JACK COLLIS
Set Decoration: JERRY WUNDERLICH
LOGAN'S RUN, A Saul David Production, Metro-Goldwyn-Mayer: DALE HENNESY
Set Decoration: ROBERT DE VESTEL

THE SHOOTIST, A Frankovich/Self Production, Dino De Laurentiis Presentation, Paramount: ROBERT F. BOYLE Set Decoration: ARTHUR JEPH PARKER

1977   Fiftieth Year

AIRPORT '77, A Jennings Lang Production, Universal: GEORGE C. WEBB Set Decoration: MICKEY S. MICHAELS

CLOSE ENCOUNTERS OF THE THIRD KIND, Close Encounter Productions, Columbia: JOE ALVES and DAN LOMINO

Set Decoration: PHIL ABRAMSON

THE SPY WHO LOVED ME, Eon Productions, United Artists: KEN ADAM and PETER LAMONT Set Decoration: HUGH SCAIFE

STAR WARS, A Twentieth Century-Fox Production, Twentieth Century-Fox: JOHN BARRY, NORMAN REYNOLDS and LESLIE DILLEY Set Decoration: ROGER CHRISTIAN

THE TURNING POINT, Hera Productions, Twentieth Century-Fox: ALBERT BRENNER Set Decoration: MARVIN MARCH

SOUND

The Academy recognized the tremendous significance of sound at the first awards ceremony by giving a special award to Warner Brothers for producing *The Jazz Singer*. No other sound pictures won an award, however, because none were eligible. Sound was judged too recent a development to permit fair competition, so the first awards were limited to silent films. By the second year sound pictures were allowed to compete, and they swept the awards. The third year a new category called Sound Recording was established. Until 1969 the Sound Recording award, or simply Sound award as it was called after 1957, went to a studio's sound department. It was accepted by the head of the department who usually carried the title Sound Director. Since 1969 the award has gone to the production mixer and supervising re-recording mixer who actually do the sound work on the film being honored. The change was made at the request of the Academy Sound Branch which pointed out that recording conditions had changed and soundtracks could now be the work of more than one studio sound department or could represent the work of non-studio technicians.

Achievements in this category are nominated by members of the Academy Sound Branch.

1929/30 Third Year
THE BIG HOUSE, Metro-Goldwyn-Mayer: DOUGLAS SHEARER
THE CASE OF SERGEANT GRISCHA, RKO Radio: JOHN TRIBBY
THE LOVE PARADE, Paramount: FRANKLIN HANSEN
RAFFLES, Goldwyn, UA: OSCAR LAGERSTROM
SONG OF THE FLAME, First National: GEORGE GROVES

1930/31 Fourth Year
METRO-GOLDWYN-MAYER STUDIO SOUND DEPARTMENT
PARAMOUNT STUDIO SOUND DEPARTMENT
RKO RADIO STUDIO SOUND DEPARTMENT
SAMUEL GOLDWYN SOUND DEPARTMENT

LARGE CAPITAL LETTERS DENOTE WINNER

1931/32 Fifth Year
PARAMOUNT STUDIO SOUND DEPARTMENT

1932/33 Sixth Year
A FAREWELL TO ARMS, Paramount: HAROLD C. LEWIS
FORTY-SECOND STREET, Warner Bros.: NATHAN LEVINSON
GOLDDIGGERS OF 1933, Warner Bros.: NATHAN LEVINSON
I AM A FUGITIVE FROM A CHAIN GANG, Warner Bros.: NATHAN LEVINSON

1934 Seventh Year
AFFAIRS OF CELLINI, 20th Century, UA. THOMAS T. MOULTON
CLEOPATRA, Paramount: FRANKLIN HANSEN
FLIRTATION WALK, First National: NATHAN LEVINSON
THE GAY DIVORCEE, RKO Radio: CARL DREHER

IMITATION OF LIFE, Universal: GILBERT KURLAND

ONE NIGHT OF LOVE, Columbia: PAUL NEAL

VIVA VILLA, Metro-Goldwyn-Mayer: DOUGLAS SHEARER

1935   Eighth Year

THE BRIDE OF FRANKENSTEIN, Universal: GILBERT KURLAND

CAPTAIN BLOOD, Warner Bros.: NATHAN LEVINSON

THE DARK ANGEL, Goldwyn, UA: Goldwyn Sound Department. THOMAS T. MOULTON

I DREAM TOO MUCH, RKO Radio: CARL DREHER

LIVES OF A BENGAL LANCER, Paramount: FRANKLIN HANSEN

LOVE ME FOREVER, Columbia: JOHN LIVADARY

NAUGHTY MARIETTA, Metro-Goldwyn-Mayer: DOUGLAS SHEARER

ONE THOUSAND DOLLARS A MINUTE, Republic: REPUBLIC SOUND DEPARTMENT

THANKS A MILLION, 20th Century-Fox: E. H. HANSEN

1936   Ninth Year

BANJO ON MY KNEE, 20th Century-Fox: E. H. HANSEN

THE CHARGE OF THE LIGHT BRIGADE, Warner Bros.: NATHAN LEVINSON

DODSWORTH, Goldwyn, UA: OSCAR LAGERSTROM

GENERAL SPANKY, Roach, M-G-M: ELMER A. RAGUSE

MR. DEEDS GOES TO TOWN, Columbia: JOHN LIVADARY

SAN FRANCISCO, Metro-Goldwyn-Mayer: DOUGLAS SHEARER

THE TEXAS RANGERS, Paramount: FRANKLIN HANSEN

THAT GIRL FROM PARIS, RKO Radio: J. O. AALBERG

THREE SMART GIRLS, Universal: HOMER G. TASKER

1937   Tenth Year

THE GIRL SAID NO, Grand National: A. E. KAYE

HITTING A NEW HIGH, RKO Radio: JOHN AALBERG

THE HURRICANE, Goldwyn, UA: THOMAS MOULTON

IN OLD CHICAGO, 20th Century-Fox: E. H. HANSEN

THE LIFE OF EMILE ZOLA, Warner Bros.: NATHAN LEVINSON

LOST HORIZON, Columbia: JOHN LIVADARY

MAYTIME, Metro-Goldwyn-Mayer: DOUGLAS SHEARER

ONE HUNDRED MEN AND A GIRL, Universal: HOMER TASKER

TOPPER, Roach, M-G-M: ELMER RAGUSE

WELLS FARGO, Paramount: L. L. RYDER

1938   Eleventh Year

ARMY GIRL, Republic: CHARLES LOOTENS

THE COWBOY AND THE LADY, Goldwyn, UA: THOMAS MOULTON

FOUR DAUGHTERS, Warner Bros.: NATHAN LEVINSON

IF I WERE KING, Paramount: L. L. RYDER

MERRILY WE LIVE, Roach, M-G-M: ELMER RAGUSE

SWEETHEARTS, Metro-Goldwyn-Mayer: DOUGLAS SHEARER

SUEZ, 20th Century-Fox: EDMUND HANSEN

THAT CERTAIN AGE, Universal: BERNARD B. BROWN

VIVACIOUS LADY, RKO Radio: JAMES WILKINSON

YOU CAN'T TAKE IT WITH YOU, Columbia: JOHN LIVADARY

Douglas Shearer, for many years head of MGM's Sound Department, received fourteen nominations and five Oscars for Sound as well as seven Scientific or Technical Awards.

1939   Twelfth Year

BALALAIKA, Metro-Goldwyn-Mayer: DOUGLAS SHEARER

GONE WITH THE WIND, Selznick, M-G-M: THOMAS T. MOULTON

GOODBYE, MR. CHIPS, Metro-Goldwyn-Mayer (British): A. W. WATKINS

THE GREAT VICTOR HERBERT, Paramount: LOREN RYDER

THE HUNCHBACK OF NOTRE DAME, RKO Radio: JOHN AALBERG

MAN OF CONQUEST, Republic: C. L. LOOTENS

MR. SMITH GOES TO WASHINGTON, Columbia: JOHN LIVADARY

OF MICE AND MEN, Roach, M-G-M: ELMER RAGUSE

THE PRIVATE LIVES OF ELIZABETH AND ESSEX, Warner Bros.: NATHAN LEVINSON

THE RAINS CAME, 20th Century-Fox: E. H. HANSEN

WHEN TOMORROW COMES, Universal: BERNARD B. BROWN

1940   Thirteenth Year

BEHIND THE NEWS, Republic: CHARLES LOOTENS

CAPTAIN CAUTION, Roach, UA: ELMER RAGUSE

THE GRAPES OF WRATH, 20th Century-Fox: E. H. HANSEN

THE HOWARDS OF VIRGINIA, Columbia: JACK WHITNEY, GENERAL SERVICE

KITTY FOYLE, RKO Radio: JOHN AALBERG

NORTH WEST MOUNTED POLICE, Paramount: LOREN RYDER

OUR TOWN, Lesser, UA: THOMAS MOULTON

THE SEA HAWK, Warner Bros.: NATHAN LEVINSON

SPRING PARADE, Universal: BERNARD B. BROWN

STRIKE UP THE BAND, Metro-Goldwyn-Mayer: DOUGLAS SHEARER

TOO MANY HUSBANDS, Columbia: JOHN LIVADARY

1941   Fourteenth Year

APPOINTMENT FOR LOVE, Universal: BERNARD B. BROWN

BALL OF FIRE, Goldwyn-RKO Radio: THOMAS MOULTON

THE CHOCOLATE SOLDIER, Metro-Goldwyn-Mayer: DOUGLAS SHEARER

CITIZEN KANE, Mercury, RKO Radio: JOHN AALBERG

THE DEVIL PAYS OFF, Republic: CHARLES LOOTENS

HOW GREEN WAS MY VALLEY, 20th Century-Fox: E. H. HANSEN

THE MEN IN HER LIFE, Columbia: JOHN LIVADARY

SERGEANT YORK, Warner Bros.: NATHAN LEVINSON

SKYLARK, Paramount: LOREN RYDER

THAT HAMILTON WOMAN, Korda, UA: JACK WHITNEY, GENERAL SERVICE

TOPPER RETURNS, Roach, UA: ELMER RAGUSE

1942   Fifteenth Year

ARABIAN NIGHTS, Universal: BERNARD BROWN

BAMBI, Disney, RKO Radio: SAM SLYFIELD

FLYING TIGERS, Republic: DANIEL BLOOMBERG

FRIENDLY ENEMIES, Small, UA: JACK WHITNEY, SOUND SERVICE, INC.

THE GOLD RUSH, Chaplin, UA: JAMES FIELDS, RCA SOUND

MRS. MINIVER, Metro-Goldwyn-Mayer: DOUGLAS SHEARER

ONCE UPON A HONEYMOON, RKO Radio: STEVE DUNN

THE PRIDE OF THE YANKEES, Goldwyn, RKO Radio: THOMAS MOULTON

ROAD TO MOROCCO, Paramount: LOREN RYDER

THIS ABOVE ALL, 20th Century-Fox: E. H. HANSEN

YANKEE DOODLE DANDY, Warner Bros. NATHAN LEVINSON

YOU WERE NEVER LOVELIER, Columbia: JOHN LIVADARY

1943   Sixteenth Year

HANGMEN ALSO DIE, Arnold, UA: JACK WHITNEY, SOUND SERVICE, INC.

IN OLD OKLAHOMA, Republic: DANIEL J. BLOOMBERG

MADAME CURIE, Metro-Goldwyn-Mayer: DOUGLAS SHEARER

THE NORTH STAR, Goldwyn, RKO Radio: THOMAS MOULTON

THE PHANTOM OF THE OPERA, Universal: BERNARD B. BROWN

RIDING HIGH, Paramount: LOREN L. RYDER

SAHARA, Columbia: JOHN LIVADARY

SALUDOS AMIGOS, Disney, RKO Radio: C. O. SLYFIELD

SO THIS IS WASHINGTON, Votion, RKO Radio: J. L. FIELDS, RCA SOUND

THE SONG OF BERNADETTE, 20th Century-Fox: E. H. HANSEN

THIS IS THE ARMY, Warner Bros.: NATHAN LEVINSON

THIS LAND IS MINE, RKO Radio: STEPHEN DUNN

1944   Seventeenth Year

BRAZIL, Republic: DANIEL J. BLOOMBERG

CASANOVA BROWN, International, RKO Radio: THOMAS T. MOULTON, Goldwyn Sound Department

COVER GIRL, Columbia: JOHN LIVADARY

DOUBLE INDEMNITY, Paramount:
  LOREN RYDER
HIS BUTLER'S SISTER, Universal: BER-
  NARD B. BROWN
HOLLYWOOD CANTEEN, Warner Bros.:
  NATHAN LEVINSON
IT HAPPENED TOMORROW, Arnold, UA:
  JACK WHITNEY, SOUND SERVICE, INC.
KISMET, Metro-Goldwyn-Mayer:
  DOUGLAS SHEARER
MUSIC IN MANHATTAN, RKO Radio:
  STEPHEN DUNN
VOICE IN THE WIND, Ripley-Monter,
  UA: W. M. DALGLEISH, RCA SOUND
WILSON, 20th Century-Fox: E. H.
  HANSEN

1945   Eighteenth Year

THE BELLS OF ST. MARY'S, Rain-
  bow, RKO Radio: STEPHEN
  DUNN
THE FLAME OF THE BARBARY COAST,
  Republic: DANIEL J. BLOOMBERG
LADY ON A TRAIN, Universal: BERNARD
  B. BROWN
LEAVE HER TO HEAVEN, 20th Century-
  Fox: THOMAS T. MOULTON
RHAPSODY IN BLUE, Warner Bros.:
  NATHAN LEVINSON
A SONG TO REMEMBER, Columbia: JOHN
  LIVADARY
THE SOUTHERNER, Loew-Hakim, UA:
  JACK WHITNEY, GENERAL SERVICE
THEY WERE EXPENDABLE, Metro-
  Goldwyn-Mayer: DOUGLAS SHEARER
THE THREE CABALLEROS, Disney, RKO
  Radio: C. O. SLYFIELD
THREE IS A FAMILY, Master Produc-
  tions, UA: W. V. WOLFE, RCA SOUND
THE UNSEEN, Paramount: LOREN L.
  RYDER
WONDER MAN, Goldwyn, RKO Radio:
  GORDON SAWYER

1946   Nineteenth Year

THE BEST YEARS OF OUR LIVES, Goldwyn, RKO Radio: GORDON SAWYER

IT'S A WONDERFUL LIFE, Liberty, RKO
  Radio: JOHN AALBERG
THE JOLSON STORY, Columbia:
  JOHN LIVADARY

1947   Twentieth Year

THE BISHOP'S WIFE, Goldwyn,
  RKO Radio: GOLDWYN SOUND
  DEPARTMENT
GREEN DOLPHIN STREET, Metro-
  Goldwyn-Mayer: METRO-GOLDWYN-
  MAYER SOUND DEPARTMENT
T-MEN, Reliance Pictures Eagle-Lion,
  SOUND SERVICES, INC.

1948   Twenty-first Year

JOHNNY BELINDA, Warner Bros.:
  WARNER BROS. SOUND DEPARTMENT
MOONRISE, Marshall Grant Prods.,
  Republic: REPUBLIC SOUND DEPART-
  MENT
THE SNAKE PIT, 20th Century-Fox:
  20TH CENTURY-FOX SOUND
  DEPARTMENT

1949   Twenty-second Year

ONCE MORE, MY DARLING, Neptune
  Films, U-I: UNIVERSAL-INTERNA-
  TIONAL SOUND DEPARTMENT
SANDS OF IWO JIMA, Republic:
  REPUBLIC SOUND DEPARTMENT
TWELVE O'CLOCK HIGH, 20th
  Century-Fox: 20TH CENTURY-
  FOX SOUND DEPARTMENT

1950   Twenty-third Year

ALL ABOUT EVE, 20th Century-Fox:
  20TH CENTURY-FOX SOUND
  DEPARTMENT
CINDERELLA, Disney, RKO Radio:
  DISNEY SOUND DEPARTMENT
LOUISA, Universal-International:
  UNIVERSAL-INTERNATIONAL SOUND
  DEPARTMENT
OUR VERY OWN, Goldwyn, RKO
  Radio: GOLDWYN SOUND DEPART-
  MENT

TRIO, Rank-Sydney Box: PARAMOUNT (British)

1951 Twenty-fourth Year

BRIGHT VICTORY, Universal-International: LESLIE I. CAREY, Sound Director

THE GREAT CARUSO, Metro-Goldwyn-Mayer: DOUGLAS SHEARER, Sound Director

I WANT YOU, Samuel Goldwyn Prods., Inc., RKO Radio: GORDON SAWYER, Sound Director

A STREETCAR NAMED DESIRE, Charles K. Feldman Group Prods., Warner Bros.: COL. NATHAN LEVINSON, Sound Director

TWO TICKETS TO BROADWAY, RKO Radio: JOHN O. AALBERG, Sound Director

1952 Twenty-fifth Year

BREAKING THE SOUND BARRIER, London Films, UA (British): LONDON FILM SOUND DEPARTMENT

HANS CHRISTIAN ANDERSEN, Goldwyn, RKO Radio. Goldwyn Sound Department: GORDON SAWYER, Sound Director

THE PROMOTER, Rank, Ronald Neame, U-I (British): PINEWOOD STUDIOS SOUND DEPARTMENT

THE QUIET MAN, Argosy, Republic. Republic Sound Department: DANIEL J. BLOOMBERG, Sound Director

WITH A SONG IN MY HEART, 20th Century-Fox. 20th Century-Fox Sound Department: THOMAS T. MOULTON, Sound Director

1953 Twenty-sixth Year

CALAMITY JANE, Warner Bros.. Warner Bros. Sound Department: WILLIAM A. MUELLER, Sound Director

FROM HERE TO ETERNITY, Columbia. Columbia Sound Department: JOHN P. LIVADARY, Sound Director

KNIGHTS OF THE ROUND TABLE, Metro-Goldwyn-Mayer: A. W. WATKINS, Sound Director

THE MISSISSIPPI GAMBLER, Universal-International. Universal-International Sound Department: LESLIE I. CAREY, Sound Director

THE WAR OF THE WORLDS, Paramount. Paramount Sound Department: LOREN L. RYDER, Sound Director

1954 Twenty-seventh Year

BRIGADOON, Metro-Goldwyn-Mayer: WESLEY C. MILLER, Sound Director

THE CAINE MUTINY, Columbia: JOHN P. LIVADARY, Sound Director

THE GLENN MILLER STORY, Universal-International: LESLIE I. CAREY, Sound Director

REAR WINDOW, Paramount: LOREN L. RYDER, Sound Director

SUSAN SLEPT HERE, RKO Radio: JOHN O. AALBERG, Sound Director

1955 Twenty-eighth Year

LOVE IS A MANY-SPLENDORED THING, 20th Century-Fox Studio Sound Department: CARL W. FAULKNER, Sound Director

LOVE ME OR LEAVE ME, Metro-Goldwyn-Mayer Studio Sound Department: WESLEY C. MILLER, Sound Director

MISTER ROBERTS, Warner Bros. Studio Sound Department: WILLIAM A. MUELLER, Sound Director

NOT AS A STRANGER, Radio Corporation of American Sound Department: WATSON JONES, Sound Director

OKLAHOMA!, Todd-AO Sound Department: FRED HYNES, Sound Director

1956 Twenty-ninth Year

THE BRAVE ONE, King Bros. Productions, Inc.: JOHN MYERS, Sound Director

THE EDDY DUCHIN STORY, Columbia Studio Sound Department: JOHN LIVADARY, Sound Director

FRIENDLY PERSUASION, Allied Artists. Westrex Sound Services, Inc.: GORDON R. GLENNAN, Sound Director; and Samuel Goldwyn Studio Sound Department: GORDON SAWYER, Sound Director

THE KING AND I, 20th Century-Fox Studio Sound Department: CARL FAULKNER, Sound Director

THE TEN COMMANDMENTS, Paramount Studio Sound Department: LOREN L. RYDER, Sound Director

1957   Thirtieth Year

Note: Name of category changed from Sound Recording to Sound.

GUNFIGHT AT THE O.K. CORRAL, Paramount Studio Sound Department: GEORGE DUTTON, Sound Director

LES GIRLS, Metro-Goldwyn-Mayer Studio Sound Department: DR. WESLEY C. MILLER, Sound Director

PAL JOEY, Columbia Studio Sound Department: JOHN P. LIVADARY, Sound Director

SAYONARA, Warner Bros. Studio Sound Department: GEORGE GROVES, Sound Director

WITNESS FOR THE PROSECUTION, Samuel Goldwyn Studio Sound Department: GORDON SAWYER, Sound Director

1958   Thirty-first Year

I WANT TO LIVE!, Samuel Goldwyn Studio Sound Department: GORDON E. SAWYER, Sound Director

SOUTH PACIFIC, Todd-AO Sound Department: FRED HYNES, Sound Director

A TIME TO LOVE AND A TIME TO DIE, Universal-International Studio Sound Department: LESLIE I. CAREY, Sound Director

VERTIGO, Paramount Studio Sound Department: GEORGE DUTTON, Sound Director

THE YOUNG LIONS, 20th Century-Fox Studio Sound Department: CARL FAULKNER, Sound Director

1959   Thirty-second Year

BEN-HUR, Metro-Goldwyn-Mayer Studio Sound Department: FRANKLIN E. MILTON, Sound Director

JOURNEY TO THE CENTER OF THE EARTH, 20th Century-Fox Studio Sound Department: CARL FAULKNER, Sound Director

LIBEL!, Metro-Goldwyn-Mayer London Sound Department (British): A. W. WATKINS, Sound Director

THE NUN'S STORY, Warner Bros. Studio Sound Department: GEORGE R. GROVES, Sound Director

PORGY AND BESS, Samuel Goldwyn Studio Sound Department: GORDON E. SAWYER, Sound Director; and Todd-AO Sound Department: FRED HYNES, Sound Director

1960   Thirty-third Year

THE ALAMO, Samuel Goldwyn Studio Sound Department: GORDON E. SAWYER, Sound Director; and Todd-AO Sound Department: FRED HYNES, Sound Director

THE APARTMENT, Samuel Goldwyn Studio Sound Department: GORDON E. SAWYER, Sound Director

CIMARRON, Metro-Goldwyn-Mayer Studio Sound Department: FRANKLIN E. MILTON, Sound Director

PEPE, Columbia Studio Sound Department: CHARLES RICE, Sound Director

SUNRISE AT CAMPOBELLO, Warner Bros. Studio Sound Department: GEORGE R. GROVES, Sound Director

1961   Thirty-fourth Year

THE CHILDREN'S HOUR, Samuel Goldwyn Studio Sound Department: GORDON E. SAWYER, Sound Director

FLOWER DRUM SONG, Revue Studio Sound Department: WALDON O. WATSON, Sound Director

THE GUNS OF NAVARONE, Shepperton Studio Sound Department: JOHN COX, Sound Director

THE PARENT TRAP, Walt Disney Studio Sound Department: ROBERT O. COOK, Sound Director

WEST SIDE STORY, Todd-AO Sound Department: FRED HYNES, Sound Director; and Samuel Goldwyn Studio Sound Department: GORDON E. SAWYER, Sound Director

1962   Thirty-fifth Year

BON VOYAGE, Walt Disney Studio Sound Department: ROBERT O. COOK, Sound Director

LAWRENCE OF ARABIA, Shepperton Studio Sound Department: JOHN COX, Sound Director

Meredith Willson's THE MUSIC MAN, Warner Bros. Studio Sound Department: GEORGE R. GROVES, Sound Director

THAT TOUCH OF MINK, Universal City Studio Sound Department: WALDON O. WATSON, Sound Director

WHAT EVER HAPPENED TO BABY JANE?, Glen Glenn Sound Department: JOSEPH KELLY, Sound Director

1963   Thirty-sixth Year

BYE BYE BIRDIE, Columbia Studio Sound Department: CHARLES RICE, Sound Director

CAPTAIN NEWMAN, M.D., Universal City Studio Sound Department: WALDON O. WATSON, Sound Director

CLEOPATRA, 20th Century-Fox Studio Sound Department: JAMES P. CORCORAN, Sound Director; and Todd A-O Sound Department: FRED HYNES, Sound Director

HOW THE WEST WAS WON, Metro-Goldwyn-Mayer Studio Sound Department: FRANKLIN E. MILTON, Sound Director

IT'S A MAD, MAD, MAD, MAD WORLD, Samuel Goldwyn Studio Sound Department: GORDON E. SAWYER, Sound Director

1964   Thirty-seventh Year

BECKET, Shepperton Studio Sound Department: JOHN COX, Sound Director

FATHER GOOSE, Universal City Studio Sound Department: WALDON O. WATSON, Sound Director

MARY POPPINS, Walt Disney Studio Sound Department: ROBERT O. COOK, Sound Director

MY FAIR LADY, Warner Bros. Studio Sound Department: GEORGE R. GROVES, Sound Director

THE UNSINKABLE MOLLY BROWN, Metro-Goldwyn-Mayer Studio Sound Department: FRANKLIN E. MILTON, Sound Director

1965   Thirty-eighth Year

THE AGONY AND THE ECSTASY, 20th Century-Fox Studio Sound Department: JAMES P. CORCORAN, Sound Director

DOCTOR ZHIVAGO, Metro-Goldwyn-Mayer British Studio Sound Department. A. W. WATKINS, Sound Director; and Metro-Goldwyn-Mayer Studio Sound Department: FRANKLIN E. MILTON, Sound Director

THE GREAT RACE, Warner Bros. Studio Sound Department: GEORGE R. GROVES, Sound Director

SHENANDOAH, Universal City Studio Sound Department: WALDON O. WATSON, Sound Director

THE SOUND OF MUSIC, 20th Cen-

tury-Fox Studio Sound Department:
JAMES P. CORCORAN, Sound
Director; and Todd-AO Sound De-
partment: FRED HYNES, Sound
Director

1966   Thirty-ninth Year

GAMBIT, Universal City Studio Sound
Department:WALDON O. WATSON,
Sound Director
GRAND PRIX, Metro-Goldwyn-Mayer
Studio Sound Department: FRANK-
LIN E. MILTON, Sound Director
HAWAII, Samuel Goldwyn Studio
Sound Department: GORDON E.
SAWYER, Sound Director
THE SAND PEBBLES, 20th Century-Fox
Studio Sound Department: JAMES P.
CORCORAN, Sound Director
WHO'S AFRAID OF VIRGINIA WOOLF?,
Warner Bros. Studio Sound Depart-
ment: GEORGE R. GROVES, Sound
Director

1967   Fortieth Year

CAMELOT, Warner Bros.-Seven Arts
Studio Sound Department
THE DIRTY DOZEN, Metro-Goldwyn-
Mayer Studio Sound Department
DOCTOR DOLITTLE, 20th Century-Fox
Studio Sound Department
IN THE HEAT OF THE NIGHT, Sam-
uel Goldwyn Studio Sound Depart-
ment
THOROUGHLY MODERN MILLIE, Univer-
sal City Studio Sound Department

1968   Forty-first Year

BULLITT, Warner Bros.-Seven Arts
Studio Sound Department
FINIAN'S RAINBOW, Warner Bros.-
Seven Arts Studio Sound Department
FUNNY GIRL, Columbia Studio Sound
Department
OLIVER!, Shepperton Studio Sound
Department

STAR!, 20th Century-Fox Studio Sound
Department

1969   Forty-second Year

ANNE OF THE THOUSAND DAYS, Hal B.
Wallis-Universal Pictures, Ltd. Pro-
duction, Universal: JOHN ALDRED
BUTCH CASSIDY AND THE SUNDANCE
KID, George Roy Hill-Paul Monash
Prod., 20th Century-Fox: WILLIAM
EDMUNDSON and DAVID DOCKENDORF
GAILY, GAILY, Mirisch-Cartier Produc-
tion, United Artists: ROBERT MARTIN
and CLEM PORTMAN
HELLO, DOLLY!, Chenault Produc-
tions, 20th Century-Fox: JACK SOL-
OMON and MURRAY SPIVACK
MAROONED, Frankovich-Sturges Pro-
duction, Columbia: LES FRESHOLTZ
and ARTHUR PIANTADOSI

1970   Forty-third Year

AIRPORT, Ross Hunter-Universal Prod.,
Universal: RONALD PIERCE and
DAVID MORIARTY
PATTON, 20th Century-Fox:
DOUGLAS WILLIAMS and DON
BASSMAN
RYAN'S DAUGHTER, Faraway Prods.,
Metro-Goldwyn-Mayer: GORDON K.
MCCALLUM and JOHN BRAMALL
TORA! TORA! TORA!, 20th Century-Fox:
MURRAY SPIVACK and HERMAN LEWIS
WOODSTOCK, Wadleigh-Maurice, Ltd.
Prod., Warner Bros: DAN WALLIN
and LARRY JOHNSON

1971   Forty-fourth Year

DIAMONDS ARE FOREVER, An Albert R.
Broccoli-Harry Saltzman Prod., UA:
GORDON K. MCCALLUM, JOHN MITCH-
ELL and ALFRED J. OVERTON
FIDDLER ON THE ROOF, Mirisch-
Cartier Prods., UA: GORDON K.
McCALLUM and DAVID HILD-
YARD

THE FRENCH CONNECTION, A Philip D'Antoni Prod. in association with Schine-Moore Prods., 20th Century-Fox: THEODORE SODERBERG and CHRISTOPHER NEWMAN

KOTCH, A Kotch Prod., ABC Pictures Presentation, Cinerama: RICHARD PORTMAN and JACK SOLOMON

MARY, QUEEN OF SCOTS, A Hal Wallis-Universal Pictures, Ltd. Prod., Universal: BOB JONES and JOHN ALDRED

1972 Forty-fifth Year

BUTTERFLIES ARE FREE, Frankovich Prods., Columbia: ARTHUR PIANTADOSI and CHARLES KNIGHT

CABARET, An ABC Pictures Production, Allied Artists: ROBERT KNUDSON and DAVID HILDYARD

THE CANDIDATE, A Redford-Ritchie Prod., Warner Bros.: RICHARD PORTMAN and GENE CANTAMESSA

THE GODFATHER, An Albert S. Ruddy Prod., Paramount: BUD GRENZBACH, RICHARD PORTMAN and CHRISTOPHER NEWMAN

THE POSEIDON ADVENTURE, An Irwin Allen Prod., 20th Century-Fox: THEODORE SODERBERG and HERMAN LEWIS

1973 Forty-sixth Year

THE DAY OF THE DOLPHIN, Icarus Prods., Avco Embassy: RICHARD PORTMAN and LAWRENCE O. JOST

THE EXORCIST, Hoya Prods., Warner Bros.: ROBERT KNUDSON and CHRIS NEWMAN

THE PAPER CHASE, Thompson-Paul Prods., 20th Century-Fox: DONALD O. MITCHELL and LAWRENCE O. JOST

PAPER MOON, A Directors Company Prod., Paramount: RICHARD PORTMAN and LES FRESHOLTZ

THE STING, A Universal-Bill/Phillips-George Roy Hill Film Prod., Zanuck/Brown Presentation, Universal: RONALD K. PIERCE and ROBERT BERTRAND

1974 Forty-seventh Year

CHINATOWN, A Robert Evans Production, Paramount: BUD GRENZBACH and LARRY JOST

THE CONVERSATION, A Directors Company Production, Paramount: WALTER MURCH and ARTHUR ROCHESTER

EARTHQUAKE, A Universal-Mark Robson-Filmakers Group Production, Universal: RONALD PIERCE and MELVIN METCALFE, SR.

THE TOWERING INFERNO, An Irwin Allen Production, 20th Century-Fox/Warner Bros.: THEODORE SODERBERG and HERMAN LEWIS

YOUNG FRANKENSTEIN, A Gruskoff/Venture Films-Crossbow Prods.-Jouer, Ltd. Production, 20th Century-Fox: RICHARD PORTMAN and GENE CANTAMESSA

1975 Forty-eighth Year

BITE THE BULLET, A Pax Enterprises Production, Columbia: ARTHUR PIANTADOSI, LES FRESHOLTZ, RICHARD TYLER and AL OVERTON, JR.

FUNNY LADY, A Rastar Pictures Production, Columbia: RICHARD PORTMAN, DON MacDOUGALL, CURLY THIRLWELL and JACK SOLOMON

THE HINDENBURG, A Robert Wise-Filmakers Group-Universal Production, Universal: LEONARD PETERSON, JOHN A. BOLGER, JR., JOHN MACK and DON K. SHARPLESS

JAWS, A Universal-Zanuck/Brown Production, Universal: ROBERT L. HOYT, ROGER HEMAN, EARL MADERY and JOHN CARTER

THE WIND AND THE LION, A Herb Jaffe Production, Metro-Goldwyn-Mayer: HARRY W. TETRICK, AARON ROCHIN,

WILLIAM MCCAUGHEY and ROY
CHARMAN

1976   Forty-ninth Year

ALL THE PRESIDENT'S MEN, A
Wildwood Enterprises Production,
Warner Bros.: ARTHUR PIAN-
TADOSI, LES FRESHOLTZ, DICK
ALEXANDER and JIM WEBB

KING KONG, A Dino De Laurentiis Pro-
duction, Paramount: HARRY WARREN
TETRICK, WILLIAM MCCAUGHEY,
AARON ROCHIN and JACK SOLOMON

ROCKY, A Robert Chartoff-Irwin
Winkler Production, United Artists:
HARRY WARREN TETRICK, WILLIAM
MCCAUGHEY, LYLE BURBRIDGE and
BUD ALPER

SILVER STREAK, A Frank Yablans Pre-
sentations Production, 20th Century-
Fox: DONALD MITCHELL, DOUGLAS
WILLIAMS, RICHARD TYLER and HAL
ETHERINGTON

A STAR IS BORN, A Barwood/Jon Peters
Production, First Artists Presentation, Warner Bros.: ROBERT KNUD-
SON, DAN WALLIN, ROBERT GLASS
and TOM OVERTON

1977   Fiftieth Year

CLOSE ENCOUNTERS OF THE THIRD
KIND, Close Encounter Productions,
Columbia: ROBERT KNUDSON, ROB-
ERT J. GLASS, DON MacDOUGALL and
GENE S. CANTAMESSA

THE DEEP, A Casablanca Filmworks
Production, Columbia: WALTER
GOSS, DICK ALEXANDER, TOM BECK-
ERT and ROBIN GREGORY

SORCERER, A William Friedkin Film
Production, Paramount-Universal:
ROBERT KNUDSON, ROBERT J. GLASS,
RICHARD TYLER and JEAN-LOUIS DU-
CARME

STAR WARS, A Twentieth Century-
Fox Production, Twentieth Century-
Fox: DON MacDOUGALL, RAY
WEST, BOB MINKLER and
DEREK BALL

THE TURNING POINT, Hera Productions,
Twentieth Century-Fox: THEODORE
SODERBERG, PAUL WELLS, DOUGLAS
O. WILLIAMS and JERRY JOST

FILM EDITING

Few persons would argue that the role of the film editor is as much creative as it is technical. By taking raw footage through a first cut to the final cut, a film editor faces a series of artistic decisions which shape the rhythm and style of the completed film and contribute substantially to how successfully the film meets the original expectations of the director.

Film editors who joined the Academy originally were assigned to the Technicians Branch. In the early 1930s they formed their own section within that branch, but it was not until 1946 that the Film Editors Branch was created.

The award for Film Editing was established in 1934. Ralph Dawson (1935, 1936, 1938) and Daniel Mandell (1942, 1946, 1960) with three awards each are the most frequent winners in this category.

Achievements in this category are nominated by members of the Academy Film Editors Branch.

1934   Seventh Year

CLEOPATRA, Paramount: ANNE BAUCHENS

ESKIMO, Metro-Goldwyn-Mayer: CONRAD NERVIG

ONE NIGHT OF LOVE, Columbia: GENE MILFORD

1935   Eighth Year

DAVID COPPERFIELD, Metro-Goldwyn-Mayer: ROBERT J. KERN

THE INFORMER, RKO Radio: GEORGE HIVELY

LES MISERABLES, 20th Century, UA: BARBARA MCLEAN

LIVES OF A BENGAL LANGER, Paramount: ELLSWORTH HOAGLAND

A MIDSUMMER NIGHT'S DREAM, Warner Bros.: RALPH DAWSON

MUTINY ON THE BOUNTY, Metro-Goldwyn-Mayer: MARGARET BOOTH

1936   Ninth Year

ANTHONY ADVERSE, Warner Bros.: RALPH DAWSON

LARGE CAPITAL LETTERS DENOTE WINNER

COME AND GET IT, Goldwyn, UA: EDWARD CURTISS

THE GREAT ZIEGFELD, Metro-Goldwyn-Mayer: WILLIAM S. GRAY

LLOYDS OF LONDON, 20th Century-Fox: BARBARA MCLEAN

A TALE OF TWO CITIES, Metro-Goldwyn-Mayer: CONRAD A. NERVIG

THEODORA GOES WILD, Columbia: OTTO MEYER

1937   Tenth Year

THE AWFUL TRUTH, Columbia: AL CLARK

CAPTAINS COURAGEOUS, Metro-Goldwyn-Mayer: ELMO VERNON

THE GOOD EARTH, Metro-Goldwyn-Mayer: BASIL WRANGELL

LOST HORIZON, Columbia: GENE HAVLICK and GENE MILFORD

100 MEN AND A GIRL, Universal: BERNARD W. BURTON

1938   Eleventh Year

THE ADVENTURES OF ROBIN HOOD, Warner Bros.: RALPH DAWSON

ALEXANDER'S RAGTIME BAND, 20th Century-Fox: BARBARA MCLEAN
THE GREAT WALTZ, Metro-Goldwyn-Mayer: TOM HELD
TEST PILOT, Metro-Goldwyn-Mayer: TOM HELD
YOU CAN'T TAKE IT WITH YOU, Columbia: GENE HAVLICK

1939 Twelfth Year

GONE WITH THE WIND, Selznick, M-G-M: HAL C. KERN and JAMES E. NEWCOM
GOODBYE, MR. CHIPS, Metro-Goldwyn-Mayer (British): CHARLES FREND
MR. SMITH GOES TO WASHINGTON, Columbia: GENE HAVLICK and AL CLARK
THE RAINS CAME, 20th Century-Fox: BARBARA MCLEAN
STAGECOACH, Wagner, UA: OTTO LOVERING and DOROTHY SPENCER

1940 Thirteenth Year

THE GRAPES OF WRATH, 20th Century-Fox: ROBERT E. SIMPSON
THE LETTER, Warner Bros.: WARREN LOW
THE LONG VOYAGE HOME, Argosy-Wanger, UA: SHERMAN TODD
NORTH WEST MOUNTED POLICE, Paramount: ANNE BAUCHENS
REBECCA, Selznick, UA: HAL C. KERN

1941 Fourteenth Year

CITIZEN KANE, Mercury-RKO Radio: ROBERT WISE
DR. JEKYLL AND MR. HYDE, Metro-Goldwyn-Mayer: HAROLD F. KRESS
HOW GREEN WAS MY VALLEY, 20th Century-Fox: JAMES B. CLARK
THE LITTLE FOXES, Goldwyn-RKO Radio: DANIEL MANDELL
SERGEANT YORK, Warner Bros.: WILLIAM HOLMES

1942 Fifteenth Year

MRS. MINIVER, Metro-Goldwyn-Mayer: HAROLD F. KRESS
THE PRIDE OF THE YANKEES, Goldwyn, RKO Radio: DANIEL MANDELL
THE TALK OF THE TOWN, Columbia: OTTO MEYER
THIS ABOVE ALL, 20th Century-Fox: WALTER THOMPSON
YANKEE DOODLE DANDY, Warner Bros.: GEORGE AMY

1943 Sixteenth Year

AIR FORCE, Warner Bros.: GEORGE AMY
CASABLANCA, Warner Bros.: OWEN MARKS
FIVE GRAVES TO CAIRO, Paramount: DOANE HARRISON
FOR WHOM THE BELL TOLLS, Paramount: SHERMAN TODD and JOHN LINK
THE SONG OF BERNADETTE, 20th Century-Fox: BARBARA MCLEAN

1944 Seventeenth Year

GOING MY WAY, Paramount: LEROY STONE
JANIE, Warner Bros.: OWEN MARKS
NONE BUT THE LONELY HEART, RKO Radio: ROLAND GROSS
SINCE YOU WENT AWAY, Selznick, UA: HAL C. KERN and JAMES E. NEWCOM
WILSON, 20th Century-Fox: BARBARA McLEAN

1945 Eighteenth Year

THE BELLS OF ST. MARY'S, Rainbow, RKO Radio: HARRY MARKER
THE LOST WEEKEND, Paramount: DOANE HARRISON
NATIONAL VELVET, Metro-Goldwyn-Mayer: ROBERT J. KERN
OBJECTIVE-BURMA, Warner Bros.: GEORGE AMY

A SONG TO REMEMBER, Columbia: CHARLES NELSON

1946 Nineteenth Year

THE BEST YEARS OF OUR LIVES, Goldwyn, RKO Radio: DANIEL MANDELL

IT'S A WONDERFUL LIFE, Liberty, RKO Radio: WILLIAM HORNBECK

THE JOLSON STORY, Columbia: WILLIAM LYON

THE KILLERS, Hellinger, Universal: ARTHUR HILTON

THE YEARLING, Metro-Goldwyn-Mayer: HAROLD KRESS

1947 Twentieth Year

THE BISHOP'S WIFE, Goldwyn, RKO Radio: MONICA COLLINGWOOD

BODY AND SOUL, Enterprise, UA: FRANCIS LYON and ROBERT PARRISH

GENTLEMAN'S AGREEMENT, 20th Century-Fox: HARMON JONES

GREEN DOLPHIN STREET, Metro-Goldwyn-Mayer: GEORGE WHITE

ODD MAN OUT, Rank-Two Cities, U-I (British): FERGUS MCDONNELL

1948 Twenty-first Year

JOAN OF ARC, Sierra Pictures, RKO Radio: FRANK SULLIVAN

JOHNNY BELINDA, Warner Bros.: DAVID WEISBART

THE NAKED CITY, Hellinger, U-I: PAUL WEATHERWAX

RED RIVER, Monterey Prods., UA: CHRISTIAN NYBY

THE RED SHOES, Rank-Archers, Eagle-Lion (British): REGINALD MILLS

1949 Twenty-second Year

ALL THE KING'S MEN, Rossen Prod., Columbia: ROBERT PARRISH and AL CLARK

BATTLEGROUND, Metro-Goldwyn-Mayer: JOHN DUNNING

CHAMPION, Screen Plays Corp., UA: HARRY GERSTAD

SANDS OF IWO JIMA, Republic: RICHARD L. VAN ENGER

THE WINDOW, RKO Radio: FREDERIC KNUDTSON

1950 Twenty-third Year

ALL ABOUT EVE, 20th Century-Fox: BARBARA MCLEAN

ANNIE GET YOUR GUN, Metro-Goldwyn-Mayer: JAMES E. NEWCOM

KING SOLOMON'S MINES, Metro-Goldwyn-Mayer: RALPH E. WINTERS and CONRAD A. NERVIG

SUNSET BOULEVARD, Paramount: ARTHUR SCHMIDT and DOANE HARRISON

THE THIRD MAN, Selznick-London Films, SRO (British): OSWALD HAFENRICHTER

1951 Twenty-fourth Year

AN AMERICAN IN PARIS, Metro-Goldwyn-Mayer: ADRIENNE FAZAN

DECISION BEFORE DAWN, 20th Century-Fox: DOROTHY SPENCER

A PLACE IN THE SUN, Paramount: WILLIAM HORNBECK

QUO VADIS, Metro-Goldwyn-Mayer: RALPH E. WINTERS

THE WELL, Popkin, UA: CHESTER SCHAEFFER

1952 Twenty-fifth Year

COME BACK, LITTLE SHEBA, Wallis, Paramount: WARREN LOW

FLAT TOP, Monogram: WILLIAM AUSTIN

THE GREATEST SHOW ON EARTH, De-Mille, Paramount: ANNE BAUCHENS

HIGH NOON, Kramer, UA: ELMO WILLIAMS and HARRY GERSTAD

MOULIN ROUGE, Romulus, UA: RALPH KEMPLEN

1953 Twenty-sixth Year

CRAZYLEGS, Bartlett, Republic: IRVINE (COTTON) WARBURTON

FROM HERE TO ETERNITY, Columbia: WILLIAM LYON

THE MOON IS BLUE, Preminger-Herbert, UA: OTTO LUDWIG

ROMAN HOLIDAY, Paramount: ROBERT SWINK

WAR OF THE WORLDS, Paramount: EVERETT DOUGLAS

1954 Twenty-seventh Year

THE CAINE MUTINY, A Stanley Kramer Prod., Columbia: WILLIAM A. LYON and HENRY BATISTA

THE HIGH AND THE MIGHTY, Wayne-Fellows Prod., Inc., Warner Bros.: RALPH DAWSON

ON THE WATERFRONT, Horizon-American Corp., Columbia: GENE MILFORD

SEVEN BRIDES FOR SEVEN BROTHERS, Metro-Goldwyn-Mayer: RALPH E. WINTERS

20,000 LEAGUES UNDER THE SEA, Walt Disney Prods., Buena Vista Film Dist. Co., Inc.: ELMO WILLIAMS

1955 Twenty-eighth Year

BLACKBOARD JUNGLE, Metro-Goldwyn-Mayer: FERRIS WEBSTER

THE BRIDGES AT TOKO-RI, Perlberg-Seaton, Paramount: ALMA MACRORIE

OKLAHOMA!, Rodgers & Hammerstein Pictures, Inc., Magna Theatre Corp.: GENE RUGGIERO and GEORGE BOEMLER

PICNIC, Columbia: CHARLES NELSON and WILLIAM A. LYON

THE ROSE TATTOO, Hal Wallis, Paramount: WARREN LOW

1956 Twenty-ninth Year

AROUND THE WORLD IN 80 DAYS, The Michael Todd Co., Inc., UA: GENE RUGGIERO and PAUL WEATHERWAX

THE BRAVE ONE, King Bros. Prods., Inc., RKO Radio: MERRILL G. WHITE

GIANT, Giant Prod., Warner Bros.: WILLIAM HORNBECK, PHILIP W. ANDERSON and FRED BOHANAN

SOMEBODY UP THERE LIKES ME, Metro-Goldwyn-Mayer: ALBERT AKST

THE TEN COMMANDMENTS, Motion Picture Assocs., Inc., Paramount: ANNE BAUCHENS

1957 Thirtieth Year

THE BRIDGE ON THE RIVER KWAI, A Horizon Picture, Columbia: PETER TAYLOR

GUNFIGHT AT THE O.K. CORRAL, A Hal Wallis Prod., Paramount: WARREN LOW

PAL JOEY, Essex-George Sidney Prod., Columbia: VIOLA LAWRENCE and JEROME THOMS

SAYONARA, William Goetz Prod., Warner Bros.: ARTHUR P. SCHMIDT and PHILIP W. ANDERSON

WITNESS FOR THE PROSECUTION, Edward Small-Arthur Hornblow Prod., UA: DANIEL MANDELL

1958 Thirty-first Year

AUNTIE MAME, Warner Bros.: WILLIAM ZIEGLER

COWBOY, Phoenix Pictures, Columbia: WILLIAM A. LYON and AL CLARK

THE DEFIANT ONES, Stanley Kramer, UA: FREDERIC KNUDTSON

GIGI, Arthur Freed Prods., Inc., M-G-M: ADRIENNE FAZAN

I WANT TO LIVE!, Figaro, Inc., UA: WILLIAM HORNBECK

1959   Thirty-second Year

ANATOMY OF A MURDER, Otto Prem-
inger, Columbia: LOUIS R. LOEFFLER
BEN-HUR, Metro-Goldwyn-Mayer:
RALPH E. WINTERS and JOHN D.
DUNNING
NORTH BY NORTHWEST, Metro-
Goldwyn-Mayer: GEORGE TOMASINI
THE NUN'S STORY, Warner Bros.:
WALTER THOMPSON
ON THE BEACH, Lomitas Prods., UA:
FREDERIC KNUDTSON

1960   Thirty-third Year

THE ALAMO, Batjac Prod., UA: STUART
GILMORE
THE APARTMENT, The Mirisch Co.,
UA: DANIEL MANDELL
INHERIT THE WIND, Stanley Kramer
Prod., UA: FREDERIC KNUDTSON
PEPE, G. S.-Posa Films International
Prod., Columbia: VIOLA LAWRENCE
and AL CLARK
SPARTACUS, Bryna Prods., Inc., U-I:
ROBERT LAWRENCE

1961   Thirty-fourth Year

FANNY, Mansfield Prod., Warner
Bros.: WILLIAM H. REYNOLDS
THE GUNS OF NAVARONE, Carl Fore-
man Prod., Columbia: ALAN OSBIS-
TON
JUDGMENT AT NUREMBERG, Stanley
Kramer Prod., UA: FREDERIC
KNUDTSON
THE PARENT TRAP, Walt Disney Prods.,
Buena Vista Dist. Co., Inc.: PHILIP
W. ANDERSON
WEST SIDE STORY, Mirisch Pic-
tures, Inc. and B and P Enterprises,
Inc., UA: THOMAS STANFORD

1962   Thirty-fifth Year

LAWRENCE OF ARABIA, Horizon
Pictures (G.B.), Ltd.-Sam Spiegel-
David Lean Prod., Columbia: ANNE
COATES

THE LONGEST DAY, Darryl F. Zanuck
Prods., 20th Century-Fox: SAMUEL
E. BEETLEY
THE MANCHURIAN CANDIDATE, M.C.
Prod., UA: FERRIS WEBSTER
Meredith Willson's THE MUSIC MAN,
Warner Bros.: WILLIAM ZIEGLER
MUTINY ON THE BOUNTY, Arcola
Prod., M-G-M: JOHN MCSWEENEY,
JR.

1963   Thirty-sixth Year

THE CARDINAL, Gamma Prod., Colum-
bia: LOUIS R. LOEFFLER
CLEOPATRA, 20th Century-Fox Ltd.-
MCL Films S.A.-WALWA Films
S.A. Prod., 20th Century-Fox:
DOROTHY SPENCER
THE GREAT ESCAPE, Mirisch-Alpha Pic-
ture Prod., UA: FERRIS WEBSTER
HOW THE WEST WAS WON, Metro-
Goldwyn-Mayer & Cinerama:
HAROLD F. KRESS
IT'S A MAD, MAD, MAD, MAD WORLD,
Casey Prod., UA: FREDERIC KNUDT-
SON, ROBERT C. JONES and GENE
FOWLER, JR.

1964   Thirty-seventh Year

BECKET, Hal Wallis Prod., Paramount:
ANNE COATES
FATHER GOOSE, Universal-Granox
Prod., Universal: TED J. KENT
HUSH . . . HUSH, SWEET CHARLOTTE,
Associates & Aldrich Prod., 20th
Century-Fox: MICHAEL LUCIANO
MARY POPPINS, Walt Disney Prods.:
COTTON WARBURTON
MY FAIR LADY, Warner Bros.: WILLIAM
ZIEGLER

1965   Thirty-eighth Year

CAT BALLOU, Harold Hecht Prod., Co-
lumbia: CHARLES NELSON
DOCTOR ZHIVAGO, Sostar S.A.-Metro-
Goldwyn-Mayer British Studios,

Ltd. Prod., M-G-M: NORMAN SAVAGE

THE FLIGHT OF THE PHOENIX, Associates & Aldrich Company Prod., 20th Century-Fox: MICHAEL LUCIANO

THE GREAT RACE, Patricia-Jalem-Reynard Prod., Warner Bros.: RALPH E. WINTERS

THE SOUND OF MUSIC, Argyle Enterprises Prod., 20th Century-Fox: WILLIAM REYNOLDS

1966   Thirty-ninth Year

FANTASTIC VOYAGE, 20th Century-Fox: WILLIAM B. MURPHY

GRAND PRIX, Douglas-Lewis-John Frankenheimer-Cherokee Prod., M-G-M: FREDRIC STEINKAMP, HENRY BERMAN, STEWART LINDER and FRANK SANTILLO

THE RUSSIANS ARE COMING THE RUSSIANS ARE COMING, Mirisch Corp. of Delaware Prod., United Artists: HAL ASHBY and J. TERRY WILLIAMS

THE SAND PEBBLES, Argyle-Solar Prod., 20th Century-Fox: WILLIAM REYNOLDS

WHO'S AFRAID OF VIRGINIA WOOLF?, Chenault Prod., Warner Bros.: SAM O'STEEN

1967   Fortieth Year

BEACH RED, Theodora Prods., United Artists: FRANK P. KELLER

THE DIRTY DOZEN, MKH Prods., Ltd., M-G-M: MICHAEL LUCIANO

DOCTOR DOLITTLE, Apjac Prods., 20th Century-Fox: SAMUEL E. BEETLEY and MARJORIE FOWLER

GUESS WHO'S COMING TO DINNER, Columbia: ROBERT C. JONES

IN THE HEAT OF THE NIGHT, Mirisch Corp. Prod., United Artists: HAL ASHBY

1968   Forty-first Year

BULLITT, Solar Prod., Warner Bros.-Seven Arts.: FRANK P. KELLER

FUNNY GIRL, Rastar Prods., Columbia: ROBERT SWINK, MAURY WINETROBE and WILLIAM SANDS

THE ODD COUPLE, Howard W. Koch Prod., Paramount: FRANK BRACHT

OLIVER!, Romulus Films, Columbia: RALPH KEMPLEN

WILD IN THE STREETS, American International: FRED FEITSHANS and EVE NEWMAN

1969   Forty-second Year

HELLO, DOLLY!, Chenault Prods., 20th Century-Fox: WILLIAM REYNOLDS

MIDNIGHT COWBOY, Jerome Hellman-John Schlesinger Prod., United Artists: HUGH A. ROBERTSON

THE SECRET OF SANTA VITTORIA, Stanley Kramer Company Prod., United Artists: WILLIAM LYON and EARLE HERDAN

THEY SHOOT HORSES, DON'T THEY?, Chartoff-Winkler-Pollack Prod., ABC Pictures Presentation Cinerama: FREDRIC STEINKAMP

Z, Reggane Films-O.N.C.I.C. Prod., Cinema V: FRANCOISE BONNOT

1970   Forty-third Year

AIRPORT, Ross Hunter-Universal Prod., Universal: STUART GILMORE

M*A*S*H, Aspen Prods., 20th Century-Fox: DANFORD B. GREENE

PATTON, 20th Century-Fox: HUGH S. FOWLER

TORA! TORA! TORA!, 20th Century-Fox: JAMES E. NEWCOM, PEMBROKE J. HERRING and INOUE CHIKAYA

WOODSTOCK, Wadleigh-Maurice, Ltd. Prod., Warner Bros.: THELMA SCHOONMAKER

1971   Forty-fourth Year

THE ANDROMEDA STRAIN, A Universal-Robert Wise Prod., Universal:

STUART GILMORE and JOHN W. HOLMES

A CLOCKWORK ORANGE, A Hawks Films, Ltd., Prod., Warner Bros.: BILL BUTLER

THE FRENCH CONNECTION, A Philip D'Antoni Prod. in association with Schine-Moore Prods., 20th Century-Fox: JERRY GREENBERG

KOTCH, A Kotch Company Prod., ABC Pictures Presentation, Cinerama: RALPH E. WINTERS

SUMMER OF '42, A Robert Mulligan-Richard Alan Roth Prod., Warner Bros.: FOLMAR BLANGSTED

1972 Forty-fifth Year

CABARET, An ABC Pictures Production, Allied Artists: DAVID BRETHERTON

DELIVERANCE, Warner Bros.: TOM PRIESTLEY

THE GODFATHER, An Albert S. Ruddy Production, Paramount: WILLIAM REYNOLDS and PETER ZINNER

THE HOT ROCK, A Landers-Roberts Production, 20th Century-Fox: FRANK P. KELLER and FRED W. BERGER

THE POSEIDON ADVENTURE, An Irwin Allen Production, 20th Century-Fox: HAROLD F. KRESS

1973 Forty-sixth Year

AMERICAN GRAFFITI, A Universal-Lucasfilm, Ltd.-Coppola Company Prod., Universal: VERNA FIELDS and MARCIA LUCAS

THE DAY OF THE JACKAL, Warwick Film Prods., Ltd.-Universal Prods. France S.A., Universal: RALPH KEMPLEN

THE EXORCIST, Hoya Prods., Warner Bros.: JORDAN LEONDOPOULOS, BUD SMITH, EVAN LOTTMAN and NORMAN GAY

JONATHAN LIVINGSTON SEAGULL, A

JLS Limited Partnership Prod., Paramount: FRANK P. KELLER and JAMES GALLOWAY

THE STING, A Universal-Bill/Phillips-George Roy Hill Film Prod., Zanuck/Brown Presentation, Universal: WILLIAM REYNOLDS

1974 Forty-seventh Year

BLAZING SADDLES, Warner Bros.: JOHN C. HOWARD and DANFORD GREENE

CHINATOWN, A Robert Evans Prod., Paramount: SAM O'STEEN

EARTHQUAKE, A Universal-Mark Robson-Filmakers Group Prod., Universal: DOROTHY SPENCER

THE LONGEST YARD, An Albert S. Ruddy Prod., Paramount: MICHAEL LUCIANO

THE TOWERING INFERNO, An Irwin Allen Prod., 20th Century-Fox/Warner Bros: HAROLD F. KRESS and CARL KRESS

1975 Forty-eighth Year

DOG DAY AFTERNOON, Warner Bros.: DEDE ALLEN

JAWS, A Universal-Zanuck/Brown Production, Universal: VERNA FIELDS

THE MAN WHO WOULD BE KING, An Allied Artists-Columbia Pictures Production, Allied Artists: RUSSELL LLOYD

ONE FLEW OVER THE CUCKOO'S NEST, A Fantasy Films Production, United Artists: RICHARD CHEW, LYNZEE KLINGMAN and SHELDON KAHN

THREE DAYS OF THE CONDOR, A Dino De Laurentiis Production, Paramount: FREDRIC STEINKAMP and DON GUIDICE

1976 Forty-ninth Year

ALL THE PRESIDENT'S MEN, A Wildwood Enterprises Production,

William Reynolds (left) receives his Oscar for editing *The Sting* (1973) from Paula Prentiss and Richard Benjamin. © *1978 A.M.P.A.S.*

Warner Bros.: ROBERT L. WOLFE

BOUND FOR GLORY, The Bound For Glory Company Production, United Artists: ROBERT JONES and PEMBROKE J. HERRING

NETWORK, A Howard Gottfried/Paddy Chayefsky Production, Metro-Goldwyn-Mayer/United Artists: ALAN HEIM

ROCKY, A Robert Chartoff-Irwin Winkler Production, United Artists:

RICHARD HALSEY and SCOTT CONRAD

TWO-MINUTE WARNING, A Filmways/Larry Peerce-Edward S. Feldman Film Production, Universal: EVE NEWMAN and WALTER HANNEMANN

1977   Fiftieth Year

CLOSE ENCOUNTERS OF THE THIRD KIND, Close Encounter Productions, Columbia: MICHAEL KAHN

JULIA, A Twentieth Century-Fox Production, Twentieth Century-Fox: WALTER MURCH and MARCEL DURHAM

SMOKEY AND THE BANDIT, A Universal/Rastar Production, Universal: WALTER HANNEMANN and ANGELO ROSS

STAR WARS, A Twentieth Century-Fox Production, Twentieth Century-Fox: PAUL HIRSCH, MARCIA LUCAS and RICHARD CHEW

THE TURNING POINT, Hera Productions, Twentieth Century-Fox: WILLIAM REYNOLDS

MUSIC: SCORING

The Music Award for Scoring was established in 1934, and for the first four years it was a Music Department Achievement with the Oscar going to the head of the studio's music department rather than to the composer. In 1938 rule changes gave the composer the award and split the category into two parts, Best Score and Original Score. Three years later these designations were changed again; this time the categories depended upon whether the film was dramatic or musical. Since then the names of the category divisions have changed several times. The present designations are, Best Original Score and Best Original Song Score or Best Adaptation Score. The Academy defines a song score as a work "consisting of not less than five original songs by the same writer or by the same identical team of writers specifically created for the film."

Entries in this category are submitted by the creators of the achievement and are screened by members of the Academy Music Branch who determine the nominees.

1934   Seventh Year
(Best Score)
THE GAY DIVORCEE, RKO Radio Studio
Music Dept.: MAX STEINER, Head.
Score by KENNETH WEBB and SAMUEL HOFFENSTEIN
THE LOST PATROL, RKO Radio Studio
Music Dept: MAX STEINER, Head.
Score by MAX STEINER
ONE NIGHT OF LOVE, Columbia
Studio Music Dept: LOUIS SILVERS, Head.
Thematic music by VICTOR SCHERTZINGER and GUS KAHN

1935   Eighth Year
(Best Score)
THE INFORMER, RKO Radio Studio
Music Dept: MAX STEINER, Head.
Score by MAX STEINER
MUTINY ON THE BOUNTY, Metro-
Goldwyn-Mayer Studio Music Dept:
NAT W. FINSTON, Head.
Score by HERBERT STOTHART

LARGE CAPITAL LETTERS DENOTE WINNER

PETER IBBETSON, Paramount Studio
Music Dept: IRVIN TALBOT, Head.
Score by ERNST TOCH

1936   Ninth Year
(Best Score)
ANTHONY ADVERSE, Warner Bros.
Studio Music Dept: LEO FORBSTEIN, Head.
Score by ERICH WOLFGANG KORNGOLD
THE CHARGE OF THE LIGHT BRIGADE,
Warner Bros. Studio Music Dept:
LEO FORBSTEIN, Head.
Score by MAX STEINER
THE GARDEN OF ALLAH, Selznick International Pictures Music Dept: MAX
STEINER, Head.
Score by MAX STEINER
THE GENERAL DIED AT DAWN, Paramount Studio Music Dept: BORIS
MORROS, Head.
Score by WERNER JANSSEN
WINTERSET, RKO Radio Studio Music
Dept: NATHANIEL SHILKRET, Head.
Score by NATHANIEL SHILKRET

1937   Tenth Year

(Best Score)

HURRICANE, Samuel Goldwyn Studio Music Dept: ALFRED NEWMAN, Head.
Score by ALFRED NEWMAN

IN OLD CHICAGO, 20th Century-Fox Studio Music Dept: LOUIS SILVERS, Head.
Score: No composer credit

THE LIFE OF EMILE ZOLA, Warner Bros. Studio Music Dept: LEO FORBSTEIN, Head.
Score by MAX STEINER

LOST HORIZON, Columbia Studio Music Dept: MORRIS STOLOFF, Head.
Score by DIMITRI TIOMKIN

MAKE A WISH, Principal Productions: DR. HUGO RIESENFELD, Musical Director.
Score by DR. HUGO RIESENFELD

MAYTIME, Metro-Goldwyn-Mayer Studio Music Dept: NAT W. FINSTON, Head.
Score by HERBERT STOTHART

ONE HUNDRED MEN AND A GIRL, Universal Studio Music Dept: CHARLES PREVIN, Head.
Score: No composer credit

PORTIA ON TRIAL, Republic Studio Music Dept: ALBERTO COLOMBO, Head.
Score by ALBERTO COLOMBO

THE PRISONER OF ZENDA, Selznick International Pictures Music Dept: ALFRED NEWMAN, Musical Director.
Score by ALFRED NEWMAN

QUALITY STREET, RKO Radio Studio Music Dept: ROY WEBB, Musical Director.
Score by ROY WEBB

SNOW WHITE AND THE SEVEN DWARFS, Walt Disney Studio Music Dept: LEIGH HARLINE, Head.
Score by FRANK CHURCHILL, LEIGH HARLINE and PAUL J. SMITH

SOMETHING TO SING ABOUT, Grand National Studio Music Dept: C. BAKALEINIKOFF, Musical Director.
Score by VICTOR SCHERTZINGER

SOULS AT SEA, Paramount Studio Music Dept: BORIS MORROS, Head.
Score by W. FRANKE HARLING and MILAN RODER

WAY OUT WEST, Hal Roach Studio Music Dept: MARVIN HATLEY, Head.
Score by MARVIN HATLEY

1938   Eleventh Year

(Best Score)

ALEXANDER'S RAGTIME BAND, 20th Century-Fox: ALFRED NEWMAN

CAREFREE, RKO Radio: VICTOR BARAVALLE

GIRLS SCHOOL, Columbia: MORRIS STOLOFF and GREGORY STONE

GOLDWYN FOLLIES, Goldwyn, UA: ALFRED NEWMAN

JEZEBEL, Warner Bros: MAX STEINER

MAD ABOUT MUSIC, Universal: CHARLES PREVIN and FRANK SKINNER

STORM OVER BENGAL, Republic: CY FEUER

SWEETHEARTS, Metro-Goldwyn-Mayer: HERBERT STOTHART

THERE GOES MY HEART, Hal Roach, UA: MARVIN HATLEY

TROPIC HOLIDAY, Paramount: BORRIS MORROS

THE YOUNG IN HEART, Selznick, UA: FRANZ WAXMAN

(Original Score)

THE ADVENTURES OF ROBIN HOOD, Warner Bros.: ERICH WOLFGANG KORNGOLD

ARMY GIRL, Republic: VICTOR YOUNG

BLOCKADE, Walter Wanger, UA: WERNER JANSSEN

BLOCKHEADS, Hal Roach, UA: MARVIN HATLEY

BREAKING THE ICE, RKO Radio: VICTOR YOUNG

THE COWBOY AND THE LADY, Goldwyn, UA: ALFRED NEWMAN

IF I WERE KING, Paramount: RICHARD
HAGEMAN

MARIE ANTOINETTE, Metro-Goldwyn-
Mayer: HERBERT STOTHART

PACIFIC LINER, RKO Radio: RUSSELL
BENNETT

SUEZ, 20th Century-Fox: LOUIS SILVERS

THE YOUNG IN HEART, Selznick, UA:
FRANZ WAXMAN

1939   Twelfth Year

(Best Score)

BABES IN ARMS, Metro-Goldwyn-
Mayer: ROGER EDENS and GEORGE E.
STOLL

FIRST LOVE, Universal: CHARLES PRE-
VIN

THE GREAT VICTOR HERBERT, Paramount: PHIL BOUTELJE and ARTHUR
LANGE

THE HUNCHBACK OF NOTRE DAME,
RKO Radio: ALFRED NEWMAN

INTERMEZZO, Selznick, UA: LOU
FORBES

MR. SMITH GOES TO WASHINGTON, Columbia: DIMITRI TIOMKIN

OF MICE AND MEN, Roach, UA: AARON
COPLAND

THE PRIVATE LIVES OF ELIZABETH AND
ESSEX, Warner Bros: ERICH
WOLFGANG KORNGOLD

SHE MARRIED A COP, Republic: CY
FEUER

STAGECOACH, Walter Wanger, UA:
RICHARD HAGEMAN, FRANK
HARLING, JOHN LEIPOLD and
LEO SHUKEN

SWANEE RIVER, 20th Century-Fox:
LOUIS SILVERS

THEY SHALL HAVE MUSIC, Goldwyn,
UA: ALFRED NEWMAN

WAY DOWN SOUTH, Lesser, RKO
Radio: VICTOR YOUNG

(Original Score)

DARK VICTORY, Warner Bros.: MAX
STEINER

ETERNALLY YOURS, Walter Wanger,
UA: WERNER JANSSEN

GOLDEN BOY, Columbia: VICTOR
YOUNG

GONE WITH THE WIND, Selznick,
M-G-M: MAX STEINER

GULLIVER'S TRAVELS, Paramount: VIC-
TOR YOUNG

THE MAN IN THE IRON MASK, Small,
UA: LUD GLUSKIN and LUCIEN
MORAWECK

MAN OF CONQUEST, Republic: VICTOR
YOUNG

NURSE EDITH CAVELL, RKO Radio:
ANTHONY COLLINS

OF MICE AND MEN, Roach, UA: AARON
COPLAND

THE RAINS CAME, 20th Century-Fox:
ALFRED NEWMAN

THE WIZARD OF OZ, Metro-
Goldwyn-Mayer: HERBERT
STOTHART

WUTHERING HEIGHTS, Goldwyn, UA:
ALFRED NEWMAN

1940   Thirteenth Year

(Best Score)

ARISE, MY LOVE, Paramount: VICTOR
YOUNG

HIT PARADE OF 1941, Republic: CY
FEUER

IRENE, Imperadio, RKO Radio: AN-
THONY COLLINS

OUR TOWN, Sol Lesser, UA: AARON
COPLAND

THE SEA HAWK, Warner Bros.: ERICH
WOLFGANG KORNGOLD

SECOND CHORUS, Paramount: ARTIE
SHAW

SPRING PARADE, Universal: CHARLES
PREVIN

STRIKE UP THE BAND, Metro-Goldwyn-
Mayer: GEORGIE STOLL and ROGER
EDENS

TIN PAN ALLEY, 20th Century-Fox:
ALFRED NEWMAN

(Original Score)

ARIZONA, Columbia: VICTOR YOUNG

THE DARK COMMAND, Republic: VICTOR YOUNG

THE FIGHT FOR LIFE, U.S. Government-Columbia: LOUIS GRUENBERG

THE GREAT DICTATOR, Chaplin, UA: MEREDITH WILLSON

THE HOUSE OF SEVEN GABLES, Universal: FRANK SKINNER

THE HOWARDS OF VIRGINIA, Columbia: RICHARD HAGEMAN

THE LETTER, Warner Bros.: MAX STEINER

THE LONG VOYAGE HOME, Argosy-Wanger, UA: RICHARD HAGEMAN

THE MARK OF ZORRO, 20th Century-Fox: ALFRED NEWMAN

MY FAVORITE WIFE, RKO Radio: ROY WEBB

NORTH WEST MOUNTED POLICE, Paramount: VICTOR YOUNG

ONE MILLION B.C., Hal Roach, UA: WERNER HEYMANN

OUR TOWN, Sol Lesser, UA: AARON COPLAND

PINOCCHIO, Disney, RKO Radio: LEIGH HARLINE, PAUL J. SMITH and NED WASHINGTON

REBECCA, Selznick, UA: FRANZ WAXMAN

THE THIEF OF BAGDAD, Korda, UA: MIKLOS ROZSA

WATERLOO BRIDGE, Metro-Goldwyn-Mayer: HERBERT STOTHART

1941   Fourteenth Year
(Scoring of a Dramatic Picture)

ALL THAT MONEY CAN BUY, RKO Radio: BERNARD HERRMANN

BACK STREET, Universal: FRANK SKINNER

BALL OF FIRE, Goldwyn, RKO Radio: ALFRED NEWMAN

CHEERS FOR MISS BISHOP, Rowland,
UA: EDWARD WARD

CITIZEN KANE, Mercury, RKO Radio: BERNARD HERRMANN

DR. JEKYLL AND MR. HYDE, Metro-Goldwyn-Mayer: FRANZ WAXMAN

HOLD BACK THE DAWN, Paramount: VICTOR YOUNG

HOW GREEN WAS MY VALLEY, 20th Century-Fox: ALFRED NEWMAN

KING OF THE ZOMBIES, Monogram: EDWARD KAY

LADIES IN RETIREMENT, Columbia: MORRIS STOLOFF and ERNST TOCH

THE LITTLE FOXES, Goldwyn, RKO Radio: MEREDITH WILLSON

LYDIA, Korda, UA: MIKLOS ROZSA

MERCY ISLAND, Republic: CY FEUER and WALTER SCHARF

SERGEANT YORK, Warner Bros.: MAX STEINER

SO ENDS OUR NIGHT, Loew-Lewin, UA: LOUIS GRUENBERG

SUNDOWN, Walter Wanger, UA: MIKLOS ROZSA

SUSPICION, RKO Radio: FRANZ WAXMAN

TANKS A MILLION, Roach, UA: EDWARD WARD

THAT UNCERTAIN FEELING, Lubitsch, UA: WERNER HEYMANN

THIS WOMAN IS MINE, Universal: RICHARD HAGEMAN

(Scoring of a Musical Picture)

ALL AMERICAN CO-ED, Roach, UA: EDWARD WARD

BIRTH OF THE BLUES, Paramount: ROBERT EMMETT DOLAN

BUCK PRIVATES, Universal: CHARLES PREVIN

THE CHOCOLATE SOLDIER, Metro-Goldwyn-Mayer: HERBERT STOTHART and BRONISLAU KAPER

DUMBO, Disney, RKO Radio: FRANK CHURCHILL and OLIVER WALLACE

ICE-CAPADES, Republic: CY FEUER

THE STRAWBERRY BLONDE, Warner Bros.: HEINZ ROEMHELD

SUN VALLEY SERENADE, 20th Century-Fox: EMIL NEWMAN

SUNNY, RKO Radio: ANTHONY COLLINS

YOU'LL NEVER GET RICH, Columbia: MORRIS STOLOFF

1942   Fifteenth Year

(Scoring of a Dramatic or Comedy Picture)

ARABIAN NIGHTS, Universal: FRANK SKINNER

BAMBI, Disney, RKO Radio: FRANK CHURCHILL and EDWARD PLUMB

THE BLACK SWAN, 20th Century-Fox: ALFRED NEWMAN

THE CORSICAN BROTHERS, Small, UA: DIMITRI TIOMKIN

FLYING TIGERS, Republic: VICTOR YOUNG

THE GOLD RUSH, Chaplin, UA: MAX TERR

I MARRIED A WITCH, Cinema Guild, UA: ROY WEBB

JOAN OF PARIS, RKO Radio: ROY WEBB

JUNGLE BOOK, Korda, UA: MIKLOS ROZSA

KLONDIKE FURY, Monogram: EDWARD KAY

NOW, VOYAGER, Warner Bros.: MAX STEINER

THE PRIDE OF THE YANKEES, Goldwyn, RKO Radio: LEIGH HARLINE

RANDOM HARVEST, Metro-Goldwyn-Mayer: HERBERT STOTHART

THE SHANGHAI GESTURE, Arnold, UA: RICHARD HAGEMAN

SILVER QUEEN, Sherman, UA: VICTOR YOUNG

TAKE A LETTER, DARLING, Paramount: VICTOR YOUNG

THE TALK OF THE TOWN, Columbia: FREDERICK HOLLANDER and MORRIS STOLOFF

TO BE OR NOT TO BE, Lubitsch, UA: WERNER HEYMANN

(Scoring of a Musical Picture)

FLYING WITH MUSIC, Roach, UA: EDWARD WARD

FOR ME AND MY GAL, Metro-Goldwyn-Mayer: ROGER EDENS and GEORGIE STOLL

HOLIDAY INN, Paramount: ROBERT EMMETT DOLAN

IT STARTED WITH EVE, Universal: CHARLES PREVIN and HANS SALTER

JOHNNY DOUGHBOY, Republic: WALTER SCHARF

MY GAL SAL, 20th Century-Fox: ALFRED NEWMAN

YANKEE DOODLE DANDY, Warner Bros.: RAY HEINDORF and HEINZ ROEMHELD

YOU WERE NEVER LOVELIER, Columbia: LEIGH HARLINE

1943   Sixteenth Year

(Scoring of a Dramatic or Comedy Picture)

THE AMAZING MRS. HOLLIDAY, Universal: HANS J. SALTER and FRANK SKINNER

CASABLANCA, Warner Bros: MAX STEINER

THE COMMANDOS STRIKE AT DAWN, Columbia: LOUIS GRUENBERG and MORRIS STOLOFF

THE FALLEN SPARROW, RKO Radio: C. BAKALEINIKOFF and ROY WEBB

FOR WHOM THE BELL TOLLS, Paramount: VICTOR YOUNG

HANGMEN ALSO DIE, Arnold, UA: HANNS EISLER

HI DIDDLE DIDDLE, Stone, UA: PHIL BOUTELJE

IN OLD OKLAHOMA, Republic: WALTER SCHARF

JOHNNY COME LATELY, Cagney, UA: LEIGH HARLINE

THE KANSAN, Sherman, UA: GERARD CARBONARA

LADY OF BURLESQUE, Stromberg, UA: ARTHUR LANGE

MADAME CURIE, Metro-Goldwyn-Mayer: HERBERT STOTHART

THE MOON AND SIXPENCE, Loew-Lewin, UA: DIMITRI TIOMKIN

THE NORTH STAR, Goldwyn, RKO Radio: AARON COPLAND

THE SONG OF BERNADETTE, 20th Century-Fox: ALFRED NEWMAN

VICTORY THROUGH AIR POWER, Disney, UA: EDWARD H. PLUMB, PAUL J. SMITH and OLIVER G. WALLACE

(Scoring of a Musical Picture)

CONEY ISLAND, 20th Century-Fox: ALFRED NEWMAN

HIT PARADE OF 1943, Republic: WALTER SCHARF

THE PHANTOM OF THE OPERA, Universal: EDWARD WARD

SALUDOS AMIGOS, Disney, RKO Radio: EDWARD H. PLUMB, PAUL J. SMITH and CHARLES WOLCOTT

THE SKY'S THE LIMIT, RKO Radio: LEIGH HARLINE

SOMETHING TO SHOUT ABOUT, Columbia: MORRIS STOLOFF

STAGE DOOR CANTEEN, Lesser, UA: FREDERIC E. RICH

STAR SPANGLED RHYTHM, Paramount: ROBERT EMMETT DOLAN

THIS IS THE ARMY, Warner Bros.: RAY HEINDORF

THOUSANDS CHEER, Metro-Goldwyn-Mayer: HERBERT STOTHART

1944   Seventeenth Year
(Scoring of a Dramatic or Comedy Picture)

ADDRESS UNKNOWN, Columbia: MORRIS STOLOFF and ERNST TOCH

THE ADVENTURES OF MARK TWAIN, Warner Bros.: MAX STEINER

THE BRIDGE OF SAN LUIS REY, Bogeaus, UA: DIMITRI TIOMKIN

CASANOVA BROWN, International, RKO Radio: ARTHUR LANGE

CHRISTMAS HOLIDAY, Universal: H. J. SALTER

DOUBLE INDEMNITY, Paramount: MIKLOS ROZSA

THE FIGHTING SEABEES, Republic: WALTER SCHARF and ROY WEBB

THE HAIRY APE, Levey, UA: MICHEL MICHELET and EDWARD PAUL

IT HAPPENED TOMORROW, Arnold, UA: ROBERT STOLZ

JACK LONDON, Bronston, UA: FREDERIC E. RICH

KISMET, Metro-Goldwyn-Mayer: HERBERT STOTHART

NONE BUT THE LONELY HEART, RKO Radio: C. BAKALEINIKOFF and HANNS EISLER

THE PRINCESS AND THE PIRATE, Regent, RKO Radio: DAVID ROSE

SINCE YOU WENT AWAY, Selznick, UA: MAX STEINER

SUMMER STORM, Angelus, UA: KARL HAJOS

THREE RUSSIAN GIRLS, R & F Prods., UA: FRANKE HARLING

UP IN MABEL'S ROOM, Small, UA: EDWARD PAUL

VOICE IN THE WIND, Ripley-Monter, UA: MICHEL MICHELET

WILSON, 20th Century-Fox: ALFRED NEWMAN

WOMAN OF THE TOWN, Sherman, UA: MIKLOS ROZSA

(Scoring of a Musical Picture)

BRAZIL, Republic: WALTER SCHARF

COVER GIRL, Columbia: CARMEN DRAGON and MORRIS STOLOFF

HIGHER AND HIGHER, RKO Radio: C. BAKALEINIKOFF

HOLLYWOOD CANTEEN, Warner Bros.: RAY HEINDORF

IRISH EYES ARE SMILING, 20th Century-

FOX: ALFRED NEWMAN

KNICKERBOCKER HOLIDAY, RCA, UA: WERNER R. HEYMANN and KURT WEILL

LADY IN THE DARK, Paramount: ROBERT EMMETT DOLAN

LADY LET'S DANCE, Monogram: EDWARD KAY

MEET ME IN ST. LOUIS, Metro-Goldwyn-Mayer: GEORGIE STOLL

THE MERRY MONAHANS, Universal: H. J. SALTER

MINSTREL MAN, PRC: LEO ERDODY and FERDE GROFE

SENSATIONS OF 1945, Stone, UA: MAHLON MERRICK

SONG OF THE OPEN ROAD, Rogers, UA: CHARLES PREVIN

UP IN ARMS, Avalon, RKO Radio: LOUIS FORBES and RAY HEINDORF

1945 Eighteenth Year

(Scoring of a Dramatic or Comedy Picture)

THE BELLS OF ST. MARY'S, Rainbow, RKO Radio: ROBERT EMMETT DOLAN

BREWSTER'S MILLIONS, Small, UA: LOU FORBES

CAPTAIN KIDD, Bogeaus, UA: WERNER JANSSEN

ENCHANTED COTTAGE, RKO Radio: ROY WEBB

FLAME OF THE BARBARY COAST, Republic: DALE BUTTS and MORTON SCOTT

G. I. HONEYMOON, Monogram: EDWARD J. KAY

G. I. JOE, Cowan, UA: LOUIS APPLEBAUM and ANN RONELL

GUEST IN THE HOUSE, Guest In The House, Inc., UA: WERNER JANSSEN

GUEST WIFE, Greentree Prods., UA: DANIELE AMFITHEATROF

THE KEYS OF THE KINGDOM, 20th Century-Fox: ALFRED NEWMAN

THE LOST WEEKEND, Paramount: MIKLOS ROZSA

LOVE LETTERS, Wallis, Paramount: VICTOR YOUNG

MAN WHO WALKED ALONE, PRC: KARL HAJOS

OBJECTIVE-BURMA, Warner Bros.: FRANZ WAXMAN

PARIS-UNDERGROUND, Bennett, UA: ALEXANDER TANSMAN

A SONG TO REMEMBER, Columbia: MIKLOS ROZSA and MORRIS STOLOFF

THE SOUTHERNER, Loew-Hakim, UA: WERNER JANSSEN

SPELLBOUND, Selznick, UA: MIKLOS ROZSA

THIS LOVE OF OURS, Universal: H. J. SALTER

VALLEY OF DECISION, Metro-Goldwyn-Mayer: HERBERT STOTHART

WOMAN IN THE WINDOW, International, RKO Radio: HUGO FRIEDHOFER and ARTHUR LANGE

(Scoring of a Musical Picture)

ANCHORS AWEIGH, Metro-Goldwyn-Mayer: GEORGIE STOLL

BELLE OF THE YUKON, International. RKO Radio: ARTHUR LANGE

CAN'T HELP SINGING, Universal: JEROME KERN and H. J. SALTER

HITCHHIKE TO HAPPINESS, Republic: MORTON SCOTT

INCENDIARY BLONDE, Paramount: ROBERT EMMETT DOLAN

RHAPSODY IN BLUE, Warner Bros.: RAY HEINDORF and MAX STEINER

STATE FAIR, 20th Century-Fox: CHARLES HENDERSON and ALFRED NEWMAN

SUNBONNET SUE, Monogram: EDWARD J. KAY

THREE CABALLEROS, Disney-RKO Radio: EDWARD PLUMB, PAUL J. SMITH and CHARLES WOLCOTT

TONIGHT AND EVERY NIGHT, Columbia: MARLIN SKILES and MORRIS STOLOFF

WHY GIRLS LEAVE HOME, PRC: WALTER GREENE

WONDER MAN, Beverly, RKO Radio: LOU FORBES and RAY HEINDORF

1946 Nineteenth Year

(Scoring of a Dramatic or Comedy Picture)

ANNA AND THE KING OF SIAM, 20th Century-Fox: BERNARD HERRMANN

THE BEST YEARS OF OUR LIVES, Goldwyn, RKO Radio: HUGO FRIEDHOFER

HENRY V, Rank, UA (British): WILLIAM WALTON

HUMORESQUE, Warner Bros.: FRANZ WAXMAN

THE KILLERS, Universal: MIKLOS ROZSA

(Scoring of a Musical Picture)

BLUE SKIES, Paramount: ROBERT EMMETT DOLAN

CENTENNIAL SUMMER, 20th Century-Fox: ALFRED NEWMAN

THE HARVEY GIRLS, Metro-Goldwyn-Mayer: LENNIE HAYTON

THE JOLSON STORY, Columbia: MORRIS STOLOFF

NIGHT AND DAY, Warner Bros.: RAY HEINDORF and MAX STEINER

1947 Twentieth Year

(Scoring of a Dramatic or Comedy Picture)

THE BISHOP'S WIFE, Goldwyn, RKO Radio: HUGO FRIEDHOFER

CAPTAIN FROM CASTILE, 20th Century-Fox: ALFRED NEWMAN

A DOUBLE LIFE, Kanin, U-I: MIKLOS ROZSA

FOREVER AMBER, 20th Century-Fox: DAVID RAKSIN

LIFE WITH FATHER, Warner Bros.: MAX STEINER

(Scoring of a Musical Picture)

FIESTA, Metro-Goldwyn-Mayer: JOHNNY GREEN

MOTHER WORE TIGHTS, 20th Century-Fox: ALFRED NEWMAN

MY WILD IRISH ROSE, Warner Bros.: RAY HEINDORF and MAX STEINER

ROAD TO RIO, Hope-Crosby, Paramount: ROBERT EMMETT DOLAN

SONG OF THE SOUTH, Disney, RKO Radio: DANIELE AMFITHEATROF, PAUL J. SMITH and CHARLES WOLCOTT

1948 Twenty-first Year

(Scoring of a Dramatic or Comedy Picture)

HAMLET, Rank-Two Cities, U-I (British): WILLIAM WALTON

JOAN OF ARC, Sierra Pictures, RKO Radio: HUGO FRIEDHOFER

JOHNNY BELINDA, Warner Bros.: MAX STEINER

THE RED SHOES, Rank-Archers-Eagle-Lion (British): BRIAN EASDALE

THE SNAKE PIT, 20th Century-Fox: ALFRED NEWMAN

(Scoring of a Musical Picture)

EASTER PARADE, Metro-Goldwyn-Mayer: JOHNNY GREEN and ROGER EDENS

THE EMPEROR WALTZ, Paramount: VICTOR YOUNG

THE PIRATE, Metro-Goldwyn-Mayer: LENNIE HAYTON

ROMANCE ON THE HIGH SEAS, Curtiz, Warner Bros: RAY HEINDORF

WHEN MY BABY SMILES AT ME, 20th Century-Fox: ALFRED NEWMAN

1949 Twenty-Second Year

(Scoring of a Dramatic or Comedy Picture)

BEYOND THE FOREST, Warner Bros.: MAX STEINER

CHAMPION, Screen Plays Corp., UA: DIMITRI TIOMKIN

THE HEIRESS, Paramount: AARON COPLAND

Composer Alfred Newman received nine Academy Awards for his music.

(Scoring of a Musical Picture)
JOLSON SINGS AGAIN, Sidney Buchman, Columbia: MORRIS STOLOFF and GEORGE DUNING
LOOK FOR THE SILVER LINING, Warner Bros.: RAY HEINDORF
ON THE TOWN, Metro-Goldwyn-Mayer: ROGER EDENS and LENNIE HAYTON

1950   Twenty-third Year
(Scoring of a Dramatic or Comedy Picture)
ALL ABOUT EVE, 20th Century-Fox: ALFRED NEWMAN
THE FLAME AND THE ARROW, Norma-

F.R., Warner Bros: MAX STEINER
NO SAD SONGS FOR ME, Columbia: GEORGE DUNING
SAMSON AND DELILAH, Paramount: VICTOR YOUNG
SUNSET BOULEVARD, Paramount: FRANZ WAXMAN

(Scoring of a Musical Picture)
ANNIE GET YOUR GUN, Metro-Goldwyn-Mayer: ADOLPH DEUTSCH and ROGER EDENS
CINDERELLA, Disney, RKO Radio: OLIVER WALLACE and PAUL J. SMITH
I'LL GET BY, 20th Century-Fox: LIONEL NEWMAN

THREE LITTLE WORDS, Metro-Goldwyn-Mayer: ANDRE PREVIN

THE WEST POINT STORY, Warner Bros.: RAY HEINDORF

1951 Twenty-fourth Year

(Scoring of a Dramatic or Comedy Picture)

DAVID AND BATHSHEBA, 20th Century-Fox: ALFRED NEWMAN

DEATH OF A SALESMAN, Kramer, Columbia: ALEX NORTH

A PLACE IN THE SUN, Paramount: FRANZ WAXMAN

QUO VADIS, Metro-Goldwyn-Mayer: MIKLOS ROZSA

A STREETCAR NAMED DESIRE, Charles K. Feldman Prods., Warner Bros: ALEX NORTH

(Scoring of A Musical Picture)

ALICE IN WONDERLAND, Disney, RKO Radio: OLIVER WALLACE

AN AMERICAN IN PARIS, Metro-Goldwyn-Mayer: JOHNNY GREEN and SAUL CHAPLIN

THE GREAT CARUSO, Metro-Goldwyn-Mayer: PETER HERMAN ADLER and JOHNNY GREEN

ON THE RIVIERA, 20th Century-Fox: ALFRED NEWMAN

SHOW BOAT, Metro-Goldwyn-Mayer: ADOLPH DEUTSCH and CONRAD SALINGER

1952 Twenty-fifth Year

(Scoring of a Dramatic or Comedy Picture)

HIGH NOON, Kramer, UA: DIMITRI TIOMKIN

IVANHOE, Metro-Goldwyn-Mayer: MIKLOS ROZSA

MIRACLE OF FATIMA, Warner Bros.: MAX STEINER

THE THIEF, Fran Prods., UA: HERSCHEL BURKE GILBERT

VIVA ZAPATA!, 20th Century-Fox: ALEX NORTH

(Scoring of a Musical Picture)

HANS CHRISTIAN ANDERSEN, Goldwyn, RKO Radio: WALTER SCHARF

THE JAZZ SINGER, Warner Bros.: RAY HEINDORF and MAX STEINER

THE MEDIUM, Transfilm-Lopert (Italian): GIAN-CARLO MENOTTI

SINGIN' IN THE RAIN, Metro-Goldwyn-Mayer: LENNIE HAYTON

WITH A SONG IN MY HEART, 20th Century-Fox: ALFRED NEWMAN

1953 Twenty-sixth Year

(Scoring of a Dramatic or Comedy Picture)

ABOVE AND BEYOND, Metro-Goldwyn-Mayer: HUGO FRIEDHOFER

FROM HERE TO ETERNITY, Columbia: MORRIS STOLOFF and GEORGE DUNING

JULIUS CAESAR, Metro-Goldwyn-Mayer: MIKLOS ROZSA

LILI, Metro-Goldwyn-Mayer: BRONISLAU KAPER

THIS IS CINERAMA, Cinerama Prods. Corp.: LOUIS FORBES

(Scoring of a Musical Picture)

THE BANDWAGON, Metro-Goldwyn-Mayer: ADOLPH DEUTSCH

CALAMITY JANE, Warner Bros.: RAY HEINDORF

CALL ME MADAM, 20th Century-Fox: ALFRED NEWMAN

5,000 FINGERS OF DR. T., Kramer-Columbia: FREDERICK HOLLANDER and MORRIS STOLOFF

KISS ME KATE, Metro-Goldwyn-Mayer: ANDRE PREVIN and SAUL CHAPLIN

1954 Twenty-seventh Year

(Scoring of a Dramatic or Comedy Picture)

THE CAINE MUTINY, A Stanley Kramer Prod., Columbia: MAX STEINER

GENEVIEVE, A J. Arthur Rank Presentation—Sirius Prods. Ltd., U-I. (British): MUIR MATHIESON

THE HIGH AND THE MIGHTY,
Wayne-Fellows Prods., Inc., Warner
Bros.: DIMITRI TIOMKIN

ON THE WATERFRONT, Horizon-
American Corp., Columbia: LEON-
ARD BERNSTEIN

THE SILVER CHALICE, A Victor Saville
Prod., Warner Bros.: FRANZ WAX-
MAN

(Scoring of a Musical Picture)

CARMEN JONES, Otto Preminger, 20th
Century-Fox: HERSCHEL BURKE GIL-
BERT

THE GLENN MILLER STORY, Universal-
International: JOSEPH GERSHENSON
and HENRY MANCINI

SEVEN BRIDES FOR SEVEN
BROTHERS, Metro-Goldwyn-
Mayer: ADOLPH DEUTSCH and
SAUL CHAPLIN

A STAR IS BORN, A Transcona Enterprises Prod., Warner Bros: RAY
HEINDORF

THERE'S NO BUSINESS LIKE SHOW BUSI-
NESS, 20th Century-Fox: ALFRED
NEWMAN and LIONEL NEWMAN

1955   Twenty-eighth Year

(Scoring of a Dramatic or
Comedy Picture)

BATTLE CRY, Warner Bros: MAX
STEINER

LOVE IS A MANY-SPLENDORED
THING, 20th Century-Fox: ALFRED
NEWMAN

THE MAN WITH THE GOLDEN ARM, Otto
Preminger Prod., UA: ELMER BERN-
STEIN

PICNIC, Columbia: GEORGE DUNING

THE ROSE TATTOO, Hal Wallis, Paramount: ALEX NORTH

(Scoring of a Musical Picture)

DADDY LONG LEGS, 20th Century-Fox:
ALFRED NEWMAN

GUYS AND DOLLS, Samuel Goldwyn
Prods., Inc., M-G-M: JAY BLACKTON
and CYRIL J. MOCKRIDGE

IT'S ALWAYS FAIR WEATHER, Metro-
Goldwyn-Mayer: ANDRÉ PREVIN

LOVE ME OR LEAVE ME, Metro-
Goldwyn-Mayer: PERCY FAITH
GEORGE STOLL

OKLAHOMA!, Rogers & Hammerstein
Pictures, Inc., Magna Theatre Corp:
ROBERT RUSSELL BENNETT,
JAY BLACKTON and ADOLPH
DEUTSCH

1956   Twenty-ninth Year

(Scoring of a Dramatic or
Comedy Picture)

ANASTASIA, 20th Century-Fox: ALFRED
NEWMAN

AROUND THE WORLD IN 80 DAYS,
The Michael Todd Co., Inc., UA:
VICTOR YOUNG

BETWEEN HEAVEN AND HELL, 20th
Century-Fox: HUGO FRIEDHOFER

GIANT, Giant Prod., Warner Bros.: DI-
MITRI TIOMKIN

THE RAINMAKER, A Hal Wallis Prod.,
Paramount: ALEX NORTH

(Scoring of a Musical Picture)

THE BEST THINGS IN LIFE ARE FREE,
20th Century-Fox: LIONEL NEWMAN

THE EDDY DUCHIN STORY, Columbia:
MORRIS STOLOFF and GEORGE DUNING

HIGH SOCIETY, Sol C. Spiegel Prod.,
M-G-M: JOHNNY GREEN and SAUL
CHAPLIN

THE KING AND I, 20th Century-Fox:
ALFRED NEWMAN and KEN
DARBY

MEET ME IN LAS VEGAS, Metro-
Goldwyn-Mayer: GEORGE STOLL and
JOHNNY GREEN

1957   Thirtieth Year

Note: Rules changed this year to one
award for Music Scoring instead
of separate awards for Scoring
Dramatic or Comedy Picture and
Scoring of a Musical Picture.

AN AFFAIR TO REMEMBER, (Dramatic or Comedy), Jerry Wald Prods., Inc., 20th Century-Fox: HUGO FRIEDHOFER

BOY ON A DOLPHIN, (Dramatic or Comedy), 20th Century-Fox: HUGO FRIEDHOFER

THE BRIDGE ON THE RIVER KWAI, (Dramatic or Comedy), A Horizon Picture, Columbia: MALCOLM ARNOLD

PERRI, (Dramatic or Comedy), Walt Disney Prods., Buena Vista Film Dist. Co., Inc: PAUL SMITH

RAINTREE COUNTY, (Dramatic or Comedy), Metro-Goldwyn-Mayer: JOHNNY GREEN

1958   Thirty-first Year

Note: Rules changed this year to two awards—one award for Scoring of a Dramatic or Comedy Picture, and one award for Scoring of a Musical Picture.

(Scoring of a Dramatic or Comedy Picture)

THE BIG COUNTRY, Anthony-Worldwide Prods., UA: JEROME MOROSS

THE OLD MAN AND THE SEA, Leland Hayward, Warner Bros: DIMITRI TIOMKIN

SEPARATE TABLES, Clifton Prods., Inc., UA: DAVID RAKSIN

WHITE WILDERNESS, Walt Disney Prods., Buena Vista Film Dist. Co., Inc.: OLIVER WALLACE

THE YOUNG LIONS, 20th Century-Fox: HUGO FRIEDHOFER

(Scoring of a Musical Picture)

THE BOLSHOI BALLET, A Rank Organization Presentation-Harmony Film, Rank Film Distributors of America, Inc. (British): YURI FAIER and G. ROZHDESTVENSKY

DAMN YANKEES, Warner Bros.: RAY HEINDORF

GIGI, Arthur Freed Prods., Inc.,

M-G-M: ANDRÉ PREVIN

MARDI GRAS, Jerry Wald Prods., Inc., 20th Century-Fox: LIONEL NEWMAN

SOUTH PACIFIC, South Pacific Enterprises, Inc., Magna Theatre Corp.: ALFRED NEWMAN and KEN DARBY

1959   Thirty-second Year

(Scoring of a Dramatic or Comedy Picture)

BEN-HUR, Metro-Goldwyn-Mayer: MIKLOS ROZSA

THE DIARY OF ANNE FRANK, 20th Century-Fox: ALFRED NEWMAN

THE NUN'S STORY, Warner Bros.: FRANZ WAXMAN

ON THE BEACH, Lomitas Prods., Inc., UA: ERNEST GOLD

PILLOW TALK, Arwin Prods., Inc., U-I: FRANK DeVOL

(Scoring of a Musical Picture)

THE FIVE PENNIES, Dena Prod., Paramount: LEITH STEVENS

LI'L ABNER, Panama and Frank, Paramount: NELSON RIDDLE and JOSEPH J. LILLEY

PORGY AND BESS, Samuel Goldwyn Prods., Columbia: ANDRÉ PREVIN and KEN DARBY

SAY ONE FOR ME, Bing Crosby Prods., 20th Century-Fox: LIONEL NEWMAN

SLEEPING BEAUTY, Walt Disney Prods., Buena Vista Film Dist. Co., Inc.: GEORGE BRUNS

1960   Thirty-third Year

(Scoring of a Dramatic or Comedy Picture)

THE ALAMO, Batjac Prod., UA: DIMITRI TIOMKIN

ELMER GANTRY, Burt Lancaster-Richard Brooks Prod., UA: ANDRÉ PREVIN

EXODUS, Carlyle-Alpina S.A. Prod., UA: ERNEST GOLD

THE MAGNIFICENT SEVEN, Mirisch-

Alpha Prod., UA: ELMER BERNSTEIN
SPARTACUS, Bryna Prods., Inc., U-I:
ALEX NORTH

(Scoring of a Musical Picture)

BELLS ARE RINGING, Arthur Freed
Prod., M-G-M: ANDRE PREVIN
CAN-CAN, Suffolk-Cummings Prods.,
20th Century-Fox: NELSON RIDDLE
LET'S MAKE LOVE, Company of Artists,
Inc., 20th Century-Fox: LIONEL
NEWMAN and EARLE H. HAGEN
PEPE, G. S.-Posa Films International
Prod., Columbia: JOHNNY GREEN
SONG WITHOUT END (THE STORY
OF FRANZ LISZT), Goetz-Vidor
Pictures Prod., Columbia: MORRIS
STOLOFF and HARRY SUKMAN

1961   Thirty-fourth Year

(Scoring of a Dramatic or
Comedy Picture)

BREAKFAST AT TIFFANY'S, Jurow-
Shepherd Prod., Paramount: HENRY
MANCINI
EL CID, Samuel Bronston Prod. in asso-
ciation with Dear Film Prod., Allied
Artists: MIKLOS ROZSA
FANNY, Mansfield Prod., Warner Bros.:
MORRIS STOLOFF and HARRY SUKMAN
THE GUNS OF NAVARONE, Carl Foreman
Prod., Columbia: DIMITRI TIOMKIN
SUMMER AND SMOKE, Hal Wallis Prod.,
Paramount: ELMER BERNSTEIN

(Scoring of a Musical Picture)

BABES IN TOYLAND, Walt Disney Prod.,
Buena Vista Dist. Co., Inc.: GEORGE
BRUNS
FLOWER DRUM SONG, Universal-Interna-
tional-Ross Hunter Prod. in associa-
tion with Joseph Fields, U-I: ALFRED
NEWMAN and KEN DARBY
KHOVANSHCHINA, Mosfilm Studios,
Artkino Pictures (Russian): DIMITRI
SHOSTAKOVICH
PARIS BLUES, Pennebaker, Inc., UA:
DUKE ELLINGTON

WEST SIDE STORY, Mirisch Pictures,
Inc. and B and P Enterprises, Inc.,
UA: SAUL CHAPLIN, JOHNNY
GREEN, SID RAMIN and IRWIN
KOSTAL

1962   Thirty-fifth Year

(Music Score—substantially original)

FREUD, Universal-International-John
Huston Prod., U-I: JERRY GOLDSMITH
LAWRENCE OF ARABIA, Horizon
Pictures (G.B.), Ltd.-Sam Spiegel-
David Lean Prod., Columbia:
MAURICE JARRE
MUTINY ON THE BOUNTY, Arcola Prod.,
M-G-M: BRONISLAU KAPER
TARAS BULBA, Harold Hecht Prod., UA:
FRANZ WAXMAN
TO KILL A MOCKINGBIRD, Universal-In-
ternational-Pakula-Mulligan-
Brentwood Prod., U-I: ELMER BERN-
STEIN

(Scoring of Music—
adaptation or treatment)

BILLY ROSE'S JUMBO, Euterpe-Arwin
Prod., M-G-M: GEORGE STOLL
GIGOT, Seven Arts Prods., 20th Cen-
tury-Fox: MICHEL MAGNE
GYPSY, Warner Bros.: FRANK PERKINS
MEREDITH WILLSON'S THE
MUSIC MAN, Warner Bros.: RAY
HEINDORF
THE WONDERFUL WORLD OF THE
BROTHERS GRIMM, Metro-Goldwyn-
Mayer & Cinerama: LEIGH HARLINE

1963   Thirty-sixth Year

(Music Score—substantially original)

CLEOPATRA, 20th Century-Fox Ltd.-
MCL Films S.A.-WALWA Films
S.A. Prod., 20th Century-Fox: ALEX
NORTH
55 DAYS AT PEKING, Samuel Bronston
Prod., Allied Artists: DIMITRI TIOM-
KIN

HOW THE WEST WAS WON, Metro-Goldwyn-Mayer & Cinerama: ALFRED NEWMAN and KEN DARBY

IT'S A MAD, MAD, MAD, MAD WORLD, Casey Prod., UA: ERNEST GOLD

TOM JONES, Woodfall Prod., UA-Lopert Pictures: JOHN ADDISON

(Scoring of Music—adaptation or treatment)

BYE BYE BIRDIE, Kohlmar-Sidney Prod., Columbia: JOHN GREEN

IRMA LA DOUCE, Mirisch-Phalanx Prod., UA: ANDRÉ PREVIN

A NEW KIND OF LOVE, Llenroc Prods., Paramount: LEITH STEVENS

SUNDAYS AND CYBELE, Terra-Fides-Orsay-Films Trocadero Prod., Columbia: MAURICE JARRE

THE SWORD IN THE STONE, Walt Disney Prods., Buena Vista Distribution Co.: GEORGE BRUNS

1964   Thirty-seventh Year

(Music Score—substantially original)

BECKET, Hal Wallis Prod., Paramount: LAURENCE ROSENTHAL

THE FALL OF THE ROMAN EMPIRE, Bronston-Roma Prod., Paramount: DIMITRI TIOMKIN

HUSH . . . HUSH, SWEET CHARLOTTE, Associates & Aldrich Prod., 20th Century-Fox: FRANK DeVOL

MARY POPPINS, Walt Disney Prods.: RICHARD M. SHERMAN and ROBERT B. SHERMAN

THE PINK PANTHER, Mirisch-G-E-Prod., United Artists: HENRY MANCINI

(Scoring of Music—adaptation or treatment)

A HARD DAY'S NIGHT, Walter Shenson Prod., United Artists: GEORGE MARTIN

MARY POPPINS, Walt Disney Prods.: IRWIN KOSTAL

MY FAIR LADY, Warner Bros.: ANDRÉ PREVIN

ROBIN AND THE 7 HOODS, P-C Prod., Warner Bros.: NELSON RIDDLE

THE UNSINKABLE MOLLY BROWN, Marten Prod., M-G-M: ROBERT ARMBRUSTER, LEO ARNAUD, JACK ELLIOTT, JACK HAYES, CALVIN JACKSON and LEO SHUKEN

1965   Thirty-eighth Year

(Music Score—substantially original)

THE AGONY AND THE ECSTASY, International Classics Prods., 20th Century-Fox: ALEX NORTH

DOCTOR ZHIVAGO, Sostar S.A.-Metro-Goldwyn-Mayer British Studios, Ltd. Prod., M-G-M: MAURICE JARRE

THE GREATEST STORY EVER TOLD, George Stevens Prod., United Artists: ALFRED NEWMAN

A PATCH OF BLUE, Pandro S. Berman-Guy Green Prod., M-G-M: JERRY GOLDSMITH

THE UMBRELLAS OF CHERBOURG, Parc-Madeleine Films Prod., American Intl.: MICHEL LEGRAND and JACQUES DEMY

(Scoring of Music—adaptation or treatment)

CAT BALLOU, Harold Hecht Prod., Columbia: DeVOL

THE PLEASURE SEEKERS, 20th Century-Fox: LIONEL NEWMAN and ALEXANDER COURAGE

THE SOUND OF MUSIC, Argyle Enterprises Prod., 20th Century-Fox: IRWIN KOSTAL

A THOUSAND CLOWNS, Harrell Prod., United Artists: DON WALKER

THE UMBRELLAS OF CHERBOURG, Parc-Madeleine Films Prod., American Intl.: MICHEL LEGRAND

1966   Thirty-ninth Year

(Original Music Score)

THE BIBLE, Thalia-A.G. Prod., 20th
Century-Fox: TOSHIRO MAYUZUMI

BORN FREE, Open Road Films, Ltd.-
Atlas Films, Ltd. Prod., Columbia:
JOHN BARRY

HAWAII, Mirisch Corp. of Delaware
Prod., UA: ELMER BERNSTEIN

THE SAND PEBBLES, Argyle-Solar Prod.,
20th Century-Fox: JERRY GOLDSMITH

WHO'S AFRAID OF VIRGINIA WOOLF?,
Chenault Prod., Warner Bros.: ALEX
NORTH

(Scoring of Music—
adaptation or treatment)

A FUNNY THING HAPPENED ON
THE WAY TO THE FORUM, Mel-
vin Frank Prod., United Artists: KEN
THORNE

THE GOSPEL ACCORDING TO ST.
MATTHEW, Arco-Lux Cie Cinemato-
grafique de France Prod., Walter
Reade-Continental Distributing: LUIS
ENRIQUE BACALOV

RETURN OF THE SEVEN, Mirisch Prod.,
United Artists: ELMER BERNSTEIN

THE SINGING NUN, Metro-Goldwyn-
Mayer: HARRY SUKMAN

STOP THE WORLD—I WANT TO GET OFF,
Warner Bros. Prods., Ltd., Warner
Bros.: AL HAM

1967   Fortieth Year

(Original Music Score)

COOL HAND LUKE, Jalem Prod., Warner
Bros.-Seven Arts: LALO SCHIFRIN

DOCTOR DOLITTLE, Apjac Prods., 20th
Century-Fox: LESLIE BRICUSSE

FAR FROM THE MADDING CROWD, Appia
Films, Ltd. Prod., M-G-M: RICHARD
RODNEY BENNETT

IN COLD BLOOD, Pax Enterprises Prod.,
Columbia: QUINCY JONES

THOROUGHLY MODERN MILLIE,

Ross Hunter-Universal Prod., Universal: ELMER BERNSTEIN

(Scoring of Music—
adaptation or treatment)

CAMELOT, Warner Bros.-Seven Arts:
ALFRED NEWMAN and KEN
DARBY

DOCTOR DOLITTLE, Apjac Productions,
20th Century-Fox: LIONEL NEWMAN
and ALEXANDER COURAGE

GUESS WHO'S COMING TO DINNER, Columbia: DeVOL

THOROUGHLY MODERN MILLIE, Ross
Hunter-Universal Production, Uni-
versal: ANDRÉ PREVIN and JOSEPH
GERSHENSON

VALLEY OF THE DOLLS, Red Lion
Prods., 20th Century-Fox: JOHN
WILLIAMS

1968   Forty-first Year

(Best Original Score—for a motion picture [not a musical])

THE FOX, Raymond Stross-Motion Pictures International Prod., Claridge
Pictures: LALO SCHIFRIN

THE LION IN WINTER, Haworth
Prods., Ltd., Avco Embassy: JOHN
BARRY

PLANET OF THE APES, Apjac Prods.,
20th Century-Fox: JERRY GOLDSMITH

THE SHOES OF THE FISHERMAN, George
Englund Prod., Metro-Goldwyn-
Mayer: ALEX NORTH

THE THOMAS CROWN AFFAIR, Mirisch-
Simkoe-Solar Prod., United Artists:
MICHEL LEGRAND

(Best Score of a Musical Picture—
[original or adaptation])

FINIAN'S RAINBOW, Warner Bros.-
Seven Arts: Adapted by RAY HEIN-
DORF

FUNNY GIRL, Rastar Prods., Columbia:
Adapted by WALTER SCHARF

OLIVER!, Romulus Films, Columbia: Adapted by JOHN GREEN

STAR!, Robert Wise Prod., 20th Century-Fox: Adapted by LENNIE HAYTON

THE YOUNG GIRLS OF ROCHEFORT, Mag Bodard-Gilbert de Goldschmidt-Parc Film-Madeleine Films Prod., Warner Bros.-Seven Arts: MICHEL LEGRAND and JACQUES DEMY

1969   Forty-second Year
(Best Original Score—for a motion picture [not a musical])

ANNE OF THE THOUSAND DAYS, Hal B. Wallis-Universal Pictures, Ltd. Prod., Universal: GEORGES DELERUE

BUTCH CASSIDY AND THE SUNDANCE KID, George Roy Hill-Paul Monash Prod., 20th Century-Fox: BURT BACHARACH

THE REIVERS, Irving Ravetch-Arthur Kramer-Solar Prods., Cinema Center Films Presentation, National General: JOHN WILLIAMS

THE SECRET OF SANTA VITTORIA, Stanley Kramer Company Prod., United Artists: ERNEST GOLD

THE WILD BUNCH, Phil Feldman Prod., Warner Bros.: JERRY FIELDING

(Best Score of a Musical Picture—[original or adaptation])

GOODBYE, MR. CHIPS, Apjac Prod., Metro-Goldwyn-Mayer: Music and lyrics by LESLIE BRICUSSE Adapted by JOHN WILLIAMS

HELLO DOLLY!, Chenault Prods., 20th Century-Fox: Adapted by LENNIE HAYTON and LIONEL NEWMAN

PAINT YOUR WAGON, Alan Jay Lerner Prod., Paramount: Adapted by NELSON RIDDLE

SWEET CHARITY, Universal: Adapted by CY COLEMAN

THEY SHOOT HORSES, DON'T THEY?,

Chartoff-Winkler-Pollack Prod., ABC Pictures Presentation, Cinerama: Adapted by JOHN GREEN and ALBERT WOODBURY

1970   Forty-third Year
(Best Original Score)

AIRPORT, Ross Hunter-Universal Prod., Universal: ALFRED NEWMAN

CROMWELL, Irving Allen, Ltd. Prod., Columbia: FRANK CORDELL

LOVE STORY, The Love Story Company Prod., Paramount: FRANCIS LAI

PATTON, 20th Century-Fox: JERRY GOLDSMITH

SUNFLOWER, Sostar Prod., Avco Embassy: HENRY MANCINI

(Best Original Song Score)

THE BABY MAKER, Robert Wise Prod., National General: Music by FRED KARLIN. Lyrics by TYLWYTH KYMRY

A BOY NAMED CHARLIE BROWN, Lee Mendelson-Melendez Features Prod., Cinema Center Films Presentation, National General: Music by ROD MCKUEN and JOHN SCOTT TROTTER. Lyrics by ROD MCKUEN, BILL MELENDEZ and AL SHEAN. Adapted by VINCE GUARALDI

DARLING LILI, Geoffrey Prods., Paramount: Music by HENRY MANCINI. Lyrics by JOHNNY MERCER

LET IT BE, Beatles-Apple Prod., UA: Music and lyrics by THE BEATLES

SCROOGE, Waterbury Films, Ltd. Prod., Cinema Center Films Presentation, National General: Music and lyrics by LESLIE BRICUSSE. Adapted by IAN FRASER and HERBERT W. SPENCER

1971   Forty-fourth Year
(Best Original Dramatic Score)

MARY, QUEEN OF SCOTS, A Hal Wallis-Universal Pictures, Ltd. Prod., Universal: JOHN BARRY

NICHOLAS AND ALEXANDRA, A Horizon Pictures Prod., Columbia: RICHARD RODNEY BENNETT

SHAFT, Shaft Prods., Ltd., M-G-M: ISAAC HAYES

STRAW DOGS, A Talent Associates, Ltd.-Amerbroco Films, Ltd. Prod., ABC Pictures Presentation, Cinerama: JERRY FIELDING

SUMMER OF '42, A Robert Mulligan-Richard Alan Roth Prod., Warner Bros: MICHEL LEGRAND

(Best Scoring: Adaptation and Original Song Score)

BEDKNOBS AND BROOMSTICKS, Walt Disney Prods., Buena Vista Distribution Company. Song Score by RICHARD M. SHERMAN and ROBERT B. SHERMAN. Adapted by IRWIN KOSTAL

THE BOY FRIEND, A Russflix, Ltd. Prod., M-G-M: Adapted by PETER MAXWELL DAVIES and PETER GREEN-WELL

FIDDLER ON THE ROOF, Mirisch-Cartier Prods., UA: Adapted by JOHN WILLIAMS

TCHAIKOVSKY, A Dimitri Tiomkin-Mosfilm Studios Prod.: Adapted by DIMITRI TIOMKIN

WILLY WONKA AND THE CHOCOLATE FACTORY, A Wolper Pictures, Ltd. Prod., Paramount: Song Score by LESLIE BRICUSSE and ANTHONY NEWLEY. Adapted by WALTER SCHARF

1972 Forty-fifth Year
(Best Original Dramatic Score)

IMAGES, A Hemdale Group, Ltd.-Lion's Gate Films Prod., Columbia: JOHN WILLIAMS

LIMELIGHT, A Charles Chaplin Prod., Columbia: CHARLES CHAPLIN, RAYMOND RASCH and LARRY RUSSELL

NAPOLEON AND SAMANTHA, A Walt Disney Prods., Buena Vista Distribution Company: BUDDY BAKER

THE POSEIDON ADVENTURE, An Irwin Allen Prod., 20th Century-Fox: JOHN WILLIAMS

SLEUTH, A Palomar Pictures International Prod., 20th Century-Fox: JOHN ADDISON

(Best Scoring: Adaptation and Original Song Score)

CABARET, An ABC Pictures Prod., Allied Artists: Adapted by RALPH BURNS

LADY SINGS THE BLUES, A Motown-Weston-Furie Prod., Paramount: Adapted by GIL ASKEY

MAN OF LA MANCHA, A PEA Produzioni Europee Associate Prod., UA: Adapted by LAURENCE ROSENTHAL

1973 Forty-sixth Year
Best Original Dramatic Score)

CINDERELLA LIBERTY, A Sanford Prod., 20th Century-Fox: JOHN WILLIAMS

THE DAY OF THE DOLPHIN, Icarus Prods., Avco Embassy: GEORGES DELERUE

PAPILLON, A Corona-General Production Company Prod., Allied Artists: JERRY GOLDSMITH

A TOUCH OF CLASS, Brut Prods., Avco Embassy: JOHN CAMERON

THE WAY WE WERE, Rastar Prods., Columbia: MARVIN HAMLISCH

(Best Scoring: Original Song Score and/or Adaptation)

JESUS CHRIST SUPERSTAR, A Universal-Norman Jewison-Robert Stigwood Prod., Universal: Adapted by ANDRÉ PREVIN, HERBERT SPENCER and ANDREW LLOYD WEBBER

THE STING, A Universal-Bill/Phillips-George Roy Hill Film Prod., Zanuck/Brown Presentation, Universal: Adapted by MARVIN HAMLISCH

TOM SAWYER, An Arthur P. Jacobs Prod., Reader's Digest Presentation, UA: Song Score by RICHARD M. SHERMAN and ROBERT B. SHERMAN. Adapted by JOHN WILLIAMS

1974   Forty-seventh Year
(Best Original Dramatic Score)
CHINATOWN, A Robert Evans Prod., Paramount: JERRY GOLDSMITH
THE GODFATHER PART II, A Coppola Company Prod., Paramount: NINO ROTA and CARMINE COPPOLA
MURDER ON THE ORIENT EXPRESS, A G.W. Films, Ltd. Prod., Paramount: RICHARD RODNEY BENNETT

SHANKS, William Castle Prods., Paramount: ALEX NORTH
THE TOWERING INFERNO, An Irwin Allen Prod., 20th Century-Fox/ Warner Bros.: JOHN WILLIAMS

(Best Scoring: Original Song Score and/or Adaptation)
THE GREAT GATSBY, A David Merrick Prod., Paramount: Adapted by NELSON RIDDLE
THE LITTLE PRINCE, A Stanley Donen Enterprises, Ltd. Prod., Paramount: Song Score by ALAN JAY LERNER and FREDERICK LOEWE. Adapted by ANGELA MORLEY and DOUGLAS GAMLEY
PHANTOM OF THE PARADISE, Harbor Prods., 20th Century-Fox: Song

Score by PAUL WILLIAMS. Adapted by PAUL WILLIAMS and GEORGE ALICESON TIPTON

1975   Forty-eighth Year

(Best Original Score)

BIRDS DO IT, BEES DO IT, A Wolper Pictures Production, Columbia: GERALD FRIED

BITE THE BULLET, A Pax Enterprises Production, Columbia: ALEX NORTH

JAWS, A Universal-Zanuck/Brown Production, Universal: JOHN WILLIAMS

ONE FLEW OVER THE CUCKOO'S NEST, A Fantasy Films Production, United Artists: JACK NITZSCHE

THE WIND AND THE LION, A Herb Jaffe Production, Metro-Goldwyn-Mayer: JERRY GOLDSMITH

(Best Scoring: Original
Song Score and/or Adaptation)

BARRY LYNDON, A Hawk Films, Ltd. Production, Warner Bros.: Adapted by LEONARD ROSENMAN

FUNNY LADY, A Rastar Pictures Production, Columbia: Adapted by PETER MATZ

TOMMY, A Robert Stigwood Organisation, Ltd. Production, Columbia: Adapted by PETER TOWNSHEND

1976   Forty-ninth Year

(Best Original Score)

OBSESSION, George Litto Productions, Columbia Pictures: BERNARD HERRMANN

THE OMEN, 20th Century-Fox Productions, Ltd., 20th Century-Fox: JERRY GOLDSMITH

THE OUTLAW JOSEY WALES, A Malpaso Company Production, Warner Bros.: JERRY FIELDING

TAXI DRIVER, A Bill/Phillips Production of a Martin Scorsese Film, Columbia Pictures: BERNARD HERRMANN

VOYAGE OF THE DAMNED, An ITC Entertainment Production, Avco Embassy: LALO SCHIFRIN

(Best Original Song Score and Its
Adaptation or Best Adaptation Score)

BOUND FOR GLORY, The Bound for Glory Company Production, United Artists: Adapted by LEONARD ROSENMAN

BUGSY MALONE, A Goodtimes Enterprises, Ltd. Production, Paramount: Song Score and Its Adaptation by PAUL WILLIAMS

A STAR IS BORN, A Barwood/Jon Peters Production, First Artists Presentation, Warner Bros.: Adapted by ROGER KELLAWAY

1977   Fiftieth Year

(Best Original Score)

CLOSE ENCOUNTERS OF THE THIRD KIND, Close Encounter Productions, Columbia: JOHN WILLIAMS

JULIA, A Twentieth Century-Fox Production, Twentieth Century-Fox: GEORGES DELERUE

MOHAMMAD-MESSENGER OF GOD, A Filmco International Production, Irwin Yablans Company: MAURICE JARRE

THE SPY WHO LOVED ME, Eon Productions, United Artists: MARVIN HAMLISCH

STAR WARS, A Twentieth Century-Fox Production, Twentieth Century-Fox: JOHN WILLIAMS

(Best Original Song Score and Its
Adaptation or Best Adaptation Score)

A LITTLE NIGHT MUSIC, A Sascha-Wien Film Production in association with Elliott Kastner, New World Pictures: Adapted by JONATHAN TUNICK

PETE'S DRAGON, Walt Disney Productions, Buena Vista Distribution Company. Song Score by AL KASHA and JOEL HIRSCHHORN. Adapted by IRWIN KOSTAL

THE SLIPPER AND THE ROSE—THE STORY OF CINDERELLA, Paradine Co-Productions, Ltd., Universal: Song Score by RICHARD M. SHERMAN and ROBERT B. SHERMAN. Adapted by ANGELA MORLEY.

MUSIC: BEST SONG

In 1934 an award for Best Song was created along with the Music Scoring award. The category has remained relatively unchanged except for a name change in 1975 to Best Original Song. The Academy defines an original song as one "consisting of original words and music specifically created for the feature motion picture for which eligibility is claimed."

Like the Scoring awards, entries for Best Original Song are submitted by the creators of the achievement and are screened by members of the Academy Music Branch who determine the nominees.

1934   Seventh Year

CARIOCA from *Flying Down to Rio,* RKO Radio
Music by VINCENT YOUMANS. Lyrics by EDWARD ELISCU and GUS KAHN
THE CONTINENTAL from *The Gay Divorcee,* RKO Radio
Music by CON CONRAD. Lyrics by HERB MAGIDSON
LOVE IN BLOOM from *She Loves Me Not,* Paramount
Music by RALPH RAINGER. Lyrics by LEO ROBIN

1935   Eighth Year

CHEEK TO CHEEK from *Top Hat,* RKO Radio
Music and Lyrics by IRVING BERLIN
LOVELY TO LOOK AT from *Roberta,* RKO Radio
Music by JEROME KERN. Lyrics by DOROTHY FIELDS and JIMMY MCHUGH
LULLABY OF BROADWAY from *Gold Diggers of 1935,* Warner Bros.
Music by HARRY WARREN. Lyrics by AL DUBIN

1936   Ninth Year

DID I REMEMBER from *Suzy,* Metro-Goldwyn-Mayer
Music by WALTER DONALDSON. Lyrics by HAROLD ADAMSON
LARGE CAPITAL LETTERS DENOTE WINNER

I'VE GOT YOU UNDER MY SKIN from *Born To Dance,* Metro-Goldwyn-Mayer
Music and Lyrics by COLE PORTER
A MELODY FROM THE SKY from *Trail Of The Lonesome Pine,* Paramount
Music by LOUIS ALTER. Lyrics by SIDNEY MITCHELL
PENNIES FROM HEAVEN from *Pennies From Heaven,* Columbia
Music by ARTHUR JOHNSTON. Lyrics by JOHNNY BURKE
THE WAY YOU LOOK TONIGHT from *Swing Time,* RKO Radio
Music by JEROME KERN. Lyrics by DOROTHY FIELDS
WHEN DID YOU LEAVE HEAVEN from *Sing Baby Sing,* 20th Century-Fox
Music by RICHARD A. WHITING. Lyrics by WALTER BULLOCK

1937   Tenth Year

REMEMBER ME from *Mr. Dodd Takes The Air,* Warner Bros.
Music by HARRY WARREN. Lyrics by AL DUBIN
SWEET LEILANI from *Waikiki Wedding,* Paramount
Music and Lyrics by HARRY OWENS
THAT OLD FEELING from *Vogues Of 1938,* Wanger, UA

Music by SAMMY FAIN. Lyrics by
LEW BROWN

THEY CAN'T TAKE THAT AWAY FROM
ME from *Shall We Dance*, RKO
Radio
Music by GEORGE GERSHWIN. Lyrics
by IRA GERSHWIN

WHISPERS IN THE DARK from *Artists
And Models*, Paramount
Music by FREDERICK HOLLANDER.
Lyrics by LEO ROBIN

1938   Eleventh Year

ALWAYS AND ALWAYS from *Man-
nequin*, Metro-Goldwyn-Mayer
Music by EDWARD WARD. Lyrics by
CHET FORREST and BOB WRIGHT

CHANGE PARTNERS AND DANCE WITH
ME from *Carefree*, RKO Radio
Music and Lyrics by IRVING BERLIN

COWBOY AND THE LADY from *The
Cowboy And The Lady*, Goldwyn,
UA
Music by LIONEL NEWMAN. Lyrics
by ARTHUR QUENZER

DUST from *Under Western Stars*, Re-
public
Music and Lyrics by JOHNNY MAR-
VIN

JEEPERS CREEPERS from *Going Places*,
Warner Bros.
Music by HARRY WARREN. Lyrics by
JOHNNY MERCER

MERRILY WE LIVE from *Merrily We
Live*, Roach, M-G-M
Music by PHIL CRAIG. Lyrics by AR-
THUR QUENZER

A MIST OVER THE MOON from *The Lady
Objects*, Columbia
Music by BEN OAKLAND. Lyrics by
OSCAR HAMMERSTEIN II

MY OWN from *That Certain Age*, Uni-
versal
Music by JIMMY MCHUGH. Lyrics by
HAROLD ADAMSON

NOW IT CAN BE TOLD from *Alexander's
Ragtime Band*, 20th Century-Fox
Music and Lyrics by IRVING BERLIN

THANKS FOR THE MEMORY from
Big Broadcast Of 1938, Paramount
Music by RALPH RAINGER.
Lyrics by LEO ROBIN

1939   Twelfth Year

FAITHFUL FOREVER from *Gulliver's
Travels*, Paramount
Music by RALPH RAINGER. Lyrics by
LEO ROBIN

I POURED MY HEART INTO A SONG from
Second Fiddle, 20th Century-Fox
Music and Lyrics by IRVING BERLIN

OVER THE RAINBOW from *The Wizard of Oz*, Metro-Goldwyn-Mayer
Music by HAROLD ARLEN. Lyrics
by E. Y. HARBURG

WISHING from *Love Affair*, RKO Radio
Music and Lyrics by BUDDY de
SYLVA

1940   Thirteenth Year

DOWN ARGENTINE WAY from *Down
Argentine Way*, 20th Century-Fox
Music by HARRY WARREN. Lyrics by
MACK GORDON

I'D KNOW YOU ANYWHERE from *You'll
Find Out*, RKO Radio
Music by JIMMY MCHUGH. Lyrics by
JOHNNY MERCER

IT'S A BLUE WORLD from *Music In My
Heart*, Columbia
Music and Lyrics by CHET FORREST
and BOB WRIGHT

LOVE OF MY LIFE from *Second Chorus*,
Paramount
Music by ARTIE SHAW. Lyrics by
JOHNNY MERCER

ONLY FOREVER from *Rhythm On The
River*, Paramount
Music by JAMES MONACO. Lyrics by
JOHN BURKE

OUR LOVE AFFAIR from *Strike Up The
Band*, Metro-Goldwyn-Mayer
Music and Lyrics by ROGER EDENS
and GEORGIE STOLL

WALTZING IN THE CLOUDS from *Spring Parade*, Universal
Music by ROBERT STOLZ. Lyrics by GUS KAHN

WHEN YOU WISH UPON A STAR from *Pinocchio*, Disney, RKO Radio
Music by LEIGH HARLINE. Lyrics by NED WASHINGTON

WHO AM I? from *Hit Parade Of 1941*, Republic
Music by JULE STYNE. Lyrics by WALTER BULLOCK

1941   Fourteenth Year

BABY MINE from *Dumbo*, Disney, RKO Radio
Music by FRANK CHURCHILL. Lyrics by NED WASHINGTON

BE HONEST WITH ME from *Ridin' On A Rainbow*, Republic
Music and Lyrics by GENE AUTRY and FRED ROSE

BLUES IN THE NIGHT from *Blues In The Night*, Warner Bros.
Music by HAROLD ARLEN. Lyrics by JOHNNY MERCER

BOOGIE WOOGIE BUGLE BOY OF COMPANY B from *Buck Privates*, Universal
Music by HUGH PRINCE. Lyrics by DON RAYE

CHATTANOOGA CHOO CHOO from *Sun Valley Serenade*, 20th Century-Fox
Music by HARRY WARREN. Lyrics by MACK GORDON

DOLORES from *Las Vegas Nights*, Paramount
Music by LOU ALTER. Lyrics by FRANK LOESSER

THE LAST TIME I SAW PARIS from *Lady Be Good*, Metro-Goldwyn-Mayer
Music by JEROME KERN. Lyrics by OSCAR HAMMERSTEIN II

OUT OF THE SILENCE from *All American Co-Ed*, Roach, UA
Music and Lyrics by LLOYD B. NORLIND

SINCE I KISSED MY BABY GOODBYE from *You'll Never Get Rich*, Columbia
Music and Lyrics by COLE PORTER

1942   Fifteenth Year

ALWAYS IN MY HEART from *Always In My Heart*, Warner Bros.
Music by ERNESTO LECUONA. Lyrics by KIM GANNON

DEARLY BELOVED from *You Were Never Lovlier*, Columbia
Music by JEROME KERN. Lyrics by JOHNNY MERCER

HOW ABOUT YOU? from *Babes On Broadway*, Metro-Goldwyn-Mayer
Music by BURTON LANE. Lyrics by RALPH FREED

IT SEEMS I HEARD THAT SONG BEFORE from *Youth On Parade*, Republic
Music by JULE STYNE. Lyrics by SAMMY CAHN

I'VE GOT A GAL IN KALAMAZOO from *Orchestra Wives*, 20th Century-Fox
Music by HARRY WARREN. Lyrics by MACK GORDON

LOVE IS A SONG from *Bambi*, Disney, RKO Radio
Music by FRANK CHURCHILL. Lyrics by LARRY MOREY

PENNIES FOR PEPPINO from *Flying With Music*, Roach UA
Music by EDWARD WARD. Lyrics by CHET FORREST and BOB WRIGHT

PIG FOOT PETE from *Hellzapoppin*, Universal
Music by GENE de PAUL. Lyrics by DON RAYE

THERE'S A BREEZE ON LAKE LOUISE from *The Mayor of 44th Street*, RKO Radio
Music by HARRY REVEL. Lyrics by MORT GREENE

WHITE CHRISTMAS from *Holiday Inn*, Paramount

Music and Lyrics by IRVING BER-
LIN

1943   Sixteenth Year

BLACK MAGIC from *Star Spangled
Rhythm*, Paramount
Music by HAROLD ARLEN. Lyrics by
JOHNNY MERCER
CHANGE OF HEART from *Hit Parade Of
1943*, Republic
Music by JULE STYNE. Lyrics by
HAROLD ADAMSON
HAPPINESS IS A THING CALLED JOE from
Cabin In The Sky, Metro-Goldwyn-
Mayer
Music by HAROLD ARLEN. Lyrics by
E. Y. HARBURG
MY SHINING HOUR from *The Sky's The
Limit*, RKO Radio
Music by HAROLD ARLEN. Lyrics by
JOHNNY MERCER
SALUDOS AMIGOS from *Saludos Amigos*,
Disney, RKO Radio
Music by CHARLES WOLCOTT. Lyrics
by NED WASHINGTON
SAY A PRAYER FOR THE BOYS OVER
THERE from *Hers To Hold*, Univer-
sal
Music by JIMMY MCHUGH. Lyrics by
HERB MAGIDSON
THEY'RE EITHER TOO YOUNG OR TOO
OLD from *Thank Your Lucky Stars*,
Warner Bros.
Music by ARTHUR SCHWARTZ. Lyrics
by FRANK LOESSER
WE MUSTN'T SAY GOOD BYE from *Stage
Door Canteen*, Lesser, UA
Music by JAMES MONACO. Lyrics by
AL DUBIN
YOU'D BE SO NICE TO COME HOME TO
from *Something To Shout About*, Co-
lumbia
Music and Lyrics by COLE PORTER
YOU'LL NEVER KNOW from *Hello,
Frisco, Hello*, 20th Century-Fox
Music by HARRY WARREN.
Lyrics by MACK GORDON

1944   Seventeenth Year

I COULDN'T SLEEP A WINK LAST NIGHT
from *Higher And Higher*, RKO
Radio
Music by JIMMY MCHUGH. Lyrics by
HAROLD ADAMSON
I'LL WALK ALONE from *Follow The
Boys*, Universal
Music by JULE STYNE. Lyrics by
SAMMY CAHN
I'M MAKING BELIEVE from *Sweet And
Lowdown*, 20th Century-Fox
Music by JAMES V. MONACO. Lyrics
by MACK GORDON
LONG AGO AND FAR AWAY from *Cover
Girl*, Columbia
Music by JEROME KERN. Lyrics by
IRA GERSHWIN
NOW I KNOW from *Up In Arms*, Ava-
lon, RKO Radio
Music by HAROLD ARLEN. Lyrics by
TED KOEHLER
REMEMBER ME TO CAROLINA from *Min-
strel Man*, PRC
Music by HARRY REVEL. Lyrics by
PAUL WEBSTER
RIO DE JANEIRO from *Brazil*, Republic
Music by ARY BARROSO. Lyrics by
NED WASHINGTON
SILVER SHADOWS AND GOLDEN DREAMS
from *Lady Let's Dance*, Monogram
Music by LEW POLLACK. Lyrics by
CHARLES NEWMAN
SWEET DREAMS SWEETHEART from *Hol-
lywood Canteen*, Warner Bros.
Music by M. K. JEROME. Lyrics by
TED KOEHLER
SWINGING ON A STAR from *Going
My Way*, Paramount
Music by JAMES VAN HEUSEN.
Lyrics by JOHNNY BURKE
TOO MUCH IN LOVE from *Song Of The
Open Road*, Rogers, UA
Music by WALTER KENT. Lyrics by
KIM GANNON
THE TROLLEY SONG from *Meet Me In
St. Louis*, Metro-Goldwyn-Mayer

Music and Lyrics by RALPH BLANE
and HUGH MARTIN

1945   Eighteenth Year

ACCENTUATE THE POSITIVE from *Here Come The Waves*, Paramount
Music by HAROLD ARLEN. Lyrics by JOHNNY MERCER

ANYWHERE from *Tonight And Every Night*, Columbia
Music by JULE STYNE. Lyrics by SAMMY CAHN

AREN'T YOU GLAD YOU'RE YOU from *The Bells Of St. Mary's*, Rainbow, RKO Radio
Music by JAMES VAN HEUSEN. Lyrics by JOHNNY BURKE

THE CAT AND THE CANARY from *Why Girls Leave Home*, PRC
Music by JAY LIVINGSTON. Lyrics by RAY EVANS

ENDLESSLY from *Earl Carroll Vanities*, Republic
Music by WALTER KENT. Lyrics by KIM GANNON

I FALL IN LOVE TOO EASILY from *Anchors Aweigh*, Metro-Goldwyn-Mayer
Music by JULE STYNE. Lyrics by SAMMY CAHN

I'LL BUY THAT DREAM from *Sing Your Way Home*, RKO Radio
Music by ALLIE WRUBEL. Lyrics by HERB MAGIDSON

IT MIGHT AS WELL BE SPRING from *State Fair*, 20th Century-Fox
Music by RICHARD RODGERS. Lyrics by OSCAR HAMMERSTEIN II

LINDA from *G. I. Joe*, Cowan, UA
Music and Lyrics by ANN RONELL

LOVE LETTERS from *Love Letters*, Wallis, Paramount
Music by VICTOR YOUNG. Lyrics by EDWARD HEYMAN

MORE AND MORE from *Can't Help Singing*, Universal
Music by JEROME KERN. Lyrics by E. Y. HARBURG

SLEIGHRIDE IN JULY from *Belle Of The Yukon*, International, RKO Radio
Music by JAMES VAN HEUSEN. Lyrics by JOHNNY BURKE

SO IN LOVE from *Wonder Man*, Beverly Prods., RKO Radio
Music by DAVID ROSE. Lyrics by LEO ROBIN

SOME SUNDAY MORNING from *San Antonio*, Warner Bros.
Music by RAY HEINDORF and M. K. JEROME. Lyrics by TED KOEHLER

1946   Nineteenth Year

ALL THROUGH THE DAY from *Centennial Summer*, 20th Century-Fox
Music by JEROME KERN. Lyrics by OSCAR HAMMERSTEIN II

I CAN'T BEGIN TO TELL YOU from *The Dolly Sisters*, 20th Century-Fox
Music by JAMES MONACO. Lyrics by MACK GORDON

OLE BUTTERMILK SKY from *Canyon Passage*, Wanger, Universal
Music by HOAGY CARMICHAEL. Lyrics by JACK BROOKS

ON THE ATCHISON, TOPEKA AND SANTA FE from *The Harvey Girls*, Metro-Goldwyn-Mayer
Music by HARRY WARREN. Lyrics by JOHNNY MERCER

YOU KEEP COMING BACK LIKE A SONG from *Blue Skies*, Paramount
Music and Lyrics by IRVING BERLIN

1947   Twentieth Year

A GAL IN CALICO from *The Time, Place And The Girl*, Warner Bros.
Music by ARTHUR SCHWARTZ. Lyrics by LEO ROBIN

I WISH I DIDN'T LOVE YOU SO from *The Perils Of Pauline*, Paramount
Music and Lyrics by FRANK LOESSER

PASS THAT PEACE PIPE from *Good News*, Metro-Goldwyn-Mayer

Music and Lyrics by RALPH BLANE,
HUGH MARTIN and ROGER EDENS
YOU DO from *Mother Wore Tights*, 20th
Century-Fox
Music by JOSEF MYROW. Lyrics by
MACK GORDON
ZIP-A-DEE-DOO-DAH from *Song Of
The South*, Disney-RKO Radio
Music by ALLIE WRUBEL. Lyrics
by RAY GILBERT

1948   Twenty-first Year
BUTTONS AND BOWS from *The
Paleface*, Paramount
Music and Lyrics by JAY LIVING-
STON and RAY EVANS
FOR EVERY MAN THERE'S A WOMAN
from *Casbah*, Marston Pictures, U-I
Music by HAROLD ARLEN. Lyrics by
LEO ROBIN
IT'S MAGIC from *Romance On The High
Seas*, Curtiz, Warner Bros.
Music by JULE STYNE. Lyrics by
SAMMY CAHN
THIS IS THE MOMENT from *That Lady In
Ermine*, 20th Century-Fox
Music by FREDERICK HOLLANDER.
Lyrics by LEO ROBIN
THE WOODY WOODPECKER SONG from
Wet Blanket Policy, Walter Lantz,
UA (Cartoon)
Music and Lyrics by RAMEY IDRISS
and GEORGE TIBBLES

1949   Twenty-second Year
BABY, IT'S COLD OUTSIDE from
Neptune's Daughter, Metro-
Goldwyn-Mayer
Music and Lyrics by FRANK LOES-
SER
IT'S A GREAT FEELING from *It's A
Great Feeling*, Warner Bros.
Music by JULE STYNE. Lyrics by
SAMMY CAHN
LAVENDER BLUE from *So Dear To My
Heart*, Disney-RKO Radio

Music by ELIOT DANIEL. Lyrics by
LARRY MOREY
MY FOOLISH HEART from *My Foolish
Heart*, Goldwyn-RKO Radio
Music by VICTOR YOUNG. Lyrics by
NED WASHINGTON
THROUGH A LONG AND SLEEPLESS
NIGHT from *Come To The Stable*,
20th Century-Fox
Music by ALFRED NEWMAN. Lyrics
by MACK GORDON

1950   Twenty-third Year
BE MY LOVE from *The Toast Of New
Orleans*, Metro-Goldwyn-Mayer
Music by NICHOLAS BRODSZKY.
Lyrics by SAMMY CAHN
BIBBIDY-BOBBIDI-BOO from *Cinderella*,
Disney, RKO Radio
Music and Lyrics by MACK DAVID,
AL HOFFMAN and JERRY LIVINGSTON
MONA LISA from *Captain Carey,
USA*, Paramount
Music and Lyrics by RAY EVANS
and JAY LIVINGSTON
MULE TRAIN from *Singing Guns*, Polo-
mar Pictures, Republic
Music and Lyrics by FRED GLICK-
MAN, HY HEATH and JOHNNY LANGE
WILHELMINA from *Wabash Avenue*,
20th Century-Fox
Music by JOSEF MYROW. Lyrics by
MACK GORDON

1951   Twenty-fourth Year
IN THE COOL, COOL, COOL OF
THE EVENING from *Here Comes
The Groom*, Paramount
Music by HOAGY CARMICHAEL.
Lyrics by JOHNNY MERCER
A KISS TO BUILD A DREAM ON from *The
Strip*, Metro-Goldwyn-Mayer
Music and Lyrics by BERT KALMAR,
HARRY RUBY and OSCAR HAMMER-
STEIN II
NEVER from *Golden Girl*, 20th Cen-
tury-Fox

Music by LIONEL NEWMAN. Lyrics
by ELIOT DANIEL
TOO LATE NOW from *Royal Wedding*,
Metro-Goldwyn-Mayer
Music by BURTON LANE. Lyrics by
ALAN JAY LERNER
WONDER WHY from *Rich, Young And
Pretty*, Metro-Goldwyn-Mayer
Music by NICHOLAS BRODSZKY.
Lyrics by SAMMY CAHN

1952   Twenty-fifth Year

AM I IN LOVE from *Son Of Paleface*,
Paramount
Music and Lyrics by JACK BROOKS
BECAUSE YOU'RE MINE from *Because
You're Mine*, Metro-Goldwyn-Mayer
Music by NICHOLAS BRODSZKY.
Lyrics by SAMMY CAHN
HIGH NOON (DO NOT FORSAKE
ME, OH MY DARLIN') from *High
Noon*, Kramer, UA
Music by DIMITRI TIOMKIN.
Lyrics by NED WASHINGTON
THUMBELINA from *Hans Christian An-
dersen*, Goldwyn, RKO Radio
Music and Lyrics by FRANK LOESSER
ZING A LITTLE ZONG from *Just For
You*, Paramount
Music by HARRY WARREN. Lyrics by
LEO ROBIN

1953   Twenty-sixth Year

THE MOON IS BLUE from *The Moon Is
Blue*, Preminger-Herbert Prod., UA
Music by HERSCHEL BURKE GILBERT.
Lyrics by SYLVIA FINE
MY FLAMING HEART from *Small Town
Girl*, Metro-Goldwyn-Mayer
Music by NICHOLAS BRODSZKY.
Lyrics by LEO ROBIN
SADIE THOMPSON'S SONG (BLUE PACIFIC
BLUES) from *Miss Sadie Thompson*,
Beckworth, Columbia
Music by LESTER LEE. Lyrics by NED
WASHINGTON

SECRET LOVE from *Calamity Jane*,
Warner Bros.
Music by SAMMY FAIN. Lyrics by
PAUL FRANCIS WEBSTER
THAT'S AMORE from *The Caddy*, York
Pictures, Paramount
Music by HARRY WARREN. Lyrics by
JACK BROOKS

1954   Twenty-seventh Year

COUNT YOUR BLESSINGS INSTEAD OF
SHEEP from *White Christmas*, Para-
mount
Music and Lyrics by IRVING BERLIN
THE HIGH AND THE MIGHTY from *The
High And The Mighty*, Wayne-
Fellows Prods., Inc., Warner Bros.
Music by DIMITRI TIOMKIN. Lyrics
by NED WASHINGTON
HOLD MY HAND from *Susan Slept Here*,
RKO Radio
Music and Lyrics by JACK LAWRENCE
and RICHARD MYERS
THE MAN THAT GOT AWAY from *A Star
Is Born*, A Transcona Enterprises
Prod., Warner Bros.
Music by HAROLD ARLEN. Lyrics by
IRA GERSHWIN
THREE COINS IN THE FOUNTAIN
from *Three Coins In The Fountain*,
20th Century-Fox
Music by JULE STYNE. Lyrics by
SAMMY CAHN

1955   Twenty-eighth Year

I'LL NEVER STOP LOVING YOU from
Love Me Or Leave Me, Metro-
Goldwyn-Mayer
Music by NICHOLAS BRODSZKY.
Lyrics by SAMMY CAHN
LOVE IS A MANY-SPLENDORED
THING from *Love Is A Many-Splen-
dored Thing*, 20th Century-Fox
Music by SAMMY FAIN. Lyrics by
PAUL FRANCIS WEBSTER
SOMETHING'S GOTTA GIVE from *Daddy
Long Legs*, 20th Century-Fox

Music and Lyrics by JOHNNY MERCER

(LOVE IS) THE TENDER TRAP from *The Tender Trap*, Metro-Goldwyn-Mayer
Music by JAMES VAN HEUSEN. Lyrics by SAMMY CAHN

UNCHAINED MELODY from *Unchained*, Hall Bartlett Prods., Inc., Warner Bros.
Music by ALEX NORTH. Lyrics by HY ZARET

1956   Twenty-ninth Year

FRIENDLY PERSUASION (THEE I LOVE) from *Friendly Persuasion*, Allied Artists
Music by DIMITRI TIOMKIN. Lyrics by PAUL FRANCIS WEBSTER

JULIE from *Julie*, Arwin Prods., M-G-M
Music by LEITH STEVENS. Lyrics by TOM ADAIR

TRUE LOVE from *High Society*, Sol C. Siegel Prod., M-G-M
Music and Lyrics by COLE PORTER

WHATEVER WILL BE, WILL BE (QUE SERA, SERA) from *The Man Who Knew Too Much*, Filwite Prods., Inc., Paramount
Music and Lyrics by JAY LIVINGSTON and RAY EVANS

WRITTEN ON THE WIND from *Written On The Wind*, Universal-International
Music by VICTOR YOUNG. Lyrics by SAMMY CAHN

1957   Thirtieth Year

AN AFFAIR TO REMEMBER from *An Affair To Remember*, Jerry Wald Prods., Inc., 20th Century-Fox
Music by HARRY WARREN. Lyrics by HAROLD ADAMSON and LEO MCCAREY

ALL THE WAY from *The Joker Is Wild*, A.M.B.L. Prod., Paramount
Music by JAMES VAN HEUSEN. Lyrics by SAMMY CAHN

APRIL LOVE from *April Love*, 20th Century-Fox
Music by SAMMY FAIN. Lyrics by PAUL FRANCIS WEBSTER

TAMMY from *Tammy And The Bachelor*, Universal-International
Music and Lyrics by RAY EVANS and JAY LIVINGSTON

WILD IS THE WIND from *Wild Is The Wind*, A Hal Wallis Prod., Paramount
Music by DIMITRI TIOMKIN. Lyrics by NED WASHINGTON

1958   Thirty-first Year

ALMOST IN YOUR ARMS (Love Song from "Houseboat") from *Houseboat*, Paramount and Scribe, Paramount
Music and Lyrics by JAY LIVINGSTON and RAY EVANS

A CERTAIN SMILE from *A Certain Smile*, 20th Century-Fox
Music by SAMMY FAIN. Lyrics by PAUL FRANCIS WEBSTER

GIGI from *Gigi*, Arthur Freed Prods., M-G-M
Music by FREDERICK LOEWE. Lyrics by ALAN JAY LERNER

TO LOVE AND BE LOVED from *Some Came Running*, Sol C. Siegel Prods., Inc., M-G-M
Music by JAMES VAN HEUSEN. Lyrics by SAMMY CAHN

A VERY PRECIOUS LOVE from *Marjorie Morningstar*, Beachwold Pictures, Warner Bros.
Music by SAMMY FAIN. Lyrics by PAUL FRANCIS WEBSTER

1959   Thirty-second Year

THE BEST OF EVERYTHING from *The Best Of Everything*, Company Of Artists, Inc., 20th Century-Fox
Music by ALFRED NEWMAN. Lyrics by SAMMY CAHN

THE FIVE PENNIES from *The Five Pennies*, Dena Prod., Paramount
Music and Lyrics by SYLVIA FINE
THE HANGING TREE from *The Hanging Tree*, Baroda Prods., Inc., Warner Bros.
Music by JERRY LIVINGSTON. Lyrics by MACK DAVID
HIGH HOPES from *A Hole In The Head*, Sincap Prods., UA
Music by JAMES VAN HEUSEN. Lyrics by SAMMY CAHN
STRANGE ARE THE WAYS OF LOVE from *The Young Land*, C. V. Whitney Pictures, Inc., Columbia
Music by DIMITRI TIOMKIN. Lyrics by NED WASHINGTON

1960   Thirty-third Year

THE FACTS OF LIFE from *The Facts Of Life*, Panama & Frank Prod., UA
Music and Lyrics by JOHNNY MERCER
FARAWAY PART OF TOWN from *Pepe*, G.S.-Posa Films International Prod., Columbia
Music by ANDRÉ PREVIN. Lyrics by DORY LANGDON
THE GREEN LEAVES OF SUMMER from *The Alamo*, Batjac Prod., UA
Music by DIMITRI TIOMKIN. Lyrics by PAUL FRANCIS WEBSTER
NEVER ON SUNDAY from *Never On Sunday*, Melinafilm Prod., Lopert Pictures Corp. (Greek)
Music and Lyrics by MANOS HADJIDAKIS
THE SECOND TIME AROUND from *High Time*, Bing Crosby Prods., 20th Century-Fox
Music by JAMES VAN HEUSEN. Lyrics by SAMMY CAHN

1961   Thirty-fourth Year

BACHELOR IN PARADISE from *Bachelor In Paradise*, Ted Richmond Prod., M-G-M
Music by HENRY MANCINI. Lyrics by MACK DAVID
LOVE THEME FROM EL CID (The Falcon And The Dove) from *El Cid*, Samuel Bronston Prod. in association with Dear Film Prod., Allied Artists
Music by MIKLOS ROZSA. Lyrics by PAUL FRANCIS WEBSTER
MOON RIVER from *Breakfast At Tiffany's*, Jurow-Shepherd Prod., Paramount
Music by HENRY MANCINI. Lyrics by JOHNNY MERCER
POCKETFUL OF MIRACLES from *Pocketful Of Miracles*, Franton Prod., UA
Music by JAMES VAN HEUSEN. Lyrics by SAMMY CAHN
TOWN WITHOUT PITY from *Town Without Pity*, Mirisch Company in association with Gloria Films, UA
Music by DIMITRI TIOMKIN. Lyrics by NED WASHINGTON

1962   Thirty-fifth Year

DAYS OF WINE AND ROSES from *Days of Wine and Roses*, Martin Manulis-Jalem Prod., Warner Bros.
Music by HENRY MANCINI. Lyrics by JOHNNY MERCER
LOVE SONG FROM MUTINY ON THE BOUNTY (FOLLOW ME) from *Mutiny On The Bounty*, Arcola Prod., M-G-M
Music by BRONISLAU KAPER. Lyrics by PAUL FRANCIS WEBSTER
SONG FROM TWO FOR THE SEESAW (SECOND CHANCE) from *Two For The Seesaw*, Mirisch-Argyle-Talbot Prod. in association with Seven Arts Productions, UA
Music by ANDRÉ PREVIN. Lyrics by DORY LANGDON
TENDER IS THE NIGHT from *Tender Is The Night*, 20th Century-Fox
Music by SAMMY FAIN. Lyrics by PAUL FRANCIS WEBSTER

WALK ON THE WILD SIDE from *Walk On The Wild Side*, Famous Artists Prods., Columbia
Music by ELMER BERNSTEIN. Lyrics by MACK DAVID.

1963   Thirty-sixth Year

CALL ME IRRESPONSIBLE from *Papa's Delicate Condition*, Amro Prods., Paramount
Music by JAMES VAN HEUSEN. Lyrics by SAMMY CAHN

CHARADE from *Charade*, Universal-Stanley Donen Prod., Universal
Music by HENRY MANCINI. Lyrics by JOHNNY MERCER

IT'S A MAD, MAD, MAD, MAD WORLD from *It's A Mad, Mad, Mad, Mad, World*, Casey Prod., UA
Music by ERNEST GOLD. Lyrics by MACK DAVID

MORE from *Mondo Cane*, Cineriz Prod., Times Film
Music by RIZ ORTOLANI and NINO OLIVIERO. Lyrics by NORMAN NEWELL

SO LITTLE TIME from *55 Days At Peking*, Samuel Bronston Prod., Allied Artists
Music by DIMITRI TIOMKIN. Lyrics by PAUL FRANCIS WEBSTER

1964   Thirty-seventh Year

CHIM CHIM CHER-EE from *Mary Poppins*, Walt Disney Prods.
Music and Lyrics by RICHARD M. SHERMAN & ROBERT B. SHERMAN

DEAR HEART from *Dear Heart*, W.B.-Out-Of-Towners Prod., Warner Bros.
Music by HENRY MANCINI. Lyrics by JAY LIVINGSTON and RAY EVANS

HUSH . . . HUSH, SWEET CHARLOTTE from *Hush . . . Hush, Sweet Charlotte*, Associates & Aldrich Prod., 20th Century-Fox
Music by FRANK DeVOL. Lyrics by MACK DAVID

MY KIND OF TOWN from *Robin And The 7 Hoods*, P-C Prod., Warner Bros.
Music by JAMES VAN HEUSEN. Lyrics by SAMMY CAHN

WHERE LOVE HAS GONE from *Where Love Has Gone*, Paramount-Embassy Pictures Prod., Paramount
Music by JAMES VAN HEUSEN. Lyrics by SAMMY CAHN

1965   Thirty-eighth Year

THE BALLAD OF CAT BALLOU from *Cat Ballou*, Harold Hecht Prod., Columbia
Music by JERRY LIVINGSTON. Lyrics by MACK DAVID

I WILL WAIT FOR YOU from *The Umbrellas Of Cherbourg*, Parc-Madeleine Films Prod., American Intl.
Music by MICHEL LEGRAND. Lyrics by JACQUES DEMY

THE SHADOW OF YOUR SMILE from *The Sandpiper*, Filmways-Venice Prod., M-G-M
Music by JOHNNY MANDEL. Lyrics by PAUL FRANCIS WEBSTER

THE SWEETHEART TREE from *The Great Race*, Patricia-Jalem-Reynard Prod., Warner Bros.
Music by HENRY MANCINI. Lyrics by JOHNNY MERCER

WHAT'S NEW PUSSYCAT? from *What's New Pussycat?*, Famous Artists-Famartists Prod., United Artists
Music by BURT BACHARACH. Lyrics by HAL DAVID

1966   Thirty-ninth Year

ALFIE from *Alfie*, Sheldrake Films, Ltd. Prod., Paramount
Music by BURT BACHARACH. Lyrics by HAL DAVID

BORN FREE from *Born Free*, Open

Road Films, Ltd.-Atlas Films, Ltd.
Prod., Columbia
Music by JOHN BARRY. Lyrics by
DON BLACK

GEORGY GIRL from *Georgy Girl*, Everglades Prods., Ltd., Columbia
Music by TOM SPRINGFIELD. Lyrics
by JIM DALE

MY WISHING DOLL from *Hawaii*,
Mirisch Corp. of Delaware Prod.,
U.A.
Music by ELMER BERNSTEIN. Lyrics
by MACK DAVID

A TIME FOR LOVE from *An American Dream*, Warner Bros.
Music by JOHNNY MANDEL. Lyrics
by PAUL FRANCIS WEBSTER

1967   Fortieth Year

THE BARE NECESSITIES from *The Jungle Book*, Walt Disney Prods., Buena
Vista Distribution Co.
Music and Lyrics by TERRY GILKYSON

THE EYES OF LOVE from *Banning*, Universal
Music by QUINCY JONES. Lyrics by
BOB RUSSELL

THE LOOK OF LOVE from *Casino Royale*, Famous Artists Prods., Ltd., Columbia
Music by BURT BACHARACH. Lyrics
by HAL DAVID

TALK TO THE ANIMALS from *Doctor Dolittle*, Apjac Prods., 20th Century-Fox
Music and lyrics by LESLIE BRICUSSE

THOROUGHLY MODERN MILLIE from
Thoroughly Modern Millie, Ross
Hunter-Universal Prod., Universal
Music and lyrics by JAMES VAN HEUSEN and SAMMY CAHN

1968   Forty-first Year

CHITTY CHITTY BANG BANG from *Chitty Chitty Bang Bang*, Warfield Prods.,

United Artists
Music and lyrics by RICHARD M.
SHERMAN and ROBERT B. SHERMAN

FOR LOVE OF IVY from *For Love Of Ivy*,
American Broadcasting Companies-
Palomar Pictures International Prod.,
Cinerama
Music by QUINCY JONES. Lyrics by
BOB RUSSELL

FUNNY GIRL from *Funny Girl*, Rastar
Prods., Columbia
Music by JULE STYNE. Lyrics by BOB
MERRILL

STAR! from *Star!*, Robert Wise Prod.,
20th Century-Fox
Music by JIMMY VAN HEUSEN.
Lyrics by SAMMY CAHN

THE WINDMILLS OF YOUR MIND
from *The Thomas Crown Affair*,
Mirisch-Simkoe-Solar Prod., United
Artists
Music by MICHEL LEGRAND.
Lyrics by ALAN and MARILYN
BERGMAN

1969   Forty-second Year

COME SATURDAY MORNING from *The Sterile Cuckoo*, Boardwalk Prods.,
Paramount
Music by FRED KARLIN. Lyrics by
DORY PREVIN

JEAN from *The Prime Of Miss Jean Brodie*, 20th Century-Fox Prods.,
Ltd., 20th Century-Fox
Music and lyrics by ROD MCKUEN

RAINDROPS KEEP FALLIN' ON
MY HEAD from *Butch Cassidy And The Sundance Kid*, George Roy Hill-
Paul Monash Prod., 20th Century-
Fox
Music by BURT BACHARACH.
Lyrics by HAL DAVID

TRUE GRIT from *True Grit*, Hal Wallis
Prod., Paramount
Music by ELMER BERNSTEIN. Lyrics
by DON BLACK

WHAT ARE YOU DOING THE REST OF

YOUR LIFE? from *The Happy Ending*,
Pax Films Prod., United Artists
Music by MICHEL LEGRAND. Lyrics
by ALAN and MARILYN BERGMAN

1970   Forty-third Year

FOR ALL WE KNOW from *Lovers
And Other Strangers*, ABC Pictures
Prod., Cinerama
Music by FRED KARLIN. Lyrics by
ROBB ROYER and JAMES GRIF-
FIN a.k.a. ROBB WILSON and
ARTHUR JAMES
PIECES OF DREAMS from *Pieces Of
Dreams*, RFB Enterprises Prod.,
United Artists
Music by MICHEL LEGRAND. Lyrics
by ALAN and MARILYN BERGMAN
THANK YOU VERY MUCH from *Scrooge*,
Waterbury Films, Ltd. Prod., Cin-
ema Center Films Presentation, Na-
tional General
Music and lyrics by LESLIE BRICUSSE
TILL LOVE TOUCHES YOUR LIFE from
Madron, Edric-Isracine-Zev Braun
Prods., Four Star-Excelsior Releas-
ing
Music by RIZ ORTOLANI. Lyrics by
ARTHUR HAMILTON
WHISTLING AWAY THE DARK from
Darling Lili, Geoffrey Prods., Para-
mount
Music by HENRY MANCINI. Lyrics by
JOHNNY MERCER

1971   Forty-fourth Year

THE AGE OF NOT BELIEVING from *Bed-
knobs And Broomsticks*, Walt Disney
Prods., Buena Vista Distribution
Company
Music and lyrics by RICHARD M.
SHERMAN and ROBERT B. SHERMAN
ALL HIS CHILDREN from *Sometimes A
Great Notion*, A Universal-Newman-
Foreman Company Prod., Universal

Music by HENRY MANCINI. Lyrics by
ALAN and MARILYN BERGMAN
BLESS THE BEASTS & CHILDREN from
Bless The Beasts & Children,
Columbia
Music and lyrics by BARRY DEVOR-
ZON and PERRY BOTKIN, JR.
LIFE IS WHAT YOU MAKE IT from
Kotch, A Kotch Company Produc-
tion, ABC Pictures Presentation,
Cinerama
Music by MARVIN HAMLISCH. Lyrics
by JOHNNY MERCER
THEME FROM SHAFT from *Shaft*,
Shaft Prods., Ltd., M-G-M
Music and lyrics by ISAAC HAYES

1972   Forty-fifth Year

BEN from *Ben*, BCP Productions, Cin-
erama
Music by WALTER SCHARF. Lyrics by
DON BLACK
COME FOLLOW, FOLLOW ME from *The
Little Ark*, Robert Radnitz Produc-
tions, Ltd., Cinema Center Films
Presentation, National General
Music by FRED KARLIN. Lyrics by
MARSHA KARLIN
MARMALADE, MOLASSES & HONEY from
*The Life And Times Of Judge Roy
Bean*, A First Artists Production
Company, Ltd. Production, National
General
Music by MAURICE JARRE. Lyrics by
MARILYN and ALAN BERGMAN
THE MORNING AFTER from *The Po-
seidon Adventure*, An Irwin Allen
Production, 20th Century-Fox
Music and lyrics by AL KASHA and
JOEL HIRSCHHORN
STRANGE ARE THE WAYS OF LOVE from
The Stepmother, Magic Eye of Hol-
lywood Productions, Crown Interna-
tional
Music by SAMMY FAIN. Lyrics by
PAUL FRANCIS WEBSTER

Issac Hayes staged a lavish production number for the 44th Awards. His "Theme From Shaft" won the 1971 Oscar for Best Song. © *1978 A.M.P.A.S.*

1973   Forty-sixth Year

ALL THAT LOVE WENT TO WASTE from
A Touch Of Class, Brut Prods.,
Avco Embassy
Music by GEORGE BARRIE. Lyrics by
SAMMY CAHN

LIVE AND LET DIE from *Live And Let Die*, Eon Prods., UA
Music and lyrics by PAUL and LINDA
MCCARTNEY

LOVE from *Robin Hood*, Walt Disney
Prods., Buena Vista Distribution
Company
Music by GEORGE BRUNS. Lyrics by
FLOYD HUDDLESTON

THE WAY WE WERE from *The Way We Were*, Rastar Prods., Columbia
Music by MARVIN HAMLISCH.
Lyrics by ALAN and MARILYN
BERGMAN

NICE TO BE AROUND from *Cinderella Liberty*, A Sanford Prod., 20th Century-Fox
Music by JOHN WILLIAMS. Lyrics by
PAUL WILLIAMS

1974   Forty-seventh Year

BENJI'S THEME (I FEEL LOVE) from
Benji, Mulberry Square
Music by EUEL BOX. Lyrics by
BETTY BOX

BLAZING SADDLES from *Blazing Saddles*, Warner Bros.
Music by JOHN MORRIS. Lyrics by
MEL BROOKS

LITTLE PRINCE from *The Little Prince*,
A Stanley Donen Enterprises, Ltd.
Prod., Paramount
Music by FREDERICK LOEWE. Lyrics
by ALAN JAY LERNER

WE MAY NEVER LOVE LIKE THIS
AGAIN from *The Towering Inferno*,

An Irwin Allen Production, 20th Century-Fox/Warner Bros.
Music and lyrics by AL KASHA and JOEL HIRSCHHORN

WHEREVER LOVE TAKES ME from *Gold,* Avton Film Productions, Ltd. Allied Artists
Music by ELMER BERNSTEIN. Lyrics by DON BLACK

1975   Forty-eighth Year

Note: Name of category changed from Best Song to Best Original Song.

HOW LUCKY CAN YOU GET from *Funny Lady,* A Rastar Pictures Production, Columbia
Music and lyrics by FRED EBB and JOHN KANDER

I'M EASY from *Nashville,* An ABC Entertainment-Jerry Weintraub-Robert Altman Production, Paramount
Music and lyrics by KEITH CARRADINE

NOW THAT WE'RE IN LOVE from *Whiffs,* Brut Productions, 20th Century-Fox
Music by GEORGE BARRIE. Lyrics by SAMMY CAHN

RICHARD'S WINDOW from *The Other Side Of The Mountain,* A Filmways-Larry Peerce-Universal Production, Universal
Music by CHARLES FOX. Lyrics by NORMAN GIMBEL

THEME FROM MAHOGANY (DO YOU KNOW WHERE YOU'RE GOING TO) from *Mahogany,* A Jobete Film Production, Paramount
Music by MICHAEL MASSER. Lyrics by GERRY GOFFIN

1976   Forty-ninth Year

AVE SATANI from *The Omen,* 20th Century-Fox Productions, Ltd., 20th Century Fox

Music and lyrics by JERRY GOLDSMITH

COME TO ME from *The Pink Panther Strikes Again,* Amjo Productions, Ltd., United Artists
Music by HENRY MANCINI. Lyrics by DON BLACK

EVERGREEN (LOVE THEME FROM A STAR IS BORN) from *A Star Is Born,* A Barwood/Jon Peters Production, First Artists Presentation, Warner Bros.
Music by BARBRA STREISAND. Lyrics by PAUL WILLIAMS

GONNA FLY NOW from *Rocky,* a Robert Chartoff-Irwin Winkler Production, United Artists
Music by BILL CONTI. Lyrics by CAROL CONNORS and AYN ROBBINS

A WORLD THAT NEVER WAS from *Half A House,* Lenro Productions, First American Films
Music by SAMMY FAIN. Lyrics by PAUL FRANCIS WEBSTER

1977   Fiftieth Year

(Best Original Song)

CANDLE ON THE WATER from *Pete's Dragon,* Walt Disney Productions, Buena Vista Distribution Company
Music and lyrics by AL KASHA and JOEL HIRSCHHORN

NOBODY DOES IT BETTER from *The Spy Who Loved Me,* Eon Productions, United Artists
Music by MARVIN HAMLISCH. Lyrics by CAROLE BAYER SAGER

THE SLIPPER AND THE ROSE WALTZ (HE DANCED WITH ME/SHE DANCED WITH ME) from *The Slipper And The Rose—The Story Of Cinderella,* Paradine Co-Productions, Ltd., Universal
Music and lyrics by RICHARD M. SHERMAN and ROBERT B. SHERMAN.

SOMEONE'S WAITING FOR YOU from *The Rescuers*, Walt Disney Productions, Buena Vista Distribution Company Music by SAMMY FAIN. Lyrics by CAROL CONNORS and AYN ROBBINS

YOU LIGHT UP MY LIFE from *You Light Up My Life*, The Session Company Production, Columbia Music and lyrics by JOSEPH BROOKS

COSTUME DESIGN

A costume designer dresses not only the actors but, in effect, the picture itself. And though costume design is frequently associated only with dressy spectacles like *Cleopatra* or *Gigi,* one must remember that all films require costumes. "More difficult, and far less likely to win applause," says Oscar-winning costume designer Julie Harris, "are the films which require dressing down, rather than dressing up."

The Academy Award for Costume Design was begun in 1948 with separate awards given for black and white films and color films. With the exception of 1957 and 1958, this division was retained until 1967 when the lack of black and white films made two separate awards impractical.

Edith Head, with an astonishing thirty-four nominations and eight Oscars, has dominated the category, though several other designers including Irene Sharaff, Orry-Kelly, Dorothy Jeakins, and Charles LeMaire have each won three or more awards.

Achievements in this category are nominated by the Costume Designer members of the Academy Art Directors Branch.

1948   Twenty-first Year
(Black-and-White)
B. F.'S DAUGHTER, Metro-Goldwyn-Mayer: IRENE
HAMLET, Rank-Two Cities, U-I (British): ROGER K. FURSE

(Color)
THE EMPEROR WALTZ, Paramount: EDITH HEAD and GILE STEELE
JOAN OF ARC, Sierra, RKO Radio: DOROTHY JEAKINS and KARINSKA

1949   Twenty-second Year
(Black-and-white)
THE HEIRESS, Paramount: EDITH HEAD and GILE STEELE
PRINCE OF FOXES, 20th Century-Fox: VITTORIO NINO NOVARESE

(Color)
ADVENTURES OF DON JUAN, Warner Bros: LEAH RHODES,
LARGE CAPITAL LETTERS DENOTE WINNER

TRAVILLA and MARJORIE BEST
MOTHER IS A FRESHMAN, 20th Century-Fox: KAY NELSON

1950   Twenty-third Year
(Black-and-white)
ALL ABOUT EVE, 20th Century-Fox: EDITH HEAD and CHARLES LE-MAIRE
BORN YESTERDAY, Columbia: JEAN LOUIS
THE MAGNIFICENT YANKEE, Metro-Goldwyn-Mayer: WALTER PLUNKETT

(Color)
THE BLACK ROSE, 20th Century-Fox: MICHAEL WHITTAKER
SAMSON AND DELILAH, DeMille, Paramount: EDITH HEAD, DOROTHY JEAKINS, ELOIS JENSSEN, GILE STEELE and GWEN WAKELING
THAT FORSYTE WOMAN, Metro-Goldwyn-Mayer: WALTER PLUNKETT and VALLES

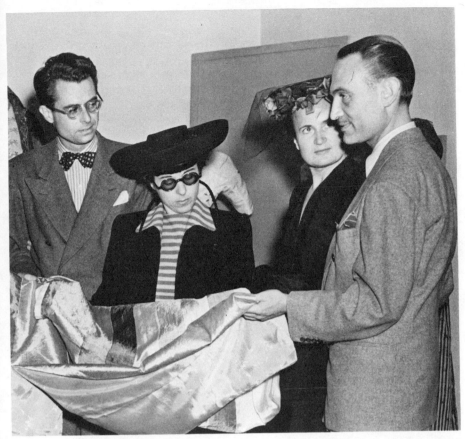

L to R: Costume designers Edward Stevenson, Edith Head, Irene, and Walter Plunkett have accounted for over fifty nominations and ten Oscars since 1948 when Costume Design became an award category.

1951 Twenty-fourth Year

(Black-and-white)

KIND LADY, Metro-Goldwyn-Mayer: WALTER PLUNKETT and GILE STEELE

THE MODEL AND THE MARRIAGE BROKER, 20th Century-Fox: CHARLES LeMARIE and RENIE

THE MUDLARK, 20th Century-Fox: EDWARD STEVENSON and MARGARET FURSE

A PLACE IN THE SUN, Paramount: EDITH HEAD

A STREETCAR NAMED DESIRE, Charles K. Feldman Group Prods., Warner Bros.: LUCINDA BALLARD

(Color)

AN AMERICAN IN PARIS, Metro-Goldwyn-Mayer: ORRY-KELLY, WALTER PLUNKETT and IRENE SHARAFF

DAVID AND BATHSHEBA, 20th Century-Fox: CHARLES LeMAIRE and EDWARD STEVENSON

THE GREAT CARUSO, Metro-Goldwyn-Mayer: HELEN ROSE and GILE STEELE

QUO VADIS, Metro-Goldwyn-Mayer: HERSCHEL MCCOY

TALES OF HOFFMANN, Powell-Pressburger, Lopert (British): HEIN HECKROTH

1952   Twenty-fifth Year
(Black-and-White)

AFFAIR IN TRINIDAD, Beckworth, Columbia: JEAN LOUIS
THE BAD AND THE BEAUTIFUL, Metro-Goldwyn-Mayer: HELEN ROSE
CARRIE, Paramount: EDITH HEAD
MY COUSIN RACHEL, 20th Century-Fox: CHARLES LeMAIRE and DOROTHY JEAKINS
SUDDEN FEAR, Joseph Kaufman, RKO Radio: SHEILA O'BRIEN

(Color)

THE GREATEST SHOW ON EARTH, De-Mille, Paramount: EDITH HEAD, DOROTHY JEAKINS and MILES WHITE
HANS CHRISTIAN ANDERSEN, Goldwyn, RKO Radio: CLAVE, MARY WILLS and MADAME KARINSKA
THE MERRY WIDOW, Metro-Goldwyn-Mayer: HELEN ROSE and GILE STEELE
MOULIN ROUGE, Romulus, UA: MARCEL VERTES
WITH A SONG IN MY HEART, 20th Century-Fox: CHARLES LeMAIRE

1953   Twenty-sixth Year
(Black-and-White)

THE ACTRESS, Metro-Goldwyn-Mayer: WALTER PLUNKETT
DREAM WIFE, Metro-Goldwyn-Mayer: HELEN ROSE and HERSCHEL MCCOY
FROM HERE TO ETERNITY, Columbia: JEAN LOUIS
THE PRESIDENT'S LADY, 20th Century-Fox: CHARLES LeMAIRE and RENIE
ROMAN HOLIDAY, Paramount: EDITH HEAD

(Color)

THE BAND WAGON, Metro-Goldwyn-Mayer: MARY ANN NYBERG
CALL ME MADAM, 20th Century-Fox: IRENE SHARAFF
HOW TO MARRY A MILLIONAIRE, 20th Century-Fox: CHARLES LeMAIRE and TRAVILLA
THE ROBE, 20th Century-Fox: CHARLES LeMAIRE and EMILE SANTIAGO
YOUNG BESS, Metro-Goldwyn-Mayer: WALTER PLUNKETT

1954   Twenty-seventh Year
(Black-and-White)

THE EARRINGS OF MADAME DE . . . , Franco-London Prods., Arlan Pictures (French): GEORGES ANNENKOV and ROSINE DELAMARE
EXECUTIVE SUITE, Metro-Goldwyn-Mayer: HELEN ROSE
INDISCRETION OF AN AMERICAN WIFE, A Vittorio DeSica Prod., Columbia: CHRISTIAN DIOR
IT SHOULD HAPPEN TO YOU, Columbia: JEAN LOUIS
SABRINA, Paramount: EDITH HEAD

(Color)

BRIGADOON, Metro-Goldwyn-Mayer: IRENE SHARAFF
DESIREE, 20th Century-Fox: CHARLES LeMAIRE and RENE HUBERT
GATE OF HELL, A Daiei Prod., Edward Harrison (Japanese): SANZO WADA
A STAR IS BORN, A Transcona Enterprises Prod., Warner Bros.: JEAN LOUIS, MARY ANN NYBERG and IRENE SHARAFF
THERE'S NO BUSINESS LIKE SHOW BUSINESS, 20th Century-Fox: CHARLES LeMAIRE, TRAVILLA and MILES WHITE

1955   Twenty-eighth Year
(Black-and-White)

I'LL CRY TOMORROW, Metro-Goldwyn-Mayer: HELEN ROSE
THE PICKWICK PAPERS, Renown Prod., Kingsley International Pictures (British): BEATRICE DAWSON

QUEEN BEE, Columbia: JEAN LOUIS
THE ROSE TATTOO, Hal Wallis, Paramount: EDITH HEAD
UGETSU, Daiei Motion Picture Co., Edward Harrison (Japanese): TADAOTO KAINOSCHO

(Color)

GUYS AND DOLLS, Samuel Goldwyn Prods., Inc., M-G-M: IRENE SHARAFF
INTERRUPTED MELODY, Metro-Goldwyn-Mayer: HELEN ROSE
LOVE IS A MANY-SPLENDORED THING, 20th Century-Fox: CHARLES LeMAIRE
TO CATCH A THIEF, Paramount: EDITH HEAD
THE VIRGIN QUEEN, 20th Century-Fox: CHARLES LeMAIRE and MARY WILLS

1956 Twenty-ninth Year
(Black-and-White)

THE MAGNIFICENT SEVEN, A Toho Prod., Kingsley International (Japanese): KOHEI EZAKI
THE POWER AND THE PRIZE, Metro-Goldwyn-Mayer: HELEN ROSE
THE PROUD AND THE PROFANE, The Perlberg-Seaton Prod., Paramount: EDITH HEAD
THE SOLID GOLD CADILLAC, Columbia: JEAN LOUIS
TEENAGE REBEL, 20th Century-Fox: CHARLES LeMAIRE and MARY WILLS

(Color)

AROUND THE WORLD IN 80 DAYS, The Michael Todd Co., Inc., UA: MILES WHITE
GIANT, Giant Prod., Warner Bros.: MOSS MABRY and MARJORIE BEST
THE KING AND I, 20th Century-Fox: IRENE SHARAFF
THE TEN COMMANDMENTS, Motion Picture Assoc., Inc., Paramount: EDITH HEAD, RALPH JESTER, JOHN JENSEN, DOROTHY JEAKINS and ARNOLD FRIBERG
WAR AND PEACE, A Ponti-De Laurentiis Prod., Paramount (Italo-American): MARIE DE MATTEIS

1957 Thirtieth Year

Note: Rules changed this year to one award for Costume Design instead of separate awards for black-and-white and color.

AN AFFAIR TO REMEMBER, Jerry Wald Prods., Inc., 20th Century-Fox: CHARLES LeMAIRE
FUNNY FACE, Paramount: EDITH HEAD and HUBERT DE GIVENCHY
LES GIRLS, Sol C. Siegel Prods., Inc., M-G-M: ORRY-KELLY
PAL JOEY, Essex-George Sidney Prod., Columbia: JEAN LOUIS
RAINTREE COUNTY, Metro-Goldwyn-Mayer: WALTER PLUNKETT

1958 Thirty-first Year

BELL, BOOK AND CANDLE, Phoenix Prods., Inc., Columbia: JEAN LOUIS
THE BUCCANEER, Cecil B. DeMille, Paramount: RALPH JESTER, EDITH HEAD and JOHN JENSEN
A CERTAIN SMILE, 20th Century-Fox: CHARLES LeMAIRE and MARY WILLS
GIGI, Arthur Freed Prods., Inc., M-G-M: CECIL BEATON
SOME CAME RUNNING, Sol C. Siegel Prods., Inc., M-G-M. WALTER PLUNKETT

1959 Thirty-second Year

Note: Rules changed this year to two awards for Costume Design: one for black-and-white and one for color.

(Black-and-White)

CAREER, Hal Wallis Prods., Paramount: EDITH HEAD

THE DIARY OF ANNE FRANK, 20th Century-Fox: CHARLES LeMAIRE and MARY WILLS

THE GAZEBO, Avon Prod., M-G-M: HELEN ROSE

SOME LIKE IT HOT, Ashton Prods. & The Mirisch Co., UA: ORRY-KELLY

THE YOUNG PHILADELPHIANS, Warner Bros.: HOWARD SHOUP

(Color)

BEN-HUR, Metro-Goldwyn-Mayer: ELIZABETH HAFFENDEN

THE BEST OF EVERYTHING, Company of Artists, Inc., 20th Century-Fox: ADELE PALMER

THE BIG FISHERMAN, Rowland V. Lee Prods., Buena Vista Film Dist. Co., Inc.: RENIE

THE FIVE PENNIES, Dena Prod., Paramount: EDITH HEAD

PORGY AND BESS, Samuel Goldwyn Prods., Columbia: IRENE SHARAFF

1960   Thirty-third Year

(Black-and-White)

THE FACTS OF LIFE, Panama & Frank Prod., UA: EDITH HEAD and EDWARD STEVENSON

NEVER ON SUNDAY, Melinafilm Prod., Lopert Pictures Corp. (Greek): DENNY VACHLIOTI

THE RISE AND FALL OF LEGS DIAMOND, United States Prod., Warner Bros.: HOWARD SHOUP

SEVEN THIEVES, 20th Century-Fox: BILL THOMAS

THE VIRGIN SPRING, Svensk Filmindustri Prod., Janus Films, Inc. (Swedish): MARIK VOS

(Color)

CAN-CAN, Suffolk-Cummings Prods., 20th Century-Fox: IRENE SHARAFF

MIDNIGHT LACE, Ross Hunter-Arwin Prod., U-I: IRENE

PEPE, G.S.-Posa Films International Prod., Columbia: EDITH HEAD

SPARTACUS, Bryna Prods., Inc., U-I: VALLES and BILL THOMAS

SUNRISE AT CAMPOBELLO, Schary Prod., Warner Bros.: MARJORIE BEST

1961   Thirty-fourth Year

(Black-and-White)

THE CHILDREN'S HOUR, Mirisch-Worldwide Prod., UA: DOROTHY JEAKINS

CLAUDELLE INGLISH, Warner Bros.: HOWARD SHOUP

JUDGMENT AT NUREMBERG, Stanley Kramer Prod., UA: JEAN LOUIS

LA DOLCE VITA, Riama Film Prod., Astor Pictures, Inc. (Italian): PIERO GHERARDI

YOJIMBO, Toho Company, Ltd. & Kurosawa Prod., Toho Company, Ltd. (Japanese): YOSHIRO MURAKI

(Color)

BABES IN TOYLAND, Walt Disney Prods., Buena Vista Distribution Co., Inc.: BILL THOMAS

BACK STREET, Universal-International-Ross Hunter Prods., Inc.-Carrollton, Inc., U-I: JEAN LOUIS

FLOWER DRUM SONG, Universal-International-Ross Hunter Prod. in association with Joseph Fields, U-I: IRENE SHARAFF

POCKETFUL OF MIRACLES, Franton Prod., UA: EDITH HEAD and WALTER PLUNKETT

WEST SIDE STORY, Mirisch Pictures, Inc. and B & P Enterprises, Inc., UA: IRENE SHARAFF

1962   Thirty-fifth Year

(Black-and-White)

DAYS OF WINE AND ROSES, Martin Manulis-Jalem Prod., Warner Bros.: DON FELD

THE MAN WHO SHOT LIBERTY VA-
LANCE, John Ford Prod., Paramount:
EDITH HEAD
THE MIRACLE WORKER, Playfilms
Prod., UA: RUTH MORLEY
PHAEDRA, Jules Dassin-Melinafilm
Prod., Lopert Pictures: DENNY
VACHLIOTI
WHAT EVER HAPPENED TO BABY
JANE?, Seven Arts-Associates &
Aldrich Co. Prod., Warner Bros.:
NORMA KOCH

(Color)

BON VOYAGE, Walt Disney Prod.,
Buena Vista Distribution Co.: BILL
THOMAS
GYPSY, Warner Bros.: ORRY-KELLY
MEREDITH WILLSON'S THE MUSIC MAN,
Warner Bros.: DOROTHY JEAKINS
MY GEISHA, Sachiko Prod., Paramount:
EDITH HEAD
THE WONDERFUL WORLD OF
THE BROTHERS GRIMM, Metro-
Goldwyn-Mayer & Cinerama:
MARY WILLS

1963   Thirty-sixty Year
(Black-and-White)
FEDERICO FELLINI'S 8½, Cineriz
Prod., Embassy Pictures: PIERO
GHERARDI
LOVE WITH THE PROPER STRANGER,
Boardwalk-Rona Prod., Paramount:
EDITH HEAD
THE STRIPPER, Jerry Wald Prods., 20th
Century-Fox: TRAVILLA
TOYS IN THE ATTIC, Mirisch-Claude
Prod., UA. BILL THOMAS
WIVES AND LOVERS, Hal Wallis Prod.,
Paramount: EDITH HEAD

(Color)

THE CARDINAL, Gamma Prod., Colum-
bia: DONALD BROOKS
CLEOPATRA, 20th Century-Fox Ltd.-
MCL Films S.A.-WALWA Films

S.A. Prod., 20th Century-Fox:
IRENE SHARAFF, VITTORIO
NINO NOVARESE and RENIE
HOW THE WEST WAS WON, Metro-
Goldwyn-Mayer & Cinerama:
WALTER PLUNKETT
THE LEOPARD, Titanus Prod., 20th
Century-Fox: PIERO TOSI
A NEW KIND OF LOVE, Llenroc Prods.,
Paramount: EDITH HEAD

1964   Thirty-seventh Year
(Black-and-White)
A HOUSE IS NOT A HOME, Clarence
Greene-Russell Rouse Prod., Em-
bassy Pictures: EDITH HEAD
HUSH . . . HUSH, SWEET CHARLOTTE,
Associates & Aldrich Prod., 20th
Century-Fox: NORMA KOCH
KISSES FOR MY PRESIDENT, Pearlayne
Prod., Warner Bros.: HOWARD
SHOUP
THE NIGHT OF THE IGUANA,
Seven Arts Prod., M-G-M:
DOROTHY JEAKINS
THE VISIT, Cinecitta-Dear Film-Les
Films du Siecle-P.E.C.S. Prod.,
20th Century-Fox: RENE HUBERT

(Color)

BECKET, Hal Wallis Prod., Paramount:
MARGARET FURSE
MARY POPPINS, Walt Disney Prods.:
TONY WALTON
MY FAIR LADY, Warner Bros.:
CECIL BEATON
THE UNSINKABLE MOLLY BROWN, Mar-
ten Prod., M-G-M: MORTON HAACK
WHAT A WAY TO GO, Apjac-Orchard
Prod., 20th Century-Fox: EDITH
HEAD and MOSS MABRY

1965   Thirty-eighth Year
(Black-and-White)
DARLING, Anglo-Amalgamated, Ltd.
Prod., Embassy: JULIE HARRIS

MORITURI, Arcola-Colony Prod., 20th Century-Fox: MOSS MABRY

A RAGE TO LIVE, Mirisch Corp. of Delaware-Araho Prod., United Artists: HOWARD SHOUP

SHIP OF FOOLS, Columbia: BILL THOMAS and JEAN LOUIS

THE SLENDER THREAD, Paramount: EDITH HEAD

(Color)

THE AGONY AND THE ECSTASY, International Classics Prod., 20th Century-Fox: VITTORIO NINO NOVARESE

DOCTOR ZHIVAGO, Sostar S.A.-Metro-Goldwyn-Mayer British Studios, Ltd. Prod., M-G-M: PHYLLIS DALTON

THE GREATEST STORY EVER TOLD, George Stevens Prod., United Artists. VITTORIO NINO NOVARESE and MARJORIE BEST

INSIDE DAISY CLOVER, Park Place Prod., Warner Bros.: EDITH HEAD and BILL THOMAS

THE SOUND OF MUSIC, Argyle Enterprises Prod., 20th Century-Fox: DOROTHY JEAKINS

1966 Thirty-ninth Year

(Black-and-White)

THE GOSPEL ACCORDING TO ST. MATTHEW, Arco-Lux Cie Cinematografique de France Prod., Walter Reade-Continental Distributing: DANILO DONATI

MANDRAGOLA, Europix-Consolidated: DANILO DONATI

MISTER BUDDWING, DDD-Cherokee Prod., M-G-M: HELEN ROSE

MORGAN!, Quintra Films, Ltd. Prod., Cinema V: JOCELYN RICKARDS

WHO'S AFRAID OF VIRGINIA WOOLF? Chenault Prod., Warner Bros.: IRENE SHARAFF

(Color)

GAMBIT, Universal: JEAN LOUIS

HAWAII, Mirisch Corp. of Delaware Prod., U.A.: DOROTHY JEAKINS

JULIET OF THE SPIRITS, Rizzoli Films S.P.A. Prod., Rizzoli Films: PIERO GHERARDI

A MAN FOR ALL SEASONS, Highland Films, Ltd. Prod., Columbia: ELIZABETH HAFFENDEN and JOAN BRIDGE

THE OSCAR, Greene-Rouse Prod., Embassy: EDITH HEAD

1967 Fortieth Year

Note: Rules changed this year to one award for Costume Design instead of separate awards for black-and-white and color.

BONNIE AND CLYDE, Tatira-Hiller Prod., Warner Bros.-Seven Arts: THEADORA VAN RUNKLE

CAMELOT, Warner Bros.-Seven Arts: JOHN TRUSCOTT

THE HAPPIEST MILLIONAIRE, Walt Disney Prods., Buena Vista Dist. Co.: BILL THOMAS

THE TAMING OF THE SHREW, Royal Films International-Films Artistici Internazionali S.r.L. Prod., Columbia: IRENE SHARAFF and DANILO DONATI

THOROUGHLY MODERN MILLIE, Ross Hunter-Universal Prod., Universal: JEAN LOUIS

1968 Forty-first Year

THE FRANCO ZEFFIRELLI PRODUCTION OF ROMEO & JULIET, B.H.E. Film-Verona Prod.-Dino De Laurentiis Cinematografica Prod., Paramount: DANILO DONATI

THE LION IN WINTER, Haworth Prods., Avco Embassy: MARGARET FURSE

OLIVER!, Romulus Films, Columbia: PHYLLIS DALTON

PLANET OF THE APES, APJAC Prods., 20th Century-Fox: MORTON HAACK

STAR!, Robert Wise Prod., 20th Century-Fox: DONALD BROOKS

1969   Forty-second Year

ANNE OF THE THOUSAND DAYS, Hal B. Wallis-Universal Pictures, Ltd. Prod., Universal: MARGARET FURSE

GAILY, GAILY, Mirisch-Cartier Prod., United Artists: RAY AGHAYAN

HELLO, DOLLY!, Chenault Prods., 20th Century-Fox: IRENE SHARAFF

SWEET CHARITY, Universal: EDITH HEAD

THEY SHOOT HORSES, DON'T THEY?, Chartoff-Winkler-Pollack Prod., ABC Pictures Presentation, Cinerama: DONFELD

1970   Forty-third Year

AIRPORT, Ross Hunter-Universal Prod., Universal: EDITH HEAD

CROMWELL, Irving Allen, Ltd. Prod., Columbia: NINO NO-VARESE

DARLING LILI, Geoffrey Prods., Paramount: DONALD BROOKS and JACK BEAR

THE HAWAIIANS, Mirisch Prods., United Artists: BILL THOMAS

SCROOGE, Waterbury Films, Ltd. Prod., Cinema Center Films Presentation, National General: MARGARET FURSE

1971   Forty-fourth Year

BEDKNOBS AND BROOMSTICKS, Walt Disney Prods., Buena Vista Distribution Company: BILL THOMAS

DEATH IN VENICE, An Alfa Cinematografica-P.E.C.F. Prod., Warner Bros.: PIERO TOSI

MARY, QUEEN OF SCOTS, A Hal Wallis-Universal Pictures, Ltd. Prod., Universal: MARGARET FURSE

NICHOLAS AND ALEXANDRA, A Horizon Pictures Prod., Columbia: YVONNE BLAKE and ANTONIO CASTILLO

WHAT'S THE MATTER WITH HELEN?, A Filmways-Raymax Prod., UA: MORTON HAACK

1972   Forty-fifth Year

THE GODFATHER, An Albert S. Ruddy Prod., Paramount: ANNA HILL JOHNSTONE

LADY SINGS THE BLUES, A Motown-Weston-Furie Prod., Paramount: BOB MACKIE, RAY AGHAYAN and NORMA KOCH

THE POSEIDON ADVENTURE, An Irwin Allen Prod., 20th Century-Fox: PAUL ZASTUPNEVICH

TRAVELS WITH MY AUNT, Robert Fryer Prods., Metro-Goldwyn-Mayer: ANTHONY POWELL

YOUNG WINSTON, An Open Road Films, Ltd. Prod., Columbia: ANTHONY MENDLESON

1973   Forty-sixth Year

CRIES AND WHISPERS, A Svenska Filminstitutet-Cinematograph AB Prod., New World Pictures: MARIK VOS

LUDWIG, A Mega Film S.p.A. Prod., Metro-Goldwyn-Mayer: PIERO TOSI

THE STING, A Universal-Bill/Phillips-George Roy Hill Film Prod., Zanuck/Brown Presentation, Universal: EDITH HEAD

TOM SAWYER, An Arthur P. Jacobs Prod., Reader's Digest Presentation, UA: DONFELD

THE WAY WE WERE, Rastar Prods., Columbia: DOROTHY JEAKINS and MOSS MABRY

1974   Forty-seventh Year

CHINATOWN, A Robert Evans Prod., Paramount: ANTHEA SYLBERT

DAISY MILLER, A Directors Company Prod., Paramount: JOHN FURNESS

THE GODFATHER PART II, A Coppola Company Prod., Paramount: THEADORA VAN RUNKLE

THE GREAT GATSBY, A David Merrick Prod., Paramount: THEONI V. ALDREDGE

Edith Head, holding her sketches for *The Sting* (1973) has an incredible thirty-four nominations and eight Costume Design Oscars to her credit. *Universal Pictures Photo*

MURDER ON THE ORIENT EXPRESS, A G.W. Films, Ltd. Prod., Paramount: TONY WALTON

1975 Forty-eighth Year

BARRY LYNDON, A Hawk Films, Ltd. Production, Warner Bros.: ULLA-BRITT SODERLUND and MILENA CANONERO

THE FOUR MUSKETEERS, A Film Trust S.A. Production, 20th Century-Fox: YVONNE BLAKE and RON TALSKY

FUNNY LADY, A Rastar Pictures Production, Columbia: RAY AGHAYAN and BOB MACKIE

THE MAGIC FLUTE, A Sveriges Radio A.B. Production, Surrogate Releasing: HENNY NOREMARK and KARIN ERSKINE

THE MAN WHO WOULD BE KING, An Allied Artists-Columbia Pictures Production, Allied Artists: EDITH HEAD

1976 Forty-ninth Year

BOUND FOR GLORY, The Bound For

Glory Company Production, United Artists: WILLIAM THEISS

FELLINI'S CASANOVA, A P.E.A.- Produzioni Europee Associate S. p.A. Production, Universal: DANILO DONATI

THE INCREDIBLE SARAH, A Helen M. Strauss-Reader's Digest Films, Ltd. Production, Seymour Borde & Associates: ANTHONY MENDLESON

THE PASSOVER PLOT, Coast Industries-Golan-Globus Productions, Ltd., Atlas Films: MARY WILLS

THE SEVEN-PER-CENT SOLUTION, A Herbert Ross Film/Winitsky-Sellers Production, A Universal Release: ALAN BARRETT

1977   Fiftieth year

AIRPORT '77, A Jennings Lang Production, Universal: EDITH HEAD and BURTON MILLER

JULIA, A Twentieth Century-Fox Production, Twentieth Century-Fox: ANTHEA SYLBERT

A LITTLE NIGHT MUSIC, A Sascha-Wien Film Production in association with Elliott Kastner, New World Pictures: FLORENCE KLOTZ

THE OTHER SIDE OF MIDNIGHT, A Frank Yablans Presentations Production, Twentieth Century-Fox: IRENE SHARAFF

STAR WARS, A Twentieth Century-Fox Production, Twentieth Century-Fox: JOHN MOLLO

SHORT FILMS

The fifth annual Academy Awards covering 1931/32 saw the introduction of a Short Subjects category. The popularity of Walt Disney's Mickey Mouse and Silly Symphony films may have played a part in the establishment of the new category, and Disney's *Flowers and Trees,* the first film ever made in three-color Technicolor, was the first winner in the cartoon division. Ten of the first eleven cartoon awards went to Disney films.

For the first four years the category was divided into cartoon, comedy, and novelty, but in 1936, spurred by the innovative use of color in short subjects, these divisions were changed to cartoon, one-reel, two-reel, and color. Within two years, however, the widespread use of Technicolor made the latter division superfluous, and it was dropped. The divisions were changed once again in 1957 to their present form, cartoon and live action. (The words "animated film" were substituted for cartoon in 1971.) The category's name was changed from Short Subjects to Short Films in 1974. Films of no more than 3000 35mm feet in length or the equivalents in 16mm or 70mm are considered short films. (At sound speed 35mm film moves at 90 feet per minute, so 3000 feet would equal 33⅓ minutes.) The distinction between Short Films—Live Actions and Documentary Short Subject is often moot. In 1971 *Sentinels of Silence* won in both categories. Rules now prevent this; if a film is eligible for either category, the producer of the film designates his choice of category when the film is submitted.

Entries in this category are submitted by the creators of the achievement and are screened by members of the Academy Short Films Branch who determine the nominees. Final voting is restricted to Academy members who attend a special screening of the nominated films.

1931/32   Fifth Year

(Cartoons)

FLOWERS AND TREES, Walt Disney, UA

MICKEY'S ORPHANS, Walt Disney, Columbia

IT'S GOT ME AGAIN, Leon Schlesinger, Warner Bros.

(Comedy)

THE LOUD MOUTH, Mack Sennett

THE MUSIC BOX, Hal Roach, M-G-M. (Laurel & Hardy)

STOUT HEARTS AND WILLING HANDS, RKO Radio. (Masquers Comedies)

LARGE CAPITAL LETTERS DENOTE WINNER

(Novelty)

SCREEN SOUVENIRS, Paramount

SWING HIGH, Metro-Goldwyn-Mayer. (Sport Champion)

WRESTLING SWORDFISH, Mack Sennett, Educational. (Cannibals Of The Deep)

1932/33   Sixth Year

(Cartoons)

BUILDING A BUILDING, Walt Disney, UA

THE MERRY OLD SOUL, Walter Lantz, Universal

206

THE THREE LITTLE PIGS, Walt Disney, UA

(Comedy)

MISTER MUGG, Universal. (Comedies)
PREFERRED LIST, RKO Radio. (Headliner Series #5)
SO THIS IS HARRIS, RKO Radio. (Special)

(Novelty)

KRAKATOA, Educational. (Three-reel Special)
MENU, Pete Smith, M-G-M. (Oddities)
THE SEA, Educational. (Battle For Life)

1934   Seventh Year

(Cartoons)

HOLIDAY LAND, Charles Mintz, Columbia
JOLLY LITTLE ELVES, Universal
THE TORTOISE AND THE HARE, Walt Disney

(Comedy)

LA CUCARACHA, RKO Radio. (Special)
MEN IN BLACK, Columbia. (Broadway Comedies)
WHAT, NO MEN!, Warner Bros. (Broadway Brevities)

(Novelty)

BOSOM FRIENDS, Educational. (Treasure Chest)
CITY OF WAX, Educational. (Battle For Life)
STRIKES AND SPARES, Metro-Goldwyn-Mayer. (Oddities)

1935. Eighth Year

(Cartoons)

THE CALICO DRAGON, Harman-Ising, M-G-M
THREE ORPHAN KITTENS, Walt Disney, UA
WHO KILLED COCK ROBIN?, Walt Disney, UA

(Comedy)

HOW TO SLEEP, Metro-Goldwyn-Mayer. (Miniature)
OH, MY NERVES, Columbia. (Broadway Comedies)
TIT FOR TAT, Hal Roach, M-G-M. (Laurel & Hardy)

(Novelty)

AUDIOSCOPIKS, Metro-Goldwyn-Mayer. (Special)
CAMERA THRILLS, Universal. (Special)
WINGS OVER MT. EVEREST, Educational. (Special)

1936   Ninth Year

(Cartoons)

COUNTRY COUSIN, Walt Disney, UA
OLD MILL POND, Harman-Ising, M-G-M
SINBAD THE SAILOR, Paramount

(One-reel)

BORED OF EDUCATION, Hal Roach, M-G-M. (Our Gang)
MOSCOW MOODS, Paramount. (Headliners)
WANTED, A MASTER, Pete Smith, M-G-M. (Pete Smith Specialties)

(Two-reel)

DOUBLE OR NOTHING, Warner Bros. (Broadway Brevities)
DUMMY ACHE, RKO Radio. (Edgar Kennedy Comedies)
THE PUBLIC PAYS, Metro-Goldwyn-Mayer. (Crime Doesn't Pay)

(Color)

GIVE ME LIBERTY, Warner Bros. (Broadway Brevities)
LA FIESTA DE SANTA BARBARA, Metro-Goldwyn-Mayer. (Musical Revues)
POPULAR SCIENCE J-6-2, Paramount.

1937   Tenth Year

(Cartoons)

EDUCATED FISH, Paramount

THE LITTLE MATCH GIRL, Charles
Mintz, Columbia
THE OLD MILL, Walt Disney, RKO
Radio

(One-Reel)

A NIGHT AT THE MOVIES, Metro-
Goldwyn-Mayer. (Robert Benchley)
PRIVATE LIFE OF THE GANNETS,
Educational
ROMANCE OF RADIUM, Pete Smith,
M-G-M. (Pete Smith Specialties)

(Two-reel)

DEEP SOUTH, RKO Radio. (Radio Musi-
cal Comedies)
SHOULD WIVES WORK, RKO Radio.
(Leon Errol Comedies)
TORTURE MONEY, Metro-Goldwyn-
Mayer. (Crime Doesn't Pay)

(Color)

THE MAN WITHOUT A COUNTRY, Warner
Bros. (Broadway Brevities)
PENNY WISDOM, Pete Smith,
M-G-M. (Pete Smith Specialties)
POPULAR SCIENCE J-7-1, Paramount

1938   Eleventh Year

(Cartoons)

BRAVE LITTLE TAILOR, Walt Disney,
RKO Radio
MOTHER GOOSE GOES HOLLYWOOD,
Walt Disney, RKO Radio
FERDINAND THE BULL, Walt Dis-
ney, RKO Radio
GOOD SCOUTS, Walt Disney, RKO
Radio
HUNKY AND SPUNKY, Paramount

(One-reel)

THE GREAT HEART, Metro-Goldwyn-
Mayer. (Miniature)
THAT MOTHERS MIGHT LIVE,
Metro-Goldwyn-Mayer. (Miniature)
TIMBER TOPPERS, 20th Century-Fox. (Ed
Thorgensen-Sports)

(Two-reel)

DECLARATION OF INDEPEN-
DENCE, Warner Bros. (Historical
Featurette)
SWINGTIME IN THE MOVIES, Warner
Bros. (Broadway Brevities)
THEY'RE ALWAYS CAUGHT, Metro-
Goldwyn-Mayer. (Crime Doesn't
Pay)

1939   Twelfth Year

(Cartoons)

DETOURING AMERICA, Warner Bros.
PEACE ON EARTH, Metro-Goldwyn-
Mayer
THE POINTER, Walt Disney, RKO Radio
THE UGLY DUCKLING, Walt Dis-
ney, RKO Radio

(One-reel)

BUSY LITTLE BEARS, Paramount.
(Paragraphics)
INFORMATION PLEASE, RKO Radio
PROPHET WITHOUT HONOR, Metro-
Goldwyn-Mayer. (Miniature)
SWORD FISHING, Warner Bros.
(Vitaphone Varieties)

(Two-reel)

DRUNK DRIVING, Metro-Goldwyn-
Mayer. (Crime Doesn't Pay)
FIVE TIMES FIVE, RKO Radio. (Special)
SONS OF LIBERTY, Warner Bros.
(Historical Featurette)

1940   Thirteenth Year

(Cartoons)

MILKY WAY, Metro-Goldwyn-
Mayer. (Rudolph Ising Series)
PUSS GETS THE BOOT, Metro-Goldwyn-
Mayer. (Cat and Mouse Series)
A WILD HARE, Leon Schlesinger,
Warner Bros.

(One-reel)

LONDON CAN TAKE IT, Warner Bros.
(Vitaphone Varieties)

MORE ABOUT NOSTRADAMUS, Metro-Goldwyn-Mayer

QUICKER 'N A WINK, Pete Smith, M-G-M

SIEGE, RKO Radio. (Reelism)

(Two-reel)

EYES OF THE NAVY, Metro-Goldwyn-Mayer. (Crime Doesn't Pay)

SERVICE WITH THE COLORS, Warner Bros. (National Defense Series)

TEDDY, THE ROUGH RIDER, Warner Bros. (Historical Featurette)

1941 Fourteenth Year

(Cartoons)

BOOGIE WOOGIE BUGLE BOY OF COMPANY B, Walter Lantz, Universal

HIAWATHA'S RABBIT HUNT, Leon Schlesinger, Warner Bros.

HOW WAR CAME, Columbia. (Raymond Gram Swing Series)

LEND A PAW, Walt Disney, RKO Radio

THE NIGHT BEFORE CHRISTMAS, Metro-Goldwyn-Mayer. (Tom and Jerry Series)

RHAPSODY IN RIVETS, Leon Schlesinger, Warner Bros.

THE ROOKIE BEAR, Metro-Goldwyn-Mayer. (Bear Series)

RHYTHM IN THE RANKS, Paramount. (George Pal Puppetoon Series)

SUPERMAN NO. 1, Paramount.

TRUANT OFFICER DONALD, Walt Disney, RKO Radio

(One-reel)

ARMY CHAMPIONS, Pete Smith, M-G-M. (Pete Smith Specialties)

BEAUTY AND THE BEACH, Paramount. (Headliner Series)

DOWN ON THE FARM, Paramount. (Speaking Of Animals)

FORTY BOYS AND A SONG, Warner Bros. (Melody Master Series)

KINGS OF THE TURF, Warner Bros. (Color Parade Series)

OF PUPS AND PUZZLES, Metro-Goldwyn-Mayer. (Passing Parade Series)

SAGEBRUSH AND SILVER, 20th Century-Fox. (Magic Carpet Series)

(Two-reel)

ALIVE IN THE DEEP, Woodard Productions, Inc.

FORBIDDEN PASSAGE, Metro-Goldwyn-Mayer. (Crime Doesn't Pay)

THE GAY PARISIAN, Warner Bros. (Miniature Featurette Series)

MAIN STREET ON THE MARCH, Metro-Goldwyn-Mayer. (Two-reel Special)

THE TANKS ARE COMING, Warner Bros. (National Defense Series)

1942 Fifteenth Year

(Cartoons)

ALL OUT FOR V, 20th Century-Fox

THE BLITZ WOLF, Metro-Goldwyn-Mayer

DER FUEHRER'S FACE, Walt Disney, RKO Radio

JUKE BOX JAMBOREE, Walt Lantz, Universal

PIGS IN A POLKA, Leon Schlesinger, Warner Bros.

TULIPS SHALL GROW, Paramount. (George Pal Puppetoon)

(One-reel)

DESERT WONDERLAND, 20th Century-Fox. (Magic Carpet Series)

MARINES IN THE MAKING, Metro-Goldwyn-Mayer. (Pete Smith Specialties)

SPEAKING OF ANIMALS AND THEIR FAMILIES. Paramount. (Speaking Of Animals)

UNITED STATES MARINE BAND, Warner Bros. (Melody Master Bands)

(Two-reel)

BEYOND THE LINE OF DUTY,
Warner Bros. (Broadway Brevities)
DON'T TALK, Metro-Goldwyn-Mayer.
(Two-reel Special)
PRIVATE SMITH OF THE U.S.A., RKO
Radio. (This Is America Series)

1943   Sixteenth Year
(Cartoons)

THE DIZZY ACROBAT, Walter Lantz,
Universal: WALTER LANTZ, Producer
THE FIVE HUNDRED HATS OF BARTHO-
LOMEW CUBBINS, Paramount.
(George Pal Puppetoon)
GREETINGS, BAIT, Warner Bros.: LEON
SCHLESINGER, Producer
IMAGINATION, Columbia: DAVE FLEI-
SCHER, Producer
REASON AND EMOTION, Walt Disney,
RKO Radio: WALT DISNEY, Producer
YANKEE DOODLE MOUSE, Metro-
Goldwyn-Mayer: FREDERICK
QUIMBY, Producer

(One-reel)

AMPHIBIOUS FIGHTERS, Para-
mount: GRANTLAND RICE, Pro-
ducer
CAVALCADE OF THE DANCE WITH VELOZ
AND YOLANDA, Warner Bros. (Mel-
ody Master Bands): GORDON HOLL-
INGSHEAD, Producer
CHAMPIONS CARRY ON, 20th Century-
Fox: (Sports Reviews) EDMUND
REEK, Producer
HOLLYWOOD IN UNIFORM, Columbia:
(Screen Snapshots #1, Series 22)
RALPH STAUB, Producer
SEEING HANDS, Metro-Goldwyn-Mayer.
(Pete Smith Specialty)

(Two-reel)

HEAVENLY MUSIC, Metro-
Goldwyn-Mayer: JERRY BRESLER
and SAM COSLOW, Producers
LETTER TO A HERO, RKO Radio: (This

Is America) FRED ULLMAN, Producer
MARDI GRAS, Paramount: (Musical Pa-
rade) WALTER MACEWEN, Producer
WOMEN AT WAR, Warner Bros.: (Tech-
nicolor Special) GORDON HOLLINGS-
HEAD, Producer

1944   Seventeenth Year
(Cartoons)

AND TO THINK I SAW IT ON MULBERRY
STREET, Paramount. (George Pal
Puppetoon)
THE DOG, CAT AND CANARY, Columbia.
(Screen Gems)
FISH FRY, Universal: WALTER LANTZ,
Producer
HOW TO PLAY FOOTBALL, Walt Disney,
RKO Radio: WALT DISNEY, Producer
MOUSE TROUBLE, Metro-Goldwyn-
Mayer: FREDERICK C. QUIMBY,
Producer
MY BOY, JOHNNY, 20th Century-Fox:
PAUL TERRY, Producer
SWOONER CROONER, Warner Bros.

(One-reel)

BLUE GRASS GENTLEMEN, 20th Century-
Fox. (Sports Review): EDMUND REEK,
Producer
JAMMIN' THE BLUES, Warner Bros.
(Melody Master Bands): GORDON
HOLLINGSHEAD, Producer
MOVIE PESTS, Metro-Goldwyn-Mayer.
(Pete Smith Specialty)
50TH ANNIVERSARY OF MOTION PIC-
TURES, Columbia. (Screen Snapshots
#9, Series 23): RALPH STAUB, Pro-
ducer
WHO'S WHO IN ANIMAL LAND,
Paramount. (Speaking Of Animals):
JERRY FAIRBANKS, Producer

(Two-reel)

BOMBALERA, Paramount. (Musical Parade): LOUIS HARRIS, Producer
I WON'T PLAY, Warner Bros: (Featurette) GORDON HOLLINGS-
HEAD, Producer

MAIN STREET TODAY, Metro-Goldwyn-Mayer: (Two-reel Special) JERRY BRESLER, Producer

1945   Eighteenth Year

(Cartoons)

DONALD'S CRIME, Walt Disney, RKO Radio. (Donald Duck): WALT DISNEY, Producer

JASPER AND THE BEANSTALK, Paramount. (Pal Puppetoon-Jasper Series): GEORGE PAL, Producer

LIFE WITH FEATHERS, Warner Bros. (Merrie Melodies): EDDIE SELZER, Producer

MIGHTY MOUSE IN GYPSY LIFE, 20th Century-Fox. (Terrytoon): PAUL TERRY, Producer

POET AND PEASANT, Universal. (Lantz Technicolor Cartune): WALTER LANTZ, Producer

QUIET PLEASE, Metro-Goldwyn-Mayer. (Tom & Jerry Series): FREDERICK QUIMBY, Producer

RIPPLING ROMANCE, Columbia. (Color Rhapsodies)

(One-reel)

ALONG THE RAINBOW TRAIL, 20th Century-Fox. (Movietone Adventure): EDMUND REEK, Producer

SCREEN SNAPSHOTS 25TH ANNIVERSARY, Columbia. (Screen Snapshots): RALPH STAUB, Producer

STAIRWAY TO LIGHT, Metro-Goldwyn-Mayer: (John Nesbitt Passing Parade): HERBERT MOULTON, Producer

STORY OF A DOG, Warner Bros.: (Vitaphone Varieties): GORDON HOLLINGSHEAD, Producer

WHITE RHAPSODY, Paramount: (Sportlights) GRANTLAND RICE, Producer

YOUR NATIONAL GALLERY, Universal: (Variety Views) JOSEPH O'BRIEN and THOMAS MEAD, Producers

(Two-reel)

A GUN IN HIS HAND, Metro-Goldwyn-Mayer: (Crime Does Not Pay) CHESTER FRANKLIN, Producer

THE JURY GOES ROUND 'N' ROUND, Columbia: (All Star Comedies) JULES WHITE, Producer

THE LITTLE WITCH, Paramount: (Musical Parade) GEORGE TEMPLETON, Producer

STAR IN THE NIGHT, Warner Bros.: (Broadway Brevities) GORDON HOLLINGSHEAD, Producer

1946   Nineteenth Year

(Cartoons)

THE CAT CONCERTO, Metro-Goldwyn-Mayer. (Tom & Jerry): FREDERICK QUIMBY, Producer

CHOPIN'S MUSICAL MOMENTS, Universal. (Musical Miniatures): WALTER LANTZ, Producer

JOHN HENRY AND THE INKY POO, Paramount. (Puppetoon): GEORGE PAL, Producer

SQUATTER'S RIGHTS, Disney-RKO Radio. (Mickey Mouse): WALT DISNEY, Producer

WALKY TALKY HAWKY, Warner Bros. (Merrie Melodies): EDWARD SELZER, Producer

(One-reel)

DIVE-HI CHAMPS, Paramount. (Sportlights) JACK EATON, Producer

FACING YOUR DANGER, Warner Bros. (Sports Parade) GORDON HOLLINGSHEAD, Producer

GOLDEN HORSES, 20th Century-Fox. (Movietone Sports Review) EDMUND REEK, Producer

SMART AS A FOX, Warner Bros. (Varieties) GORDON HOLLINGSHEAD, Producer

SURE CURES, Metro-Goldwyn-Mayer. (Pete Smith Specialty) PETE SMITH, Producer

(Two-reel)

A BOY AND HIS DOG, Warner Bros. (Featurettes) GORDON HOLLINGS-HEAD, Producer

COLLEGE QUEEN, Paramount. (Musical Parade) GEORGE TEMPLETON, Producer

HISS AND YELL, Columbia. (All Star Comedies) JULES WHITE, Producer

THE LUCKIEST GUY IN THE WORLD, Metro-Goldwyn-Mayer. (Two-reel Special) JERRY BRESLER, Producer

1947   Twentieth Year

(Cartoons)

CHIP AN' DALE, Walt Disney, RKO Radio. (Donald Duck) WALT DISNEY, Producer

DR. JEKYLL AND MR. MOUSE, Metro-Goldwyn-Mayer. (Tom & Jerry) FREDERICK QUIMBY, Producer

PLUTO'S BLUE NOTE, Walt Disney, RKO Radio. (Pluto) WALT DISNEY, Producer

TUBBY THE TUBA, Paramount. (George Pal Puppetoon) GEORGE PAL, Producer

TWEETIE PIE, Warner Bros. (Merrie Melodies) EDWARD SELZER, Producer

(One-reel)

BROOKLYN, U.S.A.., Universal-International. (Variety Series) THOMAS MEAD, Producer

GOODBYE MISS TURLOCK, Metro-Goldwyn-Mayer. (John Nesbitt Passing Parade) HERBERT MOULTON, Producer

MOON ROCKETS, Paramount. (Popular Science) Jerry Fairbanks, Producer

NOW YOU SEE IT, Metro-Goldwyn-Mayer. PETE SMITH, Producer

SO YOU WANT TO BE IN PICTURES, Warner Bros. (Joe McDoakes) GORDON HOLLINGSHEAD, Producer

(Two-reel)

CHAMPAGNE FOR TWO, Paramount. (Musical Parade Featurette) HARRY GREY, Producer

CLIMBING THE MATTERHORN, Monogram. (Color) IRVING ALLEN, Producer

FIGHT OF THE WILD STALLIONS, Universal-International. (Special) THOMAS MEAD, Producer

GIVE US THE EARTH, Metro-Goldwyn-Mayer. (Special) HERBERT MORGAN, Producer

A VOICE IS BORN, Columbia. (Musical Featurette) BEN BLAKE, Producer

1948   Twenty-first Year

(Cartoons)

THE LITTLE ORPHAN, Metro-Goldwyn-Mayer. (Tom & Jerry) FRED QUIMBY, Producer

MICKEY AND THE SEAL, Walt Disney, RKO Radio. (Pluto) WALT DISNEY, Producer

MOUSE WRECKERS, Warner Bros. (Looney Tunes) EDWARD SELZER, Producer

ROBIN HOODLUM, United Productions Of America, Columbia. (Fox & Crow) UNITED PRODUCTIONS OF AMERICA, Producer

TEA FOR TWO HUNDRED, Walt Disney, RKO Radio. (Donald Duck) WALT DISNEY, Producer

(One-reel)

ANNIE WAS A WONDER, Metro-Goldwyn-Mayer. (John Nesbitt Passing Parade) HERBERT MOULTON, Producer

CINDERELLA HORSE, Warner Bros. (Sports Parade) GORDON HOLLINGSHEAD, Producer

SO YOU WANT TO BE ON THE RADIO, Warner Bros. (Joe McDoakes) GORDON HOLLINGSHEAD, Producer

SYMPHONY OF A CITY, 20th Century-Fox. (Movietone Specialty) EDMUND H. REEK, Producer

YOU CAN'T WIN, Metro-Goldwyn-Mayer. (Pete Smith Specialty) PETE SMITH, Producer

(Two-reel)

CALGARY STAMPEDE, Warner Bros. (Technicolor Special) GORDON HOLLINGSHEAD, Producer

GOING TO BLAZES, Metro-Goldwyn-Mayer. (Special) HERBERT MORGAN, Producer

SAMBA-MANIA, Paramount. (Musical Parade) HARRY GREY, Producer

SEAL ISLAND, Walt Disney, RKO Radio. (True Life Adventure Series) WALT DISNEY, Producer

SNOW CAPERS, Universal-International. (Special Series) THOMAS MEAD, Producer

1949   Twenty-second Year

(Cartoons)

FOR SCENT-IMENTAL REASONS, Warner Bros. (Looney Tunes) EDWARD SELZER, Producer

HATCH UP YOUR TROUBLES, Metro-Goldwyn-Mayer. (Tom & Jerry) FRED QUIMBY, Producer

MAGIC FLUKE, United Productions Of America, Columbia. (Fox & Crow) STEPHEN BOSUSTOW, Producer

TOY TINKERS, Walt Disney, RKO Radio. WALT DISNEY, Producer

(One-reel)

AQUATIC HOUSE-PARTY, Paramount. (Grantland Rice Sportlights) JACK EATON, Producer

ROLLER DERBY GIRL, Paramount. (Pacemaker) JUSTIN HERMAN, Producer

SO YOU THINK YOU'RE NOT GUILTY, Warner Bros. (Joe McDoakes) GORDON HOLLINGSHEAD, Producer

SPILLS AND CHILLS, Warner Bros.

(Black-and-White Sports Review) WALTON C. AMENT, Producer

WATER TRIX, Metro-Goldwyn-Mayer. (Pete Smith Specialty) PETE SMITH, Producer

(Two-reel)

BOY AND THE EAGLE, RKO Radio. WILLIAM LASKY, Producer

CHASE OF DEATH, Irving Allen Productions. (Color Series) IRVING ALLEN, Producer

THE GRASS IS ALWAYS GREENER, Warner Bros. (Black-and-White) GORDON HOLLINGSHEAD, Producer

SNOW CARNIVAL, Warner Bros. (Technicolor) GORDON HOLLINGSHEAD, Producer

VAN GOGH, Canton-Weiner. GASTON DIEHL and ROBERT HAESSENS, Producers

1950   Twenty-third Year

(Cartoons)

GERALD McBOING-BOING, United Productions Of America, Columbia. (Joly Frolics Series) STEPHEN BOSUSTOW, Executive Producer

JERRY'S COUSIN, Metro-Goldwyn-Mayer. (Tom & Jerry) FRED QUIMBY, Producer

TROUBLE INDEMNITY, United Productions Of America, Columbia. (Mr. Magoo Series) STEPHEN BOSUSTOW, Executive Producer

(One-reel)

BLAZE BUSTERS, Warner Bros. (Vitaphone Novelties) ROBERT YOUNGSON, Producer

GRANDAD OF RACES, Warner Bros. (Sports Parade) GORDON HOLLINGSHEAD, Producer

WRONG WAY BUTCH, Metro-Goldwyn-Mayer. PETE SMITH, Producer

(Two-reel)

GRANDMA MOSES, Falcon Films, Inc.,

A.F. Films. FALCON FILMS, INC., Producer

IN BEAVER VALLEY, Walt Disney, RKO Radio. (True-Life Adventure) WALT DISNEY, Producer

MY COUNTRY 'TIS OF THEE, Warner Bros. (Featurette Series) GORDON HOLLINGSHEAD, Producer

1951   Twenty-fourth Year
(Cartoons)

LAMBERT, THE SHEEPISH LION, Walt Disney, RKO Radio. (Special) WALT DISNEY, Producer

ROOTY TOOT TOOT, United Productions of America, Columbia. (Jolly Frolics) STEPHEN BOSUSTOW, Executive Producer

TWO MOUSEKETEERS, Metro-Goldwyn-Mayer. (Tom & Jerry) FRED QUIMBY, Producer

(One-reel)

RIDIN' THE RAILS, Paramount. (Sportlights) JACK EATON, Producer

THE STORY OF TIME, A Signal Films Production by ROBERT G. LEFFINGWELL, Cornell Film Company (British)

WORLD OF KIDS, Warner Bros. (Vitaphone Novelties) ROBERT YOUNGSON, Producer

(Two-reel)

BALZAC, Les Films Du Compass, A.F. Films, Inc. (French) LES FILMS DU COMPASS, Producer

DANGER UNDER THE SEA, Universal-International. TOM MEAD, Producer

NATURE'S HALF ACRE, Walt Disney, RKO Radio. (True-Life Adventure) WALT DISNEY, Producer

1952   Twenty-fifth Year
(Cartoons)

JOHANN MOUSE, Metro-Goldwyn-Mayer. (Tom & Jerry) FRED QUIMBY, Producer

LITTLE JOHNNY JET, Metro-Goldwyn-Mayer. (M-G-M Series) FRED QUIMBY, Producer

MADELINE, UPA, Columbia. (Jolly Frolics) STEPHEN BOSUSTOW, Executive Producer

PINK AND BLUE BLUES, UPA, Columbia. (Mister Magoo) STEPHEN BOSUSTOW, Executive Producer

ROMANCE OF TRANSPORTATION, National Film Board Of Canada (Canadian). TOM DALY, Producer.

(One-reel)

ATHLETES OF THE SADDLE, Paramount. (Sportlights Series) JACK EATON, Producer

DESERT KILLER, Warner Bros. (Sports Parade) GORDON HOLLINGSHEAD, Producer

LIGHT IN THE WINDOW, Art Films Prods., 20th Century-Fox. (Art Series) BORIS VERMONT, Producer

NEIGHBOURS, National Film Board Of Canada (Canadian) NORMAN MCLAREN, Producer

ROYAL SCOTLAND, Crown Film Unit, British Information Services (British)

(Two-reel)

BRIDGE OF TIME, A London Film Prod., British Information Services (British)

DEVIL TAKE US, A Theatre Of Life Prod. (Theatre Of Life Series) HERBERT MORGAN, Producer

THAR SHE BLOWS!, Warner Bros. (Technicolor Special) GORDON HOLLINGSHEAD, Producer

WATER BIRDS, Walt Disney, RKO Radio. (True-Life Adventure) WALT DISNEY, Producer

1953   Twenty-sixth Year
(Cartoons)

CHRISTOPHER CRUMPET, UPA, Columbia. (Jolly Frolics) STEPHEN BOSUSTOW, Producer

FROM A TO Z-Z-Z-Z, Warner Bros. Cartoons, Inc., Warner Bros. (Looney Tunes) EDWARD SELZER, Producer

RUGGED BEAR, Walt Disney, RKO Radio. (Donald Duck) WALT DISNEY, Producer

THE TELL TALE HEART, UPA, Columbia. (UPA Cartoon Special) STEPHEN BOSUSTOW, Producer

TOOT, WHISTLE, PLUNK AND BOOM, Walt Disney, Buena Vista Film Distribution Co., Inc. (Special Music Series) WALT DISNEY, Producer

(One-reel)

CHRIST AMONG THE PRIMITIVES, IFE Releasing Corp. (Italian). VINCENZO LUCCI-CHIARISSI, Producer

HERRING HUNT, National Film Board Of Canada, RKO Pathe, Inc. (Canadian). (Canada Carries On Series)

JOY OF LIVING, Art Film Prods., 20th Century-Fox. (Art Film Series) BORIS VERMONT, Producer

THE MERRY WIVES OF WINDSOR OVERTURE, Metro-Goldwyn-Mayer. (Overture Series) JOHNNY GREEN, Producer

WEE WATER WONDERS, Paramount. (Grantland Rice Sportlights Series) JACK EATON, Producer

(Two-reel)

BEAR COUNTRY, Walt Disney, RKO Radio. (True-Life Adventure) WALT DISNEY, Producer

BEN AND ME, Walt Disney, Buena Vista Film Distribution Co., Inc. (Cartoon Special Series) WALT DISNEY, Producer

RETURN TO GLENNASCAUL, Dublin Gate Theatre Prod., Mayor-Kingsley Inc.

VESUVIUS EXPRESS, 20th Century-Fox. (CinemaScope Shorts Series) OTTO LANG, Producer

WINTER PARADISE, Warner Bros.

(Technicolor Special) CEDRIC FRANCIS, Producer

1954   Twenty-seventh Year
(Cartoons)

CRAZY MIXED UP PUP, Walter Lantz Prods., U-I. WALTER LANTZ, Producer

PIGS IS PIGS, Walt Disney Prods., RKO Radio. WALT DISNEY, Producer

SANDY CLAWS, Warner Bros. Cartoons, Inc. EDWARD SELZER, Producer

TOUCHE, PUSSY CAT, Metro-Goldwyn-Mayer. FRED QUIMBY, Producer

WHEN MAGOO FLEW, United Productions Of America, Columbia. STEPHEN BOSUSTOW, Producer

(One-reel)

THE FIRST PIANO QUARTETTE, 20th Century-Fox. OTTO LANG, Producer

THE STRAUSS FANTASY, Metro-Goldwyn-Mayer. JOHNNY GREEN, Producer

THIS MECHANICAL AGE, Warner Bros. ROBERT YOUNGSON, Producer

(Two-reel)

BEAUTY AND THE BULL, Warner Bros. CEDRIC FRANCIS, Producer

JET CARRIER, 20th Century-Fox. OTTO LANG, Producer

SIAM, Walt Disney Prods., Buena Vista Film Distribution Co., Inc. WALT DISNEY, Producer

A TIME OUT OF WAR, Carnival Prods., DENIS and TERRY SANDERS, Producers

1955   Twenty-eighth Year
(Cartoons)

GOOD WILL TO MEN, Metro-Goldwyn-Mayer. FRED QUIMBY, WILLIAM HANNA and JOSEPH BARBERA, Producers

THE LEGEND OF ROCK-A-BYE-POINT,

215

A Time Out of War received the 1954 Oscar for the Short Subject—Two Reel category. *Pyramid Films Photo*

Walter Lantz Prods., U-I. WALTER LANTZ, Producer

NO HUNTING, Walt Disney Prods., RKO Radio. WALT DISNEY, Producer

SPEEDY GONZALES, Warner Bros. Cartoons, Inc. EDWARD SELZER, Producer

(One-reel)

GADGETS GALORE, Warner Bros. ROBERT YOUNGSON, Producer

SURVIVAL CITY, 20th Century-Fox. EDMUND REEK, Producer

3RD AVE. EL, Carson Davidson Prods., Ardee Films. CARSON DAVIDSON, Producer

THREE KISSES, Paramount. JUSTIN HERMAN, Producer

(Two-reel)

THE BATTLE OF GETTYSBURG, Metro-Goldwyn-Mayer. DORE SCHARY, Producer

THE FACE OF LINCOLN, University Of Southern California Presentation, Cavalcade Pictures, Inc. WILBUR T. BLUME, Producer

ON THE TWELFTH DAY . . ., Go Pictures, Inc., George Brest & Assocs. GEORGE K. ARTHUR, Producer

SWITZERLAND, Walt Disney Prods., Buena Vista Film Distribution Co., Inc. WALT DISNEY, Producer

TWENTY-FOUR HOUR ALERT, Warner Bros. CEDRIC FRANCIS, Producer

1956   Twenty-ninth Year

(Cartoons)

GERALD MCBOING-BOING ON PLANET MOO, UPA Pictures, Columbia. STEPHEN BOSUSTOW, Producer

THE JAYWALKER, UPA Pictures, Columbia. STEPHEN BOSUSTOW, Producer

MISTER MAGOO'S PUDDLE JUMPER, UPA Pictures, Columbia. STEPHEN BOSUSTOW, Producer

(One-reel)

CRASHING THE WATER BARRIER, Warner Bros. KONSTANTIN KALSER, Producer

I NEVER FORGET A FACE, Warner Bros. ROBERT YOUNGSON, Producer

TIME STOOD STILL, Warner Bros. CEDRIC FRANCIS, Producer

(Two-reel)

THE BESPOKE OVERCOAT, George K. Arthur. ROMULUS FILMS, Producer

COW DOG, Walt Disney Prods., Buena Vista Film Distribution Co., Inc. LARRY LANSBURGH, Producer

THE DARK WAVE, 20th Century-Fox. JOHN HEALY, Producer

SAMOA, Walt Disney Prods., Buena Vista Film Distribution Co., Inc. WALT DISNEY, Producer

1957   Thirtieth Year

Note: Rules changed this year to two awards for Short Subjects instead of three as previously given

(Cartoons)

BIRDS ANONYMOUS, Warner Bros. EDWARD SELZER, Producer

ONE DROOPY KNIGHT, Metro-Goldwyn-Mayer. WILLIAM HANNA and JOSEPH BARBERA, Producers

TABASCO ROAD, Warner Bros. EDWARD SELZER, Producer

TREES and JAMAICA DADDY, UPA Pictures, Columbia. STEPHEN BOUSUSTOW, Producer

THE TRUTH ABOUT MOTHER GOOSE, Walt Disney Prods., Buena Vista Film Distribution Co., Inc. WALT DISNEY, Producer

(Live Action Subjects)

A CHAIRY TALE, National Film Board Of Canada, Kingsley International Pictures Corp. NORMAN MCLAREN, Producer

CITY OF GOLD, National Film Board Of Canada, Kingsley International Pictures Corp. TOM DALY, Producer

FOOTHOLD ON ANTARCTICA, World Wide Pictures, Lester A. Schoenfeld Films. JAMES CARR, Producer

PORTUGAL, Walt Disney Prods., Buena Vista Film Distribution Co., Inc. BEN SHARPSTEEN, Producer

THE WETBACK HOUND, Walt Disney Prods., Buena Vista Film Distribution Co., Inc. LARRY LANSBURGH, Producer

1958   Thirty-first Year

(Cartoons)

KNIGHTY KNIGHT BUGS, Warner Bros. JOHN W. BURTON, Producer

PAUL BUNYAN, Walt Disney Prods., Buena Vista Film Distribution Co., Inc. WALT DISNEY, Producer

SIDNEY'S FAMILY TREE, Terrytoons, 20th Century-Fox. WILLIAM M. WEISS, Producer

(Live Action Subjects)

GRAND CANYON, Walt Disney Prods., Buena Vista Film Distribution Co., Inc. WALT DISNEY, Producer

JOURNEY INTO SPRING, British Transport Films, Lester A. Schoenfeld Films. IAN FERGUSON, Producer

THE KISS, Cohay Prods., Continental Distributing, Inc. JOHN PATRICK HAYES, Producer

SNOWS OF AORANGI, New Zealand Screen Board, GEORGE BREST ASSOCIATES

T IS FOR TUMBLEWEED, Continental Distributing, Inc. JAMES A. LEBENTHAL, Producer

1959   Thirty-second Year
(Cartoons)

MEXICALI SHMOES, Warner Bros. JOHN W. BURTON, Producer

MOONBIRD, Storyboard, Inc., EDWARD HARRISON and JOHN HUBLEY, Producers

NOAH'S ARK, Walt Disney Prods., Buena Vista Film Distribution Co., Inc. WALT DISNEY, Producer

THE VIOLINIST, Pintoff Prods., Inc., Kingsley International Pictures Corp. ERNEST PINTOFF, Producer

(Live Action Subjects)

BETWEEN THE TIDES, British Transport Films, Lester A. Schoenfeld Films (British). IAN FERGUSON, Producer

THE GOLDEN FISH, Les Requins Associes, Columbia (French). JACQUES-YVES COUSTEAU, Producer

MYSTERIES OF THE DEEP, Walt Disney Prods., Buena Vista Film Distribution Co., Inc. WALT DISNEY, Producer

THE RUNNING, JUMPING AND STANDING-STILL FILM, Lion International Films, Ltd., Kingsley-Union Films (British). PETER SELLERS, Producer

SKYSCRAPER, Joseph Burstyn Film Enterprises, Inc. SHIRLEY CLARKE, WILLARD VAN DYKE and IRVING JACOBY, Producers

1960   Thirty-third Year
(Cartoons)

GOLIATH II, Walt Disney Prods., Buena Vista Distribution Co., Inc. WALT DISNEY, Producer

HIGH NOTE, Warner Bros.

MOUSE AND GARDEN, Warner Bros.

MUNRO, Rembrandt Films, Film Representations, Inc. WILLIAM L. SNYDER, Producer

A PLACE IN THE SUN, George K. Arthur-Go Pictures, Inc. (Czechoslovakian). FRANTISEK VYSTRECIL, Producer

(Live Action Subjects)

THE CREATION OF WOMAN, Trident Films, Inc., Sterling World Distributors Corp. (Indian). CHARLES F. SCHWEP and ISMAIL MERCHANT, Producers

DAY OF THE PAINTER, Little Movies, Kingsley-Union Films. EZRA R. BAKER, Producer

ISLANDS OF THE SEA, Walt Disney Prods., Buena Vista Distribution Co., Inc. WALT DISNEY, Producer

A SPORT IS BORN, Paramount. LESLIE WINIK, Producer

1961   Thirty-fourth Year
(Cartoons)

AQUAMANIA, Walt Disney Prods., Buena Vista Distribution Co., Inc. WALT DISNEY, Producer

BEEP PREPARED, Warner Bros. CHUCK JONES, Producer

ERSATZ (The Substitute), Zagreb Film, Herts-Lion International Corp.

NELLY'S FOLLY, Warner Bros. CHUCK JONES, Producer

PIED PIPER OF GUADALUPE, Warner Bros. FRIZ FRELENG, Producer

(Live Action Subjects)

BALLON VOLE (Play Ball!), Ciné-Documents, Kingsley International Pictures Corp

THE FACE OF JESUS, Dr. John D. Jennings, Harry Stern, Inc. DR. JOHN D. JENNINGS, Producer

ROOFTOPS OF NEW YORK, McCarty-Rush Prod. in association with ROBERT GAFFNEY, Columbia

SEAWARDS THE GREAT SHIPS, Templar Film Studios, LESTER A. SCHOENFELD FILMS
VERY NICE, VERY NICE, National Film Board Of Canada, KINGSLEY INTERNATIONAL PICTURES CORP

1962 Thirty-fifth Year
(Cartoons)
THE HOLE, Storyboard Inc., Brandon Films, Inc. JOHN and FAITH HUBLEY, Producers
ICARUS MONTGOLFIER WRIGHT, Format Films, United Artists. JULES ENGEL, Producer
NOW HEAR THIS, Warner Bros.
SELF DEFENSE—FOR COWARDS, Rembrandt Films, Film Representations, Inc. WILLIAM L. SNYDER, Producer
SYMPOSIUM ON POPULAR SONGS, Walt Disney Prods., Buena Vista Distribution Co. WALT DISNEY, Producer

(Live Action Subjects)
BIG CITY BLUES, Mayfair Pictures Company. MARTINA and CHARLES HUGUENOT VAN DER LINDEN, Producers
THE CADILLAC, United Producers Releasing Org. ROBERT CLOUSE, Producer
THE CLIFF DWELLERS (formerly titled "One Plus One"), Group II Film Prods., Lester A. Schoenfeld Films. HAYWARD ANDERSON, Producer
HEUREUX ANNIVERSAIRE (Happy Anniversary), CAPAC Prods., Atlantic Pictures Corp. PIERRE ETAIX and J. C. CARRIERE, Producers
PAN, Mayfair Picture Company. HERMAN VAN DER HORST, Producer

1963 Thirty-sixth Year
(Cartoons)
AUTOMANIA 2000, Halas and Batchelor

Prod., Pathe Contemporary Films. JOHN HALAS, Producer
THE CRITIC, Pintoff-Crossbow Prods., Columbia. ERNEST PINTOFF, Producer
THE GAME (Igra), Zagreb Film, Rembrandt Films-Film Representations. DUSAN VUKOTIC, Producer
MY FINANCIAL CAREER, National Film Board Of Canada, Walter Reade-Sterling-Continental Distributing. COLIN LOW and TOM DALY, Producers
PIANISSIMO, Cinema 16. CARMEN D'AVINO, Producer

(Live Action Subjects)
THE CONCERT, James A. King Corp., George K. Arthur-Go Pictures. EZRA BAKER, Producer
HOME-MADE CAR, BP (North America) Ltd., Lester A. Schoenfeld Films. JAMES HILL, Producer
AN OCCURRENCE AT OWL CREEK BRIDGE, Films Du Centaure-Filmartic, Cappagariff-Janus Films. PAUL DE ROUBAIX and MARCEL ICHAC, Producers
SIX-SIDED TRIANGLE, Milesian Film Prod. Ltd., Lion International Films. CHRISTOPHER MILES, Producer
THAT'S ME, Stuart Prods., Pathe Contemporary Films. WALKER STUART, Producer

1964 Thirty-seventh Year
(Cartoons)
CHRISTMAS CRACKER, National Film Board Of Canada, Favorite Films Of California
HOW TO AVOID FRIENDSHIP, Rembrandt Films, Film Representations. WILLIAM L. SNYDER, Producer
NUDNIK #2, Rembrandt Films, Film Representations. WILLIAM L. SNYDER, Producer

THE PINK PHINK, Mirisch-Geoffrey Prods., UA. DAVID H. DePATIE and FRIZ FRELENG, Producers

(Live Action Subjects)

CASALS CONDUCTS: 1964, Thalia Films, Beckman Film Corp. EDWARD SCHREIBER, Producer

HELP! MY SNOWMAN'S BURNING DOWN, Carson Davidson Prods., Pathe Contemporary Films. CARSON DAVIDSON, Producer

THE LEGEND OF JIMMY BLUE EYES, Robert Clouse Associates, Topaz Film Corp. ROBERT CLOUSE, Producer

1965 Thirty-eighth Year
(Cartoons)

CLAY OR THE ORIGIN OF SPECIES, Harvard University, Pathe Contemporary Films. ELIOT NOYES, JR., Producer

THE DOT AND THE LINE, Metro-Goldwyn-Mayer. CHUCK JONES and LES GOLDMAN, Producers

THE THIEVING MAGPIE (La Gazza Ladra), Giulio Gianini-Emanuele Luzzati, Allied Artists. EMANUELE LUZZATI, Producer

(Live Action Subjects)

THE CHICKEN (Le Poulet), Renn Prods., Pathe Contemporary Films. CLAUDE BERRI, Producer

FORTRESS OF PEACE, Lothar Wolff Prods. for Farner-Looser Films, Cinerama. LOTHAR WOLFF, Producer

SKATERDATER, Byway Prods., United Artists. MARSHAL BACKLAR and NOEL BLACK, Producers

SNOW, British Transport Films in association with Geoffrey Jones (Films) Ltd., Manson Distributing. EDGAR ANSTEY, Producer

TIME PIECE, Muppets, Inc., Pathe Contemporary Films. JIM HENSON, Producer

1966 Thirty-ninth Year
(Cartoons)

THE DRAG, National Film Board of Canada, Favorite Films. WOLF KOENIG and ROBERT VERRALL, Producers

HERB ALPERT AND THE TIJUANA BRASS DOUBLE FEATURE, Hubley Studio, Paramount. JOHN and FAITH HUBLEY, Producers

THE PINK BLUEPRINT, Mirisch-Geoffrey-DePatie-Freleng, U.A. DAVID H. DePATIE and FRIZ FRELENG, Producers

(Live Action Subjects)

TURKEY THE BRIDGE, Samaritan Prods., Lester A. Schoenfeld Films. DEREK WILLIAMS, Producer

WILD WINGS, British Transport Films, Manson Distributing. EDGAR ANSTEY, Producer

THE WINNING STRAIN, Winik Films, Paramount. LESLIE WINIK, Producer

1967 Fortieth Year
(Cartoons)

THE BOX, Murakami-Wolf Films, Brandon Films. FRED WOLF, Producer

HYPOTHESE BETA, Films Orzeaux, Pathe Contemporary Films. JEAN-CHARLES MEUNIER, Producer

WHAT ON EARTH!, National Film Board of Canada, Columbia. ROBERT VERRALL and WOLF KOENIG, Producers

(Live Action Subjects)

PADDLE TO THE SEA, National Film Board of Canada, Favorite Films. JULIAN BIGGS, Producer

A PLACE TO STAND, T.D.F. Prod. for The Ontario Department of Economics and Development, Columbia. CHRISTOPHER CHAPMAN, Producer

SKY OVER HOLLAND, John Ferno Prod.

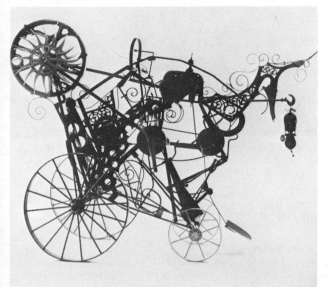

for The Netherlands, Seneca International. JOHN FERNO, Producer

STOP, LOOK AND LISTEN, Metro-Goldwyn-Mayer. LEN JANSON and CHUCK MENVILLE, Producers

1968 Forty-first Year

(Cartoons)

THE HOUSE THAT JACK BUILT, National Film Board of Canada, Columbia. WOLF KOENIG and JIM MACKAY, Producers

THE MAGIC PEAR TREE, Murakami-Wolf Prods. Bing Crosby Prods. JIMMY MURAKAMI, Producer

WINDY DAY, Hubley Studios, Paramount. JOHN and FAITH HUBLEY, Producers

WINNIE THE POOH AND THE BLUSTERY DAY, Walt Disney Prods., Buena Vista Dist. WALT DISNEY, Producer

(Live Action Subjects)

THE DOVE, Coe-Davis, Schoenfeld Film Dist. GEORGE COE, SIDNEY DAVIS and ANTHONY LOVER, Producers

DUO, National Film Board of Canada, Columbia

PRELUDE, Prelude Company, Excelsior Dist. JOHN ASTIN, Producer

ROBERT KENNEDY REMEMBERED, Guggenheim Prods., National General. CHARLES GUGGENHEIM, Producer

1969 Forty-second Year

(Cartoons)

IT'S TOUGH TO BE A BIRD, Walt Disney Prods., Buena Vista Dist.: WARD KIMBALL, Producer

OF MEN AND DEMONS, Hubley Studios, Paramount: JOHN and FAITH HUBLEY, Producers

WALKING, National Film Board of Canada, Columbia: RYAN LARKIN, Producer

(Live Action Subjects)

BLAKE, National Film Board of Canada, Vaudeo Inc.: DOUG JACKSON, Producer

THE MAGIC MACHINES, Fly-By-Night Prods., Manson Distributing: JOAN KELLER STERN, Producer

PEOPLE SOUP, Pangloss Prods., Columbia: MARC MERSON, Producer

1970   Forty-third Year
(Cartoons)

THE FURTHER ADVENTURES OF UNCLE SAM: PART TWO, The Haboush Company, Goldstone Films: ROBERT MITCHELL and DALE CASE, Producers

IS IT ALWAYS RIGHT TO BE RIGHT?, Stephen Bosustow Prods., Lester A. Schoenfeld Films: NICK BOSUSTOW, Producer

THE SHEPHERD, Cameron Guess and Associates, Brandon Films: CAMERON GUESS, Producer

(Live Action Subjects)

THE RESURRECTION OF BRONCHO BILLY, University of Southern California, Dept. of Cinema, Universal: JOHN LONGENECKER, Producer

SHUT UP . . . I'M CRYING, Robert Siegler Prods., Lester A. Schoenfeld Films: ROBERT SIEGLER, Producer

STICKY MY FINGERS . . . FLEET MY FEET, The American Film Institute, Lester A. Schoenfeld Films: JOHN HANCOCK, Producer

1971   Forty-fourth Year
Note: The designation of this category was changed from "Cartoons" to "Animated Films."

(Animated Films)

THE CRUNCH BIRD, Maxwell-Petok-Petrovich Prods., Regency Film Distributing Corp.: TED PETOK, Producer

EVOLUTION, National Film Board of Canada, Columbia: MICHAEL MILLS, Producer

THE SELFISH GIANT, Potterton Prods., Pyramid Films: PETER SANDER and MURRAY SHOSTAK, Producers

(Live Action Films)

GOOD MORNING, E/G Films, Seymour Borde & Associates: DENNY EVANS and KEN GREENWALD, Producers

THE REHEARSAL, A Cinema Verona Prod., Schoenfeld Film Distributing Corp.: STEPHEN F. VERONA, Producer

SENTINELS OF SILENCE, Producciones Concord, Paramount: MANUEL ARANGO and ROBERT AMRAM, Producers

1972   Forty-fifth Year
(Animated Films)

A CHRISTMAS CAROL, A Richard Williams Production, American Broadcasting Company Film Services: RICHARD WILLIAMS, Producer

KAMA SUTRA RIDES AGAIN, Bob Godfrey Films, Ltd., Lion International Films: BOB GODFREY, Producer

TUP TUP, A Zagreb Film-Corona Cinematografica Production, Manson Distributing Corp.: NEDELJKO DRAGIC, Producer

(Live Action Films)

FROG STORY, Gidron Productions, Schoenfeld Film Distributing Corp.: RON SATLOF and RAY GIDEON, Producers

NORMAN ROCKWELL'S WORLD . . . AN AMERICAN DREAM, A Concepts Unlimited Production, Columbia: RICHARD BARCLAY, Producer

SOLO, Pyramid Films, United Artists: DAVID ADAMS, Producer

1973   Forty-sixth Year
(Animated Films)

FRANK FILM, A Frank Mouris Production: FRANK MOURIS, Producer

THE LEGEND OF JOHN HENRY, A Stephen Bosustow-Pyramid Films Prod.:

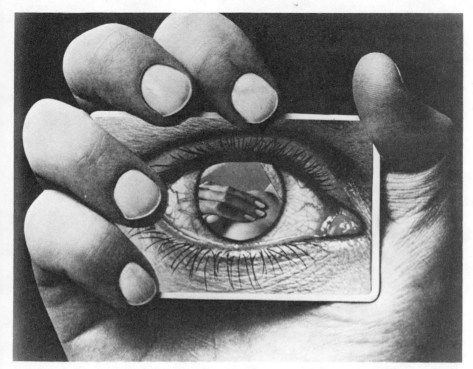

Frank Film, an animated autobiography by Frank Mouris, received a 1973 Short Subject Award. *Pyramid Films Photo*

NICK BOSUSTOW and DAVID ADAMS, Producers

PULCINELLA, A Luzzati-Gianini Prod.: EMANUELE LUZZATI and GUILIO GIANINI, Producers

(Live Action Films)

THE BOLERO, An Allan Miller Production: ALLAN MILLER and WILLIAM FERTIK, Producers

CLOCKMAKER, James Street Prods. Ltd.: RICHARD GAYER, Producer

LIFE TIMES NINE, Insight Prods. PEN DENSHAM and JOHN WATSON, Producers

1974   Forty-seventh Year

Note: Name of category changed from Short Subjects to Short Films.

(Animated Films)

CLOSED MONDAYS, Lighthouse Productions: WILL VINTON and BOB GARDINER, Producers

THE FAMILY THAT DWELT APART, National Film Board of Canada: YVON MALLETTE and ROBERT VERRALL, Producers

HUNGER, National Film Board of Canada: PETER FOLDES and RENE JODOIN, Producers

VOYAGE TO NEXT, The Hubley Studio: FAITH and JOHN HUBLEY, Producers

WINNIE THE POOH AND TIGGER TOO, Walt Disney Productions: WOLFGANG REITHERMAN, Producer

(Live Action Films)

CLIMB, Dewitt Jones Productions: DEWITT JONES, Producer

THE CONCERT, The Black And White Colour Film Company, Ltd.: JULIAN and CLAUDE CHAGRIN, Producers

The animated Short Films winner for 1974 was *Closed Mondays,* a clay animation by Will Vinton and Bob Gardiner. *Pyramid Films Photo*

ONE-EYED MEN ARE KINGS, C.A.P.A.C. Productions (Paris): PAUL CLAUDON and EDMOND SECHAN, Producers

PLANET OCEAN, Graphic Films: GEORGE V. CASEY, Producer

THE VIOLIN, A Sincinkin, Ltd. Production: ANDREW WELSH and GEORGE PASTIC, Producers

1975 Forty-eighth Year

(Animated Films)

GREAT, Grantstern Ltd. and British Lion Films Ltd.: BOB GODFREY, Producer

KICK ME, Robert Swarthe Productions: ROBERT SWARTHE Producer

MONSIEUR POINTU, National Film Board of Canada: RENÉ JODOIN, BERNARD LONGPRÉ and ANDRÉ LEDUC, Producers

SISYPHUS, Hungarofilms: MARCELL JANKOVICS, Producer

(Live Action)

ANGEL AND BIG JOE, Bert Salzman

Productions: BERT SALZMAN, Producer

CONQUEST OF LIGHT, Louis Marcus Films Ltd.: LOUIS MARCUS, Producer

DAWN FLIGHT, Lawrence M. Lansburgh Productions: LAWRENCE M. LANSBURGH and BRIAN LANSBURGH, Producers

A DAY IN THE LIFE OF BONNIE CONSOLO, Barr Films: BARRY SPINELLO, Producer

DOUBLETALK, Beattie Productions: ALAN BEATTIE, Producer

1976 Forty-ninth Year
(Animated Films)

DEDALO, A Cineteam Realizzazioni Production: MANFREDO MANFREDI, Producer

LEISURE, A Film Australia Production: SUZANNE BAKER, Producer

THE STREET, National Film Board of Canada: CAROLINE LEAF and GUY GLOVER, Producers

(Live Action)

IN THE REGION OF ICE, An American Film Institute Production: ANDRE GUTTFREUND and PETER WERNER, Producers

KUDZU, A Short Production: MARJORIE ANNE SHORT, Producer

THE MORNING SPIDER, The Black and White Colour Film Company: JULIAN CHAGRIN and CLAUDE CHAGRIN, Producers

NIGHTLIFE, Opus Films, Ltd.: CLAIRE

WILBUR and ROBIN LEHMAN, Producers

NUMBER ONE, Number One Productions: DYAN CANNON and VINCE CANNON, Producers

1977 Fiftieth Year
(Animated Films)

THE BEAD GAME, National Film Board of Canada: ISHU PATEL, Producer

THE DOONESBURY SPECIAL, The Hubley Studio: JOHN and FAITH HUBLEY and GARY TRUDEAU, Producers

JIMMY THE C, A Motionpicker Production: JIMMY PICKER and ROBERT GROSSMAN, Producers

SAND CASTLE, National Film Board of Canada: CO HOEDEMAN, Producer

(Live Action)

THE ABSENT-MINDED WAITER, The Aspen Film Society. WILLIAM E. MCEUEN, Producer

FLOATING FREE, A Trans World International Production: JERRY BUTTS, Producer

I'LL FIND A WAY, National Film Board of Canada: BEVERLY SHAFFER and YUKI YOSHIDA, Producers

NOTES ON THE POPULAR ARTS, Saul Bass Films: SAUL BASS, Producer

SPACEBORNE, A Lawrence Hall of Science Production for the Regents of the University of California with the cooperation of NASA: PHILIP DAUBER, Producer

DOCUMENTARY

The Academy honored a nonfiction film for the first time in 1936 when it voted a special award to *The March of Time,* but it was not until 1941 that a separate category for documentary film was established. The Academy defines documentary films as "those dealing with cultural, artistic, historical, social, scientific, economic or other significant subjects, photographed in actual occurrence, re-enacted or produced in animation, stop-motion or any other technique and where the emphasis is on factual content. The purely instructional film will not be considered."

World War II brought a terrific expansion in nonfiction film—newsreels, training films, and documentaries—and the 1942 Documentary awards listed four co-winners chosen from twenty-five nominations. The category was divided the following year so that feature films would not compete against short subjects. Present rules define features as films of more than 3000 35mm feet. (At sound speed 35mm film moves at 90 feet per minute, so 3000 feet would equal 33⅓ minutes.)

In 1969 for the first and only time an Oscar had to be withdrawn. When the 1968 Documentary Feature winner *Young Americans* was declared ineligible, the runner-up *Journey Into Self* was awarded an Oscar in a private ceremony at Academy headquarters. In 1971 *Sentinels of Silence* won both Documentary Short Subject and Short Subject—Live Action. The rules were then changed to permit eligible films to be entered in one or the other category but not both.

Films eligible for this award are entered by their producers and are screened by a Documentary Awards Committee which determines the nominees. Final voting is restricted to Academy members who have seen *all* nominated films.

1941   Fourteenth Year

ADVENTURES IN THE BRONX, Film Assocs.

BOMBER, U.S. Office for Emergency Management Film Unit

CHRISTMAS UNDER FIRE, British Ministry of Information, Warner Bros.

CHURCHILL'S ISLAND, Canadian Film Board, UA

LETTER FROM HOME, British Ministry of Information

LIFE OF A THOROUGHBRED, 20th Century-Fox

NORWAY IN REVOLT, March of Time, RKO Radio

LARGE CAPITAL LETTERS DENOTE WINNER

SOLDIERS OF THE SKY, 20th Century-Fox

WAR CLOUDS IN THE PACIFIC, Canadian Film Board

1942   Fifteenth Year

A SHIP IS BORN, U.S. Merchant Marine, Warner Bros.

AFRICA, PRELUDE TO VICTORY, March of Time, 20th Century-Fox

BATTLE OF MIDWAY, U.S. Navy, 20th Century-Fox

COMBAT REPORT, U.S. Army Signal Corps.

CONQUER BY THE CLOCK, Office of War Information, RKO Pathe: FREDERIC ULLMAN, JR.

THE GRAIN THAT BUILT A HEMISPHERE, Coordinator's Office, Motion Picture Society for the Americas: WALT DISNEY

HENRY BROWNE, FARMER, U.S. Department of Agriculture, Republic

HIGH OVER THE BORDERS, Canadian National Film Board

HIGH STAKES IN THE EAST, Netherlands Information Bureau

INSIDE FIGHTING CHINA, Canadian National Film Board

IT'S EVERYBODY'S WAR, Office of War Information, 20th Century-Fox

KOKODA FRONT LINE, Australian News Information Bureau

LISTEN TO BRITAIN, British Ministry of Information

LITTLE BELGIUM, Belgian Ministry of Information

LITTLE ISLES OF FREEDOM, Warner Bros.: VICTOR STOLOFF and EDGAR LOEW

MOSCOW STRIKES BACK, Artkino (Russian)

MR. BLABBERMOUTH, Office of War Information, M-G-M

MR. GARDENIA JONES, Office of War Information, M-G-M

NEW SPIRIT, U.S. Treasury Department: WALT DISNEY

PRELUDE TO WAR, U.S. Army Special Services

THE PRICE OF VICTORY, Office of War Information, Paramount: PINE-THOMAS

TWENTY-ONE MILES, British Ministry of Information

WE REFUSE TO DIE, Office of War Information, Paramount: WILLIAM C. THOMAS

WHITE EAGLE, Cocanen Films

WINNING YOUR WINGS, U.S. Army Air Force, Warner Bros.

1943   Sixteenth Year

(Short Subjects)

CHILDREN OF MARS, This is America Series, RKO Radio

DECEMBER 7TH, U.S. Navy, Field Photographic Branch, Office of Strategic Services

PLAN FOR DESTRUCTION, Metro-Goldwyn-Mayer

SWEDES IN AMERICA, Office of War Information, Overseas Motion Picture Bureau

TO THE PEOPLE OF THE UNITED STATES, U.S. Public Health Service, Walter Wanger Prods.

TOMORROW WE FLY, U.S. Navy, Bureau of Aeronautics

YOUTH IN CRISIS, March of Time, 20th Century-Fox

(Features)

BATTLE OF RUSSIA, Special Service Division of the War Department

BAPTISM OF FIRE, U.S. Army, Fighting Men Series

DESERT VICTORY, British Ministry of Information

REPORT FROM THE ALEUTIANS, U.S. Army Pictorial Service, Combat Film Series

WAR DEPARTMENT REPORT, Field Photographic Branch, Office of Strategic Services

1944   Seventeenth Year

(Short Subjects)

ARTURO TOSCANINI, Motion Picture Bureau, Overseas Branch, Office of War Information

NEW AMERICANS, This is America Series, RKO Radio

WITH THE MARINES AT TARAWA, U.S. Marine Corps.

(Features)

THE FIGHTING LADY, 20th Century-Fox and U.S. Navy

RESISTING ENEMY INTERROGATION, U.S. Army Air Force

227

1945   Eighteenth Year
(Short Subjects)
HITLER LIVES?, Warner Bros.
LIBRARY OF CONGRESS, Overseas Motion Picture Bureau, Office of War Information
TO THE SHORES OF IWO JIMA, U.S. Marine Corps.

(Features)
THE LAST BOMB, U.S. Army Air Force
THE TRUE GLORY, Governments of Great Britain and USA

1946   Nineteenth Year
(Short Subjects)
ATOMIC POWER, 20th Century-Fox
LIFE AT THE ZOO, Artkino
PARAMOUNT NEWS ISSUE #37, Paramount
SEEDS OF DESTINY, U.S. War Department
TRAFFIC WITH THE DEVIL, Metro-Goldwyn-Mayer

(No Features nominated this year)

1947   Twentieth Year
(Short Subjects)
FIRST STEPS, United Nations Division of Films and Visual Education
PASSPORT TO NOWHERE, RKO Radio (This Is America Series): FREDERIC ULLMAN, JR., Producer
SCHOOL IN THE MAILBOX, Australian News and Information Bureau

(Features)
DESIGN FOR DEATH, RKO Radio: SID ROGELL, Executive Producer; THERON WARTH and RICHARD O. FLEISCHER, Producers
JOURNEY INTO MEDICINE, U.S. Department of State, Office of Information and Educational Exchange
THE WORLD IS RICH, British Information Services: PAUL ROTHA, Producer

1948   Twenty-first Year
(Short Subjects)
HEART TO HEART, Fact Film Organization: HERBERT MORGAN, Producer
OPERATION VITTLES, U.S. Army Air Force
TOWARD INDEPENDENCE, U.S. Army

(Features)
THE QUIET ONE, Mayer-Burstyn: JANICE LOEB, Producer
THE SECRET LAND, U.S. Navy, M-G-M: O. O. DULL, Producer

1949   Twenty-second Year
(Short Subjects)
Note: Two winners this year.
A CHANCE TO LIVE, March of Time, 20th Century-Fox: RICHARD DE ROCHEMONT, Producer
1848, A. F. Films, Inc.: FRENCH CINEMA GENERAL COOPERATIVE, Producer
THE RISING TIDE, National Film Board of Canada: ST. FRANCIS-XAVIER UNIVERSITY (Nova Scotia), Producer
SO MUCH FOR SO LITTLE, Warner Bros. Cartoons, Inc.: EDWARD SELZER, Producer

(Features)
DAYBREAK IN UDI, British Information Services: CROWN FILM UNIT, Producer
KENJI COMES HOME, A Protestant Film Commission Prod.: PAUL F. HEARD, Producer

1950   Twenty-third Year
(Short Subjects)
THE FIGHT: SCIENCE AGAINST CANCER, National Film Board of Canada in cooperation with the Medical Film Institute of the Association of American Medical Colleges
THE STAIRS, Film Documents, Inc.

WHY KOREA?, 20th Century-Fox Movietone: EDMUND REEK, Producer

(Features)

THE TITAN: STORY OF MICHELANGELO, Michelangelo Co., Classics Pictures, Inc.: ROBERT SNYDER, Producer

WITH THESE HANDS, Promotional Films Co., Inc.: JACK ARNOLD and LEE GOODMAN, Producers

1951 Twenty-fourth Year

(Short Subjects)

BENJY, Made by Fred Zinnemann with the cooperation of Paramount Pictures Corp. for the Los Angeles Orthopaedic Hospital

ONE WHO CAME BACK: Owen Crump, Producer. (Film sponsored by the Disabled American Veterans, in cooperation with the United States Department of Defense and the Association of Motion Picture Producers.)

THE SEEING EYE, Warner Bros.: GORDON HOLLINGSHEAD, Producer

(Features)

I WAS A COMMUNIST FOR THE F.B.I., Warner Bros.: BRYAN FOY, Producer

KON-TIKI, An Artfilm Prod., RKO Radio (Norwegian): OLLE NORDEMAR, Producer

1952 Twenty-fifth Year

(Short Subjects)

DEVIL TAKE US, Theatre of Life Prod.: HERBERT MORGAN, Producer

THE GARDEN SPIDER (EPEIRA DIADEMA), Cristallo Films, I.F.E. Releasing Corp. (Italian): ALBERTO ANCILOTTO, Producer

MAN ALIVE!, Made by United Productions of America for the American Cancer Society: STEPHEN BOSUSTOW, Exec. Producer

NEIGHBOURS, National Film Board of Canada, Arthur Mayer-Edward Kingsley, Inc. (Canadian): NORMAN McLAREN, Producer

(Features)

THE HOAXTERS, Metro-Goldwyn-Mayer: DORE SCHARY, Producer

NAVAJO, Bartlett-Foster Prod., Lippert Pictures, Inc.: HALL BARTLETT, Producer

THE SEA AROUND US, RKO Radio: IRWIN ALLEN, Producer

1953 Twenty-sixth Year

(Short Subjects)

THE ALASKAN ESKIMO, Walt Disney Prods., RKO Radio:WALT DISNEY, Producer

THE LIVING CITY, Encyclopaedia Britannica Films, Inc.: JOHN BARNES, Producer

OPERATION BLUE JAY, U.S. Army Signal Corps

THEY PLANTED A STONE, World Wide Pictures, British Information Services (British): JAMES CARR Producer

THE WORD, 20th Century-Fox: JOHN HEALY and JOHN ADAMS, Producers

(Features)

THE CONQUEST OF EVEREST, Countryman Films, Ltd. & Group 3 Ltd., UA (British): JOHN TAYLOR, LEON CLORE and GRAHAME THARP, Producers

THE LIVING DESERT, Walt Disney Prods., Buena Vista Film Dist. Co., Inc.: WALT DISNEY, Producer

A QUEEN IS CROWNED, J. Arthur Rank Organization, Ltd., U-I (British): CASTLETON KNIGHT, Producer

1954 Twenty-seventh Year

(Short Subjects)

JET CARRIER, 20th Century-Fox: OTTO LANG, Producer

REMBRANDT: A SELF-PORTRAIT, Distributors Corp. of America: MORRIE ROIZMAN, Producer

THURSDAY'S CHILDREN, British Information Services (British): WORLD WIDE PICTURES AND MORSE FILMS, Producers

(Features)

THE STRATFORD ADVENTURE, National Film Board of Canada, Continental Dist., Inc. (Canadian): GUY GLOVER, Producer

THE VANISHING PRAIRIE, Walt Disney Prods., Buena Vista Film Dist. Co., Inc.: WALT DISNEY, Producer

1955 Twenty-eighth Year

(Short Subjects)

THE BATTLE OF GETTYSBURG, Metro-Goldwyn-Mayer: DORE SCHARY, Producer

THE FACE OF LINCOLN, University of Southern California Presentation, Cavalcade Pictures, Inc.: WILBER T. BLUME, Producer

MEN AGAINST THE ARCTIC, Walt Disney Prods., Buena Vista Film Dist. Co., Inc.: WALT DISNEY, Producer

(Features)

HEARTBREAK RIDGE, Rene Risacher Prod., Tudor Pictures (French): RENE RISACHER, Producer

HELEN KELLER IN HER STORY, Nancy Hamilton Presentation: NANCY HAMILTON, Producer

1956 Twenty-ninth Year

(Short Subjects)

A CITY DECIDES, Charles Guggenheim & Assocs., Inc. Prod.

THE DARK WAVE, 20th Century-Fox: JOHN HEALY, Producer

THE HOUSE WITHOUT A NAME, Universal-International: VALENTINE DAVIES, Producer

MAN IN SPACE, Walt Disney Prods., Buena Vista Film Dist. Co., Inc.: WARD KIMBALL, Producer

THE TRUE STORY OF THE CIVIL WAR, Camera Eye Pictures, Inc.: LOUIS CLYDE STOUMEN, Producer

(Features)

THE NAKED EYE, Camera Eye Pictures, Inc.: LOUIS CLYDE STOUMEN, Producer

THE SILENT WORLD, A Filmad-F.S.J.Y.C. Prod., Columbia (French): JACQUES-YVES COUSTEAU, Producer

WHERE MOUNTAINS FLOAT, Brandon Films, Inc. (Danish): THE GOVERNMENT FILM COMMITTEE OF DENMARK, Producer

1957 Thirtieth Year

(Note: No Short Subject Documentary Nominations voted this year.)

(Features)

ALBERT SCHWEITZER, Hill and Anderson Prod., Louis de Rochemont Assocs.: JEROME HILL, Producer

ON THE BOWERY, Lionel Rogosin Prods., Film Representations, Inc.: LIONEL ROGOSIN, Producer

TORERO!, Producciones Barbachano Ponce, Columbia (Mexican): MANUEL BARBACHANO PONCE, Producer

1958 Thirty-first Year

(Short Subjects)

AMA GIRLS, Walt Disney Prods., Buena Vista Film Dist. Co., Inc.: BEN SHARPSTEEN, Producer

EMPLOYEES ONLY, Hughes Aircraft Co.: KENNETH G. BROWN, Producer

JOURNEY INTO SPRING, British Transport Films, Lester A. Schoenfeld

Films: IAN FERGUSON, Producer

THE LIVING STONE, National Film Board of Canada: TOM DALY, Producer

OVERTURE, United Nations Film Service: THOROLD DICKINSON, Producer

(Features)

ANTARCTIC CROSSING, World Wide Pictures, Lester A. Schoenfeld Films: JAMES CARR, Producer

THE HIDDEN WORLD, Small World Co.: ROBERT SNYDER, Producer

PSYCHIATRIC NURSING, Dynamic Films, Inc.: NATHAN ZUCKER, Producer

WHITE WILDERNESS, Walt Disney Prods., Buena Vista Film Dist. Co., Inc.: BEN SHARPSTEEN, Producer

1959   Thirty-second Year

(Short Subjects)

DONALD IN MATHMAGIC LAND, Walt Disney Prods., Buena Vista Film Dist. Co., Inc.: WALT DISNEY, Producer

FROM GENERATION TO GENERATION, Cullen Assocs., Maternity Center Assoc.: EDWARD F. CULLEN, Producer

GLASS, Netherlands Government, George K. Arthur–Go Pictures, Inc. (The Netherlands): BERT HAANSTRA, Producer

(Features)

THE RACE FOR SPACE, Wolper, Inc.: DAVID L. WOLPER, Producer

SERENGETI SHALL NOT DIE, Okapia-Film Prod., Transocean Film (German): BERNHARD GRZIMEK, Producer

1960   Thirty-third Year

(Short Subjects)

BEYOND SILENCE, United States Information Agency

A CITY CALLED COPENHAGEN, Statens Filmcentral, Danish Government Film Office (Danish)

GEORGE GROSZ' INTERREGNUM, Educational Communications Corp.: CHARLES and ALTINA CAREY, Producers

GIUSEPPINA, James Hill Prod., Lester A. Schoenfeld Films (British): JAMES HILL, Producer

UNIVERSE, National Film Board of Canada, Lester A. Schoenfeld Films (Canadian): COLIN LOW, Producer

(Features)

THE HORSE WITH THE FLYING TAIL, Walt Disney Prods., Buena Vista Dist. Co., Inc.: LARRY LANSBURGH, Producer

REBEL IN PARADISE, Tiare Co.: ROBERT D. FRASER, Producer

1961   Thirty-fourth Year

(Short Subjects)

BREAKING THE LANGUAGE BARRIER, United States Air Force

CRADLE OF GENIUS, Plough Prods., An Irving M. Lesser Film Presentation (Irish): JIM O'CONNOR and TOM HAYES, Producers

KAHL, Dido-Film-GmbH., AEG-Filmdienst (German)

L'UOMO IN GRIGIO (The Man In Gray), (Italian): BENEDETTO BENEDETTI, Producer

PROJECT HOPE, MacManus, John & Adams, Inc., Ex-Cell-O Corp. A Klaeger Film Production: FRANK P. BIBAS, Producer

(Features)

LA GRANDE OLIMPIADE (Olympic Games 1960), dell'Istituto Nazionale Luce, Comitato Organizzatore dei Giochi della XVII Olimpiade. Cineriz (Italian)

LE CIEL ET LA BOUE (Sky Above And Mud Beneath), Ardennes Films and Michael Arthur Film Prods., Rank Film Distrs., Ltd. (French): ARTHUR COHN and RENÉ LAFUITE, Producers

1962   Thirty-fifth Year

(Short Subjects)

DYLAN THOMAS, TWW Ltd., Janus Films (Welsh): JACK HOWELLS, Producer

THE JOHN GLENN STORY, Department of the Navy, Warner Bros.: WILLIAM L. HENDRICKS, Producer

THE ROAD TO THE WALL, CBS Films, Inc., Department of Defense: ROBERT SAUDEK, Producer

(Features)

ALVORADA (Brazil's Changing Face), MW Filmproduktion (German): HUGO NIEBELING, Producer

BLACK FOX, Image Prods., Inc., Heritage Films, Inc.: LOUIS CLYDE STOUMEN, Producer

1963   Thirty-sixth Year

(Short Subjects)

CHAGALL, Auerbach Film Enterprises, Ltd.-Flag Films: SIMON SCHIFFRIN, Producer

THE FIVE CITIES OF JUNE, United States Information Agency: GEORGE STEVENS, JR., Producer

THE SPIRIT OF AMERICA, Spotlite News: ALGERNON G. WALKER, Producer

THIRTY MILLION LETTERS, British Transport Films: EDGAR ANSTEY, Producer

TO LIVE AGAIN, Wilding Inc.: MEL LONDON, Producer

(Features)

LE MAILLON ET LA CHAINE (The Link And The Chain), Films Du Centaure-Filmartic: PAUL DE ROUBAIX, Producer

ROBERT FROST: A LOVER'S QUARREL WITH THE WORLD, WGBH Educational Foundation: ROBERT HUGHES, Producer

THE YANKS ARE COMING, David L. Wolper Prods.: MARSHALL FLAUM, Producer

1964   Thirty-seventh Year

(Short Subjects)

BREAKING THE HABIT, American Cancer Society, Modern Talking Picture Service: HENRY JACOBS and JOHN KORTY, Producers

CHILDREN WITHOUT, National Education Association, Guggenheim Productions

KENOJUAK, National Film Board of Canada

NINE FROM LITTLE ROCK, United States Information Agency, Guggenheim Productions

140 DAYS UNDER THE WORLD, New Zealand National Film Unit, Rank Film Distributors of New Zealand: GEOFFREY SCOTT and OXLEY HUGHAN, Producers

(Features)

THE FINEST HOURS, Le Vien Films, Ltd., Columbia: JACK LE VIEN, Producer

FOUR DAYS IN NOVEMBER, David L Wolper Prods., UA: MEL STUART, Producer

THE HUMAN DUTCH, Haanstra Filmproductie: BERT HAANSTRA, Producer

JACQUES-YVES COUSTEAU'S WORLD WITHOUT SUN, Filmad-Les Requins Associes-Orsay-CEIAP, Columbia: JACQUES-YVES COUSTEAU, Producer

OVER THERE, 1914–18, Zodiac Prods., Pathe Contemporary Films: JEAN AUREL, Producer

1965   Thirty-eighth Year
(Short Subjects)

MURAL ON OUR STREET, Henry Street Settlement, Pathe Contemporary Films: KIRK SMALLMAN, Producer

OUVERTURE, Mafilm Prods., Hungarofilm-Pathe Contemporary Films

POINT OF VIEW, Vision Associates Prod., National Tuberculosis Assoc.

TO BE ALIVE!, Johnson Wax: FRANCIS THOMPSON, INC., Producer

YEATS COUNTRY, Aengus Films Ltd. for the Dept. of External Affairs of Ireland: PATRICK CAREY and JOE MENDOZA, Producers

(Features)

THE BATTLE OF THE BULGE . . . THE BRAVE RIFLES, Mascott Prods.: LAURENCE E. MASCOTT, Producer

THE ELEANOR ROOSEVELT STORY, Sidney Glazier Prod., American Intl.: SIDNEY GLAZIER, Producer

THE FORTH ROAD BRIDGE, Random Film Prods., Ltd., Shell-Mex and B.P. Film Library: PETER MILLS, Producer

LET MY PEOPLE GO, Wolper Prods.: MARSHALL FLAUM, Producer

TO DIE IN MADRID, Ancinex Prods., Altura Films Intl.: FREDERIC ROSSIF, Producer

1966   Thirty-ninth Year
(Short Subjects)

ADOLESCENCE, M.K. Prods.: MARIN KARMITZ and VLADIMIR FORGENCY, Producers

COWBOY, United States Information Agency: MICHAEL AHNEMANN and GARY SCHLOSSER, Producers.

THE ODDS AGAINST, Vision Associates Prod. for The American Foundation Institute of Corrections: LEE R. BOB-

KER and HELEN KRISTT RADIN, Producers

SAINT MATTHEW PASSION, Mafilm Studio, Hungarofilm

A YEAR TOWARD TOMORROW, Sun Dial Films, Inc. Prod. for Office of Economic Opportunity: EDMOND A. LEVY, Producer

(Features)

THE FACE OF GENIUS, WBZ-TV, Group W, Boston: ALFRED R. KELMAN, Producer

HELICOPTER CANADA, Centennial Commission, National Film Board of Canada: PETER JONES and TOM DALY, Producers

LE VOLCAN INTERDIT (The Forbidden Volcano), Cine Documents Tazieff, Athos Films: HAROUN TAZIEFF, Producer

THE REALLY BIG FAMILY, David L. Wolper Prod.: ALEX GRASSHOFF, Producer

THE WAR GAME, BBC Prod. for the British Film Institute, Pathe Contemporary Films: PETER WATKINS, Producer

1967   Fortieth Year
(Short Subjects)

MONUMENT TO THE DREAM, Guggenheim Prods.: CHARLES E. GUGGENHEIM, Producer

A PLACE TO STAND, T.D.F. Prod. for The Ontario Dept. of Economics and Development: CHRISTOPHER CHAPMAN, Producer

THE REDWOODS, King Screen Prods.: MARK HARRIS and TREVOR GREENWOOD, Producers

SEE YOU AT THE PILLAR, Associated British-Pathe Prod.: ROBERT FITCHETT, Producer

WHILE I RUN THIS RACE, Sun Dial Films for VISTA, An Economic Op-

Saul Bass received the 1968 Documentary Short Subject Oscar for *Why Man Creates. Pyramid Films Photo*

portunity Program: CARL V. RAGSDALE, Producer

(Features)

THE ANDERSON PLATOON, French Broadcasting System: PIERRE SCHOENDOERFFER, Producer

FESTIVAL, Patchke Prods.: MURRAY LERNER, Producer

HARVEST, United States Information Agency: CARROLL BALLARD, Producer

A KING'S STORY, Jack Le Vien, Prod.: JACK LE VIEN, Producer

A TIME FOR BURNING, Quest Prods. for Lutheran Film Associates: WILLIAM C. JERSEY, Producer

1968   Forty-first Year
(Short Subjects)

THE HOUSE THAT ANANDA BUILT, Films Division, Government of India: FALI BILIMORIA, Producer

THE REVOLVING DOOR, Vision Associates for The American Foundation Institute of Corrections: LEE R. BOBKER, Producer

A SPACE TO GROW, Office of Economic Opportunity for Project Upward Bound: THOMAS P. KELLY, JR., Producer

A WAY OUT OF THE WILDERNESS, John Sutherland Prods.: DAN E. WEISBURD, Producer

WHY MAN CREATES, Saul Bass & Associates: SAUL BASS, Producer

(Features)

A FEW NOTES ON OUR FOOD PROBLEM, United States Information Agency: JAMES BLUE, Producer

JOURNEY INTO SELF, Western Behavioral Sciences Institute: BILL McGAW, Producer

THE LEGENDARY CHAMPIONS, Turn Of

The Century Fights: WILLIAM CAY-TON, Producer

OTHER VOICES, DHS Films: DAVID H. SAWYER, Producer

YOUNG AMERICANS, The Young Americans Prod. ROBERT COHN and ALEX GRASSHOFF, Producers. (Declared ineligible May 7, 1969 because first released during 1967)

1969 Forty-second Year
(Short Subjects)

CZECHOSLOVAKIA 1968, Sanders-Fresco Film Makers for United States Information Agency: DENIS SANDERS and ROBERT M. FRESCO, Producers

AN IMPRESSION OF JOHN STEINBECK: WRITER, Donald Wrye Prods. for United States Information Agency: DONALD WRYE, Producer

JENNY IS A GOOD THING, A.C.I. Prod. for Project Head Start: JOAN HORVATH, Producer

LEO BEUERMAN, Centron Prod.: ARTHUR H. WOLF and RUSSELL A. MOSSER, Producers

THE MAGIC MACHINES, Fly-By-Night Prods.: JOAN KELLER STERN, Producer

(Features)

ARTHUR RUBINSTEIN—THE LOVE OF LIFE, Midem Prod.: BERNARD CHEVRY, Producer

BEFORE THE MOUNTAIN WAS MOVED, Robert K. Sharpe Prods. for The Office of Economic Opportunity: ROBERT K. SHARPE, Producer

IN THE YEAR OF THE PIG, Emile de Antonio Prod.: EMILE DE ANTONIO, Producer

THE OLYMPICS IN MEXICO, Film Section of the Organizing Committee for the XIX Olympic Games

THE WOLF MEN, MGM Documentary: IRWIN ROSTEN, Producer

1970 Forty-third Year
(Short Subjects)

THE GIFTS, Richter-McBride Prods. for the Water Quality Office of the Environmental Protection Agency: ROBERT MCBRIDE, Producer

INTERVIEWS WITH MY LAI VETERANS, Laser Film Corp.: JOSEPH STRICK, Producer

A LONG WAY FROM NOWHERE, Robert Aller Prods.: BOB ALLER, Producer

OISIN, An Aengus Film: VIVIEN and PATRICK CAREY, Producers

TIME IS RUNNING OUT, Gesellschaft fur bildende Filme: HORST DALLMAYR and ROBERT MENEGOZ, Producers

(Features)

CHARIOTS OF THE GODS, Terra-Filmkunst GmbH.: DR. HARALD REINL, Producer

JACK JOHNSON, The Big Fights: JIM JACOBS, Producer

KING: A FILMED RECORD . . . MONTGOMERY TO MEMPHIS, Commonwealth United Prod.: ELY LANDAU, Producer

SAY GOODBYE, A Wolper Prod.: DAVID H. VOWELL, Producer

WOODSTOCK, A Wadleigh-Maurice Ltd. Prod.: BOB MAURICE, Producer

1971 Forty-fourth Year
(Short Subjects)

ADVENTURES IN PERCEPTION, Han van Gelder Filmproduktie for Netherlands Information Service: HAN VAN GELDER, Producer.

ART IS . . . , Henry Strauss Associates for Sears Roebuck Foundation: JULIAN KRAININ and DEWITT L. SAGE, JR., Producers

THE NUMBERS START WITH THE RIVER, A WH Picture for United States Information Agency: DONALD WRYE, Producer

SENTINELS OF SILENCE, Producciones Concord, Paramount: MANUEL ARANGO and ROBERT AMRAM, Producers

SOMEBODY WAITING, Snider Prods. for University of California Medical Film Library: HAL RINEY, DICK SNIDER and SHERWOOD OMENS, Producers

(Features)

ALASKA WILDERNESS LAKE, Alan Landsburg Prods.: ALAN LANDSBURG, Producer

THE HELLSTROM CHRONICLE, David L. Wolper Prods., Cinema 5, Ltd.: WALON GREEN, Producer

ON ANY SUNDAY, Bruce Brown Films-Solar Prods., Cinema 5, Ltd.: BRUCE BROWN, Producer

THE RA EXPEDITIONS Swedish Broadcasting Company, Interwest Film Corp.: LENNART EHRENBORG and THOR HEYERDAHL, Producers

THE SORROW AND THE PITY, Television Rencontre-Norddeutscher Rundfunk-Television Swiss Romande, Cinema 5, Ltd.: MARCEL OPHULS, Producer

1972   Forty-fifth Year

(Short Subjects)

HUNDERTWASSER'S RAINY DAY, An Argos Films-Peter Schamoni Film Prod.: PETER SCHAMONI, Producer

K-Z, A Nexus Film Production: GIORGIO TREVES, Producer

SELLING OUT, A Unit Productions Film: TADEUSZ JAWORSKI, Producer

THIS TINY WORLD, A Charles Huguenot van der Linden Production: CHARLES and MARTINA HUGENOT VAN DER LINDEN, Producers

THE TIDE OF TRAFFIC, A BP-Greenpark Production: HUMPHREY SWINGLER, Producer

(Features)

APE AND SUPER-APE, A Bert Haanstra, Film Production, Netherlands Ministry of Culture, Recreation and Social Welfare: BERT HAANSTRA, Producer

MALCOLM X, A Marvin Worth Production, Warner Bros.: MARVIN WORTH and ARNOLD PERL, Producers

MANSON, Merrick International Pictures: ROBERT HENDRICKSON and LAURENCE MERRICK, Producers

MARJOE, A Cinema X Production, Cinema 5, Ltd.: HOWARD SMITH and SARAH KERNOCHAN, Producers

THE SILENT REVOLUTION, A Leonaris Film Production: ECKEHARD MUNCK, Producer

1973   Forty-sixth Year

(Short Subjects)

BACKGROUND, D'Avino and Fucci-Stone Prods.: CARMEN D'AVINO, Producer

CHILDREN AT WORK, (Paisti Ag Obair), Gael-Linn Films: LOUIS MARCUS, Producer

CHRISTO'S VALLEY CURTAIN, A Maysles Films Prod.: ALBERT and DAVID MAYSLES, Producers

FOUR STONES FOR KANEMITSU, A Tamarind Prod.: (Producer credit in controversy)

PRINCETON: A SEARCH FOR ANSWERS, Krainin-Sage Prods.: JULIAN KRAININ and DeWITT L. SAGE, JR., Producers

(Features)

ALWAYS A NEW BEGINNING, Goodell Motion Pictures: JOHN D. GOODELL, Producer

BATTLE OF BERLIN, Chronos Film: BENGT VON ZUR MUEHLEN, Producer

THE GREAT AMERICAN COWBOY, Keith Merrill Associates-

Rodeo Film Prods.: KEITH MER-
RILL, Producer
JOURNEY TO THE OUTER LIMITS, The
National Geographic Society and
Wolper Prods.: ALEX GRASSHOFF,
Producer
WALLS OF FIRE, Mentor Prods.: GER-
TRUDE ROSS MARKS and EDMUND F.
PENNEY, Producers.

1974   Forty-seventh Year
(Short Subjects)

CITY OUT OF WILDERNESS, Francis
Thompson Inc.: FRANCIS THOMPSON,
Producer
DON'T, R. A. Films.: ROBIN LEH-
MAN, Producer
EXPLORATORIUM, A Jon Boorstin
Prod.: JON BOORSTIN, Producer
JOHN MUIR'S HIGH SIERRA, Dewitt
Jones Prods.: DE WITT JONES and
LESLEY FOSTER, Producers
NAKED YOGA, A Filmshop Prod.: RON-
ALD S. KASS and MERVYN LLOYD,
Producers

(Features)

ANTONIA: A PORTRAIT OF THE WOMAN,
Rocky Mountain Prods.: JUDY COL-
LINS and JILL GODMILOW, Producers
THE CHALLENGE . . . A TRIBUTE TO
MODERN ART, A World View Prod.:
HERBERT KLINE, Producer
THE 81ST BLOW, A Film by Ghetto
Fighters House: JACQUOT EHRLICH,
DAVID BERGMAN and HAIM GOURI,
Producers
HEARTS AND MINDS, A Touch-
stone-Audjeff-BBS Prod., Howard
Zucker/ Henry Jaglom-Rainbow Pic-
tures Presentation: PETER DAVIS
and BERT SCHNEIDER, Producers
THE WILD AND THE BRAVE, E.S.J.
Prods. in association with Tomorrow
Entertainment Inc. & Jones/Howard
Ltd.: NATALIE R. JONES and EUGENE
S. JONES, Producers

1975   Forty-eighth Year
(Short Subjects)

ARTHUR AND LILLIE, Department of
Communication, Stanford Univer-
sity: JON ELSE, STEVEN KOVACS and
KRISTINE SAMUELSON, Producers
THE END OF THE GAME, Opus
Films Limited: CLAIRE WILBUR
and ROBIN LEHMAN, Producers
MILLIONS OF YEARS AHEAD OF MAN,
BASF.: MANFRED BAIER, Producer
PROBES IN SPACE, Graphic Films:
GEORGE V. CASEY, Producer
WHISTLING SMITH, National Film Board
of Canada: BARRIE HOWELLS and
MICHAEL SCOTT, Producers

(Features)

THE CALIFORNIA REICH, Yasny Talking
Pictures: WALTER F. PARKES and
KEITH F. CRITCHLOW, Producers
FIGHTING FOR OUR LIVES, A Farm
Worker Film: GLEN PEARCY, Pro-
ducer
THE INCREDIBLE MACHINE, The Na-
tional Geographic Society and
Wolper Prods.: IRWIN ROSTEN, Pro-
ducer
THE MAN WHO SKIED DOWN
EVEREST, A Crawley Films Pre-
sentation: F. R. CRAWLEY,
JAMES HAGER and DALE HART-
LEBEN, Producers
THE OTHER HALF OF THE SKY: A CHINA
MEMOIR, MacLaine Productions:
SHIRLEY MacLAINE Producer

1976   Forty-ninth Year
(Short Subjects)

AMERICAN SHOESHINE, Titan Films:
SPARKY GREENE, Producer
BLACKWOOD, National Film Board of
Canada: TONY IANZELO and ANDY
THOMPSON, Producers
THE END OF THE ROAD, Pelican Films:
JOHN ARMSTRONG, Producer

Harlan County U.S.A., produced and directed by Barbara Kopple, won the 1976 Documentary Feature Award. *Cinema 5 Photo*

NUMBER OUR DAYS, Community Television of Southern California. LYNNE LITTMAN, Producer

UNIVERSE, Graphic Films Corp. for NASA: LESTER NOVROS, Producer

(Features)

HARLAN COUNTY, U.S.A., Cabin Creek Films: BARBARA KOPPLE, Producer

HOLLYWOOD ON TRIAL, October Films/Cinema Associates Production: JAMES GUTMAN and DAVID HELPERN, JR., Producers

OFF THE EDGE, Pentacle Films: MICHAEL FIRTH, Producer

PEOPLE OF THE WIND, Elizabeth E. Rogers Productions: ANTHONY HOWARTH and DAVID KOFF, Producers

VOLCANO: AN INQUIRY INTO THE LIFE AND DEATH OF MALCOLM LOWRY, National Film Board of Canada: DONALD BRITTAIN and ROBERT DUNCAN, Producers

1977   Fiftieth Year

(Short Subjects)

AGUEDA MARTINEZ: OUR PEOPLE, OUR COUNTRY, A Moctesuma Esparza Production: MOCTESUMA ESPARZA, Producer

FIRST EDITION, D. L. Sage Productions: HELEN WHITNEY and DEWITT L. SAGE, JR., Producers

GRAVITY IS MY ENEMY, A John Joseph Production: JOHN JOSEPH and JAN STUSSY, Producers

OF TIME, TOMBS AND TREASURE, A Charlie/Papa Production: JAMES R. MESSENGER, Producer.

THE SHETLAND EXPERIENCE, Balfour Films: DOUGLAS GORDON, Producer

(Features)

THE CHILDREN OF THEATRE STREET, Mack-Vaganova Company: ROBERT DORNHELM and EARLE MACK, Producers

HIGH GRASS CIRCUS, National Film
Board of Canada: BILL BRIND, TOR-
BEN SCHIOLER and TONY IANZELO,
Producers

HOMAGE TO CHAGALL—THE COLOURS
OF LOVE, A CBC Production: HARRY
RASKY, Producer

UNION MAIDS, A Klein, Reichert,
Mogulescu Production: JAMES KLEIN,
JULIA REICHERT and MILES MOGU-
LESCU, Producers

WHO ARE THE DEBOLTS? AND
WHERE DID THEY GET NINE-
TEEN KIDS?, Korty Films and
Charles M. Schulz Creative Associ-
ates in association with Sanrio Films:
JOHN KORTY, DAN McCANN
and WARREN L. LOCKHART,
Producers

SPECIAL EFFECTS

In 1938 the Academy Board of Governors voted an honorary award to several individuals who had created the special photographic and sound effects in the Paramount film *Spawn of the North*. By 1939 the category of Special Effects had been officially established as an annual award. Except for three years, 1951–53, it remained an annual award until 1963 when the Academy elected to split the award into two new categories, Special Visual Effects and Sound Effects.

One should note that several achievements listed in the Scientific or Technical awards have contributed to the film industry's ability to produce special effects.

1939   Twelfth Year

GONE WITH THE WIND, Selznick, M-G-M: JOHN R. COSGROVE, FRED ALBIN and ARTHUR JOHNS

ONLY ANGELS HAVE WINGS, Columbia: ROY DAVIDSON and EDWIN C. HAHN

PRIVATE LIVES OF ELIZABETH AND ESSEX, Warner Bros.: BYRON HASKIN and NATHAN LEVINSON

THE RAINS CAME, 20th Century-Fox: E. H. HANSEN and FRED SERSEN

TOPPER TAKES A TRIP, Roach, UA: ROY SEAWRIGHT

UNION PACIFIC, Paramount: FARCIOT EDOUART, GORDON JENNINGS and LOREN RYDER

THE WIZARD OF OZ, Metro-Goldwyn-Mayer: A. ARNOLD GILLESPIE and DOUGLAS SHEARER

1940   Thirteenth Year

THE BLUE BIRD, 20th Century-Fox
Photographic: FRED SERSEN
Sound: E. H. HANSEN

BOOM TOWN, Metro-Goldwyn-Mayer
Photographic: A. ARNOLD GILLESPIE
Sound: DOUGLAS SHEARER

THE BOYS FROM SYRACUSE, Universal
Photographic: JOHN P. FULTON
Sound: BERNARD B. BROWN and JOSEPH LAPIS

LARGE CAPITAL LETTERS DENOTE WINNER

DR. CYCLOPS, Paramount
Photographic: FARCIOT EDOUART and GORDON JENNINGS
Sound: No credit listed

FOREIGN CORRESPONDENT, Wanger, UA
Photographic: PAUL EAGLER
Sound: THOMAS T. MOULTON

THE INVISIBLE MAN RETURNS, Universal
Photographic: JOHN P. FULTON
Sound: BERNARD B. BROWN and WILLIAM HEDGECOCK

THE LONG VOYAGE HOME, Argosy-Wanger, UA
Photographic: R. T. LAYTON and R. O. BINGER
Sound: THOMAS T. MOULTON

ONE MILLION B.C., Roach, UA
Photographic: ROY SEAWRIGHT
Sound: ELMER RAGUSE

REBECCA, Selznick, UA
Photographic: JACK COSGROVE
Sound: ARTHUR JOHNS

THE SEA HAWK, Warner Bros.
Photographic: BYRON HASKIN
Sound: NATHAN LEVINSON

SWISS FAMILY ROBINSON, RKO Radio
Photographic: VERNON L. WALKER
Sound: JOHN O. AALBERG

THE THIEF OF BAGDAD, Korda, UA
Photographic: LAWRENCE BUTLER

Sound: JACK WHITNEY
TYPHOON, Paramount
Photographic: FARCIOT EDOUART and GORDON JENNINGS
Sound: LOREN RYDER
WOMEN IN WAR, Republic
Photographic: HOWARD J. LYDECKER, WILLIAM BRADFORD and ELLIS J. THACKERY
Sound: HERBERT NORSCH

1941   Fourteenth Year

ALOMA OF THE SOUTH SEAS, Paramount
Photographic: FARCIOT EDOUART and GORDON JENNINGS
Sound: LOUIS MESENKOP
FLIGHT COMMAND, Metro-Goldwyn-Mayer
Photographic: A. ARNOLD GILLESPIE
Sound: DOUGLAS SHEARER
I WANTED WINGS, Paramount
Photographic: FARCIOT EDOUART and GORDON JENNINGS
Sound: LOUIS MESENKOP
THE INVISIBLE WOMAN, Universal
Photographic: JOHN FULTON
Sound: JOHN HALL
THE SEA WOLF, Warner Bros.
Photographic: BYRON HASKIN
Sound: NATHAN LEVINSON
THAT HAMILTON WOMAN, Korda, UA
Photographic: LAWRENCE BUTLER
Sound: WILLIAM H. WILMARTH
TOPPER RETURNS, Roach, UA
Photographic: ROY SEAWRIGHT
Sound: ELMER RAGUSE
A YANK IN THE R.A.F., 20th Century-Fox
Photographic: FRED SERSEN
Sound: E. H. HANSEN

1942   Fifteenth Year

THE BLACK SWAN, 20th Century-Fox
Photographic: FRED SERSEN
Sound: ROGER HEMAN and GEORGE LEVERETT
DESPERATE JOURNEY, Warner Bros.
Photographic: BYRON HASKIN
Sound: NATHAN LEVINSON
FLYING TIGERS, Republic
Photographic: HOWARD LYDECKER
Sound: DANIEL J. BLOOMBERG
INVISIBLE AGENT, Universal
Photographic: JOHN FULTON
Sound: BERNARD B. BROWN
JUNGLE BOOK, Korda, UA
Photographic: LAWRENCE BUTLER
Sound: WILLIAM H. WILMARTH
MRS. MINIVER, Metro-Goldwyn-Mayer
Photographic: A. ARNOLD GILLESPIE and WARREN NEWCOMBE
Sound: DOUGLAS SHEARER
THE NAVY COMES THROUGH, RKO Radio
Photographic: VERNON L. WALKER
Sound: JAMES G. STEWART
ONE OF OUR AIRCRAFT IS MISSING, Powell, UA (British)
Photographic: RONALD NEAME
Sound: C. C. STEVENS
PRIDE OF THE YANKEES, Goldwyn, RKO Radio
Photographic: JACK COSGROVE and RAY BINGER
Sound: THOMAS T. MOULTON
REAP THE WILD WIND, Paramount
Photographic: FARCIOT EDOUART, GORDON JENNINGS and WILLIAM L. PEREIRA
Sound: LOUIS MESENKOP

1943   Sixteenth Year

AIR FORCE, Warner Bros.
Photographic: HANS KOENEKAMP and REX WIMPY
Sound: NATHAN LEVINSON
BOMBARDIER, RKO Radio
Photographic: VERNON L. WALKER
Sound: JAMES G. STEWART and ROY GRANVILLE
CRASH DIVE, 20th Century-Fox
Photographic: FRED SERSEN
Sound: ROGER HEMAN

THE NORTH STAR, Goldwyn, RKO
Radio
Photographic: CLARENCE SLIFER and
R. O. BINGER
Sound: THOMAS T. MOULTON
SO PROUDLY WE HAIL, Paramount
Photographic: FARCIOT EDOUART and
GORDON JENNINGS
Sound: GEORGE DUTTON
STAND BY FOR ACTION, Metro-
Goldwyn-Mayer
Photographic: A. ARNOLD GILLESPIE
and DONALD JAHRAUS
Sound: MICHAEL STEINORE

1944 Seventeenth Year

THE ADVENTURES OF MARK TWAIN,
Warner Bros.
Photographic: PAUL DETLEFSEN and
JOHN CROUSE
Sound: NATHAN LEVINSON
DAYS OF GLORY, RKO Radio
Photographic: VERNON L. WALKER
Sound: JAMES G. STEWART and ROY
GRANVILLE
SECRET COMMAND, Columbia
Photographic: DAVID ALLEN, RAY
CORY and ROBERT WRIGHT
Sound: RUSSELL MALMGREN and
HARRY KUSNICK
SINCE YOU WENT AWAY, Selznick, UA
Photographic: JOHN R. COSGROVE
Sound: ARTHUR JOHNS
THE STORY OF DR. WASSELL, Paramount
Photographic: FARCIOT EDOUART and
GORDON JENNINGS
Sound: GEORGE DUTTON
THIRTY SECONDS OVER TOKYO,
Metro-Goldwyn-Mayer
Photographic: A. ARNOLD GIL-
LESPIE, DONALD JAHRAUS and
WARREN NEWCOMBE
Sound: DOUGLAS SHEARER
WILSON, 20th Century-Fox
Photographic: FRED SERSEN
Sound: ROGER HEMAN

1945 Eighteenth Year

CAPTAIN EDDIE, 20th Century-Fox
Photographic: FRED SERSEN and SOL
HALPRIN
Sound: ROGER HEMAN and HARRY
LEONARD
SPELLBOUND, Selznick, UA
Photographic: JACK COSGROVE
Sound: No credits listed
THEY WERE EXPENDABLE, Metro-
Goldwyn-Mayer
Photographic: A. ARNOLD GILLESPIE,
DONALD JAHRAUS and R. A. Mac-
DONALD
Sound: MICHAEL STEINORE
A THOUSAND AND ONE NIGHTS, Colum-
bia
Photographic: L. W. BUTLER
Sound: RAY BOMBA
WONDER MAN, Goldwyn, RKO
Radio
Photographic: JOHN FULTON
Sound: A. W. JOHNS

1946 Nineteenth Year

BLITHE SPIRIT, Rank UA (British)
Visual: THOMAS HOWARD
Audible: No credit
A STOLEN LIFE, Warner Bros.
Visual: WILLIAM MCGANN
Audible: NATHAN LEVINSON

1947 Twentieth Year

GREEN DOLPHIN STREET, Metro-
Goldwyn-Mayer
Visual: A. ARNOLD GILLESPIE
and WARREN NEWCOMBE
Audible: DOUGLAS SHEARER and
MICHAEL STEINORE
UNCONQUERED, Paramount
Visual: FARCIOT EDOUART, DEV-
EREUX JENNINGS, GORDON JEN-
NINGS, WALLACE KELLEY and PAUL
LERPAE
Audible: GEORGE DUTTON

1948   Twenty-first Year

DEEP WATERS, 20th Century-Fox
   Visual: RALPH HAMMERAS, FRED
   SERSEN and EDWARD SNYDER
   Audible: ROGER HEMAN
PORTRAIT OF JENNIE, The Selznick
   Studio
   Visual: PAUL EAGLER, J. Mc-
   MILLAN JOHNSON, RUSSELL
   SHEARMAN and CLARENCE
   SLIFER
   Audible: CHARLES FREEMAN and
   JAMES G. STEWART

1949   Twenty-second Year

MIGHTY JOE YOUNG, ARKO, RKO
   Radio
TULSA, Walter Wanger Pictures, Eagle-
   Lion

1950   Twenty-third Year

DESTINATION MOON, George Pal,
   Eagle-Lion Classics
SAMSON AND DELILAH, Cecil B. De-
   Mille, Paramount

1951   Twenty-fourth Year

Note: 1951 thru 1953 Special Effects
   classified as an "other" Award
   (not necessarily given each year)
   hence, no nominations.
WHEN WORLDS COLLIDE, Paramount

1952   Twenty-fifth Year

PLYMOUTH ADVENTURE, Metro-
   Goldwyn-Mayer

1953   Twenty-sixth Year

THE WAR OF THE WORLDS, Paramount

1954   Twenty-seventh Year

Note: Special Effects again classified
   as an Annual Award.
HELL AND HIGH WATER, 20th Century-
   Fox

THEM!, Warner Bros.
20,000 LEAGUES UNDER THE SEA,
   Walt Disney Studios

1955   Twenty-eighth Year

THE BRIDGES AT TOKO-RI, Para-
   mount
THE DAM BUSTERS, Associated British
   Picture Corp., Ltd. (British)
THE RAINS OF RANCHIPUR, 20th Cen-
   tury-Fox

1956   Twenty-ninth Year

FORBIDDEN PLANET, Metro-Goldwyn-
   Mayer: A. ARNOLD GILLESPIE, IR-
   VING RIES and WESLEY C. MILLER
THE TEN COMMANDMENTS, Mo-
   tion Picture Associates, Inc., Para-
   mount: JOHN FULTON

1957   Thirtieth Year

THE ENEMY BELOW, 20th Century-
   Fox
   Audible: WALTER ROSSI
THE SPIRIT OF ST. LOUIS, Leland Hay-
   ward-Billy Wilder, Warner Bros.
   Visual: LOUIS LICHTENFIELD

1958   Thirty-first Year

TOM THUMB, Galaxy Pictures,
   M-G-M.
   Visual: TOM HOWARD
TORPEDO RUN, Metro-Goldwyn-Mayer
   Visual: A. ARNOLD GILLESPIE
   Audible: HAROLD HUMBROCK

1959   Thirty-second Year

BEN-HUR, Metro-Goldwyn-Mayer
   Visual: A. ARNOLD GILLESPIE
   and ROBERT MacDONALD
   Audible: MILO LORY
JOURNEY TO THE CENTER OF THE
   EARTH, Joseph M. Schenck En-
   terprises, Inc. & Cooga Mooga Film
   Prods., Inc., 20th Century-Fox
   Visual: L. B. ABBOTT and JAMES B.
   GORDON

Audible: CARL FAULKNER

1960   Thirty-third Year
THE LAST VOYAGE, Andrew and
Virginia Stone Prod., M-G-M
Visual: A. J. LOHMAN
THE TIME MACHINE, Galaxy Films
Prod., M-G-M
Visual: GENE WARREN and TIM
BAAR

1961   Thirty-fourth Year
THE ABSENT MINDED PROFESSOR, Walt
Disney Prods., Buena Vista Dist.
Co.
Visual: ROBERT A. MATTEY and
EUSTACE LYCETT
THE GUNS OF NAVARONE, Carl
Foreman Prod., Columbia
Visual: BILL WARRINGTON
Audible: VIVIAN C. GREENHAM

1962   Thirty-fifth Year
THE LONGEST DAY, Darryl F. Zan-
uck Prods., 20th Century-Fox
Visual: ROBERT MacDONALD
Audible: JACQUES MAUMONT
MUTINY ON THE BOUNTY, Arcola
Prod., M-G-M
Visual: A. ARNOLD GILLESPIE
Audible: MILO LORY

For the 36th Awards Year (1963) the
Academy Board of Governors, in recognition of the fact that the best visual
effects and the best audible effects each
year did not necessarily occur in the
same picture, voted to discontinue the
Special Effects Award and created two
new Awards: The Special Visual Effects Award and the Sound Effects
Award.

SPECIAL VISUAL EFFECTS

The Special Effects award begun in 1939 had recognized persons responsible for both photographic and sound effects on a picture. For the 36th Awards, the Academy voted to eliminate the Special Effects award and create instead two new awards: Special Visual Effects and Sound Effects. This change recognized the fact that the best visual effects and best audible effects each year did not necessarily occur in the same picture. The Sound Effects award was discontinued after 1967, though Special Visual Effects remained an annual award through 1971. After that recognition in this field came through Special Achievement awards. Special Achievement awards in 1975 and 1977 honored sound effects.

1963 Thirty-sixth Year
THE BIRDS, Alfred J. Hitchcock Prod., Universal: UB IWERKS
CLEOPATRA, 20th Century-Fox Ltd.-MCL Films S.A.-WALWA Films S.A. Prod., 20th Century-Fox: EMIL KOSA, JR.

1964 Thirty-seventh Year
MARY POPPINS, Walt Disney Prods. PETER ELLENSHAW, HAMIL-TON LUSKE and EUSTACE LY-CETT.
7 FACES OF DR. LAO, Galaxy-Scarus Prod., Metro-Goldwyn-Mayer: JIM DANFORTH.

1965 Thirty-eighth Year
THE GREATEST STORY EVER TOLD, George Stevens Prod., United Artists: J. MCMILLAN JOHNSON
THUNDERBALL, Broccoli-Saltzman-McClory Prod., United Artists: JOHN STEARS

1966 Thirty-ninth Year
FANTASTIC VOYAGE, 20th Century-Fox: ART CRUICKSHANK
HAWAII, Mirisch Corp. of Delaware Prod., United Artists: LINWOOD G. DUNN

LARGE CAPITAL LETTERS DENOTE WINNER

1967 Fortieth Year
DOCTOR DOLITTLE, Apjac Prods., 20th Century-Fox: L. B. ABBOTT
TOBRUK, Gibraltar Prods.-Corman Company-Universal Prod., Universal: HOWARD A. ANDERSON, JR. and ALBERT WHITLOCK

1968 Forty-first Year
ICE STATION ZEBRA, Filmways Prod., Metro-Goldwyn-Mayer: HAL MILLAR and J. MCMILLAN JOHNSON
2001: A SPACE ODYSSEY, Polaris Prod., Metro-Goldwyn-Mayer: STANLEY KUBRICK

1969 Forty-second Year
KRAKATOA, EAST OF JAVA, American Broadcasting Companies-Cinerama Prod., Cinerama: EUGENE LOURIE and ALEX WELDON
MAROONED, Frankovich-Sturges Prod., Columbia: ROBBIE ROBERTSON

1970 Forty-third Year
PATTON, 20th Century-Fox: ALEX WELDON
TORA! TORA! TORA!, 20th Century-Fox: A. D. FLOWERS and L. B. ABBOTT

1971   Forty-fourth Year

Note: Special Visual Effects not given
as an Annual Award after 1971.

BEDKNOBS AND BROOMSTICKS,
Walt Disney Prods., Buena Vista
Distribution Company: ALAN

MALEY, EUSTACE LYCETT and
DANNY LEE

WHEN DINOSAURS RULED THE EARTH,
A Hammer Film Prod., Warner
Bros.: JIM DANFORTH and ROGER
DICKEN

SOUND EFFECTS

1963 Thirty-sixth Year

A GATHERING OF EAGLES, Universal: ROBERT L. BRATTON

IT'S A MAD, MAD, MAD, MAD WORLD, Casey Prod., UA: WALTER G. ELLIOTT

1964 Thirty-seventh Year

GOLDFINGER, Eon Prod., UA: NORMAN WANSTALL

THE LIVELY SET, Universal: ROBERT L. BRATTON

1965 Thirty-eighth Year

THE GREAT RACE, Patricia-Jalem-Reynard Prod., Warner Bros.

TREGOWETH BROWN

VON RYAN'S EXPRESS, P-R Prods., 20th Century-Fox: WALTER A. ROSSI

1966 Thirty-ninth Year

FANTASTIC VOYAGE, 20th Century-Fox: WALTER ROSSI

GRAND PRIX, Douglas-Lewis-John Frankenheimer-Cherokee Prod., M-G-M: GORDON DANIEL

1967 Fortieth Year

Note: Sound Effects award not given after 1967.

THE DIRTY DOZEN, MKH Prods., Ltd., M-G-M: JOHN POYNER

IN THE HEAT OF THE NIGHT, Mirisch Corp. Prod., UA: JAMES A. RICHARD

SPECIAL ACHIEVEMENT AWARDS

Special Achievement awards are given for work previously recognized as Special Effects, Special Visual Effects, or Sound Effects. The category was begun in 1972 when the Academy Board of Governors voted to switch Special Visual Effects from an annual to an "other" award which need not be given each year.

The Academy president appoints a Visual Effects Award Committee consisting of art directors, cinematographers, and recognized technicians who are experts in the field. The following categories of visual effects are considered:

1—Full-sized Mechanical
2—Matte Paintings
3—Miniatures
4—Optical
5—Projection Process
6—Animation

The committee reviews eligible films and grades each on a point system. Three options are possible: If two or more films achieve a predetermined score, the committee may recommend up to five nominees to be placed on the ballot for an *annual* award in Visual Effects. If only one film meets the required score, the committee may recommend that the Board of Governors vote a Special Achievement award for Visual Effects. If no film achieves the required score, the committee may decide that no award be given in this field.

1972   Forty-fifth Year
Visual Effects: L. B. ABBOTT and A. D. FLOWERS for *The Poseidon Adventure,* An Irwin Allen Production, 20th Century-Fox

1973   Forty-sixth Year
None

1974   Forty-seventh Year
Visual Effects: FRANK BRENDEL, GLEN ROBINSON and ALBERT WHITLOCK for *Earthquake,* A Universal-Mark Robson-Filmakers Group Production, Universal

1975   Forty-eighth Year
Sound Effects: PETER BERKOS for *The Hindenburg,* A Robert Wise-

LARGE CAPITAL LETTERS DENOTE WINNER

Filmakers Group-Universal Production, Universal
Visual Effects: ALBERT WHITLOCK and GLEN ROBINSON for *The Hindenburg,* A Robert-Wise Filmakers Group-Universal Production, Universal

1976   Forty-ninth Year
Visual Effects: CARLO RAMBALDI, GLEN ROBINSON and FRANK VAN DER VEER for *King Kong,* A Dino De Laurentiis Production, Paramount
Visual Effects: L. B. ABBOTT, GLEN ROBINSON and MATTHEW YURICICH for *Logan's Run,* A Saul David Production, Metro-Goldwyn-Mayer

1977   Fiftieth Year
Sound Effects: BENJAMIN BURTT, JR. for the creation of the alien, creature, and robot voices in *Star Wars,* A Twentieth Century-Fox Production, Twentieth Century-Fox

Sound Effects Editing Award: CLOSE ENCOUNTERS OF THE THIRD KIND, Close Encounter Productions, Columbia. FRANK WARNER, Supervising Sound Effects Editor

VISUAL EFFECTS

When a single achievement in visual effects is recommended for recognition by the Visual Effects Award Committee, the Academy Board of Governors votes a Special Achievement Award. But when two or more (up to five) films are designated by the committee, present rules call for these nominees to be placed in an annual award category called Visual Effects. As with all annual awards, the winner is chosen by the entire Academy membership.

Achievements for this award are judged on the basis of:
- (a) the necessity of the visual effects to overcome economic infeasibility and/or physical impracticability, and,
- (b) the skill and fidelity with which the illusion of reality and/or fantasy is achieved, and
- (c) consideration of all effects achievements and selections of those which contribute most importantly to the overall production.

1977   Fiftieth Year

CLOSE ENCOUNTERS OF THE THIRD KIND, Close Encounter Productions, Columbia: ROY ARBOGAST, DOUGLAS TRUMBULL, MATTHEW YURICICH, GREGORY JEIN and RICHARD YURICICH

STAR WARS, A Twentieth Century-Fox Production, Twentieth Century-Fox: JOHN STEARS, JOHN DYKSTRA, RICHARD EDLUND, GRANT McCUNE and ROBERT BLALACK

LARGE CAPITAL LETTERS DENOTE WINNER

FOREIGN LANGUAGE FILM AWARD

When the Academy was founded in 1927 Conrad Nagel proposed that it be named the Academy of Motion Picture Arts & Sciences International. Though the last word of his suggestion was dropped, the Academy would eventually recognize the worldwide nature of film through a foreign film award. By the end of World War II some groups such as the National Board of Review and the New York Film Critics had been recognizing foreign films for over a decade, and a special Oscar in 1946 to Laurence Olivier for *Henry V* prompted *Variety* to speculate that the Academy too would soon set up an international award. The 1947 ceremonies included a special award to the Italian neo-realist film *Shoeshine,* and Academy president Jean Hersholt called for an annual award for foreign language films. "An international award, if properly planned and carefully administered," he added, "would promote a closer relationship between American film craftsmen and those of other countries." The Academy Board of Governors continued to give honorary Oscars to foreign language films each year until 1956 when a new category was officially established, and the Best Foreign Language Film became an annual award. In 1957 rules changed to give the award to the production company rather than to the individual producers.

To be eligible a film must have a soundtrack in the original language and carry English subtitles. Each country decides what film to submit to the Academy, and only one film is accepted from each country. In the last twenty years the Academy has averaged sixteen entries per year. The entries are screened by a Foreign Language Film Award Committee which determines the five nominees. Final voting is restricted to Academy members who have seen all nominated films.

1956 Twenty-ninth Year

THE CAPTAIN OF KÖPENICK, Real-Film (Germany): GYULA TREBITSCH and WALTER KOPPEL, Producers

GERVAISE, Agnes Delahaie Productions Cinematographiques & Silver Film (France): ANNIE DORFMANN, Producer

HARP OF BURMA, Nikkatsu Corporation (Japan): MASAYUKI TAKAGI, Producer

LA STRADA, A Ponti-De Laurentiis Production (Italy). DINO DE

LARGE CAPITAL LETTERS DENOTE WINNER

LAURENTIIS and CARLO PONTI, Producers

QIVITOQ, A/S Nordisk Films Kompagni (Denmark): O. DALSGAARD-OLSEN, Producer

1957 Thirtieth Year

THE DEVIL CAME AT NIGHT, Gloria Film (Germany)

GATES OF PARIS, Filmsonor S.A. Production (France)

MOTHER INDIA, Mehboob Productions (India)

THE NIGHTS OF CABIRIA, Dino De

Ingmar Bergman's *The Virgin Spring*, the 1960 Foreign Language Film Award winner. *Janus Films Photo*

Laurentiis Production (Italy)
NINE LIVES, Nordsjofilm (Norway)

1958 Thirty-first Year

ARMS AND THE MAN, H. R. Sokal-P. Goldbaum Production, Bavaria Filmkunst A.G. (Germany)
LA VENGANZA, Guion Producciones Cinematograficas (Spain)
MY UNCLE, Specta-Gray-Alter Films in association with Films du Centaure (France)
THE ROAD A YEAR LONG, Jadran Film (Yugoslavia)
THE USUAL UNIDENTIFIED THIEVES, Lux-Vides-Cinecitta (Italy)

1959 Thirty-second Year

BLACK ORPHEUS, Dispatfilm & Gemma Cinematografica (France)
THE BRIDGE, Fono Film (Germany)
THE GREAT WAR, Dino De Laurentiis Cinematografica (Italy)

PAW, Laterna Film (Denmark)
THE VILLAGE ON THE RIVER, N. V. Nationale Filmproductie Maatschappij (The Netherlands)

1960 Thirty-third Year

KAPO, Vides-Zebrafilm-Cineriz (Italy)
LA VERITÉ, Han Productions (France)
MACARIO, Clasa Films Mundiales, S.A. (Mexico)
THE NINTH CIRCLE, Jadran Film Production (Yugoslavia)
THE VIRGIN SPRING, A. B. Svensk Filmindustri (Sweden)

1961 Thirty-fourth Year

HARRY AND THE BUTLER, Bent Christensen Production (Denmark)
IMMORTAL LOVE, Shochiku Co., Ltd. (Japan)
THE IMPORTANT MAN, Peliculas Rodriguez, S.A. (Mexico)
PLACIDO, Jet Films (Spain)

252

THROUGH A GLASS DARKLY,
A. B. Svensk Filmindustri (Sweden)

1962   Thirty-fifth Year

ELECTRA, A Michael Cacoyannis Production (Greece)

THE FOUR DAYS OF NAPLES, Titanus-
Metro (Italy)

KEEPER OF PROMISES (The Given
Word), Cinedistri (Brazil)

SUNDAYS AND CYBELE, Terra-
Fides-Orsay-Trocadero Films
(France)

TLAYUCAN, Producciones Matouk,
S.A. (Mexico)

1963   Thirty-sixth Year

FEDERICO FELLINI'S 8½, A Cineriz
Production (Italy)

KNIFE IN THE WATER, A Kamera Unit
of Film Polski Production (Poland)

LOS TARANTOS, Tecisa-Films R.B.
(Spain)

THE RED LANTERNS, Th. Damaskinos
& V. Michaelides A.E. (Greece)

TWIN SISTERS OF KYOTO, Shochiku Co.,
Ltd. (Japan)

1964   Thirty-seventh Year

RAVEN'S END, AB Europa Film (Sweden)

SALLAH, A Sallah Film Ltd. Production
(Israel)

THE UMBRELLAS OF CHERBOURG, A
Parc-Madeleine-Beta Films Production (France)

WOMAN IN THE DUNES, A Teshigahara
Production (Japan)

YESTERDAY, TODAY AND TO-
MORROW, A Champion-Concordia
Production (Italy)

1965   Thirty-eighth Year

BLOOD ON THE LAND, Th. Damaskinos
& V. Michaelides, A.E.-Finos Film
(Greece)

DEAR JOHN, A.B. Sandrew-Ateljeerna
(Sweden)

KWAIDAN, A Toho Company, Ltd. Production (Japan)

MARRIAGE ITALIAN STYLE, A Champion-Concordia Production (Italy)

THE SHOP ON MAIN STREET, A
Ceskoslovensky Film Production
(Czechoslovakia)

1966   Thirty-ninth Year

THE BATTLE OF ALGIERS, Igor Film-
Casbah Film Production (Italy)

LOVES OF A BLONDE, Barrandov Film
Production (Czechoslovakia)

A MAN AND A WOMAN, Les Films
13 Production (France)

PHARAOH, Kadr Film Unit Production
(Poland)

THREE, Avala Film Production (Yugoslavia)

1967   Fortieth Year

CLOSELY WATCHED TRAINS, Barrandov Film Studio Production
(Czechoslovakia)

EL AMOR BRUJO, Films R.B., S.A.
Production (Spain)

I EVEN MET HAPPY GYPSIES, Avala Film
Production (Yugoslavia)

LIVE FOR LIFE, Les Films Ariane-Les
Productions Artistes Associes-Vides
Films Production (France)

PORTRAIT OF CHIEKO, Shochiku Co.,
Ltd. Production (Japan)

1968   Forty-first Year

THE BOYS OF PAUL STREET, Bohgros
Films-Mafilm Studio I Production
(Hungary)

THE FIREMEN'S BALL, Barrandov Film
Studio Production (Czechoslovakia)

THE GIRL WITH THE PISTOL, Documento Film Production (Italy)

STOLEN KISSES, Les Films du Carrosse-
Les Productions Artistes Associes
Production (France)

WAR AND PEACE, Mosfilm Production (Russia)

1969   *Forty-second Year*
ADALEN'31, AB Svensk Filmindustri Production (Sweden)
THE BATTLE OF NERETVA, United Film Producers-Igor Film-Eichberg Film-Commonwealth United Production (Yugoslavia)
THE BROTHERS KARAMAZOV, Mosfilm Production (U.S.S.R.)
MY NIGHT WITH MAUD, Films du Losange-F.F.P.-Films du Carrosse-Films des Deux Mondes-Films de la Pleiade-Gueville-Renn-Simar Films Production (France)
Z, Reggane-O.N.C.I.C Production (Algeria)

1970   *Forty-third Year*
FIRST LOVE, Alfa Prods.-Seitz Film Prod. (Switzerland)
HOA-BINH, Madeleine-Parc-La Gueville-C.A.P.A.C. Prod. (France)
INVESTIGATION OF A CITIZEN ABOVE SUSPICION, Vera Films Prod. (Italy)
PAIX SUR LES CHAMPS, Philippe Collette-E.G.C. Prod. (Belgium)
TRISTANA, Forbes Films, Ltd.-United Cineworld-Epoca Films-Talia Film-Les Films Corona-Selenia Cinematografica Prod. (Spain)

1971   *Forty-fourth Year*
DODES'KA-DEN, A Toho Company, Ltd.-Yonki no Kai Prod. (Japan)
THE EMIGRANTS, A Svensk Filmindustri Prod. (Sweden)
THE GARDEN OF THE FINZI-CONTINIS, A Gianni Hecht Lucari-Arthur Cohn Prod. (Italy)
THE POLICEMAN, An Ephi-Israeli Motion Picture Studios Prod. (Israel)
TCHAIKOVSKY, A Dimitri Tiomkin-Mosfilm Studios Prod. (U.S.S.R.)

1972   *Forty-fifth Year*
THE DAWNS HERE ARE QUIET, A Gorky Film Studios Prod. (U.S.S.R.)
THE DISCREET CHARM OF THE BOURGEOISIE, A Serge Silberman Prod. (France)
I LOVE YOU ROSA, A Noah Films Ltd. Prod. (Israel)
MY DEAREST SENORITA, An El Iman Prod. (Spain)
THE NEW LAND, A Svensk Filmindustri Prod. (Sweden)

1973   *Forty-sixth Year*
DAY FOR NIGHT, A Les Films Du Carrosse-P.E.C.F. (Paris)-P.I.C. (Rome) Prod. (France)
THE HOUSE ON CHELOUCHE STREET, A Noah Films Prod. (Israel)
L 'INVITATION, A Groupe 5 Geneve-Television Suisse Romande-Citel Films-Planfilm (Paris) Prod. (Switzerland)
THE PEDESTRIAN, An ALFA Glarus-MFG-Seitz-Zev Braun Prod. (Federal Republic of West Germany)
TURKISH DELIGHT, A Rob Houwer Film Prod. (The Netherlands)

1974   *Forty-seventh Year*
AMARCORD, An F. C. (Rome)-P.E.C.F. (Paris) Prod. (Italy)
CATSPLAY, A Hunnia Studio Prod. (Hungary)
THE DELUGE, A Film Polski Prod. (Poland)
LACOMBE, LUCIEN, An NEF-UPF (Paris)-Vides Film (Rome)-Hallelujah Film (Munich) Prod. (France)
THE TRUCE, A Tamames-Zemborain Prod. (Argentina)

1975   *Forty-eighth Year*
DERSU UZALA, A Mosfilms Studios Production (U.S.S.R)

The Garden of the Finzi-Continis, directed by Vittorio De Sica, received the 1971 Oscar for Best Foreign Language Film *Cinema 5 Photo*

LAND OF PROMISE, A Film Polski Production (Poland)

LETTERS FROM MARUSIA, A Conacine Production (Mexico)

SANDAKAN NO. 8, A Toho-Haiyuza Production (Japan)

SCENT OF A WOMAN, A Dean Film Production (Italy)

1976   Forty-ninth Year

BLACK AND WHITE IN COLOR, An Arthur Cohn Production/Societe Ivoirienne De Cinema (Ivory Coast)

COUSIN, COUSINE, Les Films Pomereu-Gaumont Production (France)

JACOB, THE LIAR, A VEB/DEFA Production (German Democratic Republic)

NIGHTS AND DAYS, A Polish Corporation for Film-"KADR" Film Unit Production (Poland)

SEVEN BEAUTIES, A Medusa Distribuzione Production (Italy)

1977   Fiftieth Year

IPHIGENIA, A Greek Film Centre Production (Greece)

MADAME ROSA, A Lira Films Production (France)

OPERATION THUNDERBOLT, A Golan-Globus Production (Israel)

A SPECIAL DAY, A Canafox Films Production (Italy)

THAT OBSCURE OBJECT OF DESIRE, A Greenwich-Les Films Galaxie-In Cine Production (Spain)

HONORARY AWARDS

The Honorary Awards, known as Special Awards until 1950, are not limited to achievements from a single year and thus provide a flexibility not permitted in the annual awards. People such as D. W. Griffith, Charlie Chaplin, Lillian Gish, and Mack Sennett, whose greatest achievements in film came before the Academy Awards were established, can still be recognized by the Academy through Honorary Awards. Outstanding achievement in makeup, choreography, and other fields which fall outside the annual award categories can also be covered by Honorary Oscars. The Board of Governors has used this category to recognize service to the Academy and to honor persons whose entire career is more distinguished than single, yearly achievements which may have been overlooked by the voters. One should note that several annual award categories such as Special Effects, Documentary, Color Cinematography, and Foreign Language Film began as Honorary Awards

Honorary Awards are voted by the Academy Board of Governors.

1927/28 First Year
WARNER BROS. for producing
The Jazz Singer, the pioneer outstanding talking picture, which has
revolutionized the industry.
(statuette)
CHARLES CHAPLIN for versatility
and genius in writing, acting, directing and producing *The Circus.*
(statuette)

1928/29 Second Year
No Special Awards given this year.

1929/30 Third Year
No Special Awards given this year.

1930/31 Fourth Year
No Special Awards given this year.

1931/32 Fifth Year
WALT DISNEY for the creation of
Mickey Mouse. (statuette)

LARGE CAPITAL LETTERS DENOTE WINNER

1933 Sixth Year
No Special Awards given this year.

1934 Seventh Year
SHIRLEY TEMPLE, in grateful recognition of her outstanding contribution
to screen entertainment during the
year 1934. (miniature statuette)

1935 Eighth Year
DAVID WARK GRIFFITH, for his
distinguished creative achievements
as director and producer and his invaluable initiative and lasting contributions to the progress of the motion picture arts. (statuette)

1936 Ninth Year
MARCH OF TIME for its significance
to motion pictures and for having
revolutionized one of the most important branches of the industry—the
newsreel. (statuette)
W. HOWARD GREENE and
HAROLD ROSSON for the color
cinematography of the Selznick In-

At the first awards, Charlie Chaplin, seen here with Merna Kennedy and Henry Bergman, was given a Special Award "for versatility and genius in writing, acting, directing, and producing *The Circus*." (1928) *United Artists Photo*

ternational Production, *The Garden Of Allah*. (plaques)

1937 *Tenth Year*

MACK SENNETT, "for his lasting contribution to the comedy technique of the screen, the basic principles of which are as important today as when they were first put into practice, the Academy presents a Special Award to that master of fun, discoverer of stars, sympathetic, kindly, understanding comedy genius—Mack Sennett." (statuette)

EDGAR BERGEN for his outstanding comedy creation, Charlie McCarthy. (wooden statuette)

THE MUSEUM OF MODERN ART FILM LIBRARY for its significant work in collecting films dating from 1895 to the present and for the first time making available to the public the means of studying the historical and aesthetic development of the motion picture as one of the major arts. (scroll certificate)

W. HOWARD GREENE for the color photography of *A Star Is Born*. (This Award was recommended by a committee of leading cinematographers after viewing all the color pictures made during the year.) (plaque)

1938 *Eleventh Year*

DEANNA DURBIN and MICKEY ROONEY for their significant contribution in bringing to the screen the spirit and personification of youth, and as juvenile players setting a high standard of ability and achievement. (miniature statuette trophies)

HARRY M. WARNER in recognition of patriotic service in the production of historical short subjects presenting significant episodes in the early struggle of the American people for liberty. (scroll)

WALT DISNEY for *Snow White And The Seven Dwarfs,* recognized as a significant screen innovation which has charmed millions and pioneered a great new entertainment field for the motion picture cartoon. (one statuette—seven miniature statuettes)

OLIVER MARSH and ALLEN DAVEY for the color cinematography of the Metro-Goldwyn-Mayer production, *Sweethearts.* (plaques)

For outstanding achievement in creating Special Photographic and Sound Effects in the Paramount production, *Spawn Of The North.* Special Effects by GORDON JENNINGS, assisted by JAN DOMELA, DEV JENNINGS, IRMIN ROBERTS and ART SMITH. Transparencies by FARCIOT EDOUART, assisted by LOYAL GRIGGS. Sound Effects by LOREN RYDER, assisted by HARRY MILLS, LOUIS H. MESENKOP and WALTER OBERST. (plaques)

J. ARTHUR BALL for his outstanding contributions to the advancement of color in Motion Picture Photography. (scroll)

1939   Twelfth Year

DOUGLAS FAIRBANKS (Commemorative Award)—recognizing the unique and outstanding contribution of Douglas Fairbanks, first President of the Academy, to the international development of the motion picture. (statuette)

MOTION PICTURE RELIEF FUND—acknowledging the outstanding services to the industry during the past year of the Motion Picture Relief Fund and its progressive leadership. Presented to JEAN HERSHOLT, President; RALPH MORGAN, Chairman of the Executive Committee; RALPH BLOCK, First Vice-President; CONRAD NAGEL. (plaques)

JUDY GARLAND for her outstanding performance as a screen juvenile during the past year. (miniature statuette)

WILLIAM CAMERON MENZIES for outstanding achievement in the use of color for the enhancement of dramatic mood in the production of *Gone With The Wind.* (plaque)

TECHNICOLOR COMPANY for its contributions in successfully bringing three-color feature production to the screen. (statuette)

1940   Thirteenth Year

BOB HOPE, in recognition of his unselfish services to the Motion Picture Industry. (special silver plaque)

COLONEL NATHAN LEVINSON for his outstanding service to the industry and the Army during the past nine years, which has made possible the present efficient mobilization of the motion picture industry facilities for the production of Army Training Films. (statuette)

1941   Fourteenth Year

REY SCOTT for his extraordinary achievement in producing *Kukan,* the film record of China's struggle, including its photography with a 16mm camera under the most difficult and dangerous conditions. (certificate)

THE BRITISH MINISTRY OF INFORMATION for its vivid and dramatic presentation of the heroism of the RAF in the documentary film, *Target For Tonight*. (certificate)

LEOPOLD STOKOWSKI and his associates for their unique achievement in the creation of a new form of visualized music in Walt Disney's production *Fantasia*, thereby widening the scope of the motion picture as entertainment and as an art form. (certificate)

WALT DISNEY, WILLIAM GARITY, JOHN N. A. HAWKINS and the RCA MANUFACTURING COMPANY, for their outstanding contribution to the advancement of the use of sound in motion pictures through the production of *Fantasia*. (certificates)

1942   Fifteenth Year

CHARLES BOYER for his progressive cultural achievement in establishing the French Research Foundation in Los Angeles as a source of reference for the Hollywood Motion Picture Industry. (certificate)

NOEL COWARD for his outstanding production achievement in *In Which We Serve*. (certificate)

METRO-GOLDWYN-MAYER STUDIO for its achievement in representing the American Way of Life in the production of the *Andy Hardy* series of films. (certificate)

1943   Sixteenth Year

GEORGE PAL for the development of novel methods and techniques in the production of short subjects known as Puppetoons. (plaque)

1944   Seventeenth Year

MARGARET O'BRIEN, outstanding child actress of 1944. (miniature statuette)

BOB HOPE, for his many services to the Academy, a Life Membership in the Academy of Motion Picture Arts and Sciences

1945   Eighteenth Year

WALTER WANGER for his six years service as President of the Academy of Motion Picture Arts and Sciences. (special plaque)

PEGGY ANN GARNER, outstanding child actress of 1945. (miniature statuette)

THE HOUSE I LIVE IN, tolerance short subject; produced by Frank Ross and Mervyn LeRoy; directed by Mervyn LeRoy; screenplay by Albert Maltz; song *The House I Live In*, music by Earl Robinson, lyrics by Lewis Allen; starring Frank Sinatra; released by RKO Radio. (statuette)

REPUBLIC STUDIO, DANIEL J. BLOOMBERG and the REPUBLIC SOUND DEPARTMENT for the building of an outstanding musical scoring auditorium which provides optimum recording conditions and combines all elements of acoustic and engineering design. (certificates)

1946   Nineteenth Year

LAURENCE OLIVIER for his outstanding achievement as actor, producer and director in bringing *Henry V* to the screen. (statuette)

HAROLD RUSSELL for bringing hope and courage to his fellow veterans through his appearance in *The Best Years Of Our Lives*. (statuette)

ERNST LUBITSCH for his distinguished contributions to the art of the motion picture. (scroll)

CLAUDE JARMAN, JR., outstanding child actor of 1946. (miniature statuette)

1947   Twentieth Year

JAMES BASKETTE for his able and

heart-warming characterization of Uncle Remus, friend and story teller to the children of the world. (statuette)

BILL AND COO, in which artistry and patience blended in a novel and entertaining use of the medium of motion pictures. (plaque)

SHOE-SHINE—the high quality of this motion picture, brought to eloquent life in a country scarred by war, is proof to the world that the creative spirit can triumph over adversity. (statuette)

COLONEL WILLIAM N. SELIG, ALBERT E. SMITH, THOMAS ARMAT and GEORGE K. SPOOR (one of) the small group of pioneers whose belief in a new medium, and whose contributions to its development, blazed the trail along which the motion picture has progressed, in their lifetime, from obscurity to world-wide acclaim. (statuettes)

1948   Twenty-first Year

MONSIEUR VINCENT (French)— voted by the Academy Board of Governors as the most outstanding foreign language film released in the United States during 1948. (statuette)

IVAN JANDL, for the outstanding juvenile performance of 1948 in *The Search*. (miniature statuette)

SID GRAUMAN, master showman, who raised the standard of exhibition of motion pictures. (statuette)

ADOLPH ZUKOR, a man who has been called the father of the feature film in America, for his services to the industry over a period of forty years. (statuette)

WALTER WANGER for distinguished service to the industry in adding to its moral stature in the world community by his production of the picture *Joan Of Arc*. (statuette)

1949   Twenty-second Year

THE BICYCLE THIEF (Italian)— voted by the Academy Board of Governors as the most outstanding foreign language film released in the United States during 1949. (statuette)

BOBBY DRISCOLL, as the outstanding juvenile actor of 1949. (miniature statuette)

FRED ASTAIRE for his unique artistry and his contributions to the technique of musical pictures. (statuette)

CECIL B. DEMILLE, distinguished motion picture pioneer, for 37 years of brilliant showmanship. (statuette)

JEAN HERSHOLT, for distinguished service to the motion picture industry. (statuette)

1950   Twenty-third Year

Note: Name of category changed from Special Awards to Honorary Awards.

GEORGE MURPHY for his services in interpreting the film industry to the country at large. (statuette)

LOUIS B. MAYER for distinguished service to the motion picture industry. (statuette)

THE WALLS OF MALAPAGA (Franco-Italian)—voted by the Board of Governors as the most outstanding foreign language film released in the United States in 1950. (statuette)

1951   Twenty-fourth Year

GENE KELLY in appreciation of his versatility as an actor, singer, director and dancer, and specifically for his brilliant achievements in the art of choreography on film. (statuette)

RASHOMON (Japanese)—voted by the Board of Governors as the most outstanding foreign language film released in the United States during 1951. (statuette)

Closely identified with the Oscars is Bob Hope, a frequent host for the ceremonies and recipient of Honorary Awards in 1940, 1944, 1952, and 1965. Shown with him at the 32nd Oscar ceremonies are Hope Lange, Arthur Freed, and Olivia DeHavilland. © *1978 A.M.P.A.S.*

1952   Twenty-fifth Year

GEORGE ALFRED MITCHELL for the design and development of the camera which bears his name and for his continued and dominant presence in the field of cinematography. (statuette)

JOSEPH M. SCHENCK for long and distinguished service to the motion picture industry. (statuette)

MERIAN C. COOPER for his many innovations and contributions to the art of motion pictures. (statuette)

HAROLD LLOYD, master comedian and good citizen. (statuette)

BOB HOPE for his contribution to the laughter of the world, his service to the motion picture industry, and his devotion to the American premise. (statuette)

FORBIDDEN GAMES (French)—Best Foreign Language Film first released in the United States during 1952. (statuette)

1953   Twenty-sixth Year

PETE SMITH for his witty and pungent observations on the American scene in his series of *Pete Smith Specialties*. (statuette)

20TH CENTURY-FOX FILM CORPORATION in recognition of their imagination, showmanship and foresight in introducing the revolutionary process known as CinemaScope. (statuette)

JOSEPH I. BREEN for his conscientious, open-minded and dignified management of the Motion Picture Production Code. (statuette)

BELL AND HOWELL COMPANY for their pioneering and basic achievements in the advancement of the motion picture industry. (statuette)

1954   Twenty-seventh Year

BAUSCH & LOMB OPTICAL COM-
PANY for their contributions to the
advancement of the motion picture
industry. (statuette)

KEMP R. NIVER for the development
of the Renovare Process which has
made possible the restoration of the
Library of Congress Paper Film Collection. (statuette)

GRETA GARBO for her unforgettable
screen performances. (statuette)

DANNY KAYE for his unique talents,
his service to the Academy, the motion picture industry, and the American people. (statuette)

JON WHITELEY for his outstanding
juvenile performance in *The Little
Kidnappers.* (miniature statuette)

VINCENT WINTER for his outstanding juvenile performance in *The Little Kidnappers.* (miniature statuette)

GATE OF HELL (Japanese)—Best
Foreign Language Film first released
in the United States during 1954.
(statuette)

1955   Twenty-eighth Year

SAMURAI, THE LEGEND OF
MUSASHI, (Japanese)—Best
Foreign Language Film first released
in the United States during 1955.
(statuette)

1956   Twenty-ninth Year

EDDIE CANTOR for distinguished
service to the film industry.
(statuette)

1957   Thirtieth Year

CHARLES BRACKETT for outstanding service to the Academy.
(statuette)

B. B. KAHANE for distinguished service to the motion picture industry.
(statuette)

GILBERT M. (''Broncho Billy'') AN-
DERSON, motion picture pioneer,

for his contributions to the development of motion pictures as entertainment. (statuette)

THE SOCIETY OF MOTION PIC-
TURE AND TELEVISION ENGI-
NEERS for their contributions to the
advancement of the motion picture
industry. (statuette)

1958   Thirty-first Year

MAURICE CHEVALIER for his contributions to the world of entertainment for more than half a century.
(statuette)

1959   Thirty-second Year

LEE DE FOREST for his pioneering
inventions which brought sound to
the motion picture. (statuette)

BUSTER KEATON for his unique talents which brought immortal comedies to the screen. (statuette)

1960   Thirty-third Year

GARY COOPER for his many memorable screen performances and the international recognition he, as an individual, has gained for the motion
picture industry. (statuette)

STAN LAUREL for his creative pioneering in the field of cinema comedy. (statuette)

HAYLEY MILLS for *Pollyanna,* the
most outstanding juvenile performance during 1960. (miniature
statuette)

1961   Thirty-fourth Year

WILLIAM L. HENDRICKS for his
outstanding patriotic service in the
conception, writing and production
of the Marine Corps film, *A Force In
Readiness,* which has brought honor
to the Academy and the motion picture industry. (statuette)

FRED L. METZLER for his dedication
and outstanding service to the Acad-

emy of Motion Picture Arts and Sciences. (statuette)

JEROME ROBBINS for his brilliant achievements in the art of choreography on film. (statuette)

1962   Thirty-fifth Year

No Honorary Awards given this year.

1963   Thirty-sixth Year

No Honorary Awards given this year.

1964   Thirty-seventh Year

WILLIAM TUTTLE for his outstanding make-up achievement for *7 Faces Of Dr. Lao*. (statuette)

1965   Thirty-eighth Year

BOB HOPE for unique and distinguished service to our industry and the Academy. (gold medal)

1966   Thirty-ninth Year

Y. FRANK FREEMAN for unusual and outstanding service to the Academy during his thirty years in Hollywood. (statuette)

YAKIMA CANUTT for achievements as a stunt man and for developing safety devices to protect stunt men everywhere. (statuette)

1967   Fortieth Year

ARTHUR FREED for distinguished service to the Academy and the production of six top-rated Awards telecasts. (statuette)

1968   Forty-first Year

JOHN CHAMBERS for his outstanding make-up achievement for *Planet Of The Apes*. (statuette)

ONNA WHITE for her outstanding choreography achievement for *Oliver!*. (statuette)

1969   Forty-second Year

CARY GRANT for his unique mastery

of the art of screen acting with the respect and affection of his colleagues. (statuette)

1970   Forty-third Year

LILLIAN GISH for superlative artistry and for distinguished contribution to the progress of motion pictures.

ORSON WELLES for superlative artistry and versatility in the creation of motion pictures.

1971   Forty-fourth Year

CHARLES CHAPLIN for the incalculable effect he has had in making motion pictures the art form of this century.

1972   Forty-fifth Year

CHARLES S. BOREN, Leader for 38 years of the industry's enlightened labor relations and architect of its policy of non-discrimination. With the respect and affection of all who work in films.

EDWARD G. ROBINSON, who achieved greatness as a player, a patron of the arts and a dedicated citizen . . . in sum, a Renaissance man. From his friends in the industry he loves.

1973   Forty-sixth Year

HENRI LANGLOIS for his devotion to the art of film, his massive contributions in preserving its past and his unswerving faith in its future.

GROUCHO MARX in recognition of his brilliant creativity and for the unequalled achievements of the Marx Brothers in the art of motion picture comedy.

1974   Forty-seventh Year

HOWARD HAWKS—A master American filmmaker whose creative efforts hold a distinguished place in world cinema.

JEAN RENOIR—a genius who, with grace, responsibility and enviable devotion through silent film, sound film, feature, documentary and television, has won the world's admiration.

1975 Forty-eighth Year
MARY PICKFORD in recognition of her unique contributions to the film industry and the development of film as an artistic medium.

1976 Forty-ninth Year
No Honorary Awards given this year.

1977 Fiftieth Year
MARGARET BOOTH for sixty-two years of exceptionally distinguished service to the motion picture industry as a film editor.

GORDON E. SAWYER and SIDNEY P. SOLOW in appreciation for outstanding service and dedication in upholding the high standards of the Academy of Motion Picture Arts and Sciences (Medal of Commendation)

IRVING G. THALBERG
MEMORIAL AWARD

Irving Thalberg (1899–1936) was a motion picture producer of extraordinary ability. He went to work for Carl Laemmle at Universal and was managing the studio by the time he was twenty-one. In 1923 he became head of production for Louis B. Mayer, and, after the merger which created Metro-Goldwyn-Mayer the following year, he became second only to Mayer in charge of production at the new studio. Thalberg guided the artistic policy of MGM in the 1920s and 1930s and helped make the studio among the most powerful in Hollywood. He died of pneumonia on September 14, 1936.

At the 1936 Academy Awards banquet, held March 4, 1937, plans were announced for a memorial award to be inaugurated at the 1937 awards. The Irving G. Thalberg Memorial Award, given "to creative producers whose body of work reflects a consistently high quality of motion picture production," has been awarded twenty-five times in the past forty-one years. Darryl F. Zanuck won it three times before rules were changed limiting individuals to a single award.

The Thalberg Award is voted by the Academy Board of Governors.

1937	Tenth Year	Darryl F. Zanuck
1938	Eleventh Year	Hal B. Wallis
1939	Twelfth Year	David O. Selznick
1940	Thirteenth Year	None
1941	Fourteenth Year	Walt Disney
1942	Fifteenth Year	Sidney Franklin
1943	Sixteenth Year	Hal B. Wallis
1944	Seventeenth Year	Darryl F. Zanuck
1945	Eighteenth Year	None
1946	Nineteenth Year	Samuel Goldwyn
1947	Twentieth Year	None
1948	Twenty-first Year	Jerry Wald
1949	Twenty-second Year	None
1950	Twenty-third Year	Darryl F. Zanuck
1951	Twenty-fourth Year	Arthur Freed
1952	Twenty-fifth Year	Cecil B. DeMille
1953	Twenty-sixth Year	George Stevens
1954	Twenty-seventh Year	None
1955	Twenty-eighth Year	None
1956	Twenty-ninth Year	Buddy Adler
1957	Thirtieth Year	None

L to R: MGM mogul Louis B. Mayer, Norma Shearer, and her husband Irving G. Thalberg, for whom the Thalberg Award is named. Mayer and Thalberg were two of the founders of the Academy.

1958	Thirty-first Year	Jack L. Warner
1959	Thirty-second Year	None
1960	Thirty-third Year	None
1961	Thirty-fourth Year	Stanley Kramer
1962	Thirty-fifth Year	None
1963	Thirty-sixth Year	Sam Spiegel
1964	Thirty-seventh Year	None
1965	Thirty-eighth Year	William Wyler
1966	Thirty-ninth Year	Robert Wise
1967	Fortieth Year	Alfred Hitchcock
1968	Forty-first Year	None
1969	Forty-second Year	None
1970	Forty-third Year	Ingmar Bergman
1971	Forty-fourth Year	None

1972	Forty-fifth Year	None
1973	Forty-sixth Year	Lawrence Weingarten
1974	Forty-seventh Year	None
1975	Forty-eighth Year	Mervyn LeRoy
1976	Forty-ninth Year	Pandro S. Berman
1977	Fiftieth Year	Walter Mirisch

JEAN HERSHOLT
HUMANITARIAN AWARD

The Jean Hersholt Humanitarian Award is named for an actor whose film career spanned fifty years and 453 films. Danish-born Jean Hersholt (1886–1956) began his film career in 1906 when he was twenty. He emigrated to the United States in 1913 and became an American citizen in 1920. Despite a prolific career as an actor, Hersholt's interests were not limited to film. He made the first complete English translation of Hans Christian Andersen's fairy tales and in 1951 donated to the Library of Congress the most complete collection of Andersen's works ever assembled outside of Denmark. Hersholt received honorary awards from the Academy in 1939 and 1949 and was knighted by the King of Denmark in 1946. Much of Hersholt's fame came as a result of a radio character named Dr. Christian which he played for eighteen years.

When he died of cancer in 1956, Jean Hersholt was remembered as much for his humanitarian work as for his acting. He had headed the Motion Picture Relief Fund for eighteen years and was one of the founders of the Motion Picture Country Day Home. The award named in his honor is given to individuals "in the motion picture industry whose humanitarian efforts have brought credit to the industry."

The Hersholt Award is voted by the Academy Board of Governors.

1956	Twenty-ninth Year	Y. Frank Freeman
1957	Thirtieth Year	Samuel Goldwyn
1958	Thirty-first Year	None
1959	Thirty-second Year	Bob Hope
1960	Thirty-third Year	Sol Lesser
1961	Thirty-fourth Year	George Seaton
1962	Thirty-fifth Year	Steve Broidy
1963	Thirty-sixth Year	None
1964	Thirty-seventh Year	None
1965	Thirty-eighth Year	Edmond L. DePatie
1966	Thirty-ninth Year	George Bagnall
1967	Fortieth Year	Gregory Peck
1968	Forty-first Year	Martha Raye
1969	Forty-second Year	George Jessel
1970	Forty-third Year	Frank Sinatra
1971	Forty-fourth Year	None
1972	Forty-fifth Year	Rosalind Russell
1973	Forty-sixth Year	Lew Wasserman

Jean Hersholt, president of the Academy from 1945 to 1949, and Margaret Herrick, the Academy's executive director from 1943 to 1970. © *1978 A.M.P.A.S.*

1974	Forty-seventh Year	Arthur B. Krim
1975	Forty-eighth Year	Jules C. Stein
1976	Forty-ninth Year	None
1977	Fiftieth Year	Charlton Heston

SCIENTIFIC OR TECHNICAL AWARDS

The Academy has always been involved with the technical aspects of motion pictures, first through the Producers-Technicians Joint Committee and later through the Research Council. Among the earliest projects of the Academy were the sponsorships of studies on incandescent lighting and on motion picture sound engineering. The Scientific or Technical Awards were established in time for the 1930/31 ceremonies, and, according to the *Academy Bulletin,* nominations were solicited "from all Hollywood studios and from major manufacturing and development companies in the American motion picture industry." Then, as now, the category was divided into three classes:

Class I: For basic achievements which have a definite influence upon the advancement of the industry.

Class II: For those achievements which exhibit a high level of engineering or technical merit and which are important to the progress of the industry.

Class III: For those accomplishments which are valuable contributions to the progress of the industry.

The present rules say awards may be given "for devices, methods, formulas, discoveries, or inventions" which are applicable to the film industry.

Awards in this category are voted by the Academy Board of Governors upon the recommendation of a Scientific or Technical Awards Committee appointed by the Academy president.

1930/31   Fourth Year

Class I

ELECTRICAL RESEARCH PRODUCTS, INC., RCA-PHOTOPHONE, INC., and RKO RADIO PICTURES, INC., for noise reduction recording equipment

DuPONT FILM MANUFACTURING CORP. and EASTMAN KODAK CO. for super-sensitive panchromatic film

Class II

FOX FILM CORP. for effective use of synchro-projection composite photography

Class III

ELECTRICAL RESEARCH PRODUCTS, INC., for moving coil microphone transmitters

RKO RADIO PICTURES, INC., for reflex type microphone concentrators

RCA-PHOTOPHONE, INC., for ribbon microphone transmitters

1931/32   Fifth Year

Class I

None

Class II

TECHNICOLOR MOTION PICTURE CORP. for their color cartoon process

Class III

EASTMAN KODAK CO. for the Type II-B Sensitometer

1932/33   Sixth Year

Class I

None

Class II

ELECTRICAL RESEARCH PROD-
UCTS, INC., for their wide range
recording and reproducing system

RCA-VICTOR CO., INC., for their
high-fidelity recording and reproducing system

Class III

FOX FILM CORP., FRED JACKMAN
and WARNER BROS. PICTURES,
INC., and SIDNEY SANDERS of
RKO Studios, Inc., for their development and effective use of the
translucent cellulose screen in composite photography

1934   Seventh Year

Class I

None

Class II

ELECTRICAL RESEARCH PROD-
UCTS, INC., for their development
of the vertical cut disc method of
recording sound for motion pictures
(hill and dale recording)

Class III

COLUMBIA PICTURES CORP. for
their application of the vertical cut
disc method (hill and dale recording) to actual studio production, with
their recording of the sound on the
picture, *One Night Of Love*

BELL AND HOWELL CO. for their
development of the Bell and Howell
fully automatic sound and picture
printer

1935   Eighth Year

Class I

None

Class II

AGFA ANSCO CORP. for their development of the Agfa infra-red film

EASTMAN KODAK CO. for their development of the Eastman Pola-
Screen

Class III

METRO-GOLDWYN-MAYER STU-
DIO for the development of antidirectional negative and positive development by means of jet turbulation, and the application of the
method to all negative and print processing of the entire product of a
major producing company

WILLIAM A. MUELLER of Warner
Bros.-First National Studio Sound
Department for his method of dubbing, in which the level of the dialogue automatically controls the level
of the accompanying music and
sound effects

MOLE-RICHARDSON CO. for their
development of the "Solar-spot"
spot lamps

DOUGLAS SHEARER and METRO-
GOLDWYN-MAYER STUDIO
SOUND DEPARTMENT for their
automatic control system for cameras
and sound recording machines and
auxiliary stage equipment

ELECTRICAL RESEARCH PROD-
UCTS, INC., for their study and development of equipment to analyze
and measure flutter resulting from
the travel of the film through the
mechanisms used in the recording
and reproduction of sound

PARAMOUNT PRODUCTIONS,
INC., for the design and construction
of the Paramount transparency air
turbine developing machine

NATHAN LEVINSON, Director of
Sound Recording for Warner Bros.-
First National Studio, for the method
of intercutting variable density and

variable area sound tracks to secure an increase in the effective volume range of sound recorded for motion pictures

1936 Ninth Year

Class I

DOUGLAS SHEARER and the METRO-GOLDWYN-MAYER STUDIO SOUND DEPARTMENT for the development of a practical two-way horn system and a biased Class A push-pull recording system

Class II

E. C. WENTE and the BELL TELE-PHONE LABORATORIES for their multi-cellular high-frequency horn and receiver

RCA MANUFACTURING CO., INC., for their rotary stabilizer sound head

Class III

RCA MANUFACTURING CO., INC., for their development of a method of recording and printing sound records utilizing a restricted spectrum (known as ultra-violet light recording)

ELECTRICAL RESEARCH PROD-UCTS, INC., for the ERPI "Type Q" portable recording channel

RCA MANUFACTURING CO., INC., for furnishing a practical design and specifications for a non-slip printer

UNITED ARTISTS STUDIO CORP. for the development of a practical, efficient and quiet wind machine

1937 Tenth Year

Class I

AGFA ANSCO CORP. for Agfa Supreme and Agfa Ultra Speed pan motion picture negatives

Class II

WALT DISNEY PRODS., LTD., for the design and application to produc-tion of the Multi-Plane Camera

EASTMAN KODAK CO. for two fine-grain duplicating film stocks

FARCIOT EDOUART and PARA-MOUNT PICTURES, INC., for the development of the Paramount dual screen transparency camera setup

DOUGLAS SHEARER and the METRO-GOLDWYN-MAYER STUDIO SOUND DEPARTMENT for a method of varying the scanning width of variable density sound tracks (squeeze tracks) for the purpose of obtaining an increased amount of noise reduction

Class III

JOHN ARNOLD and the METRO-GOLDWYN-MAYER STUDIO CAMERA DEPARTMENT for their improvement of the semi-automatic follow focus device and its applica-tion to all of the cameras used by the Metro-Goldwyn-Mayer Studio

JOHN LIVADARY, Director of Sound Recording for Columbia Pictures Corp. for the application of the bi-planar light valve to motion picture sound recording

THOMAS T. MOULTON and the UNITED ARTISTS STUDIO SOUND DEPARTMENT for the ap-plication to motion picture sound re-cording of volume indicators which have peak reading response and linear decibel scales

RCA MANUFACTURING CO., INC., for the introduction of the modulated high-frequency method of determin-ing optimum photographic processing conditions for variable width sound tracks

JOSEPH E. ROBBINS and PARA-MOUNT PICTURES, INC., for an exceptional application of acoustic principles to the soundproofing of gasoline generators and water pumps

DOUGLAS SHEARER and the METRO-GOLDWYN-MAYER STUDIO SOUND DEPARTMENT for the design of the film drive mechanism as incorporated in the ERPI 1010 reproducer

1938   Eleventh Year

Class I

None

Class II

None

Class III

JOHN AALBERG and the RKO RADIO STUDIO SOUND DEPARTMENT for the application of compression to variable area recording in motion picture production

BYRON HASKIN and the SPECIAL EFFECTS DEPARTMENT of WARNER BROS. STUDIO for pioneering the development and for the first practical application to motion picture production of the triple head background projector

1939   Twelfth Year

Class I

None

Class II

None

Class III

GEORGE ANDERSON of Warner Bros. Studio for an improved positive head for sun arcs

JOHN ARNOLD of Metro-Goldwyn-Mayer Studio for the M-G-M mobile camera crane

THOMAS T. MOULTON, FRED ALBIN and the SOUND DEPARTMENT of the SAMUEL GOLDWYN STUDIO for the origination and application of the Delta db test to sound recording in motion pictures

FARCIOT EDOUART, JOSEPH E. ROBBINS, WILLIAM RUDOLPH and PARAMOUNT PICTURES, INC., for the design and construction of a quiet portable treadmill

EMERY HUSE and RALPH B. ATKINSON of Eastman Kodak Co. for their specifications for chemical analysis of photographic developers and fixing baths

HAROLD NYE of Warner Bros. Studio for a miniature incandescent spot lamp

A. J. TONDREAU of Warner Bros. Studio for the design and manufacture of an improved sound track printer

Multiple Award for important contributions in cooperative development of new improved Process Projection Equipment:

F. R. ABBOTT, HALLER BELT, ALAN COOK and BAUSCH & LOMB OPTICAL CO. for faster projection lenses

MITCHELL CAMERA CO. for a new type process projection head

MOLE-RICHARDSON CO. for a new type automatically controlled projection arc lamp

CHARLES HANDLEY, DAVID JOY and NATIONAL CARBON CO. for improved and more stable high-intensity carbons

WINTON HOCH and TECHNICOLOR MOTION PICTURE CORP. for an auxiliary optical system

DON MUSGRAVE and SELZNICK INTERNATIONAL PICTURES, INC., for pioneering in the use of coordinated equipment in the production *Gone With The Wind*

1940   Thirteenth Year

Class I

20TH CENTURY-FOX FILM CORP. for the design and construction of the

20th Century Silenced Camera, developed by DANIEL CLARK, GROVER LAUBE, CHARLES MILLER and ROBERT W. STEVENS

Class II

None

Class III

WARNER BROS. STUDIO ART DEPARTMENT and ANTON GROT for the design and perfection of the Warner Bros. water ripple and wave illusion machine

1941   Fourteenth Year

Class I

None

Class II

ELECTRICAL RESEARCH PRODUCTS DIVISION OF WESTERN ELECTRIC CO., INC., for the development of the precision integrating sphere densitometer

RCA MANUFACTURING CO. for the design and development of the MI-3043 Uni-directional microphone

Class III

RAY WILKINSON and the PARAMOUNT STUDIO LABORATORY for pioneering in the use of and for the first practical application to release printing of fine grain positive stock

CHARLES LOOTENS and the REPUBLIC STUDIO SOUND DEPARTMENT for pioneering the use of and for the first practical application to motion picture production of CLASS B push-pull variable area recording

WILBUR SILVERTOOTH and the PARAMOUNT STUDIO ENGINEERING DEPARTMENT for the design and computation of a relay

condenser system applicable to transparency process projection, delivering considerably more usable light

PARAMOUNT PICTURES, INC., and 20TH CENTURY-FOX FILM CORP. for the development and first practical application to motion picture production of an automatic scene slating device

DOUGLAS SHEARER and the METRO-GOLDWYN-MAYER STUDIO SOUND DEPARTMENT, and to LOREN RYDER and the PARAMOUNT STUDIO SOUND DEPARTMENT for pioneering the development of fine grain emulsions for variable density original sound recording in studio production

1942   Fifteenth Year

Class I

None

Class II

CARROLL CLARK, F. THOMAS THOMPSON and the RKO RADIO STUDIO ART and MINIATURE DEPARTMENTS for the design and construction of a moving cloud and horizon machine

DANIEL B. CLARK and the 20TH CENTURY-FOX FILM CORP. for the development of a lens calibration system and the application of this system to exposure control in cinematography

Class III

ROBERT HENDERSON and the PARAMOUNT STUDIO ENGINEERING and TRANSPARENCY DEPARTMENTS for the design and construction of adjustable light bridges and screen frames for transparency process photography

DANIEL J. BLOOMBERG and the REPUBLIC STUDIO SOUND DEPARTMENT for the design and application to motion picture production of a device for marking action negative for pre-selection purposes

1943   Sixteenth Year

Class I

None

Class II

FARCIOT EDOUART, EARLE MORGAN, BARTON THOMPSON and the PARAMOUNT STUDIO ENGINEERING and TRANSPARENCY DEPARTMENTS for the development and practical application to motion picture production of a method of duplicating and enlarging natural color photographs, transferring the image emulsions to glass plates and projecting these slides by especially designed stereopticon equipment

PHOTO PRODUCTS DEPARTMENT, E. I. Du PONT de NEMOURS AND CO., INC., for the development of fine-grain motion picture films

Class III

DANIEL J. BLOOMBERG and the REPUBLIC STUDIO SOUND DEPARTMENT for the design and development of an inexpensive method of converting Moviolas to Class B push-pull reproduction

CHARLES GALLOWAY CLARKE and the 20TH CENTURY-FOX STUDIO CAMERA DEPARTMENT for the development and practical application of a device for composing artificial clouds into motion picture scenes during production photography

FARCIOT EDOUART and the PARAMOUNT STUDIO TRANSPARENCY DEPARTMENT for an automatic electric transparency cueing timer

WILLARD H. TURNER and the RKO RADIO STUDIO SOUND DEPARTMENT for the design and construction of the phono-cue starter

1944   Seventeenth Year

Class I

None

Class II

STEPHEN DUNN, and the RKO RADIO STUDIO SOUND DEPARTMENT and RADIO CORPORATION OF AMERICA for the design and development of the electronic compressor-limiter

Class III

LINWOOD DUNN, CECIL LOVE and ACME TOOL MANUFACTURING CO. for the design and construction of the Acme-Dunn Optical Printer

GROVER LAUBE and the 20TH CENTURY-FOX STUDIO CAMERA DEPARTMENT for the development of a continuous loop projection device

WESTERN ELECTRIC CO. for the design and construction of the 1126A Limiting Amplifier for variable density sound recording

RUSSELL BROWN, RAY HINSDALE and JOSEPH E. ROBBINS for the development and production use of the Paramount floating hydraulic boat rocker

GORDON JENNINGS for the design and construction of the Paramount nodal point tripod

RADIO CORPORATION OF AMERICA and the RKO RADIO STUDIO SOUND DEPARTMENT for the design and construction of the RKO reverberation chamber

DANIEL J. BLOOMBERG and the REPUBLIC STUDIO SOUND DEPARTMENT for the design and development of a multi-interlock selector switch

BERNARD B. BROWN and JOHN P. LIVADARY for the design and engineering of a separate soloist and chorus recording room

PAUL ZEFF, S. J. TWINING and GEORGE SEID of the Columbia Studio Laboratory for the formula and application to production of a simplified variable area sound negative developer

PAUL LERPAE for the design and construction of the Paramount traveling matte projection and photographing device

1945   Eighteenth Year

Class I

None

Class II

None

Class III

LOREN L. RYDER, CHARLES R. DAILY and the PARAMOUNT STUDIO SOUND DEPARTMENT for the design, construction and use of the first dial controlled step-by-step sound channel line-up and test circuit

MICHAEL S. LESHING, BENJAMIN C. ROBINSON, ARTHUR B. CHATELAIN and ROBERT C. STEVENS of 20th Century-Fox Studio and JOHN G. CAPSTAFF of Eastman Kodak Co. for the 20th Century-Fox film processing machine

1946   Nineteenth Year

Class I

None

Class II

None

Class III

HARLAN L. BAUMBACH and the PARAMOUNT WEST COAST LABORATORY for an improved method for the quantitative determination of hydroquinone and metol in photographic developing baths

HERBERT E. BRITT for the development and application of formulas and equipment for producing cloud and smoke effects

BURTON F. MILLER and the WARNER BROS. STUDIO SOUND and ELECTRICAL DEPARTMENTS for the design and construction of a motion picture arc lighting generator filter

CARL FAULKNER of the 20th Century-Fox Studio Sound Department for the reversed bias method, including a double bias method for light valve and galvanometer density recording

MOLE-RICHARDSON CO. for the Type 450 super high intensity carbon arc lamp

ARTHUR F. BLINN, ROBERT O. COOK, C. O. SLYFIELD and the WALT DISNEY STUDIO SOUND DEPARTMENT for the design and development of an audio finder and track viewer for checking and locating noise in sound tracks

BURTON F. MILLER and the WARNER BROS. STUDIO SOUND DEPARTMENT for the design and application of an equalizer to eliminate relative spectral energy distortion in electronic compressors

MARTY MARTIN and HAL ADKINS of the RKO Radio Studio Miniature Department for the design and construction of equipment providing visual bullet effects

HAROLD NYE and the WARNER BROS. STUDIO ELECTRICAL DEPARTMENT for the development of the electronically controlled fire and gaslight effect

1947   Twentieth Year

Class I

None

Class II

C. C. DAVIS and ELECTRICAL RE-
SEARCH PRODUCTS, DIVISION
OF WESTERN ELECTRIC CO., for
the development and application of an
improved film drive filter mechanism

C. R. DAILY and the PARAMOUNT
STUDIO FILM LABORATORY,
STILL and ENGINEERING DE-
PARTMENTS for the development
and first practical application to motion picture and still photography of a
method of increasing film speed as
first suggested to the industry by E. I.
duPont de Nemours & Co.

Class III

NATHAN LEVINSON and the
WARNER BROS. STUDIO SOUND
DEPARTMENT for the design and
construction of a constant-speed
sound editing machine

FARCIOT EDOUART, C. R. DAILY,
HAL CORL, H. G. CARTWRIGHT
and the PARAMOUNT STUDIO
TRANSPARENCY and ENGINEER-
ING DEPARTMENTS for the first
application of a special antisolarizing
glass to high intensity background
and spot arc projectors

FRED PONEDEL of Warner Bros. Studio for pioneering the fabrication and
practical application to motion picture
color photography of large translucent photographic backgrounds

KURT SINGER and the RCA-VICTOR
DIVISION of the RADIO COR-
PORATION OF AMERICA for the
design and development of a continuously variable band elimination filter

JAMES GIBBONS of Warner Bros.
Studio for the development and pro-

duction of large dyed plastic filters for
motion picture photography

1948   Twenty-first Year

Class I

None

Class II

VICTOR CACCIALANZA,
MAURICE AYERS and the PARA-
MOUNT STUDIO SET CON-
STRUCTION DEPARTMENT for
the development and application of
"Paralite," a new lightweight plaster
process for set construction

NICK KALTEN, LOUIS J. WITTI and
the 20TH CENTURY-FOX STUDIO
MECHANICAL EFFECTS DE-
PARTMENT for a process of preserving and flame-proofing foliage

Class III

MARTY MARTIN, JACK LANNON,
RUSSELL SHEARMAN and the
RKO RADIO STUDIO SPECIAL
EFFECTS DEPARTMENT for the
development of a new method of
simulating falling snow on motion
picture sets

A. J. MORAN and the WARNER
BROS. STUDIO ELECTRICAL DE-
PARTMENT for a method of remote
control for shutters on motion picture
arc lighting equipment

1949   Twenty-second Year

Class I

EASTMAN KODAK CO. for the development and introduction of an improved safety base motion picture
film

Class II

None

Class III

LOREN L. RYDER, BRUCE H. DEN-

NEY, ROBERT CARR and the PARAMOUNT STUDIO SOUND DEPARTMENT for the development and application of the supersonic playback and public address system

M. B. PAUL for the first successful large-area seamless translucent backgrounds

HERBERT BRITT for the development and application of formulas and equipment producing artificial snow and ice for dressing motion picture sets

ANDRE COUTANT and JACQUES MATHOT for the design of the Eclair Camerette

CHARLES R. DAILY, STEVE CSILLAG and the PARAMOUNT STUDIO ENGINEERING, EDITORIAL and MUSIC DEPARTMENTS for a new precision method of computing variable tempo-click tracks

INTERNATIONAL PROJECTOR CORP. for a simplified and self-adjusting take-up device for projection machines

ALEXANDER VELCOFF for the application to production of the infrared photographic evaluator

1950   Twenty-third Year

Class I

None

Class II

JAMES B. GORDON and the 20TH CENTURY-FOX STUDIO CAMERA DEPARTMENT for the design and development of a multiple image film viewer

JOHN PAUL LIVADARY, FLOYD CAMPBELL, L. W. RUSSELL and the COLUMBIA STUDIO SOUND DEPARTMENT for the development of a multi-track magnetic re-recording system

LOREN L. RYDER and the PARAMOUNT STUDIO SOUND DEPARTMENT for the first studio-wide application of magnetic sound recording to motion picture production

Class III

None

1951   Twenty-fourth Year

Class I

None

Class II

GORDON JENNINGS, S. L. STANCLIFFE and the PARAMOUNT STUDIO SPECIAL PHOTOGRAPHIC and ENGINEERING DEPARTMENTS for the design, construction and application of a servo-operated recording and repeating device

OLIN L. DUPY of Metro-Goldwyn-Mayer Studio for the design, construction and application of a motion picture reproducing system

RADIO CORPORATION OF AMERICA, VICTOR DIVISION, for pioneering direct positive recording with anticipatory noise reduction

Class III

RICHARD M. HAFF, FRANK P. HERRNFELD, GARLAND C. MISENER and the ANSCO FILM DIVISION OF GENERAL ANILINE AND FILM CORP. for the development of the Ansco color scene tester

FRED PONEDEL, RALPH AYRES and GEORGE BROWN of Warner Bros. Studio for an air-driven water motor to provide flow, wake and white water for marine sequences in motion pictures

GLEN ROBINSON and the METRO-GOLDWYN-MAYER STUDIO CONSTRUCTION DEPARTMENT for the development of a new music wire and cable cutter

JACK GAYLORD and the METRO-GOLDWYN-MAYER STUDIO CONSTRUCTION DEPARTMENT for the development of balsa falling snow

CARLOS RIVAS of Metro-Goldwyn-Mayer Studio for the development of an automatic magnetic film splicer

1952   Twenty-fifth Year

Class I

EASTMAN KODAK CO. for the introduction of Eastman color negative and Eastman color print film

ANSCO DIVISION, GENERAL ANILINE AND FILM CORP., for the introduction of Ansco color negative and Ansco color print film

Class II

TECHNICOLOR MOTION PICTURE CORP. for an improved method of color motion picture photography under incandescent light

Class III

PROJECTION, STILL PHOTOGRAPHIC and DEVELOPMENT ENGINEERING DEPARTMENTS of METRO-GOLDWYN-MAYER STUDIO for an improved method of projecting photographic backgrounds

JOHN G. FRAYNE and R. R. SCOVILLE and WESTREX CORP. for a method of measuring distortion in sound reproduction

PHOTO RESEARCH CORP. for creating the Spectra color temperature meter

GUSTAV JIROUCH for the design of the Robot automatic film splicer

CARLOS RIVAS of Metro-Goldwyn-Mayer Studio for the development of a sound reproducer for magnetic film

1953   Twenty-sixth Year

Class I

PROFESSOR HENRI CHRETIEN and

EARL SPONABLE, SOL HALPRIN, LORIN GRIGNON, HERBERT BRAGG and CARL FAULKNER of 20th Century-Fox Studios for creating, developing and engineering the equipment, processes and techniques known as Cinema-Scope

FRED WALLER for designing and developing the multiple photographic and projection systems which culminated in Cinerama

Class II

REEVES SOUNDCRAFT CORP. for their development of a process of applying stripes of magnetic oxide to motion picture film for sound recording and reproduction

Class III

WESTREX CORP. for the design and construction of a new film editing machine

1954   Twenty-seventh Year

Class I

PARAMOUNT PICTURES, INC., LOREN L. RYDER, JOHN R. BISHOP and all the members of the technical and engineering staff for developing a method of producing and exhibiting motion pictures known as VistaVision

Class II

None

Class III

DAVID S. HORSLEY and the UNIVERSAL-INTERNATIONAL STUDIO SPECIAL PHOTOGRAPHIC DEPARTMENT for a portable remote control device for process projectors

KARL FREUND and FRANK CRANDELL of Photo Research Corp. for the design and development of a direct reading brightness meter

WESLEY C. MILLER, J. W. STAF-
FORD, K. M. FRIERSON and the
METRO-GOLDWYN-MAYER
STUDIO SOUND DEPARTMENT
for an electronic sound printing com-
parison device
JOHN P. LIVADARY, LLOYD RUS-
SELL and the COLUMBIA STUDIO
SOUND DEPARTMENT for an im-
proved limiting amplifier as applied
to sound level comparison devices
ROLAND MILLER and MAX GOEP-
PINGER of Magnascope Corp. for
the design and development of a cathode ray magnetic sound track viewer
CARLOS RIVAS, G. M. SPRAGUE
and the METRO-GOLDWYN-
MAYER STUDIO SOUND DE-
PARTMENT for the design of a magnetic sound editing machine
FRED WILSON of the Samuel Goldwyn Studio Sound Department for the
design of a variable multiple-band
equalizer
P. C. YOUNG of the Metro-Goldwyn-
Mayer Studio Projection Department
for the practical application of a variable focal length attachment to motion picture projector lenses
FRED KNOTH and ORIEN ERNEST
of the Universal-International Studio
Technical Department for the development of a hand portable, electric,
dry oil-fog machine

1955   Twenty-eighth Year
Class I
NATIONAL CARBON CO. for the de-
velopment and production of a high
efficiency yellow flame carbon for
motion picture color photography
Class II
EASTMAN KODAK CO. for Eastman
Tri-X panchromatic negative film
FARCIOT EDOUART, HAL CORL
and the PARAMOUNT STUDIO

TRANSPARENCY DEPARTMENT
for the engineering and development
of a double-frame, triple-head background projector
Class III
20TH CENTURY-FOX STUDIO and
BAUSCH & LOMB CO. for the new
combination lenses for CinemaScope
photography
WALTER JOLLEY, MAURICE LAR-
SON and R. H. SPIES of 20th Century-Fox Studio for a spraying process which creates simulated metallic
surfaces
STEVE KRILANOVICH for an improved camera dolly incorporating
multi-directional steering
DAVE ANDERSON of 20th Century-
Fox Studio for an improved spotlight
capable of maintaining a fixed circle
of light at constant intensity over
varied distances
LOREN L. RYDER, CHARLES
WEST, HENRY FRACKER and
PARAMOUNT STUDIO for a projection film index to establish proper
framing for various aspect ratios
FARCIOT EDOUART, HAL CORL
and the PARAMOUNT STUDIO
TRANSPARENCY DEPARTMENT
for an improved dual stereopticon
background projector

1956   Twenty-ninth Year
Class I
None
Class II
None
Class III
RICHARD H. RANGER of Ranger-
tone, Inc., for the development of a
synchronous recording and reproduc-
ing system for quarter-inch magnetic
tape
TED HIRSCH, CARL HAUGE and

EDWARD REICHARD of Consolidated Film Industries for an automatic scene counter for laboratory projection rooms

THE TECHNICAL DEPARTMENTS of PARAMOUNT PICTURES CORP. for the engineering and development of the Paramount lightweight horizontal-movement VistaVision camera

ROY C. STEWART AND SONS of Stewart-Trans Lux Corp., DR. C. R. DAILY and the TRANSPARENCY DEPARTMENT of PARAMOUNT PICTURES CORP. for the engineering and development of the HiTrans and Para-HiTrans rear projection screens

THE CONSTRUCTION DEPARTMENT of METRO-GOLDWYN-MAYER STUDIO for a new hand-portable fog machine

DANIEL J. BLOOMBERG, JOHN POND, WILLIAM WADE and the ENGINEERING and CAMERA DEPARTMENTS of REPUBLIC STUDIO for the Naturama adaptation to the Mitchell camera

1957 Thirtieth Year
Class I

TODD-AO CORP. and WESTREX CORP. for developing a method of producing and exhibiting wide-film motion pictures known as the Todd-AO System

MOTION PICTURE RESEARCH COUNCIL for the design and development of a high efficiency projection screen for drive-in theatres

Class II

SOCIÉTÉ D'OPTIQUE ET DE MECANIQUE DE HAUTE PRECISION for the development of a high speed vari-focal photographic lens

HARLAN L. BAUMBACH,

LORAND WARGO, HOWARD M. LITTLE and the UNICORN ENGINEERING CORP. for the development of an automatic printer light selector

Class III

CHARLES E. SUTTER, WILLIAM B. SMITH, PARAMOUNT PICTURES CORP. and GENERAL CABLE CORP. for the engineering and application to studio use of aluminum lightweight electrical cable and connectors

1958 Thirty-first Year
Class I
None

Class II

DON W. PRIDEAUX, LEROY G. LEIGHTON and the LAMP DIVISION of GENERAL ELECTRIC CO. for the development and production of an improved 10 kilowatt lamp for motion picture set lighting

PANAVISION, INC., for the design and development of the Auto Panatar anamorphic photographic lens for 35mm CinemaScope photography

Class III

WILLY BORBERG of the General Precision Laboratory, Inc., for the development of a high speed intermittent movement for 35mm motion picture theatre projection equipment

FRED PONEDEL, GEORGE BROWN and CONRAD BOYE of the Warner Bros. Special Effects Department for the design and fabrication of a new rapid fire marble gun

1959 Thirty-second Year
Class I
None
Class II
DOUGLAS G. SHEARER of Metro-

Goldwyn-Mayer, Inc., and ROBERT E. GOTTSCHALK and JOHN R. MOORE of Panavision, Inc., for the development of a system of producing and exhibiting wide-film motion pictures known as Camera 65

WADSWORTH E. POHL, WILLIAM EVANS, WERNER HOPF, S. E. HOWSE, THOMAS P. DIXON, STANFORD RESEARCH INSTITUTE and TECHNICOLOR CORP. for the design and development of the Technicolor electronic printing timer

WADSWORTH E. POHL, JACK ALFORD, HENRY IMUS, JOSEPH SCHMIT, PAUL FASSNACHT, AL LOFQUIST and TECHNICOLOR CORP. for the development and practical application of equipment for wet printing

DR. HOWARD S. COLEMAN, DR. A. FRANCIS TURNER, HAROLD H. SCHROEDER, JAMES R. BENFORD and HAROLD E. ROSENBERGER of the Bausch & Lomb Optical Co. for the design and development of the Balcold projection mirror

ROBERT P. GUTTERMAN of General Kinetics, Inc., and the LIPSNER-SMITH CORP. for the design and development of the CF-2 Ultrasonic Film Cleaner

Class III

UB IWERKS of Walt Disney Prods. for the design of an improved optical printer for special effects and matte shots

E. L. STONES, GLEN ROBINSON, WINFIELD HUBBARD and LUTHER NEWMAN of the Metro-Goldwyn-Mayer Studio Construction Department for the design of a multiple cable remote controlled winch

1960 Thirty-third Year

Class I

None

Class II

AMPEX PROFESSIONAL PRODUCTS CO. for the production of a well-engineered multi-purpose sound system combining high standards of quality with convenience of control, dependable operation and simplified emergency provisions

Class III

ARTHUR HOLCOMB, PETRO VLAHOS and COLUMBIA STUDIO CAMERA DEPARTMENT for a camera flicker indicating device.

ANTHONY PAGLIA and the 20TH CENTURY-FOX STUDIO MECHANICAL EFFECTS DEPARTMENT for the design and construction of a miniature flak gun and ammunition

CARL HAUGE, ROBERT GRUBEL and EDWARD REICHARD of Consolidated Film Industries for the development of an automatic developer replenisher system

1961 Thirty-fourth Year

Class I

None

Class II

SYLVANIA ELECTRIC PRODUCTS, INC., for the development of a hand-held high-power photographic lighting unit known as the Sun Gun Professional

JAMES DALE, S. WILSON, H. E. RICE, JOHN RUDE, LAURIE ATKIN, WADSWORTH E. POHL, H. PEASGOOD and TECHNICOLOR CORP. for a process of automatic selective printing

20TH CENTURY-FOX RESEARCH

DEPARTMENT, under the direction of E. I. SPONABLE and HERBERT E. BRAGG, and DELUXE LABORATORIES, INC., with the assistance of F. D. LESLIE, R. D. WHITMORE, A. A. ALDEN, ENDEL POOL and JAMES B. GORDON for a system of decompressing and recomposing CinemaScope pictures for conventional aspect ratios

Class III

HURLETRON, INC., ELECTRIC EYE EQUIPMENT DIVISION, for an automatic light changing system for motion picture printers

WADSWORTH E. POHL and TECHNICOLOR CORP. for an integrated sound and picture transfer process

1962   Thirty-fifth Year

Class I

None

Class II

RALPH CHAPMAN for the design and development of an advanced motion picture camera crane

ALBERT S. PRATT, JAMES L. WASSELL and HANS C. WOHLRAB of the Professional Division, Bell & Howell Co., for the design and development of a new and improved automatic motion picture additive color printer

NORTH AMERICAN PHILIPS CO., INC., for the design and engineering of the Norelco Universal 70/35mm motion picture projector

CHARLES E. SUTTER, WILLIAM BRYSON SMITH and LOUIS C. KENNELL of Paramount Pictures Corp. for the engineering and application to motion picture production of a new system of electric power distribution

Class III

ELECTRO-VOICE, INC., for a highly directional dynamic line microphone

LOUIS G. MACKENZIE for a selective sound effects repeater

1963   Thirty-sixth Year

Class I

None

Class II

None

Class III

DOUGLAS G. SHEARER and A. ARNOLD GILLESPIE of Metro-Goldwyn-Mayer Studios for the engineering of an improved Background Process Projection System

1964   Thirty-seventh Year

Class I

PETRO VLAHOS, WADSWORTH E. POHL and UB IWERKS for the conception and perfection of techniques for Color Traveling Matte Composite Cinematography

Class II

SIDNEY P. SOLOW, EDWARD H. REICHARD, CARL W. HAUGE and JOB SANDERSON of Consolidated Film Industries for the design and development of a versatile Automatic 35mm Composite Color Printer

PIERRE ANGENIEUX for the development of a ten-to-one Zoom Lens for cinematography

Class III

MILTON FORMAN, RICHARD B. GLICKMAN and DANIEL J. PEARLMAN of ColorTran Industries for advancements in the design and application to motion picture photography of lighting units using quartz iodine lamps

STEWART FILMSCREEN COR-
PORATION for a seamless translu-
cent Blue Screen for Traveling Matte
Color Cinematography
ANTHONY PAGLIA and the 20TH
CENTURY-FOX STUDIO ME-
CHANICAL EFFECTS DEPART-
MENT for an improved method of
producing Explosion Flash Effects
for motion pictures
EDWARD H. REICHARD and CARL
W. HAUGE of Consolidated Film
Industries for the design of a Proxim-
ity Cue Detector and its application
to motion picture printers
EDWARD H. REICHARD, LEON-
ARD L. SOKOLOW and CARL W.
HAUGE of Consolidated Film Indus-
tries for the design and application to
motion picture laboratory practice of
a Stroboscopic Scene Tester for color
and black-and-white film
NELSON TYLER for the design and
construction of an improved Helicopter Camera System

1965   Thirty-eighth Year

Class I

None

Class II

ARTHUR J. HATCH of The Strong
Electric Corporation, subsidiary of
General Precision Equipment Corporation, for the design and development of an Air Blown Carbon Arc
Projection Lamp
STEFAN KUDELSKI for the design
and development of the Nagra portable ¼" tape recording system for motion picture sound recording

Class III

None

1966   Thirty-ninth Year

Class I

None

Class II

MITCHELL CAMERA CORPORA-
TION for the design and development of the Mitchell Mark II 35mm
Portable Motion Picture Reflex Camera
ARNOLD & RICHTER KG for the design and development of the Arriflex
35mm Portable Motion Picture Reflex Camera

Class III

PANAVISION INCORPORATED for
the design of the Panatron Power In-
verter and its application to motion
picture camera operation
CARROLL KNUDSON for the production of a Composers Manual for Motion Picture Music Synchronization.
RUBY RAKSIN for the production of a
Composers Manual for Motion Picture Music Synchronization

1967   Fortieth Year

Class I

None

Class II

None

Class III

ELECTRO-OPTICAL DIVISION of
the KOLLMORGEN CORPORA-
TION for the design and develop-
ment of a series of Motion Picture
Projection Lenses
PANAVISION INCORPORATED for
a Variable Speed Motor for Motion
Picture Cameras
FRED R. WILSON of the SAMUEL
GOLDWYN STUDIO SOUND DE-
PARTMENT for an Audio Level
Clamper
WALDON O. WATSON and the UNI-
VERSAL CITY STUDIO SOUND
DEPARTMENT for new concepts in
the design of a Music Scoring Stage

1968   Forty-first Year

Class I

PHILIP V. PALMQUIST of MIN-NESOTA MINING AND MANU-FACTURING CO., to DR. HER-BERT MEYER of the MOTION PICTURE AND TELEVISION RE-SEARCH CENTER, and to CHARLES D. STAFFELL of the RANK ORGANISATION for the development of a successful embodiment of the reflex background projection system for composite cinematography

EASTMAN KODAK COMPANY for the development and introduction of a color reversal intermediate film for motion pictures

Class II

DONALD W. NORWOOD for the design and development of the Norwood Photographic Exposure Meters

EASTMAN KODAK COMPANY and PRODUCERS SERVICE COMPANY for the development of a new high-speed step-optical reduction printer

EDMUND M. DiGIULIO, NIELS G. PETERSEN and NORMAN S. HUGHES of the CINEMA PRODUCT DEVELOPMENT COMPANY for the design and application of a conversion which makes available the reflex viewing system for motion picture cameras

OPTICAL COATING LABORA-TORIES, INC., for the development of an improved anti-reflection coating for photographic and projection lens systems

EASTMAN KODAK COMPANY for the introduction of a new high speed motion picture color negative film

PANAVISION INCORPORATED for the conception, design and introduction of a 65mm hand-held motion picture camera

TODD-AO COMPANY and the MITCHELL CAMERA COMPANY for the design and engineering of the Todd-AO hand-held motion picture camera

Class III

CARL W. HAUGE and EDWARD H. REICHARD of CONSOLIDATED FILM INDUSTRIES and E. MICHAEL MEAHL and ROY J. RIDENOUR of RAMTRONICS for engineering an automatic exposure control for printing-machine lamps

EASTMAN KODAK COMPANY for a new direct positive film and to CONSOLIDATED FILM INDUSTRIES for the application of this film to the making of post-production work prints

1969   Forty-second Year

Class I

None

Class II

HAZELTINE CORPORATION for the design and development of the Hazeltine Color Film Analyzer

FOUAD SAID for the design and introduction of the Cinemobile series of equipment trucks for location motion picture production

JUAN DE LA CIERVA and DYNA-SCIENCES CORPORATION for the design and development of the Dynalens optical image motion compensator

Class III

OTTO POPELKA of Magna-Tech Electronics Co., Inc., for the development of an Electronically Controlled Looping System

FENTON HAMILTON of Metro-Goldwyn-Mayer Studios for the concept and engineering of a mobile battery power unit for location lighting

PANAVISION INCORPORATED for the design and development of the Panaspeed Motion Picture Camera Motor

ROBERT M. FLYNN and RUSSELL HESSY of Universal City Studios, Inc. for a machine-gun modification for motion picture photography

1970   Forty-third Year

Class I

None

Class II

LEONARD SOKOLOW and ED-WARD H. REICHARD of Consolidated Film Industries for the concept and engineering of the Color Proofing Printer for motion pictures

Class III

SYLVANIA ELECTRIC PRODUCTS INC. for the development and introduction of a series of compact tungsten halogen lamps for motion picture production

B. J. LOSMANDY for the concept, design and application of microminiature solid state amplifier modules used in motion picture recording equipment

EASTMAN KODAK COMPANY and PHOTO ELECTRONICS CORPORATION for the design and engineering of an improved video color analyzer for motion picture laboratories

ELECTRO SOUND INCORPORATED for the design and introduction of the Series 8000 Sound System for motion picture theatres

1971   Forty-fourth Year

Class I

None

Class II

JOHN N. WILKINSON of Optical Radiation Corporation for the development and engineering of a system of xenon arc lamphouses for motion picture projection

Class III

THOMAS JEFFERSON HUTCHINSON, JAMES R. ROCHESTER and FENTON HAMILTON for the development and introduction of the Sunbrute system of xenon arc lamps for location lighting in motion picture production

PHOTO RESEARCH, a Division of Kollmorgen Corporation, for the development and introduction of the film-lens balanced Three Color Meter

ROBERT D. AUGUSTE and CINEMA PRODUCTS CO. for the development and introduction of a new crystal controlled lightweight motor for the 35mm motion picture Arriflex camera

PRODUCERS SERVICE CORPORATION and CONSOLIDATED FILM INDUSTRIES; and to CINEMA RESEARCH CORPORATION and RESEARCH PRODUCTS, INC. for the engineering and implementation of fully automated blow-up motion picture printing systems

CINEMA PRODUCTS CO. for a control motor to actuate zoom lenses on motion picture cameras

1972   Forty-fifth Year

Class I

None

Class II

JOSEPH E. BLUTH for research and development in the field of electronic photography and transfer of video tape to motion picture film

EDWARD H. REICHARD and HOWARD T. LA ZARE of Consolidated Film Industries, and EDWARD EFRON of IBM for the engineering of a computerized light valve monitoring system for motion picture printing

PANAVISION INCORPORATED for the development and engineering of the Panaflex motion picture camera

Class III

PHOTO RESEARCH, a Division of Kollmorgen Corporation, and PSC TECHNOLOGY INC., Acme Products Division, for the Spectra Film Gate Photometer for motion picture printers

CARTER EQUIPMENT COMPANY, INC. and RAMTRONICS for the Ramtronics light-valve photometer for motion picture printers

DAVID DEGENKOLB, HARRY LARSON, MANFRED MICHELSON and FRED SCOBEY of DeLuxe General Incorporated for the development of a computerized motion picture printer and process control system

JIRO MUKAI and RYUSHO HIROSE of Canon, Inc. and WILTON R. HOLM of the AMPTP Motion Picture and Television Research Center for development of the Canon Macro Zoom Lens for motion picture photography

PHILIP V. PALMQUIST and LEONARD L. OLSON of the 3M Company, and FRANK P. CLARK of the AMPTP Motion Picture and Television Research Center for development of the Nextel simulated blood for motion picture color photography

E. H. GEISSLER and G. M. BERGGREN of Wil-Kin Inc. for engineering of the Ultra-Vision Motion Picture Theater Projection System

1973   Forty-sixth Year

Class I

None

Class II

JOACHIM GERB and ERICH KASTNER of The Arnold and Richter Company for the development and engineering of the Arriflex 35BL motion-picture camera

MAGNA-TECH ELECTRONIC CO., INC. for the engineering and development of a high-speed re-recording system for motion-picture production

WILLIAM W. VALLIANT of PSC Technology Inc., HOWARD F. OTT of Eastman Kodak Company, and GERRY DIEBOLD of The Richmark Camera Service Inc. for the development of a liquid-gate system for motion-picture printers

HAROLD A. SCHEIB, CLIFFORD H. ELLIS and ROGER W. BANKS of Research Products Incorporated for the concept and engineering of the Model 2101 optical printer for motion-picture optical effects

Class III

ROSCO LABORATORIES, INC. for the technical advances and the development of a complete system of light-control materials for motion-picture photography

RICHARD H. VETTER of the Todd-AO Corporation for the design of an improved anamorphic focusing system for motion-picture photography

1974   Forty-seventh Year

Class I

None

Class II

JOSEPH D. KELLY of Glen Glenn Sound for the design of new audio control consoles which have advanced the state of the art of sound recording and rerecording for motion picture production

THE BURBANK STUDIOS Sound Department for the design of new audio control consoles engineered and constructed by the Quad-Eight Sound Corporation

SAMUEL GOLDWYN STUDIOS Sound Department for the design of a new audio control console engineered and constructed by the Quad-Eight Sound Corporation

QUAD-EIGHT SOUND CORPORATION for the engineering and construction of new audio control consoles designed by The Burbank Studios Sound Department and by the Samuel Goldwyn Studios Sound Department

WALDON O. WATSON, RICHARD J. STUMPF, ROBERT J. LEONARD and the UNIVERSAL CITY STUDIOS Sound Department for the development and engineering of the Sensurround System for motion picture presentation

Class III

ELEMACK COMPANY, Rome, Italy, for the design and development of their Spyder camera dolly

LOUIS AMI of the Universal City Studios for the design and construction of a reciprocating camera platform used when photographing special visual effects for motion pictures

1975 Forty-eight Year

Class I

None

Class II

CHADWELL O'CONNOR of the O'Connor Engineering Laboratories for the concept and engineering of a fluid-damped camerahead for motion-picture photography

WILLIAM F. MINER of Universal City Studios, Inc. and the WESTINGHOUSE ELECTRIC CORPORATION for the development and engineering of a solid-state, 500 kilowatt, direct-current static rectifier for motion-picture lighting

Class III

LAWRENCE W. BUTLER and ROGER BANKS for the concept of applying low inertia and stepping electric motors to film transport systems and optical printers for motion-picture production

DAVID J. DEGENKOLB and FRED SCOBEY of Deluxe General Incorporated and JOHN C. DOLAN and RICHARD DUBOIS of the Akwaklame Company for the development of a technique for silver recovery from photographic wash-waters by ion exchange

JOSEPH WESTHEIMER for the development of a device to obtain shadowed titles on motion-picture films

CARTER EQUIPMENT CO., INC. and RAMTRONICS for the engineering and manufacture of a computerized tape punching system for programming laboratory printing machines

THE HOLLYWOOD FILM COMPANY for the engineering and manufacture of a computerized tape punching system for programming laboratory printing machines

BELL & HOWELL for the engineering and manufacture of a computerized tape punching system for programming laboratory printing machines

FREDRIK SCHLYTER for the engineering and manufacture of a computerized tape punching system for programming laboratory printing machines

1976   Forty-ninth Year

Class I

None

Class II

CONSOLIDATED FILM INDUS-
TRIES and the BARNEBEY-
CHENEY COMPANY for the development of a system for the recovery
of film-cleaning solvent vapors in a
motion-picture laboratory

WILLIAM L. GRAHAM, MANFRED
G. MICHELSON, GEOFFREY F.
NORMAN and SIEGFRIED SEI-
BERT of Technicolor for the devel-
opment and engineering of a Contin-
uous, High-Speed, Color
Motion-Picture Printing System

Class III

FRED BARTSCHER of the Koll-
morgean Corporation and to GLENN
BERGGREN of the Schneider Corporation for the design and development of a single-lens magnifier for
motion-picture projection lenses

PANAVISION INCORPORATED for
the design and development of super-
speed lenses for motion-picture photography

HIROSHI SUZUKAWA of Canon and
WILTON R. HOLM of AMPTP Motion Picture and Television Research
Center for the design and development of super-speed lenses for motion-picture photography

CARL ZEISS COMPANY for the design and development of super-speed
lenses for motion-picture photography

PHOTO RESEARCH DIVISION of
the KOLLMORGEN CORPORA-
TION for the engineering and manufacture of the spectra TriColor Meter

1977   Fiftieth Year

Class I

To GARRETT BROWN and the CIN-
EMA PRODUCTS CORP. engineering staff under the supervision of
JOHN JURGENS, for the invention
and development of Steadicam

Class II

JOSEPH D. KELLY, BARRY K.
HENLEY, HAMMOND H. HOLT
and GLEN GLENN SOUND for the
concept and development of a Post-
production Audio Processing System
for Motion Picture Films

PANAVISION, INCORPORATED,
for the concept and engineering
of the improvements incorporated
in the Panaflex Motion Picture
Camera

N. PAUL KENWORTHY, JR. and
WILLIAM R. LATADY for the invention and development of the Kenworthy Snorkel Camera System for
motion picture photography

JOHN C. DYKSTRA for the development of the Dykstraflex Camera
and to ALVAH J. MILLER and
JERRY JEFFRESS for the engineering of the Electronic Motion Control
System used in concert for multiple
exposure visual effects motion picture photography

The EASTMAN KODAK COM-
PANY for the development and introduction of a new duplicating film
for motion pictures

STEFAN KUDELSKI of Nagra
Magnetic Recorders, Incorporated,
for the engineering of the improvements
incorporated in the Nagra 4.2L
sound recorder for motion
picture production

Class III

ERNST NETTMANN of the AS-
TROVISION DIVISION of CONTI-
NENTAL CAMERA SYSTEMS,
INCORPORATED, for the engineer-

ing of its Snorkel Aerial Camera System

EECO (ELECTRONIC ENGINEERING COMPANY OF CALIFORNIA) for developing a method for interlocking non-sprocketed film and tape media used in motion picture production

DR. BERNHARD KUHL and WERNER BLOCK of OSRAM, GmbH, for the development of the HMI high-efficiency discharge lamp for motion picture lighting

PANAVISION, INCORPORATED, for the design of Panalite, a camera-mounted controllable light for motion picture photography

PANAVISION, INCORPORATED, for the engineering of the Panahead gearhead for motion picture cameras.

PICLEAR, INC., for originating and developing an attachment to motion picture projectors to improve screen image quality

ASSISTANT DIRECTOR

Achievement in film directing was recognized from the time of the first Academy Awards. Since directors frequently relied on assistants to direct second units and extras and to help maintain production schedules, a new category honoring assistant directors was announced for the 1932/33 awards.

A multiple award the first year only was given to assistant directors from the seven major studios. The award was continued for four more years and was dropped after 1937.

1932/33   Sixth Year
CHARLES BARTON, Paramount
SCOTT BEAL, Universal
CHARLES DORIAN, Metro-Goldwyn-Mayer
FRED FOX, United Artists
GORDON HOLLINGSHEAD, Warner Bros.
DEWEY STARKEY, RKO Radio
WILLIAM TUMMEL, Fox

(Multiple Award given this year only)

1934   Seventh Year
SCOTT BEAL for *Imitation Of Life*, Universal
CULLEN TATE for *Cleopatra*, Paramount
JOHN WATERS for *Viva Villa*, Metro-Goldwyn-Mayer

1935   Eighth Year
CLEM BEAUCHAMP for *Lives Of A Bengal Lancer*, Paramount
ERIC STACEY for *Les Miserables*, 20th Century, UA
PAUL WING for *Lives Of A Bengal Lancer*, Paramount

LARGE CAPITAL LETTERS DENOTE WINNER

JOSEPH NEWMAN for *David Copperfield*, Metro-Goldwyn-Mayer

1936   Ninth Year
CLEM BEAUCHAMP for *Last Of The Mohicans*, Reliance, UA
WILLIAM CANNON for *Anthony Adverse*, Warner Bros.
JOSEPH NEWMAN for *San Francisco*, Metro-Goldwyn-Mayer
ERIC G. STACEY for *Garden Of Allah*, Selznick, UA
JACK SULLIVAN for *The Charge Of The Light Brigade*, Warner Bros.

1937   Tenth Year
Note: Not given after this year
C. C. COLEMAN, JR. for *Lost Horizon*, Columbia
RUSS SAUNDERS for *The Life of Emile Zola*, Warner Bros.
ERIC STACEY for *A Star Is Born*, Selznick, UA
HAL WALKER for *Souls At Sea*, Paramount
ROBERT WEBB for *In Old Chicago*, 20th Century-Fox

Though relatively unknown to the general public, Gordon Hollingshead won twelve Oscars in his career, more than anyone else except Walt Disney. Ten of his awards came for Short Subjects, one for Documentary Short, and one for Assistant Director.© *1978 A.M.P.A.S.*

DANCE DIRECTION

Awards for Dance Direction, a short-lived category, were only given three times. The 1930s were the golden age of the American film musical, and this award honored the men who designed the memorable and frequently extravagant dance numbers. Ironically, the man most identified with Hollywood musicals of this period, Busby Berkeley, never won this Oscar, though he was nominated in each of the three years the award was given.

In the 1950s the Academy reconsidered an annual award for dancing and choreography. *Variety* noted in 1957 that Academy president George Seaton, in response to a campaign by dance fans, had agreed to form a dance award committee, but nothing came of it. The Academy has instead used honorary awards to publicize achievements in this area. Fred Astaire received an honorary Oscar in 1949, as did Gene Kelly in 1951. *West Side Story* swept the 1961 awards, and director-choreographer Jerome Robbins was given an honorary award. In 1968 Onna White was recognized for her choreography in *Oliver*.

1935   Eighth Year

BUSBY BERKELEY for *Lullaby Of Broadway* number from *Gold Diggers Of 1935*, Warner Bros. *The Words Are In My Heart* number from *Gold Diggers Of 1935*, Warner Bros.

BOBBY CONNOLLY for *Latin From Manhattan* number from *Go Into Your Dance*, Warner Bros. *Playboy From Paree* number from *Broadway Hostess*, Warner Bros.

DAVE GOULD for *I've Got A Feeling You're Fooling* number from *Broadway Melody Of 1936*, M-G-M. *Straw Hat* number from *Folies Bergere*, 20th Century, UA

SAMMY LEE for *Lovely Lady* number from *King Of Burlesque*, 20th Century-Fox. *Too Good To Be True* number from *King Of Burlesque*, 20th Century-Fox

HERMES PAN for *Piccolino* number from *Top Hat*, RKO Radio. *Top Hat* number from *Top Hat*, RKO Radio

LEROY PRINZ for *Elephant Number—*

It's The Animal In Me from *Big Broadcast Of 1936*, Paramount. *Viennese Waltz* number from *All The King's Horses*, Paramount

B. ZEMACH for *Hall Of Kings* number from *She*, RKO Radio

1936   Ninth Year

BUSBY BERKELEY for *Love And War* number from *Gold Diggers Of 1937*, Warner Bros.

BOBBY CONNOLLY for *1000 Love Songs* number from *Cain And Mabel*, Warner Bros.

SEYMOUR FELIX for *A Pretty Girl Is Like A Melody* number from *The Great Ziegfeld*, Metro-Goldwyn-Mayer

DAVE GOULD for *Swingin' The Jinx* number from *Born To Dance*, Metro-Goldwyn-Mayer

JACK HASKELL for *Skating Ensemble* number from *One In A Million*, 20th Century-Fox

RUSSELL LEWIS for *The Finale* number from *Dancing Pirate*, RKO Radio

From the MGM release *The Great Ziegfeld*. This production number, "A Pretty Girl Is Like a Melody," earned Seymour Felix the 1936 Oscar for Dance Direction. That's Virginia Bruce at the top. © *1936 Metro-Goldwyn-Mayer Corporation. Copyright renewed 1963 by Metro-Goldwyn-Mayer, Inc.*

HERMES PAN for *Bojangles* number from *Swing Time*, RKO Radio

1937   Tenth Year

Note: Not given after this year

BUSBY BERKELEY for *The Finale* number from *Varsity Show*, Warner Bros.

BOBBY CONNOLLY for *Too Marvelous For Words* number from *Ready, Willing And Able*, Warner Bros.

DAVE GOULD for *All God's Children Got Rhythm* number from *A Day At The Races*, Metro-Goldwyn-Mayer

SAMMY LEE for *Swing Is Here To Stay* number from *Ali Baba Goes To Town*, 20th Century-Fox

HARRY LOSEE for *Prince Igor Suite*
number from *Thin Ice*, 20th Century-
Fox

HERMES PAN for *Fun House* number
from *Damsel In Distress*, RKO
Radio

LEROY PRINZ for *Luau* number from
Waikiki Wedding, Paramount

ARTISTIC QUALITY
OF PRODUCTION

An award for Artistic Quality of Production was given only the first year. Academy members were asked to nominate "the Producing Company or Producer who produced the most artistic, unique and/or original motion picture without reference to cost or magnitude." As the categories underwent adjustment after the first year, this award was dropped, perhaps because it was scarcely distinguishable from the Best Picture category which honored "the most outstanding motion picture considering all elements that contribute to a picture's greatness."

1927/28   First Year
Note: Not given after this year   THE CROWD, Metro-Goldwyn-Mayer
CHANG, Paramount   SUNRISE, Fox

LARGE CAPITAL LETTERS DENOTE WINNER

George O'Brien and Janet Gaynor starred in *Sunrise* (1927) which received the only Oscar ever given for Artistic Quality of Production. *Twentieth Century-Fox Photo*

ENGINEERING EFFECTS

The Engineering Effects award was given only the first year. It went to the person who "rendered the best achievement in producing effects of whatever character obtained by engineering or mechanical means." The category was dropped after the 1927/28 awards.

1927/28   First Year

Note: Not given after this year

THE JAZZ SINGER, Warner Bros.: NUGENT SLAUGHTER

THE PRIVATE LIFE OF HELEN OF TROY, First National: RALPH HAMMERAS

WINGS, Paramount: ROY POMEROY

LARGE CAPITAL LETTERS DENOTE WINNER

CHRONOLOGICAL INDEX
OF ACADEMY AWARDS

(1927–1977)

1927 / 28

Awards Ceremony: May 16, 1929
Hollywood Roosevelt Hotel–Banquet*

Best Picture

THE LAST COMMAND, Paramount
THE RACKET, Caddo, Paramount
SEVENTH HEAVEN, Fox
THE WAY OF ALL FLESH, Paramount
WINGS, Paramount

Actor

RICHARD BARTHELMESS in *The Noose*,
First National
RICHARD BARTHELMESS in *The Patent
Leather Kid*, First National
CHARLES CHAPLIN in *The Circus*,
Chaplin, UA
EMIL JANNINGS in *The Last Com-
mand*, Paramount
EMIL JANNINGS in *The Way Of All
Flesh*, Paramount

Actress

LOUISE DRESSER in *A Ship Comes In*,
Pathe-RKO Radio
JANET GAYNOR in *Seventh Heaven*,
Fox
JANET GAYNOR in *Street Angel*, Fox
JANET GAYNOR in *Sunrise*, Fox
GLORIA SWANSON in *Sadie Thompson*,
United Artists

Directing

FRANK BORZAGE for *Seventh
Heaven*, Fox
HERBERT BRENON for *Sorrell And Son*,
United Artists

LARGE CAPITAL LETTERS DENOTE WINNER

* For the First Awards only, all nominees who did not
win Oscars were given Honorable Mention awards.

KING VIDOR for *The Crowd*, Metro-
Goldwyn-Mayer

Comedy Direction
(Not given after this year)
CHARLES CHAPLIN for *The Circus*,
Chaplin, UA
LEWIS MILESTONE for *Two Arabian
Knights*, United Artists
TED WILDE for *Speedy*, Paramount.

Writing
(Adaptation)
GLORIOUS BETSY, Warner Bros.:
ANTHONY COLDEWAY
THE JAZZ SINGER, Warner Bros.:
ALFRED COHN
SEVENTH HEAVEN, Fox: BEN-
JAMIN GLAZER

(Original Story)
THE LAST COMMAND, Paramount: LAJOS
BIRO
THE PATENT LEATHER KID, First Na-
tional: RUPERT HUGHES
UNDERWORLD, Paramount: BEN
HECHT

(Title Writing—Not given af-
ter this year)
THE PRIVATE LIFE OF HELEN OF TROY,
First National: GERALD DUFFY
THE FAIR CO-ED, Metro-Goldwyn-
Mayer: JOSEPH FARNHAM
LAUGH, CLOWN, LAUGH, Metro-
Goldwyn-Mayer: JOSEPH FARN-
HAM

TELLING THE WORLD, Metro-
Goldwyn-Mayer: JOSEPH FARN-
HAM
OH KAY!, First National: GEORGE
MARION, JR.

Cinematography

DEVIL DANCER, United Artists: GEORGE
BARNES
DRUMS OF LOVE, United Artists: KARL
STRUSS
MAGIC FLAME, United Artists: GEORGE
BARNES
MY BEST GIRL, Pickford, UA: CHARLES
ROSHER
SADIE THOMPSON, United Artists:
GEORGE BARNES
SUNRISE, Fox: CHARLES ROSHER
and KARL STRUSS
THE TEMPEST, United Artists: CHARLES
ROSHER

Interior Decoration

THE DOVE, United Artists: WIL-
LIAM CAMERON MENZIES
SEVENTH HEAVEN, Fox: HARRY OLIVER

SUNRISE, Fox: ROCHUS GLIESE
THE TEMPEST, United Artists: WIL-
LIAM CAMERON MENZIES

Artistic Quality of Production
(Not given after this year)
CHANG, Paramount
THE CROWD, Metro-Goldwyn-Mayer
SUNRISE, Fox

Engineering Effects
(Not given after this year)
THE JAZZ SINGER, Warner Bros.:
NUGENT SLAUGHTER
THE PRIVATE LIFE OF HELEN OF TROY,
First National: RALPH HAMMERAS
WINGS, Paramount: ROY POMEROY

Special Awards

WARNER BROS.: for producing
The Jazz Singer, the pioneer outstanding talking picture, which has
revolutionized the industry (statuette)
CHARLES CHAPLIN for versatility
and genius in writing, acting, directing and producing *The Circus*
(statuette)

1928 / 29

Nominations Announced: October 31, 1929
Awards Ceremony: April 3, 1930
Ambassador Hotel–Banquet

Best Picture

ALIBI, Feature Prod., UA
BROADWAY MELODY, Metro-Goldwyn-Mayer
HOLLYWOOD REVUE, Metro-Goldwyn-Mayer
IN OLD ARIZONA, Fox
THE PATRIOT, Paramount

Actor

GEORGE BANCROFT in *Thunderbolt*, Paramount
WARNER BAXTER in *In Old Arizona*, Fox
CHESTER MORRIS in *Alibi*, UA
PAUL MUNI in *The Valiant*, Fox
LEWIS STONE in *The Patriot*, Paramount

Actress

RUTH CHATTERTON in *Madame X*, Metro-Goldwyn-Mayer
BETTY COMPSON in *The Barker*, First National
JEANNE EAGELS in *The Letter*, Paramount
BESSIE LOVE in *Broadway Melody*, Metro-Goldwyn-Mayer
MARY PICKFORD in *Coquette*, Pickford, UA

Directing

LIONEL BARRYMORE for *Madame X*, Metro-Goldwyn-Mayer
HARRY BEAUMONT for *Broadway Melody*, Metro-Goldwyn-Mayer
IRVING CUMMINGS for *In Old Arizona*, Fox

LARGE CAPITAL LETTERS DENOTE WINNER

FRANK LLOYD for *The Divine Lady*, First National
FRANK LLOYD for *Weary River*, First National
FRANK LLOYD for *Drag*, First National
ERNST LUBITSCH for *The Patriot*, Paramount

Writing

(Achievement)

IN OLD ARIZONA, Fox: TOM BARRY
THE LEATHERNECK, Pathe: ELLIOTT CLAWSON
OUR DANCING DAUGHTERS, Metro-Goldwyn-Mayer: JOSEPHINE LOVETT
THE PATRIOT, Paramount: HANS KRALY
THE VALIANT, Fox: TOM BARRY
WONDER OF WOMEN, Metro-Goldwyn-Mayer: BESS MEREDYTH

Cinematography

THE DIVINE LADY, First National: JOHN SEITZ
FOUR DEVILS, Fox: ERNEST PALMER
IN OLD ARIZONA, Fox: ARTHUR EDESON
OUR DANCING DAUGHTERS, Metro-Goldwyn-Mayer: GEORGE BARNES
STREET ANGEL, Fox: ERNEST PALMER
WHITE SHADOWS IN THE SOUTH SEAS, Metro-Goldwyn-Mayer: CLYDE DE VINNA

Interior Decoration

THE BRIDGE OF SAN LUIS REY, Metro-Goldwyn-Mayer: CEDRIC GIBBONS

DYNAMITE, Pathe: MITCHELL LEISEN
HOLLYWOOD REVUE, Metro-Goldwyn-
   Mayer: CEDRIC GIBBONS
THE IRON MASK, United Artists: WIL-
LIAM CAMERON MENZIES
THE PATRIOT, Paramount: HANS DRIER
STREET ANGEL, Fox: HARRY OLIVER

1929 / 30

Nominations Announced: September 19, 1930
Awards Ceremony: November 5, 1930
Ambassador Hotel–Banquet

Best Picture

ALL QUIET ON THE WESTERN FRONT, Universal
THE BIG HOUSE, Metro-Goldwyn-Mayer
DISRAELI, Warner Bros.
THE DIVORCEE, Metro-Goldwyn-Mayer
THE LOVE PARADE, Paramount

Actor

GEORGE ARLISS in *Disraeli*, WARNER BROS.
GEORGE ARLISS in *The Green Goddess*, Warner Bros.
WALLACE BEERY in *The Big House*, Metro-Goldwyn-Mayer
MAURICE CHEVALIER in *The Love Parade*, Paramount
MAURICE CHEVALIER in *The Big Pond*, Paramount
RONALD COLMAN in *Bulldog Drummond*, Goldwyn, UA
RONALD COLMAN in *Condemned*, Goldwyn, UA
LAWRENCE TIBBETT in *The Rogue Song*, Metro-Goldwyn-Mayer

Actress

NANCY CARROLL in *The Devil's Holiday*, Paramount
RUTH CHATTERTON in *Sarah And Son*, Paramount
GRETA GARBO in *Anna Christie*, Metro-Goldwyn-Mayer
GRETA GARBO in *Romance*, Metro-Goldwyn-Mayer

LARGE CAPITAL LETTERS DENOTE WINNER

NORMA SHEARER in *The Divorcee*, Metro-Goldwyn-Mayer
NORMA SHEARER in *Their Own Desire*, Metro-Goldwyn-Mayer
GLORIA SWANSON in *The Trespasser*, Kennedy, UA

Directing

CLARENCE BROWN for *Anna Christie*, Metro-Goldwyn-Mayer
CLARENCE BROWN for *Romance*, Metro-Goldwyn-Mayer
ROBERT LEONARD for *The Divorcee*, Metro-Goldwyn-Mayer
ERNST LUBITSCH for *The Love Parade*, Paramount
LEWIS MILESTONE for *All Quiet On The Western Front*, Universal
KING VIDOR for *Hallelujah*, Metro-Goldwyn-Mayer

Writing

(Achievement—Not given after this year)

ALL QUIET ON THE WESTERN FRONT, Universal: GEORGE ABBOTT, MAXWELL ANDERSON and DELL ANDREWS
THE BIG HOUSE, Metro-Goldwyn-Mayer: FRANCES MARION
DISRAELI, Warner Bros.: JULIAN JOSEPHSON
THE DIVORCEE, Metro-Goldwyn-Mayer: JOHN MEEHAN
STREET OF CHANCE, Paramount: HOWARD ESTABROOK

Cinematography

ALL QUIET ON THE WESTERN FRONT, Universal: ARTHUR EDESON

ANNA CHRISTIE, Metro-Goldwyn-
Mayer: WILLIAM DANIELS
HELL'S ANGELS, United Artists: GAE-
TANO GAUDIO and HARRY PERRY
THE LOVE PARADE, Paramount: VICTOR
MILNER
WITH BYRD AT THE SOUTH POLE,
Paramount: JOSEPH T. RUCKER and
WILLARD VAN DER VEER

Interior Decoration
BULLDOG DRUMMOND, Goldwyn, UA:
WILLIAM CAMERON MENZIES
KING OF JAZZ, Universal: HERMAN
ROSSE
THE LOVE PARADE, Paramount: HANS
DREIER

SALLY, First National: JACK OKEY
THE VAGABOND KING, Paramount: HANS
DREIER

Sound Recording
(New Category)
THE BIG HOUSE, Metro-Goldwyn-
Mayer: DOUGLAS SHEARER
THE CASE OF SERGEANT GRISCHA, RKO
RADIO: JOHN TRIBBY
THE LOVE PARADE, Paramount: FRANK-
LIN HANSEN
RAFFLES, Goldwyn, UA: OSCAR LAGER-
STROM
SONG OF THE FLAME, First National:
GEORGE GROVES

1930 / 31

Nominations Announced: October 5, 1931
Awards Ceremony: November 10, 1931
Biltmore Hotel–Banquet
(MC: Lawrence Grant)

Best Picture
CIMARRON, RKO RADIO
EAST LYNNE, Fox
THE FRONT PAGE, Caddo, UA
SKIPPY, Paramount
TRADER HORN, Metro-Goldwyn-Mayer

Actor
LIONEL BARRYMORE in *A Free
Soul*, Metro-Goldwyn-Mayer
JACKIE COOPER in *Skippy*, Paramount
RICHARD DIX in *Cimarron*, RKO Radio
FREDRIC MARCH in *The Royal Family
Of Broadway*, Paramount
ADOLPHE MENJOU in *The Front Page*,
Caddo, UA

Actress
MARLENE DIETRICH in *Morocco*, Paramount
MARIE DRESSLER in *Min And Bill*,
Metro-Goldwyn-Mayer
IRENE DUNNE in *Cimarron*, RKO Radio
ANN HARDING in *Holiday*, RKO Pathe
NORMA SHEARER in *A Free Soul*, Metro-
Goldwyn-Mayer

Directing
CLARENCE BROWN for *A Free Soul*,
Metro-Goldwyn-Mayer
LEWIS MILESTONE for *The Front Page*,
Caddo, UA
WESLEY RUGGLES for *Cimarron*, RKO
Radio

LARGE CAPITAL LETTERS DENOTE WINNER

NORMAN TAUROG for *Skippy*, Paramount
JOSEF VON STERNBERG for *Morocco*,
Paramount

Writing
(Adaptation)
CIMARRON, RKO Radio: HOWARD
ESTABROOK
THE CRIMINAL CODE, Columbia: SETON
MILLER and FRED NIBLO, JR.
HOLIDAY, RKO Pathe: HORACE JACKSON
LITTLE CAESAR, Warner Bros.:
FRANCIS FARAGOH and ROBERT N. LEE
SKIPPY, Paramount: JOSEPH MANKIE-
WICZ and SAM MINTZ

(Original Story)
THE DAWN PATROL, Warner Bros.-
First National: JOHN MONK
SAUNDERS
DOORWAY TO HELL, Warner Bros.-First
National: ROWLAND BROWN
LAUGHTER, Paramount: HARRY D'AB-
BADIE D'ARRAST, DOUGLAS DOTY and
DONALD OGDEN STEWART
THE PUBLIC ENEMY, Warner Bros.-First
National: JOHN BRIGHT and KUBEC
GLASMON
SMART MONEY, Warner Bros.-First Na-
tional: LUCIEN HUBBARD and JOSEPH
JACKSON

Cinematography
CIMARRON, RKO Radio: EDWARD
CRONJAGER
MOROCCO, Paramount: LEE GARMES

THE RIGHT TO LOVE, Paramount: CHARLES LANG

SVENGALI, Warners-First National: BARNEY "CHICK" MCGILL

TABU, Paramount: FLOYD CROSBY

Interior Decoration

CIMARRON, RKO Radio: MAX REE

JUST IMAGINE, Fox: STEPHEN GOOSSON and RALPH HAMMERAS

MOROCCO, Paramount: HANS DREIER

SVENGALI, Warner Bros.-First National: ANTON GROT

WHOOPEE, Goldwyn, UA: RICHARD DAY

Sound Recording

METRO-GOLDWYN-MAYER STUDIO SOUND DEPARTMENT

PARAMOUNT STUDIO SOUND DE-PARTMENT

RKO RADIO STUDIO SOUND DEPARTMENT

SAMUEL GOLDWYN SOUND DEPARTMENT

Scientific Or Technical

(New Category)

Class I

ELECTRICAL RESEARCH PROD-UCTS, INC., RCA-PHOTOPHONE, INC., and RKO RADIO PICTURES, INC., for noise reduction recording equipment

DuPONT FILM MANUFACTURING CORP. and EASTMAN KODAK CO. for super-sensitive panchromatic film

Class II

FOX FILM CORP. for effective use of synchro-projection composite photography

Class III

ELECTRICAL RESEARCH PROD-UCTS, INC., for moving coil micro-phone transmitters.

RKO RADIO PICTURES, INC., for reflex type microphone concentrators

RCA-PHOTOPHONE, INC., for rib-bon microphone transmitters

1931 / 32

Nominations Announced: Otober 13, 1932
Awards Ceremony: November 18, 1932
Ambassador Hotel–Banquet
(MC: Lionel Barrymore)

Best Picture
ARROWSMITH, Goldwyn, UA
BAD GIRL, Fox
THE CHAMP Metro-Goldwyn-Mayer
FIVE STAR FINAL, First National
GRAND HOTEL, Metro-Goldwyn-Mayer
ONE HOUR WITH YOU, Paramount
SHANGHAI EXPRESS, Paramount
SMILING LIEUTENANT, Paramount

Actor (tie awards)
WALLACE BEERY in *The Champ*,
 Metro-Goldwyn-Mayer
ALFRED LUNT in *The Guardsman*,
 Metro-Goldwyn-Mayer
FREDRIC MARCH in *Dr. Jekyll And
 Mr. Hyde*, Paramount

Actress
MARIE DRESSLER in *Emma*, Metro-
 Goldwyn-Mayer
LYNN FONTANNE in *The Guardsman*,
 Metro-Goldwyn-Mayer
HELEN HAYES in *The Sin Of Madelon
 Claudet*, Metro-Goldwyn-Mayer

Directing
FRANK BORZAGE for *Bad Girl*, Fox
KING VIDOR for *The Champ*, Metro-
 Goldwyn-Mayer
JOSEF VON STERNBERG for *Shanghai
 Express*, Paramount

LARGE CAPITAL LETTERS DENOTE WINNER

Writing
(Adaptation)
ARROWSMITH, Goldwyn, UA: SIDNEY
 HOWARD
BAD GIRL, Fox: EDWIN BURKE
DR. JEKYLL AND MR. HYDE, Paramount:
 PERCY HEATH and SAMUEL HOFFEN-
 STEIN

(Original Story)
THE CHAMP, Metro-Goldwyn-Mayer:
 FRANCES MARION
LADY AND GENT, Paramount: GROVER
 JONES and WILLIAM SLAVENS MCNUTT
STAR WITNESS, Warner Bros.: LUCIEN
 HUBBARD
WHAT PRICE HOLLYWOOD, RKO Radio:
 ADELA ROGERS ST. JOHN

Cinematography
ARROWSMITH, Goldwyn, UA: RAY
 JUNE
DR. JEKYLL AND MR. HYDE, Paramount:
 KARL STRUSS
SHANGHAI EXPRESS, Paramount:
 LEE GARMES

Interior Decoration
A NOUS LA LIBERTÉ, (French): LAZARE
 MEERSON
ARROWSMITH, Goldwyn, UA: RICHARD
 DAY
TRANSATLANTIC, Fox: GORDON
 WILES

Sound Recording
PARAMOUNT STUDIO SOUND DE-
PARTMENT

Short Subjects
(New Category)

(Cartoons)
FLOWERS AND TREES, Walt Dis-
ney, UA
MICKEY'S ORPHANS, Walt Disney, Co-
lumbia
IT'S GOT ME AGAIN, Leon Schlesinger,
Warner Bros.

(Comedy)
THE LOUD MOUTH, Mack Sennett
THE MUSIC BOX, Hal Roach,
M-G-M (Laurel & Hardy)
STOUT HEARTS AND WILLING HANDS,
RKO Radio (Masquers Comedies)

(Novelty)
SCREEN SOUVENIRS, Paramount
SWING HIGH, Metro-Goldwyn-Mayer.
(Sport Champion)
WRESTLING SWORDFISH, Mack
Sennett, Educational. (Cannibals of
The Deep)

Special Award
WALT DISNEY for the creation of
Mickey Mouse. (statuette)

Scientific or Technical
Class I
None

Class II
TECHNICOLOR MOTION PICTURE
CORP. for their color cartoon process

Class III
EASTMAN KODAK CO. for the Type
II-B Sensitometer

1932 / 33

Nominations Announced: February 26, 1934
Awards Ceremony: March 16, 1934
Ambassador Hotel–Banquet
(MC: Will Rogers)

Best Picture

CAVALCADE, Fox
A FAREWELL TO ARMS, Paramount
FORTY-SECOND STREET, Warner Bros.
I AM A FUGITIVE FROM A CHAIN GANG,
Warner Bros.
LADY FOR A DAY, Columbia
LITTLE WOMEN, RKO Radio
THE PRIVATE LIFE OF HENRY VIII, London Films, UA (British)
SHE DONE HIM WRONG, Paramount
SMILIN' THRU, Metro-Goldwyn-Mayer
STATE FAIR, Fox

Actor

LESLIE HOWARD in *Berkeley Square,*
Fox
CHARLES LAUGHTON in *The Private Life Of Henry VIII*, London
Films, UA. (British)
PAUL MUNI in *I Am A Fugitive From A Chain Gang*, Warner Bros.

Actress

KATHARINE HEPBURN in *Morning Glory*, RKO Radio
MAY ROBSON in *Lady For A Day,* Columbia
DIANA WYNYARD in *Cavalcade,* Fox

Directing

FRANK CAPRA for *Lady For A Day,* Columbia
GEORGE CUKOR for *Little Women,* RKO Radio
FRANK LLOYD for *Cavalcade,* Fox

LARGE CAPITAL LETTERS DENOTE WINNER

Assistant Director

(New Category)
CHARLES BARTON, Paramount
SCOTT BEAL, Universal
CHARLES DORIAN, Metro-Goldwyn-Mayer
FRED FOX, United Artists
GORDON HOLLINGSHEAD, Warner Bros.
DEWEY STARKEY, RKO Radio
WILLIAM TUMMEL, Fox

(Multiple Award given this year only)

Writing

(Adaptation)
LADY FOR A DAY, Columbia: ROBERT RISKIN
LITTLE WOMEN, RKO Radio: VICTOR HEERMAN and SARAH Y. MASON
STATE FAIR, Fox: PAUL GREEN and SONYA LEVIEN

(Original Story)
ONE WAY PASSAGE, Warner Bros: ROBERT LORD
THE PRIZEFIGHTER AND THE LADY, Metro-Goldwyn-Mayer: FRANCES MARION
RASPUTIN AND THE EMPRESS, Metro-Goldwyn-Mayer: CHARLES MacARTHUR

Cinematography

A FAREWELL TO ARMS, Paramount: CHARLES BRYANT LANG, JR.

REUNION IN VIENNA, Metro-Goldwyn-Mayer: GEORGE J. FOLSEY, JR.
SIGN OF THE CROSS, Paramount: KARL STRUSS

Interior Decoration
CAVALCADE, Fox: WILLIAM S. DARLING
A FAREWELL TO ARMS, Paramount: HANS DREIER and ROLAND ANDERSON
WHEN LADIES MEET, Metro-Goldwyn-Mayer: CEDRIC GIBBONS

Sound Recording
A FAREWELL TO ARMS, Paramount: HAROLD C. LEWIS
FORTY-SECOND STREET, Warner Bros.: NATHAN LEVINSON
GOLDDIGGERS OF 1933, Warner Bros.: NATHAN LEVINSON
I AM A FUGITIVE FROM A CHAIN GANG, Warner Bros.: NATHAN LEVINSON

Short Subjects
(Cartoons)
BUILDING A BUILDING, Walt Disney, UA
THE MERRY OLD SOUL, Walter Lantz, Universal
THE THREE LITTLE PIGS, Walt Disney, UA

(Comedy)
MISTER MUGG, Universal: (Comedies)
PREFERRED LIST, RKO Radio: (Headliner Series #5)
SO THIS IS HARRIS, RKO Radio: (Special)

(Novelty)
KRAKATOA, Educational: (Three-reel Special)
MENU, Pete Smith, M-G-M: (Oddities)
THE SEA, Educational: (Battle For Life)

Scientific or Technical
Class I
None

Class II
ELECTRICAL RESEARCH PRODUCTS, INC., for their wide range recording and reproducing system
RCA-VICTOR CO., INC., for their high-fidelity recording and reproducing system

Class III
FOX FILM CORP., FRED JACKMAN and WARNER BROS. PICTURES, INC., and SIDNEY SANDERS of RKO STUDIOS, INC., for their development and effective use of the translucent cellulose screen in composite photography

1934

Nominations Announced: February 5, 1935
Awards Ceremony: February 27, 1935
Biltmore Hotel–Banquet
(MC: Irvin S. Cobb)

Best Picture

THE BARRETTS OF WIMPOLE STREET, Metro-Goldwyn-Mayer
CLEOPATRA, Paramount
FLIRTATION WALK, First National
THE GAY DIVORCEE, RKO Radio
HERE COMES THE NAVY, Warner Bros.
THE HOUSE OF ROTHSCHILD, 20th Century, UA
IMITATION OF LIFE, Universal
IT HAPPENED ONE NIGHT, Columbia
ONE NIGHT OF LOVE, Columbia
THE THIN MAN, Metro-Goldwyn-Mayer
VIVA VILLA, Metro-Goldwyn-Mayer
THE WHITE PARADE, Fox

Actor

CLARK GABLE in *It Happened One Night,* Columbia
FRANK MORGAN in *Affairs Of Cellini,* 20th Century, UA
WILLIAM POWELL in *The Thin Man,* Metro-Goldwyn-Mayer

Actress

CLAUDETTE COLBERT in *It Happened One Night,* Columbia
GRACE MOORE in *One Night Of Love,* Columbia
NORMA SHEARER in *The Barretts Of Wimpole Street,* Metro-Goldwyn-Mayer

LARGE CAPITAL LETTERS DENOTE WINNER

Directing

FRANK CAPRA for *It Happened One Night,* Columbia
VICTOR SCHERTZINGER for *One Night Of Love,* Columbia
W. S. VAN DYKE for *The Thin Man,* Metro-Goldwyn-Mayer

Assistant Director

SCOTT BEAL for *Imitation Of Life,* Universal
CULLEN TATE for *Cleopatra,* Paramount
JOHN WATERS for *Viva Villa,* Metro-Goldwyn-Mayer

Writing

(Adaptation)
IT HAPPENED ONE NIGHT, Columbia: ROBERT RISKIN
THE THIN MAN, Metro-Goldwyn-Mayer: FRANCES GOODRICH and ALBERT HACKETT
VIVA VILLA, Metro-Goldwyn-Mayer: BEN HECHT

(Original Story)
HIDE-OUT, Metro-Goldwyn-Mayer: MAURI GRASHIN
MANHATTAN MELODRAMA, Metro-Goldwyn-Mayer: ARTHUR CAESAR
THE RICHEST GIRL IN THE WORLD, RKO Radio: NORMAN KRASNA

Cinematography

AFFAIRS OF CELLINI, 20th Century, UA: CHARLES ROSHER

CLEOPATRA, Paramount: VICTOR MILNER

OPERATION 13, Metro-Goldwyn-Mayer: GEORGE FOLSEY

Interior Decoration

AFFAIRS OF CELLINI, 20th Century, UA: RICHARD DAY

THE GAY DIVORCEE, RKO Radio: VAN NEST POLGLASE and CARROLL CLARK

THE MERRY WIDOW, Metro-Goldwyn-Mayer: CEDRIC GIBBONS and FREDERIC HOPE

Sound Recording

AFFAIRS OF CELLINI 20th Century, UA: THOMAS T. MOULTON

CLEOPATRA, Paramount: FRANKLIN HANSEN

FLIRTATION WALK, First National: NATHAN LEVINSON

THE GAY DIVORCEE, RKO Radio: CARL DREHER

IMITATION OF LIFE, Universal: GILBERT KURLAND

ONE NIGHT OF LOVE, Columbia: PAUL NEAL

VIVA VILLA, Metro-Goldwyn-Mayer: DOUGLAS SHEARER

Film Editing

(New Category)

CLEOPATRA, Paramount: ANNE BAUCHENS

ESKIMO, Metro-Goldwyn-Mayer: CONRAD NERVIG

ONE NIGHT OF LOVE, Columbia: GENE MILFORD

Music

(New Category)

(During the years 1934 through 1937, this was a *Music Department Achievement* and the Award was presented to the departmental head instead of to the composer.)

(Best Score)

THE GAY DIVORCEE, RKO Radio Studio Music Dept.: MAX STEINER, Head
Score by KENNETH WEBB and SAMUEL HOFFENSTEIN

THE LOST PATROL, RKO Radio Studio Music Dept.: MAX STEINER, Head
Score by MAX STEINER

ONE NIGHT OF LOVE, Columbia Studio Music Dept.: LOUIS SILVERS, Head
Thematic music by VICTOR SCHERTZINGER and GUS KAHN

(Best Song)

CARIOCA from *Flying Down To Rio*, RKO Radio
Music by VINCENT YOUMANS. Lyrics by EDWARD ELISCU and GUS KAHN

THE CONTINENTAL from *The Gay Divorcee*, RKO Radio
Music by CON CONRAD. Lyrics by HERB MAGIDSON

LOVE IN BLOOM from *She Loves Me Not*, Paramount
Music by RALPH RAINGER. Lyrics by LEO ROBIN

Short Subjects

(Cartoons)

HOLIDAY LAND, Charles Mintz, Columbia

JOLLY LITTLE ELVES, Universal

THE TORTOISE AND THE HARE, Walt Disney

(Comedy)

LA CUCARACHA, RKO Radio: (Special)

MEN IN BLACK, Columbia: (Broadway Comedies)

WHAT, NO MEN!, Warner Bros.: (Broadway Brevities)

(Novelty)

BOSOM FRIENDS, Educational: (Treasure Chest)

CITY OF WAX, Educational: (Battle For Life)

STRIKES AND SPARES, Metro-Goldwyn-Mayer: (Oddities)

Special Award

SHIRLEY TEMPLE, in grateful recognition of her outstanding contribution to screen entertainment during the year 1934. (miniature statuette)

Scientific or Technical

Class I

None

Class II

ELECTRICAL RESEARCH PROD-

UCTS, INC., for their development of the vertical cut disc method of recording sound for motion pictures (hill and dale recording)

Class III

COLUMBIA PICTURES CORP. for their application of the vertical cut disc method (hill and dale recording) to actual studio production, with their recording of the sound on the picture *One Night Of Love*

BELL AND HOWELL CO. for their development of the Bell and Howell fully automatic sound and picture printer

1935

Nominations Announced: February 7, 1936
Awards Ceremony: March 5, 1936
Biltmore Hotel–Banquet

Best Picture

ALICE ADAMS, RKO Radio
BROADWAY MELODY OF 1936, Metro-
Goldwyn-Mayer
CAPTAIN BLOOD, Warner Bros.-Cos-
mopolitan
DAVID COPPERFIELD, Metro-Goldwyn-
Mayer
THE INFORMER, RKO Radio
LES MISERABLES, 20th Century, UA
LIVES OF A BENGAL LANCER, Paramount
A MIDSUMMER NIGHT'S DREAM, Warner
Bros.
MUTINY ON THE BOUNTY, Metro-
Goldwyn-Mayer.
NAUGHTY MARIETTA, Metro-Goldwyn-
Mayer
RUGGLES OF RED GAP, Paramount
TOP HAT, RKO Radio

Actor

CLARK GABLE in *Mutiny On The Bounty*,
Metro-Goldwyn-Mayer
CHARLES LAUGHTON in *Mutiny On The
Bounty*, Metro-Goldwyn-Mayer
VICTOR McLAGLEN in *The In-
former, RKO Radio*
FRANCHOT TONE in *Mutiny On The
Bounty*, Metro-Goldwyn-Mayer

Actress

ELISABETH BERGNER in *Escape Me
Never*, British & Dominions, UA
(British)
CLAUDETTE COLBERT in *Private Worlds*,
Paramount

LARGE CAPITAL LETTERS DENOTE WINNER

BETTE DAVIS in *Dangerous*, Warner
Bros.
KATHARINE HEPBURN in *Alice Adams*,
RKO Radio
MIRIAM HOPKINS in *Becky Sharp*, Pio-
neer, RKO Radio
MERLE OBERON in *The Dark Angel*,
Goldwyn, UA

Directing

JOHN FORD for *The Informer*, RKO
Radio
HENRY HATHAWAY for *Lives Of A
Bengal Lancer*, Paramount
FRANK LLOYD for *Mutiny On The Boun-
ty*, Metro-Goldwyn-Mayer.

Assistant Director

CLEM BEAUCHAMP for *Lives Of A
Bengal Lancer*, Paramount
ERIC STACEY for *Les Miserables*, 20th
Century, UA
PAUL WING for *Lives Of A Bengal
Lancer*, Paramount
JOSEPH NEWMAN for *David Copperfield*,
Metro-Goldwyn-Mayer

Writing

(Original Story)

BROADWAY MELODY OF 1936, Metro-
Goldwyn-Mayer: MOSS HART
THE GAY DECEPTION, Lasky, FOX: DON
HARTMAN and STEPHEN AVERY
THE SCOUNDREL, Paramount: BEN
HECHT and CHARLES MAC-
ARTHUR

(Screenplay)
THE INFORMER, RKO Radio: DUD-
LEY NICHOLS
LIVES OF A BENGAL LANCER, Para-
mount: ACHMED ABDULLAH, JOHN L.
BALDERSTON, GROVER JONES, WIL-
LIAM SLAVENS MCNUTT and WAL-
DEMAR YOUNG
MUTINY ON THE BOUNTY, Metro-
Goldwyn-Mayer: JULES FURTHMAN,
TALBOT JENNINGS and CAREY WILSON

Cinematography
BARBARY COAST, Goldwyn, UA: RAY
JUNE
THE CRUSADES, Paramount: VICTOR
MILNER
LES MISERABLES, 20th Century, UA:
GREGG TOLAND
A MIDSUMMER NIGHT'S DREAM,
Warner Bros: HAL MOHR

Interior Decoration
THE DARK ANGEL, Goldwyn, UA:
RICHARD DAY
LIVES OF A BENGAL LANCER, Para-
mount: HANS DREIER and ROLAND
ANDERSON
TOP HAT, RKO Radio: CARROLL CLARK
and VAN NEST POLGLASE

Sound Recording
THE BRIDE OF FRANKENSTEIN, Univer-
sal: GILBERT KURLAND
CAPTAIN BLOOD, Warner Bros: NATHAN
LEVINSON
THE DARK ANGEL, Goldwyn, UA. Gold-
wyn Sound Department: THOMAS T.
MOULTON
I DREAM TOO MUCH, RKO Radio: CARL
DREHER
LIVES OF A BENGAL LANCER, Para-
mount: FRANKLIN HANSEN
LOVE ME FOREVER, Columbia: JOHN LI-
VADARY
NAUGHTY MARIETTA, Metro-

Goldwyn-Mayer: DOUGLAS
SHEARER
ONE THOUSAND DOLLARS A MINUTE,
Republic: REPUBLIC SOUND DEPART-
MENT
THANKS A MILLION, 20th Century-Fox:
E. H. HANSEN

Film Editing
DAVID COPPERFIELD, Metro-Goldwyn-
Mayer: ROBERT J. KERN
THE INFORMER, RKO Radio: GEORGE
HIVELY
LES MISERABLES, 20th Century, UA:
BARBARA MCLEAN
LIVES OF A BENGAL LANCER, Para-
mount: ELLSWORTH HOAGLAND
A MIDSUMMER NIGHT'S DREAM,
Warner Bros.: RALPH DAWSON
MUTINY ON THE BOUNTY, Metro-
Goldwyn-Mayer: MARGARET BOOTH

Music
(Best Score)
THE INFORMER, RKO Radio Studio
Music Dept.: MAX STEINER, Head
Score by MAX STEINER
MUTINY ON THE BOUNTY, Metro-
Goldwyn-Mayer Studio Music Dept.:
NAT W. FINSTON, Head
Score by HERBERT STOTHART
PETER IBBETSON, Paramount Studio
Music Dept.: IRVIN TALBOT, Head
Score by ERNST TOCH
(Best Song)
CHEEK TO CHEEK from *Top Hat,* RKO
Radio
Music and Lyrics by IRVING BERLIN
LOVELY TO LOOK AT from *Roberta,*
RKO Radio Music by JEROME KERN.
Lyrics by DOROTHY FIELDS and
JIMMY MCHUGH
LULLABY OF BROADWAY from
Gold Diggers Of 1935, Warner Bros.
Music by HARRY WARREN. Lyrics
by AL DUBIN

Dance Direction

(New Category)

BUSBY BERKELEY for *Lullaby Of Broadway* number from *Gold Diggers Of 1935,* Warner Bros. *The Words Are In My Heart* number from *Gold Diggers Of 1935,* Warner Bros.

BOBBY CONNOLLY for *Latin From Manhattan* number from *Go Into Your Dance,* Warner Bros. *Playboy From Paree* number from *Broadway Hostess,* Warner Bros.

DAVE GOULD for *I've Got A Feeling You're Fooling* number from *Broadway Melody Of 1936,* M-G-M. *Straw Hat* number from *Folies Bergere,* 20th Century, UA

SAMMY LEE for *Lovely Lady* number from *King Of Burlesque,* 20th Century-Fox. *Too Good To Be True* number from *King Of Burlesque,* 20th Century-Fox

HERMES PAN for *Piccolino* number from *Top Hat,* RKO Radio. *Top Hat* number from *Top Hat,* RKO Radio

LEROY PRINZ for *Elephant Number— It's The Animal In Me* from *Big Broadcast Of 1936,* Paramount. *Viennese Waltz* number from *All The King's Horses,* Paramount

B. ZEMACH for *Hall Of Kings* number from *She,* RKO Radio

Short Subjects

(Cartoons)

THE CALICO DRAGON, Harman-Ising, M-G-M

THREE ORPHAN KITTENS, Walt Disney, UA

WHO KILLED COCK ROBIN?, Walt Disney, UA

(Comedy)

HOW TO SLEEP, Metro-Goldwyn-Mayer: (Miniature)

OH, MY NERVES, Columbia. (Broadway Comedies)

TIT FOR TAT, Hal Roach, M-G-M: (Laurel & Hardy)

(Novelty)

AUDIOSCOPIKS, Metro-Goldwyn-Mayer: (Special)

CAMERA THRILLS, Universal: (Special)

WINGS OVER MT. EVEREST, Educational: (Special)

Special Award

DAVID WARK GRIFFITH, for his distinguished creative achievements as director and producer and his invaluable initiative and lasting contributions to the progress of the motion picture arts. (statuette)

Scientific or Technical

Class I

None

Class II

AGFA ANSCO CORP. for their development of the Agfa infra-red film

EASTMAN KODAK CO. for their development of the Eastman Pola-Screen

Class III

METRO-GOLDWYN-MAYER STUDIO for the development of antidirectional negative and positive development by means of jet turbulation, and the application of the method to all negative and print processing of the entire product of a major producing company

WILLIAM A. MUELLER of Warner Bros.-First National Studio Sound Department for his method of dubbing, in which the level of the dialogue automatically controls the level of the accompanying music and sound effects.

MOLE-RICHARDSON CO. for their development of the "Solar-spot" spot lamps.

DOUGLAS SHEARER and METRO-GOLDWYN-MAYER STUDIO SOUND DEPARTMENT for their automatic control system for cameras and sound recording machines and auxiliary stage equipment

ELECTRICAL RESEARCH PRODUCTS, INC., for their study and development of equipment to analyze and measure flutter resulting from the travel of the film through the mechanisms used in the recording and reproduction of sound.

PARAMOUNT PRODUCTIONS, INC., for the design and construction of the Paramount transparency air turbine developing machine.

NATHAN LEVINSON, Director of Sound Recording for Warner Bros.-First National Studio, for the method of intercutting variable density and variable area sound tracks to secure an increase in the effective volume range of sound recorded for motion pictures.

1936

Nominations Announced: February 7, 1937
Awards Ceremony: March 4, 1937
Biltmore Hotel–Banquet
(MC: George Jessel)

Best Picture

ANTHONY ADVERSE, Warner Bros.
DODSWORTH, Goldwyn, UA
THE GREAT ZIEGFELD, Metro-Goldwyn-Mayer
LIBELED LADY, Metro-Goldwyn-Mayer
MR. DEEDS GOES TO TOWN, Columbia
ROMEO AND JULIET, Metro-Goldwyn-Mayer
SAN FRANCISCO, Metro-Goldwyn-Mayer
THE STORY OF LOUIS PASTEUR, Warner Bros.
A TALE OF TWO CITIES, Metro-Goldwyn-Mayer
THREE SMART GIRLS, Universal

Actor

GARY COOPER in *Mr. Deeds Goes To Town,* Columbia
WALTER HUSTON in *Dodsworth,* Goldwyn, UA
PAUL MUNI in *The Story Of Louis Pasteur,* Warner Bros.
WILLIAM POWELL in *My Man Godfrey,* Universal
SPENCER TRACY in *San Francisco,* Metro-Goldwyn-Mayer

Actress

IRENE DUNNE in *Theodora Goes Wild,* Columbia
GLADYS GEORGE in *Valiant Is The Word For Carrie,* Paramount
CAROLE LOMBARD in *My Man Godfrey,* Universal

LARGE CAPITAL LETTERS DENOTE WINNER

LUISE RAINER in *The Great Ziegfeld,* Metro-Goldwyn-Mayer
NORMA SHEARER in *Romeo And Juliet,* Metro-Goldwyn-Mayer.

Supporting Actor
(New Category)

MISCHA AUER in *My Man Godfrey,* Universal
WALTER BRENNAN in *Come And Get It,* Goldwyn, UA
STUART ERWIN in *Pigskin Parade,* 20th Century-Fox
BASIL RATHBONE in *Romeo And Juliet,* Metro-Goldwyn-Mayer
AKIM TAMIROFF in *The General Died At Dawn,* Paramount

Supporting Actress
(New Category)

BEULAH BONDI in *The Gorgeous Hussy,* Metro-Goldwyn-Mayer
ALICE BRADY in *My Man Godfrey,* Universal
BONITA GRANVILLE in *These Three,* Goldwyn, UA
MARIA OUSPENSKAYA in *Dodsworth,* Goldwyn, UA
GALE SONDERGAARD in *Anthony Adverse,* Warner Bros.

Directing

FRANK CAPRA for *Mr. Deeds Goes To Town,* Columbia
GREGORY La CAVA for *My Man Godfrey,* Universal

ROBERT Z. LEONARD for *The Great Ziegfeld,* Metro-Goldwyn-Mayer
W. S. VAN DYKE for *San Francisco,* Metro-Goldwyn-Mayer
WILLIAM WYLER for *Dodsworth,* Goldwyn, UA

Assistant Director

CLEM BEAUCHAMP for *Last Of The Mohicans,* Reliance, UA
WILLIAM CANNON for *Anthony Adverse,* Warner Bros.
JOSEPH NEWMAN for *San Francisco,* Metro-Goldwyn-Mayer
ERIC G. STACEY for *Garden Of Allah,* Selznick, UA
JACK SULLIVAN for *The Charge Of The Light Brigade,* Warner Bros.

Writing

(Original Story)
FURY, Metro-Goldwyn-Mayer: NORMAN KRASNA
THE GREAT ZIEGFELD, Metro-Goldwyn-Mayer: WILLIAM ANTHONY MCGUIRE
SAN FRANCISCO, Metro-Goldwyn-Mayer: ROBERT HOPKINS
THE STORY OF LOUIS PASTEUR, Warner Bros.: PIERRE COLLINGS and SHERIDAN GIBNEY
THREE SMART GIRLS, Universal: ADELE COMMANDINI

(Screenplay)
AFTER THE THIN MAN, Metro-Goldwyn-Mayer: FRANCES GOODRICH and ALBERT HACKETT
DODSWORTH, Goldwyn, UA: SIDNEY HOWARD
MR. DEEDS GOES TO TOWN, Columbia: ROBERT RISKIN
MY MAN GODFREY, Universal: ERIC HATCH and MORRIS RYSKIND
THE STORY OF LOUIS PASTEUR, Warner Bros.: PIERRE COLLINGS and SHERIDAN GIBNEY

Cinematography

ANTHONY ADVERSE, Warner Bros.: GAETANO GAUDIO
THE GENERAL DIED AT DAWN, Paramount: VICTOR MILNER
THE GORGEOUS HUSSY, Metro-Goldwyn-Mayer: GEORGE FOLSEY

Interior Decoration

ANTHONY ADVERSE, Warner Bros.: ANTON GROT
DODSWORTH, Goldwyn, UA: RICHARD DAY
THE GREAT ZIEGFELD, Metro-Goldwyn-Mayer: CEDRIC GIBBONS, EDDIE IMAZU and EDWIN B. WILLIS
LLOYDS OF LONDON, 20th Century-Fox: WILLIAM S. DARLING
THE MAGNIFICENT BRUTE Universal: ALBERT S. D'AGOSTINO and JACK OTTERSON
ROMEO AND JULIET, Metro-Goldwyn-Mayer: CEDRIC GIBBONS, FREDERIC HOPE and EDWIN B. WILLIS
WINTERSET, RKO Radio: PERRY FERGUSON

Sound Recording

BANJO ON MY KNEE, 20th Century-Fox: E. H. HANSEN
THE CHARGE OF THE LIGHT BRIGADE, Warner Bros.: NATHAN LEVINSON
DODSWORTH, Goldwyn, UA: OSCAR LAGERSTROM
GENERAL SPANKY, Roach, M-G-M: ELMER A. RAGUSE
MR. DEEDS GOES TO TOWN, Columbia: JOHN LIVADARY
SAN FRANCISCO, Metro-Goldwyn-Mayer: DOUGLAS SHEARER
THE TEXAS RANGERS, Paramount: FRANKLIN HANSEN
THAT GIRL FROM PARIS, RKO Radio: J. O. AALBERG
THREE SMART GIRLS, Universal: HOMER G. TASKER

Film Editing

ANTHONY ADVERSE, Warner Bros.: RALPH DAWSON

COME AND GET IT, Goldwyn, UA: EDWARD CURTISS

THE GREAT ZIEGFELD, Metro-Goldwyn-Mayer: WILLIAM S. GRAY

LLOYDS OF LONDON, 20th Century-Fox: BARBARA MCLEAN

A TALE OF TWO CITIES, Metro-Goldwyn-Mayer: CONRAD A. NERVIG

THEODORA GOES WILD, Columbia: OTTO MEYER

Music

(Best Score)

ANTHONY ADVERSE, Warner Bros. Studio Music Dept.: LEO FORBSTEIN, Head.
Score by ERICH WOLFGANG KORNGOLD

THE CHARGE OF THE LIGHT BRIGADE, Warner Bros. Studio Music Dept.: LEO FORBSTEIN, Head
Score by MAX STEINER

THE GARDEN OF ALLAH, Selznick International Pictures Music Dept.: MAX STEINER, Head
Score by MAX STEINER

THE GENERAL DIED AT DAWN, Paramount Studio Music Dept.: BORIS MORROS, Head
Score by WERNER JANSSEN

WINTERSET, RKO Radio Studio Music Dept.: NATHANIEL SHILKRET, Head
Score by NATHANIEL SHILKRET

(Best Song)

DID I REMEMBER from *Suzy*, Metro-Goldwyn-Mayer
Music by WALTER DONALDSON. Lyrics by HAROLD ADAMSON

I'VE GOT YOU UNDER MY SKIN from *Born To Dance*, Metro-Goldwyn-Mayer
Music and Lyrics by COLE PORTER

A MELODY FROM THE SKY from *Trail Of The Lonesome Pine*, Paramount
Music by LOUIS ALTER. Lyrics by SIDNEY MITCHELL

PENNIES FROM HEAVEN from *Pennies From Heaven*, Columbia
Music by ARTHUR JOHNSTON. Lyrics by JOHNNY BURKE

THE WAY YOU LOOK TONIGHT from *Swing Time*, RKO Radio.
Music by JEROME KERN. Lyrics by DOROTHY FIELDS

WHEN DID YOU LEAVE HEAVEN from *Sing Baby Sing*, 20th Century-Fox
Music by RICHARD A. WHITING. Lyrics by WALTER BULLOCK

Dance Direction

BUSBY BERKELEY for *Love And War* number from *Gold Diggers of 1937*, Warner Bros.

BOBBY CONNOLLY for *1000 Love Songs* number from *Cain And Mabel*, Warner Bros.

SEYMOUR FELIX for *A Pretty Girl Is Like A Melody* number from *The Great Ziegfeld*, Metro-Goldwyn-Mayer

DAVE GOULD for *Swingin' The Jinx* number from *Born To Dance*, Metro-Goldwyn-Mayer

JACK HASKELL for *Skating Ensemble* number from *One In A Million*, 20th Century-Fox

RUSSELL LEWIS for *The Finale* number from *Dancing Pirate*, RKO Radio

HERMES PAN for *Bojangles* number from *Swing Time*, RKO Radio

Short Subjects

(Cartoons)

COUNTRY COUSIN, Walt Disney, UA

OLD MILL POND, Harman-Ising, M-G-M

SINBAD THE SAILOR, Paramount

(One-reel)

BORED OF EDUCATION, Hal Roach, M-G-M (Our Gang)

MOSCOW MOODS, Paramount (Headliners)

WANTED, A MASTER, Pete Smith, M-G-M (Pete Smith Specialties)

(Two-reel)

DOUBLE OR NOTHING, Warner Bros. (Broadway Brevities)

DUMMY ACHE, RKO Radio (Edgar Kennedy Comedies)

THE PUBLIC PAYS, Metro-Goldwyn-Mayer (Crime Doesn't Pay)

(Color)

GIVE ME LIBERTY, Warner Bros. (Broadway Brevities)

LA FIESTA DE SANTA BARBARA, Metro-Goldwyn-Mayer (Musical Revues)

POPULAR SCIENCE J-6-2, Paramount

Special Awards

MARCH OF TIME for its significance to motion pictures and for having revolutionized one of the most important branches of the industry—the newsreel (statuette)

W. HOWARD GREENE and HAROLD ROSSON for the color cinematography of the Selznick International Production, THE GARDEN OF ALLAH (plaques)

Scientific or Technical

Class I

DOUGLAS SHEARER and the METRO-GOLDWYN-MAYER STUDIO SOUND DEPARTMENT for the development of a practical two-way horn system and a biased Class A push-pull recording system

Class II

E. C. WENTE and the BELL TELEPHONE LABORATORIES for their multi-cellular high-frequency horn and receiver

RCA MANUFACTURING CO., INC., for their rotary stabilizer sound head

Class III

RCA MANUFACTURING CO., INC., for their development of a method of recording and printing sound records utilizing a restricted spectrum (known as ultra-violet light recording)

ELECTRICAL RESEARCH PRODUCTS, INC., for the ERPI "Type Q" portable recording channel.

RCA MANUFACTURING CO., INC., for furnishing a practical design and specifications for a non-slip printer

UNITED ARTISTS STUDIO CORP. for the development of a practical, efficient and quiet wind machine.

1937

Nominations Announced: February 6, 1938
Awards Ceremony: Postponed from March 3 to March 10, 1938 because of flooding
Biltmore Hotel—Banquet
(MC: Bob Burns)

Best Picture

THE AWFUL TRUTH, Columbia
CAPTAINS COURAGEOUS, Metro-Goldwyn-Mayer
DEAD END, Goldwyn, UA
THE GOOD EARTH, Metro-Goldwyn-Mayer
IN OLD CHICAGO, 20th Century-Fox
THE LIFE OF EMILE ZOLA, Warner Bros.
LOST HORIZON, Columbia
ONE HUNDRED MEN AND A GIRL, Universal
STAGE DOOR, RKO Radio
A STAR IS BORN, Selznick International, UA

Actor

CHARLES BOYER in *Conquest,* Metro-Goldwyn-Mayer
FREDRIC MARCH in *A Star Is Born,* Selznick, UA
ROBERT MONTGOMERY in *Night Must Fall,* Metro-Goldwyn-Mayer
PAUL MUNI in *The Life Of Emile Zola,* Warner Bros.
SPENCER TRACY in *Captains Courageous,* Metro-Goldwyn-Mayer

Actress

IRENE DUNNE in *The Awful Truth,* Columbia
GRETA GARBO in *Camille,* Metro-Goldwyn-Mayer

LARGE CAPITAL LETTERS DENOTE WINNER

JANET GAYNOR in *A Star Is Born,* Selznick, UA
LUISE RAINER in *The Good Earth,* Metro-Goldwyn-Mayer
BARBARA STANWYCK in *Stella Dallas,* Goldwyn, UA

Supporting Actor

RALPH BELLAMY in *The Awful Truth,* Columbia
THOMAS MITCHELL in *Hurricane,* Goldwyn, UA
JOSEPH SCHILDKRAUT in *The Life Of Emile Zola,* Warner Bros.
H. B. WARNER in *Lost Horizon,* Columbia
ROLAND YOUNG in *Topper,* Roach, M-G-M

Supporting Actress

ALICE BRADY in *In Old Chicago,* 20th Century-Fox
ANDREA LEEDS in *Stage Door,* RKO Radio
ANNE SHIRLEY in *Stella Dallas,* Goldwyn, UA
CLAIRE TREVOR in *Dead End,* Goldwyn, UA
DAME MAY WHITTY in *Night Must Fall,* Metro-Goldwyn-Mayer

Directing

WILLIAM DIETERLE for *The Life Of Emile Zola,* Warner Bros.
SIDNEY FRANKLIN for *The Good Earth,* Metro-Goldwyn-Mayer

GREGORY LA CAVA for *Stage Door,* RKO Radio

LEO McCAREY for *The Awful Truth,* Columbia

WILLIAM WELLMAN for *A Star Is Born,* Selznick, UA

Assistant Director

(Not given after this year)

C. C. COLEMAN, JR. for *Lost Horizon,* Columbia

RUSS SAUNDERS for *The Life Of Emile Zola,* Warner Bros.

ERIC STACEY for *A Star Is Born,* Selznick, UA

HAL WALKER for *Souls At Sea,* Paramount

ROBERT WEBB for *In Old Chicago,* 20th Century-Fox

Writing

(Original Story)

BLACK LEGION, Warner Bros.: ROBERT LORD

IN OLD CHICAGO, 20th Century-Fox: NIVEN BUSCH

THE LIFE OF EMILE ZOLA, Warner Bros.: HEINZ HERALD and GEZA HERCZEG

100 MEN AND A GIRL, Universal: HANS KRALY

A STAR IS BORN, Selznick, UA: WILLIAM A. WELLMAN and ROBERT CARSON

(Screenplay)

THE AWFUL TRUTH, Columbia: VIÑA DELMAR

CAPTAINS COURAGEOUS, Metro-Goldwyn-Mayer: MARC CONNOLLY, JOHN LEE MAHIN and DALE VAN EVERY

THE LIFE OF EMILE ZOLA, Warner Bros.: HEINZ HERALD, GEZA HERCZEG and NORMAN REILLY RAINE

STAGE DOOR, RKO Radio: MORRIS RYSKIND and ANTHONY VEILLER

A STAR IS BORN, Selznick, UA: ALAN CAMPBELL, ROBERT CARSON and DOROTHY PARKER

Cinematography

DEAD END, Goldwyn, UA: GREGG TOLAND

THE GOOD EARTH, Metro-Goldwyn-Mayer: KARL FREUND

WINGS OVER HONOLULU, Universal: JOSEPH VALENTINE

Interior Decoration

CONQUEST, Metro-Goldwyn-Mayer: CEDRIC GIBBONS and WILLIAM HORNING

A DAMSEL IN DISTRESS, RKO Radio: CARROLL CLARK

DEAD END, Goldwyn, UA: RICHARD DAY

EVERY DAY'S A HOLIDAY, Major Prods., Paramount: WIARD IHNEN

THE LIFE OF EMILE ZOLA, Warner Bros.: ANTON GROT

LOST HORIZON, Columbia: STEPHEN GOOSSON

MANHATTAN MERRY-GO-ROUND, Republic: JOHN VICTOR MacKAY

THE PRISONER OF ZENDA, Selznick, UA: LYLE WHEELER

SOULS AT SEA, Paramount: HANS DREIER and ROLAND ANDERSON

VOGUES OF 1938, Wanger, UA: ALEXANDER TOLUBOFF

WEE WILLIE WINKIE, 20th Century-Fox: WILLIAM S. DARLING and DAVID HALL

YOU'RE A SWEETHEART, Universal: JACK OTTERSON

Sound Recording

THE GIRL SAID NO, Grand National: A. E. KAYE

HITTING A NEW HIGH, RKO Radio: JOHN AALBERG

THE HURRICANE, Goldwyn, UA:
THOMAS MOULTON
IN OLD CHICAGO, 20th Century-Fox:
E. H. HANSEN
THE LIFE OF EMILE ZOLA, Warner
Bros.: NATHAN LEVINSON
LOST HORIZON, Columbia: JOHN LIVA-
DARY
MAYTIME, Metro-Goldwyn-Mayer:
DOUGLAS SHEARER
ONE HUNDRED MEN AND A GIRL, Uni-
versal: HOMER TASKER
TOPPER, Roach, M-G-M: ELMER
RAGUSE
WELLS FARGO, Paramount: L. L. RYDER

Film Editing

THE AWFUL TRUTH, Columbia: AL
CLARK
CAPTAINS COURAGEOUS, Metro-
Goldwyn-Mayer: ELMO VERNON
THE GOOD EARTH, Metro-Goldwyn-
Mayer: BASIL WRANGELL
LOST HORIZON, Columbia: GENE
HAVLICK and GENE MILFORD
100 MEN AND A GIRL, Universal: BER-
NARD W. BURTON

Music
(Best Score)

HURRICANE, Samuel Goldwyn Studio
Music Dept.: ALFRED NEWMAN,
Head
Score by ALFRED NEWMAN
IN OLD CHICAGO, 20th Century-Fox
Studio Music Dept.: LOUIS SILVERS,
Head
Score: No composer credit
THE LIFE OF EMILE ZOLA, Warner Bros.
Studio Music Dept.: LEO FORBSTEIN,
Head
Score by MAX STEINER
LOST HORIZON, Columbia Studio Music
Dept.: MORRIS STOLOFF, Head
Score by DIMITRI TIOMKIN
MAKE A WISH, Principal Productions:

DR. HUGO RIESENFELD, Musical
Director
Score by DR. HUGO RIESENFELD
MAYTIME, Metro-Goldwyn-Mayer Stu-
dio Music Dept.: NAT W. FINSTON,
Head
Score by HERBERT STOTHART
ONE HUNDRED MEN AND A GIRL,
Universal Studio Music Dept.:
CHARLES PREVIN, Head
Score: No composer credit
PORTIA ON TRIAL, Republic Studio
Music Dept.: ALBERTO COLOMBO,
Head
Score by ALBERTO COLOMBO
THE PRISONER OF ZENDA, Selznick In-
ternational Pictures Music Dept.:
ALFRED NEWMAN, Musical Director
Score by ALFRED NEWMAN
QUALITY STREET, RKO Radio Studio
Music Dept.: ROY WEBB, Musical
Director
Score by ROY WEBB
SNOW WHITE AND THE SEVEN DWARFS,
Walt Disney Studio Music Dept:
LEIGH HARLINE, Head
Score by FRANK CHURCHILL, LEIGH
HARLINE and PAUL J. SMITH
SOMETHING TO SING ABOUT, Grand Na-
tional Studio Music Dept.: C. BAKA-
LEINIKOFF, Musical Director
Score by VICTOR SCHERTZINGER
SOULS AT SEA, Paramount Studio Music
Dept.: BORIS MORROS, Head
Score by W. FRANKE HARLING and
MILAN RODER
WAY OUT WEST, Hal Roach Studio
Music Dept.: MARVIN HATLEY, Head
Score by MARVIN HATLEY

(Best Song)

REMEMBER ME from *Mr. Dodd Takes
The Air*, Warner Bros.
Music by HARRY WARREN. Lyrics by
AL DUBIN
SWEET LEILANI from *Waikiki Wed-
ding*, Paramount

Music and Lyrics by HARRY
OWENS
THAT OLD FEELING from *Vogues Of
1938,* Wanger, UA
Music by SAMMY FAIN. Lyrics by
LEW BROWN
THEY CAN'T TAKE THAT AWAY FROM
ME from *Shall We Dance,* RKO
Radio
Music by GEORGE GERSHWIN. Lyrics
by IRA GERSHWIN
WHISPERS IN THE DARK from *Artists
And Models,* Paramount
Music by FREDERICK HOLLANDER
Lyrics by LEO ROBIN

Dance Direction
(Not given after this year)
BUSBY BERKELEY for *The Finale*
number from *Varsity Show,* Warner
Bros.
BOBBY CONNOLLY for *Too Marvelous
For Words* number from *Ready,
Willing And Able,* Warner Bros.
DAVE GOULD for *All God's Children
Got Rhythm* number from *A Day At
The Races,* Metro-Goldwyn-Mayer
SAMMY LEE for *Swing Is Here To Stay*
number from *Ali Baba Goes To
Town,* 20th Century-Fox
HARRY LOSEE for *Prince Igor Suite*
number from *Thin Ice,* 20th Century-
Fox
HERMES PAN for *Fun House* number
from *Damsel In Distress,* RKO
Radio
LEROY PRINZ for *Luau* number from
Waikiki Wedding, Paramount

Short Subjects
(Cartoons)
EDUCATED FISH, Paramount
THE LITTLE MATCH GIRL, Charles
Mintz, Columbia
THE OLD MILL, Walt Disney, RKO
Radio

(One-reel)
A NIGHT AT THE MOVIES, Metro-
Goldwyn-Mayer. (Robert Benchley)
PRIVATE LIFE OF THE GAN-
NETTS, Educational
ROMANCE OF RADIUM, Pete Smith,
M-G-M. (Pete Smith Specialities)

(Two-reel)
DEEP SOUTH, RKO Radio. (Radio Mu-
sical Comedies)
SHOULD WIVES WORK, RKO Radio.
(Leon Errol Comedies)
TORTURE MONEY, Metro-Goldwyn-
Mayer. (Crime Doesn't Pay)

(Color)
THE MAN WITHOUT A COUNTRY,
Warner Bros. (Broadway Brevities)
PENNY WISDOM, Pete Smith,
M-G-M. (Pete Smith Specialties)
POPULAR SCIENCE J-7-1, Paramount

Special Awards
MACK SENNETT, "for his lasting
contribution to the comedy technique
of the screen, the basic principles of
which are as important today as
when they were first put into practice, the Academy presents a Special
Award to that master of fun, discoverer of stars, sympathetic, kindly,
understanding comedy genius—
Mack Sennett." (statuette)
EDGAR BERGEN for his outstanding
comedy creation, Charlie McCarthy.
(wooden statuette)
THE MUSEUM OF MODERN ART
FILM LIBRARY for its significant
work in collecting films dating from
1895 to the present and for the first
time making available to the public
the means of studying the historical
and aesthetic development of the motion picture as one of the major arts.
(scroll certificate)
W. HOWARD GREENE for the color
photography of *A Star Is Born.*

(This Award was recommended by a committee of leading cinematographers after viewing all the color pictures made during the year.) (plaque)

Irving G. Thalberg Memorial Award (New Category)
DARRYL F. ZANUCK

Scientific or Technical
Class I
AGFA ANSCO CORP. for Agfa Supreme and Agfa Ultra Speed pan motion picture negatives
Class II
WALT DISNEY PRODS., LTD., for the design and application to production of the Multi-Plane Camera
EASTMAN KODAK CO. for two fine-grain duplicating film stocks
FARCIOT EDOUART and PARAMOUNT PICTURES, INC., for the development of the Paramount dual screen transparency camera setup
DOUGLAS SHEARER and the METRO-GOLDWYN-MAYER STUDIO SOUND DEPARTMENT for a method of varying the scanning width of variable density sound tracks (squeeze tracks) for the purpose of obtaining an increased amount of noise reduction

Class III
JOHN ARNOLD and the METRO-GOLDWYN-MAYER STUDIO CAMERA DEPARTMENT for their improvement of the semi-automatic follow focus device and its application to all of the cameras used by the Metro-Goldwyn-Mayer Studio
JOHN LIVADARY, Director of Sound Recording for Columbia Pictures Corp. for the application of the bi-planar light valve to motion picture sound recording
THOMAS T. MOULTON and the UNITED ARTISTS STUDIO SOUND DEPARTMENT for the application to motion picture sound recording of volume indicators which have peak reading response and linear decibel scales
RCA MANUFACTURING CO., INC., for the introduction of the modulated high-frequency method of determining optimum photographic processing conditions for variable width sound tracks
JOSEPH E. ROBBINS and PARAMOUNT PICTURES, INC., for an exceptional application of acoustic principles to the soundproofing of gasoline generators and water pumps
DOUGLAS SHEARER and the METRO-GOLDWYN-MAYER STUDIO SOUND DEPARTMENT for the design of the film drive mechanism as incorporated in the ERPI 1010 reproducer

1938

Nominations Announced: February 12, 1939
Awards Ceremony: February 23, 1939
Biltmore Hotel—Banquet

Best Picture

THE ADVENTURES OF ROBIN HOOD, Warner Bros.

ALEXANDER'S RAGTIME BAND, 20th Century-Fox

BOYS TOWN, Metro-Goldwyn-Mayer

THE CITADEL, Metro-Goldwyn-Mayer (British)

FOUR DAUGHTERS, Warner Bros.-First National

GRAND ILLUSION, R.A.O., World Pictures (French)

JEZEBEL, Warner Bros.

PYGMALION, Metro-Goldwyn-Mayer (British)

TEST PILOT, Metro-Goldwyn-Mayer

YOU CAN'T TAKE IT WITH YOU, Columbia

Actor

CHARLES BOYER in *Algiers*, Wanger, UA

JAMES CAGNEY in *Angels With Dirty Faces*, Warner Bros.

ROBERT DONAT in *The Citadel*, Metro-Goldwyn-Mayer (British)

LESLIE HOWARD in *Pygmalion*, Metro-Goldwyn-Mayer (British)

SPENCER TRACY in *Boys Town*, Metro-Goldwyn-Mayer

Actress

FAY BAINTER in *White Banners*, Warner Bros.

BETTE DAVIS in *Jezebel*, Warner Bros.

LARGE CAPITAL LETTERS DENOTE WINNER

WENDY HILLER in *Pygmalion*, Metro-Goldwyn-Mayer (British)

NORMA SHEARER in *Marie Antoinette*, Metro-Goldwyn-Mayer

MARGARET SULLAVAN in *Three Comrades*, Metro-Goldwyn-Mayer

Supporting Actor

WALTER BRENNAN in *Kentucky*, 20th Century-Fox

JOHN GARFIELD in *Four Daughters*, Warner Bros.

GENE LOCKHART in *Algiers*, Wanger, UA

ROBERT MORLEY in *Marie Antoinette*, Metro-Goldwyn-Mayer

BASIL RATHBONE in *If I Were King*, Paramount

Supporting Actress

FAY BAINTER in *Jezebel*, Warner Bros.

BEULAH BONDI in *Of Human Hearts*, Metro-Goldwyn-Mayer

BILLIE BURKE in *Merrily We Live*, Roach, M-G-M

SPRING BYINGTON in *You Can't Take It With You*, Columbia

MILIZA KORJUS in *The Great Waltz*, Metro-Goldwyn-Mayer

Directing

FRANK CAPRA for *You Can't Take It With You*, Columbia

MICHAEL CURTIZ for *Angels With Dirty Faces*, Warner Bros.

MICHAEL CURTIZ for *Four Daughters*, Warner Bros.

NORMAN TAUROG for *Boys Town,* Metro-Goldwyn-Mayer

KING VIDOR for *The Citadel,* Metro-Goldwyn-Mayer

Writing

(Adaptation)

PYGMALION, Metro-Goldwyn-Mayer (British): IAN DALRYMPLE, CECIL LEWIS and W. P. LIPSCOMB

(Original Story)

ALEXANDER'S RAGTIME BAND, 20th Century-Fox: IRVING BERLIN

ANGELS WITH DIRTY FACES Warner Bros.: ROWLAND BROWN

BLOCKADE, Wanger, UA: JOHN HOWARD LAWSON

BOYS TOWN, Metro-Goldwyn-Mayer: ELEANOR GRIFFIN and DORE SCHARY

MAD ABOUT MUSIC, Universal: MARCELLA BURKE and FREDERICK KOHNER

TEST PILOT, Metro-Goldwyn-Mayer: FRANK WEAD

(Screenplay)

BOYS TOWN, Metro-Goldwyn-Mayer: JOHN MEEHAN and DORE SCHARY

THE CITADEL, Metro-Goldwyn-Mayer (British): IAN DALRYMPLE, ELIZABETH HILL and FRANK WEAD

FOUR DAUGHTERS, Warner Bros.: LENORE COFFEE and JULIUS J. EPSTEIN

PYGMALION, Metro-Goldwyn-Mayer (British): GEORGE BERNARD SHAW

YOU CAN'T TAKE IT WITH YOU, Columbia: ROBERT RISKIN

Cinematography

ALGIERS, Wanger, UA: JAMES WONG HOWE

ARMY GIRL, Republic: ERNEST MILLER and HARRY WILD

THE BUCCANEER, Paramount: VICTOR MILNER

THE GREAT WALTZ, Metro-Goldwyn-Mayer: JOSEPH RUTTENBERG

JEZEBEL, Warner Bros.: ERNEST HALLER

MAD ABOUT MUSIC, Universal: JOSEPH VALENTINE

MERRILY WE LIVE, Roach, M-G-M: NORBERT BRODINE

SUEZ, 20th Century-Fox: PEVERELL MARLEY

VIVACIOUS LADY, RKO Radio: ROBERT DE GRASSE

YOU CAN'T TAKE IT WITH YOU, Columbia: JOSEPH WALKER

THE YOUNG IN HEART, Selznick, UA: LEON SHAMROY

Interior Decoration

THE ADVENTURES OF ROBIN HOOD, Warner Bros.: CARL J. WEYL

ADVENTURES OF TOM SAWYER, Selznick, UA: LYLE WHEELER

ALEXANDER'S RAGTIME BAND, 20th Century-Fox: BERNARD HERZBRUN and BORIS LEVEN

ALGIERS, Wanger UA: ALEXANDER TOLUBOFF

CAREFREE, RKO Radio: VAN NEST POLGLASE

GOLDWYN FOLLIES, Goldwyn, UA: RICHARD DAY

HOLIDAY, Columbia: STEPHEN GOOSSON and LIONEL BANKS

IF I WERE KING, Paramount: HANS DREIER and JOHN GOODMAN

MAD ABOUT MUSIC Universal: JACK OTTERSON

MARIE ANTOINETTE, Metro-Goldwyn-Mayer: CEDRIC GIBBONS

MERRILY WE LIVE, Roach, M-G-M: CHARLES D. HALL

Sound Recording

ARMY GIRL, Republic: CHARLES LOOTENS

THE COWBOY AND THE LADY, Goldwyn, UA: THOMAS MOULTON

FOUR DAUGHTERS, Warner Bros.: NATHAN LEVINSON

IF I WERE KING, Paramount: L.L. RYDER

MERRILY WE LIVE, Roach, M-G-M: ELMER RAGUSE

SWEETHEARTS, Metro-Goldwyn-Mayer: DOUGLAS SHEARER

SUEZ, 20th Century-Fox: EDMUND HANSEN

THAT CERTAIN AGE, Universal: BERNARD B. BROWN

VIVACIOUS LADY, RKO Radio: JAMES WILKINSON

YOU CAN'T TAKE IT WITH YOU, Columbia: JOHN LIVADARY

Film Editing

THE ADVENTURES OF ROBIN HOOD, Warner Bros.: RALPH DAWSON

ALEXANDER'S RAGTIME BAND, 20th Century-Fox: BARBARA MCLEAN

THE GREAT WALTZ, Metro-Goldwyn-Mayer: TOM HELD

TEST PILOT, Metro-Goldwyn-Mayer: TOM HELD

YOU CAN'T TAKE IT WITH YOU, Columbia: GENE HAVLICK

Music

(Best Score)

ALEXANDER'S RAGTIME BAND, 20th Century-Fox: ALFRED NEWMAN

CAREFREE, RKO Radio: VICTOR BARAVALLE

GIRLS SCHOOL, Columbia: MORRIS STOLOFF and GREGORY STONE

GOLDWYN FOLLIES, Goldwyn, UA: ALFRED NEWMAN

JEZEBEL, Warner Bros.: MAX STEINER

MAD ABOUT MUSIC, Universal: CHARLES PREVIN and FRANK SKINNER

STORM OVER BENGAL, Republic: CY FEUER

SWEETHEARTS, Metro-Goldwyn-Mayer: HERBERT STOTHART

THERE GOES MY HEART, Hal Roach, UA: MARVIN HATLEY

TROPIC HOLIDAY, Paramount: BORIS MORROS

THE YOUNG IN HEART, Selznick, UA: FRANZ WAXMAN

(Original Score)

THE ADVENTURES OF ROBIN HOOD, Warner Bros.: ERICH WOLFGANG KORNGOLD

ARMY GIRL, Republic: VICTOR YOUNG

BLOCKADE, Walter Wanger, UA: WERNER JANSSEN

BLOCKHEADS, Hal Roach, UA: MARVIN HATLEY

BREAKING THE ICE, RKO Radio: VICTOR YOUNG

THE COWBOY AND THE LADY, Goldwyn, UA: ALFRED NEWMAN

IF I WERE KING, Paramount: RICHARD HAGEMAN

MARIE ANTOINETTE, Metro-Goldwyn-Mayer: HERBERT STOTHART

PACIFIC LINER, RKO Radio: RUSSELL BENNETT

SUEZ, 20th Century-Fox: LOUIS SILVERS

THE YOUNG IN HEART, Selznick, UA: FRANZ WAXMAN

(Best Song)

ALWAYS AND ALWAYS from *Mannequin*, Metro-Goldwyn-Mayer Music by EDWARD WARD. Lyrics by CHET FORREST and BOB WRIGHT

CHANGE PARTNERS AND DANCE WITH ME from *Carefree*, RKO Radio Music and Lyrics by IRVING BERLIN

THE COWBOY AND THE LADY from *The*

Cowboy And The Lady, Goldwyn, UA
Music by LIONEL NEWMAN. Lyrics by ARTHUR QUENZER
DUST from *Under Western Stars,* Republic
Music and Lyrics by JOHNNY MARVIN
JEEPERS CREEPERS from *Going Places,* Warner Bros.
Music by HARRY WARREN. Lyrics by JOHNNY MERCER
MERRILY WE LIVE from *Merrily We Live,* Roach, M-G-M
Music by PHIL CRAIG. Lyrics by ARTHUR QUENZER
A MIST OVER THE MOON from *The Lady Objects,* Columbia
Music by BEN OAKLAND. Lyrics by OSCAR HAMMERSTEIN II
MY OWN from *That Certain Age,* Universal
Music by JIMMY MCHUGH. Lyrics by HAROLD ADAMSON
NOW IT CAN BE TOLD from *Alexander's Ragtime Band,* 20th Century-Fox
Music and Lyrics by IRVING BERLIN
THANKS FOR THE MEMORY from *Big Broadcast Of 1938,* Paramount
Music by RALPH RAINGER
Lyrics by LEO ROBIN

Short Subjects

(Cartoons)

BRAVE LITTLE TAILOR, Walt Disney, RKO Radio
MOTHER GOOSE GOES HOLLYWOOD, Walt Disney, RKO Radio
FERDINAND THE BULL, Walt Disney, RKO Radio
GOOD SCOUTS, Walt Disney, RKO Radio
HUNKY AND SPUNKY, Paramount

(One-reel)

THE GREAT HEART, Metro-Goldwyn-Mayer: (Miniature)

THAT MOTHERS MIGHT LIVE, Metro-Goldwyn-Mayer: (Miniature)
TIMBER TOPPERS, 20th Century-Fox: (Ed Thorgensen-Sports)

(Two-reel)

DECLARATION OF INDEPENDENCE, Warner Bros.: (Historical Featurette)
SWINGTIME IN THE MOVIES, Warner Bros.: (Broadway Brevities)
THEY'RE ALWAYS CAUGHT, Metro-Goldwyn-Mayer: (Crime Doesn't Pay)

Special Awards

DEANNA DURBIN and MICKEY ROONEY for their significant contribution in bringing to the screen the spirit and personification of youth, and as juvenile players setting a high standard of ability and achievement. (miniature statuette trophies)
HARRY M. WARNER in recognition of patriotic service in the production of historical short subjects presenting significant episodes in the early struggle of the American people for liberty. (scroll)
WALT DISNEY for *Snow White And The Seven Dwarfs,* recognized as a significant screen innovation which has charmed millions and pioneered a great new entertainment field for the motion picture cartoon. (one statuette—seven miniature statuettes)
OLIVER MARSH and ALLEN DAVEY for the color cinematography of the Metro-Goldwyn-Mayer production, *Sweethearts.* (plaques)
For outstanding achievement in creating Special Photographic and Sound Effects in the Paramount production, *Spawn Of The North.* Special Effects by GORDON JENNINGS, assisted by JAN DOMELA, DEV JENNINGS, IRMIN ROBERTS and ART

SMITH. Transparencies by FAR-
CIOT EDOUART, assisted by
LOYAL GRIGGS. Sound Effects by
LOREN RYDER, assisted by
HARRY MILLS, LOUIS H. ME-
SENKOP and WALTER OBERST.
(plaques)
J. ARTHUR BALL for his outstanding
contributions to the advancement of
color in Motion Picture Photography.
(scroll)

Irving G. Thalberg Memorial Award
HAL B. WALLIS

Scientific or Technical
Class I
None.

Class II
None

Class III
JOHN AALBERG and the RKO
    RADIO STUDIO SOUND DE-
    PARTMENT for the application of
    compression to variable area record-
    ing in motion picture production
BYRON HASKIN and the SPECIAL
    EFFECTS DEPARTMENT of
    WARNER BROS. STUDIO for
    pioneering the development and for
    the first practical application to mo-
    tion picture production of the triple
    head background projector

1939

Nominations Announced: February 12, 1940
Awards Ceremony: February 29, 1940
Ambassador Hotel—Banquet
(MC: Bob Hope for last half only)

Best Picture

DARK VICTORY, Warner Bros.
GONE WITH THE WIND, Selznick, M-G-M
GOODBYE, MR. CHIPS, Metro-Goldwyn-Mayer (British)
LOVE AFFAIR, RKO Radio
MR. SMITH GOES TO WASHINGTON, Columbia
NINOTCHKA, Metro-Goldwyn-Mayer
OF MICE AND MEN, Roach, UA
STAGECOACH, Wanger, UA
WIZARD OF OZ, Metro-Goldwyn-Mayer
WUTHERING HEIGHTS, Goldwyn, UA

Actor

ROBERT DONAT in *Goodbye, Mr. Chips,* Metro-Goldwyn-Mayer (British)
CLARK GABLE in *Gone With The Wind,* Selznick, M-G-M
LAURENCE OLIVIER in *Wuthering Heights,* Goldwyn, UA
MICKEY ROONEY in *Babes In Arms,* Metro-Goldwyn-Mayer
JAMES STEWART in *Mr. Smith Goes To Washington,* Columbia

Actress

BETTE DAVIS in *Dark Victory,* Warner Bros.
IRENE DUNNE in *Love Affair,* RKO Radio
GRETA GARBO in *Ninotchka,* Metro-Goldwyn-Mayer

LARGE CAPITAL LETTERS DENOTE WINNER

GREER GARSON in *Goodbye, Mr. Chips,* Metro-Goldwyn-Mayer (British)
VIVIEN LEIGH in *Gone With The Wind,* Selznick, M-G-M

Supporting Actor

BRIAN AHERNE in *Juarez,* Warner Bros.
HARRY CAREY in *Mr. Smith Goes To Washington,* Columbia
BRIAN DONLEVY in *Beau Geste,* Paramount
THOMAS MITCHELL in *Stagecoach,* Wanger, UA
CLAUDE RAINS in *Mr. Smith Goes To Washington,* Columbia

Supporting Actress

OLIVIA DE HAVILLAND in *Gone With The Wind,* Selznick, M-G-M
GERALDINE FITZGERALD in *Wuthering Heights,* Goldwyn, UA
HATTIE McDANIEL in *Gone With The Wind,* Selznick, M-G-M
EDNA MAY OLIVER in *Drums Along The Mohawk,* 20th Century-Fox
MARIA OUSPENSKAYA in *Love Affair,* RKO Radio

Directing

FRANK CAPRA for *Mr. Smith Goes To Washington,* Columbia
VICTOR FLEMING for *Gone With The Wind,* Selznick, M-G-M
JOHN FORD for *Stagecoach,* Wanger, UA
SAM WOOD for *Goodbye, Mr. Chips,* Metro-Goldwyn-Mayer (British)

WILLIAM WYLER for *Wuthering Heights,* Goldwyn, UA

Writing
(Original Story)
BACHELOR MOTHER, RKO Radio: FELIX JACKSON
LOVE AFFAIR, RKO Radio: MILDRED CRAM and LEO MCCAREY
MR. SMITH GOES TO WASHINGTON, Columbia: LEWIS R. FOSTER
NINOTCHKA, Metro-Goldwyn-Mayer: MELCHIOR LENGYEL
YOUNG MR. LINCOLN, 20th Century-Fox: LAMAR TROTTI

(Screenplay)
GONE WITH THE WIND, Selznick, M-G-M: SIDNEY HOWARD
GOODBYE, MR. CHIPS, Metro-Goldwyn-Mayer (British): ERIC MASCHWITZ, R. C. SHERRIFF and CLAUDINE WEST
MR. SMITH GOES TO WASHINGTON, Columbia: SIDNEY BUCHMAN
NINOTCHKA, Metro-Goldwyn-Mayer: CHARLES BRACKETT, WALTER REISCH and BILLY WILDER
WUTHERING HEIGHTS, Goldwyn, UA: BEN HECHT and CHARLES MacARTHUR

Cinematography
(Black-and-White)
STAGECOACH, Wanger, UA: BERT GLENNON
WUTHERING HEIGHTS, Goldwyn, UA: GREGG TOLAND

(Color)
GONE WITH THE WIND, Selznick, M-G-M: ERNEST HALLER and RAY RENNAHAN
THE PRIVATE LIVES OF ELIZABETH AND ESSEX, Warner Bros.: SOL POLITO and W. HOWARD GREENE

Interior Decoration
BEAU GESTE, Paramount: HANS DREIER and ROBERT ODELL
CAPTAIN FURY, Roach, UA: CHARLES D. HALL
FIRST LOVE, Universal: JACK OTTERSON and MARTIN OBZINA
GONE WITH THE WIND, Selznick, M-G-M: LYLE WHEELER
LOVE AFFAIR, RKO Radio: VAN NEST POLGLASE and AL HERMAN
MAN OF CONQUEST, Republic: JOHN VICTOR MACKAY
MR. SMITH GOES TO WASHINGTON, Columbia: LIONEL BANKS
THE PRIVATE LIVES OF ELIZABETH AND ESSEX, Warner Bros.: ANTON GROT
THE RAINS CAME, 20th Century-Fox: WILLIAM DARLING and GEORGE DUDLEY
STAGECOACH, Wanger, UA: ALEXANDER TOLUBOFF
THE WIZARD OF OZ, Metro-Goldwyn-Mayer: CEDRIC GIBBONS and WILLIAM A. HORNING
WUTHERING HEIGHTS, Goldwyn, UA: JAMES BASEVI

Sound Recording
BALALAIKA, Metro-Goldwyn-Mayer: DOUGLAS SHEARER
GONE WITH THE WIND, Selznick, M-G-M: THOMAS T. MOULTON
GOODBYE, MR. CHIPS, Metro-Goldwyn-Mayer (British): A. W. WATKINS
THE GREAT VICTOR HERBERT, Paramount: LOREN RYDER
THE HUNCHBACK OF NOTRE DAME, RKO Radio: JOHN AALBERG
MAN OF CONQUEST, Republic: C.L. LOOTENS
MR. SMITH GOES TO WASHINGTON, Columbia: JOHN LIVADARY
OF MICE AND MEN, Roach, M-G-M: ELMER RAGUSE
THE PRIVATE LIVES OF ELIZABETH AND

ESSEX, Warner Bros.: NATHAN LE-
VINSON

THE RAINS CAME, 20th Century-Fox:
E. H. HANSEN

WHEN TOMORROW COMES, Uni-
versal: BERNARD B. BROWN

Film Editing

GONE WITH THE WIND, Selznick,
M-G-M: HAL C. KERN and
JAMES E. NEWCOM

GOODBYE, MR. CHIPS, Metro-Goldwyn-
Mayer (British): CHARLES FREND

MR. SMITH GOES TO WASHINGTON, Columbia: GENE HAVLICK and AL
CLARK

THE RAINS CAME, 20th Century-Fox:
BARBARA MCLEAN

STAGECOACH, Wanger, UA: OTHO
LOVERING and DOROTHY SPENCER

Music

(Best Score)

BABES IN ARMS, Metro-Goldwyn-
Mayer: ROGER EDENS and GEORGE E.
STOLL

FIRST LOVE, Universal: CHARLES PRE-
VIN

THE GREAT VICTOR HERBERT, Paramount: PHIL BOUTELJE and ARTHUR
LANGE

THE HUNCHBACK OF NOTRE DAME,
RKO Radio: ALFRED NEWMAN

INTERMEZZO, Selznick, UA: LOU
FORBES

MR. SMITH GOES TO WASHINGTON, Columbia: DIMITRI TIOMKIN

OF MICE AND MEN, Roach, UA: AARON
COPLAND

THE PRIVATE LIVES OF ELIZABETH AND
ESSEX, Warner Bros.: ERICH
WOLFGANG KORNGOLD

SHE MARRIED A COP, Republic: CY
FEUER

STAGECOACH, Walter Wanger, UA:
RICHARD HAGEMAN, FRANK

HARLING, JOHN LEIPOLD and
LEO SHUKEN

SWANEE RIVER, 20th Century-Fox:
LOUIS SILVERS

THEY SHALL HAVE MUSIC, Goldwyn,
UA: ALFRED NEWMAN

WAY DOWN SOUTH, Lesser, RKO
Radio: VICTOR YOUNG

(Original Score)

DARK VICTORY, Warner Bros.: MAX
STEINER

ETERNALLY YOURS, Walter Wanger,
UA: WERNER JANSSEN

GOLDEN BOY, Columbia: VICTOR
YOUNG

GONE WITH THE WIND, Selznick,
M-G-M: MAX STEINER

GULLIVER'S TRAVELS, Paramount: VIC-
TOR YOUNG

THE MAN IN THE IRON MASK, Small,
UA: LUD GLUSKIN and LUCIEN
MORAWECK

MAN OF CONQUEST, Republic: VICTOR
YOUNG

NURSE EDITH CAVELL, RKO Radio:
ANTHONY COLLINS

OF MICE AND MEN, Roach, UA: AARON
COPLAND

THE RAINS CAME, 20th Century-Fox:
ALFRED NEWMAN

THE WIZARD OF OZ, Metro-
Goldwyn-Mayer: HERBERT
STOTHART

WUTHERING HEIGHTS, Goldwyn, UA:
ALFRED NEWMAN

(Best Song)

FAITHFUL FOREVER from *Gulliver's
Travels,* Paramount
Music by RALPH RAINGER. Lyrics by
LEO ROBIN

I POURED MY HEART INTO A SONG from
Second Fiddle, 20th Century-Fox
Music and Lyrics by IRVING BERLIN

OVER THE RAINBOW from *The Wizard of Oz,* Metro-Goldwyn-Mayer

Music by HAROLD ARLEN. Lyrics by E. Y. HARBURG

WISHING from *Love Affair*, RKO Radio Music and Lyrics by BUDDY DE SYLVA

Short Subjects

(Cartoons)

DETOURING AMERICA, Warner Bros.

PEACE ON EARTH, Metro-Goldwyn-Mayer

THE POINTER, Walt Disney, RKO Radio

THE UGLY DUCKLING, Walt Disney, RKO Radio

(One-reel)

BUSY LITTLE BEARS, Paramount: (Paragraphics)

INFORMATION PLEASE, RKO Radio

PROPHET WITHOUT HONOR, Metro-Goldwyn-Mayer: (Miniature)

SWORD FISHING, Warner Bros.: (Vitaphone Varieties)

(Two-reel)

DRUNK DRIVING, Metro-Goldwyn-Mayer: (Crime Doesn't Pay)

FIVE TIMES FIVE, RKO Radio: (Special)

SONS OF LIBERTY, Warner Bros.: (Historical Featurette)

Special Effects

(New Category)

GONE WITH THE WIND, Selznick, M-G-M: JOHN R. COSGROVE, FRED ALBIN and ARTHUR JOHNS

ONLY ANGELS HAVE WINGS, Columbia: ROY DAVIDSON and EDWIN C. HAHN

PRIVATE LIVES OF ELIZABETH AND ESSEX, Warner Bros.: BYRON HASKIN and NATHAN LEVINSON

THE RAINS CAME, 20th Century-Fox: E. H. HANSEN and FRED SERSEN

TOPPER TAKES A TRIP, Roach, UA: ROY SEAWRIGHT

UNION PACIFIC, Paramount: FARCIOT EDOUART, GORDON JENNINGS and LOREN RYDER

THE WIZARD OF OZ, Metro-Goldwyn-Mayer: A. ARNOLD GILLESPIE and DOUGLAS SHEARER

Special Awards

DOUGLAS FAIRBANKS (Commemorative Award)—recognizing the unique and outstanding contribution of Douglas Fairbanks, first President of the Academy, to the international development of the motion picture. (statuette)

MOTION PICTURE RELIEF FUND—acknowledging the outstanding services to the industry during the past year of the Motion Picture Relief Fund and its progressive leadership. Presented to JEAN HERSHOLT, President; RALPH MORGAN, Chairman of the Executive Committee; RALPH BLOCK, First Vice-President; CONRAD NAGEL. (plaques)

JUDY GARLAND for her outstanding performance as a screen juvenile during the past year. (miniature statuette)

WILLIAM CAMERON MENZIES for outstanding achievement in the use of color for the enhancement of dramatic mood in the production of *Gone With the Wind*. (plaque)

TECHNICOLOR COMPANY for its contributions in successfully bringing three-color feature production to the screen. (statuette)

Irving G. Thalberg Memorial Award

DAVID O. SELZNICK

Scientific or Technical

Class I

None

Class II

None

Class III

GEORGE ANDERSON of Warner Bros. Studio for an improved positive head for sun arcs

JOHN ARNOLD of Metro-Goldwyn-Mayer Studio for the M-G-M mobile camera crane

THOMAS T. MOULTON, FRED ALBIN and the SOUND DEPARTMENT of the SAMUEL GOLDWYN STUDIO for the origination and application of the Delta db test to sound recording in motion pictures

FARCIOT EDOUART, JOSEPH E. ROBBINS, WILLIAM RUDOLPH AND PARAMOUNT PICTURES, INC., for the design and construction of a quiet portable treadmill

EMERY HUSE AND RALPH B. ATKINSON of Eastman Kodak Co. for their specifications for chemical analysis of photographic developers and fixing baths

HAROLD NYE of Warner Bros. Studio for a miniature incandescent spot lamp

A. J. TONDREAU of Warner Bros. Studio for the design and manufacture of an improved sound track printer

Multiple Award for important contributions in cooperative development of new improved Process Projection Equipment:

F. R. ABBOTT, HALLER BELT, ALAN COOK and BAUSCH & LOMB OPTICAL CO. for faster projection lenses

MITCHELL CAMERA CO. for a new type process projection head

MOLE-RICHARDSON CO. for a new type automatically controlled projection arc lamp

CHARLES HANDLEY, DAVID JOY and NATIONAL CARBON CO. for improved and more stable high-intensity carbons

WINTON HOCH and TECHNICOLOR MOTION PICTURE CORP. for an auxiliary optical system

DON MUSGRAVE and SELZNICK INTERNATIONAL PICTURES, INC., for pioneering in the use of coordinated equipment in the production *Gone With the Wind*

1940

Nominations Announced: February 10, 1941
Awards Ceremony: February 27, 1941
Biltmore Hotel—Banquet
(No MC, banquet addressed via radio by President Franklin D. Roosevelt)

Best Picture

ALL THIS, AND HEAVEN TOO, Warner Bros.

FOREIGN CORRESPONDENT, Wanger, UA

THE GRAPES OF WRATH, 20th Century-Fox

THE GREAT DICTATOR, Chaplin, UA

KITTY FOYLE, RKO Radio

THE LETTER, Warner Bros.

THE LONG VOYAGE HOME, Argosy-Wanger, UA

OUR TOWN, Lesser, UA

THE PHILADELPHIA STORY, Metro-Goldwyn-Mayer

REBECCA, Selznick International, UA

Actor

CHARLES CHAPLIN in *The Great Dictator*, Chaplin, UA

HENRY FONDA in *The Grapes of Wrath*, 20th Century-Fox

RAYMOND MASSEY in *Abe Lincoln In Illinois*, RKO Radio

LAURENCE OLIVIER in *Rebecca*, Selznick-UA

JAMES STEWART in *The Philadelphia Story*, Metro-Goldwyn-Mayer

Actress

BETTE DAVIS in *The Letter*, Warner Bros.

JOAN FONTAINE in *Rebecca*, Selznick, UA

KATHARINE HEPBURN in *The Philadelphia Story*, Metro-Goldwyn-Mayer

LARGE CAPITAL LETTERS DENOTE WINNER

GINGER ROGERS in *Kitty Foyle*, RKO Radio

MARTHA SCOTT in *Our Town*, Lesser, UA

Supporting Actor

ALBERT BASSERMANN in *Foreign Correspondent*, Wanger, UA

WALTER BRENNAN in *The Westerner*, Goldwyn, UA

WILLIAM GARGAN in *They Knew What They Wanted*, RKO Radio

JACK OAKIE in *The Great Dictator*, Chaplin, UA

JAMES STEPHENSON in *The Letter*, Warner Bros.

Supporting Actress

JUDITH ANDERSON in *Rebecca*, Selznick, UA

JANE DARWELL in *The Grapes Of Wrath*, 20th Century-Fox

RUTH HUSSEY in *The Philadelphia Story*, Metro-Goldwyn-Mayer

BARBARA O'NEIL in *All This, And Heaven Too*, Warner Bros.

MARJORIE RAMBEAU in *Primrose Path*, RKO Radio

Directing

GEORGE CUKOR for *The Philadelphia Story*, Metro-Goldwyn-Mayer

JOHN FORD for *The Grapes Of Wrath*, 20th Century-Fox

ALFRED HITCHCOCK for *Rebecca*, Selznick, UA

SAM WOOD for *Kitty Foyle,* RKO Radio
WILLIAM WYLER for *The Letter,* Warner Bros.

Writing

(Original Story)

ARISE, MY LOVE, Paramount: BENJAMIN GLAZER and JOHN S. TOLDY

COMARADE X, Metro-Goldwyn-Mayer: WALTER REISCH

EDISON THE MAN, Metro-Goldwyn-Mayer: HUGO BUTLER and DORE SCHARY

MY FAVORITE WIFE, RKO Radio: LEO MCCAREY, BELLA SPEWACK & SAMUEL SPEWACK

THE WESTERNER, Goldwyn, UA: STUART N. LAKE

(Original Screenplay)

ANGELS OVER BROADWAY, Columbia: BEN HECHT

DR. EHRLICH'S MAGIC BULLET, Warner Bros.: NORMAN BURNSIDE, HEINZ HERALD and JOHN HUSTON

FOREIGN CORRESPONDENT, Wanger, UA: CHARLES BENNETT and JOAN HARRISON

THE GREAT DICTATOR, Chaplin, UA: CHARLES CHAPLIN

THE GREAT McGINTY, Paramount: PRESTON STURGES

(Screenplay)

THE GRAPES OF WRATH, 20th Century-Fox: NUNNALLY JOHNSON

KITTY FOYLE, RKO Radio: DALTON TRUMBO

THE LONG VOYAGE HOME, Argosy-Wanger, UA: DUDLEY NICHOLS

THE PHILADELPHIA STORY, Metro-Goldwyn-Mayer: DONALD OGDEN STEWART

REBECCA, Selznick, UA: ROBERT E. SHERWOOD and JOAN HARRISON

Cinematography

(Black-and-White)

ABE LINCOLN IN ILLINOIS, RKO Radio: JAMES WONG HOWE

ALL THIS, AND HEAVEN TOO, Warner Bros.: ERNEST HALLER

ARISE, MY LOVE, Paramount: CHARLES B. LANG, JR.

BOOM TOWN, Metro-Goldwyn-Mayer: HAROLD ROSSON

FOREIGN CORRESPONDENT, Wanger, UA: RUDOLPH MATE

THE LETTER, Warner Bros.: GAETANO GAUDIO

THE LONG VOYAGE HOME, Argosy-Wanger, UA: GREGG TOLAND

REBECCA, Selznick, UA: GEORGE BARNES

SPRING PARADE, Universal: JOSEPH VALENTINE

WATERLOO BRIDGE, Metro-Goldwyn-Mayer: JOSEPH RUTTENBERG

(Color)

BITTER SWEET, Metro-Goldwyn-Mayer: OLIVER T. MARSH and ALLEN DAVEY

THE BLUE BIRD, 20th Century-Fox: ARTHUR MILLER and RAY RENNAHAN

DOWN ARGENTINE WAY, 20th Century-Fox: LEON SHAMROY and RAY RENNAHAN

NORTH WEST MOUNTED POLICE, Paramount: VICTOR MILNER and W. HOWARD GREENE

NORTHWEST PASSAGE, Metro-Goldwyn-Mayer: SIDNEY WAGNER and WILLIAM V. SKALL.

THIEF OF BAGDAD, Korda, UA (British): GEORGE PERINAL

Interior Decoration

(Black-and-White)

ARISE, MY LOVE, Paramount: HANS DREIER and ROBERT USHER

ARIZONA, Columbia: LIONEL BANKS and ROBERT PETERSON

THE BOYS FROM SYRACUSE, Universal: JOHN OTTERSON

DARK COMMAND, Republic: JOHN VICTOR MACKAY

FOREIGN CORRESPONDENT, Wanger, UA: ALEXANDER GOLITZEN

LILLIAN RUSSELL, 20th Century-Fox: RICHARD DAY and JOSEPH C. WRIGHT

MY FAVORITE WIFE, RKO Radio: VAN NEST POLGLASE and MARK-LEE KIRK

MY SON, MY SON, Small, UA: JOHN DuCASSE SCHULZE

OUR TOWN, Lesser, UA: LEWIS J. RACHMIL

PRIDE AND PREJUDICE, Metro-Goldwyn-Mayer: CEDRIC GIBBONS and PAUL GROESSE

REBECCA, Selznick, UA: LYLE WHEELER

SEA HAWK, Warner Bros.: ANTON GROT

THE WESTERNER, Goldwyn, UA. JAMES BASEVI

(Color)

BITTER SWEET, Metro-Goldwyn-Mayer: CEDRIC GIBBONS and JOHN S. DETLIE

DOWN ARGENTINE WAY, 20th Century-Fox: RICHARD DAY and JOSEPH C. WRIGHT

NORTH WEST MOUNTED POLICE, Paramount: HANS DREIER and ROLAND ANDERSON

THIEF OF BAGDAD, Korda, UA. VINCENT KORDA

Sound Recording

BEHIND THE NEWS, Republic: CHARLES LOOTENS

CAPTAIN CAUTION, Roach, UA: ELMER RAGUSE

THE GRAPES OF WRATH, 20th Century-Fox: E. H. HANSEN

THE HOWARDS OF VIRGINIA, Columbia: JACK WHITNEY, GENERAL SERVICE

KITTY FOYLE, RKO Radio: JOHN AALBERG

NORTH WEST MOUNTED POLICE, Paramount: LOREN RYDER

OUR TOWN, Lesser, UA: THOMAS MOULTON

THE SEA HAWK, Warner Bros.: NATHAN LEVINSON

SPRING PARADE, Universal: BERNARD B. BROWN

STRIKE UP THE BAND, Metro-Goldwyn-Mayer: DOUGLAS SHEARER

TOO MANY HUSBANDS, Columbia: JOHN LIVADARY

Film Editing

THE GRAPES OF WRATH, 20th Century-Fox: ROBERT E. SIMPSON

THE LETTER, Warner Bros.: WARREN LOW

THE LONG VOYAGE HOME, Argosy-Wanger, UA: SHERMAN TODD

NORTH WEST MOUNTED POLICE, Paramount: ANNE BAUCHENS

REBECCA, Selznick, UA: HAL C. KERN

Music

(Best Score)

ARISE, MY LOVE, Paramount: VICTOR YOUNG

HIT PARADE OF 1941, Republic: CY FEUER

IRENE, Imperadio, RKO Radio: ANTHONY COLLINS

OUR TOWN, Sol Lesser, UA: AARON COPLAND

THE SEA HAWK, Warner Bros.: ERICH WOLFGANG KORNGOLD

SECOND CHORUS, Paramount: ARTIE SHAW

SPRING PARADE, Universal: CHARLES PREVIN

STRIKE UP THE BAND, Metro-Goldwyn-Mayer: GEORGIE STOLL and ROGER EDENS

TIN PAN ALLEY, 20th Century-Fox: ALFRED NEWMAN

very low1 9 4 0

(Original Score)
ARIZONA, Columbia: VICTOR YOUNG
THE DARK COMMAND, Republic: VICTOR YOUNG
THE FIGHT FOR LIFE, U.S. Government-Columbia: LOUIS GRUENBERG
THE GREAT DICTATOR, Chaplin, UA: MEREDITH WILLSON
THE HOUSE OF SEVEN GABLES, Universal: FRANK SKINNER
THE HOWARDS OF VIRGINIA, Columbia: RICHARD HAGEMAN
THE LETTER, Warner Bros.: MAX STEINER
THE LONG VOYAGE HOME, Argosy-Wanger, UA: RICHARD HAGEMAN
THE MARK OF ZORRO, 20th Century-Fox: ALFRED NEWMAN
MY FAVORITE WIFE, RKO Radio: ROY WEBB
NORTH WEST MOUNTED POLICE, Paramount: VICTOR YOUNG
ONE MILLION B.C., Hal Roach, UA: WERNER HEYMANN
OUR TOWN, Sol Lesser, UA: AARON COPLAND
PINOCCHIO, Disney, RKO Radio: LEIGH HARLINE, PAUL J. SMITH and NED WASHINGTON
REBECCA, Selznick, UA: FRANZ WAXMAN
THE THIEF OF BAGDAD, Korda, UA: MIKLOS ROZSA
WATERLOO BRIDGE, Metro-Goldwyn-Mayer: HERBERT STOTHART

(Best Song)
DOWN ARGENTINE WAY from Down Argentine Way, 20th Century-Fox
Music by HARRY WARREN. Lyrics by MARK GORDON
I'D KNOW YOU ANYWHERE from You'll Find Out, RKO Radio
Music by JIMMY MCHUGH. Lyrics by JOHNNY MERCER
IT'S A BLUE WORLD from Music In My Heart, Columbia

Music and Lyrics by CHET FORREST and BOB WRIGHT
LOVE OF MY LIFE from Second Chorus, Paramount
Music by ARTIE SHAW. Lyrics by JOHNNY MERCER
ONLY FOREVER from Rhythm On The River, Paramount
Music by JAMES MONACO. Lyrics by JOHN BURKE
OUR LOVE AFFAIR from Strike Up The Band, Metro-Goldwyn-Mayer
Music and Lyrics by ROGER EDENS and GEORGIE STOLL
WALTZING IN THE CLOUDS from Spring Parade, Universal
Music by ROBERT STOLZ. Lyrics by GUS KAHN
WHEN YOU WISH UPON A STAR from Pinocchio, Disney, RKO Radio
Music by LEIGH HARLINE. Lyrics by NED WASHINGTON
WHO AM I? from Hit Parade Of 1941, Republic
Music by JULE STYNE. Lyrics by WALTER BULLOCK

Short Subjects
(Cartoons)
MILKY WAY, Metro-Goldwyn-Mayer (Rudolph Ising Series)
PUSS GETS THE BOOT, Metro-Goldwyn-Mayer. (Cat and Mouse Series)
A WILD HARE, Leon Schlesinger, Warner Bros.

(One-reel)
LONDON CAN TAKE IT, Warner Bros. (Vitaphone Varieties)
MORE ABOUT NOSTRADAMUS, Metro-Goldwyn-Mayer
QUICKER 'N A WINK, Pete Smith, M-G-M
SIEGE, RKO Radio (Reelism)
(Two-reel)
EYES OF THE NAVY, Metro-Goldwyn-Mayer. (Crime Doesn't Pay)

SERVICE WITH THE COLORS, Warner Bros. (National Defense Series)
TEDDY, THE ROUGH RIDER, Warner Bros. (Historical Featurette)

Special Effects

THE BLUE BIRD, 20th Century-Fox
Photographic: FRED SERSEN
Sound: E. H. HANSEN
BOOM TOWN, Metro-Goldwyn-Mayer
Photographic: A. ARNOLD GILLESPIE
Sound: DOUGLAS SHEARER
THE BOYS FROM SYRACUSE, Universal
Photographic: JOHN P. FULTON
Sound: BERNARD B. BROWN and JOSEPH LAPIS
DR. CYCLOPS, Paramount
Photographic: FARCIOT EDOUART and GORDON JENNINGS
Sound: No credit listed
FOREIGN CORRESPONDENT, Wanger, UA
Photographic: PAUL EAGLER
Sound: THOMAS T. MOULTON
THE INVISIBLE MAN RETURNS, Universal
Photographic: JOHN P. FULTON
Sound: BERNARD B. BROWN and WILLIAM HEDGECOCK
THE LONG VOYAGE HOME, Argosy-Wanger, UA
Photographic: R. T. LAYTON and R. O. BINGER
Sound: THOMAS T. MOULTON
ONE MILLION B. C., Roach, UA
Photographic: ROY SEAWRIGHT
Sound: ELMER RAGUSE
REBECCA, Selznick, UA
Photographic: JACK COSGROVE
Sound: ARTHUR JOHNS
THE SEA HAWK, Warner Bros.
Photographic: BYRON HASKIN
Sound: NATHAN LEVINSON
SWISS FAMILY ROBINSON, RKO Radio
Photographic: VERNON L. WALKER
Sound: JOHN O. AALBERG
THE THIEF OF BAGDAD, Korda, UA

Photographic: LAWRENCE BUTLER
Sound: JACK WHITNEY
TYPHOON, Paramount
Photographic: FARCIOT EDOUART and GORDON JENNINGS
Sound: LOREN RYDER
WOMEN IN WAR, Republic
Photographic: HOWARD J. LYDECKER, WILLIAM BRADFORD and ELLIS J. THACKERY
Sound: HERBERT NORSCH

Special Awards

BOB HOPE, in recognition of his unselfish services to the Motion Picture Industry. (special silver plaque)
COLONEL NATHAN LEVINSON for his outstanding service to the industry and the Army during the past nine years, which has made possible the present efficient mobilization of the motion picture industry facilities for the production of Army Training Films. (statuette)

Irving G. Thalberg Memorial Award
None

Scientific or Technical
Class I
20TH CENTURY-FOX FILM CORP. for the design and construction of the 20th Century Silenced Camera, developed by DANIEL CLARK, GROVER LAUBE, CHARLES MILLER and ROBERT W. STEVENS

Class II
None

Class III
WARNER BROS. STUDIO ART DEPARTMENT and ANTON GROT for the design and perfection of the Warner Bros. water ripple and wave illusion machine

1941

Nominations Announced: February 9, 1942
Awards Ceremony: February 26, 1942
Biltmore Hotel—Banquet
(No MC, Wendell Willkie was principal speaker)

Best Picture

BLOSSOMS IN THE DUST, Metro-Goldwyn-Mayer
CITIZEN KANE, Mercury, RKO Radio
HERE COMES MR. JORDAN, Columbia
HOLD BACK THE DAWN, Paramount
HOW GREEN WAS MY VALLEY, 20th Century-Fox
THE LITTLE FOXES, Goldwyn, RKO Radio
THE MALTESE FALCON, Warner Bros.
ONE FOOT IN HEAVEN, Warner Bros.
SERGEANT YORK, Warner Bros.
SUSPICION, RKO Radio

Actor

GARY COOPER in *Sergeant York*, Warner Bros.
CARY GRANT in *Penny Serenade*, Columbia
WALTER HUSTON in *All That Money Can Buy*, RKO Radio
ROBERT MONTGOMERY in *Here Comes Mr. Jordan*, Columbia
ORSON WELLES in *Citizen Kane*, Mercury, RKO Radio

Actress

BETTE DAVIS in *The Little Foxes*, Goldwyn, RKO Radio
OLIVIA DE HAVILLAND in *Hold Back The Dawn*, Paramount
JOAN FONTAINE in *Suspicion*, RKO Radio

LARGE CAPITAL LETTERS DENOTE WINNER

GREER GARSON in *Blossoms In The Dust*, Metro-Goldwyn-Mayer
BARBARA STANWYCK in *Ball Of Fire*, Goldwyn, RKO Radio

Supporting Actor

WALTER BRENNAN in *Sergeant York*, Warner Bros.
CHARLES COBURN in *The Devil And Miss Jones*, RKO Radio
DONALD CRISP in *How Green Was My Valley*, 20th Century-Fox
JAMES GLEASON in *Here Comes Mr. Jordan*, Columbia
SYDNEY GREENSTREET in *The Maltese Falcon*, Warner Bros.

Supporting Actress

SARA ALLGOOD in *How Green Was My Valley*, 20th Century-Fox
MARY ASTOR in *The Great Lie*, Warner Bros.
PATRICIA COLLINGE in *The Little Foxes*, Goldwyn, RKO Radio
TERESA WRIGHT in *The Little Foxes*, Goldwyn, RKO Radio
MARGARET WYCHERLY in *Sergeant York*, Warner Bros.

Directing

JOHN FORD for *How Green Was My Valley*, 20th Century-Fox
ALEXANDER HALL for *Here Comes Mr. Jordan*, Columbia
HOWARD HAWKS for *Sergeant York*, Warner Bros.

ORSON WELLES for *Citizen Kane*, Mercury, RKO Radio

WILLIAM WYLER for *The Little Foxes*, Goldwyn, RKO Radio

Writing

(Original Story)

BALL OF FIRE, Goldwyn, RKO Radio: THOMAS MONROE and BILLY WILDER

HERE COMES MR. JORDAN, Columbia: HARRY SEGALL

THE LADY EVE, Paramount: MONCKTON HOFFE

MEET JOHN DOE, Warner Bros.: RICHARD CONNELL & ROBERT PRESNELL

NIGHT TRAIN, 20th Century-Fox: GORDON WELLESLEY

(Original Screenplay)

CITIZEN KANE, Mercury, RKO Radio: HERMAN J. MANKIEWICZ and ORSON WELLES

THE DEVIL AND MISS JONES, RKO Radio: NORMAN KRASNA

SERGEANT YORK, Warner Bros.: HARRY CHANDLEE, ABEM FINKEL, JOHN HUSTON and HOWARD KOCH

TALL, DARK AND HANDSOME, 20th Century-Fox: KARL TUNBERG and DARRELL WARE

TOM, DICK AND HARRY, RKO Radio: PAUL JARRICO

(Screenplay)

HERE COMES MR. JORDAN, Columbia: SIDNEY BUCHMAN and SETON I. MILLER

HOLD BACK THE DAWN, Paramount: CHARLES BRACKETT and BILLY WILDER

HOW GREEN WAS MY VALLEY, 20th Century-Fox: PHILIP DUNNE

THE LITTLE FOXES, Goldwyn, RKO Radio: LILLIAN HELLMAN

THE MALTESE FALCON, Warner Bros.: JOHN HUSTON

Cinematography

(Black-and-White)

THE CHOCOLATE SOLDIER, Metro-Goldwyn-Mayer: KARL FREUND

CITIZEN KANE, Mercury, RKO Radio: GREGG TOLAND

DR. JEKYLL AND MR. HYDE, Metro-Goldwyn-Mayer: JOSEPH RUTTENBERG

HERE COMES MR. JORDAN, Columbia: JOSEPH WALKER

HOLD BACK THE DAWN, Paramount: LEO TOVER

HOW GREEN WAS MY VALLEY, 20th Century-Fox: ARTHUR MILLER

SERGEANT YORK, Warner Bros.: SOL POLITO

SUN VALLEY SERENADE, 20th Century-Fox: EDWARD CRONJAGER

SUNDOWN, Wanger, UA: CHARLES LANG

THAT HAMILTON WOMAN, Korda, UA: RUDOLPH MATE

(Color)

ALOMA OF THE SOUTH SEAS, Paramount: WILFRED M. CLINE, KARL STRUSS and WILLIAM SNYDER

BILLY THE KID, Metro-Goldwyn-Mayer: WILLIAM V. SKALL and LEONARD SMITH

BLOOD AND SAND, 20th Century-Fox: ERNEST PALMER and RAY RENNAHAN

BLOSSOMS IN THE DUST, Metro-Goldwyn-Mayer: KARL FREUND and W. HOWARD GREENE

DIVE BOMBER, Warner Bros.: BERT GLENNON

LOUISIANA PURCHASE, Paramount: HARRY HALLENBERGER and RAY RENNAHAN

Interior Decoration

(Black-and-White)

CITIZEN KANE, Mercury, RKO Radio:

PERRY FERGUSON and VAN NEST POLGLASE
Interior Decoration: AL FIELDS and DARRELL SILVERA

FLAME OF NEW ORLEANS, Universal: MARTIN OBZINA and JACK OTTERSON
Interior Decoration: RUSSELL A. GAUSMAN

HOLD BACK THE DAWN, Paramount: HANS DREIER and ROBERT USHER
Interior Decoration: SAM COMER

HOW GREEN WAS MY VALLEY, 20th Century-Fox: RICHARD DAY and NATHAN JURAN
Interior Decoration: THOMAS LITTLE

LADIES IN RETIREMENT, Columbia: LIONEL BANKS
Interior Decoration: GEORGE MONTGOMERY

THE LITTLE FOXES, Goldwyn, RKO Radio: STEPHEN GOOSSON
Interior Decoration: HOWARD BRISTOL

SERGEANT YORK, Warner Bros.: JOHN HUGHES
Interior Decoration: FRED MacLEAN

SON OF MONTE CRISTO, Small, UA: JOHN DuCASSE SCHULZE
Interior Decoration: EDWARD G. BOYLE

SUNDOWN, Wanger, UA: ALEXANDER GOLITZEN
Interior Decoration: RICHARD IRVINE

THAT HAMILTON WOMAN, Korda, UA: VINCENT KORDA
Interior Decoration: JULIA HERON

WHEN LADIES MEET, Metro-Goldwyn-Mayer: CEDRIC GIBBONS and RANDALL DUELL
Interior Decoration: EDWIN B. WILLIS

(Color)

BLOOD AND SAND, 20th Century-Fox: RICHARD DAY and JOSEPH C. WRIGHT
Interior Decoration: THOMAS LITTLE

BLOSSOMS IN THE DUST, Metro-Goldwyn-Mayer: CEDRIC GIB-BONS and URIE McCLEARY
Interior Decoration: EDWIN B. WILLIS

LOUISIANA PURCHASE, Paramount: RAOUL PENE DU BOIS
Interior Decoration: STEPHEN A. SEYMOUR

Sound Recording

APPOINTMENT FOR LOVE, Universal: BERNARD B. BROWN

BALL OF FIRE, Goldwyn-RKO Radio: THOMAS MOULTON

THE CHOCOLATE SOLDIER, Metro-Goldwyn-Mayer: DOUGLAS SHEARER

CITIZEN KANE, Mercury, RKO Radio: JOHN AALBERG

THE DEVIL PAYS OFF, Republic: CHARLES LOOTENS

HOW GREEN WAS MY VALLEY, 20th Century-Fox: E. H. HANSEN

THE MEN IN HER LIFE, Columbia: JOHN LIVADARY

SERGEANT YORK, Warner Bros.: NATHAN LEVINSON

SKYLARK, Paramount: LOREN RYDER

THAT HAMILTON WOMAN, Korda, UA: JACK WHITNEY, GENERAL SERVICE

TOPPER RETURNS, Roach, UA: ELMER RAGUSE

Film Editing

CITIZEN KANE, Mercury-RKO Radio: ROBERT WISE

DR. JEKYLL AND MR. HYDE, Metro-Goldwyn-Mayer: HAROLD F. KRESS

HOW GREEN WAS MY VALLEY, 20th Century-Fox: JAMES B. CLARK

THE LITTLE FOXES, Goldwyn-RKO Radio: DANIEL MANDELL

SERGEANT YORK, Warner Bros.: WILLIAM HOLMES

Music

(Scoring of a Dramatic Picture)

ALL THAT MONEY CAN BUY, RKO Radio: BERNARD HERRMANN

BACK STREET, Universal: FRANK SKINNER

BALL OF FIRE, Goldwyn, RKO Radio: ALFRED NEWMAN

CHEERS FOR MISS BISHOP, Rowland, UA: EDWARD WARD

CITIZEN KANE, Mercury, RKO Radio: BERNARD HERRMANN

DR. JEKYLL AND MR. HYDE, Metro-Goldwyn-Mayer: FRANZ WAXMAN

HOLD BACK THE DAWN, Paramount: VICTOR YOUNG

HOW GREEN WAS MY VALLEY, 20th Century-Fox: ALFRED NEWMAN

KING OF THE ZOMBIES, Monogram: EDWARD KAY

LADIES IN RETIREMENT, Columbia: MORRIS STOLOFF and ERNST TOCH

THE LITTLE FOXES, Goldwyn, RKO Radio: MEREDITH WILLSON

LYDIA, Korda, UA: MIKLOS ROZSA

MERCY ISLAND, Republic: CY FEUER and WALTER SCHARF

SERGEANT YORK, Warner Bros.: MAX STEINER

SO ENDS OUR NIGHT, Loew-Lewin, UA: LOUIS GRUENBERG

SUNDOWN, Walter Wanger, UA: MIKLOS ROZSA

SUSPICION, RKO Radio: FRANZ WAXMAN

TANKS A MILLION, Roach, UA: EDWARD WARD

THAT UNCERTAIN FEELING, Lubitsch, UA: WERNER HEYMANN

THIS WOMAN IS MINE, Universal: RICHARD HAGEMAN

(Scoring of a Musical Picture)

ALL AMERICAN CO-ED, Roach, UA: EDWARD WARD

BIRTH OF THE BLUES, Paramount: ROBERT EMMETT DOLAN

BUCK PRIVATES, Universal: CHARLES PREVIN

THE CHOCOLATE SOLDIER, Metro-Goldwyn-Mayer: HERBERT STOTHART and BRONISLAU KAPER

DUMBO, Disney, RKO Radio: FRANK CHURCHILL and OLIVER WALLACE

ICE-CAPADES, Republic: CY FEUER

THE STRAWBERRY BLONDE, Warner Bros.: HEINZ ROEMHELD

SUN VALLEY SERENADE, 20th Century-Fox: EMIL NEWMAN

SUNNY, RKO Radio: ANTHONY COLLINS

YOU'LL NEVER GET RICH, Columbia: MORRIS STOLOFF

(Best Song)

BABY MINE from Dumbo, Disney, RKO Radio
Music by FRANK CHURCHILL. Lyrics by NED WASHINGTON

BE HONEST WITH ME from Ridin' On A Rainbow, Republic
Music and Lyrics by GENE AUTRY and FRED ROSE

BLUES IN THE NIGHT from Blues In The Night, Warner Bros.
Music by HAROLD ARLEN. Lyrics by JOHNNY MERCER

BOOGIE WOOGIE BUGLE BOY OF COMPANY B from Buck Privates, Universal
Music by HUGH PRINCE. Lyrics by DON RAYE

CHATTANOOGA CHOO CHOO from Sun Valley Serenade, 20th Century-Fox
Music by HARRY WARREN. Lyrics by MACK GORDON

DOLORES from Las Vegas Nights, Paramount
Music by LOU ALTER. Lyrics by FRANK LOESSER

THE LAST TIME I SAW PARIS from Lady Be Good, Metro-Goldwyn-Mayer
Music by JEROME KERN. Lyrics by OSCAR HAMMERSTEIN II

OUT OF THE SILENCE from All American Co-Ed, Roach, UA
Music and Lyrics by LLOYD B. NORLIND

SINCE I KISSED MY BABY GOODBYE from *You'll Never Get Rich,* Columbia Music and Lyrics by COLE PORTER

Short Subjects

(Cartoons)

BOOGIE WOOGIE BUGLE BOY OF COMPANY B, Walter Lantz, Universal

HIAWATHA'S RABBIT HUNT, Leon Schlesinger, Warner Bros.

HOW WAR CAME, Columbia. (Raymond Gram Swing Series)

LEND A PAW, Walt Disney, RKO Radio

THE NIGHT BEFORE CHRISTMAS, Metro-Goldwyn-Mayer. (Tom and Jerry Series)

RHAPSODY IN RIVETS, Leon Schlesinger, Warner Bros.

THE ROOKIE BEAR, Metro-Goldwyn-Mayer. (Bear Series)

RHYTHM IN THE RANKS, Paramount. (George Pal Puppetoon Series)

SUPERMAN NO. 1, Paramount

TRUANT OFFICER DONALD, Walt Disney, RKO Radio

(One-Reel)

ARMY CHAMPIONS, Pete Smith, M-G-M. (Pete Smith Specialties)

BEAUTY AND THE BEACH, Paramount. (Headliner Series)

DOWN ON THE FARM, Paramount. (Speaking Of Animals)

FORTY BOYS AND A SONG, Warner Bros. (Melody Master Series)

KINGS OF THE TURF, Warner Bros. (Color Parade Series)

OF PUPS AND PUZZLES, Metro-Goldwyn-Mayer. (Passing Parade Series)

SAGEBRUSH AND SILVER, 20th Century-Fox. (Magic Carpet Series)

(Two-Reel)

ALIVE IN THE DEEP, Woodard Productions, Inc.

FORBIDDEN PASSAGE, Metro-Goldwyn-Mayer. (Crime Doesn't Pay)

THE GAY PARISIAN, Warner Bros. (Miniature Featurette Series)

MAIN STREET ON THE MARCH, Metro-Goldwyn-Mayer. (Two-reel Special)

THE TANKS ARE COMING, Warner Bros. (National Defense Series)

Documentary

(New Category)

ADVENTURES IN THE BRONX, Film Assocs.

BOMBER, U.S. Office for Emergency Management Film Unit

CHRISTMAS UNDER FIRE, British Ministry of Information, Warner Bros.

CHURCHILL'S ISLAND, Canadian Film Board, UA

LETTER FROM HOME, British Ministry of Information

LIFE OF A THOROUGHBRED, 20th Century-Fox

NORWAY IN REVOLT, March of Time, RKO Radio

SOLDIERS OF THE SKY, 20th Century-Fox

WAR CLOUDS IN THE PACIFIC, Canadian Film Board

Special Effects

ALOMA OF THE SOUTH SEAS, Paramount Photographic: FARCIOT EDOUART and GORDON JENNINGS Sound: LOUIS MESENKOP

FLIGHT COMMAND, Metro-Goldwyn-Mayer Photographic: A. ARNOLD GILLESPIE Sound: DOUGLAS SHEARER

I WANTED WINGS, Paramount Photographic: FARCIOT EDOUART and GORDON JENNINGS Sound: LOUIS MESENKOP

THE INVISIBLE WOMAN, Universal Photographic: JOHN FULTON Sound: JOHN HALL

THE SEA WOLF, Warner Bros. Photographic: BYRON HASKIN

Sound: NATHAN LEVINSON
THAT HAMILTON WOMAN, Korda, UA
  Photographic: LAWRENCE BUTLER
  Sound: WILLIAM H. WILMARTH
TOPPER RETURNS, Roach, UA
  Photographic: ROY SEAWRIGHT
  Sound: ELMER RAGUSE
A YANK IN THE R.A.F., 20th Century-
  Fox
  Photographic: FRED SERSEN
  Sound: E. H. HANSEN

Special Awards
REY SCOTT for his extraordinary
  achievement in producing *Kukan,* the
  film record of China's struggle, including its photography with a 16mm
  camera under the most difficult and
  dangerous conditions. (certificate)
THE BRITISH MINISTRY OF IN-
  FORMATION for its vivid and dramatic presentation of the heroism of
  the RAF in the documentary film,
  Target For Tonight. (certificate)
LEOPOLD STOKOWSKI and his associates for their unique achievement
  in the creation of a new form of visualized music in Walt Disney's production *Fantasia,* thereby widening
  the scope of the motion picture as
  entertainment and as an art form.
  (certificate)
WALT DISNEY, WILLIAM
  GARITY, JOHN N. A. HAWKINS
  and the RCA MANUFACTURING
  COMPANY, for their outstanding
  contribution to the advancement of
  the use of sound in motion pictures
  through the production of *Fantasia.*
  (certificates)

Irving G. Thalberg Memorial Award
WALT DISNEY

Scientific or Technical
Class I
None

Class II
ELECTRICAL RESEARCH PROD-
  UCTS DIVISION OF WESTERN
  ELECTRIC CO., INC., for the development of the precision integrating sphere densitometer
RCA MANUFACTURING CO. for the
  design and development of the MI-
  3043 Uni-directional microphone

Class III
RAY WILKINSON and the PARA-
  MOUNT STUDIO LABORATORY for
  pioneering in the use of and for the
  first practical application to release
  printing of fine grain positive stock
CHARLES LOOTENS and the RE-
  PUBLIC STUDIO SOUND DE-
  PARTMENT for pioneering the use
  of and for the first practical application to motion picture production of
  Class B push-pull variable area recording
WILBUR SILVERTOOTH and the
  PARAMOUNT STUDIO EN-
  GINEERING DEPARTMENT for
  the design and computation of a
  relay condenser system applicable to
  transparency process projection, delivering considerably more usable
  light
PARAMOUNT PICTURES, INC., and
  20TH CENTURY-FOX FILM
  CORP. for the development and first
  practical application to motion picture production of an automatic
  scene slating device
DOUGLAS SHEARER and the
  METRO-GOLDWYN-MAYER
  STUDIO SOUND DEPARTMENT,
  and to LOREN RYDER and the
  PARAMOUNT STUDIO SOUND
  DEPARTMENT for pioneering the
  development of fine grain emulsions
  for variable density original sound
  recording in studio production

1942

Nominations Announced: February 8, 1943
Awards Ceremony: March 4, 1943
Ambassador Hotel–Banquet
(The custom of presenting the awards at a banquet was discontinued after 1943.
Increased attendance made it necessary to switch the ceremonies to theatres.)

Best Picture

THE INVADERS, Ortus, Columbia (British)
KINGS ROW, Warner Bros.
THE MAGNIFICENT AMBERSONS, Mercury, RKO Radio
MRS. MINIVER, Metro-Goldwyn-Mayer
THE PIED PIPER, 20th Century-Fox
THE PRIDE OF THE YANKEES, Goldwyn, RKO Radio
RANDOM HARVEST, Metro-Goldwyn-Mayer
THE TALK OF THE TOWN, Columbia
WAKE ISLAND, Paramount
YANKEE DOODLE DANDY, Warner Bros.

Actor

JAMES CAGNEY in *Yankee Doodle Dandy*, Warner Bros.
RONALD COLMAN in *Random Harvest*, Metro-Goldwyn-Mayer
GARY COOPER in *The Pride Of The Yankees*, Goldwyn, RKO Radio
WALTER PIDGEON in *Mrs. Miniver*, Metro-Goldwyn-Mayer
MONTY WOOLLEY in *The Pied Piper*, 20th Century-Fox

Actress

BETTE DAVIS in *Now, Voyager*, Warner Bros.
GREER GARSON in *Mrs. Miniver*, Metro-Goldwyn-Mayer

LARGE CAPITAL LETTERS DENOTE WINNER

KATHARINE HEPBURN in *Woman Of The Year*, Metro-Goldwyn-Mayer
ROSALIND RUSSELL in *My Sister Eileen*, Columbia
TERESA WRIGHT in *The Pride Of The Yankees*, Goldwyn, RKO Radio

Supporting Actor

WILLIAM BENDIX in *Wake Island*, Paramount
VAN HEFLIN in *Johnny Eager*, Metro-Goldwyn-Mayer
WALTER HUSTON in *Yankee Doodle Dandy*, Warner Bros.
FRANK MORGAN in *Tortilla Flat*, Metro-Goldwyn-Mayer
HENRY TRAVERS in *Mrs. Miniver*, Metro-Goldwyn-Mayer

Supporting Actress

GLADYS COOPER in *Now, Voyager*, Warner Bros.
AGNES MOOREHEAD in *The Magnificent Ambersons*, Mercury, RKO Radio
SUSAN PETERS in *Random Harvest*, Metro-Goldwyn-Mayer
DAME MAY WHITTY in *Mrs. Miniver*, Metro-Goldwyn-Mayer
TERESA WRIGHT in *Mrs. Miniver*, Metro-Goldwyn-Mayer

Directing

MICHAEL CURTIZ for *Yankee Doodle Dandy*, Warner Bros.
JOHN FARROW for *Wake Island*, Paramount

MERVYN LEROY for *Random Harvest,*
Metro-Goldwyn-Mayer
SAM WOOD for *Kings Row,* Warner
Bros.
WILLIAM WYLER for *Mrs. Miniver,*
Metro-Goldwyn-Mayer

Writing
(Original Story)
HOLIDAY INN, Paramount: IRVING BER-
LIN
THE INVADERS, Ortus, Columbia
(British): EMERIC PRESSBURGER
THE PRIDE OF THE YANKEES, Goldwyn,
RKO Radio: PAUL GALLICO
THE TALK OF THE TOWN, Columbia:
SIDNEY HARMON
YANKEE DOODLE DANDY, Warner
Bros.: ROBERT BUCKNER

(Original Screenplay)
ONE OF OUR AIRCRAFT IS MISSING, Pow-
ell, UA (British): MICHAEL POWELL
and EMERIC PRESSBURGER
THE ROAD TO MOROCCO, Paramount:
FRANK BUTLER and DON HARTMAN
WAKE ISLAND, Paramount: W. R. BUR-
NETT and FRANK BUTLER
THE WAR AGAINST MRS. HADLEY,
Metro-Goldwyn-Mayer: GEORGE
OPPENHEIMER
WOMAN OF THE YEAR, Metro-
Goldwyn-Mayer: MICHAEL
KANIN & RING LARDNER, JR.

(Screenplay)
THE INVADERS, Ortus, Columbia (Brit-
ish): RODNEY ACKLAND and EMERIC
PRESSBURGER
MRS. MINIVER, Metro-Goldwyn-
Mayer: GEORGE FROESCHEL,
JAMES HILTON, CLAUDINE
WEST and ARTHUR WIMPERIS
THE PRIDE OF THE YANKEES, Goldwyn,
RKO Radio: HERMAN J. MANKIE-
WICZ and JO SWERLING
RANDOM HARVEST, Metro-Goldwyn-
Mayer: GEORGE FROESCHEL, CLAU-
DINE WEST and ARTHUR WIMPERIS
THE TALK OF THE TOWN, Columbia:
SIDNEY BUCHMAN and IRWIN SHAW

Cinematography
(Black-and-White)
KINGS ROW, Warner Bros.: JAMES
WONG HOWE
THE MAGNIFICENT AMBERSONS, Mer-
cury, RKO Radio: STANLEY CORTEZ
MRS. MINIVER, Metro-Goldwyn-
Mayer: JOSEPH RUTTENBERG
MOONTIDE, 20th Century-Fox: CHARLES
CLARKE
THE PIED PIPER, 20th Century-Fox:
EDWARD CRONJAGER
THE PRIDE OF THE YANKEES, Goldwyn,
RKO Radio: RUDOLPH MATE
TAKE A LETTER, DARLING, Paramount:
JOHN MESCALL
THE TALK OF THE TOWN, Columbia:
TED TETZLAFF
TEN GENTLEMEN FROM WEST POINT,
20th Century-Fox: LEON SHAMROY
THIS ABOVE ALL, 20th Century-Fox:
ARTHUR MILLER

(Color)
ARABIAN NIGHTS, Wanger, Universal:
MILTON KRASNER, WILLIAM V. SKALL
and W. HOWARD GREENE
THE BLACK SWAN, 20th Century-
Fox: LEON SHAMROY
CAPTAINS OF THE CLOUDS, Warner
Bros.: SOL POLITO
JUNGLE BOOK, Korda, UA: W. HOW-
ARD GREENE
REAP THE WILD WIND, Paramount: VIC-
TOR MILNER and WILLIAM V. SKALL
TO THE SHORES OF TRIPOLI, 20th Cen-
tury-Fox: EDWARD CRONJAGER and
WILLIAM V. SKALL

Interior Decoration
(Black-and-White)
GEORGE WASHINGTON SLEPT HERE,

Warner Bros.: MAX PARKER and MARK-LEE KIRK
Interior Decoration: CASEY ROBERTS
THE MAGNIFICENT AMBERSONS, Mercury, RKO Radio: ALBERT S. D'AGOSTINO
Interior Decoration: AL FIELDS and DARRELL SILVERA
THE PRIDE OF THE YANKEES, Goldwyn, RKO Radio: PERRY FERGUSON
Interior Decoration: HOWARD BRISTOL
RANDOM HARVEST, Metro-Goldwyn-Mayer: CEDRIC GIBBONS and RANDALL DUELL
Interior Decoration: EDWIN B. WILLIS and JACK MOORE
THE SHANGHAI GESTURE, Arnold, UA: BORIS LEVEN
Interior Decoration: BORIS LEVEN
SILVER QUEEN, Sherman, UA: RALPH BERGER
Interior Decoration: EMILE KURI
THE SPOILERS, Universal: JOHN B. GOODMAN and JACK OTTERSON
Interior Decoration: RUSSELL A. GAUSMAN and EDWARD R. ROBINSON
TAKE A LETTER, DARLING, Paramount: HANS DREIER and ROLAND ANDERSON
Interior Decoration: SAM COMER
THE TALK OF THE TOWN, Columbia: LIONEL BANKS and RUDOLPH STERNAD
Interior Decoration: FAY BABCOCK
THIS ABOVE ALL, 20th Century-Fox: RICHARD DAY and JOSEPH WRIGHT
Interior Decoration: THOMAS LITTLE

(Color)
ARABIAN NIGHTS, Universal: ALEXANDER GOLITZEN and JACK OTTERSON
Interior Decoration: RUSSELL A. GAUSMAN and IRA S. WEBB
CAPTAINS OF THE CLOUDS, Warner Bros.: TED SMITH
Interior Decoration: CASEY ROBERTS
JUNGLE BOOK, Korda, UA: VINCENT KORDA
Interior Decoration: JULIA HERON
MY GAL SAL, 20th Century-Fox: RICHARD DAY and JOSEPH WRIGHT
Interior Decoration: THOMAS LITTLE
REAP THE WILD WIND, Paramount: HANS DREIER and ROLAND ANDERSON
Interior Decoration: GEORGE SAWLEY

Sound Recording
ARABIAN NIGHTS, Universal: BERNARD BROWN
BAMBI, Disney, RKO Radio: SAM SLYFIELD
FLYING TIGERS, Republic: DANIEL BLOOMBERG
FRIENDLY ENEMIES, Small, UA: JACK WHITNEY, SOUND SERVICE, INC.
THE GOLD RUSH, Chaplin, UA: JAMES FIELDS, RCA SOUND
MRS. MINIVER, Metro-Goldwyn-Mayer: DOUGLAS SHEARER
ONCE UPON A HONEYMOON, RKO Radio: STEVE DUNN
THE PRIDE OF THE YANKEES, Goldwyn, RKO Radio: THOMAS MOULTON
ROAD TO MOROCCO, Paramount: LOREN RYDER
THIS ABOVE ALL, 20th Century-Fox: E. H. HANSEN
YANKEE DOODLE DANDY, Warner Bros.: NATHAN LEVINSON
YOU WERE NEVER LOVELIER, Columbia: JOHN LIVADARY

Film Editing
MRS. MINIVER, Metro-Goldwyn-Mayer: HAROLD F. KRESS
THE PRIDE OF THE YANKEES, Goldwyn, RKO Radio: DANIEL MANDELL

THE TALK OF THE TOWN, Columbia:
OTTO MEYER
THIS ABOVE ALL, 20th Century-Fox:
WALTER THOMPSON
YANKEE DOODLE DANDY, Warner
Bros.: GEORGE AMY

Music

(Scoring of a Dramatic or Comedy Picture)

ARABIAN NIGHTS, Universal: FRANK
SKINNER
BAMBI, Disney, RKO Radio: FRANK
CHURCHILL and EDWARD PLUMB
THE BLACK SWAN, 20th Century-Fox:
ALFRED NEWMAN
THE CORSICAN BROTHERS, Small, UA:
DIMITRI TIOMKIN
FLYING TIGERS, Republic: VICTOR
YOUNG
THE GOLD RUSH, Chaplin, UA: MAX
TERR
I MARRIED A WITCH, Cinema Guild,
UA: ROY WEBB
JOAN OF PARIS, RKO Radio: ROY WEBB
JUNGLE BOOK, Korda, UA: MIKLOS
ROZSA
KLONDIKE FURY, Monogram: EDWARD
KAY
NOW, VOYAGER, Warner Bros.:
MAX STEINER
THE PRIDE OF THE YANKEES, Goldwyn,
RKO Radio: LEIGH HARLINE
RANDOM HARVEST, Metro-Goldwyn-
Mayer: HERBERT STOTHART
THE SHANGHAI GESTURE, Arnold, UA:
RICHARD HAGEMAN
SILVER QUEEN, Sherman, UA: VICTOR
YOUNG
TAKE A LETTER, DARLING, Paramount:
VICTOR YOUNG
THE TALK OF THE TOWN, Columbia:
FREDERICK HOLLANDER and MORRIS
STOLOFF
TO BE OR NOT TO BE, Lubitsch, UA:
WERNER HEYMANN

(Scoring of a Musical Picture)

FLYING WITH MUSIC, Roach, UA:
EDWARD WARD
FOR ME AND MY GAL, Metro-Goldwyn-
Mayer: ROGER EDENS and GEORGIE
STOLL
HOLIDAY INN, Paramount: ROBERT EM-
METT DOLAN
IT STARTED WITH EVE, Universal:
CHARLES PREVIN and HANS SALTER
JOHNNY DOUGHBOY, Republic: WALTER
SCHARF
MY GAL SAL, 20th Century-Fox:
ALFRED NEWMAN
YANKEE DOODLE DANDY, Warner
Bros.: RAY HEINDORF and
HEINZ ROEMHELD
YOU WERE NEVER LOVELIER, Colum-
bia: LEIGH HARLINE

(Best Song)

ALWAYS IN MY HEART from *Always In
My Heart,* Warner Bros.
Music by ERNESTO LECUONA. Lyrics
by KIM GANNON
DEARLY BELOVED from *You Were
Never Lovelier,* Columbia
Music by JEROME KERN. Lyrics by
JOHNNY MERCER
HOW ABOUT YOU? from *Babes On
Broadway,* Metro-Goldwyn-Mayer
Music by BURTON LANE. Lyrics by
RALPH FREED
IT SEEMS I HEARD THAT SONG BEFORE
from *Youth On Parade,* Republic
Music by JULE STYNE. Lyrics by
SAMMY CAHN
I'VE GOT A GAL IN KALAMAZOO from
Orchestra Wives, 20th Century-Fox
Music by HARRY WARREN. Lyrics by
MACK GORDON
LOVE IS A SONG from *Bambi,* Disney,
RKO Radio
Music by FRANK CHURCHILL. Lyrics
by LARRY MOREY
PENNIES FOR PEPPINO from *Flying With
Music,* Roach, UA

Music by EDWARD WARD. Lyrics by CHET FORREST and BOB WRIGHT

PIG FOOT PETE from *Hellzapoppin'*, Universal
Music by GENE DE PAUL. Lyrics by DON RAYE

THERE'S A BREEZE ON LAKE LOUISE from *The Mayor of 44th Street,* RKO Radio
Music by HARRY REVEL. Lyrics by MORT GREENE

WHITE CHRISTMAS from *Holiday Inn,* Paramount
Music and Lyrics by IRVING BERLIN

Short Subjects

(Cartoons)

ALL OUT FOR V, 20th Century-Fox

THE BLITZ WOLF, Metro-Goldwyn-Mayer

DER FUEHRER'S FACE, Walt Disney, RKO Radio

JUKE BOX JAMBOREE, Walt Lantz, Universal

PIGS IN A POLKA, Leon Schlesinger, Warner Bros.

TULIPS SHALL GROW, Paramount. (George Pal Puppetoon)

(One-reel)

DESERT WONDERLAND, 20th Century-Fox. (Magic Carpet Series)

MARINES IN THE MAKING, Metro-Goldwyn-Mayer. (Pete Smith Specialties)

SPEAKING OF ANIMALS AND THEIR FAMILIES, Paramount. (Speaking Of Animals)

UNITED STATES MARINE BAND, Warner Bros. (Melody Master Bands)

(Two-reel)

BEYOND THE LINE OF DUTY, Warner Bros. (Broadway Brevities)

DON'T TALK, Metro-Goldwyn-Mayer. (Two-reel Special)

PRIVATE SMITH OF THE U.S.A., RKO Radio. (This Is America Series)

Documentary

A SHIP IS BORN, U.S. Merchant Marine, Warner Bros.

AFRICA, PRELUDE TO VICTORY, March of Time, 20th Century-Fox

BATTLE OF MIDWAY, U.S. Navy, 20th Century-Fox

COMBAT REPORT, U.S. Army Signal Corps

CONQUER BY THE CLOCK, Office of War Information, RKO Pathé: FREDERIC ULLMAN, JR.

THE GRAIN THAT BUILT A HEMISPHERE, Coordinator's Office, Motion Picture Society for the Americas: WALT DISNEY

HENRY BROWNE, FARMER, U.S. Department of Agriculture, Republic

HIGH OVER THE BORDERS, Canadian National Film Board

HIGH STAKES IN THE EAST, Canadian National Film Board

INSIDE FIGHTING CHINA, Canadian National Film Board

IT'S EVERYBODY'S WAR, Office of War Information, 20th Century-Fox

KOKODA FRONT LINE, Australian News Information Bureau

LISTEN TO BRITAIN, British Ministry of Information

LITTLE BELGIUM, Belgian Ministry of Information

LITTLE ISLES OF FREEDOM, Warner Bros.: VICTOR STOLOFF and EDGAR LOEW

MOSCOW STRIKES BACK, Artkino (Russian)

MR. BLABBERMOUTH, Office of War Information, M-G-M

MR. GARDENIA JONES, Office of War Information, M-G-M

NEW SPIRIT, U.S. Treasury Department: WALT DISNEY

PRELUDE TO WAR, U.S. Army Special Services

THE PRICE OF VICTORY, Office of War Information, Paramount: PINE-THOMAS

TWENTY-ONE MILES, British Ministry of Information

WE REFUSE TO DIE, Office of War Information, Paramount: WILLIAM C. THOMAS

WHITE EAGLE, Cocanen Films

WINNING YOUR WINGS, U.S. Army Air Force, Warner Bros.

Special Effects

THE BLACK SWAN, 20th Century-Fox
Photographic: FRED SERSEN
Sound: ROGER HEMAN and GEORGE LEVERETT

DESPERATE JOURNEY, Warner Bros.
Photographic: BYRON HASKIN
Sound: NATHAN LEVINSON

FLYING TIGERS, Republic
Photographic: HOWARD LYDECKER
Sound: DANIEL J. BLOOMBERG

INVISIBLE AGENT, Universal
Photographic: JOHN FULTON
Sound: BERNARD B. BROWN

JUNGLE BOOK, Korda, UA
Photographic: LAWRENCE BUTLER
Sound: WILLIAM H. WILMARTH

MRS. MINIVER, Metro-Goldwyn .Mayer
Photographic: A. ARNOLD GILLESPIE and WARREN NEWCOMBE
Sound: DOUGLAS SHEARER

THE NAVY COMES THROUGH, RKO Radio
Photographic: VERNON L. WALKER
Sound: JAMES G. STEWART

ONE OF OUR AIRCRAFT IS MISSING, Powell, UA (British)
Photographic: RONALD NEAME
Sound: C. C. STEVENS

PRIDE OF THE YANKEES, Goldwyn, RKO Radio
Photographic: JACK COSGROVE and

RAY BINGER
Sound: THOMAS T. MOULTON

REAP THE WILD WIND, Paramount.
Photographic: FARCIOT EDOUART, GORDON JENNINGS and WILLIAM L. PEREIRA
Sound: LOUIS MESENKOP

Special Awards

CHARLES BOYER for his progressive cultural achievement in establishing the French Research Foundation in Los Angeles as a source of reference for the Hollywood Motion Picture Industry. (certificate)

NOEL COWARD for his outstanding production achievement in *In Which We Serve*. (certificate)

METRO-GOLDWYN-MAYER STUDIO for its achievement in representing the American Way of Life in the production of the *Andy Hardy* series of films. (certificate)

Irving G. Thalberg Memorial award

SIDNEY FRANKLIN

Scientific or Technical

Class I

None

Class II

CARROLL CLARK, F. THOMAS THOMPSON and the RKO RADIO STUDIO ART and MINIATURE DEPARTMENTS for the design and construction of a moving cloud and horizon machine

DANIEL B. CLARK and the 20th CENTURY-FOX FILM CORP. for the development of a lens calibration system and the application of this system to exposure control in cinematography

Class III

ROBERT HENDERSON and the PARAMOUNT STUDIO ENGINEER-

ING and TRANSPARENCY DE-
PARTMENTS for the design and
construction of adjustable light
bridges and screen frames for transparency process photography
DANIEL J. BLOOMBERG and the

REPUBLIC STUDIO SOUND DE-
PARTMENT for the design and
application to motion picture production of a device for marking
action negative for pre-selection
purposes

1943

Nominations Announced: February 7, 1944
Awards Ceremony: March 2, 1944
Grauman's Chinese Theatre
(MC: Jack Benny for overseas broadcast)

Best Picture

CASABLANCA, Warner Bros.
FOR WHOM THE BELL TOLLS, Paramount
HEAVEN CAN WAIT, 20th Century-Fox
THE HUMAN COMEDY, Metro-Goldwyn-Mayer
IN WHICH WE SERVE, Two Cities, UA (British)
MADAME CURIE, Metro-Goldwyn-Mayer
THE MORE THE MERRIER, Columbia
THE OX-BOW INCIDENT, 20th Century-Fox
THE SONG OF BERNADETTE, 20th Century-Fox
WATCH ON THE RHINE, Warner Bros.

Actor

HUMPHREY BOGART in *Casablanca*, Warner Bros.
GARY COOPER in *For Whom The Bell Tolls*, Paramount
PAUL LUKAS in *Watch On The Rhine*, Warner Bros.
WALTER PIDGEON in *Madame Curie*, Metro-Goldwyn-Mayer
MICKEY ROONEY in *The Human Comedy*, Metro-Goldwyn-Mayer

Actress

JEAN ARTHUR in *The More The Merrier*, Columbia
INGRID BERGMAN in *For Whom The Bell Tolls*, Paramount

LARGE CAPITAL LETTERS DENOTE WINNER

JOAN FONTAINE in *The Constant Nymph*, Warner Bros.
GREER GARSON in *Madame Curie*, Metro-Goldwyn-Mayer
JENNIFER JONES in *The Song Of Bernadette*, 20th Century-Fox

Supporting Actor

CHARLES BICKFORD in *The Song Of Bernadette*, 20th Century-Fox
CHARLES COBURN in *The More The Merrier*, Columbia
J. CARROL NAISH in *Sahara*, Columbia
CLAUDE RAINS in *Casablanca*, Warner Bros.
AKIM TAMIROFF in *For Whom The Bell Tolls*, Paramount

Supporting Actress

GLADYS COOPER in *The Song Of Bernadette*, 20th Century-Fox
PAULETTE GODDARD in *So Proudly We Hail*, Paramount
KATINA PAXINOU in *For Whom The Bell Tolls*, Paramount
ANNE REVERE in *The Song Of Bernadette*, 20th Century-Fox
LUCILE WATSON in *Watch On the Rhine*, Warner Bros.

Directing

CLARENCE BROWN for *The Human Comedy*, Metro-Goldwyn-Mayer
MICHAEL CURTIZ for *Casablanca*, Warner Bros.
HENRY KING for *The Song Of Bernadette*, 20th Century-Fox

ERNST LUBITSCH for *Heaven Can Wait,*
20th Century-Fox
GEORGE STEVENS for *The More The
Merrier,* Columbia

Writing
(Original Story)
ACTION IN THE NORTH ATLANTIC,
Warner Bros.: GUY GILPATRIC
DESTINATION TOKYO, Warner Bros.:
STEVE FISHER
THE HUMAN COMEDY, Metro-
Goldwyn-Mayer: WILLIAM
SAROYAN
THE MORE THE MERRIER, Columbia:
FRANK ROSS and ROBERT RUSSELL
SHADOW OF A DOUBT, Universal: GOR-
DON MCDONELL

(Original Screenplay)
AIR FORCE, Warner Bros.: DUDLEY NI-
CHOLS
IN WHICH WE SERVE, Two Cities, UA
(British): NOEL COWARD
THE NORTH STAR, Goldwyn, RKO
Radio: LILLIAN HELLMAN
PRINCESS O'ROURKE, Warner
Bros.: NORMAN KRASNA
SO PROUDLY WE HAIL, Paramount:
ALLAN SCOTT

(Screenplay)
CASABLANCA, Warner Bros.:
JULIUS J. EPSTEIN, PHILIP G.
EPSTEIN and HOWARD KOCH
HOLY MATRIMONY, 20th Century-Fox:
NUNNALLY JOHNSON
THE MORE THE MERRIER, Columbia:
RICHARD FLOURNOY, LEWIS R. FOS-
TER, FRANK ROSS and ROBERT RUS-
SELL
THE SONG OF BERNADETTE, 20th Cen-
tury-Fox: GEORGE SEATON
WATCH ON THE RHINE, Warner Bros.:
DASHIELL HAMMETT

Cinematography
(Black-and-White)

AIR FORCE, Warner Bros.: JAMES WONG
HOWE, ELMER DYER and CHARLES
MARSHALL
CASABLANCA Warner Bros.: ARTHUR
EDESON
CORVETTE K-225, Universal: TONY
GAUDIO
FIVE GRAVES TO CAIRO, Paramount:
JOHN SEITZ
THE HUMAN COMEDY, Metro-Goldwyn-
Mayer: HARRY STRADLING
MADAME CURIE, Metro-Goldwyn-
Mayer: JOSEPH RUTTENBERG
THE NORTH STAR, Goldwyn, RKO
Radio: JAMES WONG HOWE
SAHARA, Columbia: RUDOLPH MATE
SO PROUDLY WE HAIL, Paramount:
CHARLES LANG
THE SONG OF BERNADETTE, 20th
Century-Fox: ARTHUR MILLER

(Color)
FOR WHOM THE BELL TOLLS, Para-
mount: RAY RENNAHAN
HEAVEN CAN WAIT, 20th Century-Fox:
EDWARD CRONJAGER
HELLO, FRISCO, HELLO, 20th Century-
Fox: CHARLES G. CLARKE and ALLEN
DAVEY
LASSIE COME HOME, Metro-Goldwyn-
Mayer: LEONARD SMITH
PHANTOM OF THE OPERA, Univer-
sal: HAL MOHR and W. HOWARD
GREENE
THOUSANDS CHEER, Metro-Goldwyn-
Mayer: GEORGE FOLSEY

Interior Decoration
(Black-and-White)
FIVE GRAVES TO CAIRO, Paramount:
HANS DREIER and ERNST FEGTE
Interior Decoration: BERTRAM
GRANGER
FLIGHT FOR FREEDOM, RKO Radio: AL-
BERT S. D'AGOSTINO and CARROLL
CLARK
Interior Decoration: DARRELL SIL-

VERA and HARLEY MILLER
MADAME CURIE, Metro-Goldwyn-
Mayer: CEDRIC GIBBONS and PAUL
GROESSE
Interior Decoration: EDWIN B. WILLIS
and HUGH HUNT
MISSION TO MOSCOW, Warner Bros.:
CARL WEYL
Interior Decoration: GEORGE J. HOP-
KINS
THE NORTH STAR, Goldwyn, RKO
Radio: PERRY FERGUSON
Interior Decoration: HOWARD BRIS-
TOL
THE SONG OF BERNADETTE, 20th
Century-Fox: JAMES BASEVI and
WILLIAM DARLING
Interior Decoration: THOMAS LIT-
TLE

(Color)
FOR WHOM THE BELL TOLLS, Para-
mount: HANS DREIER and HALDANE
DOUGLAS
Interior Decoration: BERTRAM
GRANGER
THE GANG'S ALL HERE, 20th Century-
Fox: JAMES BASEVI and JOSEPH C.
WRIGHT
Interior Decoration: THOMAS LITTLE
PHANTOM OF THE OPERA, Univer-
sal: ALEXANDER GOLITZEN and
JOHN B. GOODMAN
Interior Decoration: RUSSELL A.
GAUSMAN and IRA S. WEBB
THIS IS THE ARMY, Warner Bros.: JOHN
HUGHES and LT. JOHN KOENIG
Interior Decoration: GEORGE J. HOP-
KINS
THOUSANDS CHEER, Metro-Goldwyn-
Mayer: CEDRIC GIBBONS and DANIEL
CATHCART
Interior Decoration: EDWIN B. WILLIS
and JACQUES MERSEREAU

Sound Recording
HANGMEN ALSO DIE, Arnold, UA: JACK

WHITNEY, SOUND SERVICE, INC.
IN OLD OKLAHOMA, Republic: DANIEL
J. BLOOMBERG
MADAME CURIE, Metro-Goldwyn-
Mayer: DOUGLAS SHEARER
THE NORTH STAR, Goldwyn, RKO
Radio: THOMAS MOULTON
THE PHANTOM OF THE OPERA, Univer-
sal: BERNARD B. BROWN
RIDING HIGH, Paramount: LOREN L.
RYDER
SAHARA, Columbia: JOHN LIVADARY
SALUDOS AMIGOS, Disney, RKO Radio:
C. O. SLYFIELD
SO THIS IS WASHINGTON, Votion, RKO
Radio: J. L. FIELDS, RCA SOUND
THE SONG OF BERNADETTE, 20th Cen-
tury-Fox: E. H. HANSEN
THIS IS THE ARMY, Warner Bros.:
NATHAN LEVINSON
THIS LAND IS MINE, RKO Radio:
STEPHEN DUNN

Film Editing
AIR FORCE, Warner Bros.: GEORGE
AMY
CASABLANCA, Warner Bros.: OWEN
MARKS
FIVE GRAVES TO CAIRO, Paramount:
DOANE HARRISON
FOR WHOM THE BELL TOLLS, Para-
mount: SHERMAN TODD and JOHN
LINK
THE SONG OF BERNADETTE, 20th Cen-
tury-Fox: BARBARA MCLEAN

Music
(Scoring of a Dramatic or Comedy Pic-
ture)
THE AMAZING MRS. HOLLIDAY, Univer-
sal: HANS J. SALTER and FRANK
SKINNER
CASABLANCA, Warner Bros.: MAX
STEINER
THE COMMANDOS STRIKE AT DAWN, Co-
lumbia: LOUIS GRUENBERG and
MORRIS STOLOFF

THE FALLEN SPARROW, RKO Radio: C. BAKALEINIKOFF and ROY WEBB

FOR WHOM THE BELL TOLLS, Paramount: VICTOR YOUNG

HANGMEN ALSO DIE, Arnold, UA: HANNS EISLER

HI DIDDLE DIDDLE, Stone, UA: PHIL BOUTELJE

IN OLD OKLAHOMA, Republic: WALTER SCHARF

JOHNNY COME LATELY, Cagney, UA: LEIGH HARLINE

THE KANSAN, Sherman, UA: GERARD CARBONARA

LADY OF BURLESQUE, Stromberg, UA: ARTHUR LANGE

MADAME CURIE, Metro-Goldwyn-Mayer: HERBERT STOTHART

THE MOON AND SIXPENCE, Loew-Lewin, UA: DIMITRI TIOMKIN

THE NORTH STAR, Goldwyn, RKO Radio: AARON COPLAND

THE SONG OF BERNADETTE, 20th Century-Fox: ALFRED NEWMAN

VICTORY THROUGH AIR POWER, Disney, UA: EDWARD H. PLUMB, PAUL J. SMITH and OLIVER G. WALLACE

(Scoring of a Musical Picture)

CONEY ISLAND, 20th Century-Fox: ALFRED NEWMAN

HIT PARADE OF 1943, Republic: WALTER SCHARF

THE PHANTOM OF THE OPERA, Universal: EDWARD WARD

SALUDOS AMIGOS, Disney, RKO Radio: EDWARD H. PLUMB, PAUL J. SMITH and CHARLES WOLCOTT

THE SKY'S THE LIMIT, RKO Radio: LEIGH HARLINE

SOMETHING TO SHOUT ABOUT, Columbia: MORRIS STOLOFF

STAGE DOOR CANTEEN, Lesser, UA: FREDERIC E. RICH

STAR SPANGLED RHYTHM, Paramount: ROBERT EMMETT DOLAN

THIS IS THE ARMY, Warner Bros.: RAY HEINDORF

THOUSANDS CHEER, Metro-Goldwyn-Mayer: HERBERT STOTHART

(Best Song)

BLACK MAGIC from *Star Spangled Rhythm,* Paramount
Music by HAROLD ARLEN. Lyrics by JOHNNY MERCER

CHANGE OF HEART from *Hit Parade Of 1943,* Republic
Music by JULE STYNE. Lyrics by HAROLD ADAMSON

HAPPINESS IS A THING CALLED JOE from *Cabin In The Sky,* Metro-Goldwyn-Mayer
Music by HAROLD ARLEN. Lyrics by E. Y. HARBURG

MY SHINING HOUR from *The Sky's The Limit,* RKO Radio
Music by HAROLD ARLEN. Lyrics by JOHNNY MERCER

SALUDOS AMIGOS from *Saludos Amigos,* Disney, RKO Radio
Music by CHARLES WOLCOTT. Lyrics by NED WASHINGTON

SAY A PRAYER FOR THE BOYS OVER THERE from *Hers To Hold,* Universal
Music by JIMMY MCHUGH. Lyrics by HERB MAGIDSON

THEY'RE EITHER TOO YOUNG OR TOO OLD from *Thank Your Lucky Stars,* Warner Bros.
Music by ARTHUR SCHWARTZ. Lyrics by FRANK LOESSER

WE MUSTN'T SAY GOOD BYE from *Stage Door Canteen,* Lesser, US
Music by JAMES MONACO. Lyrics by AL DUBIN

YOU'D BE SO NICE TO COME HOME TO from *Something To Shout About,* Columbia
Music and Lyrics by COLE PORTER

YOU'LL NEVER KNOW from *Hello, Frisco, Hello,* 20th Century-Fox

Music by HARRY WARREN.
Lyrics by MACK GORDON

Short Subjects

(Cartoons)

THE DIZZY ACROBAT, Walter Lantz,
Universal: WALTER LANTZ, Producer
THE FIVE HUNDRED HATS OF BARTHOL-
OMEW CUBBINS, Paramount. (George
Pal Puppetoon)
GREETINGS, BAIT, Warner Bros.: LEON
SCHLESINGER, Producer
IMAGINATION, Columbia: DAVE
FLEISCHER, Producer
REASON AND EMOTION, Walt Disney,
RKO Radio: WALT DISNEY, Producer
YANKEE DOODLE MOUSE, Metro-
Goldwyn-Mayer: FREDERICK
QUIMBY, Producer

(One-reel)

AMPHIBIOUS FIGHTERS, Para-
mount: GRANTLAND RICE, Pro-
ducer
CAVALCADE OF THE DANCE WITH
VELOZ AND YOLANDA, Warner
Bros.: (Melody Master Bands) GOR-
DON HOLLINGSHEAD, Producer
CHAMPIONS CARRY ON, 20th Century-
Fox: (Sports Reviews) EDMUND
REEK, Producer
HOLLYWOOD IN UNIFORM, Columbia:
(Screen Snapshots #1, Series 22)
RALPH STAUB, Producer
SEEING HANDS, Metro-Goldwyn-Mayer:
(Pete Smith Specialty)

(Two-reel)

HEAVENLY MUSIC, Metro-
Goldwyn-Mayer: JERRY BRESLER
and SAM COSLOW, Producers
LETTER TO A HERO, RKO Radio: (This
Is America) FRED ULLMAN, Producer
MARDI GRAS, Paramount: (Musical Pa-
rade) WALTER MacEWEN, Producer
WOMEN AT WAR, Warner Bros.: (Tech-

nicolor Special) GORDON HOLLINGS-
HEAD, Producer

Documentary

(Short Subjects)

CHILDREN OF MARS, This is America
Series, RKO Radio
DECEMBER 7TH, U.S. Navy, Field
Photographic Branch, Office of Stra-
tegic Services
PLAN FOR DESTRUCTION, Metro-
Goldwyn-Mayer
SWEDES IN AMERICA, Office of War In-
formation, Overseas Motion Picture
Bureau
TO THE PEOPLE OF THE UNITED STATES,
U.S. Public Health Service, Walter
Wanger Prods.
TOMORROW WE FLY, U.S. Navy,
Bureau of Aeronautics
YOUTH IN CRISIS, March of Time, 20th
Century-Fox

(Features)

BATTLE OF RUSSIA, Special Service Di-
vision of the War Department
BAPTISM OF FIRE, U.S. Army, Fighting
Men Series
DESERT VICTORY, British Ministry
of Information
REPORT FROM THE ALEUTIANS, U.S.
Army Pictorial Service, Combat
Film Series
WAR DEPARTMENT REPORT, Field Pho-
tographic Branch, Office of Strategic
Services

Special Effects

AIR FORCE, Warner Bros
Photographic: HANS KOENEKAMP and
REX WIMPY
Sound: NATHAN LEVINSON
BOMBARDIER, RKO Radio
Photographic: VERNON L. WALKER
Sound: JAMES G. STEWART and ROY
GRANVILLE
CRASH DIVE, 20th Century-Fox

Photographic: FRED SERSEN
Sound: ROGER HEMAN
THE NORTH STAR, Goldwyn, RKO
Radio
Photographic: CLARENCE SLIFER and
R. O. BINGER
Sound: THOMAS T. MOULTON
SO PROUDLY WE HAIL, Paramount
Photographic: FARCIOT EDOUART and
GORDON JENNINGS
Sound: GEORGE DUTTON
STAND BY FOR ACTION, Metro-
Goldwyn-Mayer
Photographic: A. ARNOLD GILLESPIE
and DONALD JAHRAUS
Sound: MICHAEL STEINORE

Special Awards
GEORGE PAL for the development of
novel methods and techniques in the
production of short subjects known
as Puppetoons. (plaque)

Irving G. Thalberg Memorial Award
HAL B. WALLIS

Scientific or Technical
Class I
None
Class II
FARCIOT EDOUART, EARLE
MORGAN, BARTON THOMPSON
and the PARAMOUNT STUDIO
ENGINEERING and TRANSPAR-
ENCY DEPARTMENTS for the de-
velopment and practical application
to motion picture production of a
method of duplicating and enlarging
natural color photographs, transfer-
ring the image emulsions to glass
plates and projecting these slides by
especially designed stereopticon
equipment
PHOTO PRODUCTS DEPARTMENT,
E. I. DuPONT DE NEMOURS
AND CO., INC., for the developmer
of fine-grain motion picture films
Class III
DANIEL J. BLOOMBERG and the
REPUBLIC STUDIO SOUND DE-
PARTMENT for the design and development of an inexpensive method
of converting Moviolas to Class B
push-pull reproduction.
CHARLES GALLOWAY CLARKE
and the 20TH CENTURY-FOX
STUDIO CAMERA DEPART-
MENT for the development and
practical application of a device for
composing artificial clouds into mo-
tion picture scenes during production
photography
FARCIOT EDOUART and the PARA-
MOUNT STUDIO TRANSPAR-
ENCY DEPARTMENT for an auto-
matic electric transparency cueing
timer
WILLARD H. TURNER and the RKO
RADIO STUDIO SOUND DE-
PARTMENT for the design and construction of the phono-cue starter

1944

Nominations Announced: February 5, 1945
Awards Ceremony: March 15, 1945
Grauman's Chinese Theatre
(MCs: John Cromwell and Bob Hope)

Best Picture

DOUBLE INDEMNITY, Paramount
GASLIGHT, Metro-Goldwyn-Mayer
GOING MY WAY, Paramount
SINCE YOU WENT AWAY, Selznick International, UA
WILSON, 20th Century-Fox

Actor

CHARLES BOYER in *Gaslight*, Metro-Goldwyn-Mayer
BING CROSBY in *Going My Way*, Paramount
BARRY FITZGERALD in *Going My Way*, Paramount
CARY GRANT in *None But The Lonely Heart*, RKO Radio
ALEXANDER KNOX in *Wilson*, 20th Century-Fox

Actress

INGRID BERGMAN in *Gaslight*, Metro-Goldwyn-Mayer
CLAUDETTE COLBERT in *Since You Went Away*, Selznick, UA
BETTE DAVIS in *Mr. Skeffington*, Warner Bros.
GREER GARSON in *Mrs. Parkington*, Metro-Goldwyn-Mayer
BARBARA STANWYCK in *Double Indemnity*, Paramount

Supporting Actor

HUME CRONYN in *The Seventh Cross*, Metro-Goldwyn-Mayer

LARGE CAPITAL LETTERS DENOTE WINNER

BARRY FITZGERALD in *Going My Way*, Paramount
CLAUDE RAINS in *Mr. Skeffington*, Warner Bros.
CLIFTON WEBB in *Laura*, 20th Century-Fox
MONTY WOOLLEY in *Since You Went Away*, Selznick, UA

Supporting Actress

ETHEL BARRYMORE in *None But The Lonely Heart*, RKO Radio
JENNIFER JONES in *Since You Went Away*, Selznick, UA
ANGELA LANSBURY in *Gaslight*, Metro-Goldwyn-Mayer
ALINE MacMAHON in *Dragon Seed*, Metro-Goldwyn-Mayer
AGNES MOOREHEAD in *Mrs. Parkington*, Metro-Goldwyn-Mayer

Directing

ALFRED HITCHCOCK for *Lifeboat*, 20th Century-Fox
HENRY KING for *Wilson*, 20th Century-Fox
LEO McCAREY for *Going My Way*, Paramount
OTTO PREMINGER for *Laura*, 20th Century-Fox
BILLY WILDER for *Double Indemnity*, Paramount

Writing

(Original Story)
GOING MY WAY, Paramount: LEO McCAREY

A GUY NAMED JOE, Metro-Goldwyn-Mayer: DAVID BOEHM and CHANDLER SPRAGUE

LIFEBOAT, 20th Century-Fox: JOHN STEINBECK

NONE SHALL ESCAPE, Columbia: ALFRED NEUMANN and JOSEPH THAN

THE SULLIVANS, 20th Century-Fox: EDWARD DOHERTY and JULES SCHERMER

(Original Screenplay)

HAIL THE CONQUERING HERO, Paramount: PRESTON STURGES

THE MIRACLE OF MORGAN'S CREEK, Paramount: PRESTON STURGES

TWO GIRLS AND A SAILOR, Metro-Goldwyn-Mayer: RICHARD CONNELL and GLADYS LEHMAN

WILSON, 20th Century-Fox: LAMAR TROTTI

WING AND A PRAYER, 20th Century-Fox: JEROME CADY

(Screenplay)

DOUBLE INDEMNITY, Paramount: RAYMOND CHANDLER and BILLY WILDER

GASLIGHT, Metro-Goldwyn-Mayer: JOHN L. BALDERSTON, WALTER REISCH and JOHN VAN DRUTEN

GOING MY WAY, Paramount: FRANK BUTLER and FRANK CAVETT

LAURA, 20th Century-Fox: JAY DRATLER, SAMUEL HOFFENSTEIN and BETTY REINHARDT

MEET ME IN ST. LOUIS, Metro-Goldwyn-Mayer: IRVING BRECHER and FRED F. FINKELHOFFE

Cinematography
(Black-and-White)

DOUBLE INDEMNITY, Paramount: JOHN SEITZ

DRAGON SEED, Metro-Goldwyn-Mayer: SIDNEY WAGNER

GASLIGHT, Metro-Goldwyn-Mayer: JOSEPH RUTTENBERG

GOING MY WAY, Paramount: LIONEL LINDON

LAURA, 20th Century-Fox: JOSEPH LaSHELLE

LIFEBOAT, 20th Century-Fox: GLEN MacWILLIAMS

SINCE YOU WENT AWAY, Selznick, UA: STANLEY CORTEZ and LEE GARMES

THIRTY SECONDS OVER TOKYO, Metro-Goldwyn-Mayer: ROBERT SURTEES and HAROLD ROSSON

THE UNINVITED, Paramount: CHARLES LANG

THE WHITE CLIFFS OF DOVER, Metro-Goldwyn-Mayer: GEORGE FOLSEY

(Color)

COVER GIRL, Columbia: RUDY MATE and ALLEN M. DAVEY

HOME IN INDIANA, 20th Century-Fox: EDWARD CRONJAGER

KISMET, Metro-Goldwyn-Mayer: CHARLES ROSHER

LADY IN THE DARK, Paramount: RAY RENNAHAN

MEET ME IN ST. LOUIS, Metro-Goldwyn-Mayer: GEORGE FOLSEY

WILSON, 20th Century-Fox: LEON SHAMROY

Interior Decoration
(Black-and-White)

ADDRESS UNKNOWN, Columbia: LIONEL BANKS and WALTER HOLSCHER Interior Decoration: JOSEPH KISH

THE ADVENTURES OF MARK TWAIN, Warner Bros: JOHN J. HUGHES Interior Decoration: FRED MacLEAN

CASANOVA BROWN, International, RKO Radio: PERRY FERGUSON Interior Decoration: JULIA HERON

GASLIGHT, Metro-Goldwyn-Mayer: CEDRIC GIBBONS and WILLIAM FERRARI Interior Decoration: EDWIN B. WILLIS and PAUL HULDSCHINSKY

LAURA, 20th Century-Fox: LYLE
WHEELER and LELAND FULLER
Interior Decoration: THOMAS LITTLE
NO TIME FOR LOVE, Paramount: HANS
DREIER and ROBERT USHER
Interior Decoration: SAM COMER
SINCE YOU WENT AWAY, Selznick, UA:
MARK-LEE KIRK
Interior Decoration: VICTOR A.
GANGELIN
STEP LIVELY, RKO Radio: ALBERT S.
D'AGOSTINO and CARROLL CLARK
Interior Decoration: DARRELL SIL-
VERA and CLAUDE CARPENTER

(Color)

THE CLIMAX, Universal. JOHN B.
GOODMAN and ALEXANDER GOLIT-
ZEN
Interior Decoration: RUSSELL A.
GAUSMAN and IRA S. WEBB
COVER GIRL, Columbia: LIONEL BANKS
and CARY ODELL
Interior Decoration: FAY BABCOCK
THE DESERT SONG, Warner Bros:
CHARLES NOVI
Interior Decoration: JACK MC-
CONAGHY
KISMET, Metro-Goldwyn-Mayer:
CEDRIC GIBBONS and DANIEL B.
CATHCART
Interior Decoration: EDWIN B. WILLIS
and RICHARD PEFFERLE
LADY IN THE DARK, Paramount: HANS
DREIER and RAOUL PENE DU BOIS
Interior Decoration: RAY MOYER
THE PRINCESS AND THE PIRATE, Gold-
wyn, RKO Radio: ERNST FEGTE
Interior Decoration: HOWARD BRIS-
TOL
WILSON, 20th Century-Fox: WIARD
IHNEN
Interior Decoration: THOMAS LIT-
TLE

Sound Recording

BRAZIL, Republic: DANIEL J. BLOOM-
BERG

CASANOVA BROWN, International, RKO
Radio: THOMAS T. MOULTON, Gold-
wyn Sound Department
COVER GIRL, Columbia: JOHN LIVA-
DARY
DOUBLE INDEMNITY, Paramount:
LOREN RYDER
HIS BUTLER'S SISTER, Universal: BER-
NARD B. BROWN
HOLLYWOOD CANTEEN, Warner Bros:
NATHAN LEVINSON
IT HAPPENED TOMORROW, Arnold, UA:
JACK WHITNEY, SOUND SERVICE, INC.
KISMET, Metro-Goldwyn-Mayer:
DOUGLAS SHEARER
MUSIC IN MANHATTAN, RKO Radio:
STEPHEN DUNN
VOICE IN THE WIND, Ripley-Monter,
UA: W. M. DALGLEISH, RCA Sound
WILSON, 20th Century-Fox: E. H.
HANSEN

Film Editing

GOING MY WAY, Paramount: LEROY
STONE
JANIE, Warner Bros: OWEN MARKS
NONE BUT THE LONELY HEART, RKO
Radio: ROLAND GROSS
SINCE YOU WENT AWAY, Selznick, UA:
HAL C. KERN and JAMES E. NEWCOM
WILSON, 20th Century-Fox: BAR-
BARA McLEAN

Music

(Scoring of a Dramatic or Comedy Picture)

ADDRESS UNKNOWN, Columbia: MORRIS
STOLOFF and ERNST TOCH
THE ADVENTURES OF MARK TWAIN,
Warner Bros: MAX STEINER
THE BRIDGE OF SAN LUIS REY, Bogeaus,
UA: DIMITRI TIOMKIN
CASANOVA BROWN, International, RKO
Radio: ARTHUR LANGE
CHRISTMAS HOLIDAY, Universal: H. J.
SALTER

DOUBLE INDEMNITY, Paramount: MIKLOS ROZSA

THE FIGHTING SEABEES, Republic: WALTER SCHARF and ROY WEBB

THE HAIRY APE, Levey, UA: MICHEL MICHELET and EDWARD PAUL

IT HAPPENED TOMORROW, Arnold, UA: ROBERT STOLZ

JACK LONDON, Bronston, UA: FREDERIC E. RICH

KISMET, Metro-Goldwyn-Mayer: HERBERT STOTHART

NONE BUT THE LONELY HEART, RKO Radio: C. BAKALEINIKOFF and HANNS EISLER

THE PRINCESS AND THE PIRATE, Regent, RKO Radio: DAVID ROSE

SINCE YOU WENT AWAY, Selznick, UA: MAX STEINER

SUMMER STORM, Angelus, UA: KARL HAJOS

THREE RUSSIAN GIRLS, R & F Prods., UA: FRANKE HARLING

UP IN MABEL'S ROOM, Small, UA: EDWARD PAUL

VOICE IN THE WIND, Ripley-Monter, UA: MICHEL MICHELET

WILSON, 20th Century-Fox: ALFRED NEWMAN

WOMAN OF THE TOWN, Sherman, UA: MIKLOS ROZSA

(Scoring of a Musical Picture)

BRAZIL, Republic: WALTER SCHARF

COVER GIRL, Columbia: CARMEN DRAGON and MORRIS STOLOFF

HIGHER AND HIGHER, RKO Radio: C. BAKALEINIKOFF

HOLLYWOOD CANTEEN, Warner Bros: RAY HEINDORF

IRISH EYES ARE SMILING, 20th Century-Fox: ALFRED NEWMAN

KNICKERBOCKER HOLIDAY, RCA, UA: WERNER R. HEYMANN and KURT WEILL

LADY IN THE DARK, Paramount: ROBERT EMMETT DOLAN

LADY LET'S DANCE, Monogram: EDWARD KAY

MEET ME IN ST. LOUIS, Metro-Goldwyn-Mayer: GEORGIE STOLL

THE MERRY MONAHANS, Universal: H. J. SALTER

MINSTREL MAN, PRC: LEO ERDODY and FERDE GROFÉ

SENSATIONS OF 1945, Stone, UA: MAHLON MERRICK

SONG OF THE OPEN ROAD, Rogers, UA: CHARLES PREVIN

UP IN ARMS, Avalon, RKO Radio: LOUIS FORBES and RAY HEINDORF

(Best Song)

I COULDN'T SLEEP A WINK LAST NIGHT from *Higher And Higher,* RKO Radio
Music by JIMMY MCHUGH. Lyrics by HAROLD ADAMSON

I'LL WALK ALONE from *Follow The Boys,* Universal
Music by JULE STYNE. Lyrics by SAMMY CAHN

I'M MAKING BELIEVE from *Sweet And Lowdown,* 20th Century-Fox
Music by JAMES V. MONACO. Lyrics by MACK GORDON

LONG AGO AND FAR AWAY from *Cover Girl,* Columbia
Music by JEROME KERN. Lyrics by IRA GERSHWIN

NOW I KNOW from *Up In Arms,* Avalon, RKO Radio
Music by HAROLD ARLEN. Lyrics by TED KOEHLER

REMEMBER ME TO CAROLINA from *Minstrel Man*, PRC
Music by HARRY REVEL. Lyrics by PAUL WEBSTER

RIO DE JANEIRO from *Brazil,* Republic
Music by ARY BARROSO. Lyrics by NED WASHINGTON

SILVER SHADOWS AND GOLDEN DREAMS from *Lady Let's Dance,* Monogram
Music by LEW POLLACK. Lyrics by

CHARLES NEWMAN
SWEET DREAMS SWEETHEART from *Hollywood Canteen,* Warner Bros
Music by M. K. JEROME. Lyrics by TED KOEHLER
SWINGING ON A STAR from *Going My Way,* Paramount
Music by JAMES VAN HEUSEN. Lyrics by JOHNNY BURKE
TOO MUCH IN LOVE from *Song Of The Open Road,* Rogers, UA
Music by WALTER KENT. Lyrics by KIM GANNON
THE TROLLEY SONG from *Meet Me In St. Louis,* Metro-Goldwyn-Mayer
Music and Lyrics by RALPH BLANE and HUGH MARTIN

Short Subjects

(Cartoons)

AND TO THINK I SAW IT ON MULBERRY STREET, Paramount. (George Pal Puppetoon)
THE DOG, CAT AND CANARY, Columbia. (Screen Gems)
FISH FRY, Universal: WALTER LANTZ, Producer
HOW TO PLAY FOOTBALL, Walt Disney, RKO Radio: WALT DISNEY, Producer
MOUSE TROUBLE, Metro-Goldwyn-Mayer: FREDERICK C. QUIMBY, Producer
MY BOY, JOHNNY, 20th Century-Fox: PAUL TERRY, Producer
SWOONER CROONER, Warner Bros.

(One-reel)

BLUE GRASS GENTLEMEN, 20th Century-Fox. (Sports Review): EDMUND REEK, Producer
JAMMIN'THE BLUES, Warner Bros. (Melody Master Bands): GORDON HOLLINGSHEAD, Producer
MOVIE PESTS, Metro-Goldwyn-Mayer. (Pete Smith Specialty)
50TH ANNIVERSARY OF MOTION PICTURES, Columbia. (Screen Snapshots #9, Series 23): RALPH STAUB, Producer
WHO'S WHO IN ANIMAL LAND, Paramount. (Speaking Of Animals): JERRY FAIRBANKS, Producer

(Two-reel)

BOMBALERA, Paramount. (Musical Parade) LOUIS HARRIS, Producer
I WON'T PLAY, Warner Bros. (Featurette) GORDON HOLLINGSHEAD, Producer
MAIN STREET TODAY, Metro-Goldwyn-Mayer. (Two-reel Special) JERRY BRESLER, Producer

Documentary

(Short Subjects)

ARTURO TOSCANINI, Motion Picture Bureau, Overseas Branch, Office of War Information
NEW AMERICANS, This is America Series, RKO Radio
WITH THE MARINES AT TARAWA, U.S. Marine Corps

(Features)

THE FIGHTING LADY, 20th Century-Fox and U.S. Navy
RESISTING ENEMY INTERROGATION, U.S. Army Air Force

Special Effects

THE ADVENTURES OF MARK TWAIN, Warner Bros.
Photographic: PAUL DETLEFSEN and JOHN CROUSE
Sound: NATHAN LEVINSON
DAYS OF GLORY, RKO Radio
Photographic: VERNON L. WALKER
Sound: JAMES G. STEWART and ROY GRANVILLE
SECRET COMMAND, Columbia
Photographic: DAVID ALLEN, RAY CORY and ROBERT WRIGHT
Sound: RUSSELL MALMGREN and HARRY KUSNICK

SINCE YOU WENT AWAY, Selznick, UA
  Photographic: JOHN R. COSGROVE
  Sound: ARTHUR JOHNS
THE STORY OF DR. WASSELL, Paramount
  Photographic: FARCIOT EDOUART and
  GORDON JENNINGS
  Sound: GEORGE DUTTON
THIRTY SECONDS OVER TOKYO,
  Metro-Goldwyn-Mayer
  Photographic: A. ARNOLD GILLES-
  PIE, DONALD JAHRAUS and
  WARREN NEWCOMBE
  Sound: DOUGLAS SHEARER
WILSON, 20th Century-Fox
  Photographic: FRED SERSEN
  Sound: ROGER HEMAN

Special Awards

MARGARET O'BRIEN, outstanding
child actress of 1944. (miniature
statuette)
BOB HOPE, for his many services to
the Academy, a Life Membership in
the Academy of Motion Picture Arts
and Sciences

Irving G. Thalberg Memorial Award
DARRYL F. ZANUCK

Scientific or Technical
Class I
None

Class II

STEPHEN DUNN and the RKO
  RADIO STUDIO SOUND DE-
  PARTMENT and RADIO COR-
  PORATION OF AMERICA for the
  design and development of the elec-
  tronic compressor-limiter

Class III

LINWOOD DUNN, CECIL LOVE and
  ACME TOOL MANUFACTURING
  CO. for the design and construction
  of the Acme-Dunn Optical Printer
GROVER LAUBE and the 20TH
  CENTURY-FOX STUDIO CAM-
  ERA DEPARTMENT for the devel-
  opment of a continuous loop projec-
  tion device
WESTERN ELECTRIC CO. for the
  design and construction of the 1126A
  Limiting Amplifier for variable den-
  sity sound recording
RUSSELL BROWN, RAY HINS-
  DALE and JOSEPH E. ROBBINS
  for the development and production
  use of the Paramount floating hy-
  draulic boat rocker
GORDON JENNINGS for the design
  and construction of the Paramount
  nodal point tripod
RADIO CORPORATION OF
  AMERICA and the RKO RADIO
  STUDIO SOUND DEPARTMENT
  for the design and construction of the
  RKO reverberation chamber
DANIEL J. BLOOMBERG and the
  REPUBLIC STUDIO SOUND DE-
  PARTMENT for the design and development of a multi-interlock selector switch
BERNARD B. BROWN and JOHN P.
  LIVADARY for the design and engineering of a separate soloist and
  chorus recording room
PAUL ZEFF, S. J. TWINING and
  GEORGE SEID of the Columbia
  Studio Laboratory for the formula
  and application to production of a
  simplified variable area sound negative developer
PAUL LERPAE for the design and
  construction of the Paramount traveling matte projection and photographing device

1945

Nominations Announced: Janaury 28, 1946
Awards Ceremony: March 7, 1946
Grauman's Chinese Theatre
(MCs: Bob Hope and James Stewart)

Best Picture

ANCHORS AWEIGH, Metro-Goldwyn-Mayer

THE BELLS OF ST. MARY'S, Rainbow, RKO Radio

THE LOST WEEKEND, Paramount

MILDRED PIERCE, Warner Bros.

SPELLBOUND, Selznick International, UA

Actor

BING CROSBY in *The Bells Of St. Mary's*, Rainbow, RKO Radio

GENE KELLY in *Anchors Aweigh*, Metro-Goldwyn-Mayer

RAY MILLAND in *The Lost Weekend*, Paramount

GREGORY PECK in *The Keys Of The Kingdom*, 20th Century-Fox

CORNEL WILDE in *A Song To Remember*, Columbia

Actress

INGRID BERGMAN in *The Bells Of St. Mary's*, Rainbow, RKO Radio

JOAN CRAWFORD in *Mildred Pierce*, Warner Bros.

GREER GARSON in *The Valley Of Decision*, Metro-Goldwyn-Mayer

JENNIFER JONES in *Love Letters*, Wallis, Paramount

GENE TIERNEY in *Leave Her To Heaven*, 20th Century-Fox

Supporting Actor

MICHAEL CHEKHOV in *Spellbound*, Selznick, UA

LARGE CAPITAL LETTERS DENOTE WINNER

JOHN DALL in *The Corn Is Green*, Warner Bros.

JAMES DUNN in *A Tree Grows In Brooklyn*, 20th Century-Fox

ROBERT MITCHUM in *G. I. Joe*, Cowan, UA

J. CARROL NAISH in *A Medal For Benny*, Paramount

Supporting Actress

EVE ARDEN in *Mildred Pierce*, Warner Bros.

ANN BLYTH in *Mildred Pierce*, Warner Bros.

ANGELA LANSBURY in *The Picture of Dorian Gray*, Metro-Goldwyn-Mayer

JOAN LORRING in *The Corn Is Green*, Warner Bros.

ANNE REVERE in *National Velvet*, Metro-Goldwyn-Mayer

Directing

CLARENCE BROWN for *National Velvet*, Metro-Goldwyn-Mayer

ALFRED HITCHCOCK for *Spellbound*, Selznick, UA

LEO MCCAREY for *The Bells Of St. Mary's*, Rainbow, RKO Radio

JEAN RENOIR for *The Southerner*, Loew-Hakim, UA

BILLY WILDER for *The Lost Weekend*, Paramount

Writing

(Original Story)

THE AFFAIRS OF SUSAN, Wallis, Paramount: LASZLO GOROG and THOMAS MONROE

THE HOUSE ON 92ND STREET, 20th Century-Fox: CHARLES G. BOOTH

A MEDAL FOR BENNY, Paramount: JOHN STEINBECK and JACK WAGNER

OBJECTIVE-BURMA, Warner Bros.: ALVAH BESSIE

A SONG TO REMEMBER, Columbia: ERNST MARISCHKA

(Original Screenplay)

DILLINGER, Monogram: PHILIP YORDAN

MARIE-LOUISE, Praesens Films (Swiss). RICHARD SCHWEIZER

MUSIC FOR MILLIONS, Metro-Goldwyn-Mayer: MYLES CONNOLLY

SALTY O'ROURKE, Paramount: MILTON HOLMES

WHAT NEXT, CORPORAL HARGROVE?, Metro-Goldwyn-Mayer: HARRY KURNITZ

(Screenplay)

G. I. JOE, Cowan, UA: LEOPOLD ATLAS, GUY ENDORE and PHILIP STEVENSON

THE LOST WEEKEND, Paramount: CHARLES BRACKETT and BILLY WILDER

MILDRED PIERCE, Warner Bros.: RANALD MacDOUGALL

PRIDE OF THE MARINES, Warner Bros.: ALBERT MALTZ

A TREE GROWS IN BROOKLYN, 20th Century-Fox. FRANK DAVIS and TESS SLESINGER

Cinematography

(Black-and-White)

THE KEYS OF THE KINGDOM, 20th Century-Fox: ARTHUR MILLER

THE LOST WEEKEND, Paramount: JOHN F. SEITZ

MILDRED PIERCE, Warner Bros.: ERNEST HALLER

THE PICTURE OF DORIAN GRAY, Metro-Goldwyn-Mayer: HARRY STRADLING

SPELLBOUND, Selznick, UA: GEORGE BARNES

(Color)

ANCHORS AWEIGH, Metro-Goldwyn-Mayer: ROBERT PLANCK and CHARLES BOYLE

LEAVE HER TO HEAVEN, 20th Century-Fox: LEON SHAMROY

NATIONAL VELVET, Metro-Goldwyn-Mayer: LEONARD SMITH

A SONG TO REMEMBER, Columbia: TONY GAUDIO and ALLEN M. DAVEY

THE SPANISH MAIN, RKO Radio: GEORGE BARNES

Interior Decoration

(Black-and-White)

BLOOD ON THE SUN, Cagney, UA: WIARD IHNEN
Interior Decoration: A. ROLAND FIELDS

EXPERIMENT PERILOUS, RKO Radio: ALBERT S.D'AGOSTINO and JACK OKEY
Interior Decoration: DARRELL SILVERA and CLAUDE CARPENTER

THE KEYS OF THE KINGDOM, 20th Century-Fox: JAMES BASEVI and WILLIAM DARLING
Interior Decoration: THOMAS LITTLE and FRANK E. HUGHES

LOVE LETTERS, Hal Wallis, Paramount: HANS DREIER and ROLAND ANDERSON
Interior Decoration: SAM COMER and RAY MOYER

THE PICTURE OF DORIAN GRAY, Metro-Godwyn-Mayer: CEDRIC GIBBONS and HANS PETERS
Interior Decoration: EDWIN B. WILLIS, JOHN BONAR and HUGH HUNT

(Color)

FRENCHMAN'S CREEK, Paramount:

HANS DREIER and ERNST FEGTE
Interior Decoration: SAM COMER
LEAVE HER TO HEAVEN, 20th Century-
Fox: LYLE WHEELER and MAURICE
RANSFORD
Interior Decoration: THOMAS LITTLE
NATIONAL VELVET, Metro-Goldwyn-
Mayer: CEDRIC GIBBONS and URIE
MCCLEARY
Interior Decoration: EDWIN B. WILLIS
and MILDRED GRIFFITHS
SAN ANTONIO, Warner Bros.: TED SMITH
Interior Decoration: JACK MC-
CONAGHY
A THOUSAND AND ONE NIGHTS, Colum-
bia: STEPHEN GOOSSON and RUDOLPH
STERNAD
Interior Decoration: FRANK TUTTLE

Sound Recording
THE BELLS OF ST. MARY'S, Rain-
bow, RKO Radio: STEPHEN
DUNN
THE FLAME OF THE BARBARY COAST,
Republic: DANIEL J. BLOOMBERG
LADY ON A TRAIN, Universal: BERNARD
B. BROWN
LEAVE HER TO HEAVEN, 20th Century-
Fox: THOMAS T. MOULTON
RHAPSODY IN BLUE, Warner Bros.:
NATHAN LEVINSON
A SONG TO REMEMBER, Columbia: JOHN
LIVADARY
THE SOUTHERNER, Loew-Hakim, UA:
JACK WHITNEY, GENERAL SERVICE
THEY WERE EXPENDABLE, Metro-
Goldwyn-Mayer: DOUGLAS SHEARER
THE THREE CABALLEROS, Disney, RKO
Radio: C. O. SLYFIELD
THREE IS A FAMILY, Master Produc-
tions, UA: W. V. WOLFE, RCA
SOUND
THE UNSEEN, Paramount: LOREN L.
RYDER
WONDER MAN, Goldwyn, RKO Radio:
GORDON SAWYER

Film Editing
THE BELLS OF ST. MARY'S, Rainbow,
RKO Radio: HARRY MARKER
THE LOST WEEKEND, Paramount:
DOANE HARRISON
NATIONAL VELVET, Metro-
Goldwyn-Mayer: ROBERT J. KERN
OBJECTIVE-BURMA, Warner Bros.:
GEORGE AMY
A SONG TO REMEMBER, Columbia:
CHARLES NELSON

Music
(Scoring of a Dramatic or Comedy Pic-
ture)
THE BELLS OF ST. MARY'S, Rainbow,
RKO Radio: ROBERT EMMETT DOLAN
BREWSTER'S MILLIONS, Small, UA: LOU
FORBES
CAPTAIN KIDD, Bogeaus, UA: WERNER
JANSSEN
ENCHANTED COTTAGE, RKO Radio:
ROY WEBB
FLAME OF THE BARBARY COAST, Repub-
lic: DALE BUTTS and MORTON SCOTT
G. I. HONEYMOON, Monogram: ED-
WARD J. KAY
G. I. JOE, Cowan, UA: LOUIS APPLE-
BAUM and ANN RONELL
GUEST IN THE HOUSE, Guest In The
House, Inc., UA: WERNER JANSSEN
GUEST WIFE, Greentree Prods., UA:
DANIELE AMFITHEATROF
THE KEYS OF THE KINGDOM, 20th Cen-
tury-Fox: ALFRED NEWMAN
THE LOST WEEKEND, Paramount:
MIKLOS ROZSA
LOVE LETTERS, Wallis, Paramount:
VICTOR YOUNG
MAN WHO WALKED ALONE, PRC: KARL
HAJOS
OBJECTIVE-BURMA, Warner Bros.:
FRANZ WAXMAN
PARIS-UNDERGROUND, Bennett, UA:
ALEXANDER TANSMAN
A SONG TO REMEMBER, Columbia:

MIKLOS ROZSA and MORRIS STOLOFF
THE SOUTHERNER, Loew-Hakim, UA:
WERNER JANSSEN
SPELLBOUND, Selznick, UA:
MIKLOS ROZSA
THIS LOVE OF OURS, Universal: H. J.
SALTER
VALLEY OF DECISION, Metro-Goldwyn-
Mayer: HERBERT STOTHART
WOMAN IN THE WINDOW, International,
RKO Radio: HUGO FRIEDHOFER and
ARTHUR LANGE

(Scoring of a Musical Picture)
ANCHORS AWEIGH, Metro-
Goldwyn-Mayer: GEORGIE STOLL
BELLE OF THE YUKON, International.
RKO Radio: ARTHUR LANGE
CAN'T HELP SINGING, Universal:
JEROME KERN and H. J. SALTER
HITCHHIKE TO HAPPINESS, Republic:
MORTON SCOTT
INCENDIARY BLONDE, Paramount: ROB-
ERT EMMETT DOLAN
RHAPSODY IN BLUE, Warner Bros.: RAY
HEINDORF and MAX STEINER
STATE FAIR, 20th Century-Fox:
CHARLES HENDERSON and ALFRED
NEWMAN
SUNBONNET SUE, Monogram: EDWARD
J. KAY
THREE CABALLEROS, Disney-RKO
Radio: EDWARD PLUMB, PAUL J.
SMITH and CHARLES WOLCOTT
TONIGHT AND EVERY NIGHT, Columbia:
MARLIN SKILES and MORRIS STOLOFF
WHY GIRLS LEAVE HOME, PRC.:
WALTER GREENE
WONDER MAN, Beverly, RKO Radio:
LOU FORBES and RAY HEINDORF

(Best Song)
ACCENTUATE THE POSITIVE from *Here
Come The Waves,* Paramount
Music by HAROLD ARLEN. Lyrics by
JOHNNY MERCER
ANYWHERE from *Tonight And Every
Night,* Columbia

Music by JULE STYNE. Lyrics by
SAMMY CAHN
AREN'T YOU GLAD YOU'RE YOU from
The Bells of St. Mary's, Rainbow,
RKO Radio
Music by JAMES VAN HEUSEN.
Lyrics by JOHNNY BURKE
THE CAT AND THE CANARY from *Why
Girls Leave Home,* PRC
Music by JAY LIVINGSTON. Lyrics by
RAY EVANS
ENDLESSLY from *Earl Carroll Vanities,*
Republic
Music by WALTER KENT. Lyrics by
KIM GANNON
I FALL IN LOVE TOO EASILY from *An-
chors Aweigh,* Metro-Goldwyn-
Mayer
Music by JULE STYNE. Lyrics by
SAMMY CAHN
I'LL BUY THAT DREAM from *Sing Your
Way Home,* RKO Radio
Music by ALLIE WRUBEL. Lyrics by
HERB MAGIDSON
IT MIGHT AS WELL BE SPRING
from *State Fair,* 20th Century-Fox
Music by RICHARD RODGERS.
Lyrics by OSCAR HAMMERSTEIN
II
LINDA from *G. I. Joe,* Cowan, UA
Music and Lyrics by ANN RONELL
LOVE LETTERS from *Love Letters,* Wal-
lis, Paramount
Music by VICTOR YOUNG. Lyrics by
EDWARD HEYMAN
MORE AND MORE from *Can't Help Sing-
ing,* Universal
Music by JEROME KERN. Lyrics by E.
Y. HARBURG
SLEIGHRIDE IN JULY from *Belle Of The
Yukon,* International. RKO Radio
Music by JAMES VAN HEUSEN. Lyrics
by JOHNNY BURKE
SO IN LOVE from *Wonder Man,* Beverly
Prods., RKO Radio
Music by DAVID ROSE. Lyrics by LEO
ROBIN

SOME SUNDAY MORNING from *San Antonio,* Warner Bros.
Music by RAY HEINDORF and M. K. JEROME. Lyrics by TED KOEHLER

Short Subjects
(Cartoons)
DONALD'S CRIME, Walt Disney, RKO Radio. (Donald Duck): WALT DISNEY, Producer
JASPER AND THE BEANSTALK, Paramount. (Pal Puppetoon-Jasper Series): GEORGE PAL, Producer
LIFE WITH FEATHERS, Warner Bros. (Merrie Melodies): EDDIE SELZER, Producer
MIGHTY MOUSE IN GYPSY LIFE, 20th Century-Fox. (Terrytoon): PAUL TERRY, Producer
POET AND PEASANT, Universal. (Lantz Technicolor Cartune): WALTER LANTZ, Producer
QUIET PLEASE, Metro-Goldwyn-Mayer. (Tom & Jerry Series): FREDERICK QUIMBY, Producer
RIPPLING ROMANCE, Columbia. (Color Rhapsodies)

(One-reel)
ALONG THE RAINBOW TRAIL, 20th Century-Fox. (Movietone Adventure): EDMUND REEK, Producer
SCREEN SNAPSHOTS 25TH ANNIVERSARY, Columbia. (Screen Snapshots): RALPH STAUB, Producer
STAIRWAY TO LIGHT, Metro-Goldwyn-Mayer. (John Nesbitt Passing Parade): HERBERT MOULTON, Producer
STORY OF A DOG, Warner Bros. (Vitaphone Varieties): GORDON HOLLINGSHEAD, Producer
WHITE RHAPSODY, Paramount. (Sportlights): GRANTLAND RICE, Producer
YOUR NATIONAL GALLERY, Universal. (Variety Views): JOSEPH O'BRIEN and THOMAS MEAD, Producers

(Two-reel)
A GUN IN HIS HAND, Metro-Goldwyn-Mayer. (Crime Does Not Pay): CHESTER FRANKLIN, Producer.
THE JURY GOES ROUND 'N' ROUND, Columbia. (All Star Comedies): JULES WHITE, Producer
THE LITTLE WITCH, Paramount. (Musical Parade): GEORGE TEMPLETON, Producer
STAR IN THE NIGHT, Warner Bros. (Broadway Brevities): GORDON HOLLINGSHEAD, Producer

Documentary
(Short Subjects)
HITLER LIVES?, Warner Bros.
LIBRARY OF CONGRESS, Overseas Motion Picture Bureau, Office of War Information
TO THE SHORES OF IWO JIMA, U.S. Marine Corps

(Features)
THE LAST BOMB, U.S. Army Air Force
THE TRUE GLORY, Governments of Great Britain and USA

Special Effects
CAPTAIN EDDIE, 20th Century-Fox
Photographic: FRED SERSEN and SOL HALPRIN
Sound: ROGER HEMAN and HARRY LEONARD
SPELLBOUND, Selznick, UA
Photographic: JACK COSGROVE
Sound: No credits listed
THEY WERE EXPENDABLE, Metro-Goldwyn-Mayer
Photographic: A. ARNOLD GILLESPIE, DONALD JAHRAUS and R. A. MacDONALD
Sound: MICHAEL STEINORE
A THOUSAND AND ONE NIGHTS, Columbia
Photographic: L. W. BUTLER
Sound: RAY BOMBA

WONDER MAN, Goldwyn, RKO
Radio
Photographic: JOHN FULTON
Sound: A. W. JOHNS

Special Awards
WALTER WANGER for his six years
service as President of the Academy
of Motion Picture Arts and Sciences.
(special plaque)
PEGGY ANN GARNER, outstanding
child actress of 1945. (miniature
statuette)
THE HOUSE I LIVE IN, tolerance
short subject; produced by Frank
Ross and Mervyn LeRoy; directed by
Mervyn LeRoy; screenplay by Albert
Maltz; song *The House I Live In*
music by Earl Robinson, lyrics by
Lewis Allen; starring Frank Sinatra;
released by RKO Radio. (statuette)
REPUBLIC STUDIO, DANIEL J.
BLOOMBERG and the REPUBLIC
SOUND DEPARTMENT for the
building of an outstanding musical
scoring auditorium which provides
optimum recording conditions and

combines all elements of acoustic
and engineering design. (certificates)

Irving G. Thalberg Memorial Award
None

Scientific or Technical
Class I
None.

Class II
None.

Class III
LOREN L. RYDER, CHARLES R.
DAILY and the PARAMOUNT
STUDIO SOUND DEPARTMENT
for the design, construction and use
of the first dial controlled step-by-
step sound channel line-up and test
circuit
MICHAEL S. LESHING, BENJAMIN
C. ROBINSON, ARTHUR B. CHA-
TELAIN and ROBERT C. STE-
VENS of 20th Century-Fox Studio
and JOHN G. CAPSTAFF of Eastman Kodak Co. for the 20th Century-Fox film processing machine

1946

Nominations Announced: February 10, 1947
Awards Ceremony; March 13, 1947
Shrine Auditorium
(MC: Jack Benny)

Best Picture

THE BEST YEARS OF OUR LIVES, Goldwyn, RKO Radio
HENRY V, Rank-Two Cities, UA (British)
IT'S A WONDERFUL LIFE, Liberty, RKO Radio
THE RAZOR'S EDGE, 20th Century-Fox
THE YEARLING, Metro-Goldwyn-Mayer

Actor

FREDRIC MARCH in *The Best Years Of Our Lives*, Goldwyn, RKO Radio
LAURENCE OLIVIER in *Henry V*, J. Arthur Rank-Two Cities, UA (British)
LARRY PARKS in *The Jolson Story*, Columbia
GREGORY PECK in *The Yearling*, Metro-Goldwyn-Mayer
JAMES STEWART in *It's A Wonderful Life*, Liberty Films, RKO Radio

Actress

OLIVIA DE HAVILLAND in *To Each His Own*, Paramount
CELIA JOHNSON in *Brief Encounter*, Rank, U-I. (British)
JENNIFER JONES in *Duel In The Sun*, Selznick International
ROSALIND RUSSELL in *Sister Kenny*, RKO Radio
JANE WYMAN in *The Yearling*, Metro-Goldwyn-Mayer

LARGE CAPITAL LETTERS DENOTE WINNER

Supporting Actor

CHARLES COBURN in *The Green Years*, Metro-Goldwyn-Mayer
WILLIAM DEMAREST in *The Jolson Story*, Columbia
CLAUDE RAINS in *Notorious*, RKO Radio
HAROLD RUSSELL in *The Best Years Of Our Lives*, Goldwyn, RKO Radio
CLIFTON WEBB in *The Razor's Edge*, 20th Century-Fox

Supporting Actress

ETHEL BARRYMORE in *The Spiral Staircase*, RKO Radio
ANNE BAXTER in *The Razor's Edge*, 20th Century-Fox
LILLIAN GISH in *Duel In The Sun*, Selznick International
FLORA ROBSON in *Saratoga Trunk*, Warner Bros.
GALE SONDERGAARD in *Anna And The King Of Siam*, 20th Century-Fox

Directing

CLARENCE BROWN for *The Yearling*, Metro-Goldwyn-Mayer
FRANK CAPRA for *It's A Wonderful Life*, Liberty, RKO Radio
DAVID LEAN for *Brief Encounter*, Rank, U-I (British)
ROBERT SIODMAK for *The Killers*, Hellinger, Universal
WILLIAM WYLER for *The Best Years Of Our Lives*, Goldwyn, RKO Radio

Writing

(Original Story)

THE DARK MIRROR, Universal-International: VLADIMIR POZNER

THE STRANGE LOVE OF MARTHA IVERS, Wallis, Paramount: JACK PATRICK

THE STRANGER, International, RKO Radio: VICTOR TRIVAS

TO EACH HIS OWN, Paramount: CHARLES BRACKETT

VACATION FROM MARRIAGE, London Films, M-G-M (British): CLEMENCE DANE

(Original Screenplay)

THE BLUE DAHLIA, Paramount: RAYMOND CHANDLER

CHILDREN OF PARADISE, Pathe-Cinema, Tricolore (French): JACQUES PREVERT

NOTORIOUS, RKO Radio: BEN HECHT

THE ROAD TO UTOPIA, Paramount: NORMAN PANAMA and MELVIN FRANK

THE SEVENTH VEIL, Rank, Universal (British): MURIEL BOX and SYDNEY BOX

(Screenplay)

ANNA AND THE KING OF SIAM, 20th Century-Fox: SALLY BENSON and TALBOT JENNINGS

THE BEST YEARS OF OUR LIVES, Goldwyn, RKO Radio: ROBERT E. SHERWOOD

BRIEF ENCOUNTER, Rank, U-I (British): ANTHONY HAVELOCK-ALLAN, DAVID LEAN and RONALD NEAME

THE KILLERS, Hellinger, U-I: ANTHONY VEILLER

OPEN CITY, Minerva Films (Italian): SERGIO AMIDEI and F. FELLINI

Cinematography

(Black-and-White)

ANNA AND THE KING OF SIAM, 20th Century-Fox: ARTHUR MILLER

THE GREEN YEARS, Metro-Goldwyn-Mayer: GEORGE FOLSEY

(Color)

THE JOLSON STORY, Columbia: JOSEPH WALKER

THE YEARLING, Metro-Goldwyn-Mayer: CHARLES ROSHER, LEONARD SMITH and ARTHUR ARLING

Interior Decoration

(Black-and-White)

ANNA AND THE KING OF SIAM, 20th Century-Fox: LYLE WHEELER and WILLIAM DARLING

Interior Decoration: THOMAS LITTLE and FRANK E. HUGHES

KITTY, Paramount: HANS DREIER and WALTER TYLER

Interior Decoration: SAM COMER and RAY MOYER

THE RAZOR'S EDGE, 20th Century-Fox: RICHARD DAY and NATHAN JURAN

Interior Decoration: THOMAS LITTLE and PAUL S. FOX

(Color)

CAESAR AND CLEOPATRA, Rank, UA (British): JOHN BRYAN

Interior Decoration: No credits listed

HENRY V, Rank, UA (British): PAUL SHERIFF and CARMEN DILLON

Interior Decoration: No credits listed

THE YEARLING, Metro-Goldwyn-Mayer: CEDRIC GIBBONS and PAUL GROESSE

Interior Decoration: EDWIN B. WILLIS

Sound Recording

THE BEST YEARS OF OUR LIVES, Goldwyn, RKO Radio: GORDON SAWYER

IT'S A WONDERFUL LIFE, Liberty, RKO Radio: JOHN AALBERG

THE JOLSON STORY, Columbia:
JOHN LIVADARY

Film Editing
THE BEST YEARS OF OUR LIVES,
Goldwyn, RKO Radio: DANIEL
MANDELL
IT'S A WONDERFUL LIFE, Liberty, RKO
Radio: WILLIAM HORNBECK
THE JOLSON STORY, Columbia: WIL-
LIAM LYON
THE KILLERS, Hellinger, Universal:
ARTHUR HILTON
THE YEARLING, Metro-Goldwyn-
Mayer: HAROLD KRESS

Music
(Scoring of a Dramatic or Comedy Pic-
ture)
ANNA AND THE KING OF SIAM, 20th
Century-Fox: BERNARD HERRMANN
THE BEST YEARS OF OUR LIVES,
Goldwyn, RKO Radio: HUGO
FRIEDHOFER
HENRY V, Rank, UA (British): WILLIAM
WALTON
HUMORESQUE, Warner Bros.: FRANZ
WAXMAN
THE KILLERS, Universal: MIKLOS ROZSA
(Scoring of a Musical Picture)
BLUE SKIES, Paramount: ROBERT EM-
METT DOLAN
CENTENNIAL SUMMER, 20th Century-
Fox: ALFRED NEWMAN
THE HARVEY GIRLS, Metro-Goldwyn-
Mayer: LENNIE HAYTON
THE JOLSON STORY, Columbia:
MORRIS STOLOFF
NIGHT AND DAY, Warner Bros.: RAY
HEINDORF and MAX STEINER
(Best Song)
ALL THROUGH THE DAY from *Centen-
nial Summer*, 20th Century-Fox
Music by JEROME KERN. Lyrics by
OSCAR HAMMERSTEIN II

I CAN'T BEGIN TO TELL YOU from *The
Dolly Sisters*, 20th Century-Fox
Music by JAMES MONACO. Lyrics by
MACK GORDON
OLE BUTTERMILK SKY from *Canyon
Passage*, Wanger, Universal
Music by HOAGY CARMICHAEL.
Lyrics by JACK BROOKS
ON THE ATCHISON, TOPEKA AND
SANTA FE from *The Harvey Girls*,
Metro-Goldwyn-Mayer
Music by HARRY WARREN.
Lyrics by JOHNNY MERCER
YOU KEEP COMING BACK LIKE A SONG
from *Blue Skies*, Paramount
Music and Lyrics by IRVING BERLIN

Short Subjects
(Cartoons)
THE CAT CONCERTO, Metro-
Goldwyn-Maycr. (Tom & Jerry):
FREDERICK QUIMBY, Producer
CHOPIN'S MUSICAL MOMENTS, Univer-
sal. (Musical Miniatures): WALTER
LANTZ, Producer
JOHN HENRY AND THE INKY POO, Para-
mount. (Puppetoon): GEORGE PAL,
Producer
SQUATTER'S RIGHTS, Disney-RKO
Radio. (Mickey Mouse): WALT DIS-
NEY, Producer
WALKY TALKY HAWKY, Warner Bros.
(Merrie Melodies): EDWARD SELZER,
Producer

(One-reel)
DIVE-HI CHAMPS, Paramount. (Sport-
lights): JACK EATON, Producer
FACING YOUR DANGER, Warner
Bros. (Sports Parade): GORDON
HOLLINGSHEAD, Producer
GOLDEN HORSES, 20th Century-Fox.
(Movietone Sports Review): ED-
MUND REEK, Producer
SMART AS A FOX, Warner Bros. (Varie-
ties): GORDON HOLLINGSHEAD, Pro-
ducer

SURE CURES, Metro-Goldwyn-Mayer. (Pete Smith Specialty): PETE SMITH, Producer

(Two-reel)

A BOY AND HIS DOG, Warner Bros. (Featurettes): GORDON HOLLINGS-HEAD, Producer

COLLEGE QUEEN, Paramount. (Musical Parade): GEORGE TEMPLETON, Producer

HISS AND YELL, Columbia. (All Star Comedies): JULES WHITE, Producer

THE LUCKIEST GUY IN THE WORLD, Metro-Goldwyn-Mayer. (Two-reel Special): JERRY BRESLER, Producer

Documentary

(Short Subjects)

ATOMIC POWER, 20th Century-Fox

LIFE AT THE ZOO, Artkino

PARAMOUNT NEWS ISSUE #37, Paramount

SEEDS OF DESTINY, U.S. War Department

TRAFFIC WITH THE DEVIL, Metro-Goldwyn-Mayer

(No Features nominated this year)

Special Effects

BLITHE SPIRIT, Rank UA (British)
Visual: THOMAS HOWARD
Audible: No credit

A STOLEN LIFE, Warner Bros.
Visual: WILLIAM MCGANN
Audible: NATHAN LEVINSON

Special Awards

LAURENCE OLIVIER for his outstanding achievement as actor, producer and director in bringing *Henry V* to the screen. (statuette)

HAROLD RUSSELL for bringing hope and courage to his fellow veterans through his appearance in *The Best Years Of Our Lives*. (statuette)

ERNST LUBITSCH for his distinguished contributions to the art of the motion picture. (scroll)

CLAUDE JARMAN, JR., outstanding child actor of 1946. (miniature statuette)

Irving G. Thalberg Memorial Award

SAMUEL GOLDWYN

Scientific or Technical

Class I

None

Class II

None

Class III

HARLAN L. BAUMBACH and the PARAMOUNT WEST COAST LABORATORY for an improved method for the quantitative determination of hydroquinone and metol in photographic developing baths

HERBERT E. BRITT for the development and application of formulas and equipment for producing cloud and smoke effects

BURTON F. MILLER and the WARNER BROS. STUDIO SOUND and ELECTRICAL DEPARTMENTS for the design and construction of a motion picture arc lighting generator filter

CARL FAULKNER of the 20th Century-Fox Studio Sound Department for the reversed bias method, including a double bias method for light valve and galvanometer density recording

MOLE-RICHARDSON CO. for the Type 450 super high intensity carbon arc lamp

ARTHUR F. BLINN, ROBERT O. COOK, C. O. SLYFIELD and the WALT DISNEY STUDIO SOUND DEPARTMENT for the design and development of an audio finder and

track viewer for checking and locating noise in sound tracks
BURTON F. MILLER and the WARNER BROS. STUDIO SOUND DEPARTMENT for the design and application of an equalizer to eliminate relative spectral energy distortion in electronic compressors
MARTY MARTIN and HAL ADKINS of the RKO Radio Studio Miniature Department for the design and construction of equipment providing visual bullet effects
HAROLD NYE and the WARNER BROS. STUDIO ELECTRICAL DEPARTMENT for the development of the electronically controlled fire and gaslight effect

1947

Nominations Announced: February 15, 1948
Awards Ceremony: March 20, 1948
Shrine Auditorium

Best Picture

THE BISHOP'S WIFE, Goldwyn, RKO Radio

CROSSFIRE, RKO Radio

GENTLEMAN'S AGREEMENT, 20th Century-Fox

GREAT EXPECTATIONS, Rank-Cineguild, U-I (British)

MIRACLE ON 34TH STREET, 20th Century-Fox

Actor

RONALD COLMAN in *A Double Life*, Kanin, U-I

JOHN GARFIELD in *Body And Soul*, Enterprise, UA

GREGORY PECK in *Gentleman's Agreement*, 20th Century-Fox

WILLIAM POWELL in *Life With Father*, Warner Bros.

MICHAEL REDGRAVE in *Mourning Becomes Electra*, RKO Radio

Actress

JOAN CRAWFORD in *Possessed*, Warner Bros.

SUSAN HAYWARD in *Smash Up—The Story Of a Woman*, Wanger, U-I

DOROTHY MCGUIRE in *Gentleman's Agreement*, 20th Century-Fox

ROSALIND RUSSELL in *Mourning Becomes Electra*, RKO Radio

LORETTA YOUNG in *The Farmer's Daughter*, RKO Radio

Supporting Actor

CHARLES BICKFORD in *The Farmer's Daughter*, RKO Radio

LARGE CAPITAL LETTERS DENOTE WINNER

THOMAS GOMEZ in *Ride The Pink Horse*, Universal-International

EDMUND GWENN in *Miracle On 34th Street*, 20th Century-Fox

ROBERT RYAN in *Crossfire*, RKO Radio

RICHARD WIDMARK in *Kiss Of Death*, 20th Century-Fox

Supporting Actress

ETHEL BARRYMORE in *The Paradine Case*, Selznick

GLORIA GRAHAME in *Crossfire*, RKO Radio

CELESTE HOLM in *Gentleman's Agreement*, 20th Century-Fox

MARJORIE MAIN in *The Egg And I*, Universal-International

ANNE REVERE in *Gentleman's Agreement*, 20th Century-Fox

Directing

GEORGE CUKOR for *A Double Life*, Kanin, U-I

EDWARD DMYTRYK for *Crossfire*, RKO Radio

ELIA KAZAN for *Gentleman's Agreement*, 20th Century-Fox

HENRY KOSTER for *The Bishop's Wife*, Goldwyn, RKO Radio

DAVID LEAN for *Great Expectations*, Rank-Cineguild, U-I (British)

Writing

(Original Story)

A CAGE OF NIGHTINGALES, Gaumont, Lopert Films (French): GEORGES CHAPEROT and RENE WHEELER

IT HAPPENED ON FIFTH AVENUE, Roy

Del Ruth, Allied Artists: HERBERT
CLYDE LEWIS and FREDERICK STE-
PHANI
KISS OF DEATH, 20th Century-Fox:
ELEAZAR LIPSKY
MIRACLE ON 34TH STREET, 20th
Century-Fox: VALENTINE
DAVIES
SMASH-UP—THE STORY OF A WOMAN,
Wanger, U-I: DOROTHY PARKER and
FRANK CAVETT

(Original Screenplay)
THE BACHELOR AND THE
BOBBY-SOXER, RKO Radio: SID-
NEY SHELDON
BODY AND SOUL, Enterprise, UA:
ABRAHAM POLONSKY
A DOUBLE LIFE, Kanin Prod., U-I:
RUTH GORDON and GARSON KANIN
MONSIEUR VERDOUX, Chaplin, UA:
CHARLES CHAPLIN
SHOESHINE, Lopert Films (Italian):
SERGIO AMIDEI, ADOLFO FRANCI, C.
G. VIOLA and CESARE ZAVATTINI

(Screenplay)
BOOMERANG!, 20th Century-Fox:
RICHARD MURPHY
CROSSFIRE, RKO Radio: JOHN PAXTON
GENTLEMAN'S AGREEMENT, 20th Cen-
tury-Fox: MOSS HART
GREAT EXPECTATIONS, Rank-Cineguild,
U-I (British): DAVID LEAN, RONALD
NEAME and ANTHONY HAVELOCK-
ALLAN
MIRACLE ON 34TH STREET, 20th
Century-Fox: GEORGE SEATON

Cinematography
(Black-and-White)
THE GHOST AND MRS. MUIR, 20th Cen-
tury-Fox: CHARLES LANG, JR.
GREAT EXPECTATIONS, Rank-
Cineguild, U-I (British): GUY
GREEN
GREEN DOLPHIN STREET, Metro-
Goldwyn-Mayer: GEORGE FOLSEY

(Color)
BLACK NARCISSUS, Rank-Archers,
U-I (British): JACK CARDIFF
LIFE WITH FATHER, Warner Bros.:
PEVERELL MARLEY and WILLIAM V.
SKALL
MOTHER WORE TIGHTS, 20th Century-
Fox: HARRY JACKSON

Art Direction—Set Decoration
(Prior to 1947 Known as In-
terior Decoration)
(Black-and-White)
THE FOXES OF HARROW, 20th Century-
Fox: LYLE WHEELER and MAURICE
RANSFORD
Set Decoration: THOMAS LITTLE and
PAUL S. FOX
GREAT EXPECTATIONS, Rank-
Cineguild, U-I (British): JOHN
BRYAN
Set Decoration: WILFRED SHIN-
GLETON
(Color)
BLACK NARCISSUS, Rank-Archers,
U-I (British): ALFRED JUNGE
Set Decoration: ALFRED JUNGE
LIFE WITH FATHER, Warner Bros.:
ROBERT M. HAAS
Set Decoration: GEORGE JAMES HOP-
KINS

Sound Recording
THE BISHOP'S WIFE, Goldwyn,
RKO Radio: GOLDWYN SOUND
DEPARTMENT
GREEN DOLPHIN STREET, Metro-
Goldwyn-Mayer: METRO-GOLDWYN-
MAYER SOUND DEPARTMENT
T-MEN, Reliance Pictures: Eagle-Lion,
SOUND SERVICES, INC.

Film Editing
THE BISHOP'S WIFE, Goldwyn, RKO
Radio: MONICA COLLINGWOOD
BODY AND SOUL, Enterprise, UA:

FRANCIS LYON and ROBERT PARRISH

GENTLEMAN'S AGREEMENT, 20th Century-Fox: HARMON JONES

GREEN DOLPHIN STREET, Metro-Goldwyn-Mayer: GEORGE WHITE

ODD MAN OUT, Rank-Two Cities, U-I (British): FERGUS MCDONNELL

Music

(Scoring of a Dramatic or Comedy Picture)

THE BISHOP'S WIFE, Goldwyn, RKO Radio: HUGO FRIEDHOFER

CAPTAIN FROM CASTILE, 20th Century-Fox: ALFRED NEWMAN

A DOUBLE LIFE, Kanin, U-I: MIKLOS ROZSA

FOREVER AMBER, 20th Century-Fox: DAVID RAKSIN

LIFE WITH FATHER, Warner Bros.: MAX STEINER

(Scoring of a Musical Picture)

FIESTA, Metro-Goldwyn-Mayer: JOHNNY GREEN

MOTHER WORE TIGHTS, 20th Century-Fox: ALFRED NEWMAN

MY WILD IRISH ROSE, Warner Bros.: RAY HEINDORF and MAX STEINER

ROAD TO RIO, Hope-Crosby, Paramount: ROBERT EMMETT DOLAN

SONG OF THE SOUTH, Disney, RKO Radio: DANIELE AMFITHEATROF, PAUL J. SMITH and CHARLES WOLCOTT

(Best Song)

A GAL IN CALICO from *The Time, Place And The Girl,* Warner Bros.
Music by ARTHUR SCHWARTZ. Lyrics by LEO ROBIN

I WISH I DIDN'T LOVE YOU SO from *The Perils Of Pauline,* Paramount
Music and Lyrics by FRANK LOESSER

PASS THAT PEACE PIPE from *Good News,* Metro-Goldwyn-Mayer
Music and Lyrics by RALPH BLANE, HUGH MARTIN and ROGER EDENS

YOU DO from *Mother Wore Tights,* 20th Century-Fox
Music by JOSEF MYROW. Lyrics by MACK GORDON

ZIP-A-DEE-DOO-DAH from *Song Of The South,* Disney-RKO Radio
Music by ALLIE WRUBEL. Lyrics by RAY GILBERT

Short Subjects

(Cartoons)

CHIP AN' DALE, Walt Disney, RKO Radio. (Donald Duck): WALT DISNEY, Producer

DR. JEKYLL AND MR. MOUSE, Metro-Goldwyn-Mayer. (Tom & Jerry): FREDERICK QUIMBY, Producer

PLUTO'S BLUE NOTE, Walt Disney, RKO Radio. (Pluto): WALT DISNEY, Producer

TUBBY THE TUBA, Paramount. (George Pal Puppetoon): GEORGE PAL, Producer

TWEETIE PIE, Warner Bros. (Merrie Melodies): EDWARD SELZER, Producer

(One-reel)

BROOKLYN, U.S.A., Universal-International. (Variety Series): THOMAS MEAD, Producer

GOODBYE MISS TURLOCK, Metro-Goldwyn-Mayer. (John Nesbitt Passing Parade): HERBERT MOULTON, Producer

MOON ROCKETS, Paramount. (Popular Science): JERRY FAIRBANKS, Producer

NOW YOU SEE IT, Metro-Goldwyn-Mayer: PETE SMITH, Producer

SO YOU WANT TO BE IN PICTURES, Warner Bros. (Joe McDoakes): GORDON HOLLINGSHEAD, Producer

(Two-reel)

CHAMPAGNE FOR TWO, Paramount. (Musical Parade Featurette): HARRY GREY, Producer

CLIMBING THE MATTERHORN, Monogram. (Color): IRVING ALLEN, Producer

FIGHT OF THE WILD STALLIONS, Universal-International. (Special): THOMAS MEAD, Producer

GIVE US THE EARTH, Metro-Goldwyn-Mayer. (Special): HERBERT MORGAN, Producer

A VOICE IS BORN, Columbia. (Musical Featurette): BEN BLAKE, Producer

Documentary

(Short Subjects)

FIRST STEPS, United Nations Division of Films and Visual Education

PASSPORT TO NOWHERE, RKO Radio (This Is America Series): FREDERIC ULLMAN, JR., Producer

SCHOOL IN THE MAILBOX, Australian News and Information Bureau

(Features)

DESIGN FOR DEATH, RKO Radio: SID ROGELL, Executive Producer; THERON WARTH and RICHARD O. FLEISCHER, Producers

JOURNEY INTO MEDICINE, U.S. Department of State, Office of Information and Educational Exchange

THE WORLD IS RICH, British Information Services: PAUL ROTHA, Producer

Special Effects

GREEN DOLPHIN STREET, Metro-Goldwyn-Mayer
Visual: A. ARNOLD GILLESPIE and WARREN NEWCOMBE
Audible: DOUGLAS SHEARER and MICHAEL STEINORE

UNCONQUERED, Paramount
Visual: FARCIOT EDOUART, DEVEREUX JENNINGS, GORDON JENNINGS, WALLACE KELLEY and PAUL LERPAE
Audible: GEORGE DUTTON

Special Awards

JAMES BASKETTE for his able and heart-warming characterization of Uncle Remus, friend and story teller to the children of the world. (statuette)

BILL AND COO, in which artistry and patience blended in a novel and entertaining use of the medium of motion pictures. (plaque)

SHOESHINE—the high quality of this motion picture, brought to eloquent life in a country scarred by war, is proof to the world that the creative spirit can triumph over adversity. (statuette)

COLONEL WILLIAM N. SELIG, ALBERT E. SMITH, THOMAS ARMAT and GEORGE K. SPOOR, (one of) the small group of pioneers whose belief in a new medium, and whose contributions to its development, blazed the trail along which the motion picture has progressed, in their lifetime, from obscurity to world-wide acclaim. (statuettes)

Irving G. Thalberg Memorial Award
NONE

Scientific or Technical
Class I
None

Class II

C. C. DAVIS and ELECTRICAL RESEARCH PRODUCTS, DIVISION OF WESTERN ELECTRIC CO., for the development and application of an improved film drive filter mechanism.

C. R. DAILY and the PARAMOUNT STUDIO FILM LABORATORY, STILL and ENGINEERING DEPARTMENTS for the development and first practical application to motion picture and still photography of a method of increasing film speed as first suggested to the industry by E. I. duPont de Nemours & Co.

Class III

NATHAN LEVINSON and the WARNER BROS. STUDIO SOUND DEPARTMENT for the design and construction of a constant-speed sound editing machine

FARCIOT EDOUART, C. R. DAILY, HAL CORL, H. G. CARTWRIGHT and the PARAMOUNT STUDIO TRANSPARENCY and ENGI-NEERING DEPARTMENTS for the first application of a special anti-solarizing glass to high intensity background and spot arc projectors

FRED PONEDEL of Warner Bros. Studio for pioneering the fabrication and practical application to motion picture color photography of large translucent photographic backgrounds

KURT SINGER and the RCA-VICTOR DIVISION of the RADIO CORPORATION OF AMERICA for the design and development of a continuously variable band elimination filter

JAMES GIBBONS of Warner Bros. Studio for the development and production of large dyed plastic filters for motion picture photography.

1948

Nominations Announced: February 10, 1949
Awards Ceremony: March 24, 1949
Academy Award Theatre
(MC: Robert Montgomery)

Best Picture

HAMLET, Rank-Two Cities, U-I (British)

JOHNNY BELINDA, Warner Bros.

THE RED SHOES, Rank-Archers, Eagle-Lion (British)

THE SNAKE PIT, 20th Century-Fox

TREASURE OF SIERRA MADRE, Warner Bros.

Actor

LEW AYRES in *Johnny Belinda*, Warner Bros.

MONTGOMERY CLIFT in *The Search*, Praesens Films, M-G-M. (Swiss)

DAN DAILEY in *When My Baby Smiles At Me*, 20th Century-Fox

LAURENCE OLIVIER in *Hamlet*, J. Arthur Rank-Two Cities, U-I. (British)

CLIFTON WEBB in *Sitting Pretty*, 20th Century-Fox

Actress

INGRID BERGMAN in *Joan Of Arc*, Sierra, RKO Radio

OLIVIA DE HAVILLAND in *The Snake Pit*, 20th Century-Fox

IRENE DUNNE in *I Remember Mama*, RKO Radio

BARBARA STANWYCK in *Sorry, Wrong Number*, Wallis, Paramount

JANE WYMAN in *Johnny Belinda*, Warner Bros.

LARGE CAPITAL LETTERS DENOTE WINNER

Supporting Actor

CHARLES BICKFORD in *Johnny Belinda*, Warner Bros.

JOSE FERRER in *Joan Of Arc*, Sierra, RKO Radio

OSCAR HOMOLKA in *I Remember Mama* RKO Radio

WALTER HUSTON in *Treasure Of Sierra Madre*, Warner Bros.

CECIL KELLAWAY in *The Luck Of The Irish*, 20th Century-Fox

Supporting Actress

BARBARA BEL GEDDES in *I Remember Mama*, RKO Radio

ELLEN CORBY in *I Remember Mama*, RKO Radio

AGNES MOOREHEAD in *Johnny Belinda*, Warner Bros.

JEAN SIMMONS in *Hamlet*, Rank-Two Cities, U-I. (British)

CLAIRE TREVOR in *Key Largo*, Warner Bros.

Directing

JOHN HUSTON for *Treasure Of Sierra Madre*, Warner Bros.

ANATOLE LITVAK for *The Snake Pit*, 20th Century-Fox

JEAN NEGULESCO for *Johnny Belinda*, Warner Bros.

LAURENCE OLIVIER for *Hamlet*, Rank-Two Cities, U-I (British)

FRED ZINNEMANN for *The Search*, Praesens Films, M-G-M (Swiss)

Writing

(Motion Picture Story)

THE LOUISIANA STORY, Robert Flaherty, Lopert: FRANCES FLAHERTY and ROBERT FLAHERTY

THE NAKED CITY, Hellinger, U-I: MALVIN WALD

RED RIVER, Monterey Productions, UA: BORDEN CHASE

THE RED SHOES, Rank-Archers, Eagle-Lion (British): EMERIC PRESSBURGER

THE SEARCH, Praesens Films, M-G-M (Swiss): RICHARD SCHWEIZER and DAVID WECHSLER

(Screenplay)

A FOREIGN AFFAIR, Paramount: CHARLES BRACKETT, BILLY WILDER and RICHARD L. BREEN

JOHNNY BELINDA, Warner Bros.: IRMGARD VON CUBE and ALLEN VINCENT

THE SEARCH, Praesens Films, M-G-M (Swiss): RICHARD SCHWEIZER and DAVID WECHSLER

THE SNAKE PIT, 20th Century-Fox: FRANK PARTOS and MILLEN BRAND

TREASURE OF SIERRA MADRE, Warner Bros.: JOHN HUSTON

Cinematography

(Black-and-White)

A FOREIGN AFFAIR, Paramount: CHARLES B. LANG, JR.

I REMEMBER MAMA, RKO Radio: NICHOLAS MUSURACA

JOHNNY BELINDA, Warner Bros.: TED MCCORD

THE NAKED CITY, Hellinger, U-I: WILLIAM DANIELS

PORTRAIT OF JENNIE, The Selznick Studio: JOSEPH AUGUST

(Color)

GREEN GRASS OF WYOMING, 20th Century-Fox: CHARLES G. CLARKE

JOAN OF ARC, Sierra Pictures, RKO Radio: JOSEPH VALENTINE, WILLIAM V. SKALL and WINTON HOCH

THE LOVES OF CARMEN, Beckworth Corporation, Columbia: WILLIAM SNYDER

THE THREE MUSKETEERS, Metro-Goldwyn-Mayer: ROBERT PLANCK

Art Direction—Set Decoration

(Black-and-White)

HAMLET, Rank-Two Cities, U-I (British): ROGER K. FURSE
Set Decoration: CARMEN DILLON

JOHNNY BELINDA, Warner Bros.: ROBERT HAAS
Set Decoration: WILLIAM WALLACE

(Color)

JOAN OF ARC, Sierra Pictures, RKO Radio: RICHARD DAY
Set Decoration: EDWIN CASEY ROBERTS and JOSEPH KISH

THE RED SHOES, Rank-Archers, Eagle-Lion (British): HEIN HECKROTH
Set Decoration: ARTHUR LAWSON

Sound Recording

JOHNNY BELINDA, Warner Bros.: WARNER BROS. SOUND DEPARTMENT

MOONRISE, Marshall Grant Prods., Republic: REPUBLIC SOUND DEPARTMENT

THE SNAKE PIT, 20th Century-Fox: 20TH CENTURY-FOX SOUND DEPARTMENT

Film Editing

JOAN OF ARC, Sierra Pictures, RKO Radio: FRANK SULLIVAN

JOHNNY BELINDA, Warner Bros.: DAVID WEISBART

THE NAKED CITY, Hellinger, U-I: PAUL WEATHERWAX

RED RIVER, Monterey Prods., UA: CHRISTIAN NYBY

THE RED SHOES, Rank-Archers, Eagle-Lion (British): REGINALD MILLS

Music

(Scoring of a Dramatic or Comedy Picture)

HAMLET, Rank-Two Cities, U-I (British): WILLIAM WALTON

JOAN OF ARC, Sierra Pictures, RKO Radio: HUGO FRIEDHOFER

JOHNNY BELINDA, Warner Bros.: MAX STEINER

THE RED SHOES, Rank-Archers-Eagle-Lion (British): BRIAN EASDALE

THE SNAKE PIT, 20th Century-Fox: ALFRED NEWMAN

(Scoring of a Musical Picture)

EASTER PARADE, Metro-Goldwyn-Mayer: JOHNNY GREEN and ROGER EDENS

THE EMPEROR WALTZ, Paramount: VICTOR YOUNG

THE PIRATE, Metro-Goldwyn-Mayer: LENNIE HAYTON

ROMANCE ON THE HIGH SEAS, Curtiz, Warner Bros.: RAY HEINDORF

WHEN MY BABY SMILES AT ME, 20th Century-Fox: ALFRED NEWMAN

(Best Song)

BUTTONS AND BOWS from *The Paleface,* Paramount
Music and Lyrics by JAY LIVINGSTON and RAY EVANS

FOR EVERY MAN THERE'S A WOMAN from *Casbah,* Marston Pictures, U-I
Music by HAROLD ARLEN. Lyrics by LEO ROBIN

IT'S MAGIC from *Romance On The High Seas,* Curtiz, Warner Bros.
Music by JULE STYNE. Lyrics by SAMMY CAHN

THIS IS THE MOMENT from *That Lady In Ermine,* 20th Century-Fox
Music by FREDERICK HOLLANDER. Lyrics by LEO ROBIN

THE WOODY WOODPECKER SONG from *Wet Blanket Policy,* Walter Lantz, UA (Cartoon)
Music and Lyrics by RAMEY IDRISS and GEORGE TIBBLES

Costume Design

(New Category)

(Black-and-White)

B. F.'S DAUGHTER, Metro-Goldwyn-Mayer: IRENE

HAMLET, Rank-Two Cities, U-I (British): ROGER K. FURSE

(Color)

THE EMPEROR WALTZ, Paramount: EDITH HEAD and GILE STEELE

JOAN OF ARC, Sierra, RKO Radio: DOROTHY JEAKINS and KARINSKA

Short Subjects

(Cartoons)

THE LITTLE ORPHAN, Metro-Goldwyn-Mayer. (Tom & Jerry): FRED QUIMBY, Producer

MICKEY AND THE SEAL, Walt Disney, RKO Radio. (Pluto): WALT DISNEY, Producer

MOUSE WRECKERS, Warner Bros. (Looney Tunes): EDWARD SELZER, Producer

ROBIN HOODLUM, United Productions Of America, Columbia. (Fox & Crow): UNITED PRODUCTIONS OF AMERICA, Producer

TEA FOR TWO HUNDRED, Walt Disney, RKO Radio. (Donald Duck): WALT DISNEY, Producer

(One-reel)

ANNIE WAS A WONDER, Metro-Goldwyn-Mayer. (John Nesbitt Passing Parade): HERBERT MOULTON, Producer

CINDERELLA HORSE, Warner Bros. (Sports Parade): GORDON HOLLINGS-HEAD, Producer

SO YOU WANT TO BE ON THE RADIO, Warner Bros. (Joe McDoakes): GORDON HOLLINGSHEAD, Producer

SYMPHONY OF A CITY, 20th Century-Fox. (Movietone Specialty): EDMUND H. REEK, Producer

YOU CAN'T WIN, Metro-Goldwyn-Mayer. (Pete Smith Specialty): PETE SMITH, Producer

(Two-reel)

CALGARY STAMPEDE, Warner Bros. (Technicolor Special): GORDON HOLLINGSHEAD, Producer

GOING TO BLAZES, Metro-Goldwyn-Mayer. (Special): HERBERT MORGAN, Producer

SAMBA-MANIA, Paramount. (Musical Parade): HARRY GREY, Producer

SEAL ISLAND, Walt Disney, RKO Radio. (True Life Adventure Series): WALT DISNEY, Producer.

SNOW CAPERS, Universal-International. (Special Series): THOMAS MEAD, Producer

Documentary

(Short Subjects)

HEART TO HEART, Fact Film Organization: HERBERT MORGAN, Producer

OPERATION VITTLES, U.S. Army Air Force

TOWARD INDEPENDENCE, U.S. Army

(Features)

THE QUIET ONE, Mayer-Burstyn: JANICE LOEB, Producer

THE SECRET LAND, U.S. Navy, M-G-M: O. O. DULL, Producer

Special Effects

DEEP WATERS, 20th Century-Fox Visual: RALPH HAMMERAS, FRED SERSEN and EDWARD SNYDER Audible: ROGER HEMAN

PORTRAIT OF JENNIE, The Selznick Studio Visual: PAUL EAGLER, J. McMILLAN JOHNSON, RUSSELL SHEARMAN and CLARENCE SLIFER Audible: CHARLES FREEMAN and JAMES G. STEWART

Special Awards

MONSIEUR VINCENT (French)— voted by the Academy Board of Governors as the most outstanding foreign language film released in the United States during 1948. (statuette)

IVAN JANDL, for the outstanding juvenile performance of 1948 in *The Search*. (miniature statuette)

SID GRAUMAN, master showman, who raised the standard of exhibition of motion pictures. (statuette)

ADOLPH ZUKOR, a man who has been called the father of the feature film in America, for his services to the industry over a period of forty years. (statuette)

WALTER WANGER for distinguished service to the industry in adding to its moral stature in the world community by his production of the picture *Joan Of Arc*. (statuette)

Irving G. Thalberg Memorial Award

JERRY WALD

Scientific or Technical

Class I

None

Class II

VICTOR CACCIALANZA, MAURICE AYERS and the PARAMOUNT STUDIO SET CONSTRUCTION DEPARTMENT for

the development and application of "Paralite," a new lightweight plaster process for set construction
NICK KALTEN, LOUIS J. WITTI and the 20TH CENTURY-FOX STUDIO MECHANICAL EFFECTS DE-PARTMENT for a process of preserving and flame-proofing foliage

Class III
MARTY MARTIN, JACK LANNON, RUSSELL SHEARMAN and the RKO RADIO STUDIO SPECIAL EFFECTS DEPARTMENT for the development of a new method of simulating falling snow on motion picture sets
A. J. MORAN and the WARNER BROS. STUDIO ELECTRICAL DEPARTMENT for a method of remote control for shutters on motion picture arc lighting equipment.

1949

Nominations Announced: February 14, 1950
Awards Ceremony: March 23, 1950
RKO Pantages Theatre
(MC: Paul Douglas)

Best Picture

ALL THE KING'S MEN, Rossen, Columbia

BATTLEGROUND, Metro-Goldwyn-Mayer

THE HEIRESS, Paramount

A LETTER TO THREE WIVES, 20th Century-Fox

TWELVE O'CLOCK HIGH, 20th Century-Fox

Actor

BRODERICK CRAWFORD in *All The King's Men*, Robert Rossen, Columbia

KIRK DOUGLAS in *Champion*, Screen Plays Corp., UA

GREGORY PECK in *Twelve O'Clock High*, 20th Century-Fox

RICHARD TODD in *The Hasty Heart*, Warner Bros.

JOHN WAYNE in *Sands Of Iwo Jima*, Republic

Actress

JEANNE CRAIN in *Pinky*, 20th Century-Fox

OLIVIA DE HAVILLAND in *The Heiress*, Paramount

SUSAN HAYWARD in *My Foolish Heart*, Goldwyn, RKO Radio

DEBORAH KERR in *Edward, My Son*, Metro-Goldwyn-Mayer

LORETTA YOUNG in *Come To The Stable*, 20th Century-Fox

LARGE CAPITAL LETTERS DENOTE WINNER

Supporting Actor

JOHN IRELAND in *All The King's Men*, Rossen, Columbia

DEAN JAGGER in *Twelve O'Clock High*, 20th Century-Fox

ARTHUR KENNEDY in *Champion*, Screen Plays Corp., UA

RALPH RICHARDSON in *The Heiress*, Paramount

JAMES WHITMORE in *Battleground*, Metro-Goldwyn-Mayer

Supporting Actress

ETHEL BARRYMORE in *Pinky*, 20th Century-Fox

CELESTE HOLM in *Come To The Stable*, 20th Century-Fox

ELSA LANCHESTER in *Come To The Stable*, 20th Century-Fox

MERCEDES McCAMBRIDGE in *All The King's Men*, Rossen, Columbia

ETHEL WATERS in *Pinky*, 20th Century-Fox

Directing

JOSEPH L. MANKIEWICZ for *A Letter To Three Wives*, 20th Century-Fox

CAROL REED for *The Fallen Idol*, London Films, SRO (British)

ROBERT ROSSEN for *All The King's Men*, Rossen, Columbia

WILLIAM A. WELLMAN for *Battleground*, Metro-Goldwyn-Mayer

WILLIAM WYLER for *The Heiress*, Paramount

Writing

(Motion Picture Story)

COME TO THE STABLE, 20th Century-
Fox: CLARE BOOTHE LUCE

IT HAPPENS EVERY SPRING, 20th Century-Fox: SHIRLEY W. SMITH and
VALENTINE DAVIES

SANDS OF IWO JIMA, Republic: HARRY
BROWN

THE STRATTON STORY, Metro-
Goldwyn-Mayer: DOUGLAS MOR-
ROW

WHITE HEAT, Warner Bros.: VIRGINIA
KELLOGG

(Screenplay)

ALL THE KING'S MEN, A Robert Rossen
Prod., Columbia: ROBERT ROSSEN

THE BICYCLE THIEF, De Sica, Mayer-
Burstyn (Italian): CESARE ZAVATTINI

CHAMPION, Screen Plays Corp., UA:
CARL FOREMAN

THE FALLEN IDOL, London Films, SRO
(British): GRAHAM GREENE

A LETTER TO THREE WIVES, 20th
Century-Fox: JOSEPH L. MANKIE-
WICZ

(Story and Screenplay)

BATTLEGROUND, Metro-Goldwyn-
Mayer: ROBERT PIROSH

JOLSON SINGS AGAIN, Columbia: SID-
NEY BUCHMAN

PAISAN, Roberto Rossellini, Mayer-
Burstyn (Italian): ALFRED HAYES,
FEDERICO FELLINI, SERGIO AMIDEI,
MARCELLO PAGLIERO and ROBERTO
ROSSELLINI

PASSPORT TO PIMLICO, Rank-Ealing,
Eagle-Lion (British): T. E. B. CLARKE

THE QUIET ONE, Film Documents,
Mayer-Burstyn: HELEN LEVITT,
JANICE LOEB and SIDNEY MEYERS

Cinematography

(Black-and-White)

BATTLEGROUND, Metro-Goldwyn-
Mayer: PAUL C. VOGEL

CHAMPION, Screen Plays Corp., UA:
FRANK PLANER

COME TO THE STABLE, 20th Century-
Fox: JOSEPH LaSHELLE

THE HEIRESS, Paramount: LEO TOVER

PRINCE OF FOXES, 20th Century-Fox:
LEON SHAMROY

(Color)

THE BARKLEYS OF BROADWAY, Metro-
Goldwyn-Mayer: HARRY STRADLING

JOLSON SINGS AGAIN, Columbia: WIL-
LIAM SNYDER

LITTLE WOMEN, Metro-Goldwyn-
Mayer: ROBERT PLANCK and
CHARLES SCHOENBAUM

SAND, 20th Century-Fox: CHARLES G.
CLARKE

SHE WORE A YELLOW RIBBON,
Argosy, RKO Radio: WINTON
HOCH

Art Direction—Set Decoration

(Black-and-White)

COME TO THE STABLE, 20th Century-
Fox: LYLE WHEELER and JOSEPH C.
WRIGHT
Set Decoration: THOMAS LITTLE and
PAUL S. FOX

THE HEIRESS, Paramount: JOHN
MEEHAN and HARRY HORNER
Set Decoration: EMILE KURI

MADAME BOVARY, Metro-Goldwyn-
Mayer: CEDRIC GIBBONS and JACK
MARTIN SMITH
Set Decoration: EDWIN B. WILLIS and
RICHARD A. PEFFERLE

(Color)

ADVENTURES OF DON JUAN, Warner
Bros.: EDWARD CARRERE
Set Decoration: LYLE REIFSNIDER

LITTLE WOMEN, Metro-Goldwyn-
Mayer: CEDRIC GIBBONS and
PAUL GROESSE
Set Decoration: EDWIN B. WILLIS
and JACK D. MOORE

SARABAND, Rank-Ealing, Eagle-Lion (British): JIM MORAHAN, WILLIAM KELLNER and MICHAEL RELPH
Set Decoration: No credits listed

Sound Recording

ONCE MORE, MY DARLING, Neptune Films, U-I: UNIVERSAL-INTERNATIONAL SOUND DEPARTMENT
SANDS OF IWO JIMA, Republic: REPUBLIC SOUND DEPARTMENT
TWELVE O'CLOCK HIGH, 20th Century-Fox: 20TH CENTURY-FOX SOUND DEPARTMENT

Film Editing

ALL THE KING'S MEN, Rossen Prod., Columbia: ROBERT PARRISH and AL CLARK
BATTLEGROUND, Metro-Goldwyn-Mayer: JOHN DUNNING
CHAMPION, Screen Plays Corp., UA: HARRY GERSTAD
SANDS OF IWO JIMA, Republic: RICHARD L. VAN ENGER
THE WINDOW, RKO Radio: FREDERIC KNUDTSON

Music

(Scoring of a Dramatic or Comedy Picture)
BEYOND THE FOREST, Warner Bros.: MAX STEINER
CHAMPION, Screen Plays Corp., UA: DIMITRI TIOMKIN
THE HEIRESS, Paramount: AARON COPLAND

(Scoring of a Musical Picture)
JOLSON SINGS AGAIN, Sidney Buchman, Columbia: MORRIS STOLOFF and GEORGE DUNING
LOOK FOR THE SILVER LINING, Warner Bros.: RAY HEINDORF
ON THE TOWN, Metro-Goldwyn-Mayer: ROGER EDENS and LENNIE HAYTON

(Best Song)
BABY, IT'S COLD OUTSIDE from *Neptune's Daughter,* Metro-Goldwyn-Mayer
Music and Lyrics by FRANK LOESSER
IT'S A GREAT FEELING from *It's A Great Feeling,* Warner Bros.
Music by JULE STYNE. Lyrics by SAMMY CAHN
LAVENDER BLUE from *So Dear To My Heart,* Disney-RKO Radio
Music by ELIOT DANIEL. Lyrics by LARRY MOREY
MY FOOLISH HEART from *My Foolish Heart,* Goldwyn-RKO Radio
Music by VICTOR YOUNG. Lyrics by NED WASHINGTON
THROUGH A LONG AND SLEEPLESS NIGHT from *Come To The Stable,* 20th Century-Fox
Music by ALFRED NEWMAN. Lyrics by MACK GORDON

Costume Design

(Black-and-White)
THE HEIRESS, Paramount: EDITH HEAD and GILE STEELE
PRINCE OF FOXES, 20th Century-Fox: VITTORIO NINO NOVARESE

(Color)
ADVENTURES OF DON JUAN, Warner Bros.: LEAH RHODES, TRAVILLA and MARJORIE BEST
MOTHER IS A FRESHMAN, 20th Century-Fox: KAY NELSON

Short Subjects

(Cartoons)
FOR SCENT-IMENTAL REASONS, Warner Bros. (Looney Tunes): EDWARD SELZER, Producer
HATCH UP YOUR TROUBLES, Metro-Goldwyn-Mayer. (Tom & Jerry): FRED QUIMBY, Producer

MAGIC FLUKE, United Productions of America, Columbia. (Fox & Crow): STEPHEN BOSUSTOW, Producer

TOY TINKERS, Walt Disney, RKO Radio: WALT DISNEY, Producer

(One-reel)

AQUATIC HOUSE-PARTY, Paramount. (Grantland Rice Sportlights): JACK EATON, Producer

ROLLER DERBY GIRL, Paramount. (Pacemaker): JUSTIN HERMAN, Producer

SO YOU THINK YOU'RE NOT GUILTY, Warner Bros. (Joe McDoakes): GORDON HOLLINGSHEAD, Producer

SPILLS AND CHILLS, Warner Bros. (Black-and-White Sports Review): WALTON C. AMENT, Producer

WATER TRIX, Metro-Goldwyn-Mayer. (Pete Smith Specialty): PETE SMITH, Producer

(Two-reel)

BOY AND THE EAGLE, RKO Radio: WILLIAM LASKY, Producer

CHASE OF DEATH, Irving Allen Productions. (Color Series): IRVING ALLEN, Producer

THE GRASS IS ALWAYS GREENER, Warner Bros. (Black-and-White): GORDON HOLLINGSHEAD, Producer

SNOW CARNIVAL, Warner Bros. (Technicolor): GORDON HOLLINGSHEAD, Producer

VAN GOGH, Canton-Weiner: GASTON DIEHL and ROBERT HAESSENS, Producers

Documentary

(Short Subjects, *Two Winners*)

A CHANCE TO LIVE, March of Time, 20th Century-Fox: RICHARD DE ROCHEMONT, Producer

1848, A. F. Films, Inc.: FRENCH CINEMA GENERAL COOPERATIVE, Producer

THE RISING TIDE, National Film Board of Canada: ST. FRANCIS-XAVIER UNIVERSITY (NOVA SCOTIA), Producer

SO MUCH FOR SO LITTLE, Warner Bros. Cartoons, Inc.: EDWARD SELZER, Producer

(Features)

DAYBREAK IN UDI, British Information Services: CROWN FILM UNIT, Producer

KENJI COMES HOME, A Protestant Film Commission Prod.: PAUL F. HEARD, Producer

Special Effects

MIGHTY JOE YOUNG, ARKO, RKO Radio

TULSA, Walter Wanger Pictures, Eagle-Lion

Special Awards

THE BICYCLE THIEF (Italian)— voted by the Academy Board of Governors as the most outstanding foreign language film released in the United States during 1949. (statuette)

BOBBY DRISCOLL, as the outstanding juvenile actor of 1949. (miniature statuette)

FRED ASTAIRE for his unique artistry and his contributions to the technique of musical pictures. (statuette)

CECIL B. DEMILLE, distinguished motion picture pioneer, for 37 years of brilliant showmanship. (statuette)

JEAN HERSHOLT, for distinguished service to the motion picture industry. (statuette)

Irving G. Thalberg Memorial Award
None

Scientific or Technical
Class I
EASTMAN KODAK CO. for the development and introduction of an im-

proved safety base motion picture film

Class II

None

Class III

LOREN L. RYDER, BRUCE H. DEN-NEY, ROBERT CARR and the PARAMOUNT STUDIO SOUND DEPARTMENT for the development and application of the supersonic playback and public address system

M. B. PAUL for the first successful large-area seamless translucent backgrounds

HERBERT BRITT for the development and application of formulas and equipment producing artificial snow

and ice for dressing motion picture sets

ANDRÉ COUTANT and JACQUES MATHOT for the design of the Eclair Camerette

CHARLES R. DAILY, STEVE CSIL-LAG and the PARAMOUNT STU-DIO ENGINEERING, EDITORIAL and MUSIC DEPARTMENTS for a new precision method of computing variable tempo-click tracks

INTERNATIONAL PROJECTOR CORP. for a simplified and self-adjusting take-up device for projection machines

ALEXANDER VELCOFF for the application to production of the infrared photographic evaluator

1950

Nominations Announced: February 12, 1951
Awards Ceremony: March 29, 1951
RKO Pantages Theatre
(MC: Fred Astaire)

Best Picture

ALL ABOUT EVE, 20th Century-Fox
BORN YESTERDAY, Columbia
FATHER OF THE BRIDE, Metro-
Goldwyn-Mayer
KING SOLOMON'S MINES, Metro-
Goldwyn-Mayer
SUNSET BOULEVARD, Paramount

Actor

LOUIS CALHERN in *The Magnificent
Yankee*, Metro-Goldwyn-Mayer
JOSE FERRER in *Cyrano De
Bergerac*, Stanley Kramer, UA
WILLIAM HOLDEN in *Sunset Boulevard*,
Paramount
JAMES STEWART in *Harvey*, Universal-
International
SPENCER TRACY in *Father Of The
Bride*, Metro-Goldwyn-Mayer

Actress

ANNE BAXTER in *All About Eve*, 20th
Century-Fox
BETTE DAVIS in *All About Eve*, 20th
Century-Fox
JUDY HOLLIDAY in *Born Yesterday*,
Columbia
ELEANOR PARKER in *Caged*, Warner
Bros.
GLORIA SWANSON in *Sunset Boulevard*,
Paramount

Supporting Actor

JEFF CHANDLER in *Broken Arrow*, 20th
Century-Fox

LARGE CAPITAL LETTERS DENOTE WINNER

EDMUND GWENN in *Mister 880*, 20th
Century-Fox
SAM JAFFE in *The Asphalt Jungle*,
Metro-Goldwyn-Mayer
GEORGE SANDERS in *All About Eve*,
20th Century-Fox
ERICH VON STROHEIM in *Sunset Boule-
vard*, Paramount

Supporting Actress

HOPE EMERSON in *Caged*, Warner Bros.
CELESTE HOLM in *All About Eve*, 20th
Century-Fox
JOSEPHINE HULL in *Harvey*, Uni-
versal-International
NANCY OLSON in *Sunset Boulevard*,
Paramount
THELMA RITTER in *All About Eve*, 20th
Century-Fox

Directing

GEORGE CUKOR for *Born Yesterday*,
Columbia
JOHN HUSTON for *The Asphalt Jungle*,
Metro-Goldwyn-Mayer
JOSEPH L. MANKIEWICZ for *All
About Eve*, 20th Century-Fox
CAROL REED for *The Third Man*, Selz-
nick-London Films, SRO (British)
BILLY WILDER for *Sunset Boulevard*,
Paramount

Writing

(Motion Picture Story)
BITTER RICE, Lux Films (Italian): GIU-
SEPPE DE SANTIS and CARLO LIZZANI

THE GUNFIGHTER, 20th Century-Fox: WILLIAM BOWERS and ANDRE DE TOTH

MYSTERY STREET, Metro-Goldwyn-Mayer: LEONARD SPIGELGASS

PANIC IN THE STREETS, 20th Century-Fox: EDNA ANHALT and EDWARD ANHALT

WHEN WILLIE COMES MARCHING HOME, 20th Century-Fox: SY GOMBERG

(Screenplay)

ALL ABOUT EVE, 20th Century-Fox: JOSEPH L. MANKIEWICZ

THE ASPHALT JUNGLE, Metro-Goldwyn-Mayer: BEN MADDOW and JOHN HUSTON

BORN YESTERDAY, Columbia: ALBERT MANNHEIMER

BROKEN ARROW, 20th Century-Fox: MICHAEL BLANKFORT

FATHER OF THE BRIDE, Metro-Goldwyn-Mayer: FRANCES GOODRICH and ALBERT HACKETT

(Story and Screenplay)

ADAM'S RIB, Metro-Goldwyn-Mayer: RUTH GORDON and GARSON KANIN

CAGED, Warner Bros.: VIRGINIA KELLOGG and BERNARD C. SCHOENFELD

THE MEN, Kramer, UA: CARL FOREMAN

NO WAY OUT, 20th Century-Fox: JOSEPH L. MANKIEWICZ and LESSER SAMUELS

SUNSET BOULEVARD, Paramount: CHARLES BRACKETT, BILLY WILDER and D. M. MARSHMAN, JR.

Cinematography
(Black-and-White)

ALL ABOUT EVE, 20th Century-Fox: MILTON KRASNER

THE ASPHALT JUNGLE, Metro-Goldwyn-Mayer: HAROLD ROSSON

THE FURIES, Wallis, Paramount: VICTOR MILNER

SUNSET BOULEVARD, Paramount: JOHN F. SEITZ

THE THIRD MAN, Selznick-London Films, SRO (British): ROBERT KRASKER

(Color)

ANNIE GET YOUR GUN, Metro-Goldwyn-Mayer: CHARLES ROSHER

BROKEN ARROW, 20th Century-Fox: ERNEST PALMER

THE FLAME AND THE ARROW, Norma-F.R., Warner Bros.: ERNEST HALLER

KING SOLOMON'S MINES, Metro-Goldwyn-Mayer: ROBERT SURTEES

SAMSON AND DELILAH, DeMille, Paramount: GEORGE BARNES

Art Direction—Set Decoration
(Black-and-White)

ALL ABOUT EVE, 20th Century-Fox: LYLE WHEELER and GEORGE DAVIS
Set Decoration: THOMAS LITTLE and WALTER M. SCOTT

THE RED DANUBE, Metro-Goldwyn-Mayer: CEDRIC GIBBONS and HANS PETERS
Set Decoration: EDWIN B. WILLIS and HUGH HUNT

SUNSET BOULEVARD, Paramount: HANS DREIER and JOHN MEEHAN
Set Decoration: SAM COMER and RAY MOYER

(Color)

ANNIE GET YOUR GUN, Metro-Goldwyn-Mayer: CEDRIC GIBBONS and PAUL GROESSE
Set Decoration: EDWIN B. WILLIS and RICHARD A. PEFFERLE

DESTINATION MOON, George Pal, Eagle-Lion Classics: ERNST FEGTE
Set Decoration: GEORGE SAWLEY

SAMSON AND DELILAH, DeMille-Paramount: HANS DREIER and

WALTER TYLER
Set Decoration: SAM COMER and
RAY MOYER

Sound Recording

ALL ABOUT EVE, 20th Century-Fox:
20TH CENTURY-FOX SOUND
DEPARTMENT
CINDERELLA, Disney, RKO Radio:
DISNEY SOUND DEPARTMENT
LOUISA, Universal-International: UNI-
VERSAL-INTERNATIONAL SOUND DE-
PARTMENT
OUR VERY OWN, Goldwyn, RKO
Radio: GOLDWYN SOUND DEPART-
MENT
TRIO, Rank-Sydney Box, Paramount
(British)

Film Editing

ALL ABOUT EVE, 20th Century-Fox:
BARBARA MCLEAN
ANNIE GET YOUR GUN, Metro-
Goldwyn-Mayer: JAMES E. NEWCOM
KING SOLOMON'S MINES, Metro-
Goldwyn-Mayer: RALPH E.
WINTERS and CONRAD A. NER-
VIG
SUNSET BOULEVARD, Paramount: AR-
THUR SCHMIDT and DOANE HARRISON
THE THIRD MAN, Selznick-London
Films, SRO (British): OSWALD
HAFENRICHTER

Music

(Scoring of a Dramatic or Comedy Picture)

ALL ABOUT EVE, 20th Century-Fox:
ALFRED NEWMAN
THE FLAME AND THE ARROW, Norma-
F.R., Warner Bros.: MAX STEINER
NO SAD SONGS FOR ME, Columbia:
GEORGE DUNING
SAMSON AND DELILAH, Paramount:
VICTOR YOUNG
SUNSET BOULEVARD, Paramount:
FRANZ WAXMAN

(Scoring of a Musical Picture)

ANNIE GET YOUR GUN, Metro-
Goldwyn-Mayer: ADOLPH
DEUTSCH and ROGER EDENS
CINDERELLA, Disney, RKO Radio: OL-
IVER WALLACE and PAUL J. SMITH
I'LL GET BY, 20th Century-Fox: LIONEL
NEWMAN
THREE LITTLE WORDS, Metro-Goldwyn-
Mayer: ANDRÉ PREVIN
THE WEST POINT STORY, Warner Bros.:
RAY HEINDORF

(Best Song)

BE MY LOVE from *The Toast Of New
Orleans,* Metro-Goldwyn-Mayer
Music by NICHOLAS BRODSZKY.
Lyrics by SAMMY CAHN
BIBBIDY-BOBBIDI-BOO from *Cinderella,*
Disney, RKO Radio
Music and Lyrics by MACK DAVID,
AL HOFFMAN and JERRY LIVINGSTON
MONA LISA from *Captain Carey,
USA,* Paramount
Music and Lyrics by RAY EVANS
and JAY LIVINGSTON
MULE TRAIN from *Singing Guns,* Polo-
mar Pictures, Republic
Music and Lyrics by FRED GLICK-
MAN, HY HEATH and JOHNNY LANGE
WILHELMINA from *Wabash Avenue,*
20th Century-Fox
Music by JOSEF MYROW. Lyrics by
MACK GORDON

Costume Design

(Black-and-White)

ALL ABOUT EVE, 20th Century-Fox:
EDITH HEAD and CHARLES LE-
MAIRE
BORN YESTERDAY, Columbia: JEAN
LOUIS
THE MAGNIFICENT YANKEE, Metro-
Goldwyn-Mayer: WALTER PLUNKETT

(Color)

THE BLACK ROSE, 20th Century-Fox:
MICHAEL WHITTAKER

SAMSON AND DELILAH, DeMille, Paramount: EDITH HEAD, DOROTHY JEAKINS, ELOIS JENSSEN, GILE STEELE and GWEN WAKELING

THAT FORSYTE WOMAN, Metro-Goldwyn-Mayer: WALTER PLUNKETT and VALLES

Short Subjects

(Cartoons)

GERALD McBOING-BOING, United Productions Of America, Columbia. (Jolly Frolics Series): STEPHEN BOSUSTOW, Executive Producer

JERRY'S COUSIN, Metro-Goldwyn-Mayer. (Tom & Jerry): FRED QUIMBY, Producer

TROUBLE INDEMNITY, United Productions of America, Columbia. (Mr. Magoo Series): STEPHEN BOSUSTOW, Executive Producer

(One-reel)

BLAZE BUSTERS, Warner Bros. (Vitaphone Novelties): ROBERT YOUNGSON, Producer

GRANDAD OF RACES, Warner Bros. (Sports Parade): GORDON HOLLINGSHEAD, Producer

WRONG WAY BUTCH, Metro-Goldwyn-Mayer: PETE SMITH, Producer

(Two-reel)

GRANDMA MOSES, Falcon Films, Inc., A.F. Films: FALCON FILMS, INC., Producer

IN BEAVER VALLEY, Walt Disney, RKO Radio. (True-Life Adventure): WALT DISNEY, Producer

MY COUNTRY 'TIS OF THEE, Warner Bros. (Featurette Series): GORDON HOLLINGSHEAD, Producer

Documentary

(Short Subjects)

THE FIGHT: SCIENCE AGAINST CANCER, National Film Board of Canada in cooperation with the Medical Film Institute of the Association of American Medical Colleges

THE STAIRS, Film Documents, Inc.

WHY KOREA?, 20th Century-Fox Movietone: EDMUND REEK, Producer

(Features)

THE TITAN: STORY OF MICHELANGELO, Michelangelo Co., Classics Pictures, Inc.: ROBERT SNYDER, Producer

WITH THESE HANDS, Promotional Films Co., Inc.: JACK ARNOLD and LEE GOODMAN, Producers

Special Effects

DESTINATION MOON, George Pal, Eagle-Lion Classics

SAMSON AND DELILAH, Cecil B. DeMille, Paramount

Honorary Awards

(From 1927/28 through 1949 known as Special Awards.)

GEORGE MURPHY for his services in interpreting the film industry to the country at large. (statuette)

LOUIS B. MAYER for distinguished service to the motion picture industry. (statuette)

THE WALLS OF MALAPAGA (Franco-Italian)—voted by the Board of Governors as the most outstanding foreign language film released in the United States in 1950. (statuette)

Irving G. Thalberg Memorial Award
DARRYL F. ZANUCK

Scientific or Technical
Class I
None

Class II
JAMES B. GORDON and the 20TH

CENTURY-FOX STUDIO CAMERA DEPARTMENT for the design and development of a multiple image film viewer

JOHN PAUL LIVADARY, FLOYD CAMPBELL, L. W. RUSSELL and the COLUMBIA STUDIO SOUND DEPARTMENT for the development of a multi-track magnetic recording system

LOREN L. RYDER and the PARAMOUNT STUDIO SOUND DEPARTMENT for the first studio-wide application of magnetic sound recording to motion picture production

Class III
None

1951

Nominations Announced: February 11, 1952
Awards Ceremony: March 20, 1952
RKO Pantages Theatre
(MC: Danny Kaye)

Best Picture

AN AMERICAN IN PARIS, Metro-Goldwyn-Mayer: ARTHUR FREED, Producer

DECISION BEFORE DAWN, 20th Century-Fox: ANATOLE LITVAK & FRANK MC-CARTHY, Producers

A PLACE IN THE SUN, Paramount: GEORGE STEVENS, Producer

QUO VADIS, Metro-Goldwyn-Mayer: SAM ZIMBALIST, Producer

A STREETCAR NAMED DESIRE, Charles K. Feldman Group Prods., Warner Bros.: CHARLES K. FELDMAN, Producer

Actor

HUMPHREY BOGART in *The African Queen*, Horizon, UA

MARLON BRANDO in *A Streetcar Named Desire*, Charles K. Feldman Group Prods., Warner Bros.

MONTGOMERY CLIFT in *A Place In The Sun*, Paramount

ARTHUR KENNEDY in *Bright Victory*, Universal-International

FREDRIC MARCH in *Death Of A Salesman*, Stanley Kramer, Columbia

Actress

KATHARINE HEPBURN in *The African Queen*, Horizon, UA

VIVIEN LEIGH in *A Streetcar Named Desire*, Charles K. Feldman Group Prods., Warner Bros.

LARGE CAPITAL LETTERS DENOTE WINNER

ELEANOR PARKER in *Detective Story*, Paramount

SHELLEY WINTERS in *A Place In The Sun*, Paramount

JANE WYMAN in *The Blue Veil*, Wald-Krasna, RKO Radio

Supporting Actor

LEO GENN in *Quo Vadis*, Metro-Goldwyn-Mayer

KARL MALDEN in *A Streetcar Named Desire*, Charles K. Feldman Group Prods., Warner Bros.

KEVIN MCCARTHY in *Death Of A Salesman*, Kramer, Columbia

PETER USTINOV in *Quo Vadis*, Metro-Goldwyn-Mayer

GIG YOUNG in *Come Fill The Cup*, Warner Bros.

Supporting Actress

JOAN BLONDELL in *The Blue Veil*, Wald-Krasna, RKO Radio

MILDRED DUNNOCK in *Death Of A Salesman*, Kramer, Columbia

LEE GRANT in *Detective Story*, Paramount

KIM HUNTER in *A Streetcar Named Desire*, Charles K. Feldman Group Prods., Warner Bros.

THELMA RITTER in *The Mating Season*, Paramount

Directing

JOHN HUSTON for *The African Queen*, Horizon, UA

ELIA KAZAN for *A Streetcar Named Desire*, Charles K. Feldman Group Prods., Warner Bros.

VINCENTE MINNELLI for *An American In Paris*, Metro-Goldwyn-Mayer

GEORGE STEVENS for *A Place In The Sun*, Paramount

WILLIAM WYLER for *Detective Story*, Paramount

Writing

(Motion Picture Story)

THE BULLFIGHTER AND THE LADY, Republic: BUDD BOETTICHER and RAY NAZARRO

THE FROGMEN, 20th Century-Fox: OSCAR MILLARD

HERE COMES THE GROOM, Paramount: ROBERT RISKIN and LIAM O'BRIEN

SEVEN DAYS TO NOON, Boulting Bros., Mayer-Kingsley- Distinguished Films (British): PAUL DEHN and JAMES BERNARD

TERESA, Metro-Goldwyn-Mayer: ALFRED HAYES and STEWART STERN

(Screenplay)

THE AFRICAN QUEEN, Horizon, UA: JAMES AGEE and JOHN HUSTON

DETECTIVE STORY, Paramount: PHILIP YORDAN and ROBERT WYLER

LA RONDE, Sacha Gordine, Commercial Pictures (French): JACQUES NATANSON and MAX OPHULS

A PLACE IN THE SUN, Paramount: MICHAEL WILSON and HARRY BROWN

A STREETCAR NAMED DESIRE, Charles K. Feldman Group Prods., Warner Bros.: TENNESSEE WILLIAMS

(Story and Screenplay)

AN AMERICAN IN PARIS, Metro-Goldwyn-Mayer: ALAN JAY LERNER

THE BIG CARNIVAL, Paramount: BILLY WILDER, LESSER SAMUELS and WALTER NEWMAN

DAVID AND BATHSHEBA, 20th Century-Fox: PHILIP DUNNE

GO FOR BROKE!, Metro-Goldwyn-Mayer: ROBERT PIROSH

THE WELL, Popkin, UA: CLARENCE GREENE and RUSSELL ROUSE

Cinematography

(Black-and-White)

DEATH OF A SALESMAN, Kramer, Columbia: FRANK PLANER

THE FROGMEN, 20th Century-Fox: NORBERT BRODINE

A PLACE IN THE SUN, Paramount: WILLIAM C. MELLOR

STRANGERS ON A TRAIN, Warner Bros.: ROBERT BURKS

A STREETCAR NAMED DESIRE, Charles K. Feldman Group Prods., Warner Bros.: HARRY STRADLING

(Color)

AN AMERICAN IN PARIS, Metro-Goldwyn-Mayer: ALFRED GILKS; Ballet photographed by JOHN ALTON

DAVID AND BATHSHEBA, 20th Century-Fox: LEON SHAMROY

QUO VADIS, Metro-Goldwyn-Mayer: ROBERT SURTEES and WILLIAM V. SKALL

SHOW BOAT, Metro-Goldwyn-Mayer: CHARLES ROSHER

WHEN WORLDS COLLIDE, Paramount: JOHN F. SEITZ and W. HOWARD GREENE

Art Direction—Set Decoration

(Black-and-White)

FOURTEEN HOURS, 20th Century-Fox: LYLE WHEELER and LELAND FULLER Set Decoration: THOMAS LITTLE and FRED J. RODE

HOUSE ON TELEGRAPH HILL, 20th Century-Fox: LYLE WHEELER and JOHN DeCUIR

Set Decoration: THOMAS LITTLE and PAUL S. FOX

LA RONDE, Sacha Gordine Prod., Commercial Pictures (French): D'EAUBONNE
Set Decoration: No credits listed

A STREETCAR NAMED DESIRE, Chas. K. Feldman Group Prods., Warner Bros.: RICHARD DAY
Set Decoration: GEORGE JAMES HOPKINS

TOO YOUNG TO KISS, Metro-Goldwyn-Mayer: CEDRIC GIBBONS and PAUL GROESSE
Set Decoration: EDWIN B. WILLIS and JACK D. MOORE

(Color)

AN AMERICAN IN PARIS, Metro-Goldwyn-Mayer: CEDRIC GIBBONS and PRESTON AMES
Set Decoration: EDWIN B. WILLIS and KEOGH GLEASON

DAVID AND BATHSHEBA, 20th Century-Fox: LYLE WHEELER and GEORGE DAVIS
Set Decoration: THOMAS LITTLE and PAUL S. FOX

ON THE RIVIERA, 20th Century-Fox: LYLE WHEELER and LELAND FULLER
Musical Settings: JOSEPH C. WRIGHT
Set Decoration: THOMAS LITTLE and WALTER M. SCOTT

QUO VADIS, Metro-Goldwyn-Mayer: WILLIAM A. HORNING, CEDRIC GIBBONS and EDWARD CARFAGNO
Set Decoration: HUGH HUNT

TALES OF HOFFMANN, Powell-Pressburger, Lopert (British): HEIN HECKROTH
Set Decoration: No credits listed

Sound Recording

BRIGHT VICTORY, Universal-International: LESLIE I. CAREY, Sound Director

THE GREAT CARUSO, Metro-Goldwyn-Mayer: DOUGLAS SHEARER, Sound Director

I WANT YOU, Samuel Goldwyn Prods., Inc., RKO Radio: GORDON SAWYER, Sound Director

A STREETCAR NAMED DESIRE, Charles K. Feldman Group Prods., Warner Bros.: COL. NATHAN LEVINSON, Sound Director

TWO TICKETS TO BROADWAY, RKO Radio: JOHN O. AALBERG, Sound Director

Film Editing

AN AMERICAN IN PARIS, Metro-Goldwyn-Mayer: ADRIENNE FAZAN

DECISION BEFORE DAWN, 20th Century-Fox: DOROTHY SPENCER

A PLACE IN THE SUN, Paramount: WILLIAM HORNBECK

QUO VADIS, Metro-Goldwyn-Mayer: RALPH E. WINTERS

THE WELL, Popkin, UA: CHESTER SCHAEFFER

Music

(Scoring of a Dramatic or Comedy Picture)

DAVID AND BATHSHEBA, 20th Century-Fox: ALFRED NEWMAN

DEATH OF A SALESMAN, Kramer, Columbia: ALEX NORTH

A PLACE IN THE SUN, Paramount: FRANZ WAXMAN

QUO VADIS, Metro-Goldwyn-Mayer: MIKLOS ROZSA

A STREETCAR NAMED DESIRE, Charles K. Feldman Prods., Warner Bros.: ALEX NORTH

(Scoring of a Musical Picture)

ALICE IN WONDERLAND, Disney, RKO Radio: OLIVER WALLACE

AN AMERICAN IN PARIS, Metro-Goldwyn-Mayer: JOHNNY GREEN and SAUL CHAPLIN

THE GREAT CARUSO, Metro-Goldwyn-

Mayer: PETER HERMAN ADLER and JOHNNY GREEN
ON THE RIVIERA, 20th Century-Fox: ALFRED NEWMAN
SHOW BOAT, Metro-Goldwyn-Mayer: ADOLPH DEUTSCH and CONRAD SALINGER

(Best Song)

IN THE COOL, COOL, COOL OF THE EVENING from *Here Comes The Groom,* Paramount
Music by HOAGY CARMICHAEL. Lyrics by JOHNNY MERCER
A KISS TO BUILD A DREAM ON from *The Strip,* Metro-Goldwyn-Mayer
Music and Lyrics by BERT KALMAR, HARRY RUBY and OSCAR HAMMERSTEIN II
NEVER from *Golden Girl,* 20th Century-Fox
Music by LIONEL NEWMAN. Lyrics by ELIOT DANIEL
TOO LATE NOW from *Royal Wedding,* Metro-Goldwyn-Mayer
Music by BURTON LANE. Lyrics by ALAN JAY LERNER
WONDER WHY from *Rich, Young and Pretty,* Metro-Goldwyn-Mayer
Music by NICHOLAS BRODSZKY. Lyrics by SAMMY CAHN

Costume Design

(Black-and-White)

KIND LADY, Metro-Goldwyn-Mayer: WALTER PLUNKETT and GILE STEELE
THE MODEL AND THE MARRIAGE BROKER, 20th Century-Fox: CHARLES LeMAIRE and RENIE
THE MUDLARK, 20th Century-Fox: EDWARD STEVENSON and MARGARET FURSE
A PLACE IN THE SUN, Paramount: EDITH HEAD
A STREETCAR NAMED DESIRE, Charles K. Feldman Group Prods., Warner Bros.: LUCINDA BALLARD

(Color)

AN AMERICAN IN PARIS, Metro-Goldwyn-Mayer: ORRY-KELLY, WALTER PLUNKETT and IRENE SHARAFF
DAVID AND BATHSHEBA, 20th Century-Fox: CHARLES LeMAIRE and EDWARD STEVENSON
THE GREAT CARUSO, Metro-Goldwyn-Mayer: HELEN ROSE and GILE STEELE
QUO VADIS, Metro-Goldwyn-Mayer: HERSCHEL McCOY
TALES OF HOFFMANN, Powell-Pressburger, Lopert (British): HEIN HECKROTH

Short Subjects

(Cartoons)

LAMBERT, THE SHEEPISH LION, Walt Disney, RKO Radio. (Special): WALT DISNEY, Producer
ROOTY TOOT TOOT, United Productions Of America, Columbia. (Jolly Frolics): STEPHEN BOSUSTOW, Executive Producer
TWO MOUSEKETEERS, Metro-Goldwyn-Mayer. (Tom & Jerry): FRED QUIMBY, Producer

(One-reel)

RIDIN' THE RAILS, Paramount. (Sportlights): JACK EATON, Producer
THE STORY OF TIME, A Signal Films Production by Robert G. Leffingwell, Cornell Film Company (British)
WORLD OF KIDS, Warner Bros. (Vitaphone Novelties): ROBERT YOUNGSON, Producer

(Two-reel)

BALZAC, Les Films du Compass, A.F. Films, Inc. (French): LES FILMS DU COMPASS, Producer
DANGER UNDER THE SEA, Universal-International: TOM MEAD, Producer
NATURE'S HALF ACRE, Walt Dis-

ney, RKO Radio. (True-Life Adventure): WALT DISNEY, Producer

Documentary

(Short Subjects)

BENJY, Made by Fred Zinnemann with the cooperation of Paramount Pictures Corp. for the Los Angeles Orthopaedic Hospital

ONE WHO CAME BACK. (Film sponsored by the Disabled American Veterans, in cooperation with the United States Department of Defense and the Association of Motion Picture Producers.) OWEN CRUMP, Producer.

THE SEEING EYE, Warner Bros.: GORDON HOLLINGSHEAD, Producer

(Features)

I WAS A COMMUNIST FOR THE F.B.I., Warner Bros.: BRYAN FOY, Producer

KON-TIKI, An Artfilm Prod., RKO Radio (Norwegian): OLLE NORDEMAR, Producer

Honorary Awards

GENE KELLY in appreciation of his versatility as an actor, singer, director and dancer, and specifically for his brilliant achievements in the art of choreography on film. (statuette)

RASHOMON (Japanese)—voted by the Board of Governors as the most outstanding foreign language film released in the United States during 1951. (statuette)

Special Effects

Note: 1951 thru 1953 Special Effects classified as an "other" Award (not necessarily given each year) hence, no nominations.

WHEN WORLDS COLLIDE, Paramount

Irving G. Thalberg Memorial Award

ARTHUR FREED

Scientific or Technical

Class I

None

Class II

GORDON JENNINGS, S. L. STANCLIFFE and the PARAMOUNT STUDIO SPECIAL PHOTOGRAPHIC and ENGINEERING DEPARTMENTS for the design, construction and application of a servo-operated recording and repeating device

OLIN L. DUPY of Metro-Goldwyn-Mayer Studio for the design, construction and application of a motion picture reproducing system

RADIO CORPORATION OF AMERICA, VICTOR DIVISION, for pioneering direct positive recording with anticipatory noise reduction

Class III

RICHARD M. HAFF, FRANK P. HERRNFELD, GARLAND C. MISENER and the ANSCO FILM DIVISION OF GENERAL ANILINE AND FILM CORP. for the development of the Ansco color scene tester

FRED PONEDEL, RALPH AYRES and GEORGE BROWN of Warner Bros. Studio for an air-driven water motor to provide flow, wake and white water for marine sequences in motion pictures

GLEN ROBINSON and the METRO-GOLDWYN-MAYER STUDIO CONSTRUCTION DEPARTMENT for the development of a new music wire and cable cutter

JACK GAYLORD and the METRO-GOLDWYN-MAYER STUDIO CONSTRUCTION DEPARTMENT for the development of balsa falling snow

CARLOS RIVAS of Metro-Goldwyn-Mayer Studio for the development of an automatic magnetic film splicer

1952

Nominations Announced: February 9, 1953
Awards Ceremony: March 19, 1953
RKO Pantages Theatre
(MC: Bob Hope; MC in New York: Conrad Nagel)
(Academy Awards televised for the first time. For five years—the 25th through 29th Awards—the ceremonies were held simultaneously in Los Angeles and New York.)

Best Picture

THE GREATEST SHOW ON EARTH, Cecil B. DeMille, Paramount: CECIL B. DeMILLE, Producer
HIGH NOON, Stanley Kramer Prods., UA: STANLEY KRAMER, Producer
IVANHOE, Metro-Goldwyn-Mayer: PANDRO S. BERMAN, Producer
MOULIN ROUGE, Romulus Films, UA
THE QUIET MAN, Argosy Pictures Corp., Republic: JOHN FORD and MERIAN C. COOPER, Producers

Actor

MARLON BRANDO in *Viva Zapata!*, 20th Century-Fox
GARY COOPER in *High Noon*, Stanley Kramer, UA
KIRK DOUGLAS in *The Bad And The Beautiful*, Metro-Goldwyn-Mayer
JOSE FERRER in *Moulin Rouge*, Romulus Films, UA
ALEC GUINNESS in *The Lavender Hill Mob*, J. Arthur Rank Presentation-Ealing Studios, U-I. (British)

Actress

SHIRLEY BOOTH in *Come Back, Little Sheba*, Hal Wallis, Paramount
JOAN CRAWFORD in *Sudden Fear*, Joseph Kaufman Prods., RKO Radio

LARGE CAPITAL LETTERS DENOTE WINNER

BETTE DAVIS in *The Star*, Bert E. Friedlob, 20th Century-Fox
JULIE HARRIS in *The Member Of The Wedding*, Stanley Kramer, Columbia
SUSAN HAYWARD in *With A Song In My Heart*, 20th Century-Fox

Supporting Actor

RICHARD BURTON in *My Cousin Rachel*, 20th Century-Fox
ARTHUR HUNNICUTT in *The Big Sky*, Winchester, RKO Radio
VICTOR MCLAGLEN in *The Quiet Man*, Argosy, Republic
JACK PALANCE in *Sudden Fear*, Kaufman, RKO Radio
ANTHONY QUINN in *Viva Zapata!*, 20th Century-Fox

Supporting Actress

GLORIA GRAHAME in *The Bad And The Beautiful*, Metro-Goldwyn-Mayer
JEAN HAGEN in *Singin' In The Rain*, Metro-Goldwyn-Mayer
COLETTE MARCHAND in *Moulin Rouge*, Romulus, UA
TERRY MOORE in *Come Back, Little Sheba*, Wallis, Paramount
THELMA RITTER in *With A Song In My Heart*, 20th Century-Fox

405

Directing

CECIL B. DEMILLE for *The Greatest Show On Earth,* Cecil B. DeMille, Paramount

JOHN FORD for *The Quiet Man,* Argosy, Republic

JOHN HUSTON for *Moulin Rouge,* Romulus Films, UA

JOSEPH L. MANKIEWICZ for *Five Fingers,* 20th Century-Fox

FRED ZINNEMANN for *High Noon,* Stanley Kramer, UA

Writing

(Motion Picture Story)

THE GREATEST SHOW ON EARTH, DeMille, Paramount: FREDERIC M. FRANK, THEODORE ST. JOHN and FRANK CAVETT

MY SON JOHN, Rainbow, Paramount: LEO MCCAREY

THE NARROW MARGIN, RKO Radio: MARTIN GOLDSMITH and JACK LEONARD

THE PRIDE OF ST. LOUIS, 20th Century-Fox: GUY TROSPER

THE SNIPER, Kramer, Columbia: EDNA ANHALT and EDWARD ANHALT

(Screenplay)

THE BAD AND THE BEAUTIFUL, Metro-Goldwyn-Mayer: CHARLES SCHNEE

FIVE FINGERS, 20th Century-Fox: MICHAEL WILSON

HIGH NOON, Kramer, UA: CARL FOREMAN

THE MAN IN THE WHITE SUIT, Rank-Ealing, U-I (British): ROGER MAC-DOUGALL, JOHN DIGHTON and ALEXANDER MACKENDRICK

THE QUIET MAN, Argosy, Republic: FRANK S. NUGENT

(Story and Screenplay)

THE ATOMIC CITY, Paramount: SYDNEY BOEHM

BREAKING THE SOUND BARRIER, London Films, UA (British): TERENCE RATTIGAN

THE LAVENDER HILL MOB, Rank-Ealing, U-I (British): T.E.B. CLARKE

PAT AND MIKE, Metro-Goldwyn-Mayer: RUTH GORDON and GARSON KANIN

VIVA ZAPATA!, 20th Century-Fox: JOHN STEINBECK

Cinematography

(Black-and-White)

THE BAD AND THE BEAUTIFUL, Metro-Goldwyn-Mayer: ROBERT SURTEES

THE BIG SKY, Winchester, RKO Radio: RUSSELL HARLAN

MY COUSIN RACHEL, 20th Century-Fox: JOSEPH LaSHELLE

NAVAJO, Bartlett-Foster, Lippert: VIRGIL E. MILLER

SUDDEN FEAR, Joseph Kaufman, RKO Radio: CHARLES B. LANG, JR.

(Color)

HANS CHRISTIAN ANDERSEN, Goldwyn, RKO Radio: HARRY STRADLING

IVANHOE, Metro-Goldwyn-Mayer: F.A. YOUNG

MILLION DOLLAR MERMAID, Metro-Goldwyn-Mayer: GEORGE J. FOLSEY

THE QUIET MAN, Argosy, Republic: WINTON C. HOCH and ARCHIE STOUT

THE SNOWS OF KILIMANJARO, 20th Century-Fox: LEON SHAMROY

Art Direction—Set Decoration

(Black-and-White)

THE BAD AND THE BEAUTIFUL, Metro-Goldwyn-Mayer: CEDRIC GIBBONS and EDWARD CARFAGNO

Set Decoration: EDWIN B. WILLIS and KEOGH GLEASON

CARRIE, Paramount: HAL PEREIRA and ROLAND ANDERSON
Set Decoration: EMILE KURI
MY COUSIN RACHEL, 20th Century-Fox: LYLE WHEELER and JOHN DeCUIR
Set Decoration: WALTER M. SCOTT
RASHOMON, Daiei, RKO Radio (Japanese): MATSUYAMA
Set Decoration: H. MOTSUMOTO
VIVA ZAPATA!, 20th Century-Fox: LYLE WHEELER and LELAND FULLER
Set Decoration: THOMAS LITTLE and CLAUDE CARPENTER

(Color)

HANS CHRISTIAN ANDERSEN, Goldwyn, RKO Radio: RICHARD DAY and CLAVE
Set Decoration: HOWARD BRISTOL
THE MERRY WIDOW, Metro-Goldwyn-Mayer: CEDRIC GIBBONS and PAUL GROESSE
Set Decoration: EDWIN B. WILLIS and ARTHUR KRAMS
MOULIN ROUGE, Romulus Films, UA: PAUL SHERIFF
Set Decoration: MARCEL VERTES
THE QUIET MAN, Argosy, Republic: FRANK HOTALING
Set Decoration: JOHN MCCARTHY, JR. and CHARLES THOMPSON
THE SNOWS OF KILIMANJARO, 20th Century-Fox: LYLE WHEELER and JOHN DeCUIR
Set Decoration: THOMAS LITTLE and PAUL S. FOX

Sound Recording

BREAKING THE SOUND BARRIER, London Films, UA. (British): LONDON FILM SOUND DEPARTMENT
HANS CHRISTIAN ANDERSEN, Goldwyn, RKO Radio. Goldwyn Sound Department: GORDON SAWYER, Sound Director
THE PROMOTER, Rank, Ronald Neame,

U-I (British): PINEWOOD STUDIOS SOUND DEPARTMENT
THE QUIET MAN, Argosy, Republic. Republic Sound Department: DANIEL J. BLOOMBERG, Sound Director
WITH A SONG IN MY HEART, 20th Century-Fox. 20th Century-Fox Sound Department: THOMAS T. MOULTON, Sound Director

Film Editing

COME BACK, LITTLE SHEBA, Wallis, Paramount: WARREN LOW
FLAT TOP, Monogram: WILLIAM AUSTIN
THE GREATEST SHOW ON EARTH, De-Mille, Paramount: ANNE BAUCHENS
HIGH NOON, Kramer, UA: ELMO WILLIAMS and HARRY GERSTAD
MOULIN ROUGE, Romulus, UA: RALPH KEMPLEN

Music

(Scoring of a Dramatic or Comedy Picture)
HIGH NOON, Kramer, UA: DIMITRI TIOMKIN
IVANHOE, Metro-Goldwyn-Mayer: MIKLOS ROZSA
MIRACLE OF FATIMA, Warner Bros.: MAX STEINER
THE THIEF, Fran Prods., UA: HERSCHEL BURKE GILBERT
VIVA ZAPATA!, 20th Century-Fox: ALEX NORTH

(Scoring of a Musical Picture)
HANS CHRISTIAN ANDERSEN, Goldwyn, RKO Radio: WALTER SCHARF
THE JAZZ SINGER, Warner Bros.: RAY HEINDORF and MAX STEINER
THE MEDIUM, Transfilm-Lopert (Italian): GIAN-CARLO MENOTTI
SINGIN' IN THE RAIN, Metro-Goldwyn-Mayer: LENNIE HAYTON
WITH A SONG IN MY HEART, 20th Century-Fox: ALFRED NEWMAN

(Best Song)

AM I IN LOVE from *Son Of Paleface,*
Paramount
Music and Lyrics by JACK BROOKS

BECAUSE YOU'RE MINE from *Because
You're Mine,* Metro-Goldwyn-Mayer
Music by NICHOLAS BRODSZKY.
Lyrics by SAMMY CAHN

HIGH NOON (DO NOT FORSAKE
ME, OH MY DARLIN') from *High
Noon,* Kramer, UA
Music by DIMITRI TIOMKIN.
Lyrics by NED WASHINGTON

THUMBELINA from *Hans Christian Andersen,* Goldwyn, RKO Radio
Music and Lyrics by FRANK LOESSER

ZING A LITTLE ZONG from *Just For
You,* Paramount
Music by HARRY WARREN. Lyrics by
LEO ROBIN

Costume Design

(Black-and-White)

AFFAIR IN TRINIDAD, Beckworth, Columbia: JEAN LOUIS

THE BAD AND THE BEAUTIFUL,
Metro-Goldwyn-Mayer: HELEN
ROSE

CARRIE, Paramount: EDITH HEAD

MY COUSIN RACHEL, 20th Century-Fox:
CHARLES LeMAIRE and DOROTHY
JEAKINS

SUDDEN FEAR, Joseph Kaufman, RKO
Radio: SHEILA O'BRIEN

(Color)

THE GREATEST SHOW ON EARTH, De-
Mille, Paramount: EDITH HEAD,
DOROTHY JEAKINS and MILES WHITE

HANS CHRISTIAN ANDERSEN, Goldwyn,
RKO Radio: CLAVE, MARY WILLS
and MADAME KARINSKA

THE MERRY WIDOW, Metro-Goldwyn-
Mayer: HELEN ROSE and GILE STEELE

MOULIN ROUGE, Romulus, UA:
MARCEL VERTES

WITH A SONG IN MY HEART, 20th Century-Fox: CHARLES LeMAIRE

Short Subjects

(Cartoons)

JOHANN MOUSE, Metro-Goldwyn-
Mayer. (Tom & Jerry): FRED
QUIMBY, Producer

LITTLE JOHNNY JET, Metro-Goldwyn-
Mayer. (M-G-M Series): FRED
QUIMBY, Producer

MADELINE, UPA, Columbia. (Jolly
Frolics): STEPHEN BOSUSTOW, Executive Producer

PINK AND BLUE BLUES, UPA, Columbia. (Mister Magoo): STEPHEN BO-
SUSTOW, Executive Producer

ROMANCE OF TRANSPORTATION, National Film Board of Canada (Canadian): TOM DALY, Producer

(One-reel)

ATHLETES OF THE SADDLE, Paramount.
(Sportlights Series): JACK EASTON,
Producer

DESERT KILLER, Warner Bros. (Sports
Parade): GORDON HOLLINGSHEAD,
Producer

LIGHT IN THE WINDOW, Art Films
Prods., 20th Century-Fox. (Art
Series): BORIS VERMONT, Pro-
ducer

NEIGHBOURS, National Film Board Of
Canada (Canadian): NORMAN
MCLAREN, Producer

ROYAL SCOTLAND, Crown Film Unit,
British Information Services (British)

(Two-reel)

BRIDGE OF TIME, A London Film Prod.,
British Information Services (British)

DEVIL TAKE US, A Theatre Of Life
Prod. (Theatre Of Life Series): HER-
BERT MORGAN, Producer

THAR SHE BLOWS!, Warner Bros.
(Technicolor Special): GORDON
HOLLINGSHEAD, Producer

WATER BIRDS, Walt Disney, RKO
Radio. (True-Life Adventure):

WALT DISNEY, Producer

Documentary

(Short Subjects)

DEVIL TAKE US, Theatre of Life Prod.:
HERBERT MORGAN, Producer

THE GARDEN SPIDER (EPEIRA DIADEMA),
Cristallo Films, I.F.E. Releasing
Corp. (Italian): ALBERTO ANCILOTTO,
Producer

MAN ALIVE!, Made by United Produc-
tions of America for the American
Cancer Society: STEPHEN BOSUSTOW,
Exec. Producer

NEIGHBOURS, National Film Board
of Canada, Arthur Mayer-Edward
Kingsley, Inc. (Canadian): NOR-
MAN McLAREN, Producer

(Features)

THE HOAXTERS, Metro-Goldwyn-
Mayer: DORE SCHARY, Producer

NAVAJO, Bartlett-Foster Prod., Lippert
Pictures, Inc.: HALL BARTLETT, Producer

THE SEA AROUND US, RKO Radio:
IRWIN ALLEN, Producer

Honorary Awards

GEORGE ALFRED MITCHELL for
the design and development of the
camera which bears his name and for
his continued and dominant presence
in the field of cinematography.
(statuette)

JOSEPH M. SCHENCK for long and
distinguished service to the motion
picture industry. (statuette)

MERIAN C. COOPER for his many
innovations and contributions to the
art of motion pictures. (statuette)

HAROLD LLOYD, master comedian
and good citizen. (statuette)

BOB HOPE for his contribution to the
laughter of the world, his service to
the motion picture industry, and his
devotion to the American premise.
(statuette)

FORBIDDEN GAMES (French)—Best
Foreign Language Film first released
in the United States during 1952.
(statuette)

Special Effects

PLYMOUTH ADVENTURE, Metro-
Goldwyn-Mayer

Irving G. Thalberg Memorial Award

CECIL B. DeMILLE

Scientific or Technical

Class I

EASTMAN KODAK CO. for the introduction of Eastman color negative
and Eastman color print film

ANSCO DIVISION, GENERAL ANI-
LINE AND FILM CORP., for the
introduction of Ansco color negative
and Ansco color print film

Class II

TECHNICOLOR MOTION PICTURE
CORP. for an improved method of
color motion picture photography
under incandescent light

Class III

PROJECTION, STILL PHOTO-
GRAPHIC and DEVELOPMENT
ENGINEERING DEPARTMENTS
of METRO-GOLDWYN-MAYER
STUDIO for an improved method of
projecting photographic backgrounds

JOHN G. FRAYNE and R. R. SCO-
VILLE and WESTREX CORP. for a
method of measuring distortion in
sound reproduction

PHOTO RESEARCH CORP. for creating the Spectra color temperature
meter

GUSTAV JIROUCH for the design of
the Robot automatic film splicer

CARLOS RIVAS of Metro-Goldwyn-
Mayer Studio for the development of
a sound reproducer for magnetic
film.

1953

Nominations Announced: February 15, 1954
Awards Ceremony: March 25, 1954
RKO Pantages Theatre
(MC: Donald O'Connor; MC in New York: Fredric March)

Best Picture

FROM HERE TO ETERNITY, Columbia: BUDDY ADLER, Producer

JULIUS CAESAR, Metro-Goldwyn-Mayer: JOHN HOUSEMAN, Producer

THE ROBE, 20th Century-Fox: FRANK ROSS, Producer

ROMAN HOLIDAY, Paramount: WILLIAM WYLER, Producer

SHANE, Paramount: GEORGE STEVENS, Producer

Actor

MARLON BRANDO in *Julius Caesar*, Metro-Goldwyn-Mayer

RICHARD BURTON in *The Robe*, 20th Century-Fox

MONTGOMERY CLIFT in *From Here To Eternity*, Columbia

WILLIAM HOLDEN in *Stalag 17*, Paramount

BURT LANCASTER in *From Here To Eternity*, Columbia

Actress

LESLIE CARON in *Lili*, Metro-Goldwyn-Mayer

AVA GARDNER in *Mogambo*, Metro-Goldwyn-Mayer

AUDREY HEPBURN in *Roman Holiday*, Paramount

DEBORAH KERR in *From Here To Eternity*, Columbia

LARGE CAPITAL LETTERS DENOTE WINNER

MAGGIE MCNAMARA in *The Moon Is Blue*, Preminger-Herbert, UA

Supporting Actor

EDDIE ALBERT in *Roman Holiday*, Paramount

BRANDON DE WILDE in *Shane*, Paramount

JACK PALANCE in *Shane*, Paramount

FRANK SINATRA in *From Here To Eternity*, Columbia

ROBERT STRAUSS in *Stalag 17*, Paramount

Supporting Actress

GRACE KELLY in *Mogambo*, Metro-Goldwyn-Mayer

GERALDINE PAGE in *Hondo*, Wayne-Fellows, Warner Bros.

MARJORIE RAMBEAU in *Torch Song*, Metro-Goldwyn-Mayer

DONNA REED in *From Here To Eternity*, Columbia

THELMA RITTER in *Pickup On South Street*, 20th Century-Fox

Directing

GEORGE STEVENS for *Shane*, Paramount

CHARLES WALTERS for *Lili*, Metro-Goldwyn-Mayer

BILLY WILDER for *Stalag 17*, Paramount

WILLIAM WYLER for *Roman Holiday*, Paramount

FRED ZINNEMANN for *From Here To Eternity*, Columbia

Writing

(Motion Picture Story)

ABOVE AND BEYOND, Metro-Goldwyn-Mayer: BEIRNE LAY, JR.

THE CAPTAIN'S PARADISE, London Films, Lopert-UA (British): ALEC COPPEL

LITTLE FUGITIVE, Little Fugitive Prod. Co., Joseph Burstyn, Inc.: RAY ASHLEY, MORRIS ENGEL and RUTH ORKIN

ROMAN HOLIDAY, Paramount: IAN McLELLAN HUNTER

(Screenplay)

THE CRUEL SEA, Rank-Ealing, U-I (British): ERIC AMBLER

FROM HERE TO ETERNITY, Columbia: DANIEL TARADASH

LILI, Metro-Goldwyn-Mayer: HELEN DEUTSCH

ROMAN HOLIDAY, Paramount: IAN MCLELLAN HUNTER and JOHN DIGHTON

SHANE, Paramount: A. B. GUTHRIE, JR.

(Story and Screenplay)

THE BAND WAGON, Metro-Goldwyn-Mayer: BETTY COMDEN and ADOLPH GREEN

THE DESERT RATS, 20th Century-Fox: RICHARD MURPHY

THE NAKED SPUR, Metro-Goldwyn-Mayer: SAM ROLFE and HAROLD JACK BLOOM

TAKE THE HIGH GROUND, Metro-Goldwyn-Mayer: MILLARD KAUFMAN

TITANIC, 20th Century-Fox: CHARLES BRACKETT, WALTER REISCH and RICHARD BREEN

Cinematography

(Black-and-White)

THE FOUR POSTER, Kramer, Columbia: HAL MOHR

FROM HERE TO ETERNITY, Columbia: BURNETT GUFFEY

JULIUS CAESAR, Metro-Goldwyn-Mayer: JOSEPH RUTTENBERG

MARTIN LUTHER, Louis de Rochemont Associates: JOSEPH C. BRUN

ROMAN HOLIDAY, Paramount: FRANK PLANER and HENRY ALEKAN

(Color)

ALL THE BROTHERS WERE VALIANT, Metro-Goldwyn-Mayer: GEORGE FOLSEY

BENEATH THE TWELVE-MILE REEF, 20th Century-Fox: EDWARD CRONJAGER

LILI, Metro-Goldwyn-Mayer: ROBERT PLANCK

THE ROBE, 20th Century-Fox: LEON SHAMROY

SHANE, Paramount: LOYAL GRIGGS

Art Direction—Set Decoration

(Black-and-White)

JULIUS CAESAR, Metro-Goldwyn-Mayer: CEDRIC GIBBONS and EDWARD CARFAGNO
Set Decoration: EDWIN B. WILLIS and HUGH HUNT

MARTIN LUTHER, Louis de Rochemont Assocs.: FRITZ MAURISCHAT and PAUL MARKWITZ
Set Decoration: No credits listed

THE PRESIDENT'S LADY, 20th Century-Fox: LYLE WHEELER and LELAND FULLER
Set Decoration: PAUL S. FOX

ROMAN HOLIDAY, Paramount: HAL PEREIRA and WALTER TYLER
Set Decoration: No credits listed

TITANIC, 20th Century-Fox: LYLE WHEELER and MAURICE RANSFORD
Set Decoration: STUART REISS

(Color)

KNIGHTS OF THE ROUND TABLE, Metro-Goldwyn-Mayer: ALFRED JUNGE and HANS PETERS
Set Decoration: JOHN JARVIS

LILI, Metro-Goldwyn-Mayer: CEDRIC GIBBONS and PAUL GROESSE
Set Decoration: EDWIN B. WILLIS and ARTHUR KRAMS
THE ROBE, 20th Century-Fox: LYLE WHEELER and GEORGE W. DAVIS
Set Decoration: WALTER M. SCOTT and PAUL S. FOX
THE STORY OF THREE LOVES, Metro-Goldwyn-Mayer: CEDRIC GIBBONS, PRESTON AMES, EDWARD CARFAGNO and GABRIEL SCOGNAMILLO
Set Decoration: EDWIN B. WILLIS, KEOGH GLEASON, ARTHUR KRAMS and JACK D. MOORE
YOUNG BESS, Metro-Goldwyn-Mayer: CEDRIC GIBBONS and URIE MCCLEARY
Set Decoration: EDWIN B. WILLIS and JACK D. MOORE

Sound Recording

CALAMITY JANE, Warner Bros. Warner Bros. Sound Department: WILLIAM A. MUELLER, Sound Director
FROM HERE TO ETERNITY, Columbia. Columbia Sound Department: JOHN P. LIVADARY, Sound Director
KNIGHTS OF THE ROUND TABLE, Metro-Goldwyn-Mayer: A. W. WATKINS, Sound Director
THE MISSISSIPPI GAMBLER, Universal-International. Universal-International Sound Department: LESLIE I. CAREY, Sound Director
THE WAR OF THE WORLDS, Paramount. Paramount Sound Department: LOREN L. RYDER, Sound Director

Film Editing

CRAZYLEGS, Bartlett, Republic: IRVINE (COTTON) WARBURTON
FROM HERE TO ETERNITY, Columbia: WILLIAM LYON
THE MOON IS BLUE, Preminger-Herbert, UA: OTTO LUDWIG

ROMAN HOLIDAY, Paramount: ROBERT SWINK
WAR OF THE WORLDS, Paramount: EVERETT DOUGLAS

Music

(Scoring of a Dramatic or Comedy Picture)

ABOVE AND BEYOND, Metro-Goldwyn-Mayer: HUGO FRIEDHOFER
FROM HERE TO ETERNITY, Columbia: MORRIS STOLOFF and GEORGE DUNING
JULIUS CAESAR, Metro-Goldwyn-Mayer: MIKLOS ROZSA
LILI, Metro-Goldwyn-Mayer: BRONISLAU KAPER
THIS IS CINERAMA, Cinerama Prods. Corp.: LOUIS FORBES

(Scoring of a Musical Picture)

THE BANDWAGON, Metro-Goldwyn-Mayer: ADOLPH DEUTSCH
CALAMITY JANE, Warner Bros.: RAY HEINDORF
CALL ME MADAM, 20th Century-Fox: ALFRED NEWMAN
5,000 FINGERS OF DR. T., Kramer-Columbia: FREDERICK HOLLANDER and MORRIS STOLOFF
KISS ME KATE, Metro-Goldwyn-Mayer: ANDRÉ PREVIN and SAUL CHAPLIN

(Best Song)

THE MOON IS BLUE from *The Moon Is Blue,* Preminger-Herbert Prods., UA
Music by HERSCHEL BURKE GILBERT.
Lyrics by SYLVIA FINE
MY FLAMING HEART from *Small Town Girl,* Metro-Goldwyn-Mayer
Music by NICHOLAS BRODSZKY.
Lyrics by LEO ROBIN
SADIE THOMPSON'S SONG (BLUE PACIFIC BLUES) from *Miss Sadie Thompson,* Beckworth, Columbia
Music by LESTER LEE. Lyrics by NED WASHINGTON

SECRET LOVE from *Calamity Jane,*
Warner Bros.
Music by SAMMY FAIN. Lyrics by
PAUL FRANCIS WEBSTER
THAT'S AMORE from *The Caddy,* York
Pictures, Paramount
Music by HARRY WARREN. Lyrics by
JACK BROOKS

Costume Design
(Black-and-White)
THE ACTRESS, Metro-Goldwyn-Mayer:
WALTER PLUNKETT
DREAM WIFE, Metro-Goldwyn-Mayer:
HELEN ROSE and HERSCHEL MCCOY
FROM HERE TO ETERNITY, Columbia:
JEAN LOUIS
THE PRESIDENT'S LADY, 20th Century-
Fox: CHARLES LeMAIRE and RENIE
ROMAN HOLIDAY, Paramount:
EDITH HEAD
(Color)
THE BAND WAGON, Metro-Goldwyn-
Mayer: MARY ANN NYBERG
CALL ME MADAM, 20th Century-Fox:
IRENE SHARAFF
HOW TO MARRY A MILLIONAIRE, 20th
Century-Fox: CHARLES LeMAIRE and
TRAVILLA
THE ROBE, 20th Century-Fox:
CHARLES LeMAIRE and EMILE
SANTIAGO
YOUNG BESS, Metro-Goldwyn-Mayer:
WALTER PLUNKETT

Short Subjects
(Cartoons)
CHRISTOPHER CRUMPET, UPA, Colum-
bia. (Jolly Frolics): STEPHEN BOSUS-
TOW, Producer
FROM A TO Z-Z-Z-Z, Warner Bros. Car-
toons, Inc., Warner Bros. (Looney
Tunes): EDWARD SELZER, Producer
RUGGED BEAR, Walt Disney, RKO
Radio. (Donald Duck): WALT DIS-
NEY, Producer

THE TELL TALE HEART, UPA, Colum-
bia. (UPA Cartoon Special): STE-
PHEN BOSUSTOW, Producer
TOOT, WHISTLE, PLUNK AND
BOOM, Walt Disney, Buena Vista
Film Distribution Co., Inc. (Special
Music Series): WALT DISNEY,
Producer

(One-Reel)
CHRIST AMONG THE PRIMITIVES, IFE
Releasing Corp. (Italian): VINCENZO
LUCCI-CHIARISSI, Producer
HERRING HUNT, National Film Board
Of Canada, RKO Pathe, Inc. (Cana-
dian). (Canada Carries On Series)
JOY OF LIVING, Art Film Prods., 20th
Century-Fox. (Art Film Series):
BORIS VERMONT, Producer
THE MERRY WIVES OF WINDSOR
OVERTURE, Metro-Goldwyn-
Mayer. (Overture Series): JOHNNY
GREEN, Producer
WEE WATER WONDERS, Paramount.
(Grantland Rice Sportlights Series):
JACK EATON, Producer

(Two-Reel)
BEAR COUNTRY, Walt Disney, RKO
Radio. (True-Life Adventure):
WALT DISNEY, Producer
BEN AND ME, Walt Disney, Buena
Vista Film Distribution Co., Inc.
(Cartoon Special Series): WALT DIS-
NEY, Producer
RETURN TO GLENNASCAUL, Dublin
Gate Theatre Prod., Mayer-Kingsley
Inc.
VESUVIUS EXPRESS, 20th Century-Fox.
(CinemaScope Shorts Series): OTTO
LANG, Producer
WINTER PARADISE, Warner Bros.
(Technicolor Special): CEDRIC
FRANCIS, Producer

Documentary
(Short Subjects)
THE ALASKAN ESKIMO, Walt Dis-

ney Prods., RKO Radio: WALT DISNEY, Producer

THE LIVING CITY, Encyclopaedia Britannica Films, Inc.: JOHN BARNES, Producer

OPERATION BLUE JAY, U.S. Army Signal Corps

THEY PLANTED A STONE, World Wide Pictures, British Information Services (British): JAMES CARR, Producer

THE WORD, 20th Century-Fox: JOHN HEALY and JOHN ADAMS, Producers

(Features)

THE CONQUEST OF EVEREST, Countryman Films, Ltd. & Group 3 Ltd., UA (British): JOHN TAYLOR, LEON CLORE and GRAHAME THARP, Producers

THE LIVING DESERT, Walt Disney Prods., Buena Vista Film Dist. Co., Inc.: WALT DISNEY, Producer

A QUEEN IS CROWNED, J. Arthur Rank Organization, Ltd., U-I (British): CASTLETON KNIGHT, Producer

Honorary Awards

PETE SMITH for his witty and pungent observations on the American scene in his series of *Pete Smith Specialties*. (statuette)

20TH CENTURY-FOX FILM CORPORATION in recognition of their imagination, showmanship and foresight in introducing the revolutionary process known as CinemaScope. (statuette)

JOSEPH I. BREEN for his conscientious, open-minded and dignified management of the Motion Picture Production Code. (statuette)

BELL AND HOWELL COMPANY for their pioneering and basic achievements in the advancement of the motion picture industry. (statuette)

Special Effects

THE WAR OF THE WORLDS, Paramount

Irving G. Thalberg Memorial Award

GEORGE STEVENS

Scientific or Technical

Class I

PROFESSOR HENRI CHRETIEN and EARL SPONABLE, SOL HALPRIN, LORIN GRIGNON, HERBERT BRAGG and CARL FAULKNER of 20th Century-Fox Studios for creating, developing and engineering the equipment, processes and techniques known as CinemaScope

FRED WALLER for designing and developing the multiple photographic and projection systems which culminated in Cinerama

Class II

REEVES SOUNDCRAFT CORP. for their development of a process of applying stripes of magnetic oxide to motion picture film for sound recording and reproduction

Class III

WESTREX CORP. for the design and construction of a new film editing machine

1954

Nominations Announced: February 12, 1955
Awards Ceremony: March 30, 1955
RKO Pantages Theatre
(MC: Bob Hope; MC in New York: Thelma Ritter)

Best Picture

THE CAINE MUTINY, A Stanley Kramer Prod., Columbia: STANLEY KRAMER, Producer

THE COUNTRY GIRL, Perlberg-Seaton, Paramount: WILLIAM PERLBERG, Producer

ON THE WATERFRONT, Horizon-American Corp., Columbia: SAM SPIEGEL, Producer

SEVEN BRIDES FOR SEVEN BROTHERS, Metro-Goldwyn-Mayer: JACK CUMMINGS, Producer

THREE COINS IN THE FOUNTAIN, 20th Century-Fox: SOL C. SIEGEL, Producer

Actor

HUMPHREY BOGART in *The Caine Mutiny,* Kramer, Columbia

MARLON BRANDO in *On The Waterfront,* Horizon-American, Columbia

BING CROSBY in *The Country Girl,* Perlberg-Seaton, Paramount

JAMES MASON in *A Star Is Born,* Transcona, Warner Bros.

DAN O'HERLIHY in *Adventures Of Robinson Crusoe,* Dancigers-Ehrlich, UA

Actress

DOROTHY DANDRIDGE in *Carmen Jones,* Otto Preminger, 20th Century-Fox

LARGE CAPITAL LETTERS DENOTE WINNER

JUDY GARLAND in *A Star Is Born,* Transcona, Warner Bros.

AUDREY HEPBURN in *Sabrina,* Paramount

GRACE KELLY in *The Country Girl,* Perlberg-Seaton, Paramount

JANE WYMAN in *The Magnificent Obsession,* Universal-International

Supporting Actor

LEE J. COBB in *On The Waterfront,* Horizon-American, Columbia

KARL MALDEN in *On The Waterfront,* Horizon-American, Columbia

EDMOND O'BRIEN in *The Barefoot Contessa,* Figaro, UA

ROD STEIGER in *On The Waterfront,* Horizon-American, Columbia

TOM TULLY in *The Caine Mutiny,* Kramer, Columbia

Supporting Actress

NINA FOCH in *Executive Suite,* Metro-Goldwyn-Mayer

KATY JURADO in *Broken Lance,* 20th Century-Fox

EVA MARIE SAINT in *On The Waterfront,* Horizon-American, Columbia

JAN STERLING in *The High And The Mighty,* Wayne-Fellows, Warner Bros.

CLAIRE TREVOR in *The High And The Mighty,* Wayne-Fellows, Warner Bros.

Directing

ALFRED HITCHCOCK for *Rear Window,*
Patron, Inc., Paramount

ELIA KAZAN for *On The Waterfront,*
Horizon-American, Columbia

GEORGE SEATON for *The Country Girl,*
Perlberg-Seaton, Paramount

WILLIAM WELLMAN for *The High And
The Mighty,* Wayne-Fellows, Warner
Bros.

BILLY WILDER for *Sabrina,* Paramount

Writing

(Motion Picture Story)

BREAD, LOVE AND DREAMS, Titanus,
I.F.E. Releasing Corp. (Italian): ET-
TORE MARGADONNA

BROKEN LANCE, 20th Century-Fox:
PHILIP YORDAN

FORBIDDEN GAMES, Silver Films, Times
Film Corp. (French): FRANÇOIS
BOYER

NIGHT PEOPLE, 20th Century-Fox: JED
HARRIS and TOM REED

THERE'S NO BUSINESS LIKE SHOW
BUSINESS, 20th Century-Fox: LAMAR
TROTTI

(Screenplay)

THE CAINE MUTINY, A Stanley Kramer
Prod., Columbia: STANLEY ROBERTS

THE COUNTRY GIRL, Perlberg-Seaton, Paramount: GEORGE SEATON

REAR WINDOW, Patron Inc., Paramount: JOHN MICHAEL HAYES

SABRINA, Paramount: BILLY WILDER,
SAMUEL TAYLOR and ERNEST LEH-
MAN

SEVEN BRIDES FOR SEVEN BROTHERS,
Metro-Goldwyn-Mayer: ALBERT
HACKETT, FRANCES GOODRICH and
DOROTHY KINGSLEY

(Story and Screenplay)

THE BAREFOOT CONTESSA, A Figaro,
Inc., Prod., UA: JOSEPH MANKIE-
WICZ

GENEVIEVE, A J. Arthur Rank Presentation-Sirius Prods., Ltd., U-I (British): WILLIAM ROSE

THE GLENN MILLER STORY, Universal-
International: VALENTINE DAVIES and
OSCAR BRODNEY

KNOCK ON WOOD, Dena Prods., Paramount: NORMAN PANAMA and MEL-
VIN FRANK

ON THE WATERFRONT, Horizon-
American Corp., Columbia: BUDD
SCHULBERG

Cinematography

(Black-and-White)

THE COUNTRY GIRL, Perlberg-Seaton,
Paramount: JOHN F. WARREN

EXECUTIVE SUITE, Metro-Goldwyn-
Mayer: GEORGE FOLSEY

ON THE WATERFRONT, Horizon-
American Corp., Columbia: BORIS
KAUFMAN

ROGUE COP, Metro-Goldwyn-Mayer:
JOHN SEITZ

SABRINA, Paramount: CHARLES LANG,
JR.

(Color)

THE EGYPTIAN, 20th Century-Fox:
LEON SHAMROY

REAR WINDOW, Patron Inc., Paramount: ROBERT BURKS

SEVEN BRIDES FOR SEVEN BROTHERS,
Metro-Goldwyn-Mayer: GEORGE
FOLSEY

THE SILVER CHALICE, A Victor Saville
Prod., Warner Bros.: WILLIAM V.
SKALL

THREE COINS IN THE FOUNTAIN,
20th Century-Fox: MILTON
KRASNER

Art Direction—Set Decoration

(Black-and-White)

THE COUNTRY GIRL, Perlberg-Seaton,
Paramount: HAL PEREIRA and RO-
LAND ANDERSON

Set Decoration: SAM COMER and GRACE GREGORY

EXECUTIVE SUITE, Metro-Goldwyn-Mayer: CEDRIC GIBBONS and EDWARD CARFAGNO
Set Decoration: EDWIN B. WILLIS and EMILE KURI

LE PLAISIR, Stera Film—CCFC Prod., Arthur Meyer-Edward Kingsley (French): MAX OPHULS
Set Decoration: No credits listed

ON THE WATERFRONT, Horizon-American Corp., Columbia: RICHARD DAY
Set Decoration: No credits listed

SABRINA, Paramount: HAL PEREIRA and WALTER TYLER
Set Decoration: SAM COMER and RAY MOYER

(Color)

BRIGADOON, Metro-Goldwyn-Mayer: CEDRIC GIBBONS and PRESTON AMES
Set Decoration: EDWIN B. WILLIS and KEOGH GLEASON

DESIREE, 20th Century-Fox: LYLE WHEELER and LELAND FULLER
Set Decoration: WALTER M. SCOTT and PAUL S. FOX

RED GARTERS, Paramount: HAL PEREIRA and ROLAND ANDERSON
Set Decoration: SAM COMER and RAY MOYER

A STAR IS BORN, A Transcona Enterprises Prod., Warner Bros.: MALCOLM BERT, GENE ALLEN and IRENE SHARAFF
Set Decoration: GEORGE JAMES HOPKINS

20,000 LEAGUES UNDER THE SEA, Walt Disney Prods., Buena Vista Film Dist. Co., Inc.: JOHN MEEHAN
Set Decoration: EMILE KURI

Sound Recording

BRIGADOON, Metro-Goldwyn-Mayer:

WESLEY C. MILLER, Sound Director

THE CAINE MUTINY, Columbia: JOHN P. LIVADARY, Sound Director

THE GLENN MILLER STORY, Universal-International: LESLIE I. CAREY, Sound Director

REAR WINDOW, Paramount: LOREN L. RYDER, Sound Director

SUSAN SLEPT HERE, RKO Radio: JOHN O. AALBERG, Sound Director

Film Editing

THE CAINE MUTINY, A Stanley Kramer Prod., Columbia: WILLIAM A. LYON and HENRY BATISTA

THE HIGH AND THE MIGHTY, Wayne-Fellows Prod., Inc., Warner Bros.: RALPH DAWSON

ON THE WATERFRONT, Horizon-American Corp., Columbia: GENE MILFORD

SEVEN BRIDES FOR SEVEN BROTHERS, Metro-Goldwyn-Mayer: RALPH E. WINTERS

20,000 LEAGUES UNDER THE SEA, Walt Disney Prods., Buena Vista Film Dist. Co., Inc.: ELMO WILLIAMS

Music

(Scoring of a Dramatic or Comedy Picture)

THE CAINE MUTINY, A Stanley Kramer Prod., Columbia: MAX STEINER

GENEVIEVE, A J. Arthur Rank Presentation—Sirius Prods., Ltd., U-I. (British): MUIR MATHIESON

THE HIGH AND THE MIGHTY, Wayne-Fellows Prods., Inc., Warner Bros.: DIMITRI TIOMKIN

ON THE WATERFRONT, Horizon-American Corp., Columbia: LEONARD BERNSTEIN

THE SILVER CHALICE, A Victor Saville Prod., Warner Bros.: FRANZ WAXMAN

(Scoring of a Musical Picture)

CARMEN JONES, Otto Preminger, 20th

Century-Fox: HERSCHEL BURKE GIL-
BERT

THE GLENN MILLER STORY, Universal-
International: JOSEPH GERSHENSON
and HENRY MANCINI

SEVEN BRIDES FOR SEVEN
BROTHERS, Metro-Goldwyn-
Mayer: ADOLPH DEUTSCH and
SAUL CHAPLIN

A STAR IS BORN, A Transcona Enterprises Prod., Warner Bros.: RAY
HEINDORF

THERE'S NO BUSINESS LIKE SHOW
BUSINESS, 20th Century-Fox: ALFRED
NEWMAN and LIONEL NEWMAN

(Best Song)

COUNT YOUR BLESSINGS INSTEAD OF
SHEEP from *White Christmas,* Para-
mount
Music and Lyrics by IRVING BERLIN

THE HIGH AND THE MIGHTY from *The
High And The Mighty,* Wayne-
Fellows Prods., Inc., Warner Bros.
Music by DIMITRI TIOMKIN. Lyrics
by NED WASHINGTON

HOLD MY HAND from *Susan Slept Here,*
RKO Radio
Music and Lyrics by JACK LAW-
RENCE and RICHARD MYERS

THE MAN THAT GOT AWAY from *A Star
Is Born,* A Transcona Enterprises
Prod., Warner Bros.
Music by HAROLD ARLEN. Lyrics by
IRA GERSHWIN

THREE COINS IN THE FOUNTAIN
from *Three Coins In The Fountain,*
20th Century-Fox
Music by JULE STYNE. Lyrics by
SAMMY CAHN

Costume Design
(Black-and-White)

THE EARRINGS OF MADAME DE. . . ,
Franco-London Prods., Arlan Pictures (French): GEORGES ANNENKOV
and ROSINE DELAMARE

EXECUTIVE SUITE, Metro-Goldwyn-
Mayer: HELEN ROSE

INDISCRETION OF AN AMERICAN WIFE,
A Vittorio DeSica Prod., Columbia:
CHRISTIAN DIOR

IT SHOULD HAPPEN TO YOU, Columbia:
JEAN LOUIS

SABRINA, Paramount: EDITH HEAD

(Color)

BRIGADOON, Metro-Goldwyn-Mayer:
IRENE SHARAFF

DESIREE, 20th Century-Fox: CHARLES
LeMAIRE and RENE HUBERT

GATE OF HELL, A Daiei Prod., Edward Harrison (Japanese): SANZO
WADA

A STAR IS BORN, A Transcona En-
terprises Prod., Warner Bros.: JEAN
LOUIS, MARY ANN NYBERG and IRENE
SHARAFF

THERE'S NO BUSINESS LIKE SHOW
BUSINESS, 20th Century-Fox:
CHARLES LeMAIRE, TRAVILLA and
MILES WHITE

Short Subjects
(Cartoons)

CRAZY MIXED UP PUP, Walter Lantz
Prods., U-I: WALTER LANTZ, Producer

PIGS IS PIGS, Walt Disney Prods., RKO
Radio: WALT DISNEY, Producer

SANDY CLAWS, Warner Bros. Cartoons,
Inc.: EDWARD SELZER, Producer

TOUCHÉ, PUSSY CAT, Metro-Goldwyn-
Mayer: FRED QUIMBY, Producer

WHEN MAGOO FLEW, United Productions Of America, Columbia:
STEPHEN BOSUSTOW, Producer

(One-reel)

THE FIRST PIANO QUARTETTE, 20th
Century-Fox: OTTO LANG, Producer

THE STRAUSS FANTASY, Metro-
Goldwyn-Mayer: JOHNNY GREEN,
Producer

THIS MECHANICAL AGE, Warner

Bros.: ROBERT YOUNGSON, Producer

(Two-reel)

BEAUTY AND THE BULL, Warner Bros.:
CEDRIC FRANCIS, Producer

JET CARRIER, 20th Century-Fox: OTTO
LANG, Producer

SIAM, Walt Disney Prods., Buena Vista
Film Distribution Co., Inc.: WALT
DISNEY, Producer

A TIME OUT OF WAR, Carnival
Prods.: DENIS and TERRY
SANDERS, Producers

Documentary

(Short Subjects)

JET CARRIER, 20th Century-Fox: OTTO
LANG, Producer

REMBRANDT: A SELF-PORTRAIT, Distributors Corp. of America: MORRIE
ROIZMAN, Producer

THURSDAY'S CHILDREN, British
Information Services (British):
WORLD WIDE PICTURES AND
MORSE FILMS, Producers

(Features)

THE STRATFORD ADVENTURE, National
Film Board of Canada, Continental
Dist., Inc. (Canadian): GUY GLOVER,
Producer

THE VANISHING PRAIRIE, Walt
Disney Prods., Buena Vista Film
Dist. Co., Inc.: WALT DISNEY,
Producer

Special Effects

(Back to Annual Award)

HELL AND HIGH WATER, 20th Century-Fox

THEM!, Warner Bros.

20,000 LEAGUES UNDER THE SEA,
Walt Disney Studios

Honorary Awards

BAUSCH & LOMB OPTICAL COMPANY for their contributions to the
advancement of the motion picture
industry. (statuette)

KEMP R. NIVER for the development
of the Renovare Process which has
made possible the restoration of the
Library of Congress Paper Film Collection. (statuette)

GRETA GARBO for her unforgettable
screen performances. (statuette)

DANNY KAYE for his unique talents,
his service to the Academy, the motion picture industry, and the American people. (statuette)

JON WHITELEY for his outstanding
juvenile performance in *The Little
Kidnappers*. (miniature statuette)

VINCENT WINTER for his outstanding juvenile performance in *The Little Kidnappers*. (miniature statuette)

GATE OF HELL (Japanese)—Best
Foreign Language Film first released
in the United States during 1954.
(statuette)

Irving G. Thalberg Memorial Award
None

Scientific or Technical

Class I

PARAMOUNT PICTURES, INC.,
LOREN L. RYDER, JOHN R.
BISHOP and all the members of the
technical and engineering staff for
developing a method of producing
and exhibiting motion pictures
known as VistaVision

Class II

None

Class III

DAVID S. HORSLEY and the UNIVERSAL-INTERNATIONAL STUDIO SPECIAL PHOTOGRAPHIC
DEPARTMENT for a portable remote control device for process projectors

KARL FREUND and FRANK CRAN-DELL of Photo Research Corp. for the design and development of a direct reading brightness meter

WESLEY C. MILLER, J. W. STAF-FORD, K. M. FRIERSON and the METRO-GOLDWYN-MAYER STUDIO SOUND DEPARTMENT for an electronic sound printing comparison device

JOHN P. LIVADARY, LLOYD RUS-SELL and the COLUMBIA STUDIO SOUND DEPARTMENT for an improved limiting amplifier as applied to sound level comparison devices

ROLAND MILLER and MAX GOEP-PINGER of Magnascope Corp. for the design and development of a cathode ray magnetic sound track viewer

CARLOS RIVAS, G. M. SPRAGUE and the METRO-GOLDWYN-MAYER STUDIO SOUND DE-PARTMENT for the design of a magnetic sound editing machine

FRED WILSON of the Samuel Goldwyn Studio Sound Department for the design of a variable multiple-band equalizer

P. C. YOUNG of the Metro-Goldwyn-Mayer Studio Projection Department for the practical application of a variable focal length attachment to motion picture projector lenses

FRED KNOTH and ORIEN ERNEST of the Universal-International Studio Technical Department for the development of a hand portable, electric, dry oil-fog machine

1955

Nominations Announced: February 18, 1956
Awards Ceremony: March 21, 1956
RKO Pantages Theatre
(MC: Jerry Lewis: MCs in New York: Claudette Colbert and Joseph L. Mankiewicz)

Best Picture

LOVE IS A MANY-SPLENDORED THING, 20th Century-Fox: BUDDY ADLER, Producer

MARTY, Hecht and Lancaster's Steven Prods., UA: HAROLD HECHT, Producer

MISTER ROBERTS, An Orange Prod., Warner Bros.: LELAND HAYWARD, Producer

PICNIC, Columbia: FRED KOHLMAR, Producer

THE ROSE TATTOO, Hal Wallis, Paramount: HAL B. WALLIS, Producer

Actor

ERNEST BORGNINE in *Marty,* Hecht & Lancaster's Steven Prods., UA

JAMES CAGNEY in *Love Me Or Leave Me,* Metro-Goldwyn-Mayer

JAMES DEAN in *East Of Eden,* Warner Bros.

FRANK SINATRA in *The Man With The Golden Arm,* Preminger, UA

SPENCER TRACY in *Bad Day At Black Rock,* Metro-Goldwyn-Mayer

Actress

SUSAN HAYWARD in *I'll Cry Tomorrow,* Metro-Goldwyn-Mayer

KATHARINE HEPBURN in *Summertime,* Ilya Lopert-David Lean, UA. (Anglo-American)

LARGE CAPITAL LETTERS DENOTE WINNER

JENNIFER JONES in *Love Is A Many-Splendored Thing,* 20th Century-Fox

ANNA MAGNANI in *The Rose Tattoo,* Hal B. Wallis, Paramount

ELEANOR PARKER in *Interrupted Melody,* Metro-Goldwyn-Mayer

Supporting Actor

ARTHUR KENNEDY in *Trial,* Metro-Goldwyn-Mayer

JACK LEMMON in *Mister Roberts,* An Orange Prod., Warner Bros.

JOE MANTELL in *Marty,* Hecht & Lancaster's Steven Prods., UA

SAL MINEO in *Rebel Without A Cause,* Warner Bros.

ARTHUR O'CONNELL in *Picnic,* Columbia

Supporting Actress

BETSY BLAIR in *Marty,* Hecht & Lancaster's Steven Prods., UA

PEGGY LEE in *Pete Kelly's Blues,* A Mark VII Ltd. Prod., Warner Bros.

MARISA PAVAN in *The Rose Tattoo,* Hal Wallis, Paramount

JO VAN FLEET in *East Of Eden,* Warner Bros.

NATALIE WOOD in *Rebel Without A Cause,* Warner Bros.

Directing

ELIA KAZAN for *East Of Eden,* Warner Bros.

DAVID LEAN for *Summertime,* Ilya

421

Lopert-David Lean, UA (Anglo-American)

JOSHUA LOGAN for *Picnic,* Columbia

DELBERT MANN for *Marty,* Hecht & Lancaster's Steven Prods., UA

JOHN STURGES for *Bad Day At Black Rock,* Metro-Goldwyn-Mayer

Writing

(Motion Picture Story)

LOVE ME OR LEAVE ME, Metro-Goldwyn-Mayer: DANIEL FUCHS

THE PRIVATE WAR OF MAJOR BENSON, U-I: JOE CONNELLY and BOB MOSHER

REBEL WITHOUT A CAUSE, Warner Bros.: NICHOLAS RAY

THE SHEEP HAS 5 LEGS, Raoul Ploquin, United Motion Picture Organization (French): JEAN MARSAN, HENRY TROYAT, JACQUES PERRET, HENRI VERNEUIL and RAOUL PLOQUIN

STRATEGIC AIR COMMAND, Paramount: BEIRNE LAY, JR.

(Best Screenplay)

BAD DAY AT BLACK ROCK, Metro-Goldwyn-Mayer: MILLARD KAUFMAN

BLACKBOARD JUNGLE, Metro-Goldwyn-Mayer: RICHARD BROOKS

EAST OF EDEN, Warner Bros.: PAUL OSBORN

LOVE ME OR LEAVE ME, Metro-Goldwyn-Mayer: DANIEL FUCHS and ISOBEL LENNART

MARTY, Hecht and Lancaster's Steven Prods., UA: PADDY CHAYEFSKY

(Story and Screenplay)

THE COURT-MARTIAL OF BILLY MITCH-ELL, A United States Pictures Prod., Warner Bros.: MILTON SPER-LING and EMMET LAVERY

INTERRUPTED MELODY, Metro-Goldwyn-Mayer: WILLIAM LUD-WIG and SONYA LEVIEN

IT'S ALWAYS FAIR WEATHER, Metro-Goldwyn-Mayer: BETTY COMDEN and ADOLPH GREEN

MR. HULOT'S HOLIDAY, Fred Orain Prod., GBD International Releasing Corp. (French): JACQUES TATI and HENRI MARQUET

THE SEVEN LITTLE FOYS, Hope Enterprises, Inc. and Scribe Prods.: MELVILLE SHAVELSON and JACK ROSE

Cinematography

(Black-and-White)

BLACKBOARD JUNGLE, Metro-Goldwyn-Mayer: RUSSELL HARLAN

I'LL CRY TOMORROW, Metro-Goldwyn-Mayer: ARTHUR E. ARLING

MARTY, Hecht and Lancaster's Steven Prods., UA: JOSEPH LaSHELLE

QUEEN BEE, Columbia: CHARLES LANG

THE ROSE TATTOO, Hal Wallis, Paramount: JAMES WONG HOWE

(Color)

GUYS AND DOLLS, Samuel Goldwyn Prods., Inc., M-G-M: HARRY STRADLING

LOVE IS A MANY-SPLENDORED THING, 20th Century-Fox: LEON SHAMROY

A MAN CALLED PETER, 20th Century-Fox: HAROLD LIPSTEIN

OKLAHOMA!, Rodgers & Hammerstein Pictures, Inc., Magna Theatre Corp.: ROBERT SURTEES

TO CATCH A THIEF, Paramount: ROBERT BURKS

Art Direction—Set Decoration

(Prior to 1955, Set Decorators were given plaques. Beginning in 1955, Gold Statuettes were also given to Set Decorators.)

(Black-and-White)

BLACKBOARD JUNGLE, Metro-Goldwyn-Mayer: CEDRIC GIBBONS and RAN-DALL DUELL
Set Decoration: EDWIN B. WILLIS and HENRY GRACE

I'LL CRY TOMORROW, Metro-Goldwyn-
Mayer: CEDRIC GIBBONS and MAL-
COLM BROWN
Set Decoration: EDWIN B. WILLIS and
HUGH B. HUNT
THE MAN WITH THE GOLDEN ARM, Otto
Preminger Prod., UA: JOSEPH C.
WRIGHT
Set Decoration: DARRELL SILVERA
MARTY, Hecht and Lancaster's Steven
Prods., UA: EDWARD S. HAWORTH
and WALTER SIMONDS
Set Decoration: ROBERT PRIESTLEY
THE ROSE TATTOO, Hal Wallis,
Paramount: HAL PEREIRA and
TAMBI LARSEN
Set Decoration: SAM COMER and
ARTHUR KRAMS

(Color)

DADDY LONG LEGS, 20th Century-Fox:
LYLE WHEELER and JOHN DeCUIR
Set Decoration: WALTER M. SCOTT
and PAUL S. FOX
GUYS AND DOLLS, Samuel Goldwyn
Prods., Inc., M-G-M: OLIVER SMITH
and JOSEPH C. WRIGHT
Set Decoration: HOWARD BRISTOL
LOVE IS A MANY-SPLENDORED THING,
20th Century-Fox: LYLE WHEELER
and GEORGE W. DAVIS
Set Decoration: WALTER M. SCOTT
and JACK STUBBS
PICNIC, Columbia: WILLIAM FLAN-
NERY and JO MIELZINER
Set Decoration: ROBERT PRIEST-
LEY
TO CATCH A THIEF, Paramount: HAL
PEREIRA and JOSEPH MCMILLAN
JOHNSON
Set Decoration: SAM COMER and AR-
THUR KRAMS

Sound Recording

LOVE IS A MANY-SPLENDORED THING,
20th Century-Fox Studio Sound De-
partment: CARL W. FAULKNER,
Sound Director
LOVE ME OR LEAVE ME, Metro-
Goldwyn-Mayer Studio Sound De-
partment: WESLEY C. MILLER, Sound
Director
MISTER ROBERTS, Warner Bros. Studio
Sound Department: WILLIAM A.
MUELLER, Sound Director
NOT AS A STRANGER, Radio Corpora-
tion of America Sound Department:
WATSON JONES, Sound Director
OKLAHOMA!, Todd-AO Sound De-
partment: FRED HYNES, Sound Di-
rector

Film Editing

BLACKBOARD JUNGLE, Metro-Goldwyn-
Mayer: FERRIS WEBSTER
THE BRIDGES AT TOKO-RI, Perlberg-Sea-
ton, Paramount: ALMA MACRORIE
OKLAHOMA!, Rodgers & Hammerstein
Pictures, Inc., Magna Theatre Corp.:
GENE RUGGIERO and GEORGE BOEM-
LER
PICNIC, Columbia: CHARLES NEL-
SON and WILLIAM A. LYON
THE ROSE TATTOO, Hal Wallis, Para-
mount: WARREN LOW

Music

(Scoring of a Dramatic or Comedy Picture)

BATTLE CRY, Warner Bros.: MAX
STEINER
LOVE IS A MANY-SPLENDORED
THING, 20th Century-Fox:
ALFRED NEWMAN
THE MAN WITH THE GOLDEN ARM, Otto
Preminger Prod., UA: ELMER BERN-
STEIN
PICNIC, Columbia: GEORGE DUNING
THE ROSE TATTOO, Hal Wallis, Para-
mount: ALEX NORTH

(Scoring of a Musical Picture)

DADDY LONG LEGS, 20th Century-Fox:
ALFRED NEWMAN

GUYS AND DOLLS, Samuel Goldwyn
Prods., Inc., M-G-M: JAY BLACKTON
and CYRIL J. MOCKRIDGE

IT'S ALWAYS FAIR WEATHER, Metro-
Goldwyn-Mayer: ANDRÉ PREVIN

LOVE ME OR LEAVE ME, Metro-
Goldwyn-Mayer: PERCY FAITH and
GEORGE STOLL

OKLAHOMA!, Rodgers & Hammer-
stein Pictures, Inc., Magna Theatre
Corp.: ROBERT RUSSELL BEN-
NETT, JAY BLACKTON and
ADOLPH DEUTSCH

(Best Song)

I'LL NEVER STOP LOVING YOU from
Love Me Or Leave Me, Metro-
Goldwyn-Mayer
Music by NICHOLAS BRODSZKY.
Lyrics by SAMMY CAHN

LOVE IS A MANY-SPLENDORED
THING from *Love Is A Many-Splen-
dored Thing,* 20th Century-Fox
Music by SAMMY FAIN. Lyrics by
PAUL FRANCIS WEBSTER

SOMETHING'S GOTTA GIVE from *Daddy
Long Legs,* 20th Century-Fox
Music and Lyrics by JOHNNY MER-
CER

(LOVE IS) THE TENDER TRAP from *The
Tender Trap,* Metro-Goldwyn-Mayer
Music by JAMES VAN HEUSEN. Lyrics
by SAMMY CAHN

UNCHAINED MELODY from *Unchained,*
Hall Bartlett Prods., Inc., Warner
Bros.
Music by ALEX NORTH. Lyrics by HY
ZARET

Costume Design

(Black-and-White)

I'LL CRY TOMORROW, Metro-
Goldwyn-Mayer: HELEN ROSE

THE PICKWICK PAPERS, Renown Prod.,
Kingsley International Pictures (British): BEATRICE DAWSON

QUEEN BEE, Columbia: JEAN LOUIS

THE ROSE TATTOO, Hal Wallis, Paramount: EDITH HEAD

UGETSU, Daiei Motion Picture Co., Edward Harrison (Japanese): TADAOTO
KAINOSCHO

(Color)

GUYS AND DOLLS, Samuel Goldwyn
Prods., Inc., M-G-M: IRENE
SHARAFF

INTERRUPTED MELODY, Metro-
Goldwyn-Mayer: HELEN ROSE

LOVE IS A MANY-SPLENDORED
THING, 20th Century-Fox:
CHARLES LeMAIRE

TO CATCH A THIEF, Paramount: EDITH
HEAD

THE VIRGIN QUEEN, 20th Century-Fox:
CHARLES LeMAIRE and MARY WILLS

Short Subjects

(Cartoons)

GOOD WILL TO MEN, Metro-Goldwyn-
Mayer: FRED QUIMBY, WILLIAM
HANNA and JOSEPH BARBERA, Pro-
ducers

THE LEGEND OF ROCK-A-BYE-POINT,
Walter Lantz Prods., U-I: WALTER
LANTZ, Producer

NO HUNTING, Walt Disney Prods.,
RKO Radio: WALT DISNEY, Producer

SPEEDY GONZALES, Warner Bros.
Cartoons, Inc.: EDWARD SELZER,
Producer

(One-reel)

GADGETS GALORE, Warner Bros.: ROB-
ERT YOUNGSON, Producer

SURVIVAL CITY, 20th Century-Fox:
EDMUND REEK, Producer

3RD AVE. EL, Carson Davidson Prods.,
Ardee Films: CARSON DAVIDSON,
Producer

THREE KISSES, Paramount: JUSTIN
HERMAN, Producer

(Two-reel)

THE BATTLE OF GETTYSBURG, Metro-

Goldwyn-Mayer: DORE SCHARY, Producer
THE FACE OF LINCOLN, University Of Southern California Presentation, Cavalcade Pictures, Inc.: WILBUR T. BLUME, Producer
ON THE TWELFTH DAY. . . , Go Pictures, Inc., George Brest & Assocs.: GEORGE K. ARTHUR, Producer
SWITZERLAND, Walt Disney Prods., Buena Vista Film Distribution Co., Inc.: WALT DISNEY, Producer
24 HOUR ALERT, Warner Bros.: CEDRIC FRANCIS, Producer

Documentary
(Short Subjects)
THE BATTLE OF GETTYSBURG, Metro-Goldwyn-Mayer: DORE SCHARY, Producer
THE FACE OF LINCOLN, University of Southern California Presentation, Cavalcade Pictures, Inc.: WILBUR T. BLUME, Producer
MEN AGAINST THE ARCTIC, Walt Disney Prods., Buena Vista Film Dist. Co., Inc.: WALT DISNEY, Producer

(Features)
HEARTBREAK RIDGE, Rene Risacher Prod., Tudor Pictures (French): RENE RISACHER, Producer
HELEN KELLER IN HER STORY, Nancy Hamilton Presentation: NANCY HAMILTON, Producer

Special Effects
THE BRIDGES AT TOKO-RI, Paramount
THE DAM BUSTERS, Associated British Picture Corp., Ltd. (British)
THE RAINS OF RANCHIPUR, 20th Century-Fox

Honorary Award
SAMURAI, THE LEGEND OF

MUSASHI, (Japanese)—Best Foreign Language Film first released in the United States during 1955. (statuette)

Irving G. Thalberg Memorial Award
None

Scientific or Technical
Class I
NATIONAL CARBON CO. for the development and production of a high efficiency yellow flame carbon for motion picture color photography

Class II
EASTMAN KODAK CO. for Eastman Tri-X panchromatic negative film
FARCIOT EDOUART, HAL CORL and the PARAMOUNT STUDIO TRANSPARENCY DEPARTMENT for the engineering and development of a double-frame, triple-head background projector

Class III
20TH CENTURY-FOX STUDIO and BAUSCH & LOMB CO. for the new combination lenses for CinemaScope photography
WALTER JOLLEY, MAURICE LARSON and R. H. SPIES of 20th Century-Fox Studio for a spraying process which creates simulated metallic surfaces
STEVE KRILANOVICH for an improved camera dolly incorporating multi-directional steering
DAVE ANDERSON of 20th Century-Fox Studio for an improved spotlight capable of maintaining a fixed circle of light at constant intensity over varied distances
LOREN L. RYDER, CHARLES WEST, HENRY FRACKER and PARAMOUNT STUDIO for a projection film index to establish proper framing for various aspect ratios

FARCIOT EDOUART, HAL CORL
and the PARAMOUNT STUDIO
TRANSPARENCY DEPARTMENT

for an improved dual stereopticon
background projector

1956

Nominations Announced: February 18, 1957
Awards Ceremony: March 27, 1957
RKO Pantages Theatre
(MC: Jerry Lewis; MC in New York: Celeste Holm)
(New York ceremony not held after this year.)

Best Picture

AROUND THE WORLD IN 80
DAYS, The Michael Todd Co., Inc.,
UA: MICHAEL TODD, Producer
FRIENDLY PERSUASION, Allied Artists:
WILLIAM WYLER, Producer
GIANT, Giant Prod., Warner Bros.:
GEORGE STEVENS & HENRY GINS-
BERG, Producers
THE KING AND I, 20th Century-Fox:
CHARLES BRACKETT, Producer
THE TEN COMMANDMENTS, Motion Pic-
ture Assocs., Inc., Paramount: CECIL
B. DeMILLE, Producer

Actor

YUL BRYNNER in *The King And I*,
20th Century-Fox
JAMES DEAN in *Giant*, Giant Prod.,
Warner Bros.
KIRK DOUGLAS in *Lust For Life*, Metro-
Goldwyn-Mayer
ROCK HUDSON in *Giant*, Giant Prod.,
Warner Bros.
SIR LAURENCE OLIVIER in *Richard III*,
Laurence Olivier Prod., Lopert Films
Dist. Corp. (British)

Actress

CARROLL BAKER in *Baby Doll*, A Newtown Prod., Warner Bros.
INGRID BERGMAN in *Anastasia*,
20th Century-Fox
KATHARINE HEPBURN in *The Rain-

LARGE CAPITAL LETTERS DENOTE WINNER

maker*, Hal Wallis Prods., Para-
mount
NANCY KELLY in *The Bad Seed*,
Warner Bros.
DEBORAH KERR in *The King And I*, 20th
Century-Fox

Supporting Actor

DON MURRAY in *Bus Stop*, 20th Cen-
tury-Fox
ANTHONY PERKINS in *Friendly Per-
suasion*, Allied Artists
ANTHONY QUINN in *Lust For Life*,
Metro-Goldwyn-Mayer
MICKEY ROONEY in *The Bold And The
Brave*, Filmakers Releasing Org.,
RKO Radio
ROBERT STACK in *Written On The Wind*,
Universal-International

Supporting Actress

MILDRED DUNNOCK in *Baby Doll*, A
Newtown Prod., Warner Bros.
EILEEN HECKART in *The Bad Seed*,
Warner Bros.
MERCEDES MCCAMBRIDGE in *Giant*,
Giant Prod., Warner Bros.
PATTY MCCORMACK in *The Bad Seed*,
Warner Bros.
DOROTHY MALONE in *Written On
The Wind*, Universal-International

Directing

MICHAEL ANDERSON for *Around The
World In 80 Days*, The Michael
Todd Co., Inc., UA

WALTER LANG for *The King And I,* 20th Century-Fox

GEORGE STEVENS for *Giant,* Giant Prod., Warner Bros.

KING VIDOR for *War And Peace,* A Ponti-DeLaurentiis Prod., Paramount (Italo-American)

WILLIAM WYLER for *Friendly Persuasion,* Allied Artists

Writing

(Motion Picture Story)

THE BRAVE ONE, King Bros. Prods., Inc., RKO Radio: ROBERT RICH (pseudonym for DALTON TRUMBO)

THE EDDY DUCHIN STORY, Columbia: LEO KATCHER

HIGH SOCIETY, Allied Artists: EDWARD BERNDS and ELWOOD ULLMAN. (withdrawn from final ballot)

THE PROUD AND THE BEAUTIFUL, La Compagnie Industrielle Commerciale Cinematographique, Kingsley International (French): JEAN-PAUL SARTRE

UMBERTO D., Rizzoli-De Sica-Amato Prod., Harrison & Davidson (Italian): CESARE ZAVATTINI

(Best Screenplay—adapted)

AROUND THE WORLD IN 80 DAYS, The Michael Todd Co., Inc., UA: JAMES POE, JOHN FARROW and S. J. PERELMAN

BABY DOLL, A Newtown Prod., Warner Bros.: TENNESSEE WILLIAMS

GIANT, Giant Prod., Warner Bros.: FRED GUIOL and IVAN MOFFAT

LUST FOR LIFE, Metro-Goldwyn-Mayer: NORMAN CORWIN

FRIENDLY PERSUASION, Allied Artists: (Writer MICHAEL WILSON ineligible under Academy By-laws)

(Best Screenplay—original)

THE BOLD AND THE BRAVE, Filmakers Releasing Organization, RKO

Radio: ROBERT LEWIN

JULIE, Arwin Prods., M-G-M: ANDREW L. STONE

LA STRADA, Ponti-De Laurentiis Prod., Trans-Lux Dist. Corp. (Italian): FEDERICO FELLINI and TULLIO PINELLI

THE LADY KILLERS, Ealing Studios Ltd., Continental Dist., Inc. (British): WILLIAM ROSE

THE RED BALLOON, Films Montsouris, Lopert Films Dist. Corp. (French): ALBERT LAMORISSE

Cinematography

(Black-and-White)

BABY DOLL, A Newtown Prod., Warner Bros.: BORIS KAUFMAN

THE BAD SEED, Warner Bros.: HAL ROSSON

THE HARDER THEY FALL, Columbia: BURNETT GUFFEY

SOMEBODY UP THERE LIKES ME, Metro-Goldwyn-Mayer: JOSEPH RUTTENBERG

STAGECOACH TO FURY, Regal Films, Inc. Prod., 20th Century-Fox: WALTER STRENGE

(Color)

AROUND THE WORLD IN 80 DAYS, The Michael Todd Co., Inc., UA: LIONEL LINDON

THE EDDY DUCHIN STORY, Columbia: HARRY STRADLING

THE KING AND I, 20th Century-Fox: LEON SHAMROY

THE TEN COMMANDMENTS, Motion Picture Assoc., Paramount: LOYAL GRIGGS

WAR AND PEACE, A Ponti-De Laurentiis Prod., Paramount (Italo-American): JACK CARDIFF

Art Direction—Set Decoration

(Black-and-White)

THE MAGNIFICENT SEVEN, A Toho Prod., Kingsley International (Japa-

nese): TAKASHI MATSUYAMA
Set Decoration: No credits listed
THE PROUD AND THE PROFANE, The
Perlberg-Seaton Prod., Paramount:
HAL PEREIRA and A. EARL HEDRICK
Set Decoration: SAMUEL M. COMER
and FRANK R. MCKELVY
THE SOLID GOLD CADILLAC, Columbia:
ROSS BELLAH
Set Decoration: WILLIAM R. KIERNAN
and LOUIS DIAGE
SOMEBODY UP THERE LIKES ME,
Metro-Goldwyn-Mayer: CEDRIC
GIBBONS and MALCOLM F.
BROWN
Set Decoration: EDWIN B. WILLIS
and F. KEOGH GLEASON
TEENAGE REBEL, 20th Century-Fox:
LYLE R. WHEELER and JACK MARTIN
SMITH
Set Decoration: WALTER M. SCOTT
and STUART A. REISS

(Color)
AROUND THE WORLD IN 80 DAYS, The
Michael Todd Co., Inc., UA: JAMES
W. SULLIVAN and KEN ADAM
Set Decoration: ROSS J. DOWD
GIANT, Giant Prod., Warner Bros.:
BORIS LEVEN
Set Decoration: RALPH S. HURST
THE KING AND I, 20th Century-Fox:
LYLE R. WHEELER and JOHN
DeCUIR
Set Decoration: WALTER M.
SCOTT and PAUL S. FOX
LUST FOR LIFE, Metro-Goldwyn-Mayer:
CEDRIC GIBBONS, HANS PETERS and
PRESTON AMES
Set Decoration: EDWIN B. WILLIS and
F. KEOGH GLEASON
THE TEN COMMANDMENTS, Motion Pic-
ture Assocs., Inc., Paramount: HAL
PEREIRA, WALTER H. TYLER and AL-
BERT NOZAKI
Set Decoration: SAM M. COMER and
RAY MOYER

Sound Recording
THE BRAVE ONE, King Bros. Produc-
tions, Inc.: JOHN MYERS, Sound
Director
THE EDDY DUCHIN STORY, Columbia
Studo Sound Department: JOHN LI-
VADARY, Sound Director
FRIENDLY PERSUASION, Allied Artists.
Westrex Sound Services, Inc.: GOR-
DON R. GLENNAN, Sound Director;
and Samuel Goldwyn Studio Sound
Department: GORDON SAWYER,
Sound Director
THE KING AND I, 20th Century-Fox
Studio Sound Department: CARL
FAULKNER, Sound Director
THE TEN COMMANDMENTS, Paramount
Studio Sound Department: LOREN L.
RYDER, Sound Director

Film Editing
AROUND THE WORLD IN 80
DAYS, The Michael Todd Co., Inc.,
UA: GENE RUGGIERO and PAUL
WEATHERWAX
THE BRAVE ONE, King Bros. Prods.,
Inc., RKO Radio: MERRILL G. WHITE
GIANT, Giant Prod., Warner Bros.:
WILLIAM HORNBECK, PHILIP W. AN-
DERSON and FRED BOHANAN
SOMEBODY UP THERE LIKES ME, Metro-
Goldwyn-Mayer: ALBERT AKST
THE TEN COMMANDMENTS, Motion Pic-
ture Assocs., Inc., Paramount: ANNE
BAUCHENS

Music
(Scoring of a Dramatic or Comedy Pic-
ture)
ANASTASIA, 20th Century-Fox: ALFRED
NEWMAN
AROUND THE WORLD IN 80
DAYS, The Michael Todd Co., Inc.,
UA: VICTOR YOUNG
BETWEEN HEAVEN AND HELL, 20th
Century-Fox: HUGO FRIEDHOFER

GIANT, Giant Prod., Warner Bros.:
DIMITRI TIOMKIN
THE RAINMAKER, A Hal Wallis Prod.,
Paramount: ALEX NORTH

(Scoring of a Musical Picture)

THE BEST THINGS IN LIFE ARE FREE,
20th Century-Fox: LIONEL NEWMAN
THE EDDY DUCHIN STORY, Columbia:
MORRIS STOLOFF and GEORGE DUN-
ING
HIGH SOCIETY, Sol C. Siegel Prod.,
M-G-M: JOHNNY GREEN and SAUL
CHAPLIN
THE KING AND I, 20th Century-Fox:
ALFRED NEWMAN and KEN
DARBY
MEET ME IN LAS VEGAS, Metro-
Goldwyn-Mayer: GEORGE STOLL and
JOHNNY GREEN

(Best Song)

FRIENDLY PERSUASION (THEE I LOVE)
from *Friendly Persuasion,* Allied
Artists
Music by DIMITRI TIOMKIN. Lyrics
by PAUL FRANCIS WEBSTER
JULIE from *Julie,* Arwin Prods.,
M-G-M
Music by LEITH STEVENS. Lyrics by
TOM ADAIR
TRUE LOVE from *High Society,* Sol C.
Siegel Prod., M-G-M
Music and Lyrics by COLE PORTER
WHATEVER WILL BE, WILL BE
(QUE SERA, SERA) from *The Man
Who Knew Too Much,* Filwite
Prods., Inc., Paramount
Music and Lyrics by JAY LIVING-
STON and RAY EVANS
WRITTEN ON THE WIND from *Written
On The Wind,* Universal-Interna-
tional
Music by VICTOR YOUNG. Lyrics by
SAMMY CAHN

Costume Design
(Black-and-White)

THE MAGNIFICENT SEVEN, A Toho
Prod., Kingsley International (Japa-
nese): KOHEI EZAKI
THE POWER AND THE PRIZE, Metro-
Goldwyn-Mayer: HELEN ROSE
THE PROUD AND THE PROFANE, The
Perlberg-Seaton Prod., Paramount:
EDITH HEAD
THE SOLID GOLD CADILLAC, Co-
lumbia: JEAN LOUIS
TEENAGE REBEL, 20th Century-Fox:
CHARLES LeMAIRE and MARY WILLS

(Color)

AROUND THE WORLD IN 80 DAYS, The
Michael Todd Co., Inc., UA: MILES
WHITE
GIANT, Giant Prod., Warner Bros: MOSS
MABRY and MARJORIE BEST
THE KING AND I, 20th Century-Fox:
IRENE SHARAFF
THE TEN COMMANDMENTS, Motion Pic-
ture Assoc., Inc., Paramount: EDITH
HEAD, RALPH JESTER, JOHN JENSEN,
DOROTHY JEAKINS and ARNOLD FRI-
BERG
WAR AND PEACE, A Ponti-De Laurentiis
Prod., Paramount (Italo-American):
MARIE DE MATTEIS

Short Subjects
(Cartoons)

GERALD MCBOING-BOING ON PLANET
MOO, UPA Pictures, Columbia:
STEPHEN BOSUSTOW, Producer
THE JAYWALKER, UPA Pictures, Co-
lumbia: STEPHEN BOSUSTOW, Pro-
ducer
MISTER MAGOO'S PUDDLE JUMP-
ER, UPA Pictures, Columbia: STE-
PHEN BOSUSTOW, Producer

(One-reel)

CRASHING THE WATER BARRIER,
Warner Bros. KONSTANTIN KAL-
SER, Producer
I NEVER FORGET A FACE, Warner Bros.:
ROBERT YOUNGSON, Producer

TIME STOOD STILL, Warner Bros.: CEDRIC FRANCIS, Producer

(Two-reel)

THE BESPOKE OVERCOAT, George K. Arthur. ROMULUS FILMS, Producer

COW DOG, Walt Disney Prods., Buena Vista Film Distribution Co., Inc.: LARRY LANSBURGH, Producer

THE DARK WAVE, 20th Century-Fox: JOHN HEALY, Producer

SAMOA, Walt Disney Prods., Buena Vista Film Distribution Co., Inc.: WALT DISNEY, Producer

Documentary

(Short Subjects)

A CITY DECIDES, Charles Guggenheim & Assocs., Inc. Prod.

THE DARK WAVE, 20th Century-Fox: JOHN HEALY, Producer

THE HOUSE WITHOUT A NAME, Universal-International: VALENTINE DAVIES, Producer

MAN IN SPACE, Walt Disney Prods., Buena Vista Film Dist. Co., Inc.: WARD KIMBALL, Producer

THE TRUE STORY OF THE CIVIL WAR, Camera Eye Pictures, Inc.: LOUIS CLYDE STOUMEN, Producer

(Features)

THE NAKED EYE, Camera Eye Pictures, Inc.: LOUIS CLYDE STOUMEN, Producer

THE SILENT WORLD, A Filmad-F.S.J.Y.C. Prod., Columbia (French): JACQUES-YVES COUSTEAU, Producer

WHERE MOUNTAINS FLOAT, Brandon Films, Inc. (Danish): THE GOVERNMENT FILM COMMITTEE OF DENMARK, Producer

Special Effects

FORBIDDEN PLANET, Metro-Goldwyn-Mayer: A. ARNOLD GILLESPIE, IRVING RIES and WESLEY C. MILLER

THE TEN COMMANDMENTS, Motion Picture Associates, Inc., Paramount: JOHN FULTON

Foreign Language Film Award

(New Category)

(Prior to 1956 an Honorary Award voted by Board of Governors.)

THE CAPTAIN OF KOPENICK, Real-Film (Germany): GYULA TREBITSCH and WALTER KOPPEL, Producers

GERVAISE, Agnes Delahaie Productions Cinematographiques & Silver Film (France): ANNIE DORFMANN, Producer

HARP OF BURMA, Nikkatsu Corporation (Japan): MASAYUKI TAKAGI, Producer

LA STRADA, A Ponti-De Laurentiis Production (Italy). DINO DE LAURENTIIS and CARLO PONTI, Producers

QIVITOQ, A/S Nordisk Films Kompagni (Denmark): O. DALSGAARD-OLSEN, Producer

Honorary Award

EDDIE CANTOR for distinguished service to the film industry. (statuette)

Irving G. Thalberg Memorial Award

BUDDY ADLER

Jean Hersholt Humanitarian Award

(New Category)

Y. FRANK FREEMAN

Scientific or Technical

Class I

None

Class II

None

Class III

RICHARD H. RANGER of Ranger-
tone, Inc., for the development of a
synchronous recording and reproducing system for quarter-inch magnetic
tape

TED HIRSCH, CARL HAUGE and
EDWARD REICHARD of Consolidated Film Industries for an automatic scene counter for laboratory
projection rooms

THE TECHNICAL DEPARTMENTS
of PARAMOUNT PICTURES
CORP. for the engineering and development of the Paramount lightweight horizontal-movement VistaVision camera

ROY C. STEWART AND SONS of
Stewart-Trans Lux Corp., DR. C. R.
DAILY and the TRANSPARENCY
DEPARTMENT of PARAMOUNT
PICTURES CORP. for the engineer-
ing and development of the HiTrans
and Para-HiTrans rear projection
screens

THE CONSTRUCTION DEPART-
MENT of METRO-GOLDWYN-
MAYER STUDIO for a new hand-
portable fog machine

DANIEL J. BLOOMBERG, JOHN
POND, WILLIAM WADE and the
ENGINEERING and CAMERA DE-
PARTMENTS of REPUBLIC STU-
DIO for the Naturama adaptation to
the Mitchell camera

1957

Nominations Announced: February 17, 1958
Awards Ceremony: March 26, 1958
RKO Pantages Theatre
(MCs: James Stewart, David Niven, Jack Lemmon, Rosalind Russell,
Donald Duck on film, Bob Hope)

Best Picture

THE BRIDGE ON THE RIVER KWAI, A Horizon Picture, Columbia: SAM SPIEGEL, Producer

PEYTON PLACE, Jerry Wald Prods., Inc., 20th Century-Fox: JERRY WALD, Producer

SAYONARA, William Goetz, Prod., Warner Bros.: WILLIAM GOETZ, Producer

12 ANGRY MEN, Orion-Nova Prod., UA: HENRY FONDA & REGINALD ROSE, Producers

WITNESS FOR THE PROSECUTION, Edward Small-Arthur Hornblow Prod., UA: ARTHUR HORNBLOW, JR., Producer

Actor

MARLON BRANDO in *Sayonara*, William Goetz Prod., Warner Bros.

ANTHONY FRANCIOSA in *A Hatful Of Rain*, 20th Century-Fox

ALEC GUINNESS in *The Bridge On The River Kwai*, A Horizon Picture, Columbia

CHARLES LAUGHTON in *Witness For The Prosecution*, Edward Small-Arthur Hornblow Prod., UA

ANTHONY QUINN in *Wild Is The Wind*, A Hal Wallis Prod., Paramount

Actress

DEBORAH KERR in *Heaven Knows, Mr. Allison*, 20th Century-Fox

LARGE CAPITAL LETTERS DENOTE WINNER

ANNA MAGNANI in *Wild Is The Wind*, Hal Wallis Prod., Paramount

ELIZABETH TAYLOR in *Raintree County*, Metro-Goldwyn-Mayer

LANA TURNER in *Peyton Place*, Jerry Wald Prods. Inc., 20th Century-Fox

JOANNE WOODWARD in *The Three Faces Of Eve*, 20th Century-Fox

Supporting Actor

RED BUTTONS in *Sayonara*, William Goetz Prod., Warner Bros.

VITTORIO DE SICA in *A Farewell To Arms*, The Selznick Co., Inc., 20th Century-Fox

SESSUE HAYAKAWA in *The Bridge On The River Kwai*, A Horizon Picture, Columbia

ARTHUR KENNEDY in *Peyton Place*, Jerry Wald Prods., Inc., 20th Century-Fox

RUSS TAMBLYN in *Peyton Place*, Jerry Wald Prods., Inc., 20th Century-Fox

Supporting Actress

CAROLYN JONES in *The Bachelor Party*, Norma Prod., UA

ELSA LANCHESTER in *Witness For The Prosecution*, Edward Small-Arthur Hornblow Prod., UA

HOPE LANGE in *Peyton Place*, Jerry Wald Prods., Inc., 20th Century-Fox

MIYOSHI UMEKI in *Sayonara*, William Goetz Prod., Warner Bros.

DIANE VARSI in *Peyton Place*, Jerry Wald Prods., Inc., 20th Century-Fox

Directing

DAVID LEAN for *The Bridge On The River Kwai,* A Horizon Picture, Columbia

JOSHUA LOGAN for *Sayonara,* William Goetz Prod., Warner Bros.

SIDNEY LUMET for *12 Angry Men,* Orion-Nova Prod., UA

MARK ROBSON for *Peyton Place,* Jerry Wald Prods., Inc., 20th Century-Fox

BILLY WILDER for *Witness For The Prosecution,* Edward Small-Arthur Hornblow Prod., UA

Writing

(Rules changed this year to two awards for Writing instead of three awards as previously given.)

(Best Screenplay—based on material from another medium)

THE BRIDGE ON THE RIVER KWAI, A Horizon Picture, Columbia: PIERRE BOULLE

HEAVEN KNOWS, MR. ALLISON, 20th Century-Fox: JOHN LEE MAHIN and JOHN HUSTON

PEYTON PLACE, Jerry Wald Prods., Inc., 20th Century-Fox: JOHN MICHAEL HAYES

SAYONARA, William Goetz Prod., Warner Bros.: PAUL OSBORN

12 ANGRY MEN, Orion-Nova Prod., UA: REGINALD ROSE

(Best Story and Screenplay—written directly for the screen)

DESIGNING WOMAN, Metro-Goldwyn-Mayer: GEORGE WELLS

FUNNY FACE, Paramount: LEONARD GERSHE

MAN OF A THOUSAND FACES, Universal-International: Story by RALPH WHEELRIGHT. Screenplay by R. WRIGHT CAMPBELL, IVAN GOFF and BEN ROBERTS

THE TIN STAR, The Perlberg-Seaton Prod., Paramount: Story by BARNEY SLATER and JOEL KANE. Screenplay by DUDLEY NICHOLS

VITELLONI, Peg Films/Cite Films, API-Janus Films (Italian): Story by FEDERICO FELLINI, ENNIO FLAIANO and TULLIO PINELLI. Screenplay by FEDERICO FELLINI and ENNIO FLAIANO

Cinematography

(Rules changed this year to one Award for Cinematography instead of separate awards for black-and-white and color.)

AN AFFAIR TO REMEMBER, Jerry Wald Prods., Inc., 20th Century-Fox: MILTON KRASNER

THE BRIDGE ON THE RIVER KWAI, A Horizon Picture, Columbia: JACK HILDYARD

FUNNY FACE, Paramount: RAY JUNE

PEYTON PLACE, Jerry Wald Prods., Inc., 20th Century-Fox: WILLIAM MELLOR

SAYONARA, William Goetz Prod., Warner Bros.: ELLSWORTH FREDERICKS

Art Direction—Set Decoration

(Rules changed this year to one Award for Art Direction instead of separate awards for black-and-white and color.)

FUNNY FACE, Paramount: HAL PEREIRA and GEORGE W. DAVIS
Set Decoration: SAM COMER and RAY MOYER

LES GIRLS, Sol C. Siegel Prods., Inc., M-G-M: WILLIAM A. HORNING and GENE ALLEN
Set Decoration: EDWIN B. WILLIS and RICHARD PEFFERLE

PAL JOEY, Essex-George Sidney Prod., Columbia: WALTER HOLSCHER
Set Decoration: WILLIAM KIERNAN and LOUIS DIAGE

RAINTREE COUNTY, Metro-Goldwyn-Mayer: WILLIAM A. HORNING and URIE MCCLEARY
Set Decoration: EDWIN B. WILLIS and HUGH HUNT
SAYONARA, William Goetz Prod., Warner Bros.: TED HAWORTH
Set Decoration: ROBERT PRIESTLEY

Sound

(Prior to 1957 [30th Year] known as *Sound Recording.*)

GUNFIGHT AT THE O.K. CORRAL, Paramount Studio Sound Department: GEORGE DUTTON, Sound Director
LES GIRLS, Metro-Goldwyn-Mayer Studio Sound Department: DR. WESLEY C. MILLER, Sound Director
PAL JOEY, Columbia Studio Sound Department: JOHN P. LIVADARY, Sound Director
SAYONARA, Warner Bros. Studio Sound Department: GEORGE GROVES, Sound Director
WITNESS FOR THE PROSECUTION, Samuel Goldwyn Studio Sound Department: GORDON SAWYER, Sound Director

Film Editing

THE BRIDGE ON THE RIVER KWAI, A Horizon Picture, Columbia: PETER TAYLOR
GUNFIGHT AT THE O.K. CORRAL, A Hal Wallis Prod., Paramount: WARREN LOW
PAL JOEY, Essex-George Sidney Prod., Columbia: VIOLA LAWRENCE and JEROME THOMS
SAYONARA, William Goetz Prod., Warner Bros.: ARTHUR P. SCHMIDT and PHILIP W. ANDERSON
WITNESS FOR THE PROSECUTION, Edward Small-Arthur Hornblow Prod., UA: DANIEL MANDELL

Music

(Rules changed this year to one Award for Music Scoring instead of separate Awards for Scoring Dramatic or Comedy Picture and Scoring of a Musical Picture.)

(Scoring)

AN AFFAIR TO REMEMBER (Dramatic or Comedy), Jerry Wald Prods., Inc., 20th Century-Fox: HUGO FRIEDHOFER
BOY ON A DOLPHIN (Dramatic or Comedy), 20th Century-Fox: HUGO FRIEDHOFER
THE BRIDGE ON THE RIVER KWAI (Dramatic or Comedy), A Horizon Picture, Columbia: MALCOLM ARNOLD
PERRI (Dramatic or Comedy), Walt Disney Prods., Buena Vista Film Dist. Co., Inc.: PAUL SMITH
RAINTREE COUNTY (Dramatic or Comedy), Metro-Goldwyn-Mayer: JOHNNY GREEN

(Best Song)

AN AFFAIR TO REMEMBER from *An Affair To Remember,* Jerry Wald Prods., Inc., 20th Century-Fox
Music by HARRY WARREN. Lyrics by HAROLD ADAMSON and LEO MCCAREY
ALL THE WAY from *The Joker Is Wild,* A.M.B.L. Prod., Paramount
Music by JAMES VAN HEUSEN. Lyrics by SAMMY CAHN
APRIL LOVE from *April Love,* 20th Century-Fox
Music by SAMMY FAIN. Lyrics by PAUL FRANCIS WEBSTER
TAMMY from *Tammy And The Bachelor,* Universal-International
Music and Lyrics by RAY EVANS and JAY LIVINGSTON
WILD IS THE WIND from *Wild Is The Wind,* A Hal Wallis Prod., Paramount
Music by DIMITRI TIOMKIN. Lyrics by NED WASHINGTON

Costume Design

(Rules changed this year to one Award for Costume Design instead of separate awards for black-and-white and color.)

AN AFFAIR TO REMEMBER, Jerry Wald Prods., Inc., 20th Century-Fox: CHARLES LeMAIRE

FUNNY FACE, Paramount: EDITH HEAD and HUBERT DE GIVENCHY

LES GIRLS, Sol C. Siegel Prods., Inc., M-G-M: ORRY-KELLY

PAL JOEY, Essex-George Sidney Prod., Columbia: JEAN LOUIS

RAINTREE COUNTY, Metro-Goldwyn-Mayer: WALTER PLUNKETT

Short Subjects

(Rules changed this year to two awards for Short Subjects instead of three as previously given.)

(Cartoons)

BIRDS ANONYMOUS, Warner Bros.: EDWARD SELZER, Producer

ONE DROOPY KNIGHT, Metro-Goldwyn-Mayer: WILLIAM HANNA and JOSEPH BARBERA, Producers

TABASCO ROAD, Warner Bros.: EDWARD SELZER, Producer

TREES and JAMAICA DADDY, UPA Pictures, Columbia: STEPHEN BOSUSTOW, Producer

THE TRUTH ABOUT MOTHER GOOSE, Walt Disney Prods., Buena Vista Film Distribution Co., Inc.: WALT DISNEY, Producer

(Live Action Subjects)

A CHAIRY TALE, National Film Board of Canada, Kingsley International Pictures Corp.: NORMAN MCLAREN, Producer

CITY OF GOLD, National Film Board of Canada, Kingsley International Pictures Corp.: TOM DALY, Producer

FOOTHOLD ON ANTARCTICA, World Wide Pictures, Lester A. Schoenfeld Films: JAMES CARR, Producer

PORTUGAL, Walt Disney Prods., Buena Vista Film Distribution Co., Inc.: BEN SHARPSTEEN, Producer

THE WETBACK HOUND, Walt Disney Prods., Buena Vista Film Distribution Co., Inc.: LARRY LANSBURGH, Producer

Documentary

(No Short Subject Documentary nominations voted this year.)

(Features)

ALBERT SCHWEITZER, Hill and Anderson Prod., Louis de Rochemont Assocs.: JEROME HILL, Producer

ON THE BOWERY, Lionel Rogosin Prods., Film Representations, Inc.: LIONEL ROGOSIN, Producer

TORERO!, Producciones Barbachano Ponce, Columbia (Mexican): MANUEL BARBACHANO PONCE, Producer

Special Effects

THE ENEMY BELOW, 20th Century-Fox

Audible: WALTER ROSSI

THE SPIRIT OF ST. LOUIS, Leland Hayward-Billy Wilder, Warner Bros. Visual: LOUIS LICHTENFIELD

Foreign Language Film Award

(Rules changed in 1957: Award given to the Production Company, not the individual producer.)

THE DEVIL CAME AT NIGHT, Gloria Film (Germany)

GATES OF PARIS, Filmsonor S.A. Production (France)

MOTHER INDIA, Mehboob Productions (India)

THE NIGHTS OF CABIRIA, Dino De Laurentiis Production (Italy)

NINE LIVES, Nordsjofilm (Norway)

Honorary Awards

CHARLES BRACKETT for outstanding service to the Academy. (statuette)

B. B. KAHANE for distinguished service to the motion picture industry. (statuette)

GILBERT M. ("Broncho Billy") ANDERSON, motion picture pioneer, for his contributions to the development of motion pictures as entertainment. (statuette)

THE SOCIETY OF MOTION PICTURE AND TELEVISION ENGINEERS for their contributions to the advancement of the motion picture industry. (statuette)

Irving G. Thalberg Memorial Award
None

Jean Hersholt Humanitarian Award
SAMUEL GOLDWYN

Scientific or Technical
Class I
TODD-AO CORP. and WESTREX CORP. for developing a method of producing and exhibiting wide-film motion pictures known as the Todd-AO System

MOTION PICTURE RESEARCH COUNCIL for the design and development of a high efficiency projection screen for drive-in theatres

Class II
SOCIETÉ D'OPTIQUE ET DE MECHANIQUE DE HAUTE PRECISION for the development of a high speed vari-focal photographic lens

HARLAN L. BAUMBACH, LORAND WARGO, HOWARD M. LITTLE and the UNICORN ENGINEERING CORP. for the development of an automatic printer light selector

Class III
CHARLES E. SUTTER, WILLIAM B. SMITH, PARAMOUNT PICTURES CORP. and GENERAL CABLE CORP. for the engineering and application to studio use of aluminum lightweight electrical cable and connectors

1958

Nominations Announced: February 23, 1959
Awards Ceremony: April 6, 1959
RKO Pantages Theatre
(MCs: Bob Hope, Jerry Lewis, Mort Sahl, Tony Randall, Sir Laurence Olivier, David Niven)

Best Picture

AUNTIE MAME, Warner Bros.

CAT ON A HOT TIN ROOF, Avon Prods., Inc. M-G-M: LAWRENCE WEINGARTEN, Producer

THE DEFIANT ONES, Stanley Kramer, UA: STANLEY KRAMER, Producer

GIGI, Arthur Freed Prods., Inc., M-G-M: ARTHUR FREED, Producer

SEPARATE TABLES, Clifton Prods., Inc., US: HAROLD HECHT, Producer

Actor

TONY CURTIS in *The Defiant Ones*, Stanley Kramer, UA

PAUL NEWMAN in *Cat On A Hot Tin Roof*, Avon Prods., Inc., M-G-M

DAVID NIVEN in *Separate Tables*, Clifton Prods., Inc., UA

SIDNEY POITIER in *The Defiant Ones*, Stanley Kramer, UA

SPENCER TRACY in *The Old Man And The Sea*, Leland Hayward, Warner Bros.

Actress

SUSAN HAYWARD in *I Want To Live!*, Figaro, Inc., UA

DEBORAH KERR in *Separate Tables*, Clifton Prods., Inc., UA

SHIRLEY MacLAINE in *Some Came Running*, Sol C. Siegel Prods., Inc., M-G-M

LARGE CAPITAL LETTERS DENOTE WINNER

ROSALIND RUSSELL in *Auntie Mame*, Warner Bros.

ELIZABETH TAYLOR in *Cat On A Hot Tin Roof*, Avon Prods., Inc., M-G-M

Supporting Actor

THEODORE BIKEL in *The Defiant Ones*, Stanley Kramer, UA

LEE J. COBB in *The Brothers Karamazov*, Avon Prods., Inc., M-G-M

BURL IVES in *The Big Country*, Anthony-Worldwide Prods., UA

ARTHUR KENNEDY in *Some Came Running*, Sol C. Siegel Prods., Inc., M-G-M

GIG YOUNG in *Teacher's Pet*, Perlberg-Seaton, Paramount

Supporting Actress

PEGGY CASS in *Auntie Mame*, Warner Bros.

WENDY HILLER in *Separate Tables*, Clifton Prods., Inc., UA

MARTHA HYER in *Some Came Running*, Sol C. Siegel Prods., Inc., Metro-Goldwyn-Mayer

MAUREEN STAPLETON in *Lonelyhearts*, Schary Prods., Inc., UA

CARA WILLIAMS in *The Defiant Ones*, Stanley Kramer, UA

Directing

RICHARD BROOKS for *Cat On A Hot Tin Roof*, Avon Prods., Inc., M-G-M

STANLEY KRAMER for *The Defiant Ones,* Stanley Kramer, UA

VINCENTE MINNELLI for *Gigi,* Arthur Freed Prods., Inc., M-G-M

MARK ROBSON for *The Inn Of The Sixth Happiness,* 20th Century-Fox

ROBERT WISE for *I Want To Live!,* Figaro, Inc., UA

Writing

(Best Screenplay — based on material from another medium)

CAT ON A HOT TIN ROOF, Avon Prods., Inc., M-G-M: RICHARD BROOKS and JAMES POE

GIGI, Arthur Freed Prods., Inc., M-G-M: ALAN JAY LERNER

THE HORSE'S MOUTH, Knightsbridge, UA (British): ALEC GUINNESS

I WANT TO LIVE!, Figaro, Inc., UA: NELSON GIDDING and DON MANKIEWICZ

SEPARATE TABLES, Clifton Prods., Inc., UA: TERENCE RATTIGAN and JOHN GAY

(Best Story and Screenplay — written directly for the screen)

THE DEFIANT ONES, Stanley Kramer, UA: NATHAN E. DOUGLAS and HAROLD JACOB SMITH

THE GODDESS, Carnegie Prods., Inc., Columbia: PADDY CHAYEFSKY

HOUSEBOAT, Paramount and Scribe, Paramount: MELVILLE SHAVELSON and JACK ROSE

THE SHEEPMAN, Metro-Goldwyn-Mayer: Story by JAMES EDWARD GRANT. Screenplay by WILLIAM BOWERS and JAMES EDWARD GRANT

TEACHER'S PET, Perlberg-Seaton, Paramount: FAY and MICHAEL KANIN

Cinematography

(Rules changed this year to two awards for Cinematography: one for black-and-white and one for color.)

(Black-and-White)

THE DEFIANT ONES, Stanley Kramer, UA: SAM LEAVITT

DESIRE UNDER THE ELMS, Don Hartman, Paramount: DANIEL L. FAPP

I WANT TO LIVE!, Figaro, Inc., UA: LIONEL LINDON

SEPARATE TABLES, Clifton Prods., Inc., UA: CHARLES LANG, JR.

THE YOUNG LIONS, 20th Century-Fox: JOE MacDONALD

(Color)

AUNTIE MAME, Warner Bros.: HARRY STRADLING, SR.

CAT ON A HOT TIN ROOF, Avon Prods., Inc., M-G-M: WILLIAM DANIELS

GIGI, Arthur Freed Prods., Inc., M-G-M: JOSEPH RUTTENBERG

THE OLD MAN AND THE SEA, Leland Hayward, Warner Bros.: JAMES WONG HOWE

SOUTH PACIFIC, South Pacific Enterprises, Inc., Magna Theatre Corp.: LEON SHAMROY

Art Direction—Set Decoration

AUNTIE MAME, Warner Bros.: MALCOLM BERT
Set Decoration: GEORGE JAMES HOPKINS

BELL, BOOK AND CANDLE, Phoenix Prods., Inc., Columbia: CARY ODELL
Set Decoration: LOUIS DIAGE

A CERTAIN SMILE, 20th Century-Fox: LYLE R. WHEELER and JOHN DeCUIR
Set Decoration: WALTER M. SCOTT and PAUL S. FOX

GIGI, Arthur Freed Prods., Inc., M-G-M: WILLIAM A. HORNING and PRESTON AMES
Set Decoration: HENRY GRACE and KEOGH GLEASON

VERTIGO, Alfred J. Hitchcock Prods., Inc., Paramount: HAL PEREIRA and HENRY BUMSTEAD

Set Decoration: SAM COMER and FRANK MCKELVY

Sound

I WANT TO LIVE!, Samuel Goldwyn Studio Sound Department: GORDON E. SAWYER, Sound Director

SOUTH PACIFIC, Todd-AO Sound Department: FRED HYNES, Sound Director

A TIME TO LOVE AND A TIME TO DIE, Universal-International Studio Sound Department: LESLIE I. CAREY, Sound Director

VERTIGO, Paramount Studio Sound Department: GEORGE DUTTON, Sound Director

THE YOUNG LIONS, 20th Century-Fox Studio Sound Department: CARL FAULKNER, Sound Director

Film Editing

AUNTIE MAME, Warner Bros.: WILLIAM ZIEGLER

COWBOY, Phoenix Pictures, Columbia: WILLIAM A. LYON and AL CLARK

THE DEFIANT ONES, Stanley Kramer, UA: FREDERIC KNUDTSON

GIGI, Arthur Freed Prods., Inc., M-G-M: ADRIENNE FAZAN

I WANT TO LIVE!, Figaro, Inc., UA: WILLIAM HORNBECK

Music

(Rules changed this year to two Awards —one award for Scoring of a Dramatic or Comedy Picture, and one award for Scoring of a Musical Picture.)

(Scoring of a Dramatic or Comedy Picture)

THE BIG COUNTRY, Anthony-Worldwide Prods., UA: JEROME MOROSS

THE OLD MAN AND THE SEA, Leland Hayward, Warner Bros.: DIMITRI TIOMKIN

SEPARATE TABLES, Clifton Prods., Inc., UA: DAVID RAKSIN

WHITE WILDERNESS, Walt Disney Prods., Buena Vista Film Dist. Co., Inc.: OLIVER WALLACE

THE YOUNG LIONS, 20th Century-Fox: HUGO FRIEDHOFER

(Scoring of a Musical Picture)

THE BOLSHOI BALLET, A Rank Organization Presentation-Harmony Film, Rank Film Distributors of America, Inc. (British): YURI FAIER and G. ROZHDESTVENSKY

DAMN YANKEES, Warner Bros.: RAY HEINDORF

GIGI, Arthur Freed Prods., Inc., M-G-M: ANDRÉ PREVIN

MARDI GRAS, Jerry Wald Prods., Inc., 20th Century-Fox: LIONEL NEWMAN

SOUTH PACIFIC, South Pacific Enterprises, Inc., Magna Theatre Corp.: ALFRED NEWMAN and KEN DARBY

(Best Song)

ALMOST IN YOUR ARMS (Love Song from *Houseboat*) from *Houseboat*, Paramount and Scribe, Paramount Music and Lyrics by JAY LIVINGSTON and RAY EVANS

A CERTAIN SMILE from *A Certain Smile*, 20th Century-Fox: Music by SAMMY FAIN. Lyrics by PAUL FRANCIS WEBSTER

GIGI from *Gigi*, Arthur Freed Prods., Inc., M-G-M Music by FREDERICK LOEWE. Lyrics by ALAN JAY LERNER

TO LOVE AND BE LOVED from *Some Came Running*, Sol C. Siegel Prods., Inc., M-G-M Music by JAMES VAN HEUSEN. Lyrics by SAMMY CAHN

A VERY PRECIOUS LOVE from *Marjorie Morningstar*, Beachwold Pictures, Warner Bros. Music by SAMMY FAIN. Lyrics by PAUL FRANCIS WEBSTER

Costume Design
BELL, BOOK AND CANDLE, Phoenix
Prods., Inc., Columbia: JEAN LOUIS
THE BUCCANEER, Cecil B. DeMille,
Paramount: RALPH JESTER, EDITH
HEAD and JOHN JENSEN
A CERTAIN SMILE, 20th Century-Fox:
CHARLES LeMAIRE and MARY WILLS
GIGI, Arthur Freed Prods., Inc.,
M-G-M: CECIL BEATON
SOME CAME RUNNING, Sol C. Siegel
Prods., Inc., M-G-M: WALTER
PLUNKETT

Short Subjects
(Cartoons)
KNIGHTY KNIGHT BUGS, Warner
Bros.: JOHN W. BURTON, Pro-
ducer
PAUL BUNYAN, Walt Disney Prods.,
Buena Vista Film Distribution Co.,
Inc.: WALT DISNEY, Producer
SIDNEY'S FAMILY TREE, Terrytoons,
20th Century-Fox: WILLIAM M.
WEISS, Producer

(Live Action Subjects)
GRAND CANYON, Walt Disney
Prods., Buena Vista Film Distribu-
tion Co., Inc.: WALT DISNEY, Pro-
ducer
JOURNEY INTO SPRING, British Trans-
port Films, Lester A. Schoenfeld
Films: IAN FERGUSON, Producer
THE KISS, Cohay Prods., Continental
Distributing, Inc.: JOHN PATRICK
HAYES, Producer
SNOWS OF AORANGI, New Zealand
Screen Board, George Brest Associ-
atès
T IS FOR TUMBLEWEED, Continental Dis-
tributing, Inc.: JAMES A. LEBEN-
THAL, Producer

Documentary
(Short Subjects)
AMA GIRLS, Walt Disney Prods.,

Buena Vista Film Dist. Co., Inc.:
BEN SHARPSTEEN, Producer
EMPLOYEES ONLY, Hughes Aircraft Co.:
KENNETH G. BROWN, Producer
JOURNEY INTO SPRING, British Trans-
port Films, Lester A. Schoenfeld
Films: IAN FERGUSON, Producer
THE LIVING STONE, National Film Board
of Canada: TOM DALY, Producer
OVERTURE, United Nations Film Ser-
vice: THOROLD DICKINSON, Producer

(Features)
ANTARCTIC CROSSING, World Wide Pic-
tures, Lester A. Schoenfeld Films:
JAMES CARR, Producer
THE HIDDEN WORLD, Small World Co.:
ROBERT SNYDER, Producer
PSYCHIATRIC NURSING, Dynamic Films
Inc.: NATHAN ZUCKER, Producer
WHITE WILDERNESS, Walt Disney
Prods., Buena Vista Film Dist. Co.,
Inc.: BEN SHARPSTEEN, Producer

Special Effects
TOM THUMB, Galaxy Pictures,
M-G-M:
Visual: TOM HOWARD
TORPEDO RUN, Metro-Goldwyn-Mayer
Visual: A. ARNOLD GILLESPIE
Audible: HAROLD HUMBROCK

Foreign Language Film Award
ARMS AND THE MAN, H. R. Sokal-P.
Goldbaum Production, Bavaria Film-
kunst A.G. (Germany).
LA VENGANZA, Guion Producciones
Cinematograficas (Spain).
MY UNCLE, Specta-Gray-Alter Films
in association with Films del Cen-
taure (France).
THE ROAD A YEAR LONG, Jadran Film
(Yugoslavia).
THE USUAL UNIDENTIFIED THIEVES,
Lux-Vides-Cinecitta (Italy).

Honorary Award
MAURICE CHEVALIER for his contributions to the world of entertainment for more than half a century. (statuette)

Irving G. Thalberg Memorial Award
JACK L. WARNER

Jean Hersholt Humanitarian Award
None

Scientific or Technical
Class I
None
Class II
DON W. PRIDEAUX, LEROY G. LEIGHTON and the LAMP DIVISION of GENERAL ELECTRIC CO. for the development and production of an improved 10 kilowatt lamp for motion picture set lighting.
PANAVISION, INC., for the design and development of the Auto Panatar anamorphic photographic lens for 35mm CinemaScope photography

Class III
WILLY BORBERG of the General Precision Laboratory, Inc., for the development of a high speed intermittent movement for 35mm motion picture theatre projection equipment.
FRED PONEDEL, GEORGE BROWN and CONRAD BOYE of the Warner Bros. Special Effects Department for the design and fabrication of a new rapid fire marble gun.

1959

Nominations Announced: February 22, 1960
Awards Ceremony: April 4, 1960
RKO Pantages Theatre
(MC: Bob Hope)

Best Picture

ANATOMY OF A MURDER, Otto Preminger, Columbia: OTTO PREMINGER, Producer

BEN-HUR, Metro-Goldwyn-Mayer: SAM ZIMBALIST, Producer

THE DIARY OF ANNE FRANK, 20th Century-Fox: GEORGE STEVENS, Producer

THE NUN'S STORY, Warner Bros.: HENRY BLANKE, Producer

ROOM AT THE TOP, Romulus Films, Ltd., Continental Distr., Inc., (British): JOHN & JAMES WOOLF, Producers

Actor

LAURENCE HARVEY in *Room At The Top*, Romulus Films, Ltd., Continental Dist., Inc. (British)

CHARLTON HESTON in *Ben-Hur*, Metro-Goldwyn-Mayer

JACK LEMMON in *Some Like It Hot*, Ashton Prods. & The Mirisch Co., UA

PAUL MUNI in *The Last Angry Man*, Fred Kohlmar Prods., Columbia

JAMES STEWART in *Anatomy Of A Murder*, Otto Preminger, Columbia

Actress

DORIS DAY in *Pillow Talk*, Arwin Prods., Inc., U-I

AUDREY HEPBURN in *The Nun's Story*, Warner Bros.

LARGE CAPITAL LETTERS DENOTE WINNER

KATHARINE HEPBURN in *Suddenly, Last Summer*, Horizon Prod., Columbia

SIMONE SIGNORET in *Room At The Top*, Romulus Films, Ltd., Continental Dist., Inc. (British)

ELIZABETH TAYLOR in *Suddenly, Last Summer*, Horizon Prod., Columbia

Supporting Actor

HUGH GRIFFITH in *Ben-Hur*, Metro-Goldwyn-Mayer

ARTHUR O'CONNELL in *Anatomy Of A Murder*, Otto Preminger, Columbia

GEORGE C. SCOTT in *Anatomy Of A Murder*, Otto Preminger, Columbia

ROBERT VAUGHN in *The Young Philadelphians*, Warner Bros.

ED WYNN in *The Diary Of Anne Frank*, 20th Century-Fox

Supporting Actress

HERMIONE BADDELEY in *Room At The Top*, Romulus Films, Ltd., Continental Distributing, Inc. (British)

SUSAN KOHNER in *Imitation Of Life*, Universal-International

JUANITA MOORE in *Imitation Of Life*, Universal-International

THELMA RITTER in *Pillow Talk*, Arwin Prods., Inc. U-I

SHELLEY WINTERS in *The Diary Of Anne Frank*, 20th Century-Fox

Directing

JACK CLAYTON for *Room At The Top*, Romulus Films, Ltd., Continental Dist. Inc., (British)

GEORGE STEVENS for *The Diary Of Anne Frank,* 20th Century-Fox
BILLY WILDER for *Some Like It Hot,* Ashton Prods. & The Mirisch Co., UA
WILLIAM WYLER for *Ben-Hur,* Metro-Goldwyn-Mayer
FRED ZINNEMANN for *The Nun's Story,* Warner Bros.

Writing

(Best Screenplay — based on material from another medium)

ANATOMY OF A MURDER, Otto Preminger, Columbia: WENDELL MAYES
BEN-HUR, Metro-Goldwyn-Mayer: KARL TUNBERG
THE NUN'S STORY, Warner Bros.: ROBERT ANDERSON
ROOM AT THE TOP, Romulus Films, Ltd., Continental Dist., Inc. (British): NEIL PATERSON
SOME LIKE IT HOT, Ashton Prods. & The Mirisch Co., UA: BILLY WILDER and I.A.L. DIAMOND

(Best Story and Screenplay — written directly for the screen)

THE 400 BLOWS, Les Films du Carrosse & SEDIF, Zenith International (French): FRANÇOIS TRUFFAUT and MARCEL MOUSSY
NORTH BY NORTHWEST, Metro-Goldwyn-Mayer: ERNEST LEHMAN
OPERATION PETTICOAT, Granart Co., U-I: Story by PAUL KING and JOSEPH STONE. Screenplay by STANLEY SHAPIRO and MAURICE RICHLIN
PILLOW TALK, Arwin Prods., Inc.: U-I Story by RUSSELL ROUSE and CLARENCE GREENE. Screenplay by STANLEY SHAPIRO and MAURICE RICHLIN
WILD STRAWBERRIES, Svensk Filmindustri, Janus Films (Swedish): INGMAR BERGMAN

Cinematography

(Black-and-White)

ANATOMY OF A MURDER, Otto Preminger, Columbia: SAM LEAVITT
CAREER, Hal Wallis Prods., Paramount: JOSEPH LASHELLE
THE DIARY OF ANNE FRANK, 20th Century-Fox: WILLIAM C. MELLOR
SOME LIKE IT HOT, Ashton Prods. & The Mirisch Co., UA: CHARLES LANG, JR.
THE YOUNG PHILADELPHIANS, Warner Bros.: HARRY STRADLING, SR.

(Color)

BEN-HUR, Metro-Goldwyn-Mayer: ROBERT L. SURTEES
THE BIG FISHERMAN, Rowland V. Lee Prods., Buena Vista Film Dist. Co., Inc. LEE GARMES
THE FIVE PENNIES, Dena Prod., Paramount: DANIEL L. FAPP
THE NUN'S STORY, Warner Bros.: FRANZ PLANER
PORGY AND BESS, Samuel Goldwyn Prods., Columbia: LEON SHAMROY

Art Direction—Set Decoration

(Rules changed this year to two awards for Art Direction: one for black-and-white and one for color.)

(Black-and-White)

CAREER, Hal Wallis Prods., Paramount: HAL PEREIRA and WALTER TYLER Set Decoration: SAM COMER and ARTHUR KRAMS
THE DIARY OF ANNE FRANK, 20th Century-Fox: LYLE R. WHEELER and GEORGE W. DAVIS Set Decoration: WALTER M. SCOTT and STUART A. REISS
THE LAST ANGRY MAN, Fred Kohlmar Prods., Columbia: CARL ANDERSON Set Decoration: WILLIAM KIERNAN

SOME LIKE IT HOT, Ashton Prods. &
The Mirisch Co., UA: TED
HAWORTH
Set Decoration: EDWARD G. BOYLE
SUDDENLY, LAST SUMMER, Horizon
Prod., Columbia: OLIVER MESSEL and
WILLIAM KELLNER
Set Decoration: SCOT SLIMON
(Color)
BEN-HUR, Metro-Goldwyn-Mayer:
WILLIAM A. HORNING and ED-
WARD CARFAGNO
Set Decoration: HUGH HUNT
THE BIG FISHERMAN, Rowland V. Lee
Prods., Buena Vista Film Dist. Co.,
Inc.: JOHN DeCUIR
Set Decoration: JULIA HERON
JOURNEY TO THE CENTER OF THE
EARTH, Joseph M. Schenck Enter-
prises, Inc. & Cooga Mooga Film
Prods., Inc., 20th Century-Fox:
LYLE R. WHEELER, FRANZ BACHELIN
and HERMAN A. BLUMENTHAL
Set Decoration: WALTER M. SCOTT
and JOSEPH KISH
NORTH BY NORTHWEST, Metro-
Goldwyn-Mayer: WILLIAM A. HORN-
ING, ROBERT BOYLE and MERRILL
PYE
Set Decoration: HENRY GRACE and
FRANK MCKELVY
PILLOW TALK, Arwin Prods., Inc., U-I:
RICHARD H. RIEDEL
Set Decoration: RUSSELL A.
GAUSMAN and RUBY R. LEVITT

Sound

BEN-HUR, Metro-Goldwyn-Mayer
Studio Sound Department: FRANK-
LIN E. MILTON, Sound Director
JOURNEY TO THE CENTER OF THE
EARTH, 20th Century-Fox Studio
Sound Department: CARL FAULKNER,
Sound Director
LIBEL!, Metro-Goldwyn-Mayer London
Sound Department (British): A. W.

WATKINS, Sound Director
THE NUN'S STORY, Warner Bros.
Studio Sound Department: GEORGE
R. GROVES, Sound Director
PORGY AND BESS, Samuel Goldwyn
Studio Sound Department: GORDON
E. SAWYER, Sound Director; and
Todd-AO Sound Department: FRED
HYNES, Sound Director

Film Editing

ANATOMY OF A MURDER, Otto Pre-
minger, Columbia: LOUIS R. LOEF-
FLER
BEN-HUR, Metro-Goldwyn-Mayer:
RALPH E. WINTERS and JOHN D.
DUNNING
NORTH BY NORTHWEST, Metro-
Goldwyn-Mayer: GEORGE TOMASINI
THE NUN'S STORY, Warner Bros.:
WALTER THOMPSON
ON THE BEACH, Lomitas Prods., UA:
FREDERIC KNUDTSON

Music

(Scoring of a Dramatic or Comedy Pic-
ture)
BEN-HUR, Metro-Goldwyn-Mayer:
MIKLOS ROZSA
THE DIARY OF ANNE FRANK, 20th
Century-Fox: ALFRED NEWMAN
THE NUN'S STORY, Warner Bros.:
FRANZ WAXMAN
ON THE BEACH, Lomitas Prods., Inc.,
UA: ERNEST GOLD
PILLOW TALK, Arwin Prods., Inc., U-I:
FRANK DeVOL

(Scoring of a Musical Picture)
THE FIVE PENNIES, Dena Prods.,
Paramount: LEITH STEVENS
LI'L ABNER, Panama and Frank,
Paramount: NELSON RIDDLE and
JOSEPH J. LILLEY
PORGY AND BESS, Samuel Goldwyn
Prods., Columbia: ANDRÉ PREVIN
and KEN DARBY

SAY ONE FOR ME, Bing Crosby Prods.,
20th Century-Fox: LIONEL NEWMAN
SLEEPING BEAUTY, Walt Disney Prods.,
Buena Vista Film Dist. Co., Inc.:
GEORGE BRUNS

(Best Song)

THE BEST OF EVERYTHING from *The
Best Of Everything,* Company Of Ar-
tists, Inc., 20th Century-Fox
Music by ALFRED NEWMAN. Lyrics
by SAMMY CAHN
THE FIVE PENNIES from *The Five
Pennies,* Dena Prods., Paramount:
Music and Lyrics by SYLVIA FINE
THE HANGING TREE from *The Hanging
Tree,* Baroda Prods., Inc., Warner
Bros.:
Music by JERRY LIVINGSTON. Lyrics
by MACK DAVID
HIGH HOPES from *A Hole In The
Head,* Sincap Prods., UA:
Music by JAMES VAN HEUSEN.
Lyrics by SAMMY CAHN
STRANGE ARE THE WAYS OF LOVE from
The Young Land, C. V. Whitney
Pictures, Inc., Columbia:
Music by DIMITRI TIOMKIN. Lyrics
by NED WASHINGTON

Costume Design

(Rules changed this year to two awards
for Costume Design: One for black-
and-white and one for color.)

(Black-and-White)

CAREER, Hal Wallis Prods., Paramount:
EDITH HEAD
THE DIARY OF ANNE FRANK, 20th
Century-Fox: CHARLES LeMAIRE and
MARY WILLS
THE GAZEBO, Avon Prod., M-G-M:
HELEN ROSE
SOME LIKE IT HOT, Ashton Prods.
& The Mirisch Co., UA: ORRY-
KELLY
THE YOUNG PHILADELPHIANS, Warner
Bros.: HOWARD SHOUP

(Color)

BEN-HUR, Metro-Goldwyn-Mayer:
ELIZABETH HAFFENDEN
THE BEST OF EVERYTHING, Company of
Artists, Inc., 20th Century-Fox:
ADELE PALMER
THE BIG FISHERMAN, Rowland V. Lee
Prods., Buena Vista Film Dist. Co.,
Inc.: RENIE
THE FIVE PENNIES, Dena Prod.,
Paramount: EDITH HEAD
PORGY AND BESS, Samuel Goldwyn
Prods., Columbia: IRENE SHARAFF

Short Subjects

(Cartoons)

MEXICALI SHMOES, Warner Bros.: JOHN
W. BURTON, Producer
MOONBIRD, Storyboard, Inc.: ED-
WARD HARRISON, JOHN HUB-
LEY, Producer
NOAH'S ARK, Walt Disney Prods.,
Buena Vista Film Distribution Co.,
Inc.: WALT DISNEY, Producer
THE VIOLINIST, Pintoff Prods., Inc.,
Kingsley International Pictures
Corp.: ERNEST PINTOFF, Producer

(Live Action Subjects)

BETWEEN THE TIDES, British Transport
Films, Lester A. Schoenfeld Film
(British): IAN FERGUSON, Producer
THE GOLDEN FISH, Les Requins As-
socies, Columbia (French):
JACQUES-YVES COUSTEAU,
Producer
MYSTERIES OF THE DEEP, Walt Disney
Prods., Buena Vista Film Distribu-
tion Co., Inc.: WALT DISNEY, Pro-
ducer
THE RUNNING, JUMPING AND
STANDING-STILL FILM, Lion Interna-
tional Films, Ltd., Kingsley-Union
Films (British): PETER SELLERS, Pro-
ducer
SKYSCRAPER, Joseph Burstyn Film En-
terprises, Inc.: SHIRLEY CLARKE,

WILLARD VAN DYKE and IRVING JACOBY, Producers

Documentary
(Short Subjects)
DONALD IN MATHMAGIC LAND, Walt Disney Prods., Buena Vista Film Dist. Co., Inc.: WALT DISNEY, Producer
FROM GENERATION TO GENERATION, Cullen Assocs., Maternity Center Assoc.: EDWARD F. CULLEN, Producer
GLASS, Netherlands Government, George K. Arthur–Go Pictures, Inc. (The Netherlands): BERT HAANSTRA, Producer

(Features)
THE RACE FOR SPACE, Wolper, Inc.: DAVID L. WOLPER, Producer
SERENGETI SHALL NOT DIE, Okapia-Film Prod., Transocean Film (German): BERNHARD GRZIMEK, Producer

Special Effects
BEN-HUR, Metro-Goldwyn-Mayer: Visual: A. ARNOLD GILLESPIE and ROBERT MacDONALD Audible: MILO LORY
JOURNEY TO THE CENTER OF THE EARTH, Joseph M. Schenck Enterprises, Inc. & Cooga Mooga Film Prods., Inc., 20th Century-Fox: Visual: L. B. ABBOTT and JAMES B. GORDON Audible: CARL FAULKNER

Foreign Language Film Award
BLACK ORPHEUS, Dispatfilm & Gemma Cinematografica (France)
THE BRIDGE, Fono Film (Germany)
THE GREAT WAR, Dino De Laurentiis Cinematografica (Italy)
PAW, Laterna Film (Denmark)
THE VILLAGE ON THE RIVER, N. V.

Nationale Filmproductie Maatschappij (The Netherlands)

Honorary Awards
LEE DE FOREST for his pioneering inventions which brought sound to the motion picture. (statuette)
BUSTER KEATON for his unique talents which brought immortal comedies to the screen. (statuette)

Irving G. Thalberg Memorial Award
None

Jean Hersholt Humanitarian Award
BOB HOPE

Scientific or Technical
Class I
None

Class II
DOUGLAS G. SHEARER of Metro-Goldwyn-Mayer, Inc., and ROBERT E. GOTTSCHALK and JOHN R. MOORE of Panavision, Inc., for the development of a system of producing and exhibiting wide-film motion pictures known as Camera 65
WADSWORTH E. POHL, WILLIAM EVANS, WERNER HOPF, S. E. HOWSE, THOMAS P. DIXON, STANFORD RESEARCH INSTITUTE and TECHNICOLOR CORP. for the design and development of the Technicolor electronic printing timer
WADSWORTH E. POHL, JACK ALFORD, HENRY IMUS, JOSEPH SCHMIT, PAUL FASSNACHT, AL LOFQUIST and TECHNICOLOR CORP. for the development and practical application of equipment for wet printing
DR. HOWARD S. COLEMAN, DR. A. FRANCIS TURNER, HAROLD H. SCHROEDER, JAMES R. BEN-

FORD and HAROLD E. ROSEN-BERGER of the Bausch & Lomb Optical Co. for the design and development of the Balcold projection mirror.

ROBERT P. GUTTERMAN of General Kinetics, Inc., and the LIPSNER-SMITH CORP. for the design and development of the CF-2 Ultra sonic Film Cleaner

Class III

UB IWERKS of Walt Disney Prods.

for the design of an improved optical printer for special effects and matte shots

E. L. STONES, GLEN ROBINSON, WINFIELD HUBBARD and LUTHER NEWMAN of the Metro-Goldwyn-Mayer Studio Construction Department for the design of a multiple cable remote controlled winch

1960

Nominations Announced: February 27, 1961
Awards Ceremony: April 17, 1961
Santa Monica Civic Auditorium
(MC: Bob Hope)

Best Picture

THE ALAMO, Batjac Prod., UA: JOHN WAYNE, Producer

THE APARTMENT, The Mirisch Co., Inc., UA: BILLY WILDER, Producer

ELMER GANTRY, Burt Lancaster-Richard Brooks Prod., UA: BERNARD SMITH, Producer

SONS AND LOVERS, Company of Artists, Inc., 20th Century-Fox: JERRY WALD, Producer

THE SUNDOWNERS, Warner Bros. FRED ZINNEMANN, Producer

Actor

TREVOR HOWARD in *Sons And Lovers,* Company of Artists, Inc., 20th Century-Fox

BURT LANCASTER in *Elmer Gantry,* Burt Lancaster-Richard Brooks Prod., UA

JACK LEMMON in *The Apartment,* The Mirisch Company, Inc., UA

LAURENCE OLIVIER in *The Entertainer,* Woodfall Prod., Continental Dist., Inc. (British)

SPENCER TRACY in *Inherit The Wind,* Stanley Kramer, UA

Actress

GREER GARSON in *Sunrise At Campobello,* Schary Prod., Warner Bros.

DEBORAH KERR in *The Sundowners,* Warner Bros.

SHIRLEY MacLAINE in *The Apartment,* The Mirisch Co., Inc., UA

MELINA MERCOURI in *Never On Sunday,* Melinafilm Prod., Lopert Pictures Corp. (Greek)

ELIZABETH TAYLOR in *Butterfield 8,* Afton-Linebrook Prod., M-G-M

Supporting Actor

PETER FALK in *Murder, Inc.,* 20th Century-Fox

JACK KRUSCHEN in *The Apartment,* The Mirisch Co., Inc., UA

SAL MINEO in *Exodus,* Carlyle-Alpina S.A. Prod., UA

PETER USTINOV in *Spartacus,* Bryna Prods., Inc., U-I

CHILL WILLS in *The Alamo,* Batjac Prod., UA

Supporting Actress

GLYNIS JOHNS in *The Sundowners,* Warner Bros.

SHIRLEY JONES in *Elmer Gantry,* Burt Lancaster-Richard Brooks Prod., UA

SHIRLEY KNIGHT in *The Dark At The Top Of The Stairs,* Warner Bros.

JANET LEIGH in *Psycho,* Alfred J. Hitchcock Prods., Paramount

MARY URE in *Sons And Lovers,* Company of Artists, Inc., 20th Century-Fox

Directing

JACK CARDIFF for *Sons And Lovers,*
Company of Artists, Inc., 20th
Century-Fox

JULES DASSIN for *Never On Sunday,*
Melinafilm Prod., Lopert Pictures
Corp. (Greek)

ALFRED HITCHCOCK for *Psycho,* Alfred
J. Hitchcock Prods., Paramount

BILLY WILDER for *The Apartment,*
The Mirisch Co., Inc., UA

FRED ZINNEMANN for *The Sundowners,*
Warner Bros.

Writing

(Best Screenplay—based on material
from another medium)

ELMER GANTRY, Burt Lancaster-
Richard Brooks Prod., UA: RICH-
ARD BROOKS

INHERIT THE WIND, Stanley Kramer
Prod., UA: NATHAN E. DOUGLAS and
HAROLD JACOB SMITH

SONS AND LOVERS, Company of Artists,
Inc., 20th Century-Fox: GAVIN
LAMBERT and T. E. B. CLARKE

THE SUNDOWNERS, Warner Bros.: ISO-
BEL LENNART

TUNES OF GLORY, H. M. Films Limited
Prod., Lopert Pictures Corp. (British): JAMES KENNAWAY

(Best Story and Screenplay—written
directly for the screen)

THE ANGRY SILENCE, Beaver Films
Limited Prod., JOSEPH HARRIS–SIG
SHORE (British): Story by RICHARD
GREGSON and MICHAEL CRAIG.
Screenplay by BRYAN FORBES

THE APARTMENT, The Mirisch Co.,
Inc., UA: BILLY WILDER and
I. A. L. DIAMOND

THE FACTS OF LIFE, Panama & Frank
Prod., UA: NORMAN PANAMA and
MELVIN FRANK

HIROSHIMA, MON AMOUR, Argos Films-
Como Films-Daiei Pictures, Ltd.—

Pathé Overseas Prod., Zenith International Film Corp. (French-
Japanese); MARGUERITE DURAS

NEVER ON SUNDAY, Melinafilm Prod.,
Lopert Pictures Corp. (Greek): JULES
DASSIN

Cinematography

(Black-and-White)

THE APARTMENT, The Mirisch Co.,
UA: JOSEPH LaSHELLE

THE FACTS OF LIFE, Panama & Frank
Prod., UA: CHARLES B. LANG, JR.

INHERIT THE WIND, Stanley Kramer
Prod., UA: ERNEST LASZLO

PSYCHO, Alfred J. Hitchcock Prods.,
Paramount: JOHN L. RUSSELL

SONS AND LOVERS, Company of
Artists, Inc., 20th Century-Fox:
FREDDIE FRANCIS

(Color)

THE ALAMO, Batjac Prod., UA: WIL-
LIAM H. CLOTHIER

BUTTERFIELD 8, Afton-Linebrook
Prod., M-G-M: JOSEPH RUTTENBERG
and CHARLES HARTEN

EXODUS, Carlyle-Alpina S. A. Prod.,
UA: SAM LEAVITT

PEPE, G. S.-Posa Films International
Prod., Columbia: JOE MacDONALD

SPARTACUS, Bryna Prods., Inc.,
U-I: RUSSELL METTY

Art Direction—Set Decoration

(Black-and-White)

THE APARTMENT, The Mirisch Co.,
Inc., UA: ALEXANDER TRAUN-
ER
Set Decoration: EDWARD G.
BOYLE

THE FACTS OF LIFE, Panama & Frank
Prod., UA: JOSEPH MCMILLAN
JOHNSON and KENNETH A. REID
Set Decoration: ROSS DOWD

PSYCHO, Alfred J. Hitchcock Prods., Paramount: JOSEPH HURLEY and ROBERT CLATWORTHY
Set Decoration: GEORGE MILO

SONS AND LOVERS, Company of Artists, Inc., 20th Century-Fox: TOM MORA-HAN
Set Decoration: LIONEL COUCH

VISIT TO A SMALL PLANET, Hall Wallis Prods., Paramount: HAL PEREIRA and WALTER TYLER
Set Decoration: SAM COMER and AR-THUR KRAMS

(Color)

CIMARRON, Metro-Goldwyn-Mayer: GEORGE W. DAVIS and ADDISON HEHR
Set Decoration: HENRY GRACE, HUGH HUNT and OTTO SIEGEL

IT STARTED IN NAPLES, Paramount and Capri Prod., Paramount: HAL PEREIRA and ROLAND ANDERSON
Set Decoration: SAM COMER and AR-RIGO BRESCHI

PEPE, G.S.-Posa Films International Prod., Columbia: TED HAWORTH
Set Decoration: WILLIAM KIERNAN

SPARTACUS, Bryna Prods., Inc., U-I: ALEXANDER GOLITZEN and ERIC ORBOM
Set Decoration: RUSSELL A. GAUSMAN and JULIA HERON

SUNRISE AT CAMPOBELLO, Schary Prod., Warner Bros.: EDWARD CAR-RERE
Set Decoration: GEORGE JAMES HOPKINS

Sound

THE ALAMO, Samuel Goldwyn Studio Sound Department: GOR-DON E. SAWYER, Sound Director; and Todd-AO Sound Department: FRED HYNES, Sound Director

THE APARTMENT, Samuel Goldwyn Studio Sound Department: GORDON E. SAWYER, Sound Director

CIMARRON, Metro-Goldwyn-Mayer Studio Sound Department: FRANKLIN E. MILTON, Sound Director

PEPE, Columbia Studio Sound Department: CHARLES RICE, Sound Director

SUNRISE AT CAMPOBELLO, Warner Bros. Studio Sound Department: GEORGE R. GROVES, Sound Director

Film Editing

THE ALAMO, Batjac Prod., UA: STUART GILMORE

THE APARTMENT, The Mirisch Co., UA: DANIEL MANDELL

INHERIT THE WIND, Stanley Kramer Prod., UA: FREDERIC KNUDTSON

PEPE, G. S.-Posa Films International Prod., Columbia: VIOLA LAWRENCE and AL CLARK

SPARTACUS, Bryna Prods., Inc., U-I: ROBERT LAWRENCE

Music

(Scoring of a Dramatic or Comedy Picture)

THE ALAMO, Batjac Prod., UA: DIMITRI TIOMKIN

ELMER GANTRY, Burt Lancaster-Richard Brooks Prod., UA: ANDRÉ PREVIN

EXODUS, Carlyle-Alpina S.A. Prod., UA: ERNEST GOLD

THE MAGNIFICENT SEVEN, Mirisch-Alpha Prod., UA: ELMER BERNSTEIN

SPARTACUS, Bryna Prods., Inc., U-I: ALEX NORTH

(Scoring of a Musical Picture)

BELLS ARE RINGING, Arthur Freed Prod., M-G-M: ANDRÉ PREVIN

CAN-CAN, Suffolk-Cummings Prods., 20th Century-Fox: NELSON RIDDLE

LET'S MAKE LOVE, Company of Artists, Inc., 20th Century-Fox: LIONEL NEWMAN and EARLE H. HAGEN

PEPE, G. S.-Posa Films International Prod., Columbia: JOHNNY GREEN
SONG WITHOUT END (THE STORY OF FRANZ LISZT), Goetz-Vidor Pictures Prod., Columbia: MORRIS STOLOFF and HARRY SUKMAN

(Best Song)

THE FACTS OF LIFE from *The Facts Of Life,* Panama & Frank Prod., UA: Music and Lyrics by JOHNNY MERCER
FARAWAY PART OF TOWN from *Pepe,* G. S.-Posa Films International Prod., Columbia. Music by ANDRÉ PREVIN. Lyrics by DORY LANGDON
THE GREEN LEAVES OF SUMMER from *The Alamo,* Batjac Prod., UA. Music by DIMITRI TIOMKIN. Lyrics by PAUL FRANCIS WEBSTER
NEVER ON SUNDAY from *Never On Sunday,* Melinafilm Prod., Lopert Pictures Corp. (Greek). Music and Lyrics by MANOS HADJIDAKIS
THE SECOND TIME AROUND from *High Time,* Bing Crosby Prods., 20th Century-Fox. Music by JAMES VAN HEUSEN. Lyrics by SAMMY CAHN

Costume Design

(Black-and-White)

THE FACTS OF LIFE, Panama & Frank Prod., UA: EDITH HEAD and EDWARD STEVENSON
NEVER ON SUNDAY, Melinafilm Prod., Lopert Pictures Corp. (Greek): DENNY VACHLIOTI
THE RISE AND FALL OF LEGS DIAMOND, United States Prod., Warner Bros: HOWARD SHOUP
SEVEN THIEVES, 20th Century-Fox: BILL THOMAS
THE VIRGIN SPRING, Svensk Filmindustri Prod., Janus Films, Inc. (Swedish): MARIK VOS

(Color)

CAN-CAN, Suffolk-Cummings Prods., 20th Century-Fox: IRENE SHARAFF

MIDNIGHT LACE, Ross Hunter-Arwin Prod., U-I: IRENE
PEPE, G.S.-Posa Films International Prod., Columbia: EDITH HEAD
SPARTACUS, Bryna Prods., Inc., U-I: VALLES and BILL THOMAS
SUNRISE AT CAMPOBELLO, Schary Prod., Warner Bros.: MARJORIE BEST

Short Subjects

(Cartoons)

GOLIATH II, Walt Disney Prods., Buena Vista Distribution Co., Inc.: WALT DISNEY, Producer.
HIGH NOTE, Warner Bros.
MOUSE AND GARDEN, Warner Bros.
MUNRO, Rembrandt Films, Film Representations, Inc.: WILLIAM L. SNYDER, Producer
A PLACE IN THE SUN, George K. Arthur-Go Pictures, Inc. (Czechoslovakian): FRANTISEK VYSTRECIL, Producer

(Live Action Subjects)

THE CREATION OF WOMAN, Trident Films, Inc., Sterling World Distributors Corp. (Indian): CHARLES F. SCHWEP and ISMAIL MERCHANT, Producers
DAY OF THE PAINTER, Little Movies, Kingsley-Union Films: EZRA R. BAKER, Producer
ISLANDS OF THE SEA, Walt Disney Prods., Buena Vista Distribution Co., Inc.: WALT DISNEY, Producer
A SPORT IS BORN, Paramount: LESLIE WINIK, Producer

Documentary

(Short Subjects)

BEYOND SILENCE, United States Information Agency
A CITY CALLED COPENHAGEN, Statens Filmcentral, Danish Government Film Office (Danish)
GEORGE GROSZ' INTERREGNUM, Educational Communications Corp.:

CHARLES and ALTINA CAREY, Producers

GIUSEPPINA, James Hill Prod., Lester A. Schoenfeld Films (British): JAMES HILL, Producer

UNIVERSE, National Film Board of Canada, Lester A. Schoenfeld Films (Canadian): COLIN LOW, Producer

(Features)

THE HORSE WITH THE FLYING TAIL, Walt Disney Prods., Buena Vista Dist. Co., Inc.: LARRY LANSBURGH, Producer

REBEL IN PARADISE, Tiare Co.: ROBERT D. FRASER, Producer

Special Effects

THE LAST VOYAGE, Andrew and Virginia Stone Prod., M-G-M: Visual: A. J. LOHMAN

THE TIME MACHINE, GALAXY Films Prod., M-G-M: Visual: GENE WARREN and TIM BAAR

Foreign Language Film Award

KAPO, Vides-Zebrafilm-Cineriz (Italy)

LA VERITÉ, Han Productions (France)

MACARIO, Clasa Films Mundiales, S.A. (Mexico)

THE NINTH CIRCLE, Jadran Film Production (Yugoslavia)

THE VIRGIN SPRING, A. B. Svensk Filmindustri (Sweden)

Honorary Awards

GARY COOPER for his many memorable screen performances and the international recognition he, as an individual, has gained for the motion picture industry. (statuette)

STAN LAUREL for his creative pioneering in the field of cinema comedy. (statuette)

HAYLEY MILLS for *Pollyanna*, the most outstanding juvenile performance during 1960. (miniature statuette)

Irving G. Thalberg Memorial Award
None

Jean Hersholt Humanitarian Award
SOL LESSER

Scientific or Technical
Class I
None

Class II

AMPEX PROFESSIONAL PRODUCTS CO. for the production of a well-engineered multi-purpose sound system combining high standards of quality with convenience of control, dependable operation and simplified emergency provisions

Class III

ARTHUR HOLCOMB, PETRO VLAHOS and COLUMBIA STUDIO CAMERA DEPARTMENT for a camera flicker indicating device

ANTHONY PAGLIA and the 20TH CENTURY-FOX STUDIO MECHANICAL EFFECTS DEPARTMENT for the design and construction of a miniature flak gun and ammunition

CARL HAUGE, ROBERT GRUBEL and EDWARD REICHARD of Consolidated Film Industries for the development of an automatic developer replenisher system

1961

Nominations Announced: February 26, 1962
Awards Ceremony: April 9, 1962
Santa Monica Civic Auditorium
(MC: Bob Hope)

Best Picture

FANNY, Mansfield Prod., Warner Bros: JOSHUA LOGAN, Producer

THE GUNS OF NAVARONE, Carl Foreman Prod., Columbia: CARL FOREMAN, Producer

THE HUSTLER, Robert Rossen Prod., 20th Century-Fox: ROBERT ROSSEN, Producer

JUDGMENT AT NUREMBERG, Stanley Kramer Prod., UA: STANLEY KRAMER, Producer

WEST SIDE STORY, Mirisch Pictures, Inc. and B and P Enterprises, Inc., UA: ROBERT WISE, Producer

Actor

CHARLES BOYER in *Fanny*, Mansfield Prod., Warner Bros.

PAUL NEWMAN in *The Hustler*, Robert Rossen Prod., 20th Century-Fox

MAXIMILIAN SCHELL in *Judgment At Nuremberg*, Stanley Kramer Prod., UA

SPENCER TRACY in *Judgment At Nuremberg*, Stanley Kramer Prod., UA

STUART WHITMAN in *The Mark*, Raymond Stross-Sidney Buchman Prod., Continental Dist., Inc. (British)

Actress

AUDREY HEPBURN in *Breakfast At Tiffany's*, Jurow-Shepherd Prod., Paramount

LARGE CAPITAL LETTERS DENOTE WINNER

PIPER LAURIE in *The Hustler*, Robert Rossen Prod., 20th Century-Fox

SOPHIA LOREN in *Two Women*, Champion-Les Films Marceau-Cocinor and Societé Generale De Cinematographie Prod., Embassy Pictures Corp. (Italo-French)

GERALDINE PAGE in *Summer And Smoke*, Hal Wallis Prod., Paramount

NATALIE WOOD in *Splendor In The Grass*, NBI Prod., Warner Bros.

Supporting Actor

GEORGE CHAKIRIS in *West Side Story*, Mirisch Pictures, Inc. and B and P Enterprises, Inc., UA

MONTGOMERY CLIFT in *Judgment At Nuremberg*, Stanley Kramer Prod., UA

PETER FALK in *Pocketful Of Miracles*, Franton Prod., UA

JACKIE GLEASON in *The Hustler*, Robert Rossen Prod., 20th Century-Fox

GEORGE C. SCOTT in *The Hustler*, Robert Rossen Prod., 20th Century-Fox

Supporting Actress

FAY BAINTER in *The Children's Hour*, Mirisch-Worldwide Prod., UA

JUDY GARLAND in *Judgment At Nuremberg*, Stanley Kramer Prod., UA

LOTTE LENYA in *The Roman Spring Of Mrs. Stone*, Seven Arts Presentation, Warner Bros.

UNA MERKEL in *Summer And Smoke*, Hal Wallis Prod., Paramount

RITA MORENO in *West Side Story,*
  Mirisch Pictures, Inc. and B and P
  Enterprises, Inc., UA

Directing

FEDERICO FELLINI for *La Dolce Vita,*
  Riama Film Prod., Astor Pictures,
  Inc. (Italian)

STANLEY KRAMER for *Judgment At
  Nuremberg,* Stanley Kramer Prod.,
  UA

JEROME ROBBINS for *West Side
  Story,* Mirisch Pictures, Inc. and
  B and P Enterprises, Inc., UA

ROBERT ROSSEN for *The Hustler,* Robert
  Rossen Prod., 20th Century-Fox

J. LEE THOMPSON for *The Guns of Navarone,* Carl Foreman Prod., Columbia

ROBERT WISE for *West Side Story,*
  Pictures, Inc. and B and P Enterprises, Inc., UA

Writing

(Best Screenplay—based on material
from another medium)

BREAKFAST AT TIFFANY'S, Jurow-
  Shepherd Prod., Paramount: GEORGE
  AXELROD

THE GUNS OF NAVARONE, Carl Foreman Prod., Columbia: CARL FORE-
  MAN

THE HUSTLER, Robert Rossen Prod.,
  20th Century-Fox: SIDNEY CARROLL
  and ROBERT ROSSEN

JUDGMENT AT NUREMBERG,
  Stanley Kramer Prod., UA: ABBY
  MANN

WEST SIDE STORY, Mirisch Pictures,
  Inc. and B and P Enterprises, Inc.,
  UA: ERNEST LEHMAN

(Best Story and Screenplay—written
directly for the screen)

BALLAD OF A SOLDIER, Mosfilm Studio
  Prod., Kingsley International-M.J.P.
  Enterprises, Inc. (Russian): VALEN-
  TIN YOSHOV and GRIGORI CHUKHRAI

GENERAL DELLA ROVERE, Zebra &
  S.N.E. Gaumont Prod., Continental
  Dist., Inc. (Italian): SERGIO AMIDEI,
  DIEGO FABBRI and INDRO MON-
  TANELLI

LA DOLCE VITA, Riama Film Prod.,
  Astor Pictures, Inc. (Italian): FE-
  DERICO FELLINI, TULLIO PINELLI,
  ENNIO FLAIANO and BRUNNELLO
  RONDI

LOVER COME BACK, Universal-Interna-
  tional-The 7 Pictures Corp., Nob
  Hill Prods., Inc., Arwin Prods.,
  Inc., U-I: STANLEY SHAPIRO and
  PAUL HENNING

SPLENDOR IN THE GRASS, NBI
  Prod., Warner Bros.: WILLIAM
  INGE

Cinematography

(Black-and-White)

THE ABSENT MINDED PROFESSOR, Walt
  Disney Prods., Buena Vista Distribution Co., Inc: EDWARD COLMAN

THE CHILDREN'S HOUR, Mirisch-
  Worldwide Prod., UA: FRANZ F.
  PLANER

THE HUSTLER, Robert Rossen Prod.,
  20th Century-Fox: EUGEN SHUF-
  TAN

JUDGMENT AT NUREMBERG, Stanley
  Kramer Prod., UA: ERNEST LASZLO

ONE, TWO, THREE, Mirisch Company,
  Inc. in association with Pyramid
  Prods., A. G., UA:. DANIEL L. FAPP

(Color)

FANNY, Mansfield Prod., Warner
  Bros.: JACK CARDIFF

FLOWER DRUM SONG, Universal-International-Ross Hunter Prod. in association with Joseph Fields, U-I: RUS-
  SELL METTY

A MAJORITY OF ONE, Warner Bros.:
  HARRY STRADLING, SR.

ONE-EYED JACKS, Pennebaker Prod.,
  Paramount: CHARLES LANG, JR.

WEST SIDE STORY, Mirisch Pictures, Inc. and B and P Enterprises Inc., UA: DANIEL L. FAPP

Art Direction—Set Decoration
(Black-and-White)

THE ABSENT MINDED PROFESSOR, Walt Disney Prod., Buena Vista Distribution Co., Inc.: CARROLL CLARK
Set Decoration: EMILE KURI and HAL GAUSMAN
THE CHILDREN'S HOUR, Mirisch-Worldwide Prod., UA: FERNANDO CARRERE
Set Decoration: EDWARD G. BOYLE
THE HUSTLER, Robert Rossen Prod., 20th Century-Fox: HARRY HORNER
Set Decoration: GENE CALLAHAN
JUDGMENT AT NUREMBERG, Stanley Kramer Prod., UA: RUDOLPH STERNAD
Set Decoration: GEORGE MILO
LA DOLCE VITA, Riama Film Prod., Astor Pictures, Inc. (Italian): PIERO GHERARDI

(Color)

BREAKFAST AT TIFFANY'S, Jurow-Shepherd Prod., Paramount HAL PEREIRA and ROLAND ANDERSON
Set Decoration: SAM COMER and RAY MOYER
EL CID, Samuel Bronston Prod. in association with Dear Film Prod., Allied Artists: VENIERO COLASANTI and JOHN MOORE
FLOWER DRUM SONG, Universal-International-Ross Hunter Prod. in association with Joseph Fields, U-I: ALEXANDER GOLITZEN and JOSEPH WRIGHT
Set Decoration: HOWARD BRISTOL
SUMMER AND SMOKE, Hal Wallis Prod., Paramount: HAL PEREIRA and WALTER TYLER
Set Decoration: SAM COMER and ARTHUR KRAMS

WEST SIDE STORY, Mirisch Pictures, Inc. and B and P Enterprises, Inc. UA: BORIS LEVEN
Set Decoration: VICTOR A. GANGELIN

Sound

THE CHILDREN'S HOUR, Samuel Goldwyn Studio Sound Department: GORDON E. SAWYER, Sound Director
FLOWER DRUM SONG, Revue Studio Sound Department: WALDON O. WATSON, Sound Director
THE GUNS OF NAVARONE, Shepperton Studio Sound Department: JOHN COX, Sound Director
THE PARENT TRAP, Walt Disney Studio Sound Department: ROBERT O. COOK, Sound Director
WEST SIDE STORY, Todd-AO Sound Department: FRED HYNES, Sound Director; and Samuel Goldwyn Studio Sound Department: GORDON E. SAWYER, Sound Director

Film Editing

FANNY, Mansfield Prod., Warner Bros.: WILLIAM H. REYNOLDS
THE GUNS OF NAVARONE, Carl Foreman Prod., Columbia: ALAN OSBISTON
JUDGMENT AT NUREMBERG, Stanley Kramer Prod., YA: FREDERIC KNUDTSON
THE PARENT TRAP, Walt Disney Prods., Buena Vista Dist. Co., Inc.: PHILIP W. ANDERSON
WEST SIDE STORY, Mirisch Pictures, Inc. and B and P Enterprises, Inc., UA: THOMAS STANFORD

Music
(Scoring of a Dramatic or Comedy Picture)
BREAKFAST AT TIFFANY'S, Jurow-Shepherd Prod., Paramount: HENRY MANCINI

EL CID, Samuel Bronston Prod. in association with Dear Film Prod., Allied Artists: MIKLOS ROZSA

FANNY, Mansfield Prod., Warner Bros.: MORRIS STOLOFF and HARRY SUKMAN

THE GUNS OF NAVARONE, Carl Foreman Prod., Columbia: DIMITRI TIOMKIN

SUMMER AND SMOKE, Hal Wallis Prod., Paramount: ELMER BERNSTEIN

(Scoring of a Musical Picture)

BABES IN TOYLAND, Walt Disney Prods., Buena Vista Dist. Co., Inc.: GEORGE BRUNS

FLOWER DRUM SONG, Universal-International-Ross Hunter Prod. in association with Joseph Fields, U-I: ALFRED NEWMAN and KEN DARBY

KHOVANSHCHINA, Mosfilm Studios, Artkino Pictures (Russian): DIMITRI SHOSTAKOVICH

PARIS BLUES, Pennebaker, Inc., UA: DUKE ELLINGTON

WEST SIDE STORY, Mirisch Pictures, Inc. and B and P Enterprises, Inc., UA: SAUL CHAPLIN, JOHNNY GREEN, SID RAMIN and IRWIN KOSTAL

(Best Song)

BACHELOR IN PARADISE from *Bachelor In Paradise,* Ted Richmond Prod., M-G-M
Music by HENRY MANCINI. Lyrics by MACK DAVID

LOVE THEME FROM EL CID (The Falcon And The Dove) from *El Cid,* Samuel Bronston Prod. in association with Dear Film Prod., Allied Artists
Music by MIKLOS ROZSA. Lyrics by PAUL FRANCIS WEBSTER

MOON RIVER from *Breakfast At Tiffany's,* Jurow-Shepherd Prod., Paramount
Music by HENRY MANCINI. Lyrics by JOHNNY MERCER

POCKETFUL OF MIRACLES from *Pocketful Of Miracles,* Franton Prod., UA
Music by JAMES VAN HEUSEN. Lyrics by SAMMY CAHN

TOWN WITHOUT PITY from *Town Without Pity,* Mirisch Company in association with Gloria Films, UA
Music by DIMITRI TIOMKIN. Lyrics by NED WASHINGTON

Costume Design
(Black-and-White)

THE CHILDREN'S HOUR, Mirisch-Worldwide Prod., UA: DOROTHY JEAKINS

CLAUDELLE INGLISH, Warner Bros.: HOWARD SHOUP

JUDGMENT AT NUREMBERG, Stanley Kramer Prod., UA: JEAN LOUIS

LA DOLCE VITA, Riama Film Prod., Astor Pictures, Inc. (Italian): PIERO GHERARDI

YOJIMBO, Toho Company, Ltd. & Kurosawa Prod., Toho Company, Ltd. (Japanese): YOSHIRO MURAKI

(Color)

BABES IN TOYLAND, Walt Disney Prods., Buena Vista Distribution Co., Inc.: BILL THOMAS

BACK STREET, Universal-International-Ross Hunter Prods., Inc.-Carrollton, Inc., U-I: JEAN LOUIS

FLOWER DRUM SONG, Universal-International-Ross Hunter Prod. in association with Joseph Fields, U-I: IRENE SHARAFF

POCKETFUL OF MIRACLES, Franton Prod., UA: EDITH HEAD and WALTER PLUNKETT

WEST SIDE STORY, Mirisch Pictures, Inc. and B & P Enterprises, Inc., UA: IRENE SHARAFF

Short Subjects
(Cartoons)

AQUAMANIA, Walt Disney Prods., Buena Vista Distribution Co., Inc.:

WALT DISNEY, Producer
BEEP PREPARED, Warner Bros.: CHUCK
JONES, Producer
ERSATZ (The Substitute), Zagreb
Film, Herts-Lion International Corp.
NELLY'S FOLLY, Warner Bros.: CHUCK
JONES, Producer
PIED PIPER OF GUADALUPE, Warner
Bros.: FRIZ FRELENG, Producer

(Live Action Subjects)

BALLON VOLE (Play Ball!), Ciné-
Documents, Kingsley International
Pictures Corp
THE FACE OF JESUS, Dr. John D. Jen-
nings, Harry Stern, Inc.: DR. JOHN
D. JENNINGS, Producer
ROOFTOPS OF NEW YORK, McCarty-
Rush Prod. in association with ROB-
ERT GAFFNEY, Columbia
SEAWARDS THE GREAT SHIPS,
Templar Film Studios, Lester A.
Schoenfeld Films
VERY NICE, VERY NICE, National Film
Board Of Canada, Kingsley Interna-
tional Pictures Corp.

Documentary

(Short Subjects)

BREAKING THE LANGUAGE BARRIER,
United States Air Force
CRADLE OF GENIUS, Plough Prods., An
Irving M. Lesser Film Presentation
(Irish): JIM O'CONNOR and TOM
HAYES, Producers
KAHL, Dido-Film-GmbH., AEG-Film-
dienst (German)
L'UOMO IN GRIGIO (The Man In Gray),
(Italian): BENEDETTO BENEDETTI,
Producer
PROJECT HOPE, MacManus, John &
Adams, Inc., Ex-Cell-O Corp. A
Klaeger Film Production: FRANK P.
BIBAS, Producer.

(Features)

LA GRANDE OLIMPIADE (Olympic
Games 1960), dell Istituto Nazionale

Luce, Comitato Organizzatore dei
Giochi Della XVII Olimpiade:
Cineriz (Italian)
LE CIEL ET LA BOUE (Sky Above
And Mud Beneath), Ardennes Films
and Michael Arthur Film Prods.,
Rank Film Distrs., Ltd. (French):
ARTHUR COHN and RENÉ LA-
FUITE, Producers

Special Effects

THE ABSENT MINDED PROFESSOR, Walt
Disney Prods., Buena Vista Dist.
Co.
Visual: ROBERT A. MATTEY and EUS-
TACE LYCETT
THE GUNS OF NAVARONE, Carl
Foreman Prod., Columbia
Visual: BILL WARRINGTON
Audible: VIVIAN C. GREENHAM

Foreign Language Film Award

HARRY AND THE BUTLER, Bent Chris-
tensen Production (Denmark)
IMMORTAL LOVE, Shochiku Co., Ltd.
(Japan)
THE IMPORTANT MAN, Peliculas Ro-
driguez, S.A. (Mexico)
PLACIDO, Jet Films (Spain)
THROUGH A GLASS DARKLY,
A. B. Svensk Filmindustri (Sweden)

Honorary Awards

WILLIAM L. HENDRICKS for his
outstanding patriotic service in the
conception, writing and production
of the Marine Corps film *A Force
In Readiness,* which has brought
honor to the Academy and the motion picture industry. (statuette)
FRED L. METZLER for his dedication
and outstanding service to the Academy of Motion Picture Arts and
Sciences. (statuette)
JEROME ROBBINS for his brilliant
achievements in the art of choreography on film. (statuette)

Irving G. Thalberg Memorial Award
STANLEY KRAMER

Jean Hersholt Humanitarian Award
GEORGE SEATON

Scientific or Technical

Class I

None.

Class II

SYLVANIA ELECTRIC PRODUCTS, INC., for the development of a hand-held high-power photographic lighting unit known as the Sun Gun Professional.

JAMES DALE, S. WILSON, H. E. RICE, JOHN RUDE, LAURIE ATKIN, WADSWORTH E. POHL, H. PEASGOOD and TECHNICOLOR CORP. for a process of automatic selective printing.

20TH CENTURY-FOX RESEARCH DEPARTMENT, under the direction of E. I. SPONABLE and HERBERT E. BRAGG, and DELUXE LABORATORIES, INC., with the assistance of F. D. LESLIE, R. D. WHITMORE, A. A. ALDEN, ENDEL POOL and JAMES B. GORDON for a system of decompressing and recomposing Cinema-Scope pictures for conventional aspect ratios.

Class III

HURLETRON, INC., ELECTRIC EYE EQUIPMENT DIVISION, for an automatic light changing system for motion picture printers.

WADSWORTH E. POHL and TECHNICOLOR CORP. for an integrated sound and picture transfer process.

1962

Nominations Announced: February 25, 1963
Awards Ceremony: April 8, 1963
Santa Monica Civic Auditorium
(MC: Frank Sinatra)

Best Picture

LAWRENCE OF ARABIA, Horizon Pictures (G.B.), Ltd.-Sam Spiegel-David Lean Prod., Columbia: SAM SPIEGEL, Producer

THE LONGEST DAY, Darryl F. Zanuck Prods., 20th Century-Fox: DARRYL F. ZANUCK, Producer

Meredith Willson's THE MUSIC MAN, Warner Bros.: MORTON DA COSTA, Producer

MUTINY ON THE BOUNTY, Arcola Prod., M-G-M: AARON ROSENBERG, Producer

TO KILL A MOCKINGBIRD, Universal-International-Pakula-Mulligan-Brentwood Prod., U-I: ALAN J. PAKULA, Producer

Actor

BURT LANCASTER in *Bird Man of Alcatraz*, Harold Hecht Prod., UA

JACK LEMMON in *Days Of Wine And Roses*, Martin Manulis-Jalem Prod., Warner Bros.

MARCELLO MASTROIANNI in *Divorce—Italian Style*, Lux-Vides-Galatea Film Prod., Embassy Pictures

PETER O'TOOLE in *Lawrence Of Arabia*, Horizon Pictures (G.B.), Ltd.-Sam Spiegel-David Lean Prod., Columbia

GREGORY PECK in *To Kill A Mockingbird*, Universal-International-Pakula-Mulligan-Brentwood Prod., U-I

LARGE CAPITAL LETTERS DENOTE WINNER

Actress

ANNE BANCROFT in *The Miracle Worker*, Playfilms Prod., UA

BETTE DAVIS in *What Ever Happened To Baby Jane?*, Seven Arts-Associates & Aldrich Co. Prod., Warner Bros.

KATHARINE HEPBURN in *Long Day's Journey Into Night*, Ely Landau Prods., Embassy Pictures

GERALDINE PAGE in *Sweet Bird Of Youth*, Roxbury Prod., M-G-M.

LEE REMICK in *Days Of Wine And Roses*, Martin Manulis-Jalem Prod., Warner Bros.

Supporting Actor

ED BEGLEY in *Sweet Bird Of Youth*, Roxbury Prod., M-G-M.

VICTOR BUONO in *What Ever Happened To Baby Jane?*, Seven Arts-Associates & Aldrich Co. Prod., Warner Bros.

TELLY SAVALAS in *Bird Man Of Alcatraz*, Harold Hecht Prod., UA

OMAR SHARIF in *Lawrence Of Arabia*, Horizon Pictures (G.B.), Ltd.-Sam Spiegel-David Lean Prod., Columbia

TERENCE STAMP in *Billy Budd*, Harvest Prods., Allied Artists

Supporting Actress

MARY BADHAM in *To Kill A Mockingbird*, Universal-International-Pakula-Mulligan-Brentwood Prod., U-I.

PATTY DUKE in *The Miracle Worker*, Playfilms Prod., UA

SHIRLEY KNIGHT in *Sweet Bird Of Youth,* Roxbury Prod., M-G-M.
ANGELA LANSBURY in *The Manchurian Candidate,* M. C. Prod., UA.
THELMA RITTER in *Bird Man Of Alcatraz,* Harold Hecht Prod., UA

Directing

PIETRO GERMI for *Divorce—Italian Style,* Lux-Vides-Galatea Film Prod., Embassy Pictures
DAVID LEAN for *Lawrence Of Arabia,* Horizon Pictures (G.B.), Ltd.-Sam Spiegel-David Lean Prod., Columbia
ROBERT MULLIGAN for *To Kill A Mockingbird,* Universal-International-Pakula-Mulligan-Brentwood Prod., U-I.
ARTHUR PENN for *The Miracle Worker,* Playfilms Prod., UA.
FRANK PERRY for *David And Lisa,* Heller-Perry Prods., Continental Dist.

Writing

(Best Screenplay—based on material from another medium)

DAVID AND LISA, Heller-Perry Prods., Continental Distributing: ELEANOR PERRY
LAWRENCE OF ARABIA, Horizon Pictures (G.B.), Ltd.-Sam Spiegel-David Lean Prod., Columbia: ROBERT BOLT
LOLITA, Seven Arts Prods., M-G-M: VLADIMIR NABOKOV
THE MIRACLE WORKER, Playfilms Prod., UA: WILLIAM GIBSON
TO KILL A MOCKINGBIRD, Universal-International-Pakula-Mulligan-Brentwood Prod., U-I: HORTON FOOTE

(Best Story and Screenplay—written directly for the screen)

DIVORCE—ITALIAN STYLE, Lux-Vides-Galatea Film Prod., Embassy Pictures: ENNIO DE CONCINI, ALFREDO GIANNETTI and PIETRO GERMI
FREUD, Universal-International-John Huston Prod., U-I: Story by CHARLES KAUFMAN. Screenplay by CHARLES KAUFMAN and WOLFGANG REINHARDT
LAST YEAR AT MARIENBAD, Preceitel-Terra Film Prod., Astor Pictures: ALAIN ROBBE-GRILLET
THAT TOUCH OF MINK, Universal-International-Granley-Arwin-Nob Hill Prod., U-I.: STANLEY SHAPIRO and NATE MONASTER
THROUGH A GLASS DARKLY, Svensk Filmindustri Prod., Janus Films: INGMAR BERGMAN

Cinematography

(Black-and-White)

BIRD MAN OF ALCATRAZ, Harold Hecht Prod., UA: BURNETT GUFFEY
THE LONGEST DAY, Darryl F. Zanuck Prods., 20th Century-Fox: JEAN BOURGOIN and WALTER WOTTITZ
TO KILL A MOCKINGBIRD, Universal-International-Pakula-Mulligan-Brentwood Prod., U-I: RUSSELL HARLAN
TWO FOR THE SEESAW, Mirisch-Argyle-Talbot Prod. in association with Seven Arts Prods., UA: TED MCCORD
WHAT EVER HAPPENED TO BABY JANE?, Seven Arts-Associates & Aldrich Co. Prod., Warner Bros.: ERNEST HALLER

(Color)

GYPSY, Warner Bros.: HARRY STRADLING, SR.
HATARI!, Malabar Prods., Paramount: RUSSELL HARLAN
LAWRENCE OF ARABIA, Horizon Pictures (G.B.), Ltd.-Sam Spiegel-

David Lean Prod., Columbia: FRED A. YOUNG

MUTINY ON THE BOUNTY, Arcola Prod., M-G-M: ROBERT L. SURTEES

THE WONDERFUL WORLD OF THE BROTHERS GRIMM, Metro-Goldwyn-Mayer & Cinerama: PAUL C. VOGEL

Art Direction—Set Decoration
(Black-and-White)

DAYS OF WINE AND ROSES, Martin Manulis-Jalem Prod., Warner Bros.: JOSEPH WRIGHT
Set Decoration: GEORGE JAMES HOPKINS

THE LONGEST DAY, Darryl F. Zanuck Prods., 20th Century-Fox: TED HAWORTH, LEON BARSACQ and VINCENT KORDA
Set Decoration: GABRIEL BECHIR

PERIOD OF ADJUSTMENT, Marten Prod., M-G-M: GEORGE W. DAVIS and EDWARD CARFAGNO
Set Decoration: HENRY GRACE and DICK PEFFERLE

THE PIGEON THAT TOOK ROME, Llenroc Prods., Paramount: HAL PEREIRA and ROLAND ANDERSON
Set Decoration: SAM COMER and FRANK R. MCKELVY

TO KILL A MOCKINGBIRD, Universal-International-Pakula-Mulligan-Brentwood Prod., U-I: ALEXANDER GOLITZEN and HENRY BUMSTEAD
Set Decoration: OLIVER EMERT

(Color)

LAWRENCE OF ARABIA, Horizon Pictures (G.B.), Ltd.-Sam Spiegel-David Lean Prod., Columbia: JOHN BOX and JOHN STOLL
Set Decoration: DARIO SIMONI

Meredith Willson's THE MUSIC MAN, Warner Bros.: PAUL GROESSE
Set Decoration: GEORGE JAMES HOPKINS

MUTINY ON THE BOUNTY, Arcola Prod., M-G-M: GEORGE W. DAVIS and J. MCMILLAN JOHNSON
Set Decoration: HENRY GRACE and HUGH HUNT

THAT TOUCH OF MINK, Universal-International-Granley-Arwin-Nob Hill Prod., U-I: ALEXANDER GOLITZEN and ROBERT CLATWORTHY
Set Decoration: GEORGE MILO

THE WONDERFUL WORLD OF THE BROTHERS GRIMM, Metro-Goldwyn-Mayer & Cinerama: GEORGE W. DAVIS and EDWARD CARFAGNO
Set Decoration: HENRY GRACE and DICK PEFFERLE

Sound

BON VOYAGE, Walt Disney Studio Sound Department: ROBERT O. COOK, Sound Director

LAWRENCE OF ARABIA, Shepperton Studio Sound Department: JOHN COX, Sound Director

Meredith Willson's THE MUSIC MAN, Warner Bros. Studio Sound Department: GEORGE R. GROVES, Sound Director

THAT TOUCH OF MINK, Universal City Studio Sound Department: WALDON O. WATSON, Sound Director

WHAT EVER HAPPENED TO BABY JANE?, Glen Glenn Sound Department: JOSEPH KELLY, Sound Director

Film Editing

LAWRENCE OF ARABIA, Horizon Pictures (G.B.), Ltd.-Sam Spiegel-David Lean Prod., Columbia: ANNE COATES

THE LONGEST DAY, Darryl F. Zanuck Prods., 20th Century-Fox: SAMUEL E. BEETLEY

THE MANCHURIAN CANDIDATE, M.C. Prod., UA: FERRIS WEBSTER

Meredith Willson's THE MUSIC MAN, Warner Bros.: WILLIAM ZIEGLER

MUTINY ON THE BOUNTY, Arcola
Prod., M-G-M: JOHN MCSWEENEY,
JR.

Music
(Note: Title of Awards changed.)
(Music Score—substantially original)
FREUD, Universal-International-John
Huston Prod., U-I: JERRY GOLD-
SMITH
LAWRENCE OF ARABIA, Horizon
Pictures (G.B.), Ltd.-Sam Spiegel-
David Lean Prod., Columbia:
MAURICE JARRE
MUTINY ON THE BOUNTY, Arcola
Prod., M-G-M: BRONISLAU KAPER
TARAS BULBA, Harold Hecht Prod.,
UA: FRANZ WAXMAN
TO KILL A MOCKINGBIRD, Universal-In-
ternational-Pakula-Mulligan-
Brentwood Prod., U-I: ELMER BERN-
STEIN
(Scoring of Music—adaptation or treat-
ment)
BILLY ROSE'S JUMBO, Euterpe-Arwin
Prod., M-G-M: GEORGE STOLL
GIGOT, Seven Arts Prods., 20th Cen-
tury-Fox: MICHEL MAGNE
GYPSY, Warner Bros.: FRANK PERKINS
Meredith Willson's THE MUSIC
MAN, Warner Bros.: RAY HEIN-
DORF
THE WONDERFUL WORLD OF THE
BROTHERS GRIMM, Metro-Goldwyn-
Mayer & Cinerama: LEIGH HARLINE

(Best Song)
DAYS OF WINE AND ROSES from
Days Of Wine And Roses, Martin
Manulis-Jalem Prod., Warner Bros.
Music by HENRY MANCINI.
Lyrics by JOHNNY MERCER
LOVE SONG FROM MUTINY ON THE
BOUNTY (Follow Me) from *Mutiny
On The Bounty,* Arcola Prod.,
M-G-M

Music by BRONISLAU KAPER. Lyrics
by PAUL FRANCIS WEBSTER
SONG FROM TWO FOR THE SEESAW (Sec-
ond Chance) from *Two For The See-
saw,* Mirisch-Argyle-Talbot Prod. in
association with Seven Arts Produc-
tions, UA
Music by ANDRÉ PREVIN. Lyrics by
DORY LANGDON
TENDER IS THE NIGHT from *Tender Is
The Night,* 20th Century-Fox
Music by SAMMY FAIN. Lyrics by
PAUL FRANCIS WEBSTER
WALK ON THE WILD SIDE from *Walk On
The Wild Side,* Famous Artists
Prods., Columbia
Music by ELMER BERNSTEIN. Lyrics
by MACK DAVID

Costume Design
(Black-and-White)
DAYS OF WINE AND ROSES, Martin Man-
ulis-Jalem Prod., Warner Bros.: DON
FELD
THE MAN WHO SHOT LIBERTY VA-
LANCE, John Ford Prod., Paramount:
EDITH HEAD
THE MIRACLE WORKER, Playfilms
Prod., UA: RUTH MORLEY
PHAEDRA, Jules Dassin-Melinafilm
Prod., Lopert Pictures: DENNY
VACHLIOTI
WHAT EVER HAPPENED TO BABY
JANE?, Seven Arts-Associates &
Aldrich Co. Prod., Warner Bros.:
NORMA KOCH

(Color)
BON VOYAGE, Walt Disney Prod.,
Buena Vista Distribution Co.: BILL
THOMAS
GYPSY, Warner Bros.: ORRY-KELLY
Meredith Willson's THE MUSIC MAN,
Warner Bros.: DOROTHY JEAKINS
MY GEISHA, Sachiko Prod., Paramount:
EDITH HEAD
THE WONDERFUL WORLD OF

THE BROTHERS GRIMM, Metro-Goldwyn-Mayer & Cinerama: MARY WILLS

Short Subjects
(Cartoons)
THE HOLE, Storyboard Inc., Brandon Films, Inc.: JOHN and FAITH HUBLEY, Producers
ICARUS MONTGOLFIER WRIGHT, Format Films, United Artists: JULES ENGEL, Producer
NOW HEAR THIS, Warner Bros.
SELF DEFENSE—FOR COWARDS, Rembrandt Films, Film Representations, Inc.: WILLIAM L. SNYDER, Producer
SYMPOSIUM ON POPULAR SONGS, Walt Disney Prods., Buena Vista Distribution Co.: WALT DISNEY, Producer

(Live Action Subjects)
BIG CITY BLUES, Mayfair Pictures Company: MARTINA and CHARLES HUGUENOT VAN DER LINDEN, Producers
THE CADILLAC, United Producers Releasing Org.: ROBERT CLOUSE, Producer
THE CLIFF DWELLERS (formerly titled *One Plus One*), Group II Film Prods., Lester A. Schoenfeld Films: HAYWARD ANDERSON, Producer
HEUREUX ANNIVERSAIRE (Happy Anniversary), CAPAC Prods., Atlantic Pictures Corp.: PIERRE ETAIX and J. C. CARRIERE, Producers
PAN, Mayfair Pictures Company: HERMAN VAN DER HORST, Producer

Documentary
(Short Subjects)
DYLAN THOMAS, TWW Ltd., Janus Films (Welsh): JACK HOWELLS, Producer

THE JOHN GLENN STORY, Department of the Navy, Warner Bros.: WILLIAM L. HENDRICKS, Producer
THE ROAD TO THE WALL, CBS Films, Inc., Department of Defense: ROBERT SAUDEK, Producer

(Features)
ALVORADA (Brazil's Changing Face), MW Filmproduktion (German): HUGO NIEBELING, Producer
BLACK FOX, Image Prods., Inc., Heritage Films, Inc.: LOUIS CLYDE STOUMEN, Producer

Special Effects
THE LONGEST DAY, Darryl F. Zanuck Prods., 20th Century-Fox
Visual: ROBERT MacDONALD
Audible: JACQUES MAUMONT
MUTINY ON THE BOUNTY, Arcola Prod., M-G-M
Visual: A. ARNOLD GILLESPIE
Audible: MILO LORY

Foreign Language Film Award
ELECTRA, A Michael Cacoyannis Production (Greece)
THE FOUR DAYS OF NAPLES, Titanus-Metro (Italy)
KEEPER OF PROMISES (The Given Word), Cinedistri (Brazil)
SUNDAYS AND CYBELE, Terra-Fides-Orsay-Trocadero Films (France)
TLAYUCAN, Producciones Matouk, S.A. (Mexico)

Honorary Awards
None

Irving G. Thalberg Memorial Award
None

Jean Hersholt Humanitarian Award
STEVE BROIDY

Scientific or Technical

Class I

None

Class II

RALPH CHAPMAN for the design and development of an advanced motion picture camera crane

ALBERT S. PRATT, JAMES L. WASSELL and HANS C. WOHLRAB of the Professional Division, Bell & Howell Co., for the design and development of a new and improved automatic motion picture additive color printer

NORTH AMERICAN PHILIPS CO., INC., for the design and engineering of the Norelco Universal 70/35 mm motion picture projector

CHARLES E. SUTTER, WILLIAM BRYSON SMITH and LOUIS C. KENNELL of Paramount Pictures Corp. for the engineering and application to motion picture production of a new system of electric power distribution

Class III

ELECTRO-VOICE, INC., for a highly directional dynamic line microphone.

LOUIS G. MACKENZIE for a selective sound effects repeater

1963

Nominations Announced: February 24, 1964
Awards Ceremony: April 13, 1964
Santa Monica Civic Auditorium
(MC: Jack Lemmon)

Best Picture

AMERICA AMERICA, Athena Enterprises Prod., Warner Bros.: ELIA KAZAN, Producer.

CLEOPATRA, 20th Century-Fox Ltd.-MCL Films S.A.-WALWA Films S.A. Prod., 20th Century-Fox: WALTER WANGER, Producer

HOW THE WEST WAS WON, Metro-Goldwyn-Mayer & Cinerama: BERNARD SMITH, Producer

LILIES OF THE FIELD, Rainbow Prod., UA: RALPH NELSON, Producer.

TOM JONES, Woodfall Prod., UA-Lopert Pictures: TONY RICHARDSON, Producer.

Actor

ALBERT FINNEY in *Tom Jones,* Woodfall Prod., UA-Lopert Pictures

RICHARD HARRIS in *This Sporting Life,* Julian Wintle-Leslie Parkyn Prod., Walter Reade-Sterling-Continental Dist.

REX HARRISON in *Cleopatra,* 20th Century-Fox Ltd.-MCL Films S.A.-WALWA Films S.A. Prod., 20th Century-Fox

PAUL NEWMAN in *Hud,* Salem-Dover Prod., Paramount.

SIDNEY POITIER in *Lilies Of The Field,* Rainbow Prod., UA.

Actress

LESLIE CARON in *The L-Shaped Room,* Romulus Prods., Ltd., Columbia

LARGE CAPITAL LETTERS DENOTE WINNER

SHIRLEY MacLAINE in *Irma La Douce,* Mirisch-Phalanx Prod., UA.

PATRICIA NEAL in *Hud,* Salem-Dover Prod., Paramount

RACHEL ROBERTS in *This Sporting Life,* Julian Wintle-Leslie Parkyn Prod., Walter Reade-Sterling-Continental Dist.

NATALIE WOOD in *Love With The Proper Stranger,* Boardwalk-Rona Prod., Paramount.

Supporting Actor

NICK ADAMS in *Twilight Of Honor,* Perlberg-Seaton Prod., M-G-M.

BOBBY DARIN in *Captain Newman, M.D.,* Universal-Brentwood-Reynard, Prod., Universal

MELVYN DOUGLAS in *Hud,* Salem-Dover Prod., Paramount

HUGH GRIFFITH in *Tom Jones,* Woodfall Prod., UA-Lopert Pictures.

JOHN HUSTON in *The Cardinal,* Gamma Prod., Columbia.

Supporting Actress

DIANE CILENTO in *Tom Jones,* Woodfall Prod., UA-Lopert Pictures

DAME EDITH EVANS in *Tom Jones,* Woodfall Prod., UA-Lopert Pictures

JOYCE REDMAN in *Tom Jones,* Woodfall Prod., UA-Lopert Pictures

MARGARET RUTHERFORD in *The V.I.P.s,* Metro-Goldwyn-Mayer

LILIA SKALA in *Lilies Of The Field,* Rainbow Prod., UA

Directing

FEDERICO FELLINI for *Federico Fellini's 8½,* Cineriz Prod., Embassy Pictures

ELIA KAZAN for *America America,* Athena Enterprises Prod., Warner Bros.

OTTO PREMINGER for *The Cardinal,* Gamma Prod., Columbia

TONY RICHARDSON for *Tom Jones,* Woodfall Prod., UA-Lopert Pictures

MARTIN RITT for *Hud,* Salem-Dover Prod., Paramount

Writing

(Best Screenplay—based on material from another medium)

CAPTAIN NEWMAN, M,D., Universal-Brentwood-Reynard Prod., Universal: RICHARD L. BREEN, PHOEBE and HENRY EPHRON

HUD, Salem-Dover Prod., Paramount: IRVING RAVETCH and HARRIET FRANK, JR.

LILIES OF THE FIELD, Rainbow Prod., UA: JAMES POE

SUNDAYS AND CYBELE, Terra-Fides-Orsay-Films Trocadero Prods., Columbia: SERGE BOURGUIGNON and ANTOINE TUDAL

TOM JONES, Woodfall Prod., UA-Lopert Pictures: JOHN OSBORNE

(Best Story and Screenplay—written directly for the screen)

AMERICA AMERICA, Athena Enterprises Prod., Warner Bros.: ELIA KAZAN

FEDERICO FELLINI'S 8½, Cineriz Prod., Embassy Pictures: FEDERICO FELLINI, ENNIO FLAIANO, TULLIO PINELLI and BRUNELLO RONDI

THE FOUR DAYS OF NAPLES, Titanus Prod., M-G-M.: Story by PASQUALE FESTA CAMPANILE, MASSIMO FRANCIOSA, NANNI LOY and VASCO PRATOLINI, Screenplay by CARLO BERNARI, PASQUALE FESTA CAMPANILE, MASSIMO FRANCIOSA and NANNI LOY

HOW THE WEST WAS WON, Metro-Goldwyn-Mayer & Cinerama: JAMES R. WEBB

LOVE WITH THE PROPER STRANGER, Boardwalk-Rona Prod., Paramount: ARNOLD SCHULMAN

Cinematography

(Black-and-White)

THE BALCONY, Walter Reade-Sterling-Allen-Hodgdon Prod., Walter Reade-Sterling-Continental Dist.: GEORGE FOLSEY

THE CARETAKERS, Hall Bartlett Prod., UA: LUCIEN BALLARD

HUD, Salem-Dover Prod., Paramount: JAMES WONG HOWE

LILIES OF THE FIELD, Rainbow Prod., UA: ERNEST HALLER

LOVE WITH THE PROPER STRANGER, Boardwalk-Rona Prod., Paramount: MILTON KRASNER

(Color)

THE CARDINAL, Gamma Prod., Columbia: LEON SHAMROY

CLEOPATRA, 20th Century-Fox Ltd.-MCL Films S.A.-WALWA Films S.A. Prod., 20th Century-Fox: LEON SHAMROY

HOW THE WEST WAS WON, Metro-Goldwyn-Mayer & Cinerama: WILLIAM H. DANIELS, MILTON KRASNER, CHARLES LANG, JR. and JOSEPH LaSHELLE

IRMA LA DOUCE, Mirisch-Phalanx Prod., UA: JOSEPH LaSHELLE

IT'S A MAD, MAD, MAD, MAD WORLD, Casey Prod., UA: ERNEST LASZLO

Art Direction—Set Decoration

(Black-and-White)

AMERICA AMERICA, Athena Enterprises Prod., Warner Bros.: GENE CALLAHAN

FEDERICO FELLINI'S 8½, Cineriz Prod., Embassy Pictures: PIERO GHERARDI

467

HUD, Salem-Dover Prod., Paramount:
HAL PEREIRA and TAMBI LARSEN
Set Decoration: SAM COMER and
ROBERT BENTON
LOVE WITH THE PROPER STRANGER,
Boardwalk-Rona Prod., Paramount:
HAL PEREIRA and ROLAND ANDERSON
Set Decoration: SAM COMER and
GRACE GREGORY
TWILIGHT OF HONOR, Perlberg-Seaton
Prod., M-G-M: GEORGE W. DAVIS and
PAUL GROESSE
Set Decoration: HENRY GRACE and
HUGH HUNT

(Color)

THE CARDINAL, Gamma Production,
Columbia: LYLE WHEELER
Set Decoration: GENE CALLAHAN
CLEOPATRA, 20th Century-Fox
Ltd.-MCL Films S.A.-WALWA
Films S.A. Prod., 20th Century-Fox:
JOHN DeCUIR, JACK MARTIN
SMITH, HILYARD BROWN, HER-
MAN BLUMENTHAL, ELVEN
WEBB, MAURICE PELLING and
BORIS JURAGA
Set Decoration: WALTER M.
SCOTT, PAUL S. FOX and RAY
MOYER
COME BLOW YOUR HORN, Essex-Tan-
dem Enterprises Prod., Paramount:
HAL PEREIRA and ROLAND ANDERSON
Set Decoration: SAM COMER and
JAMES PAYNE
HOW THE WEST WAS WON, Metro-
Goldwyn-Mayer & Cinerama:
GEORGE W. DAVIS, WILLIAM FERRARI
and ADDISON HEHR
Set Decoration: HENRY GRACE, DON
GREENWOOD, JR. and JACK MILLS
TOM JONES, Woodfall Production, UA-
Lopert Pictures: RALPH BRINTON, TED
MARSHALL and JOCELYN HERBERT
Set Decoration: JOSIE MacAVIN

Sound

BYE BYE BIRDIE, Columbia Studio
Sound Department: CHARLES RICE,
Sound Director
CAPTAIN NEWMAN, M.D., Universal
City Studio Sound Department:
WALDON O. WATSON, Sound Director
CLEOPATRA, 20th Century-Fox Studio
Sound Department: JAMES P. COR-
CORAN, Sound Director; and
TODD A-O Sound Department: FRED
HYNES, Sound Director
HOW THE WEST WAS WON, Metro-
Goldwyn-Mayer Studio Sound De-
partment: FRANKLIN E. MILTON,
Sound Director.
IT'S A MAD, MAD, MAD, MAD WORLD,
Samuel Goldwyn Studio Sound De-
partment. GORDON E. SAWYER, Sound
Director

Film Editing

THE CARDINAL, Gamma Prod., Colum-
bia: LOUIS R. LOEFFLER
CLEOPATRA, 20th Century-Fox Ltd.—
MCL Films S.A.—WALWA Films
S.A. Prod., 20th Century-Fox:
DOROTHY SPENCER
THE GREAT ESCAPE, Mirisch-Alpha Pic-
ture Prod., UA: FERRIS WEBSTER
HOW THE WEST WAS WON, Metro-
Goldwyn-Mayer & Cinerama:
HAROLD F. KRESS
IT'S A MAD, MAD, MAD, MAD WORLD,
Casey Prod., UA: FREDERIC KNUDT-
SON, ROBERT C. JONES and GENE
FOWLER, Jr.

Music

(Music Score—substantially original)
CLEOPATRA, 20th Century-Fox Ltd.-
MCL Films S.A.-WALWA
Films S.A. Prod., 20th Century-Fox:
ALEX NORTH
55 DAYS AT PEKING, Samuel Bronston
Prod., Allied Artists: DIMITRI TIOM-
KIN

HOW THE WEST WAS WON, Metro-Goldwyn-Mayer & Cinerama: ALFRED NEWMAN and KEN DARBY
IT'S A MAD, MAD, MAD, MAD WORLD, Casey Prod., UA: ERNEST GOLD
TOM JONES, Woodfall Prod., UA-Lopert Pictures: JOHN ADDISON

(Scoring of Music—adaptation or treatment)

BYE BYE BIRDIE, Kohlmar-Sidney Prod., Columbia: JOHN GREEN
IRMA LA DOUCE, Mirisch-Phalanx Prod., UA: ANDRÉ PREVIN
A NEW KIND OF LOVE, Llenroc Prods., Paramount: LEITH STEVENS
SUNDAYS AND CYBELE, Terra-Fides-Orsay-Films Trocadero Prod., Columbia: MAURICE JARRE
THE SWORD IN THE STONE, Walt Disney Prods., Buena Vista Distribution Co.: GEORGE BRUNS

(Best Song)

CALL ME IRRESPONSIBLE from *Papa's Delicate Condition,* Amro Prods., Paramount
Music by JAMES VAN HEUSEN. Lyrics by SAMMY CAHN
CHARADE from *Charade,* Universal-Stanley Donen Prod., Universal
Music by HENRY MANCINI. Lyrics by JOHNNY MERCER
IT'S A MAD, MAD, MAD, MAD WORLD from *It's A Mad, Mad, Mad, Mad, World,* Casey Prod., UA
Music by ERNEST GOLD. Lyrics by MACK DAVID
MORE from *Mondo Cane,* Cineriz Prod., Times Film
Music by RIZ ORTOLANI and NINO OLIVIERO, Lyrics by NORMAN NEWELL
SO LITTLE TIME from *55 Days at Peking,* Samuel Bronston Prod., Allied Artists.
Music by DIMITRI TIOMKIN. Lyrics by PAUL FRANCIS WEBSTER

Costume Design

(Black-and-White)

FEDERICO FELLINI'S 8½, Cineriz Prod., Embassy Pictures: PIERO GHERARDI
LOVE WITH THE PROPER STRANGER, Boardwalk-Rona Prod., Paramount: EDITH HEAD
THE STRIPPER, Jerry Wald Prods., 20th Century-Fox: TRAVILLA
TOYS IN THE ATTIC, Mirisch-Claude Prod., UA: BILL THOMAS
WIVES AND LOVERS, Hal Wallis Prod., Paramount: EDITH HEAD

(Color)

THE CARDINAL, Gamma Prod., Columbia: DONALD BROOKS
CLEOPATRA, 20th Century-Fox Ltd.-MCL Films S.A.-WALWA Films S.A. Prod., 20th Century-Fox: IRENE SHARAFF, VITTORIO NINO NOVARESE and RENIE
HOW THE WEST WAS WON, Metro-Goldwyn-Mayer & Cinerama: WALTER PLUNKETT
THE LEOPARD, Titanus Prod., 20th Century-Fox: PIERO TOSI
A NEW KIND OF LOVE, Llenroc Prods., Paramount: EDITH HEAD

Short Subjects

(Cartoons)

AUTOMANIA 2000, Halas and Batchelor Prod., Pathe Contemporary Films: JOHN HALAS, Producer
THE CRITIC, Pintoff-Crossbow Prods., Columbia: ERNEST PINTOFF, Producer.
THE GAME (Igra), Zagreb Film, Rembrandt Films-Film Representations: DUSAN VUKOTIC, Producer
MY FINANCIAL CAREER, National Film Board Of Canada, Walter Reade-Sterling-Continental Distributing: COLIN LOW and TOM DALY, Producers

PIANISSIMO, Cinema 16: CARMEN D'AVINO, Producer

(Live Action Subjects)

THE CONCERT, James A. King Corp., George K. Arthur–Go Pictures: EZRA BAKER, Producer

HOME-MADE CAR, BP (North America) Ltd., Lester A. Schoenfeld Films: JAMES HILL, Producer

AN OCCURRENCE AT OWL CREEK BRIDGE, Films Du Centaure-Filmartic, Cappagariff-Janus Films: PAUL DE ROUBAIX and MARCEL ICHAC, Producers

SIX-SIDED TRIANGLE, Milesian Film Prod. Ltd., Lion International Films: CHRISTOPHER MILES, Producer

THAT'S ME, Stuart Prods., Pathe Contemporary Films: WALKER STUART, Producer

Documentary

(Short Subjects)

CHAGALL, Auerbach Film Enterprises, Ltd.-Flag Films: SIMON SCHIFFRIN, Producer

THE FIVE CITIES OF JUNE, United States Information Agency: GEORGE STEVENS, JR., Producer

THE SPIRIT OF AMERICA, Spotlite News: ALGERNON G. WALKER, Producer

THIRTY MILLION LETTERS, British Transport Films: EDGAR ANSTEY, Producer

TO LIVE AGAIN, Wilding Inc: MEL LONDON, Producer

(Features)

LE MAILLON ET LA CHAINE (The Link And The Chain), Films Du Centaure-Filmartic: PAUL DE ROUBAIX, Producer

ROBERT FROST: A LOVER'S QUARREL WITH THE WORLD, WGBH Educational Foundation: ROBERT HUGHES, Producer

THE YANKS ARE COMING, David L.

Wolper Prods.: MARSHALL FLAUM, Producer

Special Visual Effects

(New Category)

(For the 36th Awards Year the Academy Board of Governors, in recognition of the fact that the best visual effects and the best audible effects each year did not necessarily occur in the same picture, voted to discontinue the Special Effects Award and created two new awards: The Special Visual Effects Award and the Sound Effects Award.)

THE BIRDS, Alfred J. Hitchcock Prod., Universal: UB IWERKS

CLEOPATRA, 20th Century-Fox Ltd.-MCL Films S.A.-WALWA Films S.A. Prod., 20th Century-Fox: EMIL KOSA, JR.

Sound Effects

(New Category)

A GATHERING OF EAGLES, Universal. ROBERT L. BRATTON

IT'S A MAD, MAD, MAD, MAD WORLD, Casey Prod., UA: WALTER G. ELLIOTT

Foreign Language Film Award

FEDERICO FELLINI'S 8½, A Cineriz Production (Italy).

KNIFE IN THE WATER, A Kamera Unit of Film Polski Production (Poland)

LOS TARANTOS, Tecisa-Films R. B. (Spain)

THE RED LANTERNS, Th. Damaskinos & V. Michaelides A.E. (Greece)

TWIN SISTERS OF KYOTO, Shochiku Co., Ltd. (Japan)

Honorary Awards

None

Irving G. Thalberg Memorial Award

SAM SPIEGEL

Jean Hersholt Humanitarian Award
None

Scientific or Technical
Class I
None
Class II
None

Class III
DOUGLAS G. SHEARER and A. AR-
NOLD GILLESPIE of Metro-
Goldwyn-Mayer Studios for the engi-
neering of an improved Background
Process Projection System

1964

Nominations Announced: February 23, 1965
Awards Ceremony: April 5, 1965
Santa Monica Civic Auditorium
(MC: Bob Hope)

Best Picture

BECKET, Hal Wallis Prod., Paramount: HAL B. WALLIS, Producer

DR. STRANGELOVE OR: HOW I LEARNED TO STOP WORRYING AND LOVE THE BOMB, Hawk Films, Ltd. Prod., Columbia: STANLEY KUBRICK, Producer

MARY POPPINS, Walt Disney Prods.: WALT DISNEY and BILL WALSH, Producers

MY FAIR LADY, Warner Bros.: JACK L. WARNER, Producer

ZORBA THE GREEK, Rochley, Ltd. Prod., International Classics: MICHAEL CACOYANNIS, Producer

Actor

RICHARD BURTON in *Becket*, Hal Wallis Prod., Paramount

REX HARRISON in *My Fair Lady*, Warner Bros.

PETER O'TOOLE in *Becket*, Hal Wallis Prod., Paramount

ANTHONY QUINN in *Zorba The Greek*, Rochley, Ltd. Prod., International Classics

PETER SELLERS in *Dr. Strangelove Or: How I Learned To Stop Worrying And Love The Bomb*, Hawk Films, Ltd. Prod., Columbia

Actress

JULIE ANDREWS in *Mary Poppins*, Walt Disney Prods.

ANNE BANCROFT in *The Pumpkin Eater*,

LARGE CAPITAL LETTERS DENOTE WINNER

Romulus Films, Ltd. Prod., Royal Films International

SOPHIA LOREN in *Marriage Italian Style*, Champion-Concordia Prod., Embassy Pictures

DEBBIE REYNOLDS in *The Unsinkable Molly Brown*, Marten Prod., M-G-M

KIM STANLEY in *Seance On A Wet Afternoon*, Richard Attenborough-Bryan Forbes Prod., Artixo Prods., Ltd.

Supporting Actor

JOHN GIELGUD in *Becket*, Hal Wallis Prod., Paramount

STANLEY HOLLOWAY in *My Fair Lady*, Warner Bros.

EDMOND O'BRIEN in *Seven Days In May*, Joel Prods., Paramount

LEE TRACY in *The Best Man*, Millar-Turman Prod., United Artists

PETER USTINOV in *Topkapi*, Filmways Prod., United Artists

Supporting Actress

GLADYS COOPER in *My Fair Lady*, Warner Bros.

DAME EDITH EVANS in *The Chalk Garden*, Quota Rentals, Ltd.-Ross Hunter Prod., Universal

GRAYSON HALL in *The Night Of The Iguana*, Seven Arts Prod., M-G-M

LILA KEDROVA in *Zorba The Greek*, Rochley, Ltd. Prod., International Classics

AGNES MOOREHEAD in *Hush . . . Hush, Sweet Charlotte*, Associates & Aldrich Co. Prod., 20th Century-Fox

Directing

MICHAEL CACOYANNIS for *Zorba The Greek,* Rochley, Ltd. Prod., Intl. Classics

GEORGE CUKOR for *My Fair Lady,* Warner Bros.

PETER GLENVILLE for *Becket,* Hal Wallis Prod., Paramount

STANLEY KUBRICK for *Dr. Strangelove Or: How I learned To Stop Worrying And Love The Bomb,* Hawk Films, Ltd. Prod., Columbia

ROBERT STEVENSON for *Mary Poppins,* Walt Disney Prods.

Writing

(Best Screenplay—based on material from another medium)

BECKET, Hal Wallis Prod., Paramount: EDWARD ANHALT

DR. STRANGELOVE OR: HOW I LEARNED TO STOP WORRYING AND LOVE THE BOMB, Hawk Films, Ltd. Prod., Columbia: STANLEY KUBRICK, PETER GEORGE and TERRY SOUTHERN

MARY POPPINS, Walt Disney Prods.: BILL WALSH and DON DaGRADI

MY FAIR LADY, Warner Bros.: ALAN JAY LERNER

ZORBA THE GREEK, Rochley, Ltd. Prod., International Classics: MICHAEL CACOYANNIS

(Best Story and Screenplay—written directly for the screen)

FATHER GOOSE, Universal-Granox Prod., Universal. Story by S.H. BARNETT. Screenplay by PETER STONE and FRANK TARLOFF

A HARD DAY'S NIGHT, Walter Shenson Prod., United Artists: ALUN OWEN

ONE POTATO, TWO POTATO, Bawalco Picture Prod., Cinema V Distributing. Story by ORVILLE H. HAMPTON. Screenplay by RAPHAEL HAYES and ORVILLE H. HAMPTON

THE ORGANIZER, Lux-Vides-Mediterranee Cinema Prod., Walter Reade-Sterling-Continental Distributing: AGE, SCARPELLI and MARIO MONICELLI

THAT MAN FROM RIO, Ariane-Les Artistes Prod., Lopert Pictures: JEAN-PAUL RAPPENEAU, ARIANE MNOUCHKINE, DANIEL BOULANGER and PHILIPPE De BROCA

Cinematography

(Black-and-White)

THE AMERICANIZATION OF EMILY, Martin Ransohoff Prod., M-G-M: PHILIP H. LATHROP

FATE IS THE HUNTER, Arcola Pictures Prod., 20th Century-Fox: MILTON KRASNER

HUSH . . . HUSH, SWEET CHARLOTTE, Associates & Aldrich Prod., 20th Century-Fox: JOSEPH BIROC

THE NIGHT OF THE IGUANA, Seven Arts Prod., M-G-M: GABRIEL FIGUEROA

ZORBA THE GREEK, Rochley, Ltd. Prod., International Classics: WALTER LASSALLY

(Color)

BECKET, Hal Wallis Prod., Paramount: GEOFFREY UNSWORTH

CHEYENNE AUTUMN, John Ford-Bernard Smith Prod., Warner Bros.: WILLIAM H. CLOTHIER

MARY POPPINS, Walt Disney Prods.: EDWARD COLMAN

MY FAIR LADY, Warner Bros.: HARRY STRADLING

THE UNSINKABLE MOLLY BROWN, Marten Prod., M-G-M: DANIEL L. FAPP

Art Direction—Set Decoration

(Black-and-White)

THE AMERICANIZATION OF EMILY, Martin Ransohoff Prod., M-G-M: GEORGE W. DAVIS, HANS PETERS and ELLIOT SCOTT

Set Decoration: HENRY GRACE and ROBERT R. BENTON

HUSH . . . HUSH, SWEET CHARLOTTE, Associates & Aldrich Prod., 20th Century-Fox: WILLIAM GLASGOW
Set Decoration: RAPHAEL BRETTON

THE NIGHT OF THE IGUANA, Seven Arts Prod., M-G-M: STEPHEN GRIMES

SEVEN DAYS IN MAY, Joel Prods., Paramount: CARY ODELL
Set Decoration: EDWARD G. BOYLE

ZORBA THE GREEK, Rochley, Ltd. Prod., International Classics: VASSILIS FOTOPOULOS

(Color)

BECKET, Hal Wallis Prod., Paramount: JOHN BRYAN and MAURICE CARTER
Set Decoration: PATRICK MCLOUGHLIN and ROBERT CARTWRIGHT

MARY POPPINS Walt Disney Prods: CARROLL CLARK and WILLIAM H. TUNTKE
Set Decoration: EMILE KURI and HAL GAUSMAN

MY FAIR LADY, Warner Bros: GENE ALLEN and CECIL BEATON
Set Decoration: GEORGE JAMES HOPKINS

THE UNSINKABLE MOLLY BROWN, Marten Prod., M-G-M: GEORGE W. DAVIS and PRESTON AMES
Set Decoration: HENRY GRACE and HUGH HUNT

WHAT A WAY TO GO, Apjac-Orchard Prod., 20th Century-Fox: JACK MARTIN SMITH and TED HAWORTH
Set Decoration: WALTER M. SCOTT and STUART A. REISS

Sound

BECKET, Shepperton Studio Sound Department: JOHN COX, Sound Director

FATHER GOOSE, Universal City Studio Sound Department: WALDON O. WATSON, Sound Director

MARY POPPINS, Walt Disney Studio Sound Department: ROBERT O. COOK, Sound Director

MY FAIR LADY, Warner Bros. Studio Sound Department: GEORGE R. GROVES, Sound Director

THE UNSINKABLE MOLLY BROWN, Metro-Goldwyn-Mayer Studio Sound Department: FRANKLIN E. MILTON, Sound Director

Film Editing

BECKET, Hal Wallis Prod., Paramount: ANNE COATES

FATHER GOOSE, Universal-Granox Prod., Universal: TED J. KENT

HUSH . . . HUSH, SWEET CHARLOTTE, Associates & Aldrich Prod., 20th Century-Fox: MICHAEL LUCIANO

MARY POPPINS, Walt Disney Prods.: COTTON WARBURTON

MY FAIR LADY, Warner Bros.: WILLIAM ZIEGLER

Music

(Music Score—Substantially Original)

BECKET, Hal Wallis Prod., Paramount: LAURENCE ROSENTHAL

THE FALL OF THE ROMAN EMPIRE, Bronston-Roma Prod., Paramount: DIMITRI TIOMKIN

HUSH . . . HUSH, SWEET CHARLOTTE, Associates & Aldrich Prod., 20th Century-Fox: FRANK DEVOL

MARY POPPINS, Walt Disney Prods.: RICHARD M. SHERMAN and ROBERT B. SHERMAN

THE PINK PANTHER, Mirisch-G-E Prod., United Artists: HENRY MANCINI

(Scoring of Music—adaptation or treatment)

A HARD DAY'S NIGHT, Walter Shenson Prod., United Artists: GEORGE MARTIN

MARY POPPINS, Walt Disney Prods.: IRWIN KOSTAL
MY FAIR LADY, Warner Bros.: ANDRÉ PREVIN
ROBIN AND THE 7 HOODS, P-C Prod., Warner Bros.: NELSON RIDDLE
THE UNSINKABLE MOLLY BROWN, Marten Prod., M-G-M: ROBERT ARMBRUSTER, LEO ARNAUD, JACK ELLIOTT, JACK HAYES, CALVIN JACKSON and LEO SHUKEN

(Best Song)

CHIM CHIM CHER-EE from *Mary Poppins,* Walt Disney Prods. Music and Lyrics by RICHARD M. SHERMAN & ROBERT B. SHERMAN
DEAR HEART from *Dear Heart,* W.B.-Out-Of-Towners Prod., Warner Bros.
Music by HENRY MANCINI. Lyrics by JAY LIVINGSTON and RAY EVANS
HUSH . . . HUSH, SWEET CHARLOTTE from *Hush . . . Hush, Sweet Charlotte,* Associates & Aldrich Prod., 20th Century-Fox
Music by FRANK DeVOL. Lyrics by MACK DAVID
MY KIND OF TOWN from *Robin And The 7 Hoods,* P-C Prod., Warner Bros.
Music by JAMES VAN HEUSEN. Lyrics by SAMMY CAHN
WHERE LOVE HAS GONE from *Where Love Has Gone,* Paramount-Embassy Pictures Prod., Paramount.
Music by JAMES VAN HEUSEN. Lyrics by SAMMY CAHN

Costume Design
(Black-and-White)

A HOUSE IS NOT A HOME, Clarence Greene–Russell Rouse Prod., Embassy Pictures: EDITH HEAD
HUSH . . . HUSH, SWEET CHARLOTTE, Associates & Aldrich Prod., 20th Century-Fox: NORMA KOCH

KISSES FOR MY PRESIDENT, Pearlayne Prod., Warner Bros.: HOWARD SHOUP
THE NIGHT OF THE IGUANA, Seven Arts Prod., M-G-M: DOROTHY JEAKINS
THE VISIT, Cinecitta-Dear Film-Les Films du Siecle-P.E.C.S. Prod., 20th Century-Fox: RENE HUBERT

(Color)

BECKET, Hal Wallis Prod., Paramount: MARGARET FURSE
MARY POPPINS, Walt Disney Prods.: TONY WALTON
MY FAIR LADY, Warner Bros.: CECIL BEATON
THE UNSINKABLE MOLLY BROWN, Marten Prod., M-G-M: MORTON HAACK
WHAT A WAY TO GO, Apjac-Orchard Prod., 20th Century-Fox: EDITH HEAD and MOSS MABRY

Short Subjects
(Cartoons)

CHRISTMAS CRACKER, National Film Board Of Canada, Favorite Films Of California
HOW TO AVOID FRIENDSHIP, Rembrandt Films, Film Representations: WILLIAM L. SNYDER, Producer
NUDNIK #2, Rembrandt Films, Film Representations: WILLIAM L. SNYDER, Producer
THE PINK PHINK, Mirisch-Geoffrey Prods., UA: DAVID H. DePATIE and FRIZ FRELENG, Producers

(Live Action Subjects)

CASALS CONDUCTS: 1964, Thalia Films, Beckman Film Corp.: EDWARD SCHREIBER, Producer
HELP! MY SNOWMAN'S BURNING DOWN, Carson Davidson Prods., Pathe Contemporary Films: CARSON DAVIDSON, Producer
THE LEGEND OF JIMMY BLUE EYES, Robert Clouse Associates, Topaz

Film Corp.: ROBERT CLOUSE, Producer

Documentary

(Short Subjects)

BREAKING THE HABIT, American Cancer Society, Modern Talking Picture Service: HENRY JACOBS and JOHN KORTY, Producers

CHILDREN WITHOUT, National Education Association, Guggenheim Productions

KENOJUAK, National Film Board of Canada

NINE FROM LITTLE ROCK, United States Information Agency, Guggenheim Productions

140 DAYS UNDER THE WORLD, New Zealand National Film Unit, Rank Film Distributors of New Zealand: GEOFFREY SCOTT and OXLEY HUGHAN, Producers

(Features)

THE FINEST HOURS, Le Vien Films, Ltd., Columbia: JACK LE VIEN, Producer

FOUR DAYS IN NOVEMEMBER, David L. Wolper Prods., UA: MEL STUART, Producer

THE HUMAN DUTCH, Haanstra Filmproductie: BERT HAANSTRA, Producer

Jacques-Yves Cousteau's WORLD WITHOUT SUN, Filmad-Les Requins Associes-Orsay-CEIAP, Columbia: JACQUES-YVES COUSTEAU, Producer

OVER THERE, 1914–18, Zodiac Prods., Pathe Contemporary Films: JEAN AUREL, Producer

Special Visual Effects

MARY POPPINS, Walt Disney Prods.: PETER ELLENSHAW, HAMILTON LUSKE and EUSTACE LYCETT

7 FACES OF DR. LAO, Galaxy-Scarus

Prod., Metro-Goldwyn-Mayer: JIM DANFORTH

Sound Effects

GOLDFINGER, Eon Prod., UA: NORMAN WANSTALL

THE LIVELY SET, Universal: ROBERT L. BRATTON

Foreign Language Film Award

RAVEN'S END, AB Europa Film (Sweden)

SALLAH, A Sallah Film Ltd. Production (Israel)

THE UMBRELLAS OF CHERBOURG, A Parc-Madeleine-Beta Films Production (France)

WOMAN IN THE DUNES, A Teshigahara Production (Japan)

YESTERDAY, TODAY AND TOMORROW, A Champion-Concordia Production (Italy)

Honorary Award

WILLIAM TUTTLE for his outstanding make-up achievement for 7 *Faces Of Dr. Lao.* (statuette)

Irving G. Thalberg Memorial Award
None

Jean Hersholt Humanitarian Award
None

Scientific or Technical
Class I
PETRO VLAHOS, WADSWORTH E. POHL and UB IWERKS for the conception and perfecton of techniques for Color Traveling Matte Composite Cinematography.

Class II
SIDNEY P. SOLOW, EDWARD H. REICHARD, CARL W. HAUGE and JOB SANDERSON of Consolidated Film Industries for the design

and development of a versatile Automatic 35mm Composite Color Printer

PIERRE ANGENIEUX for the development of a ten-to-one Zoom Lens for cinematography

Class III

MILTON FORMAN, RICHARD B. GLICKMAN and DANIEL J. PEARLMAN of ColorTran Industries for advancements in the design and application to motion picture photography of lighting units using quartz iodine lamps

STEWART FILMSCREEN CORPORATION for a seamless translucent Blue Screen for Traveling Matte Color Cinematography

ANTHONY PAGLIA and the 20TH CENTURY-FOX STUDIO MECHANICAL EFFECTS DEPARTMENT for an improved method of producing Explosion Flash Effects for motion pictures

EDWARD H. REICHARD and CARL W. HAUGE of Consolidated Film Industries for the design of a Proximity Cue Detector and its application to motion picture printers

EDWARD H. REICHARD, LEONARD L. SOKOLOW and CARL W. HAUGE of Consolidated Film Industries for the design and application to motion picture laboratory practice of a Stroboscopic Scene Tester for color and black-and-white film

NELSON TYLER for the design and construction of an improved Helicopter Camera System

1965

Nominations Announced: February 21, 1966
Awards Ceremony: April 18, 1966
Santa Monica Civic Auditorium
(MC: Bob Hope)

Best Picture

DARLING, Anglo-Amalgamated, Ltd. Prod., Embassy: JOSEPH JANNI, Producer

DOCTOR ZHIVAGO, Sostar S.A.-Metro-Goldwyn-Mayer British Studios, Ltd. Prod., M-G-M; CARLO PONTI, Producer

SHIP OF FOOLS, Columbia: STANLEY KRAMER, Producer

THE SOUND OF MUSIC, Argyle Enterprises Prod., 20th Century-Fox: ROBERT WISE, Producer

A THOUSAND CLOWNS, Harrell Prod., United Artists: FRED COE, Producer

Actor

RICHARD BURTON in *The Spy Who Came In From The Cold,* Salem Films, Ltd. Prod., Paramount

LEE MARVIN in *Cat Ballou,* Harold Hecht Prod., Columbia

LAURENCE OLIVIER in *Othello,* B.H.E. Prod., Warner Bros.

ROD STEIGER in *The Pawnbroker,* Ely Landau Prod., American Intl.

OSKAR WERNER in *Ship Of Fools,* Columbia

Actress

JULIE ANDREWS in *The Sound Of Music,* Argyle Enterprises Prod., 20th Century-Fox

JULIE CHRISTIE in *Darling,* Anglo-Amalgamated, Ltd. Prod., Embassy

LARGE CAPITAL LETTERS DENOTE WINNER

SAMANTHA EGGAR in *The Collector,* The Collector Company, Columbia

ELIZABETH HARTMAN in *A Patch Of Blue,* Pandro S. Berman-Guy Green Prod., M-G-M

SIMONE SIGNORET in *Ship Of Fools,* Columbia

Supporting Actor

MARTIN BALSAM in *A Thousand Clowns,* Harrell Prod., United Artists

IAN BANNEN in *The Flight Of The Phoenix,* Associates & Aldrich Company Prod., 20th Century-Fox

TOM COURTENAY in *Doctor Zhivago,* Sostar S.A.-Metro-Goldwyn-Mayer British Studios, Ltd. Prod., M-G-M

MICHAEL DUNN in *Ship Of Fools,* Columbia

FRANK FINLAY in *Othello,* B.H.E. Prod., Warner Bros.

Supporting Actress

RUTH GORDON in *Inside Daisy Clover,* Park Place Prod., Warner Bros.

JOYCE REDMAN in *Othello,* B.H.E. Prod., Warner Bros.

MAGGIE SMITH in *Othello,* B.H.E. Prod., Warner Bros.

SHELLEY WINTERS in *A Patch Of Blue,* Pandro S. Berman-Guy Green Prod., M-G-M

PEGGY WOOD in *The Sound Of Music,* Argyle Enterprises Prod., 20th Century-Fox

Directing

DAVID LEAN for *Doctor Zhivago,* Sostar S.A.-Metro-Goldwyn-Mayer British Studios, Ltd. Prod., M-G-M

JOHN SCHLESINGER for *Darling,* Anglo-Amalgamated, Ltd. Prod., Embassy

HIROSHI TESHIGAHARA for *Woman In The Dunes,* Teshigahara Prod., Pathe Contemporary Films

ROBERT WISE for *The Sound Of Music,* Argyle Enterprises Prod., 20th Century-Fox

WILLIAM WYLER for *The Collector,* The Collector Company, Columbia

Writing

(Best Screenplay—based on material from another medium)

CAT BALLOU, Harold Hecht Prod., Columbia: WALTER NEWMAN and FRANK R. PIERSON

THE COLLECTOR, The Collector Company, Columbia: STANLEY MANN and JOHN KOHN

DOCTOR ZHIVAGO, Sostar S.A.-Metro-Goldwyn-Mayer British Studios, Ltd. Prod., M-G-M: ROBERT BOLT

SHIP OF FOOLS, Columbia: ABBY MANN

A THOUSAND CLOWNS, Harrell Prod., United Artists: HERB GARDNER

(Best Story and Screenplay—written directly for the screen)

CASANOVA '70, C.C. Champion-Les Films Concordia Prod., Embassy: AGE, SCARPELLI, MARIO MONICELLI, TONINO GUERRA, GIORGIO SALVIONI and SUSO CECCHI D'AMICO

DARLING, Anglo-Amalgamated, Ltd. Prod., Embassy: FREDERIC RAPHAEL

THOSE MAGNIFICENT MEN IN THEIR FLYING MACHINES, 20th Century-Fox, Ltd. Prod., 20th Century-Fox: JACK DAVIES and KEN ANNAKIN

THE TRAIN Les Prods. Artistes Associes, United Artists: FRANKLIN COEN and FRANK DAVIS

THE UMBRELLAS OF CHERBOURG, Parc-Madeleine Films Prod., American International: JACQUES DEMY

Cinematography

(Black-and-White)

IN HARM'S WAY, Sigma Prods., Paramount: LOYAL GRIGGS

KING RAT, Coleytown Prod., Columbia: BURNETT GUFFEY

MORITURI, Arcola-Colony Prod., 20th Century-Fox: CONRAD HALL

A PATCH OF BLUE, Pandro S. Berman-Guy Green Prod., M-G-M.: ROBERT BURKS

SHIP OF FOOLS, Columbia: ERNEST LASZLO

(Color)

THE AGONY AND THE ECSTASY, International Classics Prod., 20th Century-Fox. LEON SHAMROY

DOCTOR ZHIVAGO, Sostar S.A.-Metro-Goldwyn-Mayer British Studios, Ltd. Prod., M-G-M: FREDDIE YOUNG

THE GREAT RACE, Patricia-Jalem-Reynard Prod., Warner Bros.: RUSSELL HARLAN

THE GREATEST STORY EVER TOLD, George Stevens Prod., United Artists: WILLIAM C. MELLOR and LOYAL GRIGGS

THE SOUND OF MUSIC, Argyle Enterprises Prod., 20th Century-Fox: TED MCCORD

Art Direction—Set Decoration

(Black-and-white)

KING RAT, Coleytown Prod., Columbia: ROBERT EMMET SMITH Set Decoration: FRANK TUTTLE

A PATCH OF BLUE, Pandro S. Berman-Guy Green Prod., M-G-M: GEORGE W. DAVIS and URIE MCCLEARY

Set Decoration: HENRY GRACE and CHARLES S. THOMPSON

SHIP OF FOOLS, Columbia: ROBERT CLATWORTHY
Set Decoration: JOSEPH KISH

THE SLENDER THREAD, Paramount: HAL PEREIRA and JACK POPLIN
Set Decoration: ROBERT BENTON and JOSEPH KISH

THE SPY WHO CAME IN FROM THE COLD, Salem Films, Ltd. Prod., Paramount: HAL PEREIRA, TAMBI LARSEN and EDWARD MARSHALL. Set Decoration: JOSIE MacAVIN

(Color)

THE AGONY AND THE ECSTASY, International Classics Prod., 20th Century-Fox: JOHN DECUIR and JACK MARTIN SMITH
Set Decoration: DARIO SIMONI

DOCTOR ZHIVAGO, Sostar S.A.-Metro-Goldwyn-Mayer British Studios, Ltd. Prod., M-G-M: JOHN BOX and TERRY MARSH
Set Decoration: DARIO SIMONI

THE GREATEST STORY EVER TOLD, George Stevens Prod., United Artists: RICHARD DAY, WILLIAM CREBER and DAVID HALL
Set Decoration: RAY MOYER, FRED MacLEAN and NORMAN ROCKETT

INSIDE DAISY CLOVER, Park Place Prod., Warner Bros.: ROBERT CLATWORTHY
Set Decoration: GEORGE JAMES HOPKINS

THE SOUND OF MUSIC, Argyle Enterprises Prod., 20th Century-Fox: BORIS LEVEN
Set Decoration: WALTER M. SCOTT and RUBY LEVITT

Sound

THE AGONY AND THE ECSTASY, 20th Century-Fox Studio Sound Department: JAMES P. CORCORAN, Sound Director

DOCTOR ZHIVAGO, Metro-Goldwyn-Mayer British Studio Sound Department: A. W. WATKINS, Sound Director; and Metro-Goldwyn-Mayer Studio Sound Department: FRANKLIN E. MILTON, Sound Director

THE GREAT RACE, Warner Bros. Studio Sound Department: GEORGE R. GROVES, Sound Director

SHENANDOAH, Universal City Studio Sound Department: WALDON O. WATSON, Sound Director

THE SOUND OF MUSIC, 20th Century-Fox Studio Sound Department: JAMES P. CORCORAN, Sound Director; and TODD-AO Sound Department. FRED HYNES, Sound Director

Film Editing

CAT BALLOU, Harold Hecht Prod., Columbia: CHARLES NELSON

DOCTOR ZHIVAGO, Sostar S.A.-Metro-Goldwyn-Mayer British Studios, Ltd. Prod., M-G-M: NORMAN SAVAGE

THE FLIGHT OF THE PHOENIX, Associates & Aldrich Company Prod., 20th Century-Fox. MICHAEL LUCIANO

THE GREAT RACE, Patricia-Jalem-Reynard Prod., Warner Bros.: RALPH E. WINTERS

THE SOUND OF MUSIC, Argyle Enterprises Prod., 20th Century-Fox: WILLIAM REYNOLDS

Music

(Music Score—substantially original)

THE AGONY AND THE ECSTASY, International Classics Prod., 20th Century-Fox: ALEX NORTH

DOCTOR ZHIVAGO, Sostar S.A.-Metro-Goldwyn-Mayer British Studios, Ltd. Prod., M-G-M: MAURICE JARRE

THE GREATEST STORY EVER TOLD, George Stevens Prod., United Artists: ALFRED NEWMAN

A PATCH OF BLUE, Pandro S. Berman-Guy Green Prod., M-G-M: JERRY GOLDSMITH

THE UMBRELLAS OF CHERBOURG, Parc-Madeleine Films Prod., American Intl. MICHEL LEGRAND and JACQUES DEMY

(Scoring of Music—adaptation or treatment)

CAT BALLOU, Harold Hecht Prod., Columbia: DEVOL

THE PLEASURE SEEKERS, 20th Century-Fox: LIONEL NEWMAN and ALEXANDER COURAGE

THE SOUND OF MUSIC, Argyle Enterprises Prod., 20th Century-Fox: IRWIN KOSTAL

A THOUSAND CLOWNS, Harrell Prod., United Artists: DON WALKER

THE UMBRELLAS OF CHERBOURG, Parc-Madeleine Films Prod., American Intl.: MICHEL LEGRAND

(Best Song)

THE BALLAD OF CAT BALLOU from *Cat Ballou,* Harold Hecht Prod., Columbia
Music by JERRY LIVINGSTON Lyrics by MACK DAVID

I WILL WAIT FOR YOU from *The Umbrellas Of Cherbourg,* Parc-Madeleine Films Prod., American Intl.
Music by MICHEL LEGRAND. Lyrics by JACQUES DEMY

THE SHADOW OF YOUR SMILE from *The Sandpiper,* Filmways-Venice Prod., M-G-M.
Music by JOHNNY MANDEL. Lyrics by PAUL FRANCIS WEBSTER

THE SWEETHEART TREE from *The Great Race,* Patricia-Jalem-Reynard Prod., Warner Bros.
Music by HENRY MANCINI. Lyrics by JOHNNY MERCER

WHAT'S NEW PUSSYCAT? from *What's New Pussycat?,* Famous Artists-Famartists Prod., United Artists.
Music by BURT BACHARACH. Lyrics by HAL DAVID

Costume Design
(Black-and-White)

DARLING, Anglo-Amalgamated, Ltd. Prod., Embassy: JULIE HARRIS

MORITURI, Arcola-Colony Prod., 20th Century Fox: MOSS MABRY

A RAGE TO LIVE, Mirisch Corp. of Delaware-Araho Prod., United Artists: HOWARD SHOUP

SHIP OF FOOLS, Columbia: BILL THOMAS and JEAN LOUIS

THE SLENDER THREAD, Paramount: EDITH HEAD

(Color)

THE AGONY AND THE ECSTASY, International Classics Prod., 20th Century-Fox: VITTORIO NINO NOVARESE

DOCTOR ZHIVAGO, Sostar S.A.-Metro-Goldwyn-Mayer British Studios, Ltd. Prod., M-G-M: PHYLLIS DALTON

THE GREATEST STORY EVER TOLD, George Stevens Prod., United Artists: VITTORIO NINO NOVARESE and MARJORIE BEST

INSIDE DAISY CLOVER, Park Place Prod., Warner Bros.: EDITH HEAD and BILL THOMAS

THE SOUND OF MUSIC, Argyle Enterprises Prod., 20th Century-Fox: DOROTHY JEAKINS

Short Subjects
(Cartoons)

CLAY OR THE ORIGIN OF SPECIES, Harvard University, Pathe Contemporary Films: ELIOT NOYES, JR., Producer

THE DOT AND THE LINE, Metro-Goldwyn-Mayer: CHUCK JONES and LES GOLDMAN, Producers

THE THIEVING MAGPIE (La Gazza Ladra), Giulio Gianini-Emanuele

Luzzati, Allied Artists: EMANUELE LUZZATI, Producer

(Live Action Subjects)

THE CHICKEN (Le Poulet), Renn Prods., Pathe Contemporary Films: CLAUDE BERRI, Producer

FORTRESS OF PEACE, Lothar Wolff Prods. for Farner-Looser Films, Cinerama: LOTHAR WOLFF, Producer

SKATERDATER, Byway Prods., United Artists: MARSHAL BACKLAR and NOEL BLACK, Producers

SNOW, British Transport Films in association with Geoffrey Jones (Films) Ltd., Manson Distributing: EDGAR ANSTEY, Producer

TIME PIECE, Muppets, Inc., Pathe Contemporary Films: JIM HENSON, Producer

Documentary

(Short Subjects)

MURAL ON OUR STREET, Henry Street Settlement, Pathe Contemporary Films: KIRK SMALLMAN, Producer

OUVERTURE, Mafilm Prods., Hungarofilm-Pathe Contemporary Films

POINT OF VIEW, Vision Associates Prod., National Tuberculosis Assoc.

TO BE ALIVE!, Johnson Wax: FRANCIS THOMPSON, INC., Producer

YEATS COUNTRY, Aengus Films Ltd. for the Dept. of External Affairs of Ireland: PATRICK CAREY and JOE MENDOZA, Producers

(Features)

THE BATTLE OF THE BULGE . . . THE BRAVE RIFLES, Mascott Prods.: LAURENCE E. MASCOTT, Producer

THE ELEANOR ROOSEVELT STORY, Sidney Glazier Prod., American Intl.: SIDNEY GLAZIER, Producer

THE FORTH ROAD BRIDGE, Random Film Prods., Ltd., Shell-Mex and

B.P. Film Library: PETER MILLS, Producer

LET MY PEOPLE GO, Wolper Prods.: MARSHALL FLAUM, Producer

TO DIE IN MADRID, Ancinex Prods., Altura Films Intl.: FREDERIC ROSSIF, Producer

Special Visual Effects

THE GREATEST STORY EVER TOLD, George Stevens Prod., United Artists: J. MCMILLAN JOHNSON

THUNDERBALL, Broccoli-Saltzman-McClory Prod., United Artists: JOHN STEARS

Sound Effects

THE GREAT RACE, Patricia-Jalem-Reynard Prod., Warner Bros.: TREGOWETH BROWN

VON RYAN'S EXPRESS, P-R Prods., 20th Century-Fox: WALTER A. ROSSI

Foreign Language Film Award

BLOOD ON THE LAND, Th. Damaskinos & V. Michaelides, A. E.-Finos Film (Greece)

DEAR JOHN, A.B. Sandrew-Ateljeerna (Sweden)

KWAIDAN, A Toho Company, Ltd. Production (Japan)

MARRIAGE ITALIAN STYLE, A Champion-Concordia Production (Italy)

THE SHOP ON MAIN STREET, A Ceskoslovensky Film Production (Czechoslovakia)

Honorary Award

BOB HOPE for unique and distinguished service to our industry and the Academy. (gold medal)

Irving G. Thalberg Memorial Award
WILLIAM WYLER

Jean Hersholt Humanitarian Award
EDMOND L. DePATIE

Scientific or Technical
Class I
None

Class II
ARTHUR J. HATCH of The Strong
   Electric Corporation, subsidiary of
   General Precision Equipment Corporation, for the design and development of an Air Blown Carbon Arc
   Projection Lamp
STEFAN KUDELSKI for the design
   and development of the Nagra portable ¼″ tape recording system for motion picture sound recording

Class III
None

1966

Nominations Announced: February 20, 1967
Awards Ceremony: April 10, 1967
Santa Monica Civic Auditorium
(MC: Bob Hope)

Best Picture

ALFIE, Sheldrake Films, Ltd. Prod., Paramount: LEWIS GILBERT, Producer

A MAN FOR ALL SEASONS, Highland Films, Ltd. Prod., Columbia: FRED ZINNEMANN, Producer

THE RUSSIANS ARE COMING THE RUSSIANS ARE COMING, Mirisch Corp. of Delaware Prod., UA: NORMAN JEWISON, Producer

THE SAND PEBBLES, Argyle-Solar Prod., 20th Century-Fox: ROBERT WISE, Producer

WHO'S AFRAID OF VIRGINIA WOOLF?, Chenault Prod., Warner Bros.: ERNEST LEHMAN, Producer

Actor

ALAN ARKIN in *The Russians Are Coming, The Russians Are Coming,* Mirisch Corp. of Delaware Prod., UA

RICHARD BURTON in *Who's Afraid of Virginia Woolf?,* Chenault Prod., Warner Bros.

MICHAEL CAINE in *Alfie,* Sheldrake Films, Ltd. Prod., Paramount

STEVE MCQUEEN in *The Sand Pebbles,* Argyle-Solar Prod., 20th Century-Fox

PAUL SCOFIELD in *A Man for All Seasons,* Highland Films, Ltd. Prod., Columbia

Actress

ANOUK AIMÉE in *A Man and a Woman,* Les Films 13 Prod., Allied Artists

LARGE CAPITAL LETTERS DENOTE WINNER

IDA KAMINSKA in *The Shop On Main Street,* Ceskoslovensky Film Company Prod., Prominent Films

LYNN REDGRAVE in *Georgy Girl,* Everglades Prods., Ltd., Columbia

VANESSA REDGRAVE in *Morgan!,* Quintra Films, Ltd. Prod., Cinema V

ELIZABETH TAYLOR in *Who's Afraid of Virginia Woolf?,* Chenault Prod., Warner Bros.

Supporting Actor

MAKO in *The Sand Pebbles,* Argyle-Solar Prod., 20th Century-Fox

JAMES MASON in *Georgy Girl,* Everglades Prods., Ltd., Columbia

WALTER MATTHAU in *The Fortune Cookie,* Phalanx-Jalem-Mirisch Corp. of Delaware Prod., UA

GEORGE SEGAL in *Who's Afraid of Virginia Woolf?,* Chenault Prod., Warner Bros.

ROBERT SHAW in *A Man for All Seasons,* Highland Films, Ltd. Prod., Columbia

Supporting Actress

SANDY DENNIS in *Who's Afraid of Virginia Woolf?,* Chenault Prod., Warner Bros.

WENDY HILLER in *A Man for All Seasons,* Highland Films, Ltd. Prod., Columbia

JOCELYNE LAGARDE in *Hawaii,* Mirisch Corp. of Delaware Prod., UA

VIVIEN MERCHANT in *Alfie,* Sheldrake Films, Ltd. Prod., Paramount

GERALDINE PAGE in *You're a Big Boy Now,* Seven Arts

Directing

MICHELANGELO ANTONIONI for *Blow-Up,* Carlo Ponti Prod., Premier Productions

RICHARD BROOKS for *The Professionals,* Pax Enterprises Prod., Columbia

CLAUDE LELOUCH for *A Man and a Woman,* Les Films 13 Prod., Allied Artists

MIKE NICHOLS for *Who's Afraid of Virginia Woolf?,* Chenault Prod., Warner Bros.

FRED ZINNEMANN for *A Man for All Seasons,* Highland Films, Ltd. Prod., Columbia

Writing

(Best Screenplay based on material from another medium)

ALFIE, Sheldrake Films, Ltd. Prod., Paramount: BILL NAUGHTON

A MAN FOR ALL SEASONS, Highland Films, Ltd. Prod., Columbia: ROBERT BOLT

THE PROFESSIONALS, Pax Enterprises Prod., Columbia: RICHARD BROOKS

THE RUSSIANS ARE COMING, THE RUSSIANS ARE COMING, Mirisch Corp. of Delaware Prod., UA: WILLIAM ROSE

WHO'S AFRAID OF VIRGINIA WOOLF?, Chenault Prod., Warner Bros.: ERNEST LEHMAN

(Best Story and Screenplay—written directly for the screen)

BLOW-UP, Carlo Ponti Prod., Premier Productions: Story by MICHELANGELO ANTONIONI. Screenplay by MICHELANGELO ANTONIONI, TONINO GUERRA and EDWARD BOND

THE FORTUNE COOKIE, Phalanx-Jalem-Mirisch Corp. of Delaware Prod., UA: BILLY WILDER and I.A. L. DIAMOND

KHARTOUM, Julian Blaustein Prod., UA: ROBERT ARDREY

A MAN AND A WOMAN, Les Films 13 Prod., Allied Artists: Story by CLAUDE LELOUCH. Screenplay by PIERRE UYTTERHOEVEN and CLAUDE LELOUCH

THE NAKED PREY, Theodora Prod., Paramount: CLINT JOHNSTON and DON PETERS

Cinematography

(Black-and-White)

THE FORTUNE COOKIE, Phalanx-Jalem-Mirisch Corp. of Delaware Prod., UA: JOSEPH LaSHELLE

GEORGY GIRL, Everglades Prods., Ltd., Columbia: KEN HIGGINS

IS PARIS BURNING?, Transcontinental Films-Marianne Prod., Paramount: MARCEL GRIGNON

SECONDS, The Seconds Company, Paramount: JAMES WONG HOWE

WHO'S AFRAID OF VIRGINIA WOOLF?, Chenault Prod., Warner Bros: HASKELL WEXLER.

(Color)

FANTASTIC VOYAGE, 20th Century-Fox: ERNEST LASZLO

HAWAII, Mirisch Corp. of Delaware Prod., UA: RUSSELL HARLAN

A MAN FOR ALL SEASONS, Highland Films, Ltd. Prod., Columbia: TED MOORE

THE PROFESSIONALS, Pax Enterprises Prod., Columbia: CONRAD HALL

THE SAND PEBBLES, Argyle-Solar Prod., 20th Century-Fox: JOSEPH MacDONALD

Art Direction—Set Decoration

(Black-and-White)

THE FORTUNE COOKIE, Phalanx-Jalem-Mirisch Corp. of Delaware Prod., UA: ROBERT LUTHARDT Set Decoration: EDWARD G. BOYLE

THE GOSPEL ACCORDING TO ST. MATTHEW, Arco-Lux Cie Cinematografique de France Prod., Walter Reade-Continental Distributing: LUIGI SCACCIANOCE

IS PARIS BURNING?, Transcontinental Films-Marianne Prod., Paramount: WILLY HOLT
Set Decoration: MARC FREDERIX and PIERRE GUFFROY

MISTER BUDDWING, DDD-Cherokee Prod., M-G-M: GEORGE W. DAVIS and PAUL GROESSE
Set Decoration: HENRY GRACE and HUGH HUNT

WHO'S AFRAID OF VIRGINIA WOOLF?, Chenault Prod., Warner Bros: RICHARD SYLBERT
Set Decoration: GEORGE JAMES HOPKINS

(Color)

FANTASTIC VOYAGE, 20th Century-Fox: JACK MARTIN SMITH and DALE HENNESY
Set Decoration: WALTER M. SCOTT and STUART A. REISS

GAMBIT, Universal: ALEXANDER GOLITZEN and GEORGE C. WEBB
Set Decoration: JOHN MCCARTHY and JOHN AUSTIN

JULIET OF THE SPIRITS, Rizzoli Films S.P.A. Prod., Rizzoli Films: PIERO GHERARDI

THE OSCAR, Greene-Rouse Prod., Embassy: HAL PEREIRA and ARTHUR LONERGAN
Set Decoration: ROBERT BENTON and JAMES PAYNE

THE SAND PEBBLES, Argyle-Solar Prod., 20th Century-Fox: BORIS LEVEN
Set Decoration: WALTER M. SCOTT, JOHN STURTEVANT and WILLIAM KIERNAN

Sound

GAMBIT, Universal City Studio Sound Department: WALDON O. WATSON, Sound Director

GRAND PRIX, Metro-Goldwyn-Mayer Studio Sound Department: FRANKLIN E. MILTON, Sound Director

HAWAII, Samuel Goldwyn Studio Sound Department: GORDON E. SAWYER, Sound Director

THE SAND PEBBLES, 20th Century-Fox Studio Sound Department: JAMES P. CORCORAN, Sound Director

WHO'S AFRAID OF VIRGINIA WOOLF?, Warner Bros. Studio Sound Department: GEORGE R. GROVES, Sound Director

Film Editing

FANTASTIC VOYAGE, 20th Century-Fox: WILLIAM B. MURPHY

GRAND PRIX, Douglas-Lewis-John Frankenheimer-Cherokee Prod., M-G-M: FREDRIC STEINKAMP, HENRY BERMAN, STEWART LINDER and FRANK SANTILLO

THE RUSSIANS ARE COMING, THE RUSSIANS ARE COMING, Mirisch Corp. of Delaware Prod., United Artists: HAL ASHBY and J. TERRY WILLIAMS

THE SAND PEBBLES, Argyle-Solar Prod., 20th Century-Fox: WILLIAM REYNOLDS

WHO'S AFRAID OF VIRGINIA WOOLF?, Chenault Prod., Warner Bros.: SAM O'STEEN

Music

(Original Music Score)

THE BIBLE, Thalia-A.G. Prod., 20th Century-Fox: TOSHIRO MAYUZUMI

BORN FREE, Open Road Films, Ltd.-Atlas Films, Ltd. Prod., Columbia: JOHN BARRY

HAWAII, Mirisch Corp. of Delaware Prod., UA: ELMER BERNSTEIN

THE SAND PEBBLES, Argyle-Solar Prod., 20th Century-Fox: JERRY GOLDSMITH

WHO'S AFRAID OF VIRGINIA WOOLF?, Chenault Prod., Warner Bros.: ALEX NORTH

(Scoring of Music—adaptation or treatment)

A FUNNY THING HAPPENED ON THE WAY TO THE FORUM, Melvin Frank Prod., United Artists: KEN THORNE

THE GOSPEL ACCORDING TO ST. MATTHEW, Arco-Lux Cie Cinematografique de France Prod., Walter Reade-Continental Distributing: LUIS ENRIQUE BACALOV

RETURN OF THE SEVEN, Mirisch Prods., United Artists: ELMER BERNSTEIN

THE SINGING NUN, Metro-Goldwyn-Mayer: HARRY SUKMAN

STOP THE WORLD—I WANT TO GET OFF, Warner Bros. Prods., Ltd., Warner Bros.: AL HAM

(Best Song)

ALFIE from *Alfie,* Sheldrake Films, Ltd. Prod., Paramount
Music by BURT BACHARACH. Lyrics by HAL DAVID

BORN FREE from *Born Free,* Open Road Films, Ltd.-Atlas Films, Ltd. Prod., Columbia
Music by JOHN BARRY. Lyrics by DON BLACK

GEORGY GIRL from *Georgy Girl,* Everglades Prods., Ltd., Columbia
Music by TOM SPRINGFIELD. Lyrics by JIM DALE

MY WISHING DOLL from *Hawaii,* Mirisch Corp. of Delaware Prod., UA
Music by ELMER BERNSTEIN. Lyrics by MACK DAVID

A TIME FOR LOVE from *An American Dream,* Warner Bros.

Music by JOHNNY MANDEL. Lyrics by PAUL FRANCIS WEBSTER

Costume Design

(Black-and-White)

THE GOSPEL ACCORDING TO ST. MATTHEW, Arco-Lux Cie Cinematografique de France Prod., Walter Reade-Continental Distributing: DANILO DONATI

MANDRAGOLA, Europix-Consolidated: DANILO DONATI

MISTER BUDDWING, DDD-Cherokee Prod., M-G-M: HELEN ROSE

MORGAN!, Quintra Films, Ltd. Prod., Cinema V: JOCELYN RICKARDS

WHO'S AFRAID OF VIRGINIA WOOLF?, Chenault Prod., Warner Bros.: IRENE SHARAFF

(Color)

GAMBIT, Universal: JEAN LOUIS

HAWAII, Mirisch Corp. of Delaware Prod., UA: DOROTHY JEAKINS

JULIET OF THE SPIRITS, Rizzoli Films S.P.A. Prod., Rizzoli Films: PIERO GHERARDI

A MAN FOR ALL SEASONS, Highland Films, Ltd. Prod., Columbia: ELIZABETH HAFFENDEN and JOAN BRIDGE

THE OSCAR, Greene-Rouse Prod., Embassy: EDITH HEAD

Short Subjects

(Cartoons)

THE DRAG, National Film Board of Canada, Favorite Films: WOLF KOENIG and ROBERT VERRALL, Producers

HERB ALPERT AND THE TIJUANA BRASS DOUBLE FEATURE, Hubley Studio, Paramount: JOHN and FAITH HUBLEY, Producers

THE PINK BLUEPRINT, Mirisch-Geoffrey-DePatie-Freleng, UA:

DAVID H. DePATIE and FRIZ FRELENG, Producers

(Live Action Subjects)

TURKEY THE BRIDGE, Samaritan Prods., Lester A. Schoenfeld Films: DEREK WILLIAMS, Producer

WILD WINGS, British Transport Films, Manson Distributing: EDGAR ANSTEY, Producer

THE WINNING STRAIN, Winik Films, Paramount: LESLIE WINIK, Producer

Documentary

(Short Subjects)

ADOLESCENCE, M.K. Prods.: MARIN KARMITZ and VLADIMIR FORGENCY, Producers

COWBOY, United States Information Agency: MICHAEL AHNEMANN and GARY SCHLOSSER, Producers

THE ODDS AGAINST, Vision Associates Prod. for The American Foundation Institute of Corrections: LEE R. BOBKER and HELEN KRISTT RADIN, Producers

SAINT MATTHEW PASSION, Mafilm Studio, Hungarofilm

A YEAR TOWARD TOMORROW, Sun Dial Films, Inc. Prod. for Office of Economic Opportunity: EDMOND A. LEVY, Producer

(Features)

THE FACE OF GENIUS, WBZ-TV, Group W, Boston: ALFRED R. KELMAN, Producer

HELICOPTER CANADA, Centennial Commission, National Film Board of Canada: PETER JONES and TOM DALY, Producers

LE VOLCAN INTERDIT (The Forbidden Volcano), Cine Documents Tazieff, Athos Films: HAROUN TAZIEFF, Producer

THE REALLY BIG FAMILY, David L. Wolper, Prod.: ALEX GRASSHOFF, Producer

THE WAR GAME, BBC Prod. for the British Film Institute, Pathe Contemporary Films: PETER WATKINS, Producer

Special Visual Effects

FANTASTIC VOYAGE, 20th Century Fox: ART CRUICKSHANK

HAWAII, Mirisch Corp. of Delaware Prod., United Artists: LINWOOD G. DUNN

Sound Effects

FANTASTIC VOYAGE, 20th Century-Fox: WALTER ROSSI

GRAND PRIX, Douglas-Lewis-John Frankenheimer-Cherokee Prod., M-G-M: GORDON DANIEL

Foreign Language Film Award

THE BATTLE OF ALGIERS, Igor Film-Casbah Film Production (Italy)

LOVES OF A BLONDE, Barrandov Film Production (Czechoslovakia)

A MAN AND A WOMAN, Les Films 13 Production (France)

PHARAOH, Kadr Film Unit Production (Poland)

THREE, Avala Film Production (Yugoslavia)

Honorary Awards

Y. FRANK FREEMAN for unusual and outstanding service to the Academy during his thirty years in Hollywood. (statuette)

YAKIMA CANUTT for achievements as a stunt man and for developing safety devices to protect stunt men everywhere. (statuette)

Irving G. Thalberg Memorial Award
ROBERT WISE

Jean Hersholt Humanitarian Award
GEORGE BAGNALL

Scientific or Technical

Class I

None

Class II

MITCHELL CAMERA CORPORA-
TION for the design and development of the Mitchell Mark II 35mm
Portable Motion Picture Reflex Camera

ARNOLD & RICHTER KG for the design and development of the Arriflex
35mm Portable Motion Picture Reflex Camera

Class III

PANAVISION INCORPORATED for
the design of the Panatron Power In-
verter and its application to motion
picture camera operation

CARROLL KNUDSON for the production of a Composers Manual for Motion Picture Music Synchronization

RUBY RAKSIN for the production of a
Composers Manual for Motion Picture Music Synchronization.

1967

Nominations Announced: February 19, 1968
Awards Ceremony: Postponed from April 8 to April 10, 1968
because of the death of Dr. Martin Luther King, Jr.
Santa Monica Civic Auditorium
(MC: Bob Hope)

Best Picture

BONNIE AND CLYDE, Tatira-Hiller Prod., Warner Bros.-Seven Arts: WARREN BEATTY, Producer

DOCTOR DOLITTLE, Apjac Prods., 20th Century-Fox: ARTHUR P. JACOBS, Producer

THE GRADUATE, Mike Nichols-Lawrence Turman Prod., Embassy: LAWRENCE TURMAN, Producer

GUESS WHO'S COMING TO DINNER, Columbia: STANLEY KRAMER, Producer

IN THE HEAT OF THE NIGHT, Mirisch Corp. Prod., United Artists: WALTER MIRISCH, Producer

Actor

WARREN BEATTY in *Bonnie And Clyde*, Tatira-Hiller Prod., Warner Bros.-Seven Arts

DUSTIN HOFFMAN in *The Graduate*, Mike Nichols-Lawrence Turman Prod., Embassy

PAUL NEWMAN in *Cool Hand Luke*, Jalem Prod., Warner Bros.-Seven Arts

ROD STEIGER in *In The Heat Of The Night*, Mirisch Corp. Prod., United Artists

SPENCER TRACY in *Guess Who's Coming To Dinner*, Columbia

Actress

ANNE BANCROFT in *The Graduate*, Mike Nichols-Lawrence Turman Prod., Embassy

FAYE DUNAWAY in *Bonnie And Clyde*, Tatira-Hiller Prod., Warner Bros.-Seven Arts

DAME EDITH EVANS in *The Whisperers*, Seven Pines Prods., Ltd., United Artists

AUDREY HEPBURN in *Wait Until Dark*, Warner Bros.-Seven Arts

KATHARINE HEPBURN in *Guess Who's Coming To Dinner*, Columbia

Supporting Actor

JOHN CASSAVETES in *The Dirty Dozen*, MKH Prods., Ltd., Metro-Goldwyn-Mayer

GENE HACKMAN in *Bonnie And Clyde*, Tatira-Hiller Prod., Warner Bros.-Seven Arts

CECIL KELLAWAY in *Guess Who's Coming To Dinner*, Columbia

GEORGE KENNEDY in *Cool Hand Luke*, Jalem Prod., Warner Bros.-Seven Arts

MICHAEL J. POLLARD in *Bonnie And Clyde*, Tatira-Hiller Prod., Warner Bros.-Seven Arts

Supporting Actress

CAROL CHANNING in *Thoroughly Modern Millie*, Ross Hunter-Universal Prod., Universal

MILDRED NATWICK in *Barefoot In The Park*, Hal Wallis Prod., Paramount

ESTELLE PARSONS in *Bonnie And*

LARGE CAPITAL LETTERS DENOTE WINNER

Clyde, Tatira-Hiller Prod., Warner Bros.-Seven Arts

BEAH RICHARDS in *Guess Who's Coming To Dinner,* Columbia

KATHARINE ROSS in *The Graduate,* Mike Nichols-Lawrence Turman Prod., Embassy

Directing

RICHARD BROOKS for *In Cold Blood,* Pax Enterprises Prod., Columbia

NORMAN JEWISON for *In The Heat Of The Night,* Mirisch Corp. Prod., United Artists

STANLEY KRAMER for *Guess Who's Coming To Dinner,* Columbia

MIKE NICHOLS for *The Graduate,* Mike Nichols-Lawrence Turman Prod., Embassy

ARTHUR PENN for *Bonnie And Clyde,* Tatira-Hiller Prod., Warner Bros. Seven Arts

Writing

(Best Screenplay—based on material from another medium)

COOL HAND LUKE, Jalem Prod., Warner Bros.-Seven Arts: DONN PEARCE and FRANK R. PIERSON

THE GRADUATE, Mike Nichols-Lawrence Turman Prod., Embassy: CALDER WILLINGHAM and BUCK HENRY

IN COLD BLOOD, Pax Enterprises Prod., Columbia: RICHARD BROOKS

IN THE HEAT OF THE NIGHT, Mirisch Corp. Prod., United Artists: STIRLING SILLIPHANT

ULYSSES, Walter Reade, Jr.-Joseph Strick Prod., Walter Reade-Continental Distributing: JOSEPH STRICK and FRED HAINES

(Best Story and Screenplay—written directly for the screen)

BONNIE AND CLYDE, Tatira-Hiller Prod., Warner Bros.-Seven Arts:

DAVID NEWMAN and ROBERT BENTON

DIVORCE AMERICAN STYLE, Tandem Prods. for National General Prods., Columbia: Story by ROBERT KAUFMAN. Screenplay by NORMAN LEAR

GUESS WHO'S COMING TO DINNER, Columbia: WILLIAM ROSE

LA GUERRE EST FINIE, Sofracima and Europa-Film Prod., Brandon Films: JORGE SEMPRUN

TWO FOR THE ROAD, Stanley Donen Films Prod., 20th Century-Fox: FREDERIC RAPHAEL

Cinematography

(Rules changed this year to one Award for Cinematography instead of separate awards for black-and-white and color.)

BONNIE AND CLYDE, Tatira-Hiller Prod., Warner Bros.-Seven Arts: BURNETT GUFFEY

CAMELOT, Warner Bros.-Seven Arts: RICHARD H. KLINE

DOCTOR DOLITTLE, Apjac Prods., 20th Century-Fox: ROBERT SURTEES

THE GRADUATE, Mike Nichols-Lawrence Turman Prod., Embassy: ROBERT SURTEES

IN COLD BLOOD, Pax Enterprises Prod., Columbia: CONRAD HALL

Art Direction—Set Decoration

(Rules changed this year to one Award for Art Direction instead of separate awards for black-and-white and color.)

CAMELOT, Warner Bros.-Seven Arts: JOHN TRUSCOTT and EDWARD CARRERE
Set Decoration: JOHN W. BROWN

DOCTOR DOLITTLE, Apjac Prods., 20th Century-Fox: MARIO CHIARI, JACK MARTIN SMITH and ED GRAVES
Set Decoration: WALTER M. SCOTT and STUART A. REISS

GUESS WHO'S COMING TO DINNER, Columbia: ROBERT CLATWORTHY
Set Decoration: FRANK TUTTLE

THE TAMING OF THE SHREW, Royal
Films International-Films Artistici
Internazionali S.r.L. Prod., Colum-
bia: RENZO MONGIARDINO, JOHN
DeCUIR, ELVEN WEBB and GIUSEPPE
MARIANI
Set Decoration: DARIO SIMONI and
LUIGI GERVASI
THOROUGHLY MODERN MILLIE, ROSS
Hunter-Universal Prod., Universal:
ALEXANDER GOLITZEN and GEORGE
C. WEBB
Set Decoration: HOWARD BRISTOL

Sound
CAMELOT, Warner Bros.-Seven Arts
Studio Sound Department
THE DIRTY DOZEN, Metro-Goldwyn-
Mayer Studio Sound Department
DOCTOR DOLITTLE, 20th Century-Fox
Studio Sound Department
IN THE HEAT OF THE NIGHT, Sam-
uel Goldwyn Studio Sound Depart-
ment
THOROUGHLY MODERN MILLIE, Univer-
sal City Studio Sound Department

Film Editing
BEACH RED, Theodora Prods., United
Artists: FRANK P. KELLER
THE DIRTY DOZEN, MKH Prods., Ltd.,
M-G-M: MICHAEL LUCIANO
DOCTOR DOLITTLE, Apjac Prods., 20th
Century-Fox: SAMUEL E. BEETLEY
and MARJORIE FOWLER
GUESS WHO'S COMING TO DINNER, Co-
lumbia: ROBERT C. JONES
IN THE HEAT OF THE NIGHT,
Mirisch Corp. Prod., United Artists:
HAL ASHBY

Music
(Original Music Score)
COOL HAND LUKE, Jalem Prod.,
Warner Bros.-Seven Arts: LALO
SCHIFRIN

DOCTOR DOLITTLE, Apjac Prods., 20th
Century-Fox: LESLIE BRICUSSE
FAR FROM THE MADDING CROWD, Appia
Films, Ltd. Prod., M-G-M: RICHARD
RODNEY BENNETT
IN COLD BLOOD, Pax Enterprises Prod.,
Columbia: QUINCY JONES
THOROUGHLY MODERN MILLIE,
Ross Hunter-Universal Prod., Uni-
versal: ELMER BERNSTEIN

(Scoring of Music—adaptation or treat-
ment)
CAMELOT, Warner Bros.-Seven Arts:
ALFRED NEWMAN and KEN
DARBY
DOCTOR DOLITTLE, Apjac Productions,
20th Century-Fox: LIONEL NEWMAN
and ALEXANDER COURAGE
GUESS WHO'S COMING TO DINNER, Co-
lumbia: DeVOL
THOROUGHLY MODERN MILLIE, Ross-
Hunter-Universal Production, Uni-
versal: ANDRÉ PREVIN and JOSEPH
GERSHENSON
VALLEY OF THE DOLLS, Red Lion
Prods., 20th Century-Fox: JOHN
WILLIAMS

(Best Song)
THE BARE NECESSITIES from *The Jungle
Book,* Walt Disney Prods., Buena
Vista Distribution Co.
Music and Lyrics by TERRY GILKY-
SON
THE EYES OF LOVE from *Banning,* Uni-
versal
Music by QUINCY JONES. Lyrics by
BOB RUSSELL
THE LOOK OF LOVE from *Casino
Royale,* Famous Artists Prods., Ltd.,
Columbia
Music by BURT BACHARACH. Lyrics
by HAL DAVID
TALK TO THE ANIMALS from *Doc-
tor Dolittle,* Apjac Prods., 20th Cen-
tury-Fox

Music and Lyrics by LESLIE BRI-
CUSSE
HOROUGHLY MODERN MILLIE from
Thoroughly Modern Millie, Ross
Hunter-Universal Prod., Universal
Music and Lyrics by JAMES VAN
HEUSEN and SAMMY CAHN

Costume Design
Rules changed this year to one Award
or Costume Design instead of Separate
awards for black-and-white and color.)

BONNIE AND CLYDE, Tatira-Hiller
Prod., Warner Bros.-Seven Arts:
THEADORA VAN RUNKLE
CAMELOT, Warner Bros.-Seven Arts:
JOHN TRUSCOTT
THE HAPPIEST MILLIONAIRE, Walt Dis-
ney Prods., Buena Vista Dist. Co.:
BILL THOMAS
THE TAMING OF THE SHREW, Royal
Films International-Films Artistici
Internazionali S.r.L. Prod., Colum-
bia: IRENE SHARAFF and DANILO
DONATI
THOROUGHLY MODERN MILLIE, Ross
Hunter-Universal Prod., Universal:
JEAN LOUIS

Short Subjects
(Cartoons)
THE BOX, Murakami-Wolf Films,
Brandon Films: FRED WOLF, Pro-
ducer
HYPOTHESE BETA, Films Orzeaux,
Pathe Contemporary Films: JEAN-
CHARLES MEUNIER, Producer
WHAT ON EARTH!, National Film Board
of Canada, Columbia: ROBERT VER-
RALL and WOLF KOENIG, Producers
(Live Action Subjects)
PADDLE TO THE SEA, National Film
Board of Canada, Favorite Films:
JULIAN BIGGS, Producer

A PLACE TO STAND, T.D.F. Prod.
for The Ontario Department of Economics and Development, Columbia:
CHRISTOPHER CHAPMAN, Pro-
ducer
SKY OVER HOLLAND, John Ferno Prod.
for The Netherlands, Seneca International: JOHN FERNO, Producer
STOP, LOOK AND LISTEN, Metro-
Goldwyn-Mayer: LEN JANSON and
CHUCK MENVILLE, Producers

Documentary
(Short Subjects)
MONUMENT TO THE DREAM, Guggen-
heim Prods.: CHARLES E. GUGGEN-
HEIM, Producer
A PLACE TO STAND, T.D.F. Prod. for
The Ontario Dept. of Economics and
Development: CHRISTOPHER CHAP-
MAN, Producer
THE REDWOODS, King Screen
Prods.: MARK HARRIS and TRE-
VOR GREENWOOD, Producers
SEE YOU AT THE PILLAR, Associated
British-Pathe Prod.: ROBERT FITCH-
ETT, Producer
WHILE I RUN THIS RACE, Sun Dial
Films for VISTA, An Economic Op-
portunity Program: CARL V. RAGS-
DALE, Producer

(Features)
THE ANDERSON PLATOON, French
Broadcasting System: PIERRE
SCHOENDOERFFER, Producer
FESTIVAL, Patchke Prods.: MURRAY
LERNER, Producer
HARVEST, United States Information
Agency: CARROLL BALLARD, Pro-
ducer
A KING'S STORY, Jack Le Vien Prod.:
JACK LE VIEN, Producer
A TIME FOR BURNING, Quest Prods. for
Lutheran Film Associates: WILLIAM
C. JERSEY, Producer

Special Visual Effects
DOCTOR DOLITTLE, Apjac Prods.,
20th Century-Fox: L. B. ABBOTT
TOBRUK, Gibraltar Prods.-Corman
Company-Universal Prod., Universal: HOWARD A. ANDERSON, JR. and
ALBERT WHITLOCK

Sound Effects
(Not given as an Annual Award after
this year.)
THE DIRTY DOZEN, MKH Prods.,
Ltd., M-G-M: JOHN POYNER
IN THE HEAT OF THE NIGHT, Mirisch
Corp. Prod., UA: JAMES A. RICHARD

Foreign Language Film Award
CLOSELY WATCHED TRAINS, Barrandov Film Studio Production
(Czechoslovakia)
EL AMOR BRUJO, Films R.B., S.A. Production (Spain)
I EVEN MET HAPPY GYPSIES, Avala Film
Production (Yugoslavia)
LIVE FOR LIFE, Les Films Ariane-Les
Productions Artistes Associes-Vides
Films Production (France)
PORTRAIT OF CHIEKO, Shochiku Co.,
Ltd. Production (Japan)

Honorary Awards
ARTHUR FREED for distinguished

service to the Academy and the production of six top-rated Awards telecasts. (statuette)

Irving G. Thalberg Memorial Award
ALFRED HITCHCOCK

Jean Hersholt Humanitarian Award
GREGORY PECK

Scientific or Technical
Class I
None

Class II
None

Class III
ELECTRO-OPTICAL DIVISION of
the KOLLMORGEN CORPORATION for the design and development of a series of Motion Picture
Projection Lenses
PANAVISION INCORPORATED for
a Variable Speed Motor for Motion
Picture Cameras
FRED R. WILSON of the SAMUEL
GOLDWYN STUDIO SOUND DEPARTMENT for an Audio Level
Clamper
WALDON O. WATSON and the UNIVERSAL CITY STUDIO SOUND
DEPARTMENT for new concepts in
the design of a Music Scoring Stage

1968

Nominations Announced: February 24, 1969
Awards Ceremony: April 14, 1969
Dorothy Chandler Pavilion, Los Angeles County Music Center

Best Picture
The Franco Zeffirelli production of
ROMEO & JULIET, B.H.E. Film-
Verona Prod.-Dino De Laurentiis
Cinematografica Prod., Paramount:
ANTHONY HAVELOCK-ALLAN and
JOHN BRABOURNE, Producers
FUNNY GIRL, Rastar Prods., Columbia:
RAY STARK, Producer
THE LION IN WINTER, Haworth Prods.,
Avco Embassy: MARTIN POLL, Pro-
ducer
OLIVER!, Romulus Films, Columbia:
JOHN WOOLF, Producer
RACHEL, RACHEL, Kayos Prod.,
Warner Bros.-Seven Arts: PAUL
NEWMAN, Producer

Actor
ALAN ARKIN in *The Heart Is A Lonely
Hunter,* Warner Bros.-Seven Arts
ALAN BATES in *The Fixer,* John Fran-
kenheimer-Edward Lewis Prods.,
Metro-Goldwyn-Mayer
RON MOODY in *Oliver!,* Romulus Films,
Ltd., Columbia
PETER O'TOOLE in *The Lion In Winter,*
Haworth Prods., Ltd., Avco Em-
bassy
CLIFF ROBERTSON in *Charly,*
American Broadcasting Companies-
Selmur Pictures Prod., Cinerama

Actress (tie awards)
KATHARINE HEPBURN in *The Lion*

LARGE CAPITAL LETTERS DENOTE WINNER

In Winter, Haworth Prods., Ltd.,
Avco Embassy
PATRICIA NEAL in *The Subject Was
Roses,* Metro-Goldwyn-Mayer
VANESSA REDGRAVE in *Isadora,* Robert
and Raymond Hakim-Universal, Ltd.
Prod., Universal
BARBRA STREISAND in *Funny Girl,*
Rastar Prods., Columbia
JOANNE WOODWARD in *Rachel, Rachel,*
Kayos Prod., Warner Bros.-Seven
Arts

Supporting Actor
JACK ALBERTSON in *The Subject
Was Roses,* Metro-Goldwyn-Mayer
SEYMOUR CASSEL in *Faces,* John Cas-
savetes Prod., Walter Reade-Con-
tinental Distributing
DANIEL MASSEY in *Star!,* Robert Wise
Prod., 20th Century-Fox
JACK WILD in *Oliver!,* Romulus Films,
Ltd., Columbia
GENE WILDER in *The Producers,* Sid-
ney Glazier Prod., Avco Embassy

Supporting Actress
LYNN CARLIN in *Faces,* John Cas-
savetes Prod., Walter Reade-Con-
tinental Distributing
RUTH GORDON in *Rosemary's Baby,*
William Castle Enterprises Prod.,
Paramount
SONDRA LOCKE in *The Heart Is A
Lonely Hunter,* Warner Bros.-Seven
Arts

KAY MEDFORD in *Funny Girl,* Rastar Prods., Columbia

ESTELLE PARSONS in *Rachel, Rachel,* Kayos Prod., Warner Bros.-Seven Arts

Directing

ANTHONY HARVEY for *The Lion In Winter,* Haworth Prods., Avco Embassy

STANLEY KUBRICK for *2001: A Space Odyssey,* Polaris Prod., Metro-Goldwyn-Mayer

GILLO PONTECORVO for *The Battle Of Algiers,* Igor-Casbah Film Prod., Allied Artists

CAROL REED for *Oliver!,* Romulus Films, Columbia

FRANCO ZEFFIRELLI for *The Franco Zeffirelli production of Romeo & Juliet,* B.H.E. Film-Verona Prod.-Dino De Laurentiis Cinematografica Prod., Paramount

Writing

(Best Screenplay—based on material from another medium)

THE LION IN WINTER, Haworth Prods., Avco Embassy: JAMES GOLDMAN

THE ODD COUPLE, Howard W. Koch Prod., Paramount: NEIL SIMON

OLIVER!, Romulus Films, Columbia: VERNON HARRIS

RACHEL, RACHEL, Kayos Prod., Warner Bros.-Seven Arts: STEWART STERN

ROSEMARY'S BABY, William Castle Enterprises Prod., Paramount: ROMAN POLANSKI

(Best Story and Screenplay—written directly for the screen)

THE BATTLE OF ALGIERS, Igor-Casbah Film Prod., Allied Artists: FRANCO SOLINAS and GILLO PONTECORVO

FACES, John Cassavetes Prod., Walter Reade-Continental Dist.: JOHN CASSAVETES

HOT MILLIONS, Mildred Freed Albert Prod., Metro-Goldwyn-Mayer: IRA WALLACH and PETER USTINOV

THE PRODUCERS, Sidney Glazier Prod., Avco Embassy: MEL BROOKS

2001: A SPACE ODYSSEY, Polaris Prod., Metro-Goldwyn-Mayer: STANLEY KUBRICK and ARTHUR C. CLARKE

Cinematography

The Franco Zeffirelli production of ROMEO & JULIET, B.H.E. Film-Verona Prod.-Dino De Laurentiis Cinematografica Prod., Paramount: PASQUALINO DE SANTIS

FUNNY GIRL, Rastar Prods., Columbia: HARRY STRADLING

ICE STATION ZEBRA, Filmways Prod., Metro-Goldwyn-Mayer: DANIEL L. FAPP

OLIVER!, Romulus Films, Columbia: OSWALD MORRIS

STAR!, Robert Wise Prod., 20th Century-Fox: ERNEST LASZLO

Art Direction—Set Decoration

OLIVER!, Romulus Films, Ltd., Columbia: JOHN BOX and TERENCE MARSH
Set Decoration: VERNON DIXON and KEN MUGGLESTON

THE SHOES OF THE FISHERMAN, George Englund Prod., Metro-Goldwyn-Mayer: GEORGE W. DAVIS and EDWARD CARFAGNO

STAR!, Robert Wise Prod., 20th Century-Fox: BORIS LEVEN
Set Decoration: WALTER M. SCOTT and HOWARD BRISTOL

2001: A SPACE ODYSSEY, Polaris Prod., Metro-Goldwyn-Mayer: TONY MASTERS, HARRY LANGE and ERNIE ARCHER

WAR AND PEACE, Mosfilm Prod.,

Walter Reade-Continental Dist.:
MIKHAIL BOGDANOV and GENNADY
MYASNIKOV
Set Decoration: G. KOSHELEV and V.
UVAROV

Sound

BULLITT, Warner Bros.-Seven Arts
Studio Sound Department
FINIAN'S RAINBOW, Warner Bros.-
Seven Arts Studio Sound Department
FUNNY GIRL, Columbia Studio Sound
Department
OLIVER!, Shepperton Studio Sound
Department
STAR!, 20th Century-Fox Studio Sound
Department

Film Editing

BULLITT, Solar Prod., Warner Bros.-
Seven Arts: FRANK P. KELLER
FUNNY GIRL, Rastar Prods., Columbia:
ROBERT SWINK, MAURY WINETROBE
and WILLIAM SANDS
THE ODD COUPLE, Howard W. Koch
Prod., Paramount: FRANK BRACHT
OLIVER!, Romulus Films, Columbia:
RALPH KEMPLEN
WILD IN THE STREETS, American Inter-
national: FRED FEITSHANS and EVE
NEWMAN

Music

(Best Original Score—for a motion picture [not a musical])

THE FOX, Raymond Stross-Motion Pic-
tures International Prod., Claridge
Pictures: LALO SCHIFRIN
THE LION IN WINTER, Haworth
Prods., Ltd., Avco Embassy: JOHN
BARRY
PLANET OF THE APES, APJAC Prods.,
20th Century-Fox: JERRY GOLDSMITH
THE SHOES OF THE FISHERMAN, George
Englund Prod., Metro-Goldwyn-
Mayer: ALEX NORTH

THE THOMAS CROWN AFFAIR, Mirisch-
Simkoe-Solar Prod., United Artists:
MICHEL LEGRAND

(Best Score of a Musical Picture—
[original or adaptation])

FINIAN'S RAINBOW, Warner Bros.-
Seven Arts: Adapted by RAY HEIN-
DORF
FUNNY GIRL, Rastar Prods., Columbia:
Adapted by WALTER SCHARF
OLIVER!, Romulus Films, Columbia:
Adapted by JOHN GREEN
STAR!, Robert Wise Prod., 20th Cen-
tury-Fox: Adapted by LENNIE HAY-
TON
THE YOUNG GIRLS OF ROCHEFORT, Mag
Bodard-Gilbert de Goldschmidt-Parc
Film-Madeleine Films Prod., Warner
Bros.-Seven Arts: MICHEL LEGRAND
and JACQUES DEMY

(Best Song)

CHITTY CHITTY BANG BANG from *Chitty
Chitty Bang Bang,* Warfield Prods.,
United Artists
Music and lyrics by RICHARD M.
SHERMAN and ROBERT B. SHERMAN
FOR LOVE OF IVY from *For Love Of Ivy,*
American Broadcasting Companies-
Palomar Pictures International Prod.,
Cinerama
Music by QUINCY JONES. Lyrics by
BOB RUSSELL
FUNNY GIRL from *Funny Girl,* Rastar
Prods., Columbia
Music by JULE STYNE. Lyrics by BOB
MERRILL
STAR! from *Star!,* Robert Wise Prod.,
20th Century-Fox
Music by JIMMY VAN HEUSEN.
Lyrics by SAMMY CAHN
THE WINDMILLS OF YOUR MIND
from *The Thomas Crown Affair,*
Mirisch-Simkoe-Solar Prod., United
Artists Music by MICHEL LE-
GRAND. Lyrics by ALAN and
MARILYN BERGMAN

Costume Design

The Franco Zeffirelli production of
ROMEO & JULIET, B.H.E. Film-
Verona Prod.-Dino De Laurentiis
Cinematografica Prod., Paramount:
DANILO DONATI

THE LION IN WINTER, Haworth Prods.,
Avco Embassy: MARGARET FURSE

OLIVER!, Romulus Films, Columbia:
PHYLLIS DALTON

PLANET OF THE APES, APJAC Prods.,
20th Century-Fox: MORTON HAACK

STAR!, Robert Wise Prod., 20th Century-Fox: DONALD BROOKS

Short Subjects

(Cartoons)

THE HOUSE THAT JACK BUILT, National
Film Board of Canada, Columbia:
WOLF KOENIG and JIM MACKAY, Pro-
ducers

THE MAGIC PEAR TREE, Murakami-Wolf
Prods., Bing Crosby Prods.: JIMMY
MURAKAMI, Producer

WINDY DAY, Hubley Studios, Paramount: JOHN and FAITH HUBLEY,
Producers

WINNIE THE POOH AND THE
BLUSTERY DAY, Walt Disney
Prods., Buena Vista Dist.: WALT
DISNEY, Producer

(Live Action Subjects)

THE DOVE, Coe-Davis, Schoenfeld
Film Dist.: GEORGE COE, SIDNEY
DAVIS and ANTHONY LOVER, Pro-
ducers

DUO, National Film Board of Canada,
Columbia

PRELUDE, Prelude Company, Excelsior
Dist.: JOHN ASTIN, Producer

ROBERT KENNEDY REMEM-
BERED, Guggenheim Prods., Na-
tional General: CHARLES
GUGGENHEIM, Producer

Documentary

(Short Subjects)

THE HOUSE THAT ANANDA BUILT,
Films Division, Government of
India: FALI BILIMORIA, Producer

THE REVOLVING DOOR, Vision Associ-
ates for The American Foundation
Institute of Corrections: LEE R. BOB-
KER, Producer

A SPACE TO GROW, Office of Economic
Opportunity for Project Upward
Bound: THOMAS P. KELLY, JR., Pro-
ducer

A WAY OUT OF THE WILDERNESS, John
Sutherland Prods.: DAN E. WEIS-
BURD, Producer

WHY MAN CREATES, Saul Bass &
Associates: SAUL BASS, Producer

(Features)

A FEW NOTES ON OUR FOOD PROBLEM,
United States Information Agency:
JAMES BLUE, Producer

JOURNEY INTO SELF, Western Behavioral Sciences Institute: BILL
McGAW, Producer

THE LEGENDARY CHAMPIONS, Turn Of
The Century Fights: WILLIAM CAY-
TON, Producer

OTHER VOICES, DHS Films: DAVID H.
SAWYER, Producer

YOUNG AMERICANS, The Young Americans Prod.: ROBERT COHN and ALEX
GRASSHOFF, Producers. (Declared ineligible May 7, 1969 because first released during 1967.)

Special Visual Effects

ICE STATION ZEBRA, Filmways Prod.,
Metro-Goldwyn-Mayer: HAL MILLAR
and J. MCMILLAN JOHNSON

2001: A SPACE ODYSSEY, Polaris
Prod., Metro-Goldwyn-Mayer:
STANLEY KUBRICK

Foreign Language Film Award

THE BOYS OF PAUL STREET, Bohgros

Films-Mafilm Studio I Production (Hungary)

THE FIREMEN'S BALL, Barrandov Film Studio Production (Czechoslovakia)

THE GIRL WITH THE PISTOL, Documento Film Production (Italy)

STOLEN KISSES, Les Films du Carrosse-Les Productions Artistes Associes Production (France)

WAR AND PEACE, Mosfilm Production (Russia)

Honorary Awards

JOHN CHAMBERS for his outstanding make-up achievement for *Planet Of The Apes*. (statuette)

ONNA WHITE for her outstanding choreography achievement for *Oliver!*. (statuette)

Irving G. Thalberg Memorial Award
None

Jean Hersholt Humanitarian Award
MARTHA RAYE

Scientific or Technical
Class I

PHILIP V. PALMQUIST of MINNESOTA MINING AND MANUFACTURING CO., to DR. HERBERT MEYER of the MOTION PICTURE AND TELEVISION RESEARCH CENTER, and to CHARLES D. STAFFELL of the RANK ORGANISATION for the development of a successful embodiment of the reflex background projection system for composite cinematography.

EASTMAN KODAK COMPANY for the development and introduction of a color reversal intermediate film for motion pictures

Class II
DONALD W. NORWOOD for the design and development of the Norwood Photographic Exposure Meters

EASTMAN KODAK COMPANY and PRODUCERS SERVICE COMPANY for the development of a new high-speed step-optical reduction printer

EDMUND M. DiGIULIO, NIELS G. PETERSEN and NORMAN S. HUGHES of the CINEMA PRODUCT DEVELOPMENT COMPANY for the design and application of a conversion which makes available the reflex viewing system for motion picture cameras

OPTICAL COATING LABORATORIES, INC., for the development of an improved anti-reflection coating for photographic and projection lens systems

EASTMAN KODAK COMPANY for the introduction of a new high-speed motion picture color negative film

PANAVISION INCORPORATED for the conception, design and introduction of a 65mm hand-held motion picture camera

TODD-AO COMPANY and the MITCHELL CAMERA COMPANY for the design and engineering of the Todd-AO hand-held motion picture camera

Class III

CARL W. HAUGE and EDWARD H. REICHARD of CONSOLIDATED FILM INDUSTRIES and E. MICHAEL MEAHL and ROY J. RIDENOUR of RAMTRONICS for engineering an automatic exposure control for printing-machine lamps

EASTMAN KODAK COMPANY for a new direct positive film and to CONSOLIDATED FILM INDUSTRIES for the application of this film to the making of post-production work prints

1969

Nominations Announced: February 16, 1970
Awards Ceremony: April 7, 1970
Dorothy Chandler Pavilion, Los Angeles County Music Center

Best Picture

ANNE OF THE THOUSAND DAYS, Hal B. Wallis-Universal Pictures, Ltd. Production, Universal: HAL B. WALLIS, Producer

BUTCH CASSIDY AND THE SUNDANCE KID, George Roy Hill-Paul Monash Prod., 20th Century-Fox: JOHN FOREMAN, Producer

HELLO, DOLLY!, Chenault Productions, 20th Century-Fox: ERNEST LEHMAN, Producer

MIDNIGHT COWBOY, Jerome Hellman-John Schlesinger Production. United Artists: JEROME HELLMAN, Producer

Z, Reggane Films-O.N.C.I.C. Production, Cinema V: JACQUES PERRIN and HAMED RACHEDI, Producers

Actor

RICHARD BURTON in *Anne Of The Thousand Days,* Hal B. Wallis-Universal Pictures, Ltd. Prod., Universal

DUSTIN HOFFMAN in *Midnight Cowboy,* Jerome Hellman-John Schlesinger Prod., United Artists

PETER O'TOOLE in *Goodbye, Mr. Chips,* APJAC Prod., Metro-Goldwyn-Mayer

JON VOIGHT in *Midnight Cowboy,* Jerome Hellman-John Schlesinger Prod., United Artists

JOHN WAYNE in *True Grit,* Hal Wallis Prod., Paramount

LARGE CAPITAL LETTERS DENOTE WINNER

Actress

GENEVIEVE BUJOLD in *Anne Of The Thousand Days,* Hal B. Wallis-Universal Pictures, Ltd. Prod., Universal

JANE FONDA in *They Shoot Horses, Don't They?,* Chartoff-Winkler-Pollack Prod., ABC Pictures Presentation, Cinerama

LIZA MINNELLI in *The Sterile Cuckoo,* Boardwalk Prods., Paramount

JEAN SIMMONS in *The Happy Ending,* Pax Films Prod., United Artists

MAGGIE SMITH in *The Prime Of Miss Jean Brodie,* 20th Century-Fox Prods., Ltd., 20th Century-Fox

Supporting Actor

RUPERT CROSSE in *The Reivers,* Irving Ravetch-Arthur Kramer-Solar Prods., Cinema Center Films Presentation, National General

ELLIOTT GOULD in *Bob & Carol & Ted & Alice,* Frankovich Prods., Columbia

JACK NICHOLSON in *Easy Rider,* Pando-Raybert Prods., Columbia

ANTHONY QUAYLE in *Anne Of The Thousand Days,* Hal B. Wallis-Universal Pictures, Ltd. Prod., Universal

GIG YOUNG in *They Shoot Horses, Don't They?,* Chartoff-Winkler-Pollack Prod., ABC Pictures Presentation, Cinerama

Supporting Actress

CATHERINE BURNS in *Last Summer,*

Frank Perry-Alsid Prod., Allied Artists

DYAN CANNON in *Bob & Carol & Ted & Alice*, Frankovich Prods., Columbia

GOLDIE HAWN in *Cactus Flower*, Frankovich Prods., Columbia

SYLVIA MILES in *Midnight Cowboy*, A Jerome Hellman-John Schlesinger Prod., United Artists

SUSANNAH YORK in *They Shoot Horses, Don't They?*, Chartoff-Winkler-Pollack Prod., ABC Pictures Presentation, Cinerama

Directing

COSTA-GAVRAS for *Z*, Reggane Films-O.N.C.I.C. Prod., Cinema V

GEORGE ROY HILL for *Butch Cassidy And The Sundance Kid*, George Roy Hill-Paul Monash Prod., 20th Century-Fox

ARTHUR PENN for *Alice's Restaurant*, Florin Prod., United Artists

SYDNEY POLLACK for *They Shoot Horses, Don't They?*, Chartoff-Winkler-Pollack Prod., ABC Pictures Presentation, Cinerama

JOHN SCHLESINGER for *Midnight Cowboy*, Jerome Hellman-John Schlesinger Prod., United Artists

Writing

(Best Screenplay-based on material from another medium)

ANNE OF THE THOUSAND DAYS, Hal B. Wallis-Universal Pictures, Ltd. Prod., Universal: JOHN HALE and BRIDGET BOLAND. Adaptation by RICHARD SOKOLOVE

GOODBYE, COLUMBUS, Willow Tree Prods., Paramount: ARNOLD SCHULMAN

MIDNIGHT COWBOY, Jerome Hellman-John Schlesinger Prod., United Artists: WALDO SALT

THEY SHOOT HORSES, DON'T THEY?,

Chartoff-Winkler-Pollack Prod., ABC Pictures Presentation, Cinerama: JAMES POE and ROBERT E. THOMPSON

Z, Reggane Films-O.N.C.I.C. Prod., Cinema V: JORGE SEMPRUN and COSTA-GAVRAS

(Best Story and Screenplay—based on material not previously published or produced.)

BOB & CAROL & TED & ALICE, Frankovich Prods., Columbia: PAUL MAZURSKY and LARRY TUCKER

BUTCH CASSIDY AND THE SUNDANCE KID, George Roy Hill-Paul Monash Prod., 20th Century-Fox: WILLIAM GOLDMAN

THE DAMNED, Pegaso-Praesidens Film Prod., Warner Bros.: Story by NICOLA BADALUCCO. Screenplay by NICOLA BADALUCCO, ENRICO MEDIOLI and LUCHINO VISCONTI

EASY RIDER, Pando-Raybert Prods., Columbia: PETER FONDA, DENNIS HOPPER and TERRY SOUTHERN

THE WILD BUNCH, Phil Feldman Prod., Warner Bros.: Story by WALON GREEN and ROY N. SICKNER. Screenplay by WALON GREEN and SAM PECKINPAH

Cinematography

ANNE OF THE THOUSAND DAYS, Hal B. Wallis-Universal Pictures, Ltd. Prod., Universal: ARTHUR IBBETSON

BOB & CAROL & TED & ALICE, Frankovich Prods., Columbia: CHARLES B. LANG

BUTCH CASSIDY AND THE SUNDANCE KID, George Roy Hill-Paul Monash Prod., 20th Century-Fox: CONRAD HALL

HELLO, DOLLY!, Chenault Prods., 20th Century-Fox: HARRY STRADLING

MAROONED, Frankovich-Sturges Prod., Columbia: DANIEL FAPP

Art Direction—Set Decoration

ANNE OF THE THOUSAND DAYS, Hal B. Wallis-Universal Pictures, Ltd. Prod., Universal: MAURICE CARTER and LIONEL COUCH Set Decoration: PATRICK MCLOUGHLIN

GAILY, GAILY, Mirisch-Cartier Prod., United Artists: ROBERT BOYLE and GEORGE B. CHAN Set Decoration: EDWARD BOYLE and CARL BIDDISCOMBE

HELLO, DOLLY!, Chenault Prods., 20th Century-Fox: JOHN DeCUIR, JACK MARTIN SMITH and HERMAN BLUMENTHAL Set Decoration: WALTER M. SCOTT, GEORGE HOPKINS and RAPHAEL BRETTON

SWEET CHARITY, Universal: ALEXANDER GOLITZEN and GEORGE C. WEBB Set Decoration: JACK D. MOORE

THEY SHOOT HORSES, DON'T THEY?, Chartoff-Winkler-Pollack Prod., ABC Pictures Presentation, Cinerama: HARRY HORNER Set Decoration: FRANK MCKELVY

Sound

ANNE OF THE THOUSAND DAYS, Hal B. Wallis—Universal Pictures, Ltd. Production, Universal: JOHN ALDRED

BUTCH CASSIDY AND THE SUNDANCE KID, George Roy Hill-Paul Monash Prod., 20th Century-Fox: WILLIAM EDMUNDSON and DAVID DOCKENDORF

GAILY, GAILY, Mirisch-Cartier Production, United Artists: ROBERT MARTIN and CLEM PORTMAN

HELLO, DOLLY!, Chenault Productions, 20th Century-Fox: JACK SOLOMON and MURRAY SPIVACK

MAROONED, Frankovich-Sturges Production, Columbia: LES FRESHOLTZ and ARTHUR PIANTADOSI

Film Editing

HELLO, DOLLY!, Chenault Prods., 20th Century-Fox: WILLIAM REYNOLDS

MIDNIGHT COWBOY, Jerome Hellman-John Schlesinger Prod., United Artists: HUGH A. ROBERTSON

THE SECRET OF SANTA VITTORIA, Stanley Kramer Company Prod., United Artists: WILLIAM LYON and EARLE HERDAN

THEY SHOOT HORSES, DON'T THEY?, Chartoff-Winkler-Pollack Prod., ABC Pictures Presentation, Cinerama: FREDRIC STEINKAMP

Z, Reggane Films-O.N.C.I.C. Prod., Cinema V: FRANÇOISE BONNOT

Music

(Best Original Score—for a motion picture [not a musical])

ANNE OF THE THOUSAND DAYS, Hal B. Wallis-Universal Pictures, Ltd. Prod., Universal: GEORGES DELERUE

BUTCH CASSIDY AND THE SUNDANCE KID, George Roy Hill-Paul Monash Prod., 20th Century-Fox: BURT BACHARACH

THE REIVERS, Irving Ravetch-Arthur Kramer-Solar Prods., Cinema Center Films Presentation, National General: JOHN WILLIAMS

THE SECRET OF SANTA VITTORIA, Stanley Kramer Company Prod., United Artists: ERNEST GOLD

THE WILD BUNCH, Phil Feldman Prod., Warner Bros.: JERRY FIELDING

(Best Score of a Musical Picture— [original or adaptation])

GOODBYE, MR. CHIPS, APJAC Prod., Metro-Goldwyn-Mayer. Music and Lyrics by LESLIE BRICUSSE Adapted by JOHN WILLIAMS

HELLO, DOLLY!, Chenault Prods., 20th Century-Fox Adapted by LENNIE HAYTON and LIONEL NEWMAN

PAINT YOUR WAGON, Alan Jay Lerner
Prod., Paramount
Adapted by NELSON RIDDLE
SWEET CHARITY, Universal. Adapted
by CY COLEMAN
THEY SHOOT HORSES, DON'T THEY?,
Chartoff-Winkler-Pollack Prod.,
ABC Pictures Presentation, Cin-
erama
Adapted by JOHN GREEN and ALBERT
WOODBURY

(Best Song)

COME SATURDAY MORNING from *The
Sterile Cuckoo,* Boardwalk Prods.,
Paramount
Music by FRED KARLIN. Lyrics by
DORY PREVIN
JEAN from *The Prime Of Miss Jean
Brodie,* 20th Century-Fox Prods.,
Ltd., 20th Century-Fox
Music and lyrics by ROD McKUEN
RAINDROPS KEEP FALLIN' ON
MY HEAD from *Butch Cassidy And
The Sundance Kid,* George Roy Hill-
Paul Monash Prod., 20th Century-
Fox
Music by BURT BACHARACH.
Lyrics by HAL DAVID
TRUE GRIT from *True Grit,* Hal Wallis
Prod., Paramount
Music by ELMER BERNSTEIN. Lyrics
by DON BLACK
WHAT ARE YOU DOING THE REST OF
YOUR LIFE? from *The Happy Ending,*
Pax Films Prod., United Artists
Music by MICHEL LEGRAND
Lyrics by ALAN and MARILYN BERG-
MAN

Costume Design

ANNE OF THE THOUSAND DAYS,
Hal B. Wallis-Universal Pictures,
Ltd. Prod., Universal: MARGARET
FURSE
GAILY, GAILY, Mirisch-Cartier Prod.,
United Artists: RAY AGHAYAN

HELLO, DOLLY!, Chenault Prods., 20th
Century-Fox: IRENE SHARAFF
SWEET CHARITY, Universal: EDITH
HEAD
THEY SHOOT HORSES, DON'T THEY?,
Chartoff-Winkler-Pollack Prod.,
ABC Pictures Presentation, Cinera-
ma: DONFELD

Short Subjects

(Cartoons)

IT'S TOUGH TO BE A BIRD, Walt
Disney Prods., Buena Vista Dist.:
WARD KIMBALL, Producer
OF MEN AND DEMONS, Hubley Studios,
Paramount: JOHN and FAITH HUB-
LEY, Producers
WALKING, National Film Board of Can-
ada, Columbia: RYAN LARKIN, Pro-
ducer

(Live Action Subjects)

BLAKE, National Film Board of Can-
ada, Vaudeo Inc.: DOUG JACKSON,
Producer
THE MAGIC MACHINES, Fly-By-
Night Prods., Manson Distributing:
JOAN KELLER STERN, Producer
PEOPLE SOUP, Pangloss Prods., Colum-
bia: MARC MERSON, Producer

Documentary

(Short Subjects)

CZECHOSLOVAKIA 1968, Sanders-
Fresco Film Makers for United
States Information Agency: DENIS
SANDERS and ROBERT M. FRES-
CO, Producers
AN IMPRESSION OF JOHN STEINBECK:
WRITER, Donald Wrye Prods. for
United States Information Agency:
DONALD WRYE, Producer
JENNY IS A GOOD THING, A.C.I. Prod.
for Project Head Start: JOAN HOR-
VATH, Producer
LEO BEUERMAN, Centron Prod.: AR-
THUR H. WOLF and RUSSELL A. MOS-
SER, Producers

THE MAGIC MACHINES, Fly-By-Night Prods.: JOAN KELLER STERN, Producer

(Features)

ARTHUR RUBINSTEIN—THE LOVE OF LIFE, Midem Prod.: BERNARD CHEVRY, Producer

BEFORE THE MOUNTAIN WAS MOVED, Robert K. Sharpe Prods. for The Office of Economic Opportunity: ROBERT K. SHARPE, Producer

IN THE YEAR OF THE PIG, Emile de Antonio Prod.: EMILE DE ANTONIO, Producer

THE OLYMPICS IN MEXICO, Film Section of the Organizing Committee for the XIX Olympic Games

THE WOLF MEN, MGM Documentary: IRWIN ROSTEN, Producer

Special Visual Effects

KRAKATOA, EAST OF JAVA, American Broadcasting Companies-Cinerama Prod., Cinerama: EUGENE LOURIE and ALEX WELDON

MAROONED, Frankovich-Sturges Prod., Columbia: ROBBIE ROBERTSON

Foreign Language Film Award

ADALEN '31, AB Svensk Filmindustri Production (Sweden)

THE BATTLE OF NERETVA, United Film Producers-Igor Film-Eichberg Film-Commonwealth United Production (Yugoslavia)

THE BROTHERS KARAMAZOV, Mosfilm Production (U.S.S.R.)

MY NIGHT WITH MAUD, Films du Losange-F.F.P-Films du Carrosse-Films des Deux Mondes-Films de la Pleiade-Gueville-Renn-Simar Films Production (France)

Z, Reggane-O.N.C.I.C. Production (Algeria)

Honorary Award

CARY GRANT for his unique mastery of the art of screen acting with the respect and affection of his colleagues. (statuette)

Irving G. Thalberg Memorial Award

None

Jean Hersholt Humanitarian Award

GEORGE JESSEL

Scientific or Technical

Class I

None

Class II

HAZELTINE CORPORATION for the design and development of the Hazeltine Color Film Analyzer

FOUAD SAID for the design and introduction of the Cinemobile series of equipment trucks for location motion picture production

JUAN DE LA CIERVA and DYNASCIENCES CORPORATION for the design and development of the Dynalens optical image motion compensator

Class III

OTTO POPELKA of Magna-Tech Electronics Co., Inc., for the development of an Electronically Controlled Looping System

FENTON HAMILTON of Metro-Goldwyn-Mayer Studios for the concept and engineering of a mobile battery power unit for location lighting

PANAVISION INCORPORATED for the design and development of the Panaspeed Motion Picture Camera Motor

ROBERT M. FLYNN and RUSSELL HESSY of Universal City Studios, Inc. for a machine-gun modification for motion picture photography

1970

Nominations Announced: February 22, 1971
Awards Ceremony: April 15, 1971
Dorothy Chandler Pavilion, Los Angeles County Music Center

Best Picture

AIRPORT, Ross-Hunter-Universal Prod., Universal: ROSS HUNTER, Producer

FIVE EASY PIECES, BBS Prods., Columbia: BOB RAFELSON and RICHARD WECHSLER, Producers

LOVE STORY, The Love Story Company Prod., Paramount: HOWARD G. MINSKY, Producer

M*A*S*H, Aspen Prods., 20th Century-Fox: INGO PREMINGER, Producer

PATTON, 20th Century-Fox: FRANK McCARTHY, Producer

Actor

MELVYN DOUGLAS in *I Never Sang For My Father*, Jamel Prods., Columbia

JAMES EARL JONES in *The Great White Hope*, Lawrence Turman Films Prod., 20th Century-Fox

JACK NICHOLSON in *Five Easy Pieces*, BBS Prods., Columbia

RYAN O'NEAL in *Love Story*, The Love Story Company Prod., Paramount

GEORGE C. SCOTT in *Patton*, 20th Century-Fox

Actress

JANE ALEXANDER in *The Great White Hope*, Lawrence Turman Films Prod., 20th Century-Fox

GLENDA JACKSON in *Women In Love*, Larry Kramer–Martin Rosen Prod., United Artists

ALI MacGRAW in *Love Story*, The Love Story Company Prod., Paramount

LARGE CAPITAL LETTERS DENOTE WINNER

SARAH MILES in *Ryan's Daughter*, Faraway Prods., Metro-Goldwyn-Mayer

CARRIE SNODGRESS in *Diary Of A Mad Housewife*, Frank Perry Films Prod., Universal

Supporting Actor

RICHARD CASTELLANO in *Lovers And Other Strangers*, ABC Pictures Prod., Cinerama

CHIEF DAN GEORGE in *Little Big Man*, Hiller Prods., Ltd.-Stockbridge Prods., Cinema Center Films Presentation, National General

GENE HACKMAN in *I Never Sang For My Father*, Jamel Prods., Columbia

JOHN MARLEY in *Love Story*, The Love Story Company Prod., Paramount

JOHN MILLS in *Ryan's Daughter*, Faraway Prods., Metro-Goldwyn-Mayer

Supporting Actress

KAREN BLACK in *Five Easy Pieces*, BBS Prods., Columbia

LEE GRANT in *The Landlord*, A Mirisch-Cartier II Prod., United Artists

HELEN HAYES in *Airport*, Ross-Hunter-Universal Prod., Universal

SALLY KELLERMAN in *M*A*S*H*, Aspen Prods., 20th Century-Fox

MAUREEN STAPLETON in *Airport*, Ross Hunter-Universal Prod., Universal

Directing

ROBERT ALTMAN for *M*A*S*H*, Aspen Prods., 20th Century-Fox

FEDERICO FELLINI for *Fellini Satyricon,* Alberto Grimaldi Prod., United Artists

ARTHUR HILLER for *Love Story,* The Love Story Company Prod., United Artists

KEN RUSSELL for *Women in Love,* Larry Kramer-Martin Rosen Prod., United Artists.

FRANKLIN J. SCHAFFNER for *Patton,* 20th Century-Fox

Writing

(Best Screenplay—based on material from another medium)

AIRPORT, Ross Hunter-Universal Prod., Universal: GEORGE SEATON

I NEVER SANG FOR MY FATHER, Jamel Prods., Columbia: ROBERT ANDERSON

LOVERS AND OTHER STRANGERS, ABC Pictures Prod., Cinerama: RENEE TAYLOR, JOSEPH BOLOGNA and DAVID ZELAG GOODMAN

M*A*S*H, Aspen Prods., 20th Century-Fox: RING LARDNER, JR.

WOMEN IN LOVE, Larry Kramer-Martin Rosen Prod., UA: LARRY KRAMER

(Best Story and Screenplay—based on factual material or material not previously published or produced)

FIVE EASY PIECES, BBS Prods., Columbia: Story by BOB RAFELSON and ADRIEN JOYCE. Screenplay by ADRIEN JOYCE

JOE, Group Prod., Cannon Releasing: NORMAN WEXLER

LOVE STORY, The Love Story Company Prod., Paramount: ERICH SEGAL

MY NIGHT AT MAUD'S, Films du Losange-Carrosse-Renn-Deux Mondes-La Gueville-Simar-La Pleiade-F.F.P. Prod., Pathe Contemporary: ERIC ROHMER

PATTON, 20th Century-Fox: FRANCIS FORD COPPOLA and EDMUND H. NORTH

Cinematography

AIRPORT, Ross Hunter-Universal Prod., Universal: ERNEST LASZLO

PATTON, 20th Century-Fox: FRED KOENEKAMP

RYAN'S DAUGHTER, Faraway Prods., Metro-Goldwyn-Mayer: FREDDIE YOUNG

TORA! TORA! TORA!, 20th Century-Fox: CHARLES F. WHEELER, OSAMI FURUYA, SINSAKU HIMEDA and MASAMICHI SATOH

WOMEN IN LOVE, Larry Kramer-Martin Rosen Prod., United Artists: BILLY WILLIAMS

Art Direction—Set Decoration

AIRPORT, Ross Hunter-Universal Prod., Universal: ALEXANDER GOLITZEN and E. PRESTON AMES Set Decoration: JACK D. MOORE and MICKEY S. MICHAELS

THE MOLLY MAGUIRES, Tamm Prods., Paramount: TAMBI LARSEN Set Decoration: DARRELL SILVERA

PATTON, 20th Century-Fox: URIE McCLEARY and GIL PARRONDO Set Decoration: ANTONIO MATEOS and PIERRE-LOUIS THEVENET

SCROOGE, Waterbury Films, Ltd. Prod., Cinema Center Films Presentation, National General: TERRY MARSH and BOB CARTWRIGHT Set Decoration PAMELA CORNELL

TORA! TORA! TORA!, 20th Century-Fox: JACK MARTIN SMITH, YOSHIRO MURAKI, RICHARD DAY and TAIZOH KAWASHIMA Set Decoration: WALTER M. SCOTT, NORMAN ROCKETT and CARL BIDDISCOMBE

Sound

AIRPORT, Ross Hunter-Universal Prod., Universal: RONALD PIERCE and DAVID MORIARTY

PATTON, 20th Century-Fox:

DOUGLAS WILLIAMS and DON
BASSMAN
RYAN'S DAUGHTER, Faraway Prods.,
  Metro-Goldwyn-Mayer: GORDON K.
  MCCALLUM and JOHN BRAMALL
TORA! TORA! TORA!, 20th Century-Fox:
  MURRAY SPIVACK and HERMAN LEWIS
WOODSTOCK, Wadleigh-Maurice, Ltd.
  Prod., Warner Bros.: DAN WALLIN
  and LARRY JOHNSON

Film Editing
AIRPORT, Ross Hunter-Universal Prod.,
  Universal: STUART GILMORE
M*A*S*H, Aspen Prods., 20th Century-
  Fox: DANFORD B. GREENE
PATTON, 20th Century-Fox: HUGH
  S. FOWLER
TORA! TORA! TORA!, 20th Century-Fox:
  JAMES E. NEWCOM, PEMBROKE J.
  HERRING and INOUE CHIKAYA
WOODSTOCK, Wadleigh-Maurice, Ltd.
  Prod., Warner Bros.: THELMA
  SCHOONMAKER

Music
(Best Original Score)
AIRPORT, Ross Hunter-Universal Prod.,
  Universal: ALFRED NEWMAN
CROMWELL, Irving Allen, Ltd. Prod.,
  Columbia: FRANK CORDELL
LOVE STORY, The Love Story Com-
  pany Prod., Paramount: FRANCIS
  LAI
PATTON, 20th Century-Fox: JERRY
  GOLDSMITH
SUNFLOWER, Sostar Prod., Avco Em-
  bassy: HENRY MANCINI

(Best Original Song Score)
THE BABY MAKER, Robert Wise Prod.,
  National General
  Music by FRED KARLIN. Lyrics by
  TYLWYTH KYMRY
A BOY NAMED CHARLIE BROWN, Lee
  Mendelson-Melendez Features
  Prod., Cinema Center Films Presen-
tation, National General
  Music by ROD MCKUEN and JOHN
  SCOTT TROTTER
  Lyrics by ROD MCKUEN, BILL ME-
  LENDEZ and AL SHEAN. Adapted by
  VINCE GUARALDI
DARLING LILI, Geoffrey Prods., Para-
mount
  Music by HENRI MANCINI. Lyrics by
  JOHNNY MERCER
LET IT BE, Beatles-Apple Prod., UA
  Music and lyrics by THE BEATLES
SCROOGE, Waterbury Films, Ltd. Prod.,
  Cinema Center Films Presentation,
  National General
  Music and lyrics by LESLIE BRICUSSE
  Adapted by IAN FRASER and HERBERT
  W. SPENCER

(Best Song)
FOR ALL WE KNOW from *Lovers
  And Other Strangers,* ABC Pictures
  Prod., Cinerama
  Music by FRED KARLIN. Lyrics by
  ROBB ROYER and JAMES GRIF-
  FIN (aka ROBB WILSON and AR-
  THUR JAMES)
PIECES OF DREAMS from *Pieces Of
  Dreams,* RFB Enterprises Prod.,
  United Artists
  Music by MICHEL LEGRAND
  Lyrics by ALAN and MARILYN BERG-
  MAN
THANK YOU VERY MUCH from *Scrooge,*
  Waterbury Films, Ltd. Prod., Cin-
  ema Center Films Presentation, Na-
  tional General
  Music and lyrics by LESLIE BRICUSSE
TILL LOVE TOUCHES YOUR LIFE from
  Madron, Edric-Isracine-Zev Braun
  Prods., Four Star-Excelsior Releas-
  ing
  Music by RIZ ORTOLANI. Lyrics by
  ARTHUR HAMILTON
WHISTLING AWAY THE DARK from
  Darling Lili, Geoffrey Prods., Para-
  mount

Music by HENRI MANCINI. Lyrics by
JOHNNY MERCER

Costume Design

AIRPORT, Ross Hunter-Universal Prod.,
Universal: EDITH HEAD
CROMWELL, Irving Allen, Ltd.
Prod., Columbia: NINO NO-
VARESE
DARLING LILI, Geoffrey Prods., Para-
mount: DONALD BROOKS and JACK
BEAR
THE HAWAIIANS, Mirisch Prods.,
United Artists: BILL THOMAS
SCROOGE, Waterbury Films, Ltd. Prod.,
Cinema Center Films Presentation,
National General: MARGARET FURSE

Short Subjects

(Cartoons)

THE FURTHER ADVENTURES OF UNCLE
SAM: PART TWO, The Haboush Com-
pany, Goldstone Films: ROBERT
MITCHELL and DALE CASE, Producers
IS IT ALWAYS RIGHT TO BE
RIGHT?, Stephen Bosustow Prods.,
Lester A. Schoenfeld Films: NICK
BOSUSTOW, Producer
THE SHEPHERD, Cameron Guess and
Associates, Brandon Films: CAM-
ERON GUESS, Producer.

(Live Action Subjects)

THE RESURRECTION OF BRON-
CHO BILLY, University of Southern
California, Dept. of Cinema, Univer-
sal: JOHN LONGENECKER, Pro-
ducer
SHUT UP . . . I'M CRYING, Robert
Siegler Prods., Lester A. Schoenfeld
Films: ROBERT SIEGLER, Producer
STICKY MY FINGERS . . . FLEET MY
FEET, The American Film Institute,
Lester A. Schoenfeld Films: JOHN
HANCOCK, Producer

Documentary

(Short Subjects)

THE GIFTS, Richter-McBride Prods. For
the Water Quality Office of the Envi-
ronmental Protection Agency: ROB-
ERT MCBRIDE, Producer
INTERVIEWS WITH MY LAI VET-
ERANS, Laser Film Corp.: JOSEPH
STRICK, Producer
A LONG WAY FROM NOWHERE, Robert
Aller Prods.: BOB ALLER, Producer
OISIN, An Aengus Film: VIVIEN and
PATRICK CAREY, Producers
TIME IS RUNNING OUT, Gesellschaft für
bildende Filme: HORST DALLMAYR
and ROBERT MENEGOZ, Producers

(Features)

CHARIOTS OF THE GODS, Terra-
Filmkunst GmbH.; DR. HARALD
REINL, Producer
JACK JOHNSON, The Big Fights: JIM
JACOBS, Producer
KING: A FILMED RECORD . . .
MONTGOMERY TO MEMPHIS, Com-
monwealth United Prod.: ELY LAN-
DAU, Producer
SAY GOODBYE, A Wolper Prod.: DAVID
H. VOWELL, Producer
WOODSTOCK, A Wadleigh-Maurice
Ltd. Prod.: BOB MAURICE, Pro-
ducer

Special Visual Effects

PATTON, 20th Century-Fox: ALEX
WELDON
TORA! TORA! TORA!, 20th Century-
Fox: A. D. FLOWERS and L. B.
ABBOTT

Foreign Language Film Award

FIRST LOVE, Alfa Prods.-Seitz Film
Prod. (Switzerland)
HOA-BINH, Madeleine-Parc-La Gue-
ville-C.A.P.A.C. Prod. (France)
INVESTIGATION OF A CITIZEN

ABOVE SUSPICION, Vera Films Prod. (Italy)
PAIX SUR LES CHAMPS, Philippe Collette-E.G.C. Prod. (Belgium)
TRISTANA, Forbes Films, Ltd.-United Cineworld-Epoca Films-Talia Film-Les Films Corona-Selenia Cinematografica Prod. (Spain)

Honorary Awards
LILLIAN GISH for superlative artistry and for distinguished contribution to the progress of motion pictures
ORSON WELLES for superlative artistry and versatility in the creation of motion pictures

Irving G. Thalberg Memorial Award
INGMAR BERGMAN

Jean Hersholt Humanitarian Award
FRANK SINATRA

Scientific or Technical
Class I
None

Class II
LEONARD SOKOLOW and EDWARD H. REICHARD of Consolidated Film Industries for the concept and engineering of the Color Proofing Printer for motion pictures

Class III
SYLVANIA ELECTRIC PRODUCTS INC. for the development and introduction of a series of compact tungsten halogen lamps for motion picture production
B. J. LOSMANDY for the concept, design and application of microminiature solid state amplifier modules used in motion picture recording equipment
EASTMAN KODAK COMPANY and PHOTO ELECTRONICS CORPORATION for the design and engineering of an improved video color analyzer for motion picture laboratories
ELECTRO SOUND INCORPORATED for the design and introduction of the Series 8000 Sound System for motion picture theatres

1971

Nominations Announced: February 22, 1972
Awards Ceremony: April 10, 1972
Dorothy Chandler Pavilion, Los Angeles County Music Center
(MCs: Helen Hayes, Alan King, Sammy Davis, Jr., and Jack Lemmon)

Best Picture

A CLOCKWORK ORANGE, A Hawks Films, Ltd. Prod., Warner Bros.: STANLEY KUBRICK, Producer

FIDDLER ON THE ROOF, Mirisch-Cartier Prods., UA: NORMAN JEWISON, Producer

THE FRENCH CONNECTION, A Phillip D'Antoni Prod. in association with Schine-Moore Prods., 20th Century-Fox: PHILIP D'ANTONI, Producer

THE LAST PICTURE SHOW, BBS Prods., Columbia: STEPHEN J. FRIEDMAN, Producer

NICHOLAS AND ALEXANDRA, A Horizon Pictures Prod., Columbia: SAM SPIEGEL, Producer

Actor

PETER FINCH in *Sunday Bloody Sunday*, A Joseph Janni Prod., UA

GENE HACKMAN in *The French Connection*, A Philip D'Antoni Prod. in association with Schine-Moore Prods., 20th Century-Fox

WALTER MATTHAU in *Kotch*, A Kotch Company Prod., ABC Pictures Presentation, Cinerama

GEORGE C. SCOTT in *The Hospital*, A Howard Gottfried-Paddy Chayefsky Prod. in association with Arthur Hiller, UA

TOPOL in *Fiddler On The Roof*, A Mirisch-Cartier Prods., UA

LARGE CAPITAL LETTERS DENOTE WINNER

Actress

JULIE CHRISTIE in *McCabe & Mrs. Miller*, A Robert Altman-David Foster Prod., Warner Bros.

JANE FONDA in *Klute*, A Gus Prod., Warner Bros.

GLENDA JACKSON in *Sunday Bloody Sunday*, A Joseph Janni Prod., UA

VANESSA REDGRAVE in *Mary, Queen Of Scots*, A Hal Wallis-Universal Pictures, Ltd. Prod., Universal

JANET SUZMAN in *Nicholas And Alexandra*, A Horizon Pictures Prod., Columbia

Supporting Actor

JEFF BRIDGES in *The Last Picture Show*, BBS Prods., Columbia

LEONARD FREY in *Fiddler On the Roof*, Mirisch-Cartier Prods., UA

RICHARD JAECKEL in *Sometimes A Great Notion*, A Universal-Newman-Foreman Company Prod., Universal

BEN JOHNSON in *The Last Picture Show*, BBS Prods., Columbia

ROY SCHEIDER in *The French Connection*, A Philip D'Antoni Prod. in association with Schine-Moore Prods., 20th Century-Fox

Supporting Actress

ELLEN BURSTYN in *The Last Picture Show*, BBS Prods., Columbia

BARBARA HARRIS in *Who Is Harry Kellerman, And Why Is He Saying Those Terrible Things About Me?*, A Who Is Harry Kellerman Company

Prod., Cinema Center Films Presentation, National General

CLORIS LEACHMAN in *The Last Picture Show*, BBS Prods., Columbia

MARGARET LEIGHTON in *The Go-Between*, A World Film Services, Ltd. Prod., Columbia

ANN-MARGRET in *Carnal Knowledge*, Icarus Prods., Avco Embassy

Directing

PETER BOGDANOVICH for *The Last Picture Show*, BBS Prods., Columbia

WILLIAM FRIEDKIN for *The French Connection*, A Phillip D'Antoni Prod. in association with Schine-Moore Prods., 20th Century-Fox

NORMAN JEWISON for *Fiddler On The Roof*, Mirisch-Cartier Prods., UA

STANLEY KUBRICK for *A Clockwork Orange*, A Hawks Films, Ltd., Prod., Warner Bros.

JOHN SCHLESINGER for *Sunday Bloody Sunday*, A Joseph Janni Prod., UA

Writing

(Best Screenplay—based on material from another medium)

A CLOCKWORK ORANGE, A Hawks Films, Ltd. Prod., Warner Bros.: STANLEY KUBRICK

THE CONFORMIST, Mars Film Produzione, S.P.A.-Marianne Prods., Paramount: BERNARDO BERTOLUCCI

THE FRENCH CONNECTION, A Philip D'Antoni Prod. in association with Schine-Moore Prods., 20th Century-Fox: ERNEST TIDYMAN

THE GARDEN OF THE FINZI-CONTINIS, A Gianni Hecht Lucari-Arthur Cohn Prod., Cinema 5, Ltd.: UGO PIRRO and VITTORIO BONICELLI

THE LAST PICTURE SHOW, BBS Prods., Columbia: LARRY MCMURTRY and PETER BOGDANOVICH

(Best Story and Screenplay—based on factual material or material not previously published or produced)

THE HOSPITAL, A Howard Gottfried-Paddy Chayefsky Prod. in association with Arthur Hiller, UA: PADDY CHAYEFSKY

INVESTIGATION OF A CITIZEN ABOVE SUSPICION, A Vera Films, S.P.A. Prod., Columbia: ELIO PETRI and UGO PIRRO

KLUTE, A Gus Prod., Warner Bros.: ANDY and DAVE LEWIS

SUMMER OF '42, A Robert Mulligan-Richard Alan Roth Prod., Warner Bros.: HERMAN RAUCHER

SUNDAY BLOODY SUNDAY, A Joseph Janni Prod., UA: PENELOPE GILLIATT

Cinematography

FIDDLER ON THE ROOF, Mirisch-Cartier Prods., UA: OSWALD MORRIS

THE FRENCH CONNECTION, A Philip D'Antoni Prod. in association with Schine-Moore Prods., 20th Century-Fox: OWEN ROIZMAN

THE LAST PICTURE SHOW, BBS Prods., Columbia: ROBERT SURTEES

NICHOLAS AND ALEXANDRA, A Horizon Pictures Prod., Columbia: FREDDIE YOUNG

SUMMER OF '42, A Robert Mulligan-Richard Alan Roth Prod., Warner Bros.: ROBERT SURTEES

Art Direction—Set Decoration

THE ANDROMEDA STRAIN, A Universal-Robert Wise Prod., Universal: BORIS LEVEN and WILLIAM TUNTKE Set Decoration: RUBY LEVITT

BEDKNOBS AND BROOMSTICKS, Walt Disney Prods., Buena Vista Distribution Company: JOHN B. MANSBRIDGE and PETER ELLENSHAW

Set Decoration: EMILE KURI and HAL GAUSMAN

FIDDLER ON THE ROOF, Mirisch-Cartier Prods., UA: ROBERT BOYLE and MICHAEL STRINGER
Set Decoration: PETER LAMONT

MARY, QUEEN OF SCOTS, A Hal Wallis-Universal Pictures, Ltd. Prod., Universal: TERENCE MARSH and ROBERT CARTWRIGHT
Set Decoration: PETER HOWITT

NICHOLAS AND ALEXANDRA, A Horizon Pictures Prod., Columbia: JOHN BOX, ERNEST ARCHER, JACK MAXSTED and GIL PARRONDO
Set Decoration: VERNON DIXON

Sound

DIAMONDS ARE FOREVER, An Albert R. Broccoli-Harry Saltzman Prod., UA: GORDON K. MCCALLUM, JOHN MITCHELL and ALFRED J. OVERTON

FIDDLER ON THE ROOF, Mirisch-Cartier Prods., UA: GORDON K. McCALLUM and DAVID HILDYARD

THE FRENCH CONNECTION, A Philip D'Antoni Prod. in association with Schine-Moore Prods., 20th Century-Fox: THEODORE SODERBERG and CHRISTOPHER NEWMAN

KOTCH, A Kotch Prod., ABC Pictures Presentation, Cinerama: RICHARD PORTMAN and JACK SOLOMON

MARY, QUEEN OF SCOTS, A Hal Wallis-Universal Pictures, Ltd. Prod., Universal: BOB JONES and JOHN ALDRED

Film Editing

THE ANDROMEDA STRAIN, A Universal-Robert Wise Prod., Universal: STUART GILMORE and JOHN W. HOLMES

A CLOCKWORK ORANGE, A Hawks Films, Ltd., Prod., Warner Bros.: BILL BUTLER

THE FRENCH CONNECTION, A Philip D'Antoni Prod. in association with Schine-Moore Prods., 20th Century-Fox: JERRY GREENBERG

KOTCH, A Kotch Company Prod., ABC Pictures Presentation, Cinerama: RALPH E. WINTERS

SUMMER OF '42, A Robert Mulligan-Richard Alan Roth Prod., Warner Bros.: FOLMAR BLANGSTED

Music

(Best Original Dramatic Score)

MARY, QUEEN OF SCOTS, A Hal Wallis-Universal Pictures, Ltd. Prod., Universal: JOHN BARRY

NICHOLAS AND ALEXANDRA, A Horizon Pictures Prod., Columbia: RICHARD RODNEY BENNETT

SHAFT, Shaft Prods., Ltd., M-G-M: ISAAC HAYES

STRAW DOGS, A Talent Associates, Ltd.-Amerbroco Films, Ltd. Prod., ABC Pictures Presentation, Cinerama: JERRY FIELDING

SUMMER OF '42, A Robert Mulligan-Richard Alan Roth Prod., Warner Bros.: MICHEL LEGRAND

(Best Scoring: Adaptation and Original Song Score)

BEDKNOBS AND BROOMSTICKS, Walt Disney Prods., Buena Vista Distribution Company
Song Score by RICHARD M. SHERMAN and ROBERT B. SHERMAN
Adapted by IRWIN KOSTAL

THE BOY FRIEND, A Russflix, Ltd. Prod., M-G-M
Adapted by PETER MAXWELL DAVIES and PETER GREENWELL

FIDDLER ON THE ROOF, Mirisch-Cartier Prods., UA
Adapted by JOHN WILLIAMS

TCHAIKOVSKY, A Dimitri Tiomkin-Mosfilm Studios Prod.
Adapted by DIMITRI TIOMKIN

WILLY WONKA AND THE CHOCOLATE FACTORY, A Wolper Pictures, Ltd. Prod., Paramount
Song Score by LESLIE BRICUSSE and ANTHONY NEWLEY
Adapted by WALTER SCHARF

(Best Song)

THE AGE OF NOT BELIEVING from *Bedknobs And Broomsticks*, Walt Disney Prods., Buena Vista Distribution Company. Music and lyrics by RICHARD M. SHERMAN and ROBERT B. SHERMAN

ALL HIS CHILDREN from *Sometimes A Great Notion*, A Universal-Newman-Foreman Company Prod., Universal
Music by HENRY MANCINI
Lyrics by ALAN and MARILYN BERGMAN

BLESS THE BEASTS & CHILDREN from *Bless The Beasts & Children*, Columbia.
Music and lyrics by BARRY DeVORZON and PERRY BOTKIN, JR.

LIFE IS WHAT YOU MAKE IT from *Kotch*, A Kotch Company Production, ABC Pictures Presentation, Cinerama.
Music by MARVIN HAMLISCH
Lyrics by JOHNNY MERCER

THEME FROM SHAFT from *Shaft*, Shaft Prods., Ltd., M-G-M
Music and lyrics by ISAAC HAYES

Costume Design

BEDKNOBS AND BROOMSTICKS, Walt Disney Prods., Buena Vista Distribution Company: BILL THOMAS

DEATH IN VENICE, An Alfa Cinematografica-P.E.C.F. Prod., Warner Bros.: PIERO TOSI

MARY, QUEEN OF SCOTS, A Hal Wallis-Universal Pictures, Ltd. Prod., Universal: MARGARET FURSE

NICHOLAS AND ALEXANDRA, A Horizon Pictures Prod., Columbia:

YVONNE BLAKE and ANTONIO CASTILLO
WHAT'S THE MATTER WITH HELEN?, A Filmways-Raymax Prod., UA: MORTON HAACK

Short Subjects

(The designation of this category was changed from *Cartoons* to *Animated Films*.)

(Animated Films)

THE CRUNCH BIRD, Maxwell-Petok-Petrovich Prods., Regency Film Distributing Corp.: TED PETOK, Producer

EVOLUTION, National Film Board of Canada, Columbia: MICHAEL MILLS, Producer

THE SELFISH GIANT, Potterton Prods., Pyramid Films: PETER SANDER and MURRAY SHOSTAK, Producers

(Live Action Films)

GOOD MORNING, E/G Films, Seymour Borde & Associates: DENNY EVANS and KEN GREENWALD, Producers

THE REHEARSAL, A Cinema Verona Prod., Schoenfeld Film Distributing Corp.: STEPHEN F. VERONA, Producer

SENTINELS OF SILENCE, Producciones Concord, Paramount: MANUEL ARANGO and ROBERT AMRAM, Producers

Documentary

(Short Subjects)

ADVENTURES IN PERCEPTION, Han van Gelder Filmproduktie for Netherlands Information Service: HAN VAN GELDER, Producer

ART IS . . . , Henry Strauss Associates for Sears Roebuck Foundation: JULIAN KRAININ and DeWITT L. SAGE, JR., Producers

THE NUMBERS START WITH THE RIVER, A WH Picture for United States Information Agency: DONALD WRYE, Producer

SENTINELS OF SILENCE, Producciones Concord, Paramount: MANUEL ARANGO and ROBERT AMRAM, Producers

SOMEBODY WAITING, Snider Prods. for University of California Medical Film Library: HAL RINEY, DICK SNIDER and SHERWOOD OMENS, Producers

(Features)

ALASKA WILDERNESS LAKE, Alan Landsburg Prods.: ALAN LANDSBURG, Producer

THE HELLSTROM CHRONICLE, David L. Wolper Prods., Cinema 5, Ltd.: WALON GREEN, Producer

ON ANY SUNDAY, Bruce Brown Films-Solar Prods., Cinema 5, Ltd.: BRUCE BROWN, Producer

THE RA EXPEDITIONS, Swedish Broadcasting Company, Interwest Film Corp.: LENNART EHRENBORG and THOR HEYERDAHL, Producers

THE SORROW AND THE PITY, Television Rencontre-Norddeutscher Rundfunk-Television Swiss Romande, Cinema 5, Ltd.: MARCEL OPHULS, Producer

Special Visual Effects
(Not given as an Annual Award after this year)

BEDKNOBS AND BROOMSTICKS, Walt Disney Prods., Buena Vista Distribution Company: ALAN MALEY, EUSTACE LYCETT and DANNY LEE

WHEN DINOSAURS RULED THE EARTH, A Hammer Film Prod., Warner Bros.: JIM DANFORTH and ROGER DICKEN

Foreign Language Film Award
DODES'KA-DEN, A Toho Company, Ltd.-Yonki no Kai Prod. (Japan)

THE EMIGRANTS, A Svensk Filmindustri Prod. (Sweden)

THE GARDEN OF THE FINZI-CONTINIS, A Gianni Hecht Lucari-Arthur Cohn Prod. (Italy)

THE POLICEMAN, An Ephi-Israeli Motion Picture Studios Prod. (Israel)

TCHAIKOVSKY, A Dimitri Tiomkin-Mosfilm Studios Prod. (U.S.S.R.)

Honorary Award
CHARLES CHAPLIN for the incalculable effect he has had in making motion pictures the art form of this century

Irving G. Thalberg Memorial Award
None

Jean Hersholt Humanitarian Award
None

Scientific or Technical
Class I
None

Class II
JOHN N. WILKINSON of Optical Radiation Corporation for the development and engineering of a system of xenon arc lamphouses for motion picture projection

Class III
THOMAS JEFFERSON HUTCHINSON, JAMES R. ROCHESTER and FENTON HAMILTON for the development and introduction of the Sunbrute system of xenon arc lamps for location lighting in motion picture production

PHOTO RESEARCH, a Division of Kollmorgen Corporation, for the development and introduction of the film-lens balanced Three Color Meter

ROBERT D. AUGUSTE and CINEMA PRODUCTS CO. for the development and introduction of a new crystal controlled lightweight motor for the 35mm motion picture Arriflex camera

PRODUCERS SERVICE CORPORATION and CONSOLIDATED FILM INDUSTRIES; and to CINEMA RESEARCH CORPORATION and RESEARCH PRODUCTS, INC. for the engineering and implementation of fully automated blow-up motion picture printing systems

CINEMA PRODUCTS CO. for a control motor to actuate zoom lenses on motion picture cameras

1972

Nominations Announced: February 12, 1973
(Song nominations: March 5, 1973)
Awards Ceremony: March 27, 1973
Dorothy Chandler Pavilion, Los Angeles County Music Center
(MCs: Carol Burnett, Michael Caine, Charlton Heston, and Rock Hudson)

Best Picture

CABARET, An ABC Pictures Production, Allied Artists: CY FEUER, Producer

DELIVERANCE, Warner Bros.: JOHN BOORMAN, Producer

THE EMIGRANTS, A Svensk Filmindustri Production, Warner Bros.: BENGT FORSLUND, Producer

THE GODFATHER, An Albert S. Ruddy Production, Paramount: ALBERT S. RUDDY, Producer

SOUNDER, Radnitz/Mattel Productions, 20th Century-Fox: ROBERT B. RADNITZ, Producer

Actor

MARLON BRANDO in *The Godfather,* An Albert S. Ruddy Production, Paramount

MICHAEL CAINE in *Sleuth,* A Palomar Pictures International Production, 20th Century-Fox

LAURENCE OLIVIER in *Sleuth,* A Palomar Pictures International Production, 20th Century-Fox

PETER O'TOOLE in *The Ruling Class,* A Keep Films, Ltd. Production, Avco Embassy

PAUL WINFIELD in *Sounder,* Radnitz/Mattel Productions, 20th Century-Fox

Actress

LIZA MINNELLI in *Cabaret,* An

LARGE CAPITAL LETTERS DENOTE WINNER

ABC Pictures Production, Allied Artists

DIANA ROSS in *Lady Sings The Blues,* A Motown-Weston-Furie Production, Paramount

MAGGIE SMITH in *Travels With My Aunt,* Robert Fryer Productions, Metro-Goldwyn-Mayer

CICELY TYSON in *Sounder,* Radnitz/Mattel Productions, 20th Century-Fox

LIV ULLMANN in *The Emigrants,* A Svensk Filmindustri Production, Warner Bros.

Supporting Actor

EDDIE ALBERT in *The Heartbreak Kid,* A Palomar Pictures International Production, 20th Century-Fox

JAMES CAAN in *The Godfather,* An Albert S. Ruddy Production, Paramount

ROBERT DUVALL in *The Godfather,* An Albert S. Ruddy Production, Paramount

JOEL GREY in *Cabaret,* An ABC Pictures Production, Allied Artists

AL PACINO in *The Godfather,* An Albert S. Ruddy Production, Paramount

Supporting Actress

JEANNIE BERLIN in *The Heartbreak Kid,* A Palomar Pictures International Production, 20th Century-Fox

EILEEN HECKART in *Butterflies Are Free,* Frankovich Productions, Columbia

GERALDINE PAGE in *Pete 'N' Tillie,* A Universal-Martin Ritt-Julius J. Epstein Production, Universal

SUSAN TYRRELL in *Fat City,* Rastar Productions, Columbia

SHELLEY WINTERS in *The Poseidon Adventure,* An Irwin Allen Production, 20th Century-Fox

Directing

JOHN BOORMAN for *Deliverance,* Warner Bros.

FRANCIS FORD COPPOLA for *The Godfather,* An Albert S. Ruddy Production, Paramount

BOB FOSSE for *Cabaret,* An ABC Pictures Production, Allied Artists

JOSEPH L. MANKIEWICZ for *Sleuth,* A Palomar Pictures International Production, 20th Century-Fox

JAN TROELL for *The Emigrants,* A Svensk Filmindustri Production, Warner Bros.

Writing

(Best Screenplay—based on material from another medium)

CABARET, An ABC Pictures Prod., Allied Artists: JAY ALLEN

THE EMIGRANTS, A Svensk Filmindustri Prod., Warner Bros.: JAN TROELL and BENGT FORSLUND

THE GODFATHER, An Albert S. Ruddy Prod., Paramount: MARIO PUZO and FRANCIS FORD COPPOLA

PETE 'N' TILLIE, A Universal-Martin Ritt-Julius J. Epstein Prod., Universal: JULIUS J. EPSTEIN

SOUNDER, Radnitz/Mattel Prods., 20th Century-Fox: LONNE ELDER, III

(Best Story and Screenplay—based on factual material or material not previously published or produced)

THE CANDIDATE, A Redford-Ritchie Prod., Warner Bros.: JEREMY LARNER

THE DISCREET CHARM OF THE BOURGEOISIE, A Serge Silberman Prod., 20th Century-Fox: LUIS BUÑUEL in collaboration with JEAN-CLAUDE CARRIERE

LADY SINGS THE BLUES, A Motown-Weston-Furie Prod., Paramount: TERENCE MCCLOY, CHRIS CLARK and SUZANNE DE PASSE

MURMUR OF THE HEART, A Nouvelles Editions De Films-Marianne Productions-Vides Cinematografica-Franz Seitz Filmproduktion, Continental Distributing: LOUIS MALLE

YOUNG WINSTON, An Open Road Films, Ltd. Prod., Columbia: CARL FOREMAN

Cinematography

BUTTERFLIES ARE FREE, Frankovich Productions, Columbia: CHARLES B. LANG

CABARET, An ABC Pictures Production, Allied Artists: GEOFFREY UNSWORTH

THE POSEIDON ADVENTURE, An Irwin Allen Production, 20th Century-Fox: HAROLD E. STINE

"1776," A Jack L. Warner Production, Columbia: HARRY STRADLING, JR.

TRAVELS WITH MY AUNT, Robert Fryer Productions, Metro-Goldwyn-Mayer: DOUGLAS SLOCOMBE

Art Direction—Set Decoration

CABARET, An ABC Pictures Production, Allied Artists: ROLF ZEHETBAUER and JURGEN KIEBACH Set Decoration: HERBERT STRABEL

LADY SINGS THE BLUES, A Motown-Weston-Furie Production, Paramount: CARL ANDERSON Set Decoration: REG ALLEN

THE POSEIDON ADVENTURE, An Irwin Allen Production, 20th Century-Fox: WILLIAM CREBER

Set Decoration: RAPHAEL BRETTON
TRAVELS WITH MY AUNT, Robert Fryer
Productions, Metro-Goldwyn-Mayer:
JOHN BOX, GIL PARRONDO and ROB-
ERT W. LAING
YOUNG WINSTON, An Open Road
Films, Ltd. Production, Columbia:
DON ASHTON, GEOFFREY DRAKE,
JOHN GRAYSMARK and WILLIAM
HUTCHINSON
Set Decoration: PETER JAMES

Sound

BUTTERFLIES ARE FREE, Frankovich
Prods., Columbia: ARTHUR PIAN-
TADOSI and CHARLES KNIGHT
CABARET, An ABC Pictures Produc-
tion, Allied Artists: ROBERT
KNUDSON and DAVID
HILDYARD
THE CANDIDATE, A Redford-Ritchie
Prod., Warner Bros.: RICHARD
PORTMAN and GENE CANTAMESSA
THE GODFATHER, An Albert S. Ruddy
Prod., Paramount: BUD GRENZBACH,
RICHARD PORTMAN and CHRISTOPHER
NEWMAN
THE POSEIDON ADVENTURE, An Irwin
Allen Prod., 20th Century-Fox:
THEODORE SODERBERG and HERMAN
LEWIS

Film Editing

CABARET, An ABC Pictures Produc-
tion, Allied Artists: DAVID
BRETHERTON
DELIVERANCE, Warner Bros.: TOM
PRIESTLEY
THE GODFATHER, An Albert S. Ruddy
Production, Paramount: WILLIAM
REYNOLDS and PETER ZINNER
THE HOT ROCK, A Landers-Roberts
Production, 20th Century-Fox:
FRANK P. KELLER and FRED W.
BERGER
THE POSEIDON ADVENTURE, An Irwin

Allen Production, 20th Century-Fox:
HAROLD F. KRESS

Music

(Best Original Dramatic Score)

IMAGES, A Hemdale Group, Ltd.-
Lion's Gate Films Prod., Columbia:
JOHN WILLIAMS
LIMELIGHT, A Charles Chaplin
Prod., Columbia: CHARLES CHAP-
LIN, RAYMOND RASCH and
LARRY RUSSELL
NAPOLEON AND SAMANTHA, A Walt
Disney Prods., Buena Vista Dis-
tribution Company: BUDDY BAKER
THE POSEIDON ADVENTURE, An Irwin
Allen Prod., 20th Century-Fox: JOHN
WILLIAMS
SLEUTH, A Palomar Pictures Interna-
tional Prod., 20th Century-Fox:
JOHN ADDISON

(Best Scoring: Adaptation and
Original Song Score)

CABARET, An ABC Pictures Prod.,
Allied Artists. Adapted by RALPH
BURNS
LADY SINGS THE BLUES, A Motown-
Weston-Furie Prod., Paramount.
Adapted by GIL ASKEY
MAN OF LA MANCHA, A PEA Produ-
zioni Europee Associate Prod., UA.
Adapted by LAURENCE ROSENTHAL

(Best Song)

BEN from *Ben,* BCP Productions, Cin-
erama
Music by WALTER SCHARF
Lyrics by DON BLACK
COME FOLLOW, FOLLOW ME from *The
Little Ark,* Robert Radnitz Produc-
tions, Ltd., Cinema Center Films
Presentation, National General
Music by FRED KARLIN
Lyrics by MARSHA KARLIN
MARMALADE, MOLASSES & HONEY from
The Life And Times Of Judge Roy

Bean, A First Artists Production Company, Ltd. Production, National General
Music by MAURICE JARRE
Lyrics by MARILYN and ALAN BERGMAN
THE MORNING AFTER from *The Poseidon Adventure,* An Irwin Allen Production, 20th Century-Fox
Music and lyrics by AL KASHA and JOEL HIRSCHHORN
STRANGE ARE THE WAYS OF LOVE from *The Stepmother,* Magic Eye of Hollywood Productions, Crown International
Music by SAMMY FAIN
Lyrics by PAUL FRANCIS WEBSTER

Costume Design

THE GODFATHER, An Albert S. Ruddy Prod., Paramount: ANNA HILL JOHNSTONE
LADY SINGS THE BLUES, A Motown-Weston-Furie Prod., Paramount: BOB MACKIE, RAY AGHAYAN and NORMA KOCH
THE POSEIDON ADVENTURE, An Irwin Allen Prod., 20th Century-Fox: PAUL ZASTUPNEVICH
TRAVELS WITH MY AUNT, Robert Fryer Prods., Metro-Goldwyn-Mayer: ANTHONY POWELL
YOUNG WINSTON, An Open Road Films, Ltd. Prod., Columbia: ANTHONY MENDLESON

Short Subjects

(Animated Films)
A CHRISTMAS CAROL, A Richard Williams Production, American Broadcasting Company Film Services: RICHARD WILLIAMS, Producer
KAMA SUTRA RIDES AGAIN, Bob Godfrey Films, Ltd., Lion International Films: BOB GODFREY, Producer

TUP TUP, A Zagreb Film-Corona Cinematografica Production, Manson Distributing Corp: NEDELJKO DRAGIC, Producer

(Live Action Films)
FROG STORY, Gidron Productions, Schoenfeld Film Distributing Corp: RON SATLOF and RAY GIDEON, Producers
NORMAN ROCKWELL'S WORLD . . . AN AMERICAN DREAM, A Concepts Unlimited Production, Columbia: RICHARD BARCLAY, Producer
SOLO, Pyramid Films, United Artists: DAVID ADAMS, Producer

Documentary

(Short Subjects)
HUNDERTWASSER'S RAINY DAY, an Argos Films-Peter Schamoni Film Prod: PETER SCHAMONI, Producer
K-Z, A Nexus Film Production: GIORGIO TREVES, Producer
SELLING OUT, A Unit Productions Film: TADEUSZ JAWORSKI, Producer
THIS TINY WORLD, A Charles Huguenot van der Linden Production: CHARLES and MARTINA HUGUENOT VAN DER LINDEN, Producers
THE TIDE OF TRAFFIC, A BP-Greenpark Production: HUMPHREY SWINGLER, Producer

(Features)
APE AND SUPER-APE, A Bert Haanstra Film Production, Netherlands Ministry of Culture, Recreation and Social Welfare: BERT HAANSTRA, Producer
MALCOLM X, A Marvin Worth Production, Warner Bros: MARVIN WORTH and ARNOLD PERL, Producers
MANSON, Merrick International Pictures: ROBERT HENDRICKSON and

LAURENCE MERRICK, Producers
MARJOE, A Cinema X Production, Cinema 5, Ltd: HOWARD SMITH and SARAH KERNOCHAN, Producers
THE SILENT REVOLUTION, A Leonaris Film Production: ECKEHARD MUNCK, Producer

Foreign Language Film Award
THE DAWNS HERE ARE QUIET, A Gorky Film Studios Prod. (U.S.S.R.).
THE DISCREET CHARM OF THE BOURGEOISIE, A Serge Silberman Prod. (France)
I LOVE YOU ROSA, A Noah Films Ltd. Prod. (Israel)
MY DEAREST SEÑORITA, An El Iman Prod. (Spain)
THE NEW LAND, A Svensk Filmindustri Prod. (Sweden)

Honorary Awards
CHARLES S. BOREN, Leader for 38 years of the industry's enlightened labor relations and architect of its policy of non-discrimination. With the respect and affection of all who work in films.
EDWARD G. ROBINSON who achieved greatness as a player, a patron of the arts and a dedicated citizen . . . in sum, a Renaissance man. From his friends in the industry he loves.

Special Achievement
(New Category)

(Created as an "other" Award—not necessarily given each year and hence no nominations—to honor achievements formerly recognized in the Special Visual Effects and Sound Effects categories.)
Visual Effects: L.B. ABBOTT and A.D. FLOWERS for *The Poseidon*
Adventure, an Irwin Allen Production, 20th Century-Fox

Irving G. Thalberg Memorial Award
None

Jean Hersholt Humanitarian Award
ROSALIND RUSSELL

Scientific or Technical
Class I
None
Class II
JOSEPH E. BLUTH for research and development in the field of electronic photography and transfer of video tape to motion picture film
EDWARD H. REICHARD and HOWARD T. LA ZARE of Consolidated Film Industries, and EDWARD EFRON of IBM for the engineering of a computerized light valve monitoring system for motion picture printing
PANAVISION INCORPORATED for the development and engineering of the Panaflex motion picture camera
Class III
PHOTO RESEARCH, a Division of Kollmorgen Corporation, and PSC TECHNOLOGY INC., Acme Products Division, for the Spectra Film Gate Photometer for motion picture printers
CARTER EQUIPMENT COMPANY, INC. and *RAM*TRONICS for the RAMtronics light-valve photometer for motion picture printers
DAVID DEGENKOLB, HARRY LARSON, MANFRED MICHELSON and FRED SCOBEY of De-Luxe General Incorporated for the development of a computerized motion picture printer and process control system

JIRO MUKAI and RYUSHO HIROSE of Canon, Inc. and WILTON R. HOLM of the AMPTP Motion Picture and Television Research Center for development of the Canon Macro Zoom Lens for motion picture photography

PHILIP V. PALMQUIST and LEONARD L. OLSON of the 3M Company, and FRANK P. CLARK of the AMPTP Motion Picture and Television Research Center for development of the Nextel simulated blood for motion picture color photography

E. H. GEISSLER and G. M. BERGGREN of Wil-Kin Inc. for engineering of the Ultra-Vision Motion Picture Theater Projection System

1973

Nominations Announced: February 19, 1974
Awards Ceremony: April 2, 1974
Dorothy Chandler Pavilion, Los Angeles County Music Center
(MCs: John Huston, David Niven, Burt Reynolds, and Diana Ross)

Best Picture

AMERICAN GRAFFITI, A Universal-Lucasfilm, Ltd.-Coppola Company Prod., Universal: FRANCIS FORD COPPOLA, Producer. GARY KURTZ, Co-Producer

CRIES AND WHISPERS, A Svenska Film-institutet-Cinematograph AB Prod., New World Pictures: INGMAR BERGMAN, Producer

THE EXORCIST, Hoya Prods., Warner Bros: WILLIAM PETER BLATTY, Producer

THE STING, A Universal-Bill/Phillips-George Roy Hill Film Prod., Zanuck/Brown Presentation, Universal: TONY BILL, MICHAEL and JULIA PHILLIPS, Producers

A TOUCH OF CLASS, Brut Prods., Avco Embassy: MELVIN FRANK, Producer

Actor

MARLON BRANDO in *Last Tango In Paris,* A PEA Produzioni Europee Associate S.A.S.-Les Productions Artistes Associes S.A. Prod., UA

JACK LEMMON in *Save The Tiger,* Filmways-Jalem-Cirandinha Prods., Paramount

JACK NICHOLSON in *The Last Detail,* An Acrobat Films Prod., Columbia

AL PACINO in *Serpico,* A Produzioni De Laurentiis International Manufacturing Company S.p.A. Prod., Paramount

LARGE CAPITAL LETTERS DENOTE WINNER

ROBERT REDFORD in *The Sting,* A Universal-Bill/Phillips-George Roy Hill Film Production, Zanuck/Brown Presentation, Universal

Actress

ELLEN BURSTYN in *The Exorcist,* Hoya Prods., Warner Bros.

GLENDA JACKSON in *A Touch Of Class,* Brut Prods., Avco Embassy

MARSHA MASON in *Cinderella Liberty,* A Sanford Prod., 20th Century-Fox

BARBRA STREISAND in *The Way We Were,* Rastar Prods., Columbia

JOANNE WOODWARD in *Summer Wishes, Winter Dreams,* A Rastar Pictures Prod., Columbia

Supporting Actor

VINCENT GARDENIA in *Bang The Drum Slowly,* A Rosenfield Production, Paramount

JACK GILFORD in *Save The Tiger,* Filways-Jalem-Cirandinha Productions, Paramount

JOHN HOUSEMAN in *The Paper Chase,* Thompson-Paul Productions, 20th Century-Fox

JASON MILLER in *The Exorcist,* Hoya Productions, Warner Bros.

RANDY QUAID in *The Last Detail,* An Acrobat Films Prod., Columbia

Supporting Actress

LINDA BLAIR in *The Exorcist,* Hoya Prods., Warner Bros.

CANDY CLARK in *American Graffiti,* A

Universal-Lucasfilm, Ltd.-Coppola
Company Prod., Universal

MADELINE KAHN in *Paper Moon,* A
Directors Company Prod., Paramount

TATUM O'NEAL in *Paper Moon,* A
Directors Company Prod., Paramount

SYLVIA SIDNEY in *Summer Wishes,
Winter Dreams,* A Rastar Pictures
Prod., Columbia

Directing

INGMAR BERGMAN for *Cries And Whis-
pers,* A Svenska Filminstitutet-
Cinematograph AB Prod., New
World Pictures

BERNARDO BERTOLUCCI for *Last Tango
In Paris,* A PEA Produzioni Europee
Associate S.A.S.-Les Productions
Artistes Associes S.A. Prod., UA

WILLIAM FRIEDKIN for *The Exorcist,*
Hoya Prods., Warner Bros.

GEORGE ROY HILL for *The Sting,* A
Universal-Bill/Phillips-George Roy
Hill Film Prod., Zanuck/Brown Pre-
sentation, Universal

GEORGE LUCAS for *American Graffiti,* A
Universal-Lucasfilm, Ltd.-Coppola
Company Prod., Universal

Writing

(Best Screenplay—based on material
from another medium)

THE EXORCIST, Hoya Prods.,
Warner Bros: WILLIAM PETER
BLATTY

THE LAST DETAIL, An Acrobat Films
Prod., Columbia: ROBERT TOWNE

THE PAPER CHASE, Thompson-Paul
Prods., 20th Century-Fox: JAMES
BRIDGES

PAPER MOON, A Directors Company
Prod., Paramount: ALVIN SARGENT

SERPICO, A Produzioni De Laurentiis
International Manufacturing Com-

pany S.p.A. Prod., Paramount:
WALDO SALT and NORMAN WEXLER

(Best Story and Screenplay—based on
factual material or material not previously published or produced)

AMERICAN GRAFFITI, A Universal-
Lucasfilm, Ltd.-Coppola Company
Prod., Universal: GEORGE LUCAS,
GLORIA KATZ and WILLARD HUYCK

CRIES AND WHISPERS, A Svenska Film-
institutet-Cinematograph AB Prod.,
New World Pictures: INGMAR BERG-
MAN

SAVE THE TIGER, Filmways-Jalem-
Cirandinha Prods., Paramount:
STEVE SHAGAN

THE STING, A Universal-Bill/Phillips-
George Roy Hill Film Prod., Zan-
uck/Brown Presentation, Universal:
DAVID S. WARD

A TOUCH OF CLASS, Brut Productions,
Avco Embassy: MELVIN FRANK and
JACK ROSE

Cinematography

CRIES AND WHISPERS, A Svenska
Filminstitutet-Cinematograph AB
Prod., New World Pictures: SVEN
NYKVIST

THE EXORCIST, Hoya Prods., Warner
Bros: OWEN ROIZMAN

JONATHAN LIVINGSTON SEAGULL, A
JLS Limited Partnership Prod., Paramount: JACK COUFFER

THE STING, A Universal-Bill/Phillips-
George Roy Hill Film Prod., Zan-
uck/Brown Presentation, Universal:
ROBERT SURTEES

THE WAY WE WERE, Rastar Prods., Columbia: HARRY STRADLING, JR

Art Direction—Set Decoration

BROTHER SUN SISTER MOON, Euro Inter-
national Films-Vic Film (Prods.),
Ltd., Paramount:LORENZO MONGI-
ARDINO and GIANNI QUARANTA

Set Decoration: CARMELO PATRONO
THE EXORCIST, Hoya Prods., Warner
Bros: BILL MALLEY
Set Decoration: JERRY WUNDERLICH
THE STING, A Universal-Bill/Phillips-
George Roy Hill Film Prod., Zan-
uck/Brown Presentation, Universal:
HENRY BUMSTEAD
Set Decoration: JAMES PAYNE
TOM SAWYER, An Arthur P. Jacobs
Prod., Reader's Digest Presentation,
UA: PHILIP JEFFERIES
Set Decoration: ROBERT DE VESTEL
THE WAY WE WERE, Rastar Prods., Co-
lumbia: STEPHEN GRIMES
Set Decoration: WILLIAM KIERNAN

Sound

THE DAY OF THE DOLPHIN, Icarus
Prods., Avco Embassy: RICHARD
PORTMAN and LAWRENCE O. JOST
THE EXORCIST, Hoya Prods.,
Warner Bros.: ROBERT KNUDSON
and CHRIS NEWMAN
THE PAPER CHASE, Thompson-Paul
Prods., 20th Century-Fox: DONALD
O. MITCHELL and LAWRENCE O. JOST
PAPER MOON, A Directors Company
Prod., Paramount: RICHARD PORT-
MAN and LES FRESHOLTZ
THE STING, A Universal-Bill/Phillips-
George Roy Hill Film Prod., Zan-
uck/Brown Presentation, Universal:
RONALD K. PIERCE and ROBERT BER-
TRAND

Film Editing

AMERICAN GRAFFITI, A Universal-
Lucasfilm, Ltd.-Coppola Company
Prod., Universal: VERNA FIELDS and
MARCIA LUCAS
THE DAY OF THE JACKAL, Warwick
Film Prods., Ltd.-Universal Prods.
France S.A., Universal: RALPH
KEMPLEN
THE EXORCIST, Hoya Prods., Warner
Bros: JORDAN LEONDOPOULOS, BUD

SMITH, EVAN LOTTMAN and NORMAN
GAY
JONATHAN LIVINGSTON SEAGULL, A
JLS Limited Partnership Prod., Para-
mount: FRANK P. KELLER and JAMES
GALLOWAY
THE STING, A Universal-Bill/Phillips-
George Roy Hill Film Prod., Zan-
uck/Brown Presentation, Universal:
WILLIAM REYNOLDS

Music

(Best Original Dramatic Score)

CINDERELLA LIBERTY, A Sanford
Prod., 20th Century-Fox: JOHN
WILLIAMS
THE DAY OF THE DOLPHIN, Icarus
Prods., Avco Embassy: GEORGES
DELERUE
PAPILLON, A Corona-General Produc-
tion Company Prod., Allied Artists:
JERRY GOLDSMITH
A TOUCH OF CLASS, Brut Prods., Avco
Embassy: JOHN CAMERON
THE WAY WE WERE, Rastar Prods.,
Columbia: MARVIN HAMLISCH

(Best Scoring: Original Song Score
and/or Adaptation)

JESUS CHRIST SUPERSTAR, A Universal-
Norman Jewison-Robert Stigwood
Prod., Universal:
Adapted by ANDRÉ PREVIN, HERBERT
SPENCER and ANDREW LLOYD WEB-
BER
THE STING, A Universal-Bill/Phillips-
George Roy Hill Film Prods., Zan-
uck/Brown Presentation, Universal:
Adapted by MARVIN HAMLISCH
TOM SAWYER, An Arthur P. Jacobs
Prod., Reader's Digest Presentation,
UA:
Song Score by RICHARD M. SHERMAN
and ROBERT B. SHERMAN. Adapted
by JOHN WILLIAMS

(Best Song)

ALL THAT LOVE WENT TO WASTE from

A Touch Of Class, Brut Prods.,
Avco Embassy
Music by GEORGE BARRIE
Lyrics by SAMMY CAHN
LIVE AND LET DIE from *Live And Let Die,* Eon Prods., UA
Music and lyrics by PAUL and LINDA MCCARTNEY
LOVE from *Robin Hood,* Walt Disney Prods., Buena Vista Distribution Company
Music by GEORGE BRUNS
Lyrics by FLOYD HUDDLESTON
THE WAY WE WERE from *The Way We Were,* Rastar Prods., Columbia
Music by MARVIN HAMLISCH
Lyrics by ALAN and MARILYN BERGMAN
NICE TO BE AROUND from *Cinderella Liberty,* A Sanford Prod., 20th Century-Fox
Music by JOHN WILLIAMS
Lyrics by PAUL WILLIAMS

Costume Design

CRIES AND WHISPERS, A Svenska Filminstitutet-Cinematograph AB Prod., New World Pictures: MARIK VOS
LUDWIG, A Mega Film S.p.A. Prod., Metro-Goldwyn-Mayer: PIERO TOSI
THE STING, A Universal-Bill/Phillips-George Roy Hill Film Prod., Zanuck/Brown Presentation, Universal: EDITH HEAD
TOM SAWYER, An Arthur P. Jacobs Prod., Reader's Digest Presentation, UA: DONFELD
THE WAY WE WERE Rastar Prods., Columbia: DOROTHY JEAKINS and MOSS MABRY

Short Subjects
(Animated Films)
FRANK FILM, A Frank Mouris Production: FRANK MOURIS, Producer
THE LEGEND OF JOHN HENRY, A Ste-

phen Bosustow-Pyramid Films Prod: NICK BOSUSTOW and DAVID ADAMS, Producers
PULCINELLA, A Luzzati-Gianini Prod: EMANUELE LUZZATI and GUILIO GIANINI, Producers

(Live Action Films)
THE BOLERO, An Allan Miller Production: ALLAN MILLER and WILLIAM FERTIK, Producers
CLOCKMAKER, James Street Prods. Ltd: RICHARD GAYER, Producer
LIFE TIMES NINE, Insight Prods: PEN DENSHAM and JOHN WATSON, Producers

Documentary
(Short Subjects)
BACKGROUND, D'Avino and Fucci-Stone Prods.: CARMEN D'AVINO, Producer
CHILDREN AT WORK, (Paisti Ag Obair), Gael-Linn Films: LOUIS MARCUS, Producer
CHRISTO'S VALLEY CURTAIN, A Maysles Films Prod: ALBERT and DAVID MAYSLES, Producers
FOUR STONES FOR KANEMITSU, A Tamarind Prod: (Producer credit in controversy)
PRINCETON: A SEARCH FOR ANSWERS, Krainin-Sage Prods. JULIAN KRAININ and DeWITT L. SAGE, JR., Producers

(Features)
ALWAYS A NEW BEGINNING, Goodell Motion Pictures: JOHN D. GOODELL, Producer
BATTLE OF BERLIN, Chronos Film: BENGT VON ZUR MUEHLEN, Producer
THE GREAT AMERICAN COWBOY, Kieth Merrill Associates-Rodeo Film Prods: KIETH MERRILL, Producer
JOURNEY TO THE OUTER LIMITS, the National Geographic Society and

Wolper Prods: ALEX GRASSHOFF, Producer

WALLS OF FIRE, Mentor Prods.: GER-TRUDE ROSS MARKS and EDMUND F. PENNEY, Producers

Foreign Language Film Award

DAY FOR NIGHT, A Les Films Du Carrosse-P.E.C.F. (Paris)-P.I.C. (Rome) Prod. (France)

THE HOUSE ON CHELOUCHE STREET, A Noah Films Prod. (Israel)

L'INVITATION, A Groupe 5 Geneve-Television Suisse Romande-Citel Films-Planfilm (Paris) Prod. (Switzerland)

THE PEDESTRIAN, An ALFA Glarus-MFG-Switz-Zev Braun Prod. (Federal Republic of Germany)

TURKISH DELIGHT, A Rob Houwer Film Prod. (The Netherlands)

Honorary Awards

HENRI LANGLOIS for his devotion to the art of film, his massive contributions in preserving its past and his unswerving faith in its future

GROUCHO MARX in recognition of his brilliant creativity and for the unequalled achievements of the Marx Brothers in the art of motion picture comedy

Special Achievement
None

Irving G. Thalberg Memorial Award
LAWRENCE WEINGARTEN

Jean Hersholt Humanitarian Award
LEW WASSERMAN

Scientific or Technical
Class I
None

Class II

JOACHIM GERB and ERICH KASTNER of The Arnold and Richter Company for the development and engineering of the Arriflex 35BL motion-picture camera

MAGNA-TECH ELECTRONIC CO., INC. for the engineering and development of a high-speed re-recording system for motion-picture production

WILLIAM W. VALLIANT of PSC Technology Inc., HOWARD F. OTT of Eastman Kodak Company, and GERRY DIEBOLD of The Richmark Camera Service Inc. for the development of a liquid-gate system for motion-picture printers

HAROLD A. SCHEIB, CLIFFORD H. ELLIS and ROGER W. BANKS of Research Products Incorporated for the concept and engineering of the Model 2101 optical printer for motion-picture optical effects

Class III

ROSCO LABORATORIES, INC. for the technical advances and the development of a complete system of light-control materials for motion-picture photography

RICHARD H. VETTER of the Todd-AO Corporation for the design of an improved anamorphic focusing system for motion-picture photography

1974

Nominations Announced: February 24, 1975
Awards Ceremony: April 8, 1975
Dorothy Chandler Pavilion, Los Angeles County Music Center
(MCs: Sammy Davis, Jr., Bob Hope, Shirley MacLaine, and Frank Sinatra)

Best Picture

CHINATOWN, A Robert Evans Production, Paramount: ROBERT EVANS, Producer

THE CONVERSATION, A Directors Company Production, Paramount: FRANCIS FORD COPPOLA, Producer. FRED ROOS, Co-Producer

THE GODFATHER PART II, A Coppola Company Production, Paramount: FRANCIS FORD COPPOLA, Producer. GRAY FREDERICKSON and FRED ROOS, Co-Producers

LENNY, A Marvin Worth Production, United Artists: MARVIN WORTH, Producer

THE TOWERING INFERNO, An Irwin Allen Production, 20th Century-Fox/Warner Bros: IRWIN ALLEN, Producer

Actor

ART CARNEY in *Harry and Tonto,* 20th Century-Fox

ALBERT FINNEY in *Murder On The Orient Express,* A G.W. Films, Ltd. Production, Paramount

DUSTIN HOFFMAN in *Lenny,* A Marvin Worth Production, United Artists

JACK NICHOLSON in *Chinatown,* A Robert Evans Production, Paramount

AL PACINO in *The Godfather Part II,* A Coppola Company Production, Paramount

LARGE CAPITAL LETTERS DENOTE WINNER

Actress

ELLEN BURSTYN in *Alice Doesn't Live Here Anymore,* Warner Bros.

DIAHANN CARROLL in *Claudine,* Third World Cinema Productions in association with Joyce Selznick and Tina Pine, 20th Century-Fox

FAYE DUNAWAY in *Chinatown,* A Robert Evans Production, Paramount

VALERIE PERRINE in *Lenny,* A Marvin Worth Production, United Artists

GENA ROWLANDS in *A Woman Under The Influence,* A Faces International Films Production

Supporting Actor

FRED ASTAIRE in *The Towering Inferno,* An Irwin Allen Production, 20th Century-Fox/Warner Bros.

JEFF BRIDGES in *Thunderbolt And Lightfoot,* A Malpaso Company Film Production, United Artists

ROBERT DE NIRO in *The Godfather Part II,* A Coppola Company Production, Paramount

MICHAEL V. GAZZO in *The Godfather Part II,* A Coppola Company Production, Paramount

LEE STRASBERG in *The Godfather Part II,* A Coppola Company Production, Paramount

Supporting Actress

INGRID BERGMAN in *Murder On The Orient Express,* A G.W. Films, Ltd. Production, Paramount

527

VALENTINA CORTESE in *Day For Night,* A Les Films Du Carrosse and P.E.C.F., Paris; P.I.C., Rome Prod., Warner Bros.

MADELINE KAHN in *Blazing Saddles,* Warner Bros.

DIANE LADD in *Alice Doesn't Live Here Anymore,* Warner Bros.

TALIA SHIRE in *The Godfather Part II,* A Coppola Company Prod., Paramount

Directing

JOHN CASSAVETES for *A Woman Under The Influence,* A Faces International Films Prod.

FRANCIS FORD COPPOLA for *The Godfather Part II,* A Coppola Company Prod., Paramount

BOB FOSSE for *Lenny,* A Marvin Worth Prod., United Artists

ROMAN POLANSKI for *Chinatown,* A Robert Evans Prod., Paramount

FRANÇOIS TRUFFAUT for *Day For Night,* A Les Films Du Carrosse and P.E.C.F., Paris; P.I.C., Rome Prod., Warner Bros.

Writing

(Best Original Screenplay)

ALICE DOESN'T LIVE HERE ANYMORE, Warner Bros.: ROBERT GETCHELL

CHINATOWN, A Robert Evans Production, Paramount: ROBERT TOWNE

THE CONVERSATION, A Directors Company Production, Paramount: FRANCIS FORD COPPOLA

DAY FOR NIGHT, A Les Films Du Carrosse and P.E.C.F., Paris; P.I.C., Rome Production, Warner Bros.: FRANÇOIS TRUFFAUT, JEAN-LOUIS RICHARD, and SUZANNE SCHIFFMAN

HARRY AND TONTO, 20th Century-Fox: PAUL MAZURSKY and JOSH GREEN-FELD

(Best Screenplay adapted from other material)

THE APPRENTICESHIP OF DUDDY KRAVITZ, An International Cinemedia Centre, Ltd. Prod., Paramount. Screenplay by MORDECAI RICHLER. Adaptation by LIONEL CHETWYND.

THE GODFATHER PART II, A Coppola Company Prod., Paramount. Screenplay by FRANCIS FORD COPOLA and MARIO PUZO

LENNY, A Marvin Worth Production, United Artists. Screenplay by JULIAN BARRY

MURDER ON THE ORIENT EXPRESS, A G.W. Films, Ltd. Prod., Paramount. Screenplay by PAUL DEHN

YOUNG FRANKENSTEIN, A Gruskoff/Venture Films-Crossbow Prods.-Jouer, Ltd. Production, 20th Century-Fox. Screenplay by GENE WILDER and MEL BROOKS

Cinematography

CHINATOWN, A Robert Evans Prod., Paramount: JOHN A. ALONZO

EARTHQUAKE, A Universal-Mark Robson-Filmakers Group Prod., Universal: PHILIP LATHROP

LENNY, A Marvin Worth Prod., United Artists: BRUCE SURTEES

MURDER ON THE ORIENT EXPRESS, A G.W. Films, Ltd. Prod., Paramount: GEOFFREY UNSWORTH

THE TOWERING INFERNO, An Irwin Allen Prod., 20th Century-Fox/Warner Bros.: FRED KOENE-KAMP and JOSEPH BIROC

Art Direction—Set Decoration

CHINATOWN, A Robert Evans Prod., Paramount: RICHARD SYLBERT and W. STEWART CAMPBELL Set Decoration: RUBY LEVITT

EARTHQUAKE, A Universal-Mark Robson-Filmakers Group Prod., Uni-

versal: ALEXANDER GOLITZEN and E. PRESTON AMES
Set Decoration: FRANK MCKELVY
THE GODFATHER PART II, A Coppola Company Prod., Paramount. DEAN TAVOULARIS and ANGELO GRAHAM
Set Decoration: GEORGE R. NELSON
THE ISLAND AT THE TOP OF THE WORLD, Walt Disney Prods., Buena Vista Distribution Company: PETER ELLENSHAW, JOHN B. MANSBRIDGE, WALTER TYLER and AL ROELOFS
Set Decoration: HAL GAUSMAN
THE TOWERING INFERNO, An Irwin Allen Prod., 20th Century-Fox/Warner Bros.: WILLIAM CREBER and WARD PRESTON
Set Decoration: RAPHAEL BRETTON

Sound

CHINATOWN, A Robert Evans Production, Paramount: BUD GRENZBACH and LARRY JOST
THE CONVERSATION, A Directors Company Production, Paramount: WALTER MURCH and ARTHUR ROCHESTER
EARTHQUAKE, A Universal-Mark Robson-Filmakers Group Production, Universal: RONALD PIERCE and MELVIN METCALFE, SR.
THE TOWERING INFERNO, An Irwin Allen Production, 20th Century-Fox/Warner Bros.: THEODORE SODERBERG and HERMAN LEWIS
YOUNG FRANKENSTEIN, A Gruskoff/Venture Films-Crossbow Prods.-Jouer, Ltd. Production, 20th Century-Fox: RICHARD PORTMAN and GENE CANTAMESSA

Film Editing

BLAZING SADDLES Warner Bros.: JOHN C. HOWARD and DANFORD GREENE
CHINATOWN, A Robert Evans Prod.,

Paramount: SAM O'STEEN
EARTHQUAKE, A Universal-Mark Robson-Filmakers Group Prod., Universal: DOROTHY SPENCER
THE LONGEST YARD, An Albert S. Ruddy Prod., Paramount: MICHAEL LUCIANO
THE TOWERING INFERNO, An Irwin Allen Prod., 20th Century-Fox/Warner Bros.: HAROLD F. KRESS and CARL KRESS

Music

(Best Original Dramatic Score)
CHINATOWN, A Robert Evans Prod., Paramount: JERRY GOLDSMITH
THE GODFATHER PART II, A Coppola Company Prod., Paramount: NINO ROTA and CARMINE COPPOLA
MURDER ON THE ORIENT EXPRESS, A G.W. Films, Ltd. Prod., Paramount: RICHARD RODNEY BENNETT
SHANKS, William Castle Prods., Paramount: ALEX NORTH
THE TOWERING INFERNO, An Irwin Allen Prod., 20th Century-Fox/Warner Bros.: JOHN WILLIAMS

(Best Scoring: Original Song Score and/or Adaptation)
THE GREAT GATSBY, A David Merrick Prod., Paramount. Adapted by NELSON RIDDLE
THE LITTLE PRINCE, A Stanley Donen Enterprises, Ltd. Prod., Paramount. Song Score by ALAN JAY LERNER and FREDERICK LOEWE. Adapted by ANGELA MORLEY and DOUGLAS GAMLEY
PHANTOM OF THE PARADISE, Harbor Prods., 20th Century-Fox. Song Score by PAUL WILLIAMS. Adapted by PAUL WILLIAMS and GEORGE ALICESON TIPTON

(Best Song)
BENJI'S THEME (I FEEL LOVE) from

Benji, Mulberry Square
Music by EUEL BOX
Lyrics by BETTY BOX
BLAZING SADDLES from *Blazing Saddles,* Warner Bros.
Music by JOHN MORRIS
Lyrics by MEL BROOKS
LITTLE PRINCE from *The Little Prince,* A Stanley Donen Enterprises, Ltd. Prod., Paramount
Music by FREDERICK LOEWE
Lyrics by ALAN JAY LERNER
WE MAY NEVER LOVE LIKE THIS AGAIN from *The Towering Inferno,* An Irwin Allen Production, 20th Century-Fox/Warner Bros.
Music and lyrics by AL KASHA and JOEL HIRSCHHORN
WHEREVER LOVE TAKES ME from *Gold,* Avton Film Productions, Ltd. Allied Artists
Music by ELMER BERNSTEIN
Lyrics by DON BLACK

Costume Design

CHINATOWN, A Robert Evans Prod., Paramount: ANTHEA SYLBERT
DAISY MILLER, A Directors Company Prod., Paramount: JOHN FURNESS
THE GODFATHER PART II, A Coppola Company Prod., Paramount: THEADORA VAN RUNKLE
THE GREAT GATSBY, A David Merrick Prod., Paramount: THEONI V. ALDREDGE
MURDER ON THE ORIENT EXPRESS, A G. W. Films, Ltd. Prod., Paramount: TONY WALTON

Short Films
(Name changed from *Short Subjects*)

(Animated Films)

CLOSED MONDAYS, Lighthouse Productions: WILL VINTON and BOB GARDINER, Producers

THE FAMILY THAT DWELT APART, National Film Board of Canada: YVON MALLETTE and ROBERT VERRALL, Producers
HUNGER, National Film Board of Canada: PETER FOLDES and RENE JODOIN, Producers
VOYAGE TO NEXT, The Hubley Studio: FAITH and JOHN HUBLEY, Producers
WINNIE THE POOH AND TIGGER TOO, Walt Disney Productions: WOLFGANG REITHERMAN, Producer

(Live Action Films)

CLIMB, Dewitt Jones Productions: DEWITT JONES, Producer
THE CONCERT, The Black And White Colour Film Company, Ltd.: JULIAN and CLAUDE CHAGRIN, Producers
ONE-EYED MEN ARE KINGS, C.A.P.A.C. Productions (Paris): PAUL CLAUDON and EDMOND SECHAN, Producers
PLANET OCEAN, Graphic Films: GEORGE V. CASEY, Producer
THE VIOLIN, A Sincinkin, Ltd. Production: ANDREW WELSH and GEORGE PASTIC, Producers

Documentary
(Short Subjects)

CITY OUT OF WILDERNESS, Francis Thompson Inc.: FRANCIS THOMPSON, Producer
DON'T, R. A. Films: ROBIN LEHMAN, Producer
EXPLORATORIUM, A Jon Boorstin Prod; JON BOORSTIN, Producer
JOHN MUIR'S HIGH SIERRA, Dewitt Jones Prods: DEWITT JONES and LESLEY FOSTER, Producers
NAKED YOGA, A Filmshop Prod.: RONALD S. KASS and MERVYN LLOYD, Producers

(Features)

ANTONIA: A PORTRAIT OF THE WOMAN, Rocky Mountain Prods:

JUDY COLLINS and JILL GODMILOW, Producers

THE CHALLENGE . . . . A TRIBUTE TO MODERN ART, A World View Prod: HERBERT KLINE, Producer

THE 81ST BLOW, A Film by Ghetto Fighters House: JACQUOT EHRLICH, DAVID BERGMAN and HAIM GOURI, Producers

HEARTS AND MINDS, A Touchstone-Audjeff-BBS Prod., Howard Zucker/Henry Jaglom-Rainbow Pictures Presentation: PETER DAVIS and BERT SCHNEIDER, Producers

THE WILD AND THE BRAVE, E.S.J. Prods. in association with Tomorrow Entertainment Inc. & Jones/Howard Ltd.: NATALIE R. JONES and EUGENE S. JONES, Producers

Foreign Language Film Award

AMARCORD, An F.C. (Rome)-P.E.C.F. (Paris) Prod. (Italy).

CATSPLAY, A Hunnia Studio Prod. (Hungary)

THE DELUGE, A Film Polski Prod. (Poland)

LACOMBE, LUCIEN, An NEF-UPF (Paris)—Vides Film (Rome)—Hallelujah Film (Munich) Prod. (France)

THE TRUCE, A Tamames-Zemborain Prod. (Argentina)

Honorary Awards

HOWARD HAWKS—A master American filmmaker whose creative efforts hold a distinguished place in world cinema

JEAN RENOIR—a genius who, with grace, responsibility and enviable devotion through silent film, sound film, feature, documentary and television, has won the world's admiration

Special Achievement

Visual Effects: FRANK BRENDEL, GLEN ROBINSON and ALBERT WHITLOCK for *Earthquake,* A Universal-Mark Robson-Filmakers Groups Production, Universal

Irving G. Thalberg Memorial Award
None

Jean Hersholt Humanitarian Award
ARTHUR B. KRIM

Scientific or Technical
Class I
None
Class II

JOSEPH D. KELLY of Glen Glenn Sound for the design of new audio control consoles which have advanced the state of the art of sound recording and rerecording for motion picture production

THE BURBANK STUDIOS Sound Department for the design of new audio control consoles engineered and constructed by the Quad-Eight Sound Corporation

SAMUEL GOLDWYN STUDIOS Sound Department for the design of a new audio control console engineered and constructed by the Quad-Eight Sound Corporation

QUAD-EIGHT SOUND CORPORATION for the engineering and construction of new audio control consoles designed by The Burbank Studios Sound Department and by the Samuel Goldwyn Studios Sound Department

WALDON O. WATSON, RICHARD J. STUMPF, ROBERT J. LEONARD and the UNIVERSAL CITY STUDIOS Sound Department for the development and engineering of the Sensurround System for motion picture presentation

Class III

ELEMACK COMPANY, Rome, Italy, for the design and development of their Spyder camera dolly

LOUIS AMI of the Universal City Studios for the design and construction of a reciprocating camera platform used when photographing special visual effects for motion pictures

1975

Nominations Announced: February 17, 1976
Awards Ceremony: March 29, 1976
Dorothy Chandler Pavilion, Los Angeles County Music Center
(MCs: Goldie Hawn, Gene Kelly, Walter Matthau, George Segal, and Robert Shaw)

Best Picture

BARRY LYNDON, A Hawk Films, Ltd. Production, Warner Bros.: STANLEY KUBRICK Producer

DOG DAY AFTERNOON, Warner Bros.: MARTIN BREGMAN and MARTIN ELFAND, Producers

JAWS, A Universal-Zanuck/Brown Production, Universal: RICHARD D. ZANUCK and DAVID BROWN, Producers

NASHVILLE, An ABC Entertainment-Jerry Weintraub-Robert Altman Production, Paramount: ROBERT ALTMAN, Producer

ONE FLEW OVER THE CUCKOO'S NEST, A Fantasy Films Production, United Artists: SAUL ZAENTZ and MICHAEL DOUGLAS, Producers

Actor

WALTER MATTHAU in *The Sunshine Boys,* A Ray Stark Production, Metro-Goldwyn-Mayer

JACK NICHOLSON in *One Flew Over The Cuckoo's Nest,* A Fantasy Films Production, United Artists

AL PACINO in *Dog Day Afternoon,* Warner Bros.

MAXIMILIAN SCHELL in *The Man In The Glass Booth,* An Ely Landau Organization Production, AFT Distributing

JAMES WHITMORE in *Give 'em Hell,*

LARGE CAPITAL LETTERS DENOTE WINNERS

Harry!, A Theatrovision Production, Avco Embassy

Actress

ISABELLE ADJANI in *The Story Of Adele H.,* A Les Films du Carrosse-Les Productions Artistes Associes Production, New World Pictures

ANN-MARGRET in *Tommy,* A Robert Stigwood Organisation, Ltd. Production, Columbia

LOUISE FLETCHER in *One Flew Over The Cuckoo's Nest,* A Fantasy Films Production, United Artists

GLENDA JACKSON in *Hedda,* A Royal Shakespeare-Brut Productions—George Barrie/Robert Enders Film Production, Brut Productions

CAROL KANE in *Hester Street,* Midwest Film Productions

Supporting Actor

GEORGE BURNS in *The Sunshine Boys,* A Ray Stark Production, Metro-Goldwyn-Mayer

BRAD DOURIF in *One Flew Over The Cuckoo's Nest,* A Fantasy Films Production, United Artists

BURGESS MEREDITH in *The Day Of The Locust,* A Jerome Hellman Production, Paramount

CHRIS SARANDON in *Dog Day Afternoon,* Warner Bros.

JACK WARDEN in *Shampoo,* Rubeeker Productions, Columbia

Supporting Actress

RONEE BLAKLEY in *Nashville,* An ABC Entertainment-Jerry Weintraub-Robert Altman Production, Paramount

LEE GRANT in *Shampoo,* Rubeeker Productions, Columbia

SYLVIA MILES in *Farewell, My Lovely,* An Elliott Kastner-ITC Production, Avco Embassy

LILY TOMLIN in *Nashville,* An ABC Entertainment-Jerry Weintraub-Robert Altman Production, Paramount

BRENDA VACCARO in *Jacqueline Susann's Once Is Not Enough,* A Howard W. Koch Production, Paramount

Directing

ROBERT ALTMAN for *Nashville,* An ABC Entertainment-Jerry Weintraub-Robert Altman Production, Paramount

FEDERICO FELLINI for *Amarcord,* An F.C. Productions-P.E.C.F. Production, New World Pictures

MILOS FORMAN for *One Flew Over The Cuckoo's Nest,* A Fantasy Films Production, United Artists

STANLEY KUBRICK for *Barry Lyndon,* A Hawk Films, Ltd. Production, Warner Bros.

SIDNEY LUMET for *Dog Day Afternoon,* Warner Bros.

Writing

(Best Original Screenplay)

AMARCORD, An F.C. Productions-P.E.C.F. Production, New World Pictures: FEDERICO FELLINI and TONINO GUERRA

AND NOW MY LOVE, A Rizzoli Film-Les Films 13 Production, Avco Embassy: CLAUDE LELOUCH and PIERRE UYTTERHOEVEN

DOG DAY AFTERNOON, Warner Bros.: FRANK PIERSON

LIES MY FATHER TOLD ME, Pentimento Productions, Ltd.-Pentacle VIII Productions, Ltd., Columbia: TED ALLAN

SHAMPOO, Rubeeker Productions, Columbia: ROBERT TOWNE and WARREN BEATTY

(Best Screenplay adapted from other material)

BARRY LYNDON, A Hawk Films, Ltd. Production, Warner Bros. Screenplay by STANLEY KUBRICK

THE MAN WHO WOULD BE KING, An Allied Artists-Columbia Pictures Production, Allied Artists. Screenplay by JOHN HUSTON and GLADYS HILL

ONE FLEW OVER THE CUCKOO'S NEST, A Fantasy Films Production, United Artists. Screenplay by LAWRENCE HAUBEN and BO GOLDMAN

SCENT OF A WOMAN, A Dean Film Production, 20th Century-Fox. Screenplay by RUGGERO MACCARI and DINO RISI

THE SUNSHINE BOYS, A Ray Stark Production, Metro-Goldwyn-Mayer. Screenplay by NEIL SIMON

Cinematography

BARRY LYNDON, A Hawk Films, Ltd. Production, Warner Bros.: JOHN ALCOTT

THE DAY OF THE LOCUST, A Jerome Hellman Production, Paramount: CONRAD HALL

FUNNY LADY, A Rastar Pictures Production, Columbia: JAMES WONG HOWE

THE HINDENBURG, A Robert Wise-Filmakers Group-Universal Production, Universal: ROBERT SURTEES

ONE FLEW OVER THE CUCKOO'S NEST, A Fantasy Films Production, United Artists: HASKELL WEXLER and BILL BUTLER

Art Direction—Set Decoration

BARRY LYNDON, A Hawk Films, Ltd. Production, Warner Bros.: KEN ADAM and ROY WALKER
Set Decoration: VERNON DIXON

THE HINDENBURG, A Robert Wise-Filmakers Group-Universal Production, Universal: EDWARD CARFAGNO
Set Decoration: FRANK MCKELVY

THE MAN WHO WOULD BE KING, An Allied Artists-Columbia Pictures Production, Allied Artists: ALEXANDER TRAUNER and TONY INGLIS
Set Decoration: PETER JAMES

SHAMPOO, Rubeeker Productions, Columbia: RICHARD SYLBERT and W. STEWART CAMPBELL
Set Decoration: GEORGE GAINES

THE SUNSHINE BOYS, A Ray Stark Production, Metro-Goldwyn-Mayer: ALBERT BRENNER
Set Decoration: MARVIN MARCH

Sound

BITE THE BULLET, A Pax Enterprises Production, Columbia: ARTHUR PIANTADOSI, LES FRESHOLTZ, RICHARD TYLER and AL OVERTON, JR.

FUNNY LADY, A Rastar Pictures Production, Columbia: RICHARD PORTMAN, DON MacDOUGALL, CURLY THIRLWELL and JACK SOLOMON

THE HINDENBURG, A Robert Wise-Filmakers Group Universal Production, Universal: LEONARD PETERSON, JOHN A. BOLGER, JR., JOHN MACK and DON K. SHARPLESS

JAWS, A Universal-Zanuck/Brown Production, Universal: ROBERT L. HOYT, ROGER HEMAN, EARL MADERY and JOHN CARTER

THE WIND AND THE LION, A Herb Jaffe Production, Metro-Goldwyn-Mayer: HARRY W. TETRICK, AARON ROCHIN, WILLIAM MCCAUGHEY and ROY CHARMAN

Film Editing

DOG DAY AFTERNOON, Warner Bros.: DEDE ALLEN

JAWS, A Universal-Zanuck/Brown Production, Universal: VERNA FIELDS

THE MAN WHO WOULD BE KING, An Allied Artists-Columbia Pictures Production, Allied Artists: RUSSELL LLOYD

ONE FLEW OVER THE CUCKOO'S NEST, A Fantasy Films Production, United Artists: RICHARD CHEW, LYNZEE KLINGMAN and SHELDON KAHN

THREE DAYS OF THE CONDOR, A Dino De Laurentiis Production, Paramount: FREDRIC STEINKAMP and DON GUIDICE

Music

(Best Original Score)

BIRDS DO IT, BEES DO IT, A Wolper Pictures Production, Columbia: GERALD FRIED

BITE THE BULLET, A Pax Enterprises Production, Columbia: ALEX NORTH

JAWS, A Universal-Zanuck/Brown Production, Universal: JOHN WILLIAMS

ONE FLEW OVER THE CUCKOO'S NEST, A Fantasy Films Production, United Artists: JACK NITZSCHE

THE WIND AND THE LION, A Herb Jaffe Production, Metro-Goldwyn-Mayer: JERRY GOLDSMITH

(Best Scoring: Original Song Score and/or Adaptation)

BARRY LYNDON, A Hawk Films, Ltd. Production, Warner Bros.: Adapted by LEONARD ROSENMAN

FUNNY LADY, A Rastar Pictures Production, Columbia: Adapted by PETER MATZ

TOMMY, A Robert Stigwood Organisation, LTD. Production, Columbia:

Adapted by PETER TOWNSHEND

(Best Original Song)

HOW LUCKY CAN YOU GET from *Funny Lady,* A Rastar Pictures Production, Columbia
Music and lyrics by FRED EBB and JOHN KANDER

I'M EASY from *Nashville,* An ABC Entertainment-Jerry Weintraub-Robert Altman Production, Paramount
Music and lyrics by KEITH CAR-RADINE

NOW THAT WE'RE IN LOVE from *Whiffs,* Brut Productions, 20th Century-Fox
Music by GEORGE BARRIE. Lyrics by SAMMY CAHN

RICHARD'S WINDOW from *The Other Side Of The Mountain,* A Filmways-Larry Peerce-Universal Production, Universal
Music by CHARLES FOX. Lyrics by NORMAN GIMBEL

THEME FROM MAHOGANY (DO YOU KNOW WHERE YOU'RE GOING TO) from *Mahogany,* A Jobete Film Production, Paramount.
Music by MICHAEL MASSER. Lyrics by GERRY GOFFIN

Costume Design

BARRY LYNDON, A Hawk Films, Ltd. Production, Warner Bros.: ULLA-BRITT SODERLUND and MILENA CANONERO

THE FOUR MUSKETEERS, A Film Trust S.A. Production, 20th Century-Fox: YVONNE BLAKE and RON TALSKY

FUNNY LADY, A Rastar Pictures Production, Columbia: RAY AGHAYAN and BOB MACKIE

THE MAGIC FLUTE, A Sveriges Radio A.B. Production, Surrogate Releasing: HENNY NOREMARK and KARIN ERSKINE

THE MAN WHO WOULD BE KING, An Allied Artists-Columbia Pictures Production, Allied Artists: EDITH HEAD

Short Films

(Animated Films)

GREAT, Grantstern Ltd. and British Lion Films Ltd.: BOB GODFREY, Producer

KICK ME, Robert Swarthe Productions: ROBERT SWARTHE, Producer

MONSIEUR POINTU, National Film Board of Canada: RENÉ JODOIN, BERNARD LONGPRÉ and ANDRÉ LEDUC, Producers

SISYPHUS, Hungarofilms MARCELL JANKOVICS, Producer

(Live Action)

ANGEL AND BIG JOE, Bert Salzman Productions: BERT SALZMAN, Producer

CONQUEST OF LIGHT, Louis Marcus Films Ltd.: LOUIS MARCUS, Producer

DAWN FLIGHT, Lawrence M. Lansburgh Productions: LAWRENCE M. LANSBURGH and BRIAN LANSBURGH, Producers

A DAY IN THE LIFE OF BONNIE CONSOLO, Barr Films: BARRY SPINELLO, Producer

DOUBLETALK, Beattie Productions: ALAN BEATTIE, Producer

Documentary

(Short Subjects)

ARTHUR AND LILLIE, Department of Communication, Stanford University: JON ELSE, STEVEN KOVACS and KRISTINE SAMUELSON, Producers

THE END OF THE GAME, Opus Films Limited: CLAIRE WILBUR and ROBIN LEHMAN, Producers

MILLIONS OF YEARS AHEAD OF MAN, BASF: MANFRED BAIER, Producer

PROBES IN SPACE, Graphic Films:

GEORGE V. CASEY, Producer
WHISTLING SMITH, National Film Board of Canada: BARRIE HOWELLS and MICHAEL SCOTT, Producers

(Features)

THE CALIFORNIA REICH, Yasny Talking Pictures: WALTER F. PARKES and KEITH F. CRITCHLOW, Producers

FIGHTING FOR OUR LIVES, A Farm Worker Film: GLEN PEARCY, Producer

THE INCREDIBLE MACHINE, The National Geographic Society and Wolper Prods: IRWIN ROSTEN, Producer

THE MAN WHO SKIED DOWN EVEREST, A Crawley Films Presentation: F. R. CRAWLEY, JAMES HAGER and DALE HARTLEBEN, Producers

THE OTHER HALF OF THE SKY: A CHINA MEMOIR, MacLaine Productions: SHIRLEY MacLAINE Producer

Foreign Language Film Award
DERSU UZALA, A Mosfilms Studio Production (U.S.S.R.)

LAND OF PROMISE, A Film Polski Production (Poland)

LETTERS FROM MARUSIA, A Conacine Production (Mexico)

SANDAKAN NO. 8, A Toho-Haiyuza Production (Japan)

SCENT OF A WOMAN, A Dean Film Production (Italy)

Honorary Award
MARY PICKFORD in recognition of her unique contributions to the film industry and the development of film as an artistic medium.

Special Achievement
Sound Effects: PETER BERKOS for *The Hindenburg,* A Robert Wise-Filmakers Group-Universal Production, Universal

Visual Effects: ALBERT WHITLOCK and GLEN ROBINSON for *The Hindenburg* A Robert Wise-Filmakers Group-Universal Production, Universal

Irving G. Thalberg Memorial Award
MERVYN LEROY

Jean Hersholt Humanitarian Award
JULES C. STEIN

Scientific or Technical
Class I
None

Class II
CHADWELL O'CONNOR of the O'Connor Engineering Laboratories for the concept and engineering of a fluid-damped camerahead for motion-picture photography

WILLIAM F. MINER of Universal City Studios, Inc. and the WESTINGHOUSE ELECTRIC CORPORATION for the development and engineering of a solid-state, 500 kilowatt, direct-current static rectifier for motion-picture lighting.

Class III
LAWRENCE W. BUTLER and ROGER BANKS for the concept of applying low inertia and stepping electric motors to film transport systems and optical printers for motion-picture production.

DAVID J. DEGENKOLB and FRED SCOBEY of Deluxe General Incorporated and JOHN C. DOLAN and RICHARD DUBOIS of the Akwaklame Company for the development of a technique for silver recovery from photographic wash-waters by ion exchange.

JOSEPH WESTHEIMER for the development of a device to obtain shadowed titles on motion-picture films.

CARTER EQUIPMENT CO., INC. and RAMTRONICS for the engineering and manufacture of a computerized tape punching system for programming laboratory printing machines.

THE HOLLYWOOD FILM COMPANY for the engineering and manufacture of a computerized tape punching system for programming laboratory printing machines.

BELL & HOWELL for the engineering and manufacture of a computerized tape punching system for programming laboratory printing machines.

FREDRIK SCHLYTER for the engineering and manufacture of a computerized tape punching system for programming laboratory printing machines.

1976

Nominations Announced: February 10, 1977
Awards Ceremony: March 28, 1977
Dorothy Chandler Pavilion, Los Angeles County Music Center
(MCs: Warren Beatty, Ellen Burstyn, Jane Fonda, and Richard Pryor)

Best Picture

ALL THE PRESIDENT'S MEN, A Wildwood Enterprises Production, Warner Bros.: WALTER COBLENZ, Producer

BOUND FOR GLORY, The Bound For Glory Company Production, United Artists: ROBERT F. BLUMOFE and HAROLD LEVENTHAL, Producers

NETWORK, A Howard Gottfried/Paddy Chayefsky Production, Metro-Goldwyn-Mayer/United Artists: HOWARD GOTTFRIED, Producer

ROCKY, A Robert Chartoff-Irwin Winkler Production, United Artists: IRWIN WINKLER and ROBERT CHARTOFF, Producers

TAXI DRIVER, A Bill/Phillips Production of a Martin Scorsese Film, Columbia Pictures: MICHAEL PHILLIPS and JULIA PHILLIPS, Producers

Actor

ROBERT DE NIRO in *Taxi Driver,* A Bill/Phillips Production of a Martin Scorsese Film, Columbia Pictures

PETER FINCH in *Network,* A Howard Gottfried/Paddy Chayefsky Production, Metro-Goldwyn-Mayer/United Artists

GIANCARLO GIANNINI in *Seven Beauties,* A Medusa Distribuzione Production, Cinema 5, Ltd.

WILLIAM HOLDEN in *Network,* A Howard Gottfried/Paddy Chayefsky

LARGE CAPITAL LETTERS DENOTE WINNER

Production, Metro-Goldwyn-Mayer/United Artists

SYLVESTER STALLONE in *Rocky,* A Robert Chartoff-Irwin Winkler Production, United Artists

Actress

MARIE-CHRISTINE BARRAULT in *Cousin, Cousine,* Les Films Pomereu-Gaumont Production, Northal Film Distributors Ltd.

FAYE DUNAWAY in *Network,* A Howard Gottfried/Paddy Chayefsky Production, Metro-Goldwyn-Mayer/United Artists

TALIA SHIRE in *Rocky,* A Robert Chartoff-Irwin Winkler Production, United Artists

SISSY SPACEK in *Carrie,* A Redbank Films Production, United Artists

LIV ULLMANN in *Face to Face,* A Cinematograph A.B. Production, Paramount

Supporting Actor

NED BEATTY in *Network,* A Howard Gottfried/Paddy Chayefsky Production, Metro-Goldwyn-Mayer/United Artists

BURGESS MEREDITH in *Rocky,* A Robert Chartoff-Irwin Winkler Production, United Artists

LAURENCE OLIVIER in *Marathon Man,* A Robert Evans-Sidney Beckerman Production, Paramount

JASON ROBARDS in *All The Presi-*

539

dent's Men, A Wildwood Enterprises Production, Warner Bros.

BURT YOUNG in *Rocky,* A Robert Chartoff-Irwin Winkler Production, United Artists

Supporting Actress

JANE ALEXANDER in *All The President's Men,* A Wildwood Enterprises Production, Warner Bros.

JODIE FOSTER in *Taxi Driver,* A Bill/Phillips Production of a Martin Scorsese Film, Columbia Pictures

LEE GRANT in *Voyage Of The Damned,* An ITC Entertainment Production, Avco Embassy

PIPER LAURIE in *Carrie,* A Redbank Films Production, United Artists.

BEATRICE STRAIGHT in *Network,* A Howard Gottfried/Paddy Chayefsky Production, Metro-Goldwyn-Mayer/United Artists

Directing

JOHN G. AVILDSEN for *Rocky,* A Robert Chartoff-Irwin Winkler Production, United Artists

INGMAR BERGMAN for *Face To Face,* A Cinematograph A.B. Production, Paramount

SIDNEY LUMET for *Network,* A Howard Gottfried/Paddy Chayefsky Production, Metro-Goldwyn-Mayer/United Artists

ALAN J. PAKULA for *All The President's Men,* A Wildwood Enterprises Production, Warner Bros.

LINA WERTMULLER for *Seven Beauties,* A Medusa Distribuzione Production, Cinema 5, Ltd.

Writing

(Best Screenplay—Written Directly For The Screen)

COUSIN, COUSINE, Les Films Pomereu-Gaumont Production, Northal Film Distributors Ltd.

Story and Screenplay by JEAN-CHARLES TACCHELLA
Adaptation by DANIELE THOMPSON

THE FRONT, Columbia Pictures
Story and Screenplay by WALTER BERNSTEIN

NETWORK, A Howard Gottfried/ Paddy Chayefsky Production, Metro-Goldwyn-Mayer/United Artists
Story and Screenplay by PADDY CHAYEFSKY

ROCKY, A Robert Chartoff-Irwin Winkler Production, United Artists
Story and Screenplay by SYLVESTER STALLONE

SEVEN BEAUTIES, A Medusa Distribuzione Production, Cinema 5, Ltd.
Story and Screenplay by LINA WERTMULLER

(Best Screenplay Based On Material From Another Medium)

ALL THE PRESIDENT'S MEN, A Wildwood Enterprises Production, Warner Bros.
Screenplay by WILLIAM GOLDMAN

BOUND FOR GLORY, The Bound For Glory Production, United Artists
Screenplay by ROBERT GETCHELL

FELLINI'S CASANOVA, A P.E.A.-Produzioni Europee Associate S.p.A. Production, Universal
Screenplay by FEDERICO FELLINI and BERNADINO ZAPPONI

THE SEVEN-PER-CENT SOLUTION, A Herbert Ross Film/Winitsky-Sellers Production, A Universal Release
Screenplay by NICHOLAS MEYER

VOYAGE OF THE DAMNED, An ITC Entertainment Production, Avco Embassy
Screenplay by STEVE SHAGAN and DAVID BUTLER

Cinematography

BOUND FOR GLORY, The Bound

For Glory Company Production, United Artists: HASKELL WEXLER

KING KONG, A Dino De Laurentiis Production, Paramount: RICHARD H. KLINE

LOGAN'S RUN, A Saul David Production, Metro-Goldwyn-Mayer: ERNEST LASZLO

NETWORK, A Howard Gottfried/Paddy Chayefsky Production, Metro-Goldwyn-Mayer/United Artists: OWEN ROIZMAN

A STAR IS BORN, A Barwood/Jon Peters Production, First Artists Presentation, Warner Bros.: ROBERT SURTEES

Art Direction—Set Decoration

ALL THE PRESIDENT'S MEN, A Wildwood Enterprises Production, Warner Bros.: GEORGE JENKINS Set Decoration: GEORGE GAINES

THE INCREDIBLE SARAH, A Helen M. Strauss-Reader's Digest Films, Ltd. Production, Seymour Borde & Associates: ELLIOT SCOTT and NORMAN REYNOLDS

THE LAST TYCOON, A Sam Spiegel–Elia Kazan Film Production, Paramount: GENE CALLAHAN and JACK COLLIS Set Decoration: JERRY WUNDERLICH

LOGAN'S RUN, A Saul David Production, Metro-Goldwyn-Mayer: DALE HENNESY Set Decoration: ROBERT DE VESTEL

THE SHOOTIST, A Frankovich/Self Production, Dino De Laurentiis Presentation, Paramount: ROBERT F. BOYLE Set Decoration: ARTHUR JEPH PARKER

Sound

ALL THE PRESIDENT'S MEN, A Wildwood Enterprises Production, Warner Bros.: ARTHUR PIANTADOSI, LES FRESHOLTZ, DICK ALEXANDER and JIM WEBB

KING KONG, A Dino De Laurentiis Production, Paramount: HARRY WARREN TETRICK, WILLIAM MCCAUGHEY, AARON ROCHIN and JACK SOLOMON

ROCKY, A Robert Chartoff-Irwin Winkler Production United Artists: HARRY WARREN TETRICK, WILLIAM MCCAUGHEY, LYLE BURBRIDGE and BUD ALPER

SILVER STREAK, A Frank Yablans Presentations Production, 20th Century-Fox: DONALD MITCHELL, DOUGLAS WILLIAMS, RICHARD TYLER and HAL ETHERINGTON

A STAR IS BORN, A Barwood/Jon Peters Production, First Artists Presentation, Warner Bros.: ROBERT KNUDSON, DAN WALLIN, ROBERT GLASS and TOM OVERTON

Film Editing

ALL THE PRESIDENT'S MEN, A Wildwood Enterprises Production, Warner Bros.: ROBERT L. WOLFE

BOUND FOR GLORY, The Bound For Glory Company Production, United Artists: ROBERT JONES and PEMBROKE J. HERRING

NETWORK, A Howard Gottfried/Paddy Chayefsky Production, Metro-Goldwyn-Mayer/United Artists: ALAN HEIM

ROCKY, A Robert Chartoff-Irwin Winkler Production, United Artists: RICHARD HALSEY and SCOTT CONRAD

TWO-MINUTE WARNING, A Filmways/Larry Peerce-Edward S. Feldman Film Production, Universal: EVE NEWMAN AND WALTER HANNEMANN

Music

(Best Original Score)

OBSESSION, George Litto Productions, Columbia Pictures: BERNARD HERRMANN

THE OMEN, 20th Century-Fox Productions, Ltd., 20th Century-Fox: JERRY GOLDSMITH

THE OUTLAW JOSEY WALES, A Malpaso Company Production, Warner Bros.: JERRY FIELDING

TAXI DRIVER, A Bill/Phillips Production of a Martin Scorsese Film, Columbia Pictures: BERNARD HERRMANN

VOYAGE OF THE DAMNED, An ITC Entertainment Production, Avco Embassy: LALO SCHIFRIN

(Best Original Song Score and Its Adaptation or Best Adaptation Score)

BOUND FOR GLORY, The Bound For Glory Company Production, United Artists: Adapted by LEONARD ROSENMAN

BUGSY MALONE, A Goodtimes Enterprises, Ltd. Production, Paramount: Song Score and Its Adaptation by PAUL WILLIAMS

A STAR IS BORN, A Barwood/Jon Peters Production, First Artists Presentation, Warner Bros.: Adapted by ROGER KELLAWAY

(Best Original Song)

AVE SATANI from *The Omen,* 20th Century-Fox Productions, Ltd., 20th Century Fox
Music and lyrics by JERRY GOLDSMITH

COME TO ME from *The Pink Panther Strikes Again,* Amjo Productions, Ltd., United Artists
Music by HENRY MANCINI
Lyrics by DON BLACK

EVERGREEN (LOVE THEME FROM A STAR IS BORN) from *A Star Is Born,* A Barwood/Jon Peters Production, First Artists Presentation, Warner Bros.
Music by BARBRA STREISAND
Lyrics by PAUL WILLIAMS

GONNA FLY NOW from *Rocky,* a Robert Chartoff-Irwin Winkler Production, United Artists
Music by BILL CONTI
Lyrics by CAROL CONNORS and AYN ROBBINS

A WORLD THAT NEVER WAS from *Half A House,* Lenro Productions, First American Films
Music by SAMMY FAIN
Lyrics by PAUL FRANCIS WEBSTER

Costume Design

BOUND FOR GLORY, The Bound For Glory Company Production, United Artists: WILLIAM THEISS

FELLINI'S CASANOVA, A P.E.A.-Produzioni Europee Associate S.p.A. Production, Universal: DANILO DONATI

THE INCREDIBLE SARAH, A Helen M. Strauss-Reader's Digest Films, Ltd. Production, Seymour Borde & Associates: ANTHONY MENDLESON

THE PASSOVER PLOT, Coast Industries-Golan-Globus Productions, Ltd., Atlas Films: MARY WILLS

THE SEVEN-PER-CENT SOLUTION, A Herbert Ross Film/Winitsky-Sellers Production, A Universal Release: ALAN BARRETT

Short Films

(Animated Films)

DEDALO, A Cineteam Realizzazioni Production. MANFREDO MANFREDI, Producer

LEISURE, A Film Australia Production: SUZANNE BAKER, Producer

THE STREET, National Film Board of Canada: CAROLINE LEAF and GUY GLOVER, Producers

(Live Action)

IN THE REGION OF ICE, An American Film Institute Production: ANDRE GUTTFREUND and PETER WERNER, Producers

KUDZU, A Short Production: MARJORIE

ANNE SHORT, Producer

THE MORNING SPIDER, The Black and White Colour Film Company: JULIAN CHAGRIN and CLAUDE CHAGRIN, Producers

NIGHTLIFE, Opus Films, Ltd.: CLAIRE WILBUR and ROBIN LEHMAN, Producers

NUMBER ONE, Number One Productions: DYAN CANNON and VINCE CANNON, Producers

Documentary

(Short Subjects)

AMERICAN SHOESHINE, Titan Films: SPARKY GREENE, Producer

BLACKWOOD, National Film Board of Canada: TONY IANZELO and ANDY THOMPSON, Producers

THE END OF THE ROAD, Pelican Films: JOHN ARMSTRONG, Producer

NUMBER OUR DAYS, Community Television of Southern California: LYNNE LITTMAN, Producer

UNIVERSE, Graphic Films Corp. for NASA: LESTER NOVROS, Producer

(Features)

HARLAN COUNTY, U.S.A., Cabin Creek Films: BARBARA KOPPLE, Producer

HOLLYWOOD ON TRIAL, October Films/Cinema Associates Production: JAMES GUTMAN and DAVID HELPERN, JR., Producers

OFF THE EDGE, Pentacle Films: MICHAEL FIRTH, Producer

PEOPLE OF THE WIND, Elizabeth E. Rogers Productions: ANTHONY HOWARTH and DAVID KOFF, Producers

VOLCANO: AN INQUIRY INTO THE LIFE AND DEATH OF MALCOLM LOWRY, National Film Board of Canada: DONALD BRITTAIN and ROBERT DUNCAN, Producers

Foreign Language Film Award

BLACK AND WHITE IN COLOR, An Arthur Cohn Production/Societé Ivoirienne de Cinema (Ivory Coast)

COUNSIN, COUSINE, Les Films Pomereu-Gaumont Production (France)

JACOB, THE LIAR, A VEB/DEFA Production (German Democratic Republic)

NIGHTS AND DAYS, A Polish Corporation for Film-"KADR" Film Unit Production (Poland)

SEVEN BEAUTIES, A Medusa Distribuzione Production (Italy)

Honorary Awards

None

Special Achievement

Visual Effects: CARLO RAMBALDI, GLEN ROBINSON and FRANK VAN DER VEER for *King Kong,* A Dino De Laurentiis Production, Paramount

Visual Effects: L.B. ABBOTT, GLEN ROBINSON and MATTHEW YURICICH for *Logan's Run,* A Saul David Production, Metro-Goldwyn-Mayer

Irving G. Thalberg Memorial Award

PANDRO S. BERMAN

Jean Hersholt Humanitarian Award

None

Scientific or Technical

Class I

None

Class II

CONSOLIDATED FILM INDUSTRIES and the BARNEBEY-CHENEY COMPANY for the development of a system for the recovery of film-cleaning solvent vapors in a motion-picture laboratory

WILLIAM L. GRAHAM, MANFRED G. MICHELSON, GEOFFREY F. NORMAN and SIEGFRIED SEIBERT of Technicolor for the development and engineering of a Continuous, High-Speed, Color Motion-Picture Printing System

Class III

FRED BARTSCHER of the Kollmorgen Corporation and to GLENN BERGGREN of the Schneider Corporation for the design and development of a single-lens magnifier for motion-picture projection lenses

PANAVISION INCORPORATED for the design and development of super-speed lenses for motion-picture photography

HIROSHI SUZUKAWA of Canon and WILTON R. HOLM of AMPTP Motion Picture and Television Research Center for the design and development of super-speed lenses for motion-picture photography

CARL ZEISS COMPANY for the design and development of super-speed lenses for motion-picture photography

PHOTO RESEARCH DIVISION of the KOLLMORGEN CORPORATION For the engineering and manufacture of the spectra TriColor Meter

1977

Nominations Announced: February 21, 1978
Awards Ceremony: April 3, 1978
Dorothy Chandler Pavilion, Los Angeles County Music Center
(MC: Bob Hope)

Best Picture

ANNIE HALL, Jack Rollins-Charles H. Joffe Productions, United Artists: CHARLES H. JOFFE, Producer

THE GOODBYE GIRL, A Ray Stark Production, Metro-Goldwyn-Mayer/Warner Bros.: RAY STARK, Producer

JULIA, A Twentieth Century-Fox Production, Twentieth Century-Fox: RICHARD ROTH, Producer

STAR WARS, A Twentieth Century-Fox Production, Twentieth Century-Fox: GARY KURTZ, Producer

THE TURNING POINT, Hera Productions, Twentieth Century-Fox: HERBERT ROSS and ARTHUR LAURENTS, Producers

Actor

WOODY ALLEN in *Annie Hall,* Jack Rollins-Charles H. Joffe Productions, United Artists

RICHARD BURTON in *Equus,* A Winkast Company, Ltd./P.B., Ltd. Production, United Artists

RICHARD DREYFUSS in *The Goodbye Girl,* A Ray Stark Production, Metro-Goldwyn-Mayer/Warner Bros.

MARCELLO MASTROIANNI in *A Special Day,* A Canafox Films Production, Cinema 5, Ltd.

JOHN TRAVOLTA in *Saturday Night Fever,* A Robert Stigwood Production, Paramount

LARGE CAPITAL LETTERS DENOTE WINNERS

Actress

ANNE BANCROFT in *The Turning Point,* Hera Productions, Twentieth Century-Fox

JANE FONDA in *Julia,* A Twentieth Century-Fox Production, Twentieth Century-Fox

DIANE KEATON in *Annie Hall,* Jack Rollins-Charles H. Joffe Productions, United Artists

SHIRLEY MacLAINE in *The Turning Point,* Hera Productions, Twentieth Century-Fox

MARSHA MASON in *The Goodbye Girl,* A Ray Stark Production, Metro-Goldwyn-Mayer/Warner Bros.

Supporting Actor

MIKHAIL BARYSHNIKOV in *The Turning Point,* Hera Productions, Twentieth Century-Fox

PETER FIRTH in *Equus,* A Winkast Company, Ltd./P.B., Ltd. Production, United Artists

ALEC GUINNESS in *Star Wars,* A Twentieth Century-Fox Production, Twentieth Century-Fox

JASON ROBARDS in *Julia,* A Twentieth Century-Fox Production, Twentieth Century-Fox

MAXIMILIAN SCHELL in *Julia,* A Twentieth Century-Fox Production, Twentieth Century-Fox

Supporting Actress

LESLIE BROWNE in *The Turning Point,*

Hera Productions, Twentieth Century-Fox

QUINN CUMMINGS in *The Goodbye Girl,* A Ray Stark Production, Metro-Goldwyn-Mayer/Warner Bros.

MELINDA DILLON in *Close Encounters Of The Third Kind,* Close Encounter Productions, Columbia

VANESSA REDGRAVE in *Julia,* A Twentieth Century-Fox Production, Twentieth Century-Fox

TUESDAY WELD in *Looking For Mr. Goodbar,* A Freddie Fields Production, Paramount

Directing

WOODY ALLEN, for ANNIE HALL Jack Rollins-Charles H. Joffe Productions, United Artists.

STEVEN SPIELBERG for CLOSE ENCOUNTERS OF THE THIRD KIND, Close Encounter Productions, Columbia.

FRED ZINNEMANN for JULIA, A Twentieth Century-Fox Production, Twentieth Century-Fox.

GEORGE LUCAS for STAR WARS, A Twentieth Century-Fox Production, Twentieth Century-Fox.

HERBERT ROSS for THE TURNING POINT, Hera Productions, Twentieth Century-Fox.

Writing

(Best Screenplay—written directly for the screen)

ANNIE HALL, Jack Rollins-Charles H. Joffe Productions, United Artists: Story and screenplay by WOODY ALLEN and MARSHALL BRICKMAN

THE GOODBYE GIRL, A Ray Stark Production, Metro-Goldwyn-Mayer/Warner Bros. Story and screenplay by NEIL SIMON

THE LATE SHOW, A Lion's Gate Film Production, Warner Bros: Story and screenplay by ROBERT BENTON

STAR WARS, A Twentieth Century-Fox Production, Twentieth Century-Fox: Story and screenplay by GEORGE LUCAS

THE TURNING POINT, Hera Productions, Twentieth Century-Fox: Story and screenplay by ARTHUR LAURENTS

(Best Screenplay—based on material from another medium)

EQUUS, A Winkast Company, Ltd./P.B., Ltd. Production, United Artists: Screenplay by PETER SHAFFER

I NEVER PROMISED YOU A ROSE GARDEN, A Scherick/Blatt Production, New World Pictures: Screenplay by GAVIN LAMBERT and LEWIS JOHN CARLINO

JULIA, A Twentieth Century-Fox Production, Twentieth Century-Fox: Screenplay by ALVIN SARGENT

OH, GOD!, A Warner Bros. Production, Warner Bros.: Screenplay by LARRY GELBART

THAT OBSCURE OBJECT OF DESIRE, A Greenwich-Les Films Galaxie-In Cine Production, First Artists: Screenplay by LUIS BUÑUEL and JEAN-CLAUDE CARRIERE

Cinematography

CLOSE ENCOUNTERS OF THE THIRD KIND, Close Encounter Productions, Columbia: VILMOS ZSIGMOND

ISLANDS IN THE STREAM, A Peter Bart/Max Palevsky Production, Paramount: FRED J. KOENEKAMP

JULIA, A Twentieth Century-Fox Production, Twentieth Century-Fox: DOUGLAS SLOCOMBE

LOOKING FOR MR. GOODBAR, A Freddie Fields Production, Paramount: WILLIAM A. FRAKER

THE TURNING POINT, Hera Productions,

Twentieth Century-Fox: ROBERT SURTEES

Art Direction—Set Decoration

AIRPORT '77, A Jennings Lang Production, Universal
Art Direction: GEORGE C. WEBB
Set Decoration: MICKEY S. MICHAELS
CLOSE ENCOUNTERS OF THE THIRD KIND, Close Encounter Productions, Columbia:
Art Direction: JOE ALVES and DAN LOMINO
Set Decoration: PHIL ABRAMSON
THE SPY WHO LOVED ME, Eon Productions, United Artists
Art Direction: KEN ADAM and PETER LAMONT
Set Decoration: HUGH SCAIFE
STAR WARS, A Twentieth Century-Fox Production, Twentieth Century-Fox
Art Direction: JOHN BARRY, NORMAN REYNOLDS and LESLIE DILLEY
Set Decoration: ROGER CHRISTIAN
THE TURNING POINT, Hera Productions, Twentieth Century-Fox
Art Direction: ALBERT BRENNER
Set Decoration: MARVIN MARCH

Sound

CLOSE ENCOUNTERS OF THE THIRD KIND, Close Encounter Productions, Columbia: ROBERT KNUDSON, ROBERT J. GLASS, DON MacDOUGALL and GENE S. CANTAMESSA
THE DEEP, A Casablanca Filmworks Production, Columbia: WALTER GOSS, DICK ALEXANDER, TOM BECKERT and ROBIN GREGORY
SORCERER, A William Friedkin Film Production, Paramount-Universal: ROBERT KNUDSON, ROBERT J. GLASS,

RICHARD TYLER and JEAN-LOUIS DUCARME
STAR WARS, A Twentieth Century-Fox Production, Twentieth Century-Fox: DON MacDOUGALL, RAY WEST, BOB MINKLER and DEREK BALL
THE TURNING POINT, Hera Productions, Twentieth Century-Fox: THEODORE SODERBERG, PAUL WELLS, DOUGLAS O. WILLIAMS and JERRY JOST

Film Editing

CLOSE ENCOUNTERS OF THE THIRD KIND, Close Encounter Productions, Columbia: MICHAEL KAHN
JULIA, A Twentieth Century-Fox Production, Twentieth Century-Fox: WALTER MURCH and MARCEL DURHAM
SMOKEY AND THE BANDIT, A Universal/Rastar Production, Universal: WALTER HANNEMANN and ANGELO ROSS
STAR WARS, A Twentieth Century-Fox Production, Twentieth Century-Fox: PAUL HIRSCH, MARCIA LUCAS and RICHARD CHEW
THE TURNING POINT, Hera Productions, Twentieth Century-Fox: WILLIAM REYNOLDS

Music

(Best Original Score)

CLOSE ENCOUNTERS OF THE THIRD KIND, Close Encounter Productions, Columbia: JOHN WILLIAMS
JULIA, A Twentieth Century-Fox Production, Twentieth Century-Fox: GEORGES DELERUE
MOHAMMAD—MESSENGER OF GOD, A Filmco International Production, Irwin Yablans Company: MAURICE JARRE
THE SPY WHO LOVED ME, Eon Productions, United Artists: MARVIN HAMLISCH

STAR WARS, A Twentieth Century-
Fox Production, Twentieth Century-
Fox: JOHN WILLIAMS

(Best Original Song Score And Its Adaptation or Best Adaptation Score)

A LITTLE NIGHT MUSIC, A Sascha-
Wien Film Production in association
with Elliott Kastner, New World
Pictures
Adapted by JONATHAN TUNICK

PETE'S DRAGON, Walt Disney Produc-
tions, Buena Vista Distribution
Company
Song Score by AL KASHA and JOEL
HIRSCHHORN
Adapted by IRWIN KOSTAL

THE SLIPPER AND THE ROSE—THE
STORY OF CINDERELLA, Paradine Co-
Productions, Ltd., Universal
Song Score by RICHARD M. SHERMAN
and ROBERT B. SHERMAN
Adapted by ANGELA MORLEY

(Best Original Song)

CANDLE ON THE WATER from *Pete's
Dragon,* Walt Disney Productions,
Buena Vista Distribution Company
Music and lyrics by AL KASHA and
JOEL HIRSCHHORN

NOBODY DOES IT BETTER from *The Spy
Who Loved Me,* Eon Productions,
United Artists
Music by MARVIN HAMLISCH
Lyrics by CAROLE BAYER SAGER

THE SLIPPER AND THE ROSE WALTZ (HE
DANCED WITH ME/SHE DANCED WITH
ME) from *The Slipper and The
Rose—The Story of Cinderella,*
Pardine Co-Productions, Ltd., Uni-
versal:
Music and lyrics by RICHARD M.
SHERMAN and ROBERT B. SHERMAN

SOMEONE'S WAITING FOR YOU from
The Rescuers, Walt Disney Produc-
tions, Buena Vista Distribution
Company:
Music by SAMMY FAIN

Lyrics by CAROL CONNORS and AYN
ROBBINS

YOU LIGHT UP MY LIFE from *You
Light Up My Life,* The Session
Company Production, Columbia
Music and lyrics by JOSEPH
BROOKS

Costume Design

AIRPORT '77, A Jennings Lang Production, Universal: EDITH HEAD and
BURTON MILLER

JULIA, A Twentieth Century-Fox Production, Twentieth Century-Fox:
ANTHEA SYLBERT

A LITTLE NIGHT MUSIC, A Sascha-Wien
Film Production in association with
Elliott Kastner, New World Pic-
tures: FLORENCE KLOTZ

THE OTHER SIDE OF MIDNIGHT, A Frank
Yablans Presentations Production,
Twentieth Century-Fox: IRENE
SHARAFF

STAR WARS, A Twentieth Century-
Fox Production, Twentieth Century-
Fox: JOHN MOLLO

Short Films

(Animated)

THE BEAD GAME, National Film Board
of Canada: ISHU PATEL, Producer

THE DOONESBURY SPECIAL, The Hubley
Studio: JOHN and FAITH HUBLEY and
GARY TRUDEAU, Producers

JIMMY THE C, A Motionpicker Production: JIMMY PICKER and ROBERT
GROSSMAN, Producers

SAND CASTLE, National Film Board
of Canada: CO HOEDEMAN, Producer

(Live Action)

THE ABSENT-MINDED WAITER, The
Aspen Film Society: WILLIAM E.
MCEUEN, Producer

FLOATING FREE, A Trans World International Production: JERRY BUTTS,

Producer

I'LL FIND A WAY, National Film Board of Canada: BEVERLY SHAFFER and YUKI YOSHIDA, Producers

NOTES ON THE POPULAR ARTS, Saul Bass Films: SAUL BASS, Producer

SPACEBORNE, A Lawrence Hall of Science Production for the Regents of the University of California with the cooperation of NASA: PHILIP DAUBER, Producer

Documentary

(Short Subjects)

AGUADA MARTINEZ: OUR PEOPLE, OUR COUNTRY, A Moctesuma Esparza Production: MOCTESUMA ESPARZA, Producer

FIRST EDITION, D. L. Sage Productions: HELEN WHITNEY and DeWITT L. SAGE, JR., Producers

GRAVITY IS MY ENEMY, A John Joseph Production: JOHN JOSEPH and JAN STUSSY, Producers

OF TIME, TOMBS AND TREASURE, A Charlie/Papa Production: JAMES R. MESSENGER, Producer

THE SHETLAND EXPERIENCE, Balfour Films: DOUGLAS GORDON, Producer

(Features)

THE CHILDREN OF THEATRE STREET, Mack-Vaganova Company: ROBERT DORNHELM and EARLE MACK, Producers

HIGH GRASS CIRCUS, National Film Board of Canada: BILL BRIND, TORBEN SCHIOLER and TONY IANZELO, Producers

HOMAGE TO CHAGALL—THE COLOURS OF LOVE, A CBC Production: HARRY RASKY, Producer

UNION MAIDS, A Klein, Reichert, Mogulescu Production: JAMES KLEIN, JULIA REICHERT and MILES MOGULESCU, Producers

WHO ARE THE DeBOLTS? AND

WHERE DID THEY GET NINETEEN KIDS?, Korty Films and Charles M. Schulz Creative Associates in association with Sanrio Films: JOHN KORTY, DAN McCANN and WARREN L. LOCKHART, Producers

Foreign Language Film Award

IPHIGENIA, A Greek Film Centre Production (Greece)

MADAME ROSA, A Lira Films Production (France)

OPERATION THUNDERBOLT, A Golan-Globus Production (Israel)

A SPECIAL DAY, A Canafox Films Production (Italy)

THAT OBSCURE OBJECT OF DESIRE, A Greenwich-Les Films Galaxie-In Cine Production (Spain).

Visual Effects

CLOSE ENCOUNTERS OF THE THIRD KIND, Close Encounter Productions, Columbia. ROY ARBOGAST, DOUGLAS TRUMBULL, MATTHEW YURICICH, GREGORY JEIN and RICHARD YURICICH

STAR WARS, A Twentieth Century-Fox Production, Twentieth Century-Fox: JOHN STEARS, JOHN DYKSTRA, RICHARD EDLUND, GRANT McCUNE and ROBERT BLALACK

Honorary Award

MARGARET BOOTH for sixty-two years of exceptionally distinguished service to the motion picture industry as a film editor

Medal of Commendation

GORDON E. SAWYER and SIDNEY P. SOLOW in appreciation for outstanding service and dedication in upholding the high standards of the Academy of Motion Picture Arts and Sciences

Special Achievement Awards

Sound Effects: BENJAMIN BURTT, JR. for the creation of the alien, creature, and robot voices in *Star Wars,* A Twentieth Century-Fox Production, Twentieth Century-Fox.

Sound Effects Editing Award: CLOSE ENCOUNTERS OF THE THIRD KIND, Close Encounter Productions, Columbia. FRANK WARNER, Supervising Sound Effects Editor.

Irving G. Thalberg Memorial Award
WALTER MIRISCH

Jean Hersholt Humanitarian Award
CHARLTON HESTON

Scientific or Technical
Class I

GARRETT BROWN and the CINEMA PRODUCTS CORP. engineering staff under the supervision of JOHN JURGENS, for the invention and development of Steadicam

Class II

JOSEPH D. KELLY, BARRY K. HENLEY, HAMMOND H. HOLT and GLEN GLENN SOUND for the concept and development of a Postproduction Audio Processing System for Motion Picture Films

PANAVISION, INCORPORATED, for the concept and engineering of the improvements incorporated in the Panaflex Motion Picture Camera

N. PAUL KENWORTHY, JR. and WILLIAM R. LATADY for the invention and development of the Kenworthy Snorkel Camera System for motion picture photography

JOHN C. DYKSTRA for the development of the Dykstraflex Camera and to ALVAH J. MILLER and

JERRY JEFFRESS for the engineering of the Electronic Motion Control System used in concert for multiple exposure visual effects motion picture photography

EASTMAN KODAK COMPANY for the development and introduction of a new duplicating film for motion pictures

STEPHAN KUDELSKI of NAGRA MAGNETIC RECORDERS, INCORPORATED, for the engineering of the improvements incorporated in the Nagra 4.2L sound recorder for motion picture production

Class III

ERNST NETTMANN of the ASTROVISION DIVISION of CONTINENTAL CAMERA SYSTEMS, INCORPORATED, for the engineering of its Snorkel Aerial Camera System

EECO (ELECTRONIC ENGINEERING COMPANY OF CALIFORNIA) for developing a method for interlocking non-sprocketed film and tape media used in motion picture production

DR. BERNHARD KUHL and WERNER BLOCK of OSRAM, GmbH, for the development of the HMI high-efficiency discharge lamp for motion picture lighting

PANAVISION, INCORPORATED, for the design of Panalite, a camera-mounted controllable light for motion picture photography

PANAVISION, INCORPORATED, for the engineering of the Panahead gearhead for motion picture cameras

PICLEAR, INC., for originating and developing an attachment to motion picture projectors to improve screen image quality

APPENDICES

Academy Founders

On the evening of January 11, 1927, thirty-six persons who represented a cross section of the film industry held a dinner at the Ambassador Hotel in Los Angeles to discuss the formation of an organization which would benefit the motion picture industry. These people became the founders of the Academy of Motion Picture Arts and Sciences.

The branch of the Academy which each member joined is indicated after the name.

J. ARTHUR BALL (1895–1951) Technicians Branch. Pioneer color film engineer. Cameraman and later technical director of Technicolor.

RICHARD BARTHELMESS (1895–1963) Actors Branch. Leading man for First National whose most memorable films were *Broken Blossoms* and *Tol'able David*. Formed his own company in 1921.

FRED BEETSON (1879–1953) Producers Branch. Came to Hollywood in 1923 at the request of Will Hays. An officer of the Association of Motion Picture Producers for nearly twenty years, also organizer and president of the Central Casting Corporation and a founder and vice-president of the Motion Picture Relief Fund.

CHARLES H. CHRISTIE (1880–1955) Producers Branch. Co-producer with brother Al of the Christie Comedies. Vice-president and general manager of Christie Studios.

GEORGE W. COHEN (1895–1971) Special member. Known as the "father of motion picture contracts." As a member of the law firm of Loeb, Walker, and Loeb, he represented several studios and, with Edwin Loeb, drew up the Constitution and By-laws of the Academy.

CECIL B. DeMILLE (1881–1959) Directors Branch. Pioneer Hollywood producer and director. In 1913, with Jesse Lasky, Samuel Goldwyn, and Arthur Friend, formed the Jesse L. Lasky Feature Play Company. Later founded his own production company. Active in the Association of Motion Picture Producers.

DOUGLAS FAIRBANKS, SR. (1883–1939) Actors Branch. Swashbuckling leading man. Began film career in 1914 with D.W.

Griffith. In 1919, with Mary Pickford, Charlie Chaplin, and Griffith, formed United Artists. Married Pickford in 1920. First president of the Academy of Motion Picture Arts & Sciences.

JOSEPH WHITE FARNHAM (1884–?) Writers Branch. After varied career as writer, independent exhibitor, and advertising manager for Lubin, came to Hollywood as a free lance editor and writer. In 1924 joined MGM as title writer and editor.

CEDRIC GIBBONS (1895–1960) Technicians Branch. Came to Hollywood with the Goldwyn Company. Became head of MGM's art department when Goldwyn merged with Metro.

BENJAMIN F. GLAZER (1888–1956) Writers Branch. Screenwriter who worked for several studios including Paramount, Fox, and MGM. In 1928 became head of production for Pathe.

SID GRAUMAN (1879–1950) Producers Branch. Veteran movie exhibitor. Built the Million Dollar Theatre in Los Angeles, also the Metropolitan, Egyptian, and Chinese. Credited by *Variety* with originating the gala Hollywood premiere.

MILTON E. HOFFMAN (1880–1952) Producers Branch. Started with Paramount in 1916, later worked for MGM and for Cecil B. DeMille. In 1924 became executive studio manager for Paramount.

JACK HOLT (1888–1951) Actors Branch. Broke into pictures as a stunt man in 1913, eventually became a star for Columbia.

HENRY KING (1888–   ) Directors Branch. Entered films as an actor for the Lubin Company in 1912. Began directing in 1916 for Pathe. In the 1920s directed for First

National, Paramount, Goldwyn, and United Artists. From 1930 on directed for Fox.

JESSE L. LASKY (1880–1958) Producers Branch. In 1913, with DeMille, Goldwyn, and Arthur Friend, formed Jesse L. Lasky Feature Play Company. Became vice-president in charge of production after merger with Adolph Zukor's Famous Players in 1916.

M. C. LEVEE (1891–1972) Producers Branch. Began with Fox in 1917. Senior executive with Paramount, vice-president of United Studios, then vice-president and executive business manager of First National. First treasurer of the Academy of Motion Picture Arts & Sciences.

FRANK LLOYD (1889–1960) Directors Branch. Began directing in 1913. Formed his own production company in 1923 and worked as a producer-director releasing through First National.

HAROLD LLOYD (1893–1971) Actors Branch. Comedian best known for perilous comic situations involving dangerous stunts. Began film work in 1916. First contract was with Hal Roach. Formed his own production company in 1923.

EDWIN LOEB (1887–1970) Special member. Founder of a law firm widely known for motion picture contract work. In 1927 the Academy expressed its indebtedness to Loeb and George Cohen of Loeb, Walker, and Loeb "for their untiring and able services, voluntarily tendered in drafting the Constitution and By-laws, and for other legal work and advice."

JEANIE MACPHERSON (1887–1946) Writers Branch. Began as an actress with Florence Lawrence and Mary Pickford. Later had her own unit at Universal where she wrote, directed, and acted in two-reelers. Fired for taking seven days on a production. Hired by Cecil B. DeMille and became best known as a screenwriter for him.

LOUIS B. MAYER (1885–1957) Producers Branch. Vice-president in charge of production for MGM. Began producing films in 1916. Formed his own company which he merged with Loew's Metro and Goldwyn's company to form MGM in 1924.

BESS MEREDYTH (1890–1969) Writers Branch. Started as an extra for Biograph.

Began writing screenplays for Griffith in 1913, later worked for several studios. Co-scripted (with Carey Wilson) *Ben Hur* for MGM.

CONRAD NAGEL (1897–1970) Actors Branch. Leading man for MGM. Active in Actors' Equity and then the Academy in trying to negotiate a standard contract for actors.

FRED NIBLO (1874–1948) Directors Branch. After much stage experience, entered films in 1917 as actor, director, and producer. Directed *The Mark of Zorro, Blood and Sand, Ben Hur*. Became one of MGM's top directors in the 1920s. First vice-president of the Academy of Motion Picture Arts & Sciences.

MARY PICKFORD (1893–) Producers Branch. Started in films with Griffith at Biograph. Organized her own company in 1916 and became an independent producer in 1918. The following year she founded United Artists with Fairbanks, Chaplin, and Griffith.

ROY J. POMEROY (1893–1947) Technicians Branch. Joined Lasky in 1922 and became head of special photographic effects department for Paramount. Parted the Red Sea for DeMille's *Ten Commandments*. Later worked on sound production and directed Paramount's first all-talking picture, *Interference*.

HARRY RAPF (1881–1949) Producers Branch. Joined Mayer in 1924 and became producer, later production executive for MGM.

JOSEPH M. SCHENCK (1878–1961) Producers Branch. Veteran showman and movie mogul. In 1924 became chairman of the board of United Artists. Later founded Twentieth Century Productions.

MILTON SILLS (1882–1930) Actors Branch. Leading man for First National. One of the founders of Actors' Equity.

JOHN M. STAHL (1886–1950) Directors Branch. Began directing films in 1914. Directed for First National, then MGM in the 1920s. In 1928 became vice-president supervising production for Tiffany-Stahl Productions.

IRVING G. THALBERG (1899–1936) Producers Branch. Started with Universal in 1917, became studio manager at age twenty-one. Became head of production for Louis B. Mayer's company in 1923. When MGM was formed, became second only to Mayer in charge of production.

RAOUL WALSH (1887–) Directors Branch. Joined Biograph in 1912 as an actor and assistant to D.W. Griffith. Directed films for various companies including Fox and Paramount.

HARRY WARNER (1881–1958) Producers Branch. Eldest of the four Warner brothers. Named president when the studio was founded in 1923.

JACK L. WARNER (1892–1978) Producers Branch. Youngest of the four Warner brothers. Active in film exhibition and distribution from 1905. Began film production with brother Sam in 1912. Named vice-president in charge of production when Warner Brothers Studio was founded in 1923.

CAREY WILSON (1889–1962) Writers Branch. Top screenwriter for Thalberg at MGM. Co-scripted (with Bess Meredyth) *Ben Hur* and many other MGM hits.

FRANK WOODS (1860–1939) Writers Branch. Film critic for the New York *Dramatic Mirror*. In 1911 joined D.W. Griffith as a story editor. Convinced Griffith to film *The Clansman*. Became scenario chief at Famous Players-Lasky. First secretary of the Academy of Motion Picture Arts & Sciences.

Academy Presidents

Douglas Fairbanks, Sr.	May 4, 1927–October 1929
William C. DeMille	October 1929–October 1931
M. C. Levee	October 1931–October 1932
Conrad Nagel (resigned)	October 1932–April 1933
J. Theodore Reed	April 1933–October 1934
Frank Lloyd	October 1934–October 1935
Frank Capra (no elections held 1936/37 and 1937/38)	October 1935–December 1939
Walter Wanger	December 1939–October 1941
Bette Davis (resigned)	October 1941–December 1941
Walter Wanger	December 1941–October 1945
Jean Hersholt	October 1945–May 1949
Charles Brackett	May 1949–May 1955
George Seaton	June 1955–May 1958
George Stevens	June 1958–May 1959
B. B. Kahane	June 1959–September 1960
Valentine Davies	September 1960–July 1961
Wendell R. Corey	August 1961–June 1963
Arthur Freed	June 1963–May 1967
Gregory Peck	June 1967–May 1970
Daniel Taradash	June 1970–June 1973
Walter Mirisch	June 1973–May 1977
Howard W. Koch	June 1977–

Directors of Best Picture

Year	Film	Director
1927/28	Wings	William A. Wellman
1928/29	Broadway Melody	Harry Beaumont
1929/30	All Quiet On the Western Front	Lewis Milestone*
1930/31	Cimarron	Wesley Ruggles
1931/32	Grand Hotel	Edmund Goulding
1932/33	Cavalcade	Frank Lloyd*
1934	It Happened One Night	Frank Capra*
1935	Mutiny On the Bounty	Frank Lloyd
1936	The Great Ziegfeld	Robert Z. Leonard
1937	The Life of Emile Zola	William Dieterle
1938	You Can't Take It With You	Frank Capra*
1939	Gone With The Wind	Victor Fleming*
1940	Rebecca	Alfred Hitchcock
1941	How Green Was My Valley	John Ford*
1942	Mrs. Miniver	William Wyler*
1943	Casablanca	Michael Curtiz*
1944	Going My Way	Leo McCarey*
1945	The Lost Weekend	Billy Wilder*
1946	The Best Years of Our Lives	William Wyler*
1947	Gentlemen's Agreement	Elia Kazan*
1948	Hamlet	Laurence Olivier
1949	All the King's Men	Robert Rossen
1950	All About Eve	Joseph L. Mankiewicz*
1951	An American In Paris	Vincente Minnelli
1952	The Greatest Show On Earth	Cecil B. DeMille
1953	From Here To Eternity	Fred Zinnemann*
1954	On the Waterfront	Elia Kazan*
1955	Marty	Delbert Mann*
1956	Around the World In Eighty Days	Michael Anderson
1957	The Bridge On the River Kwai	David Lean*
1958	Gigi	Vincente Minnelli*
1959	Ben-Hur	William Wyler*
1960	The Apartment	Billy Wilder*
1961	West Side Story	Robert Wise,* Jerome Robbins*
1962	Lawrence of Arabia	David Lean*
1963	Tom Jones	Tony Richardson*
1964	My Fair Lady	George Cukor*
1965	The Sound of Music	Robert Wise*
1966	A Man For All Seasons	Fred Zinnemann*

* Also won Oscar for Directing

1967	In the Heat of the Night	Norman Jewison*
1968	Oliver	Carol Reed*
1969	Midnight Cowboy	John Schlesinger*
1970	Patton	Franklin J. Schaffner*
1971	The French Connection	William Friedkin*
1972	The Godfather	Francis Ford Coppola
1973	The Sting	George Roy Hill*
1974	The Godfather II	Francis Ford Coppola*
1975	One Flew Over the Cuckoo's Nest	Milos Forman*
1976	Rocky	John G. Avildsen*
1977	Annie Hall	Woody Allen*

*Also won Oscar for Directing

Selected Bibliography

The following list includes all books published by the Academy of Motion Picture Arts and Sciences, all books specifically about the Oscars, and those film histories, biographies, and other works which mention the Academy in a historical context.

Most of the articles cited address questions of Academy policy rather than the Oscars. I have not included citations for accounts of specific Awards shows. The reader is encouraged to check the specific dates of the Awards presentations (given in the chronological index) and consult the major Hollywood trade papers such as *Daily Variety, Hollywood Reporter, Motion Picture Herald,* and *Film Daily.*

My intention has been to acknowledge the sources which have proved useful to me and to offer to readers who wish to examine the subject more carefully a guide for further research.

BOOKS

Academy of Motion Picture Arts and Sciences. *Academy War Film Library Catalog of Prints: May 1942–May 1944.* Hollywood, California: AMPAS, 1944. 109 pp., indexed. A list of over four hundred films from the United States, Great Britain, Canada, Australia, and Belgium which the Academy collected during the war "primarily as an aid to studio production."

————. *Motion Picture Sound Engineering.* New York: D. Van Nostrand Company, 1938. 547 pp., indexed. Reprint of lectures sponsored by the Research Council. Updates the Academy's 1931 book on sound and includes an appendix list of members who have served on Research Council committees.

————. *Press Clipping File On the Senate Sub-Committee War Film Hearings, Volume One, August 1st–October 15, 1941.* 294 pp., indexed. Fascinating collection of cartoons and clippings from newspapers, studio publicity releases, trade papers, and the Congressional Record concerning the investigation by Senate isolationists who complained of Hollywood war propaganda. Limited edition of 175 copies printed.

Capra, Frank. *The Name Above the Title.* New York: Macmillan, 1971. 562 pp., indexed. Autobiography of the director who won three Oscars and served as president of the Academy from 1935 to 1939. An insider's view on the most crisis-ridden period of the Academy's history.

Clark, Henry. *Academy Award Diary: 1928–1955.* New York: Pageant Press, 1959. 188 pp., no index. Year by year account of the awards with little analysis or critical comment. The design of the book makes the material nearly inaccessible.

Cowan, Lester, ed. *Recording Sound For Motion Pictures.* New York: McGraw-Hill, 1931. 404 pp., indexed. Reprint of lectures first published in the Academy's Technical Digest series. In his preface, Academy president William DeMille wrote, "If the Academy had not been organized to make such cooperation [between studio sound technicians] possible this book would never have been written, and we offer it to the craft with a certain paternal glow."

Crowther, Bosley. *Hollywood Rajah: The Life and Times of Louis B. Mayer.* New York: Henry Holt and Company, 1960. 339 pp., indexed. Some brief references to the founding of the Academy.

Eder, Shirley. *Not This Time, Cary Grant!* Garden City, NY: Doubleday and Company, 1973. 295 pp., no index. A short section called "Oscar Memories" is a personal glimpse of the 1971 Awards by a veteran Hollywood gossip columnist.

Frederik, Nathalie. *The New Hollywood and the Academy Awards*. Beverly Hills, CA: Hollywood Awards Publications, 1971. 208 pp., no index. Heavily illustrated paperback reference book on the Oscars. Emphasis is on the Best Picture and Acting Awards with all other winners listed after each decade. The major shortcoming is the failure to include an index and the names of nominees, though some may still find it handy as a quick reference.

Likeness, George. *The Oscar People: From Wings To My Fair Lady*. Mendota, Illinois: The Wayside Press, 1965, 432 pp., indexed but does not include all winners' names. The Best Picture and Acting Awards are emphasized at the expense of the other categories. Very little history or explanation of the categories.

Manfull, Helen, ed. *Additional Dialogue: Letters of Dalton Trumbo, 1942–1962*. New York: M. Evans and Company, 1970. 576 pp., indexed. Includes some fascinating letters on the Academy's role during the blacklist period.

Mayer, Michael F. *Foreign Films On American Screens*. New York: Arco, 1965. 119 pp., no index. Discusses the rising interest in foreign films in postwar America. Eighteen appendices list foreign films which have won Oscars, New York Film Critics awards, and numerous festival prizes.

Michael, Paul. *The Academy Awards: A Pictorial History*. New York: Crown, 1975. 390 pp., indexed. A standard reference book on the Oscars, arranged chronologically with emphasis on the picture and acting categories. Excellent illustrations. Lists nominees only for Picture, Actor, and Actress.

Michael, Paul, ed. *The American Movies Reference Book: The Sound Era*. Englewood Cliffs, N.J.: Prentice-Hall, 1969. The section called "The Awards" is useful for comparing Oscar-winning achievements with the awards of several other groups including the New York Film Critics, Film Daily, Photoplay, and the National Board of Review.

Osborne, Robert. *The Academy Awards Illustrated*. La Habra, CA: Ernest Schworck, 1969. 321 pp., no index. A standard work on the Oscars, far superior to Michael or Frederik. Updated each year, though no attempt has been made to revise or correct any of the pre-1970 material. The readable, informative text is factual though not critical, with much of the material apparently taken from the Hollywood trade papers. Nominees for all categories are listed, and the book offers an excellent selection of illustrations. Major shortcomings are the absence of an index and a rather skimpy, one-page history of the Academy. Osborne has also published several paperback spin-offs of this volume.

Osborne, Robert. *50 Golden Years of Oscar: The Official History of the Academy of Motion Picture Arts and Sciences*. La Habra, California: ESE California, 1978.

Perry, Louis B. and Richard S. Perry. *A History of the Los Angeles Labor Movement, 1911–1941*. Berkeley and Los Angeles: University of California Press, 1963. 622 pp., indexed. The chapter on "Union Success In the Movie Industry" is a detailed account of the labor relations with which the Academy involved itself for the first decade of its existence. The authors say the Academy was established by the producers as a means of frustrating the bargaining attempts by the talent groups and forestalling unionization.

Pickard, Roy. *The Oscar Movies: From A To Z*. New York: Taplinger, 1978. 247 pp., indexed. Alphabetical listings of every feature film to win an Oscar in any category.

Reed, Rex. *Conversations In the Raw*. Cleveland and New York: World Publishing Company, 1969. 312 pp., no index. One small section includes an amusing, vitriolic, and jaundiced account of the 40th Awards ceremony, which the author calls a "night of back-stabbing and utter stupidity."

Ross, Murray. *Stars and Strikes: Unionization of Hollywood*. New York: Columbia

University Press, 1941. 233 pp., indexed. Essential reading for anyone interested in learning how the motion picture industry became unionized. Includes many references to the role played by the Academy in this struggle.

Sands, Pierre Norman. *A Historical Study of the Academy of Motion Picture Arts and Sciences (1927–1947)*. New York: Arno Press, 1973. 262 pp., no index. Reprint of a 1966 University of Southern California Ph.D. dissertation. Easily the most comprehensive study of the Academy's early history yet published, though the material lacks any critical objectivity and is arranged to please a committee of academicians rather than a general readership. The inclusion of an index would have made this volume far more valuable.

Sklar, Robert. *Movie-Made America: A Cultural History of American Movies*. New York: Random House, 1975. 340 pp., indexed. Calls the Academy a company union set up by the producers in response to Equity's drive to organize actors. Mentions the Academy's role in the 1933 bank holiday studio crisis and the work of the Research Council in World War II. Many other minor references to the Academy.

Who Wrote the Movie and What Else Did He Write? An Index of Screenwriters and Their Film Works, 1936–1969. Los Angeles: Academy of Motion Picture Arts and Sciences and the Writers Guild of America-West, 1970. 491 pp., indexed. The Awards index includes the winners and nominees for the Academy Awards for writing and the awards of the Screen Writers' Guild. A good, helpful research tool.

ARTICLES

"Abandoned Oscar." *Newsweek,* April 11, 1949, p. 90. A brief article which says the decision by the five major studios to withdraw financial support for the Oscar ceremonies was not a hasty reaction to the foreign film *Hamlet* winning Best Picture but was decided months before the 1948 Awards.

"Academy Talent Up In Arms." *Motion Picture Herald* III (April 29, 1933): 10. Trade paper account of the Academy talent groups' opposition to the producers' proposed Artists' Service Bureau. Says AMPAS champions the workers' cause against the producers.

"The Academy Writer-Producer Agreement . . . Another Attempt To Destroy the Guild." *Screen Guilds' Magazine* 2 (October 1935): 1–2. Militant accusation by the actor and writer guilds that the Academy is a company union and tool of the producers. Academy founder Frank Woods confirmed some allegations, corrected others in an article in the following issue.

Alpert, Hollis. "A Matter of Opinion." *Saturday Review,* April 11, 1953, p. 55. A brief complaint that the Oscars reflect "an inability to distinguish between the pretentious and the real, a nostalgia for the past, a fear of the future." Mentions the general dismay registered when *The Greatest Show On Earth* was named Best Picture over *High Noon.*

"An Award Worth Winning." *The Screen Guilds' Magazine* 3 (March 1936): 1. A reprint of screenwriter Dudley Nichols' letter to the Academy refusing his Oscar for *The Informer.*

Beaton, Welford. "Industry Fashioning Weapon of Defence." *The Film Spectator* III (May 28, 1927): 3. Laudatory editorial noting the formation of the Academy as a means for the motion picture industry to answer unjust criticism with a unified voice.

———. "Is Entitled To Support of All." *The Film Spectator* III (May 28, 1927): 4. More praise for the newly founded Academy. Quotes at length the declaration of aims printed on the invitations to the Academy's organizational banquet.

Bickerstaff, Isaac. "The Oscars—By Radio." *Films in Review* 3 (April 1952): 164–70. Useless account of listening to the 1952 Oscar ceremonies on the radio.

Bower, Anthony. "Academy Awards."

Nation 152 (March 15, 1941): 305. Some historical background but mostly an account of the 1940 Awards banquet which was addressed via radio by President Roosevelt.

Champlin, Charles. "The Academy At Fifty." *American Film,* March 1978, pp. 16–19. A look at the Academy's year-round activities.

Chandler, Raymond. "Oscar Night In Hollywood." *Atlantic* 181 (March 1948): 24–27. Stylish, iconoclastic piece which characterizes the Oscar ceremony as a "grotesque ritual." "If we permit noise, ballyhoo and bad theatre to influence us in the selection of the people who are to run the country, why should we object to the same methods in the selection of meritorious achievement in the film business?"

———. "Oscar Night In Hollywood." *Sight and Sound* 19 (June 1950): 157–61. Identical to Chandler's 1948 *Atlantic* article.

Daily Variety. 1933–present. Major trade paper in Hollywood and a constant source of news about the Academy and the motion picture industry.

Elliot, Paul. "Looking Over the Oscars." *Atlantic* 174 (August 1944): 103–7. Inconsequential; mostly a complaint about *Casablanca* winning the Best Picture award.

Garringer, Nelson E. "Academy Award Nominations." *Films In Review* 8 (March 1957): 111–15. Oscar trivia culled from lists of nominations, now too dated to be of value.

Gledhill, Donald. "The Motion Picture Academy, A Cooperative In Hollywood." *Journal of Educational Sociology* 13 (January 1940). Brief overview of Academy achievements by the organization's executive secretary. Part of a special issue on "Some Educational Aspects of Motion Pictures."

———. "Screen Academy and the Field It Covers." *Hollywood Spectator,* March 1, 1940. Virtually identical to Gledhill's article in the *Journal of Educational Sociology* published two months earlier.

Hersholt, Jean. "The Academy Speaks." *Atlantic* 181 (May 1948): 43–45. The president of the Academy responds to Chandler's anti-Academy article which appeared two months earlier. Hersholt describes the other Academy activities besides the Oscars and defends the Academy against charges of arbitrary voting, politicking, and discrimination against foreign films.

Hollywood Reporter. 1930–present. Another major Hollywood trade paper which reports the news of the motion picture industry.

Hubler, Richard G. "Pulitzer Prize For Motion Pictures." *Screen Writer* 2 (January 1947): 7–10. A plea from a screenwriter for an impartial judge outside the industry to bestow awards of merit for motion picture achievement. Complains that the "inbred praise and inhibited exhibitionism" of the Academy Awards lower the standards of movies.

Hurd, Reggie, Jr. "Academy Award Mistakes." *Films In Review* 6 (May 1955): 209–15. Lists performances which should have won Oscars but didn't. Nearly everyone who scans the winner's list plays this game sooner or later.

Joseph, Robert. "Re: Unions In Hollywood." *Films* 1 (Summer 1940): 35–40. Claims that the founding of the Academy was a plot by producers "to sell the talent groups down the river." Characterizes the Academy's involvement in labor relations as "a twelve year history of chicanery and malfeasance, broken faith and double-crossing."

Kline, Herbert. "Academy's Last Supper." *New Theatre* 3 (April 1936): 32–33. An account of the tumultuous battle by Hollywood talent groups to win recognition and bargaining power from the producers. The title refers to the successful boycott of the Awards banquet in 1936 by the Screen Actors' and Screen Writers' Guilds.

Lavery, Emmet. "Mr. Shakespeare's Earthquake: Much Ado About the Oscars." *Saturday Review,* April 16, 1949, p. 13. The author, a member of the Academy

Board of Governors, contends that by picking *Hamlet* as Best Picture, Academy voters have demonstrated that the balloting is free from studio influence and Hollywood chauvinism.

Logan, Somerset. "The Battle of Hollywood." *The New Republic* 59 (August 7, 1929): 308. A pro-Actors Equity article about the attempt to unionize actors. The Academy is not mentioned.

———. "Revolt In Hollywood." *Nation* 129 (July 17, 1929): 61. Cites poor conditions for actors and their need for a union. No mention of the Academy. "Equity will prevail in Hollywood."

"The Menace of the Academy." *The Screen Player* 1 (April 15, 1934): 1. Editorial published by the Screen Actors Guild which claims that the producer-controlled Academy is trying to destroy the Guild.

New York Times, April 21, 1933, p. 24. Brief news story of Conrad Nagel's resignation as AMPAS president in the stormy aftermath of Hollywood's 1933 salary-cut crisis. "Created originally by the film executives to protect themselves from Actors Equity and the A.F. of L., [the Academy] has risen to the defense of the actors and now finds itself in the ironical position of opposing the producers who have given it their financial support."

Niver, Kemp R. "From Film To Paper To Film." *Quarterly Journal of the Library of Congress* 21 (October 1964): 248–64. Excellent article on the restoration of the paper prints collection, a joint project of the Academy and the Library of Congress.

"Organized Hosts." *Screen Guilds' Magazine* 3 (March 1936): 3. "The fight of the Guilds against the Academy is a fight between honest employees' organizations and a company union." Calls for the Academy to be destroyed and forgotten.

"Oscar." *Films and Filming* 1 (June 1955): 3. Worthless article purportedly on the history of the Academy Awards.

"Oscar On TV." *Life,* March 30, 1953, p. 39+. A mostly pictorial essay on the first Awards show to be televised. Wryly notes that television "bought the right to the ceremony for $100,000, used it for a one and a half hour show which presumably kept millions of TV-viewers from going to the movies that night."

"Sadder But Braver." *Nation* 188 (January 24, 1959): 62. Brief item noting the Academy's repeal of its controversial "blacklist" amendment which prevented suspected Communists from receiving Oscar recognition. See also *Daily Variety,* January 14, 1959.

Schickel, Richard. "Measuring Oscar." *American Film,* March 1978, p. 3. Academy voters, despite some occasional lapses, have honored some memorable achievements in the past fifty years. If these Academy Awards "don't quite represent the ultimate in motion picture achievement as their industry apologists and hired flacks annually insist, they are not quite the monument to bad taste and faulty judgment that their critics insist on telling us each spring."

Simon, John. "Oscars . . . They Shun the Best, Don't They?" *New York Times,* March 1, 1970, II, p. 1. Simon complains that the Academy is not a suitable judge. He favors a small jury to select the winners rather than a "large, unwieldy, semi-anonymous and influenceable body." See *N.Y.Times,* April 5, 1970, II, p. 11 for several rebuttals.

Skolsky, Sidney. "What Goes On at the Academy Awards." *McCall's,* April 1962, p. 74+. Entertaining reminiscences of memorable Oscar ceremonies by a veteran observer of the Hollywood scene. It is in this article that Skolsky defends his claim that he, not Margaret Herrick or Bette Davis, named the statuette "Oscar."

Stanley, Fred M. "Oscar: His Life and Times." *New York Times Magazine,* March 18, 1945, p. 18. Explodes some myths, such as the story of Cedric Gibbons sketching the Oscar design on a tablecloth, but perpetuates other inaccuracies.

Thalberg, Irving. "Technical Activities of the Academy of Motion Picture Arts and

Sciences." *Journal of the Society of Motion Picture Engineers* 15 (July 1930): 3–16. A good summary of the projects of the Academy's Producers-Technicians Committee which supervised AMPAS technical activities before the Research Council was founded.

"That's Me." *Newsweek,* January 26, 1959, p. 25. As soon as the Academy repealed its blacklist amendment, Screenwriter Dalton Trumbo identified himself as the "Robert Rich" who had won the 1956 Oscar for writing *The Brave One.*

Trumbo, Dalton. "The Graven Image." *Theatre Arts* 34 (July 1950): 32–35. Humorous tongue-in-cheek account of awards (not just Oscars) bestowed in Hollywood.

Wald, Jerry and Norman Krasna. "Oscar Fever." *Films In Review* 3 (March 1952): 102–4. A very minor article advocating greater use of original scripts rather than adaptations.

"What Makes Simon Snicker?" *New York Times,* April 5, 1970, II, p. 11. Several letters to the editor responding to John Simon's March 1, 1970 *Times* piece criticizing the Oscars. Simon then replies to all of his critics.

Woods, Frank. "History of Producer-Talent Relations In the Academy." *Screen Guilds' Magazine* 2 (November 1935): 4. An intelligent response to the article "The Academy Writer-Producer Agreement . . . Another Attempt To Destroy the Guild" which appeared in the previous issue. Woods writes from the unique perspective of being a founder and former officer of both the Academy and the original Screen Writers' Guild.

OTHER SOURCES

Academy of Motion Picture Arts and Sciences. *Academy Leader.* April 1972, July 1972, November 1972. A fourth attempt by the Academy to publish a widely circulated film periodical; the venture lasted for three issues.

———. *Annual Reports.* 1929–1930, 1941.

Helpful information on the internal affairs of the Academy.

———. *Bulletin.* 1927–1935. Published by the Academy for its members, this monthly report is one of the finest sources of information about the formative years of the Academy.

———. *By-laws.* 1927–present. These articles, revised periodically, define the purposes, structure, and operating rules of the Academy.

———. *Motion Picture Arts and Sciences.* Vol. 1, #1 (November 1927). The Academy's first attempt to publish a mass circulation film periodical. Only one issue was ever printed.

———. *A Report—The Academy In Wartime.* May 1, 1943. Academy president Walter Wanger's four-page report deals mainly with the activities of the Research Council.

Bertrand, Daniel. *Evidence Study No. 25 of the Motion Picture Industry.* Office of the National Recovery Administration, Division of Review. November 1935. These government studies were originally planned as a means of collecting information bearing on legal issues which arose under the National Industrial Recovery Act.

———. *Work Materials No. 34: The Motion Picture Industry.* Office of the National Recovery Administration, Division of Review. February 1936. Good source of information about the movie industry in the 1930s, includes Bertrand's *Evidence Study No. 25* as an appendix. This 169-page study concludes that "The Motion Picture Industry and the public welfare could effectively be served by the continuation of a measure, at least, of governmental interest."

Emanuel, Itzhak. *A Descriptive History of the Academy of Motion Picture Arts and Sciences Annual Awards: The Television Productions, 1953–1970.* 416 pp., no index. A 1971 UCLA Master's thesis. Extremely detailed and technical, with charts, illustrations, and thirty-six appendices. Unpublished.

U.S. Congress, House. Committee on Appropriations. *Hearings Before the Subcommittee of the Committee on Appropriations, House of Representatives, 86th Congress, 1st Session, 1960.* Brief discussion of funding for the restoration of the Library of Congress Paper Print Collection, a project with which the Academy was greatly involved.

U.S. Congress, Senate. *Investigation of*

Concentration of Economic Power. Monograph No. 43: The Motion Picture Industry—A Pattern of Control. Temporary National Economic Committee, 76th Congress, 3rd Sessions, 1941. This 92-page pamphlet, written by the committee's administrative assistant Daniel Bertrand, covers such issues as block booking, blind selling, and overbuying.

Note on the Index

Entries in the index are alphabetized according to a lettery-by-letter system. For example, *Alaskan Eskimo, The* comes before *Alaska Wilderness Lake*. Titles beginning with *Doctor* or *Dr.* will be found under *Do* or *Dr*, respectively, depending upon the spelling used in the official Academy listing. A similar system has been used in alphabetizing titles beginning with *Mister* or *Mr*. Those unsure of the official spelling should check both places.

Index